1,000,000 Books
are available to read at

www.ForgottenBooks.com

Read online
Download PDF
Purchase in print

ISBN 978-0-365-85763-1
PIBN 11345723

This book is a reproduction of an important historical work. Forgotten Books uses state-of-the-art technology to digitally reconstruct the work, preserving the original format whilst repairing imperfections present in the aged copy. In rare cases, an imperfection in the original, such as a blemish or missing page, may be replicated in our edition. We do, however, repair the vast majority of imperfections successfully; any imperfections that remain are intentionally left to preserve the state of such historical works.

Forgotten Books is a registered trademark of FB &c Ltd.
Copyright © 2018 FB &c Ltd.
FB &c Ltd, Dalton House, 60 Windsor Avenue, London, SW19 2RR.
Company number 08720141. Registered in England and Wales.

For support please visit www.forgottenbooks.com

1 MONTH OF FREE READING

at

www.ForgottenBooks.com

By purchasing this book you are eligible for one month membership to ForgottenBooks.com, giving you unlimited access to our entire collection of over 1,000,000 titles via our web site and mobile apps.

To claim your free month visit: www.forgottenbooks.com/free1345723

* Offer is valid for 45 days from date of purchase. Terms and conditions apply.

English
Français
Deutsche
Italiano
Español
Português

www.forgottenbooks.com

Mythology Photography **Fiction**
Fishing Christianity **Art** Cooking
Essays Buddhism Freemasonry
Medicine **Biology** Music **Ancient Egypt** Evolution Carpentry Physics
Dance Geology **Mathematics** Fitness
Shakespeare **Folklore** Yoga Marketing
Confidence Immortality Biographies
Poetry **Psychology** Witchcraft
Electronics Chemistry History **Law**
Accounting **Philosophy** Anthropology
Alchemy Drama Quantum Mechanics
Atheism Sexual Health **Ancient History**
Entrepreneurship Languages Sport
Paleontology Needlework Islam
Metaphysics Investment Archaeology
Parenting Statistics Criminology
Motivational

A BOOK OF STRATTONS
VOLUME II

"Genealogical data is often buried in a mass of material so deep as well-nigh to discourage all ambition to bring it to light; but when the fragments are gathered and connected to form a record, there emerges from apparent chaos a story of surprising interest."—MILLS.

ENSIGN SAMUEL STRATTON (1720-1803)
Page 23.

A BOOK OF STRATTONS

A COLLECTION OF RECORDS OF THE DESCENDANTS OF
THE EARLY COLONIAL STRATTONS IN AMERICA
FROM THE FIFTH GENERATION TO
THE PRESENT DAY

COMPILED BY

HARRIET RUSSELL STRATTON

CHATTANOOGA, TENNESSEE

Volume II

FREDERICK H. HITCHCOCK
GENEALOGICAL PUBLISHER

NEW YORK   MCMXVIII

Ensign Samuel Stratton (1720-1803)
Page 23.

A BOOK OF STRATTONS

A COLLECTION OF RECORDS OF THE DESCENDANTS OF
THE EARLY COLONIAL STRATTONS IN AMERICA
FROM THE FIFTH GENERATION TO
THE PRESENT DAY

COMPILED BY

HARRIET RUSSELL STRATTON

CHATTANOOGA, TENNESSEE

Volume II

FREDERICK H. HITCHCOCK
GENEALOGICAL PUBLISHER

NEW YORK   MCMXVIII

Copyright, 1918,
BY HARRIET RUSSELL STRATTON

JUL 24 1919

©CLA529345

DEDICATED
TO
THE STRATTONS

"If you could see your ancestors
 All standing in a row,
Would you be proud of them or not,
 Or don't you really know?

  * * * * * *

"But here's another question, which
 Requires a different view—
If you could meet your ancestors
 Would they be proud of you?"

	PAGE
PREFACE	xiii
EXPLANATION	xvii

PART III.—STRATTONS IN THE OLD WORLD

STRATTONS IN ENGLAND	3
Abstracts of Wills	4
Bills of Complaint	7
Court Records	9
Places Called Stratton	10

PART IV.—STRATTONS IN AMERICA

COLONIAL STRATTONS	17
STRATTONS OF MASSACHUSETTS	20
Samuel of Watertown, His Descendants	20
Caleb of Boston, His Descendants	176
John of Watertown, His Descendants	191
Joseph of Waltham	228
STRATTONS OF LONG ISLAND	229
Richard of Easthampton, His Descendants	229
David of Millville	256
Jonathan of Philadelphia	265
Benjamin of Pittsgrove	269
John of Easthampton, His Descendants	273
STRATTONS OF CONNECTICUT	313
John of Woodbury, His Descendants	313
William of Windsor, His Descendants	321
STRATTONS OF VIRGINIA	341
Thomas of the Eastern Shore, His Descendants	341
Thomas of Pittsylvania Co.	351
Edward of Bermuda Hundred, His Descendants	358
Strattons of Eastern Kentucky	399

Contents

	PAGE
STRATTONS OF NEW JERSEY	410
Mark of Evesham, His Descendants	410
Seth of Frederick Co.	458
William of Spottsylvania Co.	462
Absolom of Amherst Co.	465
Emanuel of Evesham, His Descendants	468
Strattons of Sussex Co.	477
INDEXES	497

LIST OF ILLUSTRATIONS

Ensign Samuel Stratton	*Frontispiece*
	FACING PAGE
Stratton House, England	2
Stratton's Folly, Village and Hall	6
Some Stratton Coats of Arms	10
An Old Stratton Bible	14
Stratton Village and Stratton Tavern	40
Rev. Ebenezer H. Stratton	50
Charles River and Stratton Park	62
Sons of Shuball C. Stratton	72
Sons of Shuball C. Stratton	76
A Page of Stratton Autographs	106
Albert G. Stratton and Paul Stratton	112
Five Children of John Stratton	116
Mrs. Louisa (Stratton) Russell	130
A Group of Athol Strattons	150
Rufus, Daniel and Lorenzo Stratton	164
Latham Stratton and Sons	178
Rev. William O. Stratton	184
Some Old Stratton Autographs	190
James and Elizabeth (Wheeler) Stratton	194
Children of James and Elizabeth Stratton	206
Stratton Homestead, Little Valley	212
Asa E. Stratton and Lorenzo Stratton	216
A Summer Morning at Cactus Cottage	220
Some Stratton Homes, Tennessee	224
Rev. Daniel Stratton	228
Nathan L. Stratton and Dr. Joseph B. Stratton	236
Myron Stratton and Gov. C. C. Stratton	242
Stratton Chapel, Library, Mountain and Other Views	248
James T. Stratton and Dr. C. C. Stratton	302
George W. Stratton and Samuel E. Stratton	312
Timothy Stratton, Sr.	322
Catherine (Stratton) Snow and Asa E. Stratton	330

	FACING PAGE
SENATOR JOHN STRATTON AND DAUGHTER	340
SOME STRATTON HOMES AND AN OLD CHURCH	346
A GROUP OF STRATTONS	350
STRATTON SPRING, STRATTON HOMES AND SOME STRATTON BURIAL PLACES	358
EARLY STRATTON HOMES IN EIGHT STATES	364
A GROUP OF STRATTONS	380
TWO SILHOUETTES. GEORGE W. STRATTON AND GRANDDAUGHTER RUTH	410
FIVE STRATTONS	420
WILLIAM L. STRATTON, JOHN STRATTON AND ELI STRATTON	430
FIVE STRATTON HOMES	440
JOHN R. STRATTON AND MARK STRATTON	450
JOHN AND RACHEL STRATTON AND THEIR NINE CHILDREN	476

PREFACE

VOLUME I of *A Book of Strattons* (published nearly ten years ago), after giving sixty-six pages concerning Strattons in England and Scotland, gives all that the compiler has found of the early Strattons in America and their descendants to the fifth generation. This second volume is a continuation of Vol. I, beginning where that left off and coming down to the present time. This volume is complete in itself to this extent—it contains a brief sketch of the first Stratton of each Colonial line in America, and then as the descendant's name appears on the page his ancestry is given through all the generations back to the first Stratton of the line to which he belongs. But the full records of the first generation, and the details concerning the second, third and fourth generations, which form so large a part of Vol. I, are not repeated here, and of course none of the English data is here repeated.

To the compiler it has been a matter of exceeding interest to trace the movements of the different generations of Strattons, to study their characteristics and conditions from the time when our English ancestors settled on the Atlantic coast of the New World down through more than two hundred and fifty years to the time when their descendants are found in every state of the Union, in every trade, profession and line of business, and in many varied conditions of life.

To trace the descendants of the different lines and branches as they have remained for many generations within a few miles of the first homestead or have steadily migrated westward; to locate the different families, and different members of the same family, as they have moved from place to place; to ferret out connecting links which had long been lost; to study the source of family traditions, adjust conflicting data and solve puzzling genealogical problems—all this has long been a work of unfailing interest and now the compiler has the satisfaction of feeling that many records have thus been preserved which otherwise would soon have become obscure or irretrievably lost.

It would be impossible to give the authority for all the data which this volume contains but the utmost care has been taken to give nothing as fact that has not been verified by the best authorities obtainable. All available printed matter has been consulted and information secured from church, town, court and military records, from wills, deeds, society and college catalogues, from family Bibles, gravestones, old letters and aged people. Many hundreds of letters have been written and often there have been months, even years of waiting for replies to inquiries (some of which have not yet arrived!) and hours spent in deciphering almost illegible handwriting (in which the Strattons seem proficient!) and in endeavoring to read between the lines what the writers have failed to express in words. Often only the barest genealogical data has been sent—birth, marriage, death—where some items of biographical and historical interest concerning the older Strattons could easily have been contributed. That the volume gives more about some than others is due often to the fact that the compiler knew more about them, or was furnished more biographical material by her correspondents.

No doubt there are many whose lives deserve a more lengthy notice, but the compiler did not know of it. In some instances a biographical sketch has served to preserve historical and geographical items of interest concerning some section of our country. Some family records are incomplete, and perhaps inaccurate, owing to the silence of those who might have contributed complete and correct data.

The aim has been not to laud the living (that is left to some future genealogist) but "to gather up the traditions that still exist; to show the world that if we are not called upon to follow the example of our fathers, we are at least not insensible to the worth of their characters, nor indifferent to the sacrifices and trials by which they purchased our prosperity." *Edward Everett.*

As the manuscript for this second volume goes to the press no one realizes more fully than the compiler the errors that such a book must necessarily contain and the incompleteness of the work, yet it seems best not to longer delay publication. As more complete data accumulates, a supplement to this volume— a small third volume—should be issued. If then, errors are here found will not those better informed supply corrections, and if any reader possesses data which would render the genealogical record of any family more complete, or biographical and historical items which would add to the interest of Stratton history, why not forward same to the compiler at once?

Above all it is most earnestly hoped that the way may soon open for an extended research in England, seeking to establish there the ancestry of each line of Strattons in America. If our Colonial ancestors belonged to armigerous lines of Strattons, as seems very probable, would it not be of interest to their descendants to know the arms to which they are entitled and the act of bravery, or chivalry for which this right was conferred upon their ancestor? Among the many descendants living in various parts of our country to-day may there not be some who would be willing to help direct and finance such a research, and thus add interesting material not only to Stratton lore but to early Colonial history as well?

And now to the many Strattons who have kindly contributed data and pictures, and who from time to time have sent words of encouragement and appreciation the compiler would here extend grateful and heart-felt thanks.

Cactus Cottage,
Grand View, Tenn.,
1918.

Hattie R. Stratton.

EXPLANATIONS

THE arrangement here is the same as in *Volume* I, and the system of tracing from one generation to another is so clear and easily understood it is hoped that each Stratton into whose hands the book falls will acquaint himself with it. The few abbreviations used will be readily understood.

As in *Volume* I, and other genealogical works, the small figure following the name and placed above the line indicates the generation from the emigrant ancestor.

The number preceding the name is an individual number and denotes the person's place in the line of Strattons to which he belongs.

The minus sign (—) placed before a number in the lists of children's names shows that this individual is not traced further.

The plus sign (+) preceding a number denotes that the number and name are repeated on a succeeding page (the number in black-faced type) where a more extended account of that individual is given. If, as in a few cases, the individual number in black-faced type is enclosed in brackets [thus] it denotes that the parentage of that individual is not positively established.

The compiler had hoped to continue in this volume the charts of Volume I, pages 310-325, but finding this impractical, at present, has left this feature for some future volume.

Vol. I. contains the names of Strattons in Colonial Wars and in the Revolution.

The lists which have been collected of Strattons who served in the War of 1812, the Mexican War, the Civil War and the Spanish-American War must also wait for some future publication. They would fill many pages. In most cases the service has been included in the individual biography.

As this volume comes from the press more than two million of our country's young men are enrolled in the great World War. Among them are many Strattons. It is the desire of the compiler to secure a list of all Strattons in Military and Navy service in this War. By all means let us make this list complete for a future volume and so do our bit toward honoring those of our own name who are giving their service and their lives for us, for our country and for the world.

Special care has been taken with the indexes. A son marked with a plus sign (+) in a list of children is indexed but once and then on the page giving his fullest record. His parentage, with place and date of birth (if given) may be readily found by tracing back his individual number. Conceding to many requests the compiler has refrained (in most cases) from giving dates of birth later than 1850. Names of children who died young are not indexed. In other families than Strattons only the family name is given in the index, even though several members of the family may be found on the pages indicated. Sometimes a name appears on a page several times although indexed but once.

The names of those whom Strattons have married are in black-faced type, while the parentage of the wives of Strattons is in italics.

In Volume I, Part II, the Colonial Strattons are arranged in the order of their first appearance in America or their connection with English records. In this volume, Part IV, they are grouped according to the colony in which they lived, or in which has been found the earliest records of them.

PART III

STRATTONS IN THE OLD WORLD

"Without genealogy the study of history is comparatively lifeless."
JOHN FISKE.

"Enquire, I pray thee, of the former age, and prepare thyself to the search of their fathers." JOB viii, 8.

"These things ought not to be forgotten; for the benefit of our children and those that follow them, they should be recorded." FRANKLIN.

A BOOK OF STRATTONS

STRATTONS IN ENGLAND

"Writ in remembrance of things long passed." IVIN.

THE little additional research which the author has been able to make in England since the first volume of this work was issued has not resulted in establishing our ancestry there. It has, however, discovered clews which will probably help to bring about the desired result whenever a more extended research is undertaken.

There seems no reason to doubt that among the great amount of material on the Strattons in England in the seventeenth and eighteenth centuries may be found the ancestry of most, if not all, the lines in America to-day.

Possibly some may be traced back to the places where the name originated—Stratton being a "place-name" from Street-town (*stræt-tûn*), the early Anglo-Saxon settlements made on the old Roman roads in Great Britain (see *p. 3, Vol. I*). These street-towns were widely scattered and from them many families took the name Stratton (Stretton, Straton, &c.) when surnames began to come into use about the eleventh century. Thus in **1148** we find Richard filius Roberti of Street-town whose son was later known as Robert de Stratton and whose grandson, in **1210**, was Thomas Stratton.

The records of baptisms, marriages and burials in many of the old parish registers are so complete, and the Stratton wills and administrations so numerous and so easily accessible, that a more extended research could hardly fail to reveal much of interest to the Strattons in America.*

---

* In a letter of Mr. Sherley's to Gov. Bradford of Plymouth, dated Jan. 2, 1631, he mentions that "Straton & Fogge" were above a month trying to straighten out the accounts of two vessels, the *White Angel* and the *Friendship*, both evidently Bristol ships. Ralph Fogg had dealings with N. E. early. These ships sailed to Plymouth with supplies and then to the Maine coast for fishing trips. Bristol men sent ships to Monhegan Isle, on the coast of Maine, for cod fish as early as **1616**, perhaps earlier. John Stratton of Suffolk was in N. E. in **1628**.

A Book of Strattons

ABSTRACTS OF WILLS

The following abstracts of Stratton wills (in addition to those given in Vol. I) from the Prerogative Court of Canterbury, London, will serve to show the character of the genealogical material from this source:

Will of Julian Stratton of the parish of Dale, dated 5 July, 1462. To be buried in the churchyard of Dale. Legacies to the high altar, the parish clerk, and for masses to be sung in the church of Dale at my month's mind and my year's mind. To John Browne my servant all my small utensils. Residue to John Trary and Walter Sayer, whom executors. Overseer, Richard Baker alias Barbor. I will that all my lands and tenements in Dale shall be sold, and that the money so arising, my debts and legacies paid, shall remain to Johan my daughter, except 20s., which I will that John Browne my servant shall have. Witnesses: None. Proved 6 July, 1463, by the executors. (From the Latin.)

Will of John Stretton of All Hallows (co. Kent), fisherman, dated 19 Oct., 1592. Being sicke in bodie. To be buried in the Chauncell of the parish church of All Hallows, neere unto my mother. And as touching such goods as God here in this vale of miserie hath endewed me withall, I give to my eldest son Robert my fishing boate, with the occupying of the fishing grounds; to my daughter Agnes Stretton £5; to my daughter Jane Stretton 26s.8d.; to my son William £5 at 18; to my daughter Elizabeth £6-13-3 at 16; to my sister Alice Stretton of Rochester one ewe lamb; to my wife's sister Elizabeth Clarke another ewe lamb; and to the poor of All Hallows, where I am parishioner, two bushells of wheat to be made in white bread, and a kilderkin of good beere, with some cheese, on the day of my funerall. The residue I give to my wife Joan, whom I ordain executrix, and my brothers William Stretton, citizen of Rochester, and Henry Awsten of St. Marie's, yeoman, overseers. Witnesses: Francis Lomelyn, vicar of All Hallows, John Newman, clerk of the same church, and John Wright, parishioner there. Proved 7 Nov., 1592, by the executrix.

Will of William Stretton * of Tenterden (co. Kent), Jurat,

---

* This abstract, exactly as here given, was furnished the compiler from London by the well-known genealogist, J. Henry Lea, since the publication of Vol. I. of this work.

dated 31 May, 1647. Being in health of bodie. To my wife Margaret Stretton £1045 as agreed upon between us before our marriage. Also I give unto her her wearing apparell and her dwelling in the house wherein I now live, for the space of half a year without paying for it. To my son Joseph £100 at his age of 23 years, my best Bible, my best backsworde, and one of the books of the writings of Mr. Perkins. To my son Benjamin £100 at his age of 23, my rapier, and one of the said books. To my son Bartholomew fourscore and ten pounds at his age of 23, my black-hilted backsword and the book of Acts and Monuments written by Mr Foxe. To my daughter Elizabeth £140 at 20 or marriage and a trunk of linen appointed her by her mother. To my son Samuel £100 at 23 and one of the books of the Acts and Monuments. To my son Caleb £110 at 23 and one of the said books. My three youngest sons Thomas, John and Nathaniel each £120 at 23. To my daughter Sarah Pickering, to be divided amongst her children, £10. Overseers, my wife and Mr Thomas Brett. Son William my best bedstede and money due to me from the Parliament. My wife's two daughters Rose and Margaret each 10s in gould. Executor, son William, whom residuary legatee. Witnesses: William Stretton, Tho: Brett, Tho: Manton. Proved 11 Jan., 1647-8, by the executor.

Will of Robert Stratton of the parish of St. Martins in the Fields, co. Middlesex, gent, dated 16 July, 1640. To my wife Elizabeth Stratton £100 and my leases of certain tenements and forges which I hold of the Lord of Lexington, now Earl of Monmouth, and his now Countess, situate in Long-acre and Drewry-lane in the parish of St. Giles in the Fields, co. Middlesex; and after her death to my three sons, Edward Stratton, Samuel Stratton, and William Stratton. To my eldest son Edward Stratton £500. To my second son Samuel Stratton £300. To my youngest son William Stratton £500, to be put out for his use during his minority. All my wearing apparel to my said son William. My wife Elizabeth Stratton, out of the means and estate I leave, shall maintain, educate and bring up my son William. To my two daughters in law, my two eldest sons' wives, 20s. each for rings. To my cousin Matthew Billinge's daughter 20s. To my cousins Christian Hurle, Phrissey her sister, and Joan Browne her sister, and to my cousin Robert Hurle, my godson, £5 amongst them. To my kinswoman Katherine White £5. I give £5 towards the repayringe and beawtyfyinge of the Cathedrall

Church of St. Paul in London. Residue to Elizabeth my wife, whom executrix. Overseers, my sons Edward Stratton and Samuel Stratton. Witnesses: William Foster, Richard Hatherington, Mathew Billinge, scr. Proved 9 Sept., 1640, by the executrix.

Will of Samuel Stratton of the parish of St. Clement Danes, co. Middlesex, gent, dated 10 July, 1652. Sick in body. I will that such leases as I have lately assigned to certain friends, and one assignment of a house in Ficketts Field to my mother Elizabeth Stratton, widow, shall remain as expressed in the deeds. To my mother Elizabeth Stratton one gold ring with an onix stone in it. To my mother in law Adelina Smith, widow, two twenty-shilling pieces of Queene Elizabeth coyne. To my brother Edward Stratton, gent, one gold ring set with a fair table diamond. To my brother William Stratton one skie coloured enamelled ring with gold starrs in it. To my cousin Walter Stratton and his wife 20s. each, and 10s. to their son John. To my friend Mr Dawson a ring of gold with five rubies in it. To my friend Mr Domville my gimmoll ring of gold with three lincks in it. To Mrs Baker, wife of Stephen Baker, taylor, £5. To Mr Clarke the chirurgeon one agate knife and fork of silver typt with gold. To Walley Browne the Scotch boy my grey cloth suit. Executrix and residuary legatee, my wife Duckett Stratton. Witnesses: Nich: Horsinell, Humphrey Tuckey, E. Straton, Nicho: Dumvill, scr. Proved 21 Oct, 1652, by the executrix.

Will of John Stratton of the parish of St. Olaves Southwark, co. Surrey, wheelwright, dated 18 May, 1700. "Now going beyond the seas." To my wife Ellen Stratton £200. To my son John Stratton £300 at his age of 21 years, and he to be apprenticed to a wine-cooper in the meantime. To my daughter Susannah Stratton £300 at 18. Residuary legatees, my said son and daughter, John and Susan (sic.) Executors, friends Richard Tilden and Daniel Tilden of London, merchants. Witnesses: Alex: Walrond, Geo: Tilden, Jos: Mayner. 24 Sept., 1706, commission to Ellenor Stratton, relict and principal legatary named in the will of John Stratton, late of the parish of St. Olave Southwark, co. Surrey, but at the Barbadoes deceased, the executors refusing.

Will of William Stretton, citizen and goldsmith of London dated 7 Feb., 1690-91. To my mother Mrs Rebecca Stretton all

— Stratton Hall, Suffolk, Eng.
Built before 1329.
From a photograph, 1908
See Vol. I, page 48.

1. "Stratton's Folly," Hertshire, Eng. *Page* 13.
2. A glimpse of the quaint little town of Stratton, Cornwall. *Page* 12.

my estate whatsoever, with all my lands and tenements wheresoever, and her I appoint my executrix. Whereas my grandfather William Greaves of Lymehouse, in the parish of Stebunheath alias Stepney, co. Middlesex, shipwright, did bequeath to my mother Rebecca Stretton, wife of Samuel Stretton, after the death of my grandmother Elizabeth Greaves, one third part of all his messuages, etc. in Limehouse for the term of her life, and afterwards to me, now I do devise the same to my said mother and her heirs. Witnesses: Tho: Collett, Hen: Minchard, Not. Pub., Tim: Smith, clerk to said Notary. Proved 13 March, 1690-91, by the executrix.

Will of William Stratton of Hoo, co. Kent, belonging to H.M. ship Falmouth, mariner, dated 10 March, 1700-01. Sole legatee and executor, my kinsman John Banks of Chatham, co. Kent, cordwainer. Witnesses: Thomas Barr, John King, John Martin. Proved 18 Nov., 1703.

Will of John Stratton, steward and taylor, now outward bound to the East Indies in the good ship Fleet Frygate, Capt. Charles Newton, commander, dated 2 Jan., 1707-8. To my friend John Coben of Black Fryars, London, taylor, £5-10. Residue to my sister Anne Patterson, wife of George Patterson of St. John Wapping, barber chirurgeon. Executors, John Coben and my said sister. Witnesses: John Wyndham, Richard Colyer, Linthwt Farrant. Proved 18 Oct., 1711, by Anne Patterson, power reserved to John Coben.

BILLS OF COMPLAINTS

The following "complaints" from Duchy of Lancaster Court records are given merely to show the quaint old language of that period:

In most humble wise complayninge shewen vnto yor honnor (Sir Ralph Sadler, Knight, Chancellor of the Duchy) your poore and daylie orators Thomas Balles and Elizabeth his wyef That whereas one Willm Mere was in his leif tyme lawfullye seased as of fee tail generall to him and the heires of his bodye by coppie of Court Rolle accordinge to the custome of the Manner of New Castell in the countye of Staff of and in divers copiehold messuages and landes lying and beynge in Shelton in the said countye and had yssue Alice who was maryed to one Thomas

Stratton And after the said Willm Mere died of such estate seased by whose death the right of the same premisses discended and came vnto the said Alice his daughter and beire By vertew whereof the said Thomas Stratton and Alice as in the right of the said Alice ought to have been thereof seased accordingly And had yssue Thomas Stratton and both died After whose death the right of the same premisses discended and came vnto the said Thomas Stratton the sonne as sonne and heir of the said Thomas Stratton the father and Alice By vertew whereof the said Thomas Stratton the sonne ought thereof to have been seased accordingly And had yssue the said Elizabeth Balles one of your honnors said orators and dyed After whose death the right of the same premisses discended and came vnto the said Elizabeth as daughter and heir of the said Thomas Stratton the sonne By vertew whereof the said Elizabeth ought thereof to have been seased accordingly And took to husband the said Thomas Balles By vertew whereof the said Thomas Balles and Elizabeth as in right of the said Elizabeth ought to have the said premisses But so yt ys that by reason that divers copies of Court Rolls munyments and wrytinges touching the premisses and rightfullye belonging vnto your orators are by casuall meanes comen to the handes of one Henry Meare and Robert Hill they by collor of having thereof have wrongfullye entered into the premisses and deteine and keepe the possession thereof from your said orators. Dated 28 April, 1586.

Bill of complaint of John Stratton the elder of Compton Bassett, co. Wilts, John Stratton the younger, and Edith Phelpes, widow, sworn 10 June, 1594 (or 10 Jan., 1594-5: the date is almost illegible):—Sir James Marvin, Knt., being seized in his demesne as of fee of and in the Manor of Compton Bassett, co. Wilts, did, about the 32nd year of the Queen's reign that now is, in consideration of £10 to him paid by William Stratton, father of the aforesaid John Stratton the elder, grant one messuage and one yardland and a half unto the said William and John Stratton, to be holden for the term of their two lives successively. In due course William Stratton the father was taken tenant and did his fealty. He afterwards died, and orator was in turn admitted tenant, but was enforced to give for his admittance two third parts of twelve acres of corn which he and his brother John (sic) Stratton had sown, and to enter into bond to keep and sustain two poor children. But now of late one

Elizabeth Stratton, widow, and others, pretending title to the said premises, have commenced suit at Common Law against orator for the recovery thereof. Sir James, countenancing this attempt, caused a Court to be holden for the Manor, at which all tenants were enjoined to appear upon pain of 40s. Orator accordingly appeared, leaving in his house only a woman servant, a young child, and one Smith, a tailor. Elizabeth Stratton, acting on the advice of Sir James, took advantage of this opportunity to dispossess orator of his goods and to expell him from his tenement; for her servant, coming to the house, and finding the doors fast shut, thrust at the fore door and desisted not until it was unbolted, when he entered and expelled orator's servant and others being there, and presently delivered the said house and goods to the said Elizabeth Stratton, being near at hand redie to receive the same. Sir James now refuses to restore possession of the tenement.

COURT RECORDS

These two records from Co. Suffolk are of interest as connected with John Stratton of Shotley, Eng., and Salem, Mass. (See *p. 77, Vol. I.*)

Final Concord made in the King's Court at Westminster, Easter, 3 Charles I. (1628), Between John Leman Knt. and John Leman gent, plaintiffs, and John Stratton senior gent and Ann his wife, and John Stratton junior gent, son and heir apparent of the said John Stratton, senior, and Thomas Thorne, clerk, and Cecily his wife, deforciants, of the Manor of Kirketon with appurtenances, and of three messuages, one cottage, 2 tofts, 3 gardens, 2 orchards, 160 acres of land, 10 acres of meadow, 30 acres of pasture, 4 acres of wood and 20s. rent with appurtenances in Kirketon alias Shotley, Erwarton alias Arwarton and Chelmondeston, whereupon a plea was summoned between them in the same Court, to wit, that the aforesaid John Stratton and Ann, John Stratton and Thomas and Cecily acknowledged the said Manor and tenements to be the right of the said John Leman Knt. as those which the said John and John Leman gent had of the gift of the aforesaid John Stratton and Ann, John Stratton and Thomas and Cecily and those which were remised and quitclaimed of them the said John Stratton and Ann, John Stratton and Thomas and Cecily, and their heirs to the aforesaid John Leman and John Leman and to the heirs of the same John Leman Knt. for ever. Consideration, £200.

Final Concord made in the King's Court at Westminster, Easter, 5 Charles I., Between Edmund Trench and John Cock, plaintiffs, and John Stratton, gent, and William Stratton, gent, deforciants, of the Manor of Thurkolton alias Shurkolton alias Thurcalton alias Shurcalton with appurtenances, and of 2 messuages, one toft, one garden, one orchard, 100 acres of land, 12 acres of meadow, 60 acres of pasture, 2 acres of wood, 4 acres of moor, 3 acres of gorse, 8 acres of marsh, and free fishing with appurtenances in Kerketon alias Shotley, whereupon a plea was summoned between them in the same Court, to wit, that the aforesaid John Stratton and William have acknowledged the aforesaid Manor, tenements and fishing to be the right of the said Edmund as those which the said Edmund and John Cock had of the gift of the aforesaid John Stratton and William, and as those remised and quitclaimed of the said John Stratton and William and their heirs to the aforesaid Edmund and John Cock and the heirs of the said Edmund for ever. Consideration, £160.

PLACES CALLED STRATTON

Among the places of interest now called Stratton (or Stretton) in England may be especially noted the following:

Stratton, Dorsetshire, is a village on the river Frome. Near it are traces of an old Roman road. The church of St. Mary, a stone building in the Perpendicular style, has a fine embattled tower and windows still retaining fragments of ancient stained glass. The register dates from 1561. There is in this parish a farm called Strattonfield. The following are Stratton items from this old register:

- 1600: Johanna Stratton sepulta 21 April
    Thomas Stratton et Christiana Carpenter matrimonio copulabantur 28 Oct.
- 1600–01: Johannes Stratton et Elizabetha Norfolke matrimonio copulabantur 15 Jan.
- 1601: Elizabetha Stratton bapitzata est 25 Aug.
- 1601–2: Johannes Stratton baptizatus est 20 Mar.
- 1604–5: Jedion Stratton baptised 24 March
- 1615: Walter Stratton, son of John, bapt 26 March.
- 1617: Mary Stratton, daughter of John, bapt 3 Aug.
- 1630: Robert Stratton and Susan Boore married 4 Nov.
- 1632: Bridget Stratton buried 15 July
    Robert, son of Robert Stratton, bapt 16 Dec.

SOME COATS OF ARMS
FOUND IN
STRATTON HOMES

———

For other
Stratton Arms
See Vol. I of
"A Book of Strattons"
Pages 11-13

1637: John Jones and Anne Stratton married 29 June
1638: Elizabeth, daughter of Robert and Susan Stratton, bapt 17 June
1639: Susan Stratton buried 13 May
1640: Sarah Stretton, daughter of Robert and Frances, bapt 19 May
1643: Mary, wife of Robert Straton, buried 6 Nov.

Stretton, Staffordshire, is a parish and small village on the river Penk. The church of St. John, originally erected as a chapel of ease to Penkridge, is a small edifice of stone in the Norman and Early English styles, consisting of chancel, nave, transepts, south porch and a western turret containing one bell. The nave is Early English; the chancel Norman, and part of the original structure. The register dates from 1659. Stretton Hall, a fine old mansion built from designs by Inigo Jones, is the seat of the lord of the manor.

Stratton, Wiltshire, takes its name from the old Roman road that runs through the parish. It was originally divided into three tithings, called the Street, the Green, and Upper Stratton. The church, dedicated to St. Margaret, is an ancient edifice of stone, in the Early English style, consisting of chancel, nave, aisles separated from the nave by arcades of four bays, south porch and a western tower. The oldest monumental tablet dates back to 1645; the register to 1608.

Stratton, Gloucestershire, is a parish and village on the river Churn. The church of St. Peter is in the Early English style, and the register dates from 1601. Stratton House in this parish is the residence of the Firebraces.

East Stratton, Hampshire, is a parish and small village eight miles north-east from Winchester. The church of All Saints is of modern erection. The registers, incorporated with those of Micheldever, date from 1540. Stratton House stands in a park of some 300 acres adjoining the village. The mansion is of ancient erection, but has been added to at different dates, and is consequently of mixed architecture. It was formerly a seat of the Russell family, dukes of Bedford, and was once occupied by the Lady Rachell, widow of Lord William Russell, who was beheaded in Lincoln's Inn Fields, 18 July, 1683. About 1825 it was the residence of Sir Thomas Baring, Bart., and later was the seat of the Earl of Northbrook.

Stretton-Baskerville, Warwickshire, in Domesday called

"stratone," is a parish four miles south-east of Nuneaton, on the border of Leicestershire. It takes its name from Watling Street, an old Roman road, which lies on the north side of it, and from the ancient family of Baskerville, by whom it was anciently held. At one time it was a place of some consequence, but in the reign of Henry VII eighty tenants were evicted from some twenty-three cottages, and the church, falling into decay, became "as a shelter for cattle." The site of the ancient village, the church, manor house and pools, may still be traced in what is now called the "Township."

Stratton, Cornwall, is an ancient market town one and a half miles from Bude on the Cornish coast. This "Street-town" was built on the old Roman road between Devon and Cornwall, and a little bit of the old way yet remains in the vicinity. Some one in writing of it says, "Imagine a little town built in a thimble —there you have Stratton. At the bottom runs the river (frequently called the Strat) crossed by a bridge, and so picturesque on either side that you will want a camera or a sketch book at once. From the bridge the steep street rises to the church, perched, as it were, on the thimble's edge, while here a corner, and there a roof forms more pictures as the town goes clustering up the hill. It is this steepness that makes Stratton the dearest, quaintest little town imaginable." Of late years the church has been effectively restored. A figure of St. Andrew, to whom the building is dedicated, occupies the ancient niche. Within the church is beautiful. The Norman font is circular; the pulpit is Jacobean. The altar tomb of Sir John Arundel occupies the south chancel aisle; on its top are fine brasses of the knight and his two wives, with smaller brasses for their twelve children, and armorial bearings.*

In a window of the north aisle lies the battered but very ancient effigy of a knight in chained armor of the thirteenth century. This is supposed to be Sir Ralph de Blanchminister whose name is attached to the Stratton parish charity founded as early as 1249.†

---

* Sir John was esquire of the body of Henry VIII and was knighted at the Battle of the Spurs. He died in 1561.

† Centuries have elapsed, yet this charity in the hands of trustees has prospered and increased, enabling the present trustees not only to give each year (the Sunday after Christmas) the "dole" in the church, but to assist deserving cases in the parish and to establish scholarships for young people.

Stratton Tower in the Village of Little Berkhampshire (Hertshire) was built by John Stratton in 1789 at a cost of £3,000. His father (whose residence near The Tower was called "The Gage" and is still known by that name) was a large trader having offices in London and The Tower was built that from it one might get an extensive view over the beautiful surrounding country, watch the shipping on the Thames, and for astronomical purposes.* It proved, however, to be unsafe, and it stands to-day just as it was built more than a century ago, a picturesque landmark known as "Stratton's Folly."

---

*The property is now owned, and the Gage occupied, by his grandson, Col. J. H. Stratton, with whom the compiler has had some pleasant correspondence and who kindly furnished the photograph of "The Tower."

TITLE PAGE OF THE "JOHN STRATTON BIBLE"
Brought from England about 1649, passed down through eight generations to its present owner. *Page 274.*

PART IV

STRATTONS IN AMERICA

"Of all literature biography is the most interesting." DR. ELMORE.

"Records of well lived lives are legacies to mankind, which should be handed down from generation to generation." ADDISON.

"Those who do not treasure up the memory of their ancestors, do not deserve to be remembered by posterity." EDMUND BURKE.

COLONIAL STRATTONS

"And so it was in the days of old." SHAKESPERE.

THE Strattons traced in this volume are the descendants of the following eleven colonial lines:

CALEB STRATTON,[1] born in England in 1635, came to America about 1660. He married Mary Adams of Boston. His son William settled in Nantucket.

RICHARD STRATTON [1] and JOHN STRATTON [1] (brothers) settled at Easthampton, L. I., about 1650, and were closely connected with the early history of that town. Richard married Elizabeth Edwards. His sons were Richard, Thomas, Isaac and Benjamin. John's sons were John, Joseph, Stephen and Cornelius.

THOMAS STRATTON [1] died before 1632 when his widow, Alice Stratton, was living on the Eastern Shore, Va., where she was granted 200 acres of land. Upon this land the descendants of their son Thomas Stratton, Jr., lived for several generations.

EDWARD STRATTON, in 1674, was living in Bermuda Hundred, Va., where he owned a plantation. His son Edward was born about 1655, whether in England or America we know not.

SAMUEL STRATTON,[1] born in England in 1592, settled in Watertown, Mass., some time before 1647 with wife Alice and sons Samuel, John and Richard.

JOHN STRATTON, in 1667, at the age of twenty-five years, married Mary Smith in Watertown, Mass. Their sons were John, Thomas, James, Jonathan and Samuel.

JOHN STRATTON bought land in Woodbury, Conn., in 1682. His estate was settled there in 1716. His son Thomas settled in Stratford, Conn.

WILLIAM STRATTON married Abigail Moore in Winsor, Conn., in 1705. He was one of the company sent to invade Canada, in the old French War. He died while in the service in 1709. His sons were Serajah and William.

MARK STRATTON and EMANUEL STRATTON were brothers, of whom the earliest record we have is in 1713 when they were living in Evesham, N. J. The sons of Emanuel were Jacob and Emanuel.

The sons of Mark were David, Daniel, John, Enoch and Isaac.*

Five of the above colonial Strattons are known to have been emigrants—each the first of his line in the New World. Of the other six it can only be said that a most painstaking research has failed to reveal their parentage here. A research in England might find them there.†

Three other Strattons came early to the New World:

JOSEPH STRATTON from Shotley, Eng., was a member of the House of Burgesses at James City, Va., in 1629.

JOHN STRATTON, a nephew of Joseph, was granted 2,000 acres of land along the coast of Maine in 1631, including an island at the mouth of the Saco River which is still known as "Stratton Island."

BARTHOLOMEW STRATTON from Tenterden, Eng., came to America in 1658. He had sons and grandsons living in Boston but no record of them has been found later than 1698.‡

These three emigrants were men of considerable wealth, prominence and standing in those early days. Although the com-

---

* Daniel and Thomas Stratton of Sussex Co., N. J., in 1779, are supposed to belong to this line, although no *actual proof* of this connection has yet been found.

† For an extended account of these eleven early Strattons in America, and records of their descendants to the fifth generation, see *A Book of Strattons,* Vol. I, pp. 92-299.

More than five thousand of their descendants from the fifth generation to the present day are traced in this volume.

‡ See pages 69-91, *Vol. I.*

Dec. 2, 1696, a William Stratton had a case in court in Boston concerning the brigantine *Tryal* of which he was master. The case was continued for more than a year (see page 73, *Vol. I*). The many papers in this and other cases prove that he was a citizen of Boston. In 1691 he was mate of the ship *Providence,* of London. From 1694 to 1696 he fought a case about his management of the ship *Friends' Adventure.* June 8, 1696, he was on a jury of inquest in a Maine town about a child found drowned near a wharf. Dec. 18, 1695, he had a judgment in his favor in the suit over the *Friends' Adventure.* Sept. 5, 1696, he signed a receipt for the cash for his judgment against John Cary of Bristol (now in R. I.). Dec. 2, 1696, he was on trial for bringing the ship *Tryal* into Boston and refusing to deliver her up to those who claimed her. (Probably a Newcastle, Del., man who had bought the *Tryal* from the French privateer who seized her in Newfoundland waters.) So many of these papers bear Wm. Stratton's signature, and he is so often called "of Boston," that there seems to be no question of his being Bartholomew's son. The question of great interest is what became of him after 1698 and what became of his sons William[3] and John[3]?

piler has thus far failed to trace any Strattons of the present generation back to them, it is not impossible that this may yet be done through some still undiscovered sources of information.*

---

* In the course of many years of correspondence with Strattons here and abroad, the compiler has come across several families of Strattons who have come more recently to America—who have not been traced back to colonial days here, though a search in Great Britain might show a kinship between them and the earlier emigrants:

Samuel D. Stratton, Willapa, Wash., is a son of John Stratton of Queens Co., N. B., and grandson of Stephen Stratton born in England in 1794. His eight sons and daughters are living in Washington and Oregon.

A John Stratton, born in Wiltshire, England, in 1811 (son of James, Jr., and Charlotte Stratton), settled in Ontario while a young man. Several of his sons settled in the States.

Thomas C. Stratton, son of George and Charlotte Stratton of Montreal, married Caroline, daughter of Dr. Elbridge Simpson of Ashfield, Mass., and Hudson, N. Y. Their children are:

a. Albert Elbridge, Mfg. Chemist, Bronxville, N. Y., served 8 yrs. in 7th Regt., N. G., N. Y., m. Clara I. Reynolds; chn. Helen Esther, Elbridge.
b. May Simpson, m. Asa Wynkoop of Albany; ch. Stratton.
c. Alice Louise.
d. Gerald, Lieut. 7th Regt., N. G., N. Y., m. Bertha MacFarlane.
e. Dorothy Beatrice, m. William Frederick May.
f. Frank Lawrence, m. Nancy Shaw.

Roland Reed Stratton, Littleton, Colo., is only son of Charles J. Stratton, grandson of William J. Stratton (Co. D. 3rd Wis. Regt.) and great-grandson of James Stratton, b. Feb. 14, 1804, in Wiltshire, Eng.

Joseph Stratton, born in 1804 (in England?), was one of the very early settlers of Fort Wayne, Ind., being there in 1835. Had three sons in U. S. Army. His son, Walter Stratton, is Supt. of Sewers in Milwaukee; his grandson, Walter (son of John), is a civil engineer at Mariette, Wis.

Albert J. Stratton of Seattle is son of Richard Y. Stratton of Ontario, and grandson of William and Hannah (Yates) Stratton of Co. Leitram, Ireland.

In Providence, R. I., are Strattons who are grandchildren of a Thomas Stratton, born in 1803 in Co. Leitram, Ire.

In Hingham, Mass., are Strattons who came from Scotland thirty years ago.

Dr. John Roach Straton, noted Baptist divine of Baltimore, is son of Rev. Henry D. Straton and grandson of David Straton of Bannockburn, Scotland.

STRATTONS OF MASSACHUSETTS
SAMUEL STRATTON OF WATERTOWN
(*Chart G, Vol.* I)

"I do not object to a wholesome pride in ancestry." LOWELL.

TO the descendants of Samuel Stratton [1] it is interesting to note that "Elmwood," the home of James Russell Lowell in Cambridge, purchased by his father, Rev. Charles Lowell, from the heirs of Lt.-Gov. Oliver, was by him (Oliver) bought from John, Abigail and Eunice, only surviving children and heirs of John Stratton [4] (*John,*[3] *John,*[2] *Samuel*[1]). From the boundaries of the land and description of the homestead there can be no doubt that this is the land of Samuel Stratton,[1] which, in his will dated **1672**, he left to his son, John Stratton,[2] and it is quite probable that "Elmwood" may be the "mansion house" of the early Stratton wills, though much changed, improved and embellished.

Notice also the following. In the courthouse at Cambridge is an original paper (in package under 1649-1652, secondary package marked "miscellaneous") containing these words:

"Let the honored court know that the traine-band of Watertown have chosen Lieutenant Mason to be our Captain and Sergeant Perse to be our Lieutenant, here is also the names of certain men whom upon this occasion have taken the oath of Fidelity." In the list that follows are the names of Samuel Stratton, Sr., Samuel Stratton, Jr., and John Stratton.*

FIFTH GENERATION

60. HEZEKIAH STRATTON [5] (*Samuel,*[4] *Samuel,*[3] *Samuel,*[2] *Samuel*[1]) was born in Concord, Mass., **Sept. 8, 1714.** He married

---

* In the book on *Military Watertown* this company, or "traine-band," is not mentioned, probably because the compiler did not know of its existence. At the court house the above paper is indexed "List of persons who had taken the oath of fidelity in 1652," and so it is not surprising that the train-band was overlooked.

Dorothy Hubbard in 1737. She was daughter of *Daniel* and *Dorothy (Dakin) Hubbard,* born Mar. 24, 1719, and died May 30, 1768. He was a soldier in the French and Indian war in 1758, marching 128 miles to the relief of Ft. Williams, under Ensign Jonathan Brooks.

Children:—*Born in Concord, Mass.*
- —144 Dorothy,⁶ b. Sept. 26, 1738; m. **Joseph Goodnough,** 1768.
- +145 Josiah,⁶ b. June 7, 1741.
- +146 Daniel,⁶ b. Oct. 13, 1743.
- +147 Hezekiah,⁶ b. July 24, 1746.
- —148 Mary,⁶ b. June 26, 1748.
- —149 Rebecca,⁶ b. May 25, 1750; m. **Isaac Stearns,** 1768.
- —150 Betsey,⁶ b. Mar. 29, 1752.
- —151 Jane,⁶ b. Mar. 28, 1754; m. in Lincoln, **Nathaniel Colborn,** Feb. 26, 1776.
- —152 Sarah,⁶ b. June 28, 1758.
- +153 Nehemiah,⁶ b. June 15, 1759.

61. JONATHAN STRATTON⁵ (*Samuel,*⁴ *Samuel,*³ *Samuel,*² *Samuel*¹) was born in Concord, Mass., June 29, 1716. For full account of him and his children, with copy of his will, and his autograph, see *Vol. I,* p. 197, 200-207.*

Children:—*Born in Weston, Mass.*

—154	Lucy.⁶	+158	Jonathan.⁶
—155	Mary.⁶	+159	Daniel.⁶
—156	Mary.⁶	+160	Isaac.⁶
—157	Beulah.⁶	+161	Elisha.⁶

---

*On page 171, *Vol. I,* of "A Book of Strattons" Jonathan,⁵ son of Samuel and Sarah (Allen) Stratton, is marked by a note as follows: ("This may be the Jonathan who was killed by a falling tree . . . in 1774.") More recent investigation shows that it was not Jonathan but Lieut. Jonas Stratton⁵ (No. 87) who was killed in 1774. That Jonathan⁵ of Weston, who married Dinah Bemis Nov. 1, 1738 (p. 200, *Vol. I*) was son of Samuel and Sarah is now clear. Original deeds show that this Jonathan bought three lots of land in Holden in 1737, '38 and '41. These lots were not far from the land in Rutland bought in 1737 by his father Samuel,⁴ where he and Sarah lived to a good old age, honored and respected citizens. Sarah died Mar. 15, 1789, at the home of her daughter, Mrs. Watson, aged 99 yrs. 10 mos. and 19 days. Jonathan sold all his holdings in Holden in 1743 and thereafter was identified with Weston for more than half a century. Deeds show, also, that his older brother, Thomas, bought a lot in Rutland, which he sold in 1737. What became of Thomas after this date is not known.

—162 Sarah.⁶
—163 Elizabeth.⁶
+164 John.⁶
—165 Braddyl.⁶

64. SAMUEL STRATTON⁵ (*Samuel*,⁴ *Samuel*,³ *Samuel*,² *Samuel*¹) was born in Concord, Feb. 1, 1721. He went to Rutland and there married **Mary Eaton**, daughter of *Samuel Eaton* of Sudbury. The "Intention of marriage" was published in Rutland Nov. 15, 1749. He bought a farm in Rutland and built a house, where he lived the remainder of his life. In 1794 he sold the farm to his son Alpheus. He and his sons were among the substantial, respected citizens of the town. He died July 18, 1809. His wife died Jan. 18, 1819, aged 90 years.

Children:—*Born in Rutland, Mass.*
+166 Ebenezer,⁶ b. Nov. 2, 1751.
—167 Ruth,⁶ b. Dec. 24, 1753; m. **Samuel Herring**, June 18, 1784.
+168 David,⁶ b. Apr. 20, 1756.
—169 Mary,⁶ b. Aug. 17, 1758; m. **Calvin Killborne**, Oct. 9, 1783.
—170 Relief,⁶ b. Feb. 13, 1761; m. **Jeremiah Morse**, of Holden, July 1, 1781.
+171 Samuel,⁶ b. Dec. 2, 1763.
+172 Alpheus,⁶ b. May 30, 1769.
+173 Thomas,⁶ b. Jan., 1772.
—174 Sarah,⁶ b. Apr. 30, 1776.

Did they have, also, a son Asa, b. June 1, 1766? If so, what became of him?

68. EBENEZER STRATTON⁵ (*Hezekiah*,⁴ *Samuel*,³ *Samuel*,² *Samuel*¹) was born in Northfield, Mass., Dec. 1, 1718. He was a soldier in King George's war, and in 1749 was Captain in charge of Fort Colevain. He served in the French and Indian war, where he did good service in Col. William Williams' regiment in 1758. He married **Tamer Allen**, June, 1752. He was selectman in Northfield in 1769. His wife died July 23, 1797. He died Nov. 29, 1801. His will is recorded at Northampton.*

---

* Hezekiah Stratton,⁴ who came from Concord to Northfield in about 1713, inherited from his father £111 18s. 9d., and from his mother £18 8s. 10d.

In the terrible struggles with the Indians in 1747-1750 no men of Northfield took a more active, brave and intelligent part than the sons of Hezekiah. The names of Ensign Samuel Stratton, Lieut. Hezekiah Stratton, Capt. Eleazer Stratton, Capt. Ebenezer Stratton, Ensign John

Children:—Born in *Northfield, Mass.*

—175 Hannah,[6] b. Mar. 17, 1753; d. Oct. 29, 1733; m. **Samuel Healy.**
—176 Elizabeth,[6] b. Oct. 21, 1754; m. **Nathaniel Steames,** Feb. 23, 1778.
—177 Asseneth,[6] b. Aug. 17, 1756; m. 1st, **Selah Morton,** Jan. 10, 1791; m. 2nd, **Elisha Lane.**
—178 Tamer,[6] b. Mar. 25, 1758; d. July 17, 1759.
—179 Tamer,[6] b. Mar. 28, 1760; d. aged 2 years.
+180 Ebenezer,[6] b. Feb. 14, 1762.
—181 Martha,[6] b. Apr. 30, 1764; d. Aug. 19, 1767.
—182 Calvin,[6] b. Aug. 9, 1769. Was in the war of 1812; m. **Sarah Cushman,** d. of *Consider Cushman.* Kept tavern at mouth of Miller's River. She m. 2nd, Capt. Howes. She had a son Albah. Was he by 1st marriage, or 2nd?

69. Ensign SAMUEL STRATTON [5] (*Hezekiah,*[4] *Samuel,*[3] *Samuel,*[2] *Samuel* [1]) was born in Northfield Feb. 8, 1720. He served his country in the French and Indian war, and was known as Ensign Samuel Stratton. He settled in Vernon, Vt., where he bought a large tract of land which was occupied by himself and his descendants for six generations. The earliest deed to land in that section was made to Ensign Stratton in 1749, "in His Majesty's Reign, King George II." "As an intrepid and courageous man Ensign Stratton was well calculated to cope with the hardships and dangers incident to a pioneer's life." He married **Ruth Wright,** daughter of B*enoni Wright.* She died in Vernon, Dec. 16, 1800, aged 61 years. He died in 1803. Both are buried in Whithed burial ground, at Vernon. A collection of thirty-five "Deeds of Land" to him, amounting to nearly 2,000 acres, are in possession of his descendants. An oil portrait, taken in his advanced years, is an heirloom treasured by the family. (See Frontispiece.*)

Stratton, Lieut. Asa Stratton appear again and again in the history of these troublous times. They were among the true heroes of the day and their brave conduct did much to keep up the spirits of the garrison at Northfield, to inspire confidence and give a sense of safety. They were among the first to offer their services in every perilous undertaking.

*Permission to reproduce this portrait for *A Book of Strattons* was kindly given the author by Mr. Frank W. Cone of Boston, a descendant of Ensign Stratton.

Child:—*Born in Vernon.*
+183 John,[6] b. June 28, 1756.

71. ELEAZER STRATTON[5] (*Hezekiah,*[4] *Samuel,*[3] *Samuel,*[2] *Samuel*[1]) was born in Northfield Apr. 30, 1722. With his father and brother he served in the French and Indian war. He married Lydia Allen, daughter of *Caleb Allen,* granddaughter of *Edward Allen,* who was one of the founders of Suffield, Conn. They lived for a short while at Endfield, Conn., and then returned to Northfield. She died Apr. 13, 1783, aged 56 years, and he died six years later, Sept. 24, 1789.

Children:—*Born in Northfield, Mass.*
+184 Caleb,[6] b. Feb. 24, 1753.
—185 Submit,[6] b. Sept. 8, 1755; m. 1st, **Asa Briggs**; 2nd, **Wm. Maltby, Esq.**
+186 Asa,[6] b. 1758.
—187 Eliphalet,[6] b. Jan. 8, 1760; served in the Revolution; marched on an alarm Apr. 22, 1776; served until Sept. 30, 1777. "Statue 5 ft. 9 in., dark complection." m. **Elizabeth Stebbins**, daughter of *Joseph Stebbins* of Deerfield. No record of children.
+188 Eleazer,[6] b. Jan., 1762.
—189 Lydia,[6] b. Feb. 29, 1767; m. **James Knox**, Feb. 2, 1786.
—190 Sarah,[6] b. July 2, 1769; m. **Elisha Pomroy**.

72. HEZEKIAH STRATTON[5] (*Hezekiah,*[4] *Samuel,*[3] *Samuel,*[2] *Samuel*[1]) was born in Northfield Jan. 17, 1724. He was Selectman at Northfield, 1772 to 1777, and 1780 to 1787. Served on Committee of Correspondence, and was appointed to "look after the families of soldiers." He married **Mary Smith**, daughter of *Deacon Samuel Smith*. He died Jan. 25, 1800. His will is recorded at Northampton. His widow married Simon Lyman, and died Dec. 24, 1824, aged 91 years.

Children:—*Born in Northfield, Mass.*
—191 Elijah,[6] b. July 24, 1751; a Revolutionary soldier; a physician; m. **Abigail Stebbins**, daughter of *Joseph Stebbins.*
—192 Sarah,[6] b. Dec. 26, 1752; d. Aug. 25, 1770.
+193 Rufus,[6] b. Mar. 19, 1755.
—194 Mary,[6] b. Sept. 17, 1757; m. **Eldad Alexander**, Mar. 18. 1783.
—195 Eunice,[6] b. Jan. 9, 1760; m. **Medad Alexander**.

—196 Jerusha,⁶ b. June 9, 1760; m. **Simeon Alexander**, Mar. 2, 1780.
—197 Rhodah,⁶ b. Oct. 18, 1761; m. **Henry Field**, Feb. 3, 1783.
+198 Hezekiah,⁶ b. Jan. 26, 1766.
—199 Samuel,⁶ b. Apr. 11, 1773; d. aged 3 years.
—200 Cynthia Woody,⁶ adopted daughter; bapt. July 27, 1783.

81. JOSEPH STRATTON ⁵ (*Joseph,⁴ Samuel,³ Samuel,² Samuel¹*) was born in Concord, Mass., Nov. 18, 1717. Mar. 4th, 1740, he married **Elizabeth Dudley**. He died Dec. 7, 1754. His will is recorded in Cambridge. The administration of his estate names but four children.

Children:—*Born in Concord, Mass.*
—201 Elizabeth,⁶ b. July 17, 1742; m. **Daniel Cray**, of Concord, Feb. 1, 1763.
—202 Joseph,⁶ b. Jan. 10, 1744; d. Aug. 26, 1746.
—203 Lucy,⁶ b. Aug. 1, 1749; m. —— **Dudly**.
—204 Sarah,⁶ b. Apr. 17, 1750; m. **Reuben Hodgman**.
—205 Joseph,⁶ b. May 7, 1753; m. **Sarah Whitmore** May 23, 1780, who married again after his death; d. in Concord Nov. 16, 1784; child, Joseph,⁷ b. Dec. 4, 1781, in Concord.

83. NATHAN STRATTON ⁵ (*Joseph,⁴ Samuel,³ Samuel,² Samuel¹*) was born in Concord "Feb. ye 15 day 1722." Oct. 27, 1748, he married **Hannah Brooks**, daughter of *Job* and *Elizabeth Brooks*. She died in Concord May 7, 1750. He seems to have been still living in Concord in 1756 and 1757 when he deeded land to Thos. Fox and Benjamin Pratt. The compiler failed to find later information of him.

87. JONAS STRATTON ⁵ (*Joseph,⁴ Samuel,³ Samuel,² Samuel,¹*) was born in Concord Sept. 18, 1732. He married **Elizabeth Hartwell** of Lincoln, Sept. 3, 1764. He was in the French and Indian war, Corporal in 1755, 1st Lieut., 1760-1762. In 1774 he was killed by a falling tree near Concord.*

Children:—*Born in Concord, Mass.*

---

* A recently found paper among Concord administrations is this:
To the Honʳ. Samuel Danforth Esq, judge of Probate for the County of Middlesex. This is to Inform your Honʳ. That my husband was

—206 Lydia,⁶ b. June 21, 1769; m. **Caleb Campbell** of New Ipswich, Apr. 22, 1794.
+207 Jonas,⁶ b. Aug. 20, 1771.

90. JOHN STRATTON ⁵ (*Joseph,⁴ Samuel,³ Samuel,² Samuel¹*) was born in Concord, Feb. 3, 1740. Dec. 1, 1768, he married **Ruth Wright** of Concord. He was in the Revolution in 1780 and in 1781 enlisted for three years. He died in Concord Feb. 18, 1785. What became of his family after his death?
Children:—*Born in Concord, Mass.*
—208 Abigail,⁶ b. Feb. 30, 1769.
—209 Hannah,⁶ b. Feb. 26, 1771.
—210 John,⁶ b. Oct. 21, 1772.

93. RICHARD STRATTON ⁵ (*Ichabod,⁴ Samuel,³ Samuel,² Samuel¹*) was born in Chelmsford, Mass., June 21, 1712. He bought land in Brookfield in 1733. Dec. 21, 1737, he married **Mary (Dormer?)** and settled in Warren (Western), where he lived until 1760, when he moved to Williamstown, where he bought land and built a house which is still standing. He was deacon in the Baptist church.
Children:—*Born in Warren, Mass.*
+211 Isaac,⁶ b. Nov. 25, 1739.
+212 Daniel,⁶ b. July 9, 1743.
+213 Ebenezer,⁶ b. Dec. 15, 1745.
—214 Ruth,⁶ b. Feb. 29, 1747; m. **William Foster**.
—215 Abner,⁶ b. Dec. 20, 1751; d. before 1769.
—216 Lucy,⁶ b. July 10, 1753; m. **Seth Luce,** son of Ebenezer Luce.
—217 Rachel,⁶ b. Aug. 13, 1756, twin.
—218 Phœbe,⁶ b. Aug. 13, 1756, twin.
+219 David,⁶ b. June 14, 1759.

95. FRANCIS STRATTON ⁵ (*Ichabod,⁴ Richard,³ Samuel,² Samuel¹*) was born in Chelmsford, Mass., Dec. 8. He served in the Revolutionary War as Corporal in 1776 and Sergeant in 1778. He married **Eunice Corley**, Apr. 29, 1740.

Killed by a falling tree at a place called Eleclzander about a Fortnight agoe and I Desire your Honʳ. would Put Capt. Eleazer Brooks of Lincoln administrator to my husband Jonas Stratton Decesed Estate.
               ELIZABETH STRATTON.
Test SAMUEL HARTWELL
 Concord, July 4, 1774.

Children:—Born in Herdwick, Mass.
—220 Sarah,⁶ b. Feb. 4, 1741.
—221 Martha,⁶ b. June 19, 1743.
—222 Eunice,⁶ b. Aug. 18, 1746.
Born in Warren, Mass.
—223 Thankful,⁶ b. Nov. 21, 1748.
+224 John,⁶ b. Jan. 4, 1755.

97. ICHABOD STRATTON ⁵ (*Ichabod,⁴ Richard,³ Samuel,² Samuel¹*) was born, Jan. 11, 1722, in Chelmsford, Mass. He married, first, **Abigail Church** of Hadley, Oct. 8, 1743, second, **Hannah Goodman** (or **Goodnough**), July 1, 1755. His name appears on a folio at Bennington dated 1754, but he returned to Hardwick and probably lived there until after 1777 and then settled in Vermont. He was living at Rutland, Vt., in 1790.
Children:—Born in Hardwick, Mass.
By first marriage.
+225 Asa,⁶ b. July 15, 1744 (bapt. July 22).
—226 Elihu,⁶ b. Feb. 25, 1746.
—227 John,⁶ b. Apr. 20, 1748.*
—228 Mary,⁶ b. Feb. 2, 1750.
By second marriage.
+229 Jonathan,⁶ b. Apr. 6, 1756.
—230 Abigail,⁶ b. Apr. 9, 1757.
+231 Joel,⁶ b. Oct. 16, 1758.

99. DAVID STRATTON ⁵ (*Ichabod,⁴ Richard,³ Samuel,² Samuel¹*) was born Apr. 5, 1728. His birth is recorded at Brookfield, and he is probably the David who was in Brookfield in 1764, with wife **Martha** and children Ann and Martha. He is supposed to have settled in Vermont, but the writer has failed to find any later record of him.

101. JOSHUA STRATTON ⁵ (*John,⁴ John,³ John² Samuel¹*) was born Nov. 14, 1722, at Cambridge, Mass. Apr. 6, 1749, he married **Mercy Coolidge**, who died within a year. He died three

---

* The author found a James Stratton, b. in Ohio (Ashtabula Co.?) abt. 1800; m. **Mary Losie** in 1827 and d. in Minnesota in 1869, who is thought to be a son of John,⁶ son of Ichabod. A family record gives his children: Rowena Charity (b. 1829; m. Richard **Shephard,** in 1847), Riley, Hiram, Albert, John, Martin, and Emma. Perhaps some reader may be able to supply more exact data.

years later. Stones mark their graves in Arlington Cemetery. His estate was administered by Joseph Coolidge.

105. JOHN STRATTON⁵ (*John*,⁴ *John*,³ *John*,² *Samuel*¹) was born in Cambridge, Mass., Oct. 14, 1732. He married **Mary Coolidge**, Sept. 28, 1752, Rev. Seth Storer officiating. She was daughter of *Nathaniel* and *Grace* (*Bowman*) *Coolidge*, born in 1734. She died in Cambridge, Nov. 2, 1814, aged 81 years. Nathaniel Coolidge was born in Watertown in 1702 and was son of *Richard Coolidge*. Dec. 29, 1753, John and Mary Stratton "Owned ye covenant" in the church at Cambridge. He died in Cambridge in June, 1787.

Children:—*Born in Cambridge, Mass.*
—232 Joshua,⁶ b. Dec. 29, 1753;. d. in 1754.
—233 Nathaniel,⁶ b. Dec. 14, 1755; m. Susannah Champney; d. in Cambridge, July 7, 1827; child, John,⁷ b. 1792. What became of him?
—234 Lucy,⁶ bapt. April 29, 1759; m. Jan. 11, 1798, **Rev. Clement A. Sumner** of Keene and rec'd letter from the Cambridge church to the church at Keene.
—235 Susannah,⁶ b. Dec. 2, 1760; m. **Major John Palmer**, Nov. 23 1781.
—236 William,⁶ b. July 4, 1762.*
+237 Richard Coolidge,⁶ b. Feb. 28, 1766.
—238 Isaac,⁶ b. Feb. 20, 1770.
—239 Mary,⁶ bapt. Nov. 10, 1771.

112. JOHN STRATTON⁵ (*Ebenezer*,⁴ *John*,³ *John*,² *Samuel*¹) was born in Cambridge in 1727.. He married **Mercy Narcross**, May 3, 1750. They were both received into full membership in the church at Cambridge April 5, 1751. They lived on the south side of Charles river, called "Little Cambridge," which, in 1807, became the town of Brighton and is now Ward 25 of the city of Boston. His will is recorded at E. Cambridge, made Nov. 25, 1791; proved Dec. 7 of the same year. It mentions only daughter Abigail, son-in-law Silas Robins, children of daughter

---

* The writer has found three mentions of William Strattons in the Revolution, but cannot definitely place any of them. William Stratton of Woburn is said to have died at Ticonderoga in 1776. In 1778 William Stratton, a soldier, was detailed from 1st Cambridge Co. as guard. When the brig *Phœnix* at Boston was taken by the British, July 1781, a William Stratton was among the men made prisoners.

Mercy, and "my good friend Nathaniel Champney" to whom he gave one-half the estate.

Children:—*Born in Cambridge.**

—240 Mary (or Mercy),[6] b. 1752; m. Silas Robins, May 7, 1772.
—241 Abigail,[6] bapt. May 11, 1755; m. William Richards of Dedham, Oct. 27, 1774.
—242 Lydia,[6] bapt. Feb. 27, 1757; prob. d. in childhood.
—243 John,[6] bapt. Apr. 13, 1759. Did he die in infancy?

114. ABIJAH STRATTON [5] (*Jabez,*[4] *John,*[3] *John,*[2] *Samuel*[1]) was born in Watertown, Mass., May 4, 1726, and died in Sherborn March 16, 1769. June 3, 1747, he was married to **Mary Learned** by Rev. G. Porter, and settled in Natick. He served in the Revolution. In the administration of his estate, Apr. 11, 1769, only two sons are mentioned, Abijah, "oldest son," and Daniel. March 15, 1775, his widow married Capt. Thomas Savin of Natick.

Children:—*Born in Natick, Mass.*

—244 Jonathan,[6] b. Oct. 28, 1748; d. Oct. 6, 1756.
—245 Abigail,[6] m. —— Warren.
+246 Abijah,[6] b. Apr. 10, 1751.
+247 Daniel,[6] b. Sept. 28, 1753.
—248 Samuel,[6] b. May 27, 1756; d. Aug. 24, 1757.
—249 Elizabeth,[6] m. —— Adams.

115. NATHAN STRATTON [5] (*Jabez,*[4] *John,*[3] *John,*[2] *Samuel*[1]) was born in Watertown, Mass., Oct. 7, 1726. He bought land in Sherborn in 1748, and purchased other lands there in 1755, 1756, 1761 and 1769. He died in Sherborn Feb. 7, 1805. He married, Apr. 12, 1760, **Mary Boleyn** (written also Bullen), daughter of *Ruth (Morse)* and *Ephraim Boleyn, Jr.* They settled on the farm left her by her father on Chestnut Brook. She died in 1810, aged 81 years.

Child:—*Born in Sherborn.*

+250 Nathan, Jr.,[6] b. May 1, 1761.

---

* Prior to 1780 the little church at Cambridge Village, or "Little Cambridge" (later known as Third Church), was supplied by ministers from Cambridge, Watertown, Boston and other towns. These ministers usually recorded the baptisms in their own books, hence we find the baptisms of John Stratton's children on the books of these towns, although he lived all the time in Cambridge Village. Nathaniel Champney, son of Solomon, came to live with John Stratton when he was seven years old and became as a son to the family.

116. ELIAS STRATTON⁵ (*Jabez,⁴ John,³ John,² Samuel¹*) was born in Watertown, Mass., Oct. 22, 1730. In 1757 his name was on the alarm list in the French and Indian war. He married Millicent —— in 1754, and settled in Athol, Mass., about 1775. The date of her death is not known. The early records of Athol were destroyed by fire. In Sherborn, in 1761, he was a "house wright." He married, second, Mar. 25, 1796, widow **Joanna Brooks**. He died Oct. 4, 1796, and was buried on that part of his own farm which later became a public cemetery.

Children:—*Born in Sherborn, Mass.*
—251 Millicent,⁶ b. 1755.
—252 Sarah,⁶ b. 1757.
+253 Ebenezer,⁶ b. Aug. 27, 1759.
+254 Elias,⁶ b. Dec. 20, 1761.
—255 Jonathan,⁶ b. Jan., 1765; m. **Ruth Foster**, Nov. 10, 1788; went to Ithaca or Sangerfield, N. Y., and then to Penn. Had a son who was a teacher in San Francisco.
—256 Hannah,⁶ b. 1766; m. **John Stone**, a Revolutionary soldier.
+257 Joseph,⁶ b. July 11, 1768.
+258 Jabez,⁶ b. Apr. 2, 1770.
—259 Abigail,⁶ b. 1772; m. **Josiah Stebbins**, July 27, 1797.
—260 Mary,⁶ b. 1773; m. **Bezabel Gleason**, Feb. 22, 1795.

119. JONATHAN STRATTON⁵ (*Jonathan,⁴ Joseph,³ John,² Samuel¹*) was born in Marlboro, Mass., Sept. 29, 1742. He married **Abigail Barnes**, Sept. 10, 1765, daughter of *Jonathan* and *Rachel Barnes*.* He was the administrator of his mother's estate, Mar. 11, 1794. Abigail, widow of Jonathan Stratton, died in Marlboro, Dec. 30, 1794. In 1800 a suit against Wm. Boyd was withdrawn "because Jonathan Stratton was dead."

Children:—*Born in Marlboro, Mass.*
—261 Abigail,⁶ b. Sept. 22, 1766; d. June 11, 1771.
—262 Jonathan,⁶ b. Feb. 8, 1769. What became of him?
—263 Abigail,⁶ b. Nov. 27, 1771.
—264 Aaron,⁶ b. Nov. 16, 1773. (This may be the Col. Aaron Stratton who, with his wife **Lavina**, was living in Kentucky in 1814.

---

* Her brother, Rev. Jonathan Barnes, was the first minister and one of the first settlers of Hillsboro, N. H.

+265 Moses,⁶ b. Nov. 16, 1776.
—266 Sarah,⁶ m. Moses Eager, Dec. 29, 1793 (another record says she married —— **Payne** and settled in Conn.).
+267 Lemuel,⁶ b. Nov. 9, 1779.
+268 Samuel,⁶ b. Sept. 6, 1781.
—269 Lydia,⁶ b. Apr. 20, 1785; m. **William Hadden**.
—270 Anna,⁶ b. Aug. 27, 1787; a teacher in Charlestown, became the 2nd wife of **Dr. Reuben Hatch** of Hillsboro, N. H.
—271 Phœbe,⁶ b. Feb. 27, 1790; m. **Isaac Saltmarsh** of Antrim, N. H., Nov. 13, 1808.

122. SAMUEL STRATTON⁵ (*Jonathan,*⁴ *Joseph,*³ *John,*² *Samuel*¹) was born in Marlboro, Mass., Dec. 30, 1748. He lived in Marlboro and Southboro. He married **Lucy Brigham**, daughter of *Joseph* and *Comfort (Biglow) Brigham.** She was born in Marlboro Aug. 19, 1752. In 1794 he signed a paper releasing any farther interest in dower estate of his mother, Betty (Brigham) Stratton.

Children:—B*irths recorded in Marlboro.*
+272 Winsor.⁶
—273 Jonah Brigham,⁶ b. March 20, 1771. What became of him?
—274 Lucy,⁶ b. Sept. 13, 1772; m. **Winsor Morse**, May 2, 1792.
—275 Elizabeth,⁶ b. Sept. 11, 1774; m. **Moses Temple**, July 14, 1793.

128. SAMUEL STRATTON⁵ (*Samuel,*⁴ *Samuel,*³ *John,*² *Samuel*¹) settled in Natick about 1766, where he owned a mill and later bought other land. He was a soldier in the Revolution, at the battle of Bunker Hill and later enlisted in Capt. Nathaniel Wade's Co. He married **Beulah Parker** of Needham, Feb. 28, 1763. He and his sons Samuel, Jr., James and Elijah were brickmakers in Natick. He died Aug. 26, 1801.†

---

*Comfort Biglow's father, John Biglow, was taken captive by the Indians and held for some time. After his liberation he named his first daughter Comfort, and his second Freedom.

† March 18, 1766, the selectmen of Natick warned out Samuel Stratton, Jr., his wife Beulah and one child called Elijah, who came from Needham in April 1765. After this "warning out" Samuel Stratton, Jr., and his

Children:—*Born in Needham, Mass.*
+276 Elijah,⁶ b. July 15, 1764.
  Born in Natick, Mass.
—277 Sarah,⁶ b. Sept. 13, 1765; m., Oct. 27, 1784, **Nathan Stratton,** her second cousin.

---

family continued to live in Natick for about forty years, respected, well-to-do people, owning three tracts of land.

This "warning out" was simply a legal notice that they had recently come into the town and not yet been officially recognized as citizens.

Samuel Stratton⁴ (No. 46, *Vol. I*) of Watertown was a miller and in 1759 he bought "37 acres and a grist mill" in Natick. To the compiler there seems no reason to doubt that the Samuel Stratton who settled in Natick four years later was his son, born in Watertown June 29, 1739.

There was, however, another Samuel Stratton at this time whom the compiler has not been able to place, even after years of research. Perhaps some reader can give some clew to his parentage.

He was in Brookfield in 1769 and there married **Sarah Parker** Nov. 30, 1769. To them were born in Brookfield, Aug. 28, 1770, twins, Sallie, who m. **John Reese** in 1763, and Samuel, Jr. This Samuel, Jr., married in Worcester, Jan. 1, 1799, **Betsey Smith,** and settled in Craftsbury, Vt., the same year. The house which he built about 1806 is still standing in a good state of preservation. He was a well-to-do farmer. After the death of his wife (April 16, 1841, aged 61 years) he married **Martha Harrington.** He died Oct. 28, 1857. Following are his descendants, some of whom are still living in Craftsbury. His gravestone gives dates of birth and death. Children:

1. Samuel, b. July 25, 1800; m. **Abigail Harrington.**
    A. Horace D., m. Elizabeth **Ramwold.**
        a. Arthur, res., Craftsbury.
        b. Fannie.
2. Asa, b. 1802; left home while a young man, was a teacher in Alabama, several years before the Civil War.
3. Eliza, d. unm.
4. Horace, b. May 18, 1806; m. **Abigail** Chase June 2, 1831; d. April 4, 1897.
    A. Edwin Smith, b. 1833, m. **Ann S. Cass.**
        a. Carlton Cass, m. Augusta **Gage,** 1882.
            (1) Carlton Cass, Jr.
            (2) Samuel Wesley.
        b. Elmer Chase, m. Belle Davidson, 1883.
    B. Samuel, m. Sarah **Cramer,** d. in Bell Plain, N. J.
        a. Horace, res., Pleasantville, N. J.
        b. Maurice, res., Ocean View, N. J.
        c. Mary Ellen, m. **Jerry Hampton.**
        d. Cordelia, m. **Charles Lee.**
        e. Etta E.
    C. Mary E., m. **J. S. Warren,** 1865; res., Morrisville, Vt.
5. Maria, m. Henry Whitney; d. in Craftsbury.

—278 Beulah.⁶
+279 Samuel.⁶
—280 Lydia.⁶
—281 James,⁶ b. Aug. 27, 1774; m. Abigail ——, who died in Natick, Sept. 16, 1823; child, Anna,⁷ b. Feb. 14, 1799.
—282 Betsey.⁶
—283 David.⁶
—284 Anna,⁶ m. **Jabez White**.

6. Daniel, b. 1812, m. **Mary Scott**; d. in Johnson, Vt., 1857.
   A. Emeline, m. and moved West.
   B. Hiram, a Baptist minister.
   C. Jane, m. **George Bagley**.
7. William, b. 1814; m. **Mary Ellen Powers**; d. in Craftsbury, 1880.
   A. Asa Powers, b. 1849.
8. Lucy, b. 1816, m. **Jefferson Robbins**.

Then, the compiler has also the following records from an old family Bible of a Samuel Stratton who was born Dec. 10, 1769—no place given. There is a tradition among his descendants that he was the son of a Samuel Stratton who was killed at the Battle of Bunker Hill. He married **Naomi Emery** March 5, 1789; married, second, Lois Daniels Feb. 1809. Children:

By First Marriage.
1. Lydia, b. Apr. 8, 1790
2. Pheneus, b. May 15, 1792
3. Stephen, b. July 20, 1794
4. Sarah, b. May 15, 1797
5. Samuel, b. Mar. 1, 1801
6. John (twin), b. Mar. 1, 1801
7. Jacob, b. Mar. 26, 1803
8. Adah, b. Aug. 12, 1805
9. Nathaniel, b. Sept. 17, 1807

By Second Marriage.
10. Susan, b. Dec. 16, 1812
11. William, b. Aug. 7, 1814
12. Ephraim, b. June 11, 1817
13. Abigail, b. Apr. 8, 1819
14. Lois, b. Apr. 18, 1821
15. Elias, b. Apr. 23, 1823
16. Jonathan, b. Dec. 30, 1824
17. Enoch (twin), b. Dec. 3, 1824
18. Theodore, b. Mar. 25, 1826
19. Sarah, b. Oct. 2, 1828

2. Pheneus (b. May 15, 1792) was a soldier in the War of 1812. He married **Susanna** —— Nov. 20, 1817 and moved first to Allegany Co., N. Y., later to Potter Co., Pa., then to Onondaga Co., N. Y., and about 1836 to Barren Co., Mich. Children:
   Samuel, b. Nov. 19, 1818; m. **Eliza Whitman**.
   Nathaniel, b. Oct. 31, 1819; m. **Mary Murdock**.
   John H., b. Nov. 9, 1821; m. **Martha Miller**.
   Emeline, b. March 7, 1823; m. **John Manly**, near Buffalo.
   Sarah Ann, b. July 21, 1824; m. **Henry Pike**.
   James, b. June 4, 1825; m. **Elizabeth Abley**.
   Ephraim, b. Sept. 1, 1829; m. **Margaret Carson**; d. in Chicago.
   Charles D., b. June 8, 1833; d. unm.
   Henry, b. Jan. 1, 1835; m. **Emma** ——.
   Mary, b. April 7, 1848; m. **Fred Abley**; residence, Hemmingford, Neb.
   William Emery, d. in childhood.

131. NATHANIEL STRATTON [5] (*Samuel,*[4] *Samuel,*[3] *John,*[2] *Samuel*[1]) was born in Watertown, Oct. 16, 1748. This is probably the Nathaniel Stratton who, as one of Capt. Josiah Parker's Co., joined the army of Ticonderoga and received "travel expense" of £10 18s. He is thought to have settled in New Hampshire or Vermont.

134. JOHN STRATTON [5] (*Enoch,*[4] *Samuel,*[3] *Richard,*[2] *Samuel*[1]) was born in Weston, Mass., May 4, 1725. He married **Mary** —— and settled with his father's family in Glastonbury, Conn., where he bought land in 1757, and where he died in 1761. Apr. 1, 1759, he enlisted in the French and Indian war, serving 37 weeks. Enlisted again in 1760 and for his service in this year he was to receive £11 19s, but he died before the amount was paid. The administration of his estate is recorded in Hartford.
Children:
—285 John,[6] b. 1753.
—286 Lemuel,[6] b. May, 1755; served in Revolution, Aug. and Sept., 1776.
—287 Rebecca,[6] b. Feb., 1757; m. David **Andrews**.
—288 Mary,[6] b. March, 1759.

136. SAMUEL STRATTON [5] (*Enoch,*[4] *Richard,*[3] *Samuel,*[2] *Samuel*[1]) was born in Concord, Mass., Nov. 6, 1728. He went to Connecticut and married **Mehitable (Hollister)**, her second husband. He was in Eastbury in 1752, where he subscribed £2 for the support of his pastor. In 1757 he bought land in Glastonbury. He married, second, **Mrs. Sarah Bidwell**, who died Aug. 26, 1822, aged 88 years. Samuel died Aug. 7, 1810.
Children:—*Born in Glastonbury.*
+289 Samuel,[6] b. 1758; d. in Glastonbury, 1807.
—290 Ann,[6] m. Jacob **Stevens**.
—291 Isaac,[6] b. 1763; d. aged 22 years.
—292 Hannah,[6] m. Roger **Hollister**, Oct. 11, 1792. Settled at Marietta, Ohio.

---

12. Ephraim (b. June 11, 1817) married Elizabeth —— March 11, 1842, and settled in Barrington, N. H. Children:
Amanda.
Sarah.
Samuel C., d. in childhood.
Elizabeth H., d. in childhood.
Henrietta.
Henry (twin).
Samuel C., residence, Barrington, N. H. (Dover R. F. D.).

+293 William,⁶ b. Mar. 9, 1766.
—294 Ruth,⁶ m., Sept. 6, 1790, **Asa Goodrich**.
—295 Elizabeth,⁶ m. **Roswell Hollister**.

137. ISAAC STRATTON⁵ (*Enoch*,⁴ *Samuel*,³ *Richard*,² *Samuel*¹) married Lucy —— and settled in Glastonbury, Conn., where he bought land in 1757. He was a soldier in the French and Indian war, March, October, 1759, and died in Glastonbury before Dec. 26 of the same year.

Child:—B*orn in Glastonbury, Conn.*
—296 Honour,⁶ m., Mar. 10, 1776, **Hezekiah Wright**.

139. BENJAMIN STRATTON⁵ (*Jabez*,⁴ *Samuel*,³ *Richard*,² *Samuel*¹) was born in Concord, Oct. 24, 1725. He married **Sarah Simmons** of Bedford, May 24, 1750. He was then living in Lexington where his father settled about 1730. In Feb., 1784, he moved to Fairlee, Vermont, with his son, Benjamin Stratton, Jr. Between 1754 and 1784 he seems to have lived in Woburn, Waltham and Roxbury. He was a Revolutionary soldier, answering the alarm, Apr. 19, 1775, and enlisting again in 1776. He died in Fairlee in 1808.

Children:
—297 Sarah,⁶ b. Aug. 24, 1752; d. in Lexington, Jan. 14, 1754.
+298 Benjamin,⁶ b. 1754.
+299 John,⁶ b. 1767.

There may have been other children; if so, the author would be very glad to know of them.

141. JABEZ STRATTON⁵ (*Jabez*,⁴ *Samuel*,³ *Richard*,² *Samuel*¹) was born in Lexington, Mass., Jan. 2, 1733. The church records at Lexington show that he was baptized on the 6th of the same month. He married **Lucy Wooley** of Rutland, Dec. 5, 1758, and lived in Princeton and Greenwich. He enlisted in the Revolutionary army from Greenwich in 1780, "aged 46 years, five feet 10 in., light complexion." The family seem to have left Massachusetts soon after the Revolution.*

---

*It is thought that Jabez⁵ had a brother Isaac, born about 1741, and that this was the Isaac Stratton of Rutland who received a bounty for three years' service in the Revolution. He was about thirty-eight years old in 1779. Also, in the administration in 1770 of the estate of Jabez,⁴ who died in Lincoln about 1745 (see p. 181, Vol. I), "Isaac and Jabez now living in Princeton and John Jones of Concord" were bound to care for the widow, Margaret Stratton (widow of Jabez⁴).

Children:—*Born in Princeton, Mass.*
—300   Jonathan,⁶ b. July 16, 1759.*
—301   Isaac,⁶ b. Nov. 21, 1761.†
+302   Jabez,⁶ b. Sept. 26, 1763.
+303   Samuel,⁶ b. July 6, 1765.
—304   Lucy,⁶ b. 1767.

---

* The compiler believes this to be the Jonathan Stratton of Addison, Vt., who had son David who m. Eunice Biglow in 1803, was a soldier in the War of 1812, and moved to Licking Co., O., about 1818, where he d. in 1862.

Children:—*Born in Addison, Vt.*
Cynthia, b. 1804; m. **John Wheeler.**
James H., b. 1806; m. **Betsey Jett**; d. in Ohio.
David, b. 1808; m. **Adelia Critchett**; d. New Way, O.
Ira, b. 1810; m. **Grace Turner**; d. New Way, O.
Harrison, b. 1818; m. **Clara H. Conger,** 1841; d. in Lutsville, Mich. His children: Mary T., Eunice A., David W., Ezra B., Dennis C., John C., Arletta A.

† This is believed to be the Isaac Stratton who enlisted in the Revolutionary Army from Greenwich in 1781, and in 1784 was at Clarenden, Vt., where he bought twenty-seven acres of land in 1795. He died before 1810. He married **Abigail** ———, who survived him but a short time, dying while the children were still young.

Children:—*Born in Clarenden, Vt.*
Amos, b. Jan. 16, 1784.
Phœbe, b. Nov. 5, 1786; per. m. ——— **Simmons.**
Isaac, b. Oct. 11, 1788.
Hiram, became a minister and settled in New York State.
Ezra, moved to New York State.
Catherine, m. ——— **Sawyer.**
Levi.
Truman.
Orin, b. May 5, 1800; m. **Weatha B. Miller,** Nov. 14, 1821, of Castleton, Vt. Died in Johnson, Vt., Oct. 12, 1882. Their only child was James Albert Stratton, b. in Castleton, Vt., July 8, 1822; m. in 1844, Hannah F. Hayford; lived in Johnson, Hyde Park and Morristown, Vt.; a farmer, also held several town offices; d. in Burlington, Jan. 16, 1913. Children:
Annie E., m. **Loomis G. Terrill**; res., Jericho, Vt.
George E., b. at Hyde Park, Vt., Oct. 5, 1859; m. **Ettie May Allen,** in 1882; d. in Burlington, Nov. 11, 1914, where he was a well-known business man.
Children:
Ralph Orcutt, m. **Ada H. Lehr,** July 12, 1911; chn. Allen L., George E.
Gladys E.
Dorothy H., d. May 5, 1911, aged 18 yrs.
Donald Allen.

There may have been other children, born elsewhere. The descendants of Jabez[6] believe that he had a brother Benjamin who settled at Crown Point, N. Y., and a brother Joseph who lived in Pittsfield, Vt.

145. JOSIAH STRATTON[6] (*Hezekiah,*[5] *Samuel,*[4] *Samuel,*[3] *Samuel,*[2] *Samuel*[1]) married **Mary Davis** of Holden, Oct. 31, 1765, and settled in Holden. At the time of his marriage he was "of Brookfield," and was a miller. April 9, 1775, he was one of Major Paul Raymond's Company that marched from Holden to Cambridge. He was Selectman of Holden in 1782, 1788-9, 1790-1. In 1787 he was representative in General Court.* April 2, 1800, he married **Olive Adams** (widow).

Children:—*Born in Holden, Mass.*
—305   Mary,[7] b. Aug. 15, 1766; d. Sept. 19, 1766.
+306   James,[7] b. July 11, 1767.
+307   Paul,[7] b. Mar. 26, 1769.
+308   Israel,[7] b. Dec. 10, 1770.
—309   John Hubbard,[7] b. Nov. 21, 1772; d. Jan. 21, 1773.
+310   John Hubbard,[7] b. Mar. 26, 1774.
—311   Simon Davis,[7] b. Mar. 1, 1776. What became of him?
+312   Frink,[7] b. Jan. 8, 1778.
—313   Josiah,[7] b. Mar. 29, 1780; m. **Elizabeth Cheney**; d. in Holden in 1883; prob. left no children.
—314   Hezekiah,[7] b. June 4, 1783, of whom the author could learn nothing more.

146. DANIEL STRATTON[6] (*Hezekiah,*[5] *Samuel,*[4] *Samuel,*[3] *Samuel,*[2] *Samuel*[1]) when twenty-three years old bought land in New Ipswich, N. H., on what is now known as Knight's Hill. This farm remained in the possession of his descendants for about one hundred years. He was one of the men who marched from New Ipswich for Cambridge before daylight on the morning of Apr. 20, 1775, on the alarm of the battle of Concord. He married **Sarah Stark**, who died in New Ipswich, July 1, 1784, aged 39 years.† He married, second, **Sarah Warner** in 1785. She died

---

* At Brookfield is recorded the "intention of marriage" of Josiah Stratton and Eliza Wood, July 1763. No record of marriage has been found.

† Sarah Stark, d. of George and Sarah (Wilds) Stark, was born Feb. 4, 1745. She was granddaughter of William and Deborah (Loud) Stark. William was a "mariner resident" of New Ipswich.

Oct. 5, 1825, aged 72 years.* Daniel died in New Ipswich, July 22, 1832.

Children:—*Born in New Ipswich, N. H.*
By first marriage.
- −315   Sarah,[7] b. May 15, 1771; d. May 27, 1790.
- +316   Daniel,[7] b. Mar. 23, 1773.
- +317   John,[7] b. Mar. 28, 1775.
- −318   Asa,[7] b. Nov. 8, 1777; d. in New Ipswich, Nov. 9, 1802, unm.
- −319   Dolly,[7] b. Mar. 16, 1780; d. Oct. 26, 1780.
- −320   Dolly,[7] b. Dec. 1, 1781; m. **Jonathan Weber**, Dec. 21, 1806.
- −321   Lucy,[7] b. Jan. 16, 1784; d. Apr. 29, 1784.

By second marriage.
- +322   William,[7] b. Jan. 17, 1786, a twin.
- −323   Elizabeth,[7] b. Jan. 17, 1786, a twin.
- −324   Lydia,[7] b. Dec. 7, 1787.
- −325   Polly,[7] b. July 5, 1789; d. Apr. 17, 1790.
- +326   Jeremiah.[7]

147. HEZEKIAH STRATTON [6] (*Hezekiah*,[5] *Samuel*,[4] *Samuel*,[3] *Samuel*,[2] *Samuel* [1]) went to Maine where, in 1768, he began clearing a farm in the primeval forest on the banks of the Sebasicook, near a small settlement called Kingsfield, made four years earlier on the Kenebeck. Three years later this settlement was incorporated and named Winslow in honor of Gen. John Winslow. Here besides being a farmer Hezekiah was a hunter and trapper, as were nearly all the early Maine settlers. When Arnold in the fall of 1775, with his one thousand picked men from the army at Cambridge, marched on his expedition against Quebec, he passed through Fort Weston (now Augusta), stopping a day or two to organize for the trip. Here several Winslow men were taken along as guides and helpers. Among these was Hezekiah Stratton. Hezekiah's farm was about sixteen miles north of Fort Western and the expedition passed his home on its way up the river.

July 8, 1776, the town of Winslow called a town meeting at which was appointed a "Committee of Safety." It also voted to

---

*Sarah Warner, b. March 27, 1753, d. of Caleb and Elizabeth (Brown) Warner of "Warner's Mills," New Ipswich. Her ancestry is as follows: Caleb,[5] Daniel,[4] Daniel,[3] Daniel,[2] William Warner,[1] b. in England, settled in Ipswich, Mass., about 1637.

hire three men to go up the river on scout duty to see whether any British force was approaching, and a committee to petition the General Court for defence against Canada. Among the names of the men who served on these committees during the Revolution are Hezekiah Stratton and Zimri Heywood. April 20, 1778, Hezekiah married **Eunice Heywood**, a daughter of *Zimri Heywood.** She was born in 1760 and died in 1836. He died two years later. Gravestones stand to their memory in the family burial ground on the old Stratton farm at Winslow. This farm is still owned and occupied by his descendants.

Children:—*Born in Winslow, Me.*
+327 Samuel,⁷ b. Jan. 20, 1779.
+328 William,⁷ b. May 9, 1781.
—329 Jane,⁷ b. June 29, 1783; m. **Owen Folger Smith** at Hallowell, Me., in 1803.
—330 Hezekiah, Jr.,⁷ b. Mar. 25, 1786; d. unm. Apr. 3, 1821, in Winslow. The young lady whom he was to marry died the day before the day set for the wedding.

153. NEHIMIAH STRATTON ⁶ (*Hezekiah,*⁵ *Samuel,*⁴ *Samuel,*³ *Samuel,*² *Samuel* ¹) served ten weeks in the Continental Army in 1775, and six months in 1776. Jan. 29, 1777, he was in Capt. Josiah Brown's Co., Col. Nathan Hale's Regt., marching from New Ipswich to reinforce the garrison at Ticonderoga, but the regiment was ordered back by Col. Fellows and returned to Rutland. In Aug., 1778, he belonged to a regiment which marched from New Hampshire and joined the Continental Army on Rhode Island. In Jan., 1781, he enlisted as a private for three years, was promoted to a Sergeant, and then became one of Washington's Life Guards, and was honorably discharged in Dec., 1783, on Constitution Island opposite West Point.†

In 1780 he bought land at New Ipswich and was a taxpayer

---

* Zimri Heywood (spelled Howard and Hawood on the Revolutionary War Rolls) was captain of the 6th Co., Lincoln Co. Militia, and later captain of a company in Col. Timothy Healds regiment. He descended from the Heywoods who came from Odell, Eng., in the *Susan & Ellen* and settled in Concord, Mass., in 1635. On the Concord town books the name is variously spelled Heywood, Haywood, Harwood, Howard. He married Jane Foster, lived in Ashburnham, then Lunenburg, and then settled at Winslow.

† To the Honorable E. Thompson, Secretary of State of New Hampshire:
Honorable Sir, in compliance with a clause of an Art. of this state passed the present year, for raising and completing this state's quota of the Continental Army, we have raised in this Town twelve new recruits,

there until 1795. In 1784 he married **Sarah Prichard**. She was born Apr. 17, 1762, and died Jan. 22, 1789. Nehemiah married, second, **Lois Newell**, and in 1789 settled in Albion, Me., on a farm, where as a farmer he spent the remainder of his life. In 1840 he was granted a pension. Mr. Stratton died Nov. 25, 1843. His widow died Dec. 8, 1846, aged 77 years.

Children:—*Born in New Ipswich, N. H.*

By first marriage.

—331   Sarah,[7] b. Feb. 7, 1785; m. **Benjamin Kidder** of Albion and became the mother of 12 children.

—332   Hannah,[7] b. Jan. 17, 1786; m. 1st, **Dr. Sprague** of Boston, 2d, **Stephen Wheeler** of Ipswich.

By second marriage.

+333   Ebenezer,[7] b. June 29, 1788.

Born in Albion, Me.

—334   George,[7] b. Feb. 10, 1790; d. in Pike Co., Ill.; left no heirs.

+335   Charles,[7] b. Dec. 29, 1792.

+336   James,[7] b. Nov. 21, 1794.

—337   Onesimus,[7] b. Nov. 16, 1796; d. aged 17 years.

+338   William,[7] b. 1799.

—339   Nancy,[7] b. Jan. 1, 1801; m. **Joseph Tuck**.

+340   Jonas,[7] b. June 1, 1803.

—341   Roxey,[7] b. Apr. 20, 1805; m. **Benjamin Webb**; went to Ill.

—342   Mehitable,[7] b. Mar. 13, 1807; m. **Joel Miller,** a Universalist minister.

+343   Newell,[7] b. June 2, 1809.

—344   Almond,[7] b. 1811; m. **Sarah Dow**. Lived and died at Searsport, Me. Left a son and daughter of whom information is desired.

---

for three years' service, and they have all passed muster, before Gen. Nichols, at Amherst the first passed was Feb. 14, and the last March 13 (Viz.) Nehemiah Stratton, John Adams, Samuel Walker, Jesse Walker, Peter Bullard, Phineas Adams, Joseph Proctor, Amos Baker, John Bullard, Stephen Adams, Joel Baker, and John Thomas, we expect we have five men in the Continental Army from this Town, but I cannot with safety mention the names at present.

New Ipswich, May 5, 1781. By Order of the Selectment of said N. Ipswich.

BENJAMIN ADAMS, Town Clerk.

Also see Dr. Charles E. Godfrey's *Washington's Life Guards* and records at War Dept. at Washington, D. C.

Stratton Village, Stratton Brook and Biglow Mountain, Maine.
Page 9, Vol I

"Stratton Tavern," a well-known landmark for more than a century at Waltham, Mass., burned to the ground in 1893. *Page 106.*

158. Jonathan Stratton [6] (*Jonathan*,[5] *Samuel*,[4] *Samuel*,[3] *Samuel*,[2] *Samuel*[1]) was born in Weston, Mass. For full account of him see *Vol. I*, p. 207, No. 6.

Children:—*Born in Weston, Mass.*
+345   Shubael,[7] b. Dec. 6, 1768.
—346   Sarah,[7] b. Oct. 20, 1770; m. William Rice.*
+347   Braddyll,[7] b. July 20, 1772.
—348   Relief,[7] b. May 25, 1774; m. **George How.**
—349   Lucy,[7] b. Nov. 7, 1778; d. Oct. 31, 1779.

Born in Gerry (now Phillipston), Mass.
+350   Jonathan,[7] b. Nov. 25, 1780.
+351   Isaac,[7] b. Jan. 10, 1783.
+352   Nathan,[7] b. Dec. 12, 1784.
—353   Mary,[7] b. Oct. 10, 1786.
—354   Susan,[7] b. Jan. 17, 1789; d. Oct. 14, 1817.

159. Daniel Stratton [6] (*Jonathan*,[5] *Samuel*,[4] *Samuel*,[3] *Samuel*,[2] *Samuel*[1]), for full data concerning him, see *Vol. I*, pp. 208, No. 7.

Children:—*Born in Weston, Mass.*
+355   Daniel,[7] b. Apr. 22, 1777.
—356   Elizabeth,[7] b. Nov. 24, 1778; m. **Jeddo Thayer.**
—357   Martha,[7] b. July 31, 1780; m. **Henry Coggin.**
—358   Nancy [7] (twin), b. July 31, 1780; m. **Robert Fiske.**
+359   Josiah,[7] b. Oct. 20, 1782, and was bapt. the same day.
+360   Dana,[7] b. Dec. 13, 1784.
—361   Samuel,[7] b. Dec. 5, 1787.
—362   Myranda,[7] b. May 1, 1790; m. **Enoch Jones.**
—363   Sarah,[7] b. June 24, 1794; d. unm.
—364   Dorcas,[7] b. Aug. 23, 1796; m. **Francis Garfield.**
—365   Calvin,[7] b. Nov. 30, 1798; m. **Martha** —— and d. May 17, 1823, leaving an "only child," Martha Ann.[8]

160. Isaac Stratton [6] (*Jonathan*,[5] *Samuel*,[4] *Samuel*,[3] *Samuel*,[2] *Samuel*[1]) was born in Weston. See *Vol. I*, p. 209, No. 8, for data concerning him, and his children.

---

*It was at the home of Sarah and William Rice in Woodstock, Vt., that Justin Morgan died, the owner of the famous horse "Morgan,"—the head of the Morgan stock of horses. Just before his death he gave the horse to his friends, Mr. and Mrs. Rice. This was in the spring of 1798. The horse "Morgan" died in 1819, at the age of twenty-seven years.

Children:
- —366 Louisa,⁷ b. Dec. 9, 1786; m. **Cyrus Russell**.
- +367 Nahum,⁷ b. 1788.
- —368 Elizabeth,⁷ d. in infancy.
- +369 Henry,⁷ b. Jan. 8, 1792.
- —370 Mary,⁷ m. **Woodbury Hill**.
- —371 Martha,⁷ m. **Samuel Smith**.
- —372 Priscilla,⁷ m. **Daniel Bemis**.
- —373 Louis, d. unm. in Richmond, Va.

161. ELISHA STRATTON⁶ (*Jonathan,⁵ Samuel,⁴ Samuel,³ Samuel,² Samuel¹*). See *Vol. I*, p. 210, No. 9, for full records of him. He died in Weston, Nov. 19, 1817.

Children:—*Born in Weston, Mass.*
- —374 Susan,⁷ b. Oct. 7, 1780; m. **Joseph Cheney**.
- +375 Thomas,⁷ b. Oct. 7, 1782.
- +376 Charles,⁷ b. June 1, 1785.
- —377 Harriet,⁷ b. Jan. 4, 1790; m. **Jonathan F. Hurd**.
- +378 Elisha,⁷ b. Mar., 1795.
- +379 George,⁷ b. June 3, 1798.

164. JOHN STRATTON⁶ (*Jonathan,⁵ Samuel,⁴ Samuel,³ Samuel,² Samuel¹*). See *Vol. I*, p. 211, No. 12, for full data concerning him.

Child—*Born in Weston, Mass.*
- —380 Abigail,⁷ b. Oct. 28, 1791; m. **David Viles**.

166. EBENEZER STRATTON⁶ (*Samuel,⁵ Samuel,⁴ Samuel,³ Samuel,² Samuel¹*) married **Tabitha Davis**, Jan. 11, 1776. They lived for one year after their marriage in Princeton, Mass.; about six years in Jaffrey, N. H., and then moved to Rindge, N. H. He was selectman for seven years. He was a leading Baptist of the town, contributing generously to the support of the church, and preaching was sometimes had at his own house. He died Mar. 22, 1837. His widow died in 1851. His will is recorded at Keene.

Children:—*Born in Princeton, Mass.*
- —381 Ebenezer,⁷ b. July 15, 1777; d. Oct. 8, 1785.
  Born in Jeffrey, N. H.
- +382 Asa,⁷ b. July 25, 1778.
- +383 Josiah,⁷ b. Feb. 24, 1781.

—384 Tabitha,[7] b. 1783; d. 1786.
B*orn in Rindge, N. H.*
—385 Polly,[7] b. 1785; d., unm., 1857.
+386 Ebenezer,[7] b. Mar. 12, 1787; m. **Mary U. Bonner.**
—387 Raymond,[7] b. Apr. 6, 1790; died in New Ipswich, N. H., Sept. 14, 1838; left one daughter, Susan M.,[8] who m. **O. J. Prescott.**
—388 Tabitha,[7] b. 1792; d., unm., 1879.
—389 Samuel,[7] b. Apr. 12, 1795; m. **Louisa Gibson**, daughter of *Reuben Gibson*, in 1818; d. Aug. 21, 1840; children, Julia A.,[8] Emeline,[8] Mary,[8] Lyman.[8]

168. DAVID STRATTON [6] (*Samuel,[5] Samuel,[4] Samuel,[3] Samuel,[2] Samuel[1]*) was a soldier in the Revolution, enlisting "for the war" at Rutland in 1779. In 1786 he married **Mary Leland** and settled in Jeffrey, N. H., where he died in 1837. His widow survived him fourteen years, dying in 1851.

Children:—B*orn in Jeffrey, N. H.*
+390 Samuel,[7] b. 1787.
+391 Isaac,[7] b. 1789.
—392 Nathan,[7] b. about 1795; m. **Susan Carter**, and d. in New York state.
—393 Polly,[7] b. 1797; m. **John Town.**
—394 Jabez,[7] died young.

171. DEACON SAMUEL STRATTON [6] (*Samuel,[5] Samuel,[4] Samuel,[3] Samuel,[2] Samuel[1]*) bought land in Princeton, Mass., and married Nov. 14, 1782, **Martha Davis**, daughter of *Ephraim Davis, Jr.* She was born Jan. 13, 1764, and died in Princeton June 24, 1858. He was a "cord wainer" by trade, a deacon in the church, an influential man in the town. In 1790 he sold fifty-six acres in Princeton to Phelps Davis. In 1808-9 he was a selectman. He died Jan. 13, 1838. A gravestone stands to the memory of Samuel and Martha Stratton at Rutland.

Children:—B*orn in Princeton, Mass.*
+395 John,[7] b. Mar. 31, 1784.
—396 Martha,[7] b. Jan. 25, 1785; d. Jan. 27, 1785.
—397 Patty,[7] b. Feb. 7, 1786; m. **Stephen Stearns**, Sept. 18, 1806.
—398 Sarah,[7] b. Dec. 25, 1788; d. Mar. 13, 1835.
—399 Mary,[7] b. Oct. 1, 1791; d. Oct. 7, 1800.
—400 Nancy,[7] b. June 17, 1802.

—401 Lucy,⁷ b. Sept. 16, 1793; m. Lieut. **Benjamin Roper,** and lived at Hubbardstown, Mass. They were the parents of sixteen children. He died and she married, 2d, Richard Bull.
—402 Samuel,⁷ b. Sept. 4, 1795; d. Nov. 5, 1795.
+403 Samuel,⁷ b. Nov. 24, 1796.
—404 Elizabeth,⁷ b. July 16, 1798; m. **Amos Ball,** Dec. 2, 1819.
—405 Calvin,⁷ b. June 14, 1800; a teacher; d. in Georgia where he settled many years before; married; did he leave children?
—406 Nancy,⁷ b. June 17, 1802; m. **Charles Pratt** of Grafton, Apr. 5, 1825; d. in 1892.
—407 Marianne,⁷ b. Apr. 17, 1805; m. **Edward A. Pratt** of Shrewsbury, Apr. 2, 1827; d. 1868.
—408 Eliza,⁷ b. Nov. 20, 1807; d. 1815.

172. ALPHEUS STRATTON ⁶ (*Samuel,⁵ Samuel,⁴ Samuel,³ Samuel,² Samuel¹*) married Lucy Keys of Princeton, Nov. 26, 1789. In 1794 he bought his father's farm in Rutland, where he lived the rest of his life. He died Nov. 9, 1827. His wife died June 6, 1826, aged 56 years.

Children:—*Born in Rutland, Mass.*
+409 Alpheus,⁷ b. Nov. 4, 1790.
+410 Cyprian,⁷ b. Sept. 8, 1791.
+411 Samuel,⁷ b. Mar. 29, 1793.
—412 Lucy,⁷ b. Mar. 16, 1795; m. **Wm. Henshaw** of Leichester.
—413 Clarissa,⁷ b. Oct. 5, 1796; d. Aug. 28, 1813.
—414 Melissa,⁷ b. Oct. 11, 1798; m. **Abijah Brigham,** Oct. 19, 1817.
—415 Lovina,⁷ b. Nov. 26, 1800; m. **Silas Skinner,** July 3, 1828; d. Mar. 29, 1833.
—416 Harriet,⁷ b. Oct. 2, 1803.
—417 Mary,⁷ b. Apr. 16, 1805; m. **Jacob R. Davis,** Dec. 30, 1824.
—418 Martha,⁷ b. June 18, 1806; d. Sept. 4, 1813.
—419 Ruth,⁷ b. Sept. 23, 1809.
—420 Luke,⁷ b. Aug. 16, 1811.* Is this the Luke Stratton

---

* Feb. 28, 1828, Cyprian Stratton was appointed guardian for Ruth and Luke Stratton and sold two undivided tenths of the estate for their benefit.

of Enfield who married **Julia M. Robinson** at Barre, Aug. 12, 1833?

173. Thomas Stratton[6] (*Samuel,*[5] *Samuel,*[4] *Samuel,*[3] *Samuel,*[2] *Samuel*[1]) was a cord wainer in Holden. He married **Eunice Cutting**, Nov. 20, 1794.
Children:—*Born in Holden, Mass.*
—421 Mary,[7] b. May 28, 1795.
—422 Simon,[7] b. Nov. 23, 1795.
—423 Roxey,[7] b. Oct. 10, 1798.
—424 Charles,[7] b. Dec. 28, 1800; d. Aug. 20, 1801.
—425 Eunice,[7] b. June 28, 1802.
What became of the family after 1802?

180. Ebenezer Stratton[6] (*Ebenezer,*[5] *Hezekiah,*[4] *Samuel,*[3] *Samuel,*[2] *Samuel*[1]) married, first, **Sarah Smith**, daughter of *Reuben Smith*, Feb. 20, 1811. He married, second, **Mrs. McKinze**. He settled in Brookfield, Vt., where he kept a tavern long kept by his descendants. He died Jan. 14, 1814.
Children:—*Born in Brookfield, Vt.*
By first marriage.
—426 Patty,[7] b. July 6, 1784; d. unm.
—427 Sarah,[7] b. Feb. 15, 1789; m. **Luthur Wheatley**.
—428 Alpha,[7] b. Feb. 26, 1792; d. in 1811.
+429 Caleb Allen,[7] b. Dec. 22, 1797.
—430 Harriet,[7] b. Nov. 1, 1800; m. **Jesse Wheatley**.
By second marriage.
—431 Sophrona,[7] b. Oct. 18, 1813; m. **Cyrus Perkins**.

183. John Stratton[6] (*Samuel,*[5] *Hezekiah,*[4] *Samuel,*[3] *Samuel,*[2] *Samuel*[1]) was the only child of Ensign Samuel Stratton. He married **Roxana P. Field**, daughter of *Paul Field* of Northfield. June 1, 1785, while out with a party of young men to spear salmon, he was drowned in the Connecticut River at Bellow's Falls. The following year, Aug. 14, 1786, his widow, Roxana, died, aged 30 years. Their three little daughters were brought up by Mr. Stratton's parents.*

---

*In a small ancient burial ground in Vernon, Vt., is a gravestone with this inscription:

Memento Mori
Here lie interr'ed where Silence reigns
Mr. John Strattons Sad Remains

Children:—*Born at Vernon, Vt.*

—432 Thankful,⁷ b. May 9, 1776; m., Aug. 20, 1795, **Lieut. Job Wright**, son of *Rev. Job Wright* of Bernardstown, Mass., who died Apr. 26, 1806, at the early age of 34. She inherited the homestead of her grandfather, Ensign Samuel Stratton, and beneath this rooftree her children grew to manhood and womanhood. She died May 24, 1849. She was a woman of great worth and ability.*

—433 Electa,⁷ m. **Cyrus Washburn.**

—434 Roxana,⁷ d. in 1803, aged 21 years.

184. CALEB STRATTON ⁶ (*Eleazer,*⁵ *Hezekiah,*⁴ *Samuel,*³ *Samuel,*² *Samuel* ¹) owned land in Northfield in 1795. Later he settled in Shelburne, Mass. He married **Elizabeth Strong.**

Children:—*Born in Shelburne, Mass.*

>   Samuel & Ruth once happy were
>   In Him their only Son & Heir
>   In January e'er the Sun
>   Had eight & Twenty Circuits run
>   In Seventeen Hundred Fifty Six
>   With mortals here on earth to mix
>   He first begun, but lost his life
>   In seventeen hundred eighty five
>   The first of June as on his Tour
>   Where Walpole Rapids foam & roar
>   He to a Rock went down too nigh
>   To pierce the Salmon passing by
>   The Rock's Smooth Glossy Sloping Side
>   His feet betray'd and let him slide
>   Plump down into a watry tomb
>   No more to see his native Home
>   His tender Parents lovely Spouse
>   Or those bright beauties of his House
>   Three little hapless female Heirs
>   Left to bedew his Grave with Tears.
>   Alas who can their loss repair
>   Or ease the Widows Soul of Care
>   Or furnish adequate Relief
>   To cure the Parents pungent Grief
>   Father of Mercies hear our call
>   Extend thy Pity to them all
>   Let momentary Ills like this
>   Issue in everlasting bliss.

*Among her descendants the name Stratton has been continued as a "middle name." Her daughter Ruth m. Marshall Whithed, and their daughter Adaline m. Charles F. Cone of Boston.

—435 Sarah,[7] b. 1801; d. 1885; m. **John Hardy.**
+436 Caleb Strong,[7] b. 1802.
—437 Elizabeth,[7] b. 1803; d. Nov. 13, 1852.
—438 Samuel,[7] b. 1807; m. **Roxana Miller.** Moved to Ohio, where he died in 1894; had two daughters, no sons.

186. ASA STRATTON [6] (*Eleazer,*[5] *Hezekiah,*[4] *Samuel,*[3] *Samuel,*[2] *Samuel*[1]) married **Lucy Woodbury** of Barre, Nov. 30, 1780. He owned a farm of 400 acres near Northfield, some parts of which are retained in the family to-day. He was a Revolutionary soldier under Burgoyne; serving at Bennington, under Gen. Stark; at Saratoga and other points. The gun which he carried is still in the possession of his descendants at Greenfield. He died Mar. 17, 1818.

Children:—*Born in Northfield, Mass.*
—439 Mary,[7] b. Feb. 18, 1781; m. **Samuel Holton,** 1809.
—440 Charlotte,[7] b. Sept. 10, 1782; m. **Jonathan Lyman;** d. Apr. 7, 1788.
+441 Roswell,[7] b. June 7, 1784; m. **Rhoda Wright,** who died Aug. 30, 1857.
+442 Asa,[7] b. Sept. 10, 1786.
—443 Chester,[7] b. 1790; d. Apr. 14, 1815, in Penbrook.
+444 Seth,[7] b. Aug. 9, 1792.
—445 Charles,[7] b. Dec. 1, 1794; a dentist; d. in Brattleboro, Vt., Jan. 4, 1869.
+446 Alonzo,[7] b. Dec. 1, 1798.
+447 Albert,[7] b. Apr. 28, 1801. (Written Alberto Stratton in some records.)

188. ELEAZER STRATTON [6] (*Eleazer,*[5] *Hezekiah,*[4] *Samuel,*[3] *Samuel,*[2] *Samuel*[1]) married **Submit Field,** Aug. 31, 1790. In March, 1797, he was one of a corporation known as "The Proprietors of the Aqueduct" in Northfield. This aqueduct was for the purpose of conveying water by subterraneous pipes through the town.

Children:—*Born in Northfield.*
—448 Clark,[7] b. Aug., 1792; d. Nov. 27, 1883; m. Dec. 13, 1835, **Sophrona White,** who died Dec. 11, 1855, aged 48 years. They lived and died in Heath, Mass. He was a good man, a thrifty, industrious farmer; his estate inventoried $8,000. He had but one child, Mariah,[8] b. 1837; m. **Norris D. Taintor.**

—449 Mariah.⁷
—450 Mary⁷ (Polly).
+451 Eleazer,⁷ b. 1798.
+452 Alvin,⁷ b. Aug. 15, 1802.
      Born in Chelsea, Vt.
—453 Eliphalet,⁷ b. July 4, 1803; went to Perry, Ohio, about 1828; m. **Eliza Belknap**. She d. in 1876, and he m. 2nd, **Mrs. Maria Tyler**. He d. in 1885. He was lieutenant-colonel of militia, and a man greatly respected by his townsmen. He had no children, but Eliphalet Stratton Belknap, his wife's nephew, was his legally adopted son.

193. RUFUS STRATTON⁶ (*Hezekiah,⁵ Hezekiah,⁴ Samuel,³ Samuel,² Samuel¹*) married **Asenette Field**, Nov. 19, 1778, daughter of *Capt. Samuel Field,* and lived in Northfield, where he owned a farm. He was selectman in 1790, 1796, 1798, 1799. In 1800 he was one of a committee on inspection of schools. In 1820 he built a grist mill at the falls on Four Mile Creek. He died March 18, 1827. His widow died two years later, Apr., 1829, aged 71 years. He was a prosperous and successful man.
Children:—*Born in Northfield, Mass.*
—454 Sarah, b. Dec. 2, 1779; m. **Dr. Stephen Batchelor** of Athol.
—455 Lucy, b. May 25, 1781; d. in infancy.
+456 Samuel, b. July 30, 1782.
+457 Elihu, b. Nov. 28, 1784 (date of baptism).
—458 John, b. Apr. 5, 1787; d. aged 3 years.
+459 Rufus, b. Sept. 3, 1789 (bapt. Sept. 12).
—460 John, b. Aug. 8, 1791; d. aged 14 years.
—461 Elijah, b. Aug. 22, 1793; killed by lightning, 1809.
—462 Lucy, b. Mar. 9, 1796; m. May 11, 1820, **Allured Benjamin**.
+463 Lorenzo, b. Dec. 16, 1798.

198. HEZEKIAH STRATTON⁶ (*Hezekiah,⁵ Hezekiah,⁴ Samuel,³ Samuel,² Samuel¹*) married **Hannah Wright**, daughter of *Reuben Wright,* Mar. 5, 1789. She died Jan. 5, 1846, aged 81 years. He kept a tavern at Northfield Farms, which for many years was kept by his father and later by his son Arad. In the Memorial Hall at Deerfield is preserved the sign which hung in front of his tavern for three generations. He was town treasurer in 1812. He died Oct. 24, 1825. In the cemetery at Northfield are tombstones to the two Hezekiahs.

Children:—*Born in Northfield, Mass.*
+464 Charles,[7] b. May 28, 1790.
+465 Harris,[7] b. Nov. 29, 1791.
+466 Arad,[7] b. Oct. 19, 1795.
—467 Hannah, b. Apr. 25, 1801; m. **Asabel Sawyer.**
+468 Hezekiah,[7] b. June 26, 1804.
—469 Fannie,[7] b. 1811; d. 1822.

207. JONAS STRATTON [6] (*Jonas,*[5] *Joseph,*[4] *Samuel,*[3] *Samuel,*[2] *Samuel* [1]) married **Nancy Smith** in Lincoln, Dec. 5, 1802 (per. d. in Hillsboro Co., N. H., in 1820).

Children:—*Born in Lincoln, Mass.*
—470 Laurinda,[7] b. Feb. 12, 1803.
—471 Mary,[7] b. Feb. 20, 1805.
—472 Eliza,[7] b. Nov. 11, 1808.
—473 Charles,[7] b. Nov. 20, 1810; m. **Sarah J. Brown,** d. of *Abel P. Brown;* d. in Lexington, July 4, 1891, aged 70 years.
—474 Jonas S.,[7] b. Dec. 20, 1812. What became of him?
—475 Caroline,[7] b. May 15, 1815.

211. ISAAC STRATTON [6] (*Richard,*[5] *Ichabod,*[4] *Richard,*[3] *Samuel,*[2] *Samuel* [1]) married **Mary Fox.** They lived at Williamstown, where he owned a house and land, and where his will is recorded. He was a Revolutionary soldier. He died in Williamstown April 3, 1789. His widow married Clark Rogers, and died Mar. 20, 1812.

Children:—*Born in Williamstown, Mass.**
—476 Phœbe,[7] b. Apr. 9, 1762; m. **James Sloan** in Williamstown in 1780.
—477 Moses,[7] b. June, 1764; d. aged 3 years.
—478 Mary,[7] b. Apr. 6, 1769; m. **Cyrus Starkweather,** May 17, 1788.
—479 Huldah,[7] b. Mar. 14, 1772; m. **James Sherwood,** June 1, 1789.
—480 Rachel,[7] b. Sept., 1775.
—481 Clara.[7]
—482 Olive.[7]
—483 Isaac.[7]

---

* The last three names are not recorded at Williamstown, but were given the writer by a descendant of Richard.[5]

212. DANIEL STRATTON [6] (*Richard,*[5] *Ichabod,*[4] *Richard,*[3] *Samuel,*[2] *Samuel*[1]) married **Mary** ——, and lived in Williamstown; more complete records of this family desired.

Children:—*Born in Williamstown, Mass.*
- —484 Abner,[7] b. Aug. 18, 1769; m. **Eunice Phelps,** Oct. 3, 1791. They had a daughter, Miranda,[8] b. Oct. 10, 1792.
- —485 Richard Alger,[7] b. Sept. 1, 1771.
- —486 Daniel,[7] b. Apr. 7, 1775; d. in infancy.
- —487 Silvanus,[7] b. Nov. 26, 1778.
- —488 Andrew,[7] b. Oct. 5, 1780.
- +489 Isaac Johnson,[7] b. Nov. 13, 1782.
- —490 Lydia,[7] b. 1784.
- —491 Harvey,[7] b. Sept. 3, 1786.
- —492 Cyrenius,[7] b. Dec. 15, 1788.

213. Deacon EBENEZER STRATTON [6] (*Richard,*[5] *Ichabod,*[4] *Richard,*[3] *Samuel,*[2] *Samuel*[1]) owned a valuable tract of land near the eastern end of Wiliamstown, a part of his father's estate, on what is still called the "Stratton Road." On this farm he led a very useful life. Was public spirited and prominent in many good works, highly respected, a deacon for many years. He married **Mabel Noble,** daughter of *Daniel Noble* of Williamstown, who died in 1777. He married, second, **Mary Blair.**

Children:—*Born in Williamstown.*
By first marriage.
- —493 Sarah,[7] b. Oct. 13, 1771; d. in childhood.
- —494 Mary,[7] b. Aug. 31, 1773; m. June 19, 1492, **Edward Foster.**
- —495 Cyrus,[7] b. June 7, 1776; m. **Rachel Smedley;** moved to Ohio and died there.

By second marriage.
- —496 Mabel,[7] b. July 19, 1779; m. —— **Burrett.**
- +497 Ebenezer,[7] b. Nov. 7, 1783.
- —498 Lena,[7] b. Oct. 27, 1789; lived in Troy, N. Y.
- —499 Julia,[7] b. Aug. 10, 1793; m. —— **Willey.**

219. DAVID STRATTON [6] (*Richard,*[5] *Ichabod,*[4] *Richard,*[3] *Samuel,*[2] *Samuel*[1]) married **Ruth** ——, Nov. 22, 1781. To what place did this family remove from Williamstown?

Children:—*Born in Williamstown, Mass.*
- —500 Erasmus,[7] b. Sept. 14, 1782.

REV. EBENEZER H. STRATTON; *Page* 136.
In 1899 the oldest minister in General Assembly and oldest graduate of Williams College, aged 93 years.

—501 Anna,⁷ b. Mar. 1, 1784.
—502 Moses,⁷ b. Oct. 25, 1785.
—503 Phœbe,⁷ b. Mar. 9, 1787.
—504 Ruth,⁷ b. Feb. 9, 1789.
—505 Mary,⁷ b. Nov. 20, 1790.
—506 David,⁷ b. Nov. 24, 1792.
—507 Lucy,⁷ b. Jan. 10, 1795.
—508 Ervin (Alvin),⁷ b. May 10, 1797.

224. JOHN STRATTON ⁶ (*Francis*,⁵ Ichabod,⁴ Richard,³ Samuel,² Samuel¹) married **Anna Carpenter**. Lived in Warren, Mass., until about 1799, then moved to Oneida Co., N. Y., where he soon died. Mrs. Stratton died in 1823 at her daughter's home in Trenton, N. J. She had been blind for many years.
Children:—*Born in Warren, Mass.*
+509 Francis,⁷ b. Feb. 7, 1780.
—510 John,⁷ b. May 5, 1782; d. prob. unm.
—511 Lydia,⁷ b. Mar. 9, 1785; m. **Thomas Converse**, Jefferson Co., N. Y.
+512 Richard,⁷ b. Aug., 1792.

225. ASA STRATTON ⁶ (*Ichabod*,⁵ Ichabod,⁴ Richard,³ Samuel,² Samuel¹) was born in Hardwick, Mass., July 14, 1744. He married Lydia **Johnson** in Worcester Co., Mass., and about 1795 moved to Chester, Vt. In Chester he bought land in 1799, which he sold in 1803. He then went to Cavendish, Vt., and lived here, or in this vicinity, the rest of his life. He died in 1845 at the age of 101 years.
Children:
—513 Abigail,⁷ m. —— Parker.
—514 Sarah,⁷ m. —— Kenney, and moved to New York state.
—515 Lucy,⁷ m. —— Everett.
+516 Asa,⁷ b. Sept. 1, 1787.
—517 Lucettia,⁷ m. —— Webber, lived and died in Cavendish.

229. JONATHAN STRATTON ⁶ (*Ichabod*,⁵ Ichabod,⁴ Richard,³ Samuel,² Samuel¹) was born in Hardwick, Mass., Apr. 6, 1756. He was a soldier in the Revolution in 1779.
Children:
—518 Venlory.⁷
—519 Matilda.⁷
—520 Tryphena.⁷
—521 Lucinda.⁷

—522   Olive.⁷
—523   Rebecca.⁷
—524   Amanda.⁷
—525   Eunice.⁷
—526   Philada.⁷
—527   Hannah.⁷
—528   Jefferson.⁷

Information concerning this family is desired. Jefferson is said to have had a son who settled in Michigan.

231.   JOEL STRATTON ⁶ (*Ichabod,*⁵ *Ichabod,*⁴ *Richard,*³ *Samuel,*² *Samuel* ¹) was a soldier in the Revolution at the age of 19, in Capt. Tim Page's Co., Col. James Convers's Regt. The company arrived at Bennington, Vt., Aug. 17, 1777, the day after the battle.* Joel, when the company was discharged, after several months of good service, remained in Vermont. Sept. 25, 1782, he married **Rhoda Beeman**, who was born in Kent, Conn., and was a daughter of *Joseph Beeman* ³ (*Thomas,*² *Simon* ¹). He brought his bride on horseback to the log house he had previously built for her. In this log house, more than 130 years ago, they began housekeeping, with "one pewter spoon, and one pewter basin, as the sole contents of their china closet." It was not long before they had a larger house well furnished for that time and place, and here they lived to a good old age. This farm is still in possession of his descendants, and they are among the thrifty, prosperous, well-to-do people of that section. Mrs. Stratton died Oct. 15, 1836, and Mr. Stratton eleven years later, Jan. 7, 1847.

Children—*Born in Bennington, Vt.*
—529   Daniel,⁷ b. July 6, 1783; d. 1802, unm.
—530   Joel,⁷ b. July 9, 1786; d. in Bennington; left several children.†
+531   Sheldon,⁷ b. Sept. 3, 1789 (another record says July 8).
—532   Rhoda,⁷ b. Sept. 27, 1791; m. **Newman Harrington**.
—533   Susan,⁷ b. Mar. 3, 1794; m. **Eunice Wellman**; d. in Bennington.

---

* His descendants still have a bell which came into his possession that day. It was taken from one of the cows which were being driven over the country by Burgoyne's army to furnish milk for the officers' table. He brought it into the village and it was used to assist in the noise-making in the celebration of the victory.

† The compiler has been unable to find the descendants of Joel Stratton.⁷ Although he died in his native town, he is said to have lived most of his married life in the northern part of the state—perhaps at Fairfax, Vt.

+534   Elhanan,⁷ b. Sept. 17, 1797.
+535   Joseph B.,⁷ b. Mar. 14, 1800.
+536   Freeman,⁷ b. Nov. 12, 1802.

237. RICHARD STRATTON ⁶ (*John,⁵ John,⁴ John,³ John,² Samuel* ¹) married **Hannah Wheat** in Watertown, Mass., Sept. 19, 1785.* Soon after his marriage he went to Swanzey, N. H., where he bought land in 1789, in 1796 and 1799, and became quite a prominent man. In 1788 his wife died and Nov. 13, 1794, he married **Desire Norton** of Swanzey. He was a dyer and dresser of cloth and carried on an extensive business. He died Mar. 9, 1827, and his two sons, John and Richard, Jr., succeeded him in owning and operating large cotton and woollen mills in Swanzey. In 1866, the "Stratton Mill Co." was formed. In the old cemetery at Swanzey is a gravestone with this inscription:

> Mr. Richard Stratton
> Died March 9, 1827
> aged 61 years
> Death is a debt to nature due
> Which I have paid and so must you.

His homestead in West Swanzey, long known as the "Old Mansion" and still called the Stratton Place' was built about the time of his marriage. It is one of the fine old historic places of the town, though it has been considerably remodeled, first by his son John Stratton, and then by George E. Whitcome, the present owner.

Children:—B*orn in Swanzey, N. H.*
   By first marriage.
—537   Hannah,⁷ b. Dec. 3, 1786; m. **Tilly Marvin.**
+538   John,⁷ b. Apr. 2, 1788.
   By second marriage.

---

* He was baptised "Richard Coolidge," but seems never to have used the middle name. Mr. Benjamin Read, the historian of Swanzey, makes him a son of Nathaniel Stratton. Mr. Read got his information from the older Swanzey Strattons, and they gave it from memory. The error probably arose from the fact that Richard, while a young man, received a legacy from his maternal grandfather, *Nathaniel Coolidge,* and so the name *Nathaniel* was remembered by his descendants, who came to believe that it was his father's name. An "intention of marriage" of Richard Stratton of Swanzey and Polly Eustis was "published" in Newton, Mass., Oct. 2, 1790. Two years later she married Oliver Fuller of Newton.

—539 Lucy,⁷ b. Nov. 23, 1795; m. 1st, **Abijah Whitcome;** 2nd, **Seth Belding.**
+540 Richard,⁷ b. Nov. 10, 1798.

246. ABIJAH STRATTON⁶ (*Abijah,⁵ Jabez,⁴ John,³ John,² Samuel¹*) married **Sarah Kendall,** July 3, 1773, and lived in Natick, where he inherited a part of his father's estate, including the homestead. He was a Revolutionary soldier from 1776 to 1780; first as sergeant, then lieutenant, then captain. His will, made Feb. 28, 1825, was proved June 29, 1830. He died May 1, 1830.

Children:—*Born in Natick, Mass.*
+541 Abijah,⁷ b. May 25, 1775.
—542 Mary,⁷ b. May 2, 1778; m. **Jonas Greenwood,** May 17, 1798.
—543 Sarah,⁷ b. May 21, 1780; d. before 1806; unm.
—544 Elizabeth,⁷ b. Mar. 13, 1783; m. **Ezra Morse** of Sherborn, Apr. 2, 1806.

It is possible there were other children, but the author has found no record of them.

247. DANIEL STRATTON⁶ (*Abijah,⁵ Jabez,⁴ John,³ John,² Samuel¹*) marched from Natick with Capt. Morse's Co. on the alarm on the morning of Apr. 19, 1775, and later was at Horse Neck, under command of Col. Brooks. He married, first, **Susannah Morse,** May 9, 1773. In 1774 he sold his part of his father's estate to his brother Abijah for £78-16-8, and bought land in Sherborn. He married, second, **Sarah Bullard,** who survived him. There is a monument to his memory in South Natick cemetery.

Children:—*Born in Sherborn, Mass.*
+545 Jonathan,⁷ b. Nov. 28, 1773.
—546 Hannah,⁷ b. Feb. 28, 1776.
—547 Rebecca,⁷ b. Dec. 1, 1777.
—548 Abigail,⁷ b. Aug. 13, 1780.
—549 Daniel,⁷ b. Nov. 22, 1783.* What became of him?
+550 John.⁷
—551 Martha.⁷
+552 William.⁷
—553 Eliza,⁷ m. —— Hobson.
—554 Susan,⁷ m. —— Steele.

The five older children, at least, were by the first marriage.

---

* The writer has been given some family records of a Daniel Stratton who was in the Mexican War and who m., first, **Zelpha Phippen** and had

250. NATHAN STRATTON [6] (*Nathan*,[5] *Jabez*,[4] *John*,[3] *John*,[2] *Samuel*[1]) married **Sarah Stratton**, Oct. 27, 1784 (No. 277), daughter of *Samuel* and *Beulah* (*Parker*) *Stratton*. Their descendants understand that they were second cousins. They lived in Sherborn for nearly thirty years, then in Ringe, N. H., for six years, and in 1821 moved to Leominister, where Mr. Stratton died May 2, 1842, and Mrs. Stratton Oct. 28, 1852.

Children:—B*orn in Sherborn, Mass.*
- —555 Ruth,[7] b. Nov. 12, 1784; m. **Joseph Coggins**, Dec. 19, 1802; lived in Holliston.
- —556 Amelia,[7] b. Mar. 13, 1787; m. **Luther Guy**.
- —557 Mary,[7] b. Feb. 12, 1789; m. **Lawson Walker**; d. Aug. 28, 1835.
- —558 Joannah,[7] b. Aug. 5, 1791; d. in infancy.
- —559 Ephraim,[7] b. Nov. 27, 1793; d. in childhood.
- —560 Jabez,[7] b. Nov. 12, 1896; m. **Sarah Devoll**; d. Oct. 30, 1858. No issue.
- +561 John,[7] b. May 17, 1798.
- —562 Sarah,[7] b. Dec. 2, 1800; m. **Lawson Walker** (his second wife).
- —563 Almira,[7] b. Mar. 13, 1804; m. —— **Sawin**; d. 1842.
- +564 Albert,[7] b. Apr. 4, 1807.

253. EBENEZER STRATTON [6] (*Elias*,[5] *Jabez*,[4] *John*,[3] *John*,[2] *Samuel*[1]) was a soldier in the Revolution. Wounded at the battle of White Plains; enlisted at the age of sixteen, substituting for his father; was in Capt. Oliver's Co., Col. Grout's Regt. He was a farmer of Athol. He married, first, **Abigail Hill** in Sherborn, June 5, 1788. She died July 30, 1801, aged 31 years. He married, second, **Hannah Wilder** of Sterling, Mar. 19, 1802. She died in Athol Dec. 30, 1850. Mr. Stratton died Sept. 14, 1835.

---

a son Daniel b. Feb. 14, 1810, in Surry, N. H., who m. Elizabeth Childs in 1840. Children, born at Westminster, Vt.:

James W., m. Phœbe Bemis; res., Walpole, N. H.
Charles Henry, m. Lucy M. Phillips; res., West Townshead, Vt. Children:
    Flora E., m. Orin B. Burnap.
    Hugh Ernest.
    Henry Clay. Children:

Ralph Harland.	Esther Evelyn.
Aubrey Edward.	Charles Henry.
Florence Isabella.	Maynard Nelson.

Perhaps some reader can give more complete records.

Children:—Born in Athol, Mass.
  By first marriage.
+565 Walter,⁷ b. Oct. 20, 1788.
−566 Clarissa,⁷ b. Aug. 4, 1790; m. **Abel Stevens,** May 8, 1811.
−567 Mary,⁷ b. 1792; m. **Wm. Meacham.**
−568 Abigail,⁷ b. 1794; m. **Josephus Bardwell,** Feb. 25, 1816.
−569 Abijah,⁷ b. May 20, 1797; d. in Athol, Aug. 1, 1830; unm.
  By second marriage.
−570 Wilder,⁷ b. Apr. 3, 1803; d. Oct. 3, 1806.
+571 Ebenezer,⁷ b. June 6, 1806.
−572 Ann,⁷ b. Jan. 10, 1808; m. in Barre, **Mason Amsworth,** Mar. 12, 1836.
−573 Hannah,⁷ b. Apr. 21, 1813; m. **Reuben Stratton.**
+574 Wilder,⁷ b. June 17, 1815.*

254. Elias Stratton ⁶ (*Elias,*⁵ *Jabez,*⁴ *John,*³ *John,*² *Samuel* ¹) lived and died in Athol. He married, May 23, 1786, **Caroline Richardson,** daughter of *Samuel Richardson.* She died in Athol Feb. 21, 1829, aged 71 years. His will, recorded in Worcester, dated June 12, 1830, names his five sons, of whom Elisha and Samuel were administrators.

Children:—Born in Athol, Mass.
+575 Elisha,⁷ b. Aug. 3, 1789.
+576 Samuel,⁷ b. Aug. 30, 1790.
−577 Asa,⁷ b. Oct. 29, 1792; m. in Petersham, 1821, **Elizabeth Rogers;** no children.
−578 Harris,⁷ b. May 25, 1795; went South; m. in Tuscaloosa, Ala. He and his wife were both teachers in Claiborne Academy, Ala. Did they leave children?
−579 Lydia,⁷ m. **Hubbard Taft.**
−580 Daniel,⁷ b. Jan. 10, 1799; a shoemaker; lived in Wendall; d. leaving no children; per. m. **Eunice Oliver** in Pellam May 1, 1828.

257. Joseph Stratton ⁶ (*Elias,*⁵ *Jabez,*⁴ *John,*³ *John,*² *Samuel* ¹) was a farmer at Athol. He married **Mary (or Dolly) Wheeler** in Petersham, May 28, 1793. She died Feb. 25, 1854. Mr. Stratton died in Athol April 13, 1834.

* On the town record of births this name is written "Phenehas Wilder Stratton." Neither he nor his family seem to have used the double name. By all who knew him he was known as Wilder Stratton.

Children:—Born in Athol, Mass.
+581   Joel,[7] b. Feb. 14, 1794.
+582   Jonathan,[7] b. Oct. 5, 1795.
+583   Joseph, Jr.,[7] b. May 3, 1798.
—584   Sarah,[7] b. Nov. 14, 1799.
—585   Jacob,[7] b. July 28, 1804; d. aged 4 days.
—586   Mary (Dolly),[7] b. Nov. 16, 1807.

258. JABEZ STRATTON [6] (*Elias,*[5] *Jabez,*[4] *John,*[3] *John,*[2] *Samuel*[1]) married **Mary Dudley** of Petersham, Mar. 18, 1800. He died Oct. 4, 1816. Mrs. Stratton died Oct. 23, 1848, aged 76 years.
Children:—Born in Athol, Mass.
—587   Betsey,[7] b. Dec. 25, 1801; m. **Benjamin Cook** in Athol, May 29, 1829.
—588   Mary,[7] b. Dec. 3, 1803; d. unm.
—589   Jabez,[7] b. Apr. 7, 1806; m. **Electa Littlefield**, who d. in 1849; ch. Charles H.,[8] d. young.
—590   Charles,[7] b. Aug. 14, 1808; d. aged 17.
+591   Lyman,[7] b. Nov. 8, 1812.

265. MOSES STRATTON [6] (*Jonathan,*[5] *Jonathan,*[4] *Joseph,*[3] *John,*[2] *Samuel*[1]) married **Elizabeth Hervey**, Aug. 4, 1794. They lived for awhile at the old homestead in Marlboro, and then moved to Hopkinton. He died June 10, 1832.
Children:—Born in Marlboro.
—592   Lambert,[7] b. Feb. 28, 1795; d. in Marlboro in 1875.
—593   Betsey,[7] b. Apr. 12, 1798.
—594   Lucy,[7] b. May 13, 1801; m. **Otis Brigham**, July 1, 1819.
—595   Lyman,[7] b. Aug. 9, 1803.
—596   George Washington,[7] b. June 22, 1805.
—597   Harriet Frink,[7] b. Nov. 10, 1809.

267. LEMUEL STRATTON [6] (*Jonathan,*[5] *Jonathan,*[4] *Joseph,*[3] *John,*[2] *Samuel*[1]) married **Phillippa Jackman**, June 4, 1804, in Bradford, N. H. They spent the last years of their lives in the home of their eldest daughter, Mrs. Reed, in Brighton, Ill. She died in 1857, and he a few years earlier.
Children:—Born in Bradford, N. H.
—598   Marianna,[7] b. Oct. 14, 1806; m. **Wm. Reed**; d. in Brighton, Ill.
+599   Lemuel Page,[7] b. Dec. 18, 1808.

+600 Stephen Jackman,[7] b. Jan. 16, 1811.
—601 John Herrick,[7] b. Nov. 25, 1813; d. unm. Apr. 26, 1851. Congregational minister; grad. Amherst College, 1840; Andover Theo. Seminary, 1843; pastor at Pittston, Me., 1844-5; at Erving, Mass., 1849-51.
+602 Levi Woodbury,[7] b. Apr. 25, 1816.
—603 Caroline,[7] b. Nov. 6, 1818; m. Elijah Kimball; d. in Auburn, N. H.
—604 Lucy,[7] b. Feb. 23, 1821.
—605 Horace,[7] b. Sept. 1, 1823; m. **Mrs. Baxter**; resided in Brighton; left no children; d. abt. 1888.
—606 Maria,[7] b. Mar. 23, 1826; d. Aug. 8, 1830.

268. SAMUEL STRATTON[6] (*Jonathan,*[5] *Jonathan,*[4] *Joseph,*[3] *John,*[2] *Samuel*[1]) married Lydia **Adams** of Bradford, and lived there until after 1815, then moved to New York state (perhaps near Hoosick, N. Y.).

Children:—*Born in Bradford, N. H.*
—607 Nabby,[7] b. Feb. 14, 1804.
—608 Jonathan,[7] b. Feb. 17, 1806.
—609 Phœbe Andrews,[7] b. Feb. 18, 1808.
—610 Lydia,[7] b. July 29, 1810.
—611 Anna,[7] b. Feb. 14, 1814.

272. WINSOR STRATTON[6] (*Samuel,*[5] *Jonathan,*[4] *Joseph,*[3] *John,*[2] *Samuel*[1]) was born in Marlboro, Oct. 27, 1770. His baptism on June 23 of the following year is recorded in the church records there. Feb. 22, 1791, he married **Anna Wood**. She was born Nov. 8, 1773, daughter of *Peter* and *Sybil* (*Howe*) *Wood*. They lived in Northboro on a farm at the foot of Rock Hill, and this farm was in possession of some member of the Stratton family for more than one hundred years. It is quite probable that it was a part of the original estate of Joseph Stratton,[3] which he bought in Marlboro about 1695. The present line between Northboro and Marlboro was not fully established until 1807. He died Apr. 30, 1837.

Children:—*Born in Northboro, Mass.*
+612 Jonah Brigham,[7] b. Mar. 20, 1791.
—613 Loring,[7] b. 1795; d. Nov. 24, 1798.
—614 Sarah,[7] b. 1799; d. Nov. 20, 1719.
—615 Lucy,[7] b. Aug. 29, 1802; d. Aug. 14, 1840.

—616 Marina,⁷ b. Sept. 23, 1806; d. June 24, 1839; m. **Samuel Maynard**, who m. 2nd, Sally Rice.
+617 William,⁷ b. Jan. 16, 1809.
—618 Winsor Wood,⁷ b. 1811; d. aged 3 years.
—619 Levi,⁷ b. 1816; m. **Martha Brigham**, Apr. 12, 1848; d. June 2, 1872; no children.

276. ELIJAH STRATTON ⁶ (*Samuel*,⁵ *Samuel*,⁴ *Samuel*,³ *John*,² *Samuel* ¹) married **Thankful Rice** in Natick, Mar. 15, 1790. He was a brickmaker in Natick in 1801.*

Children:—*Born in Natick, Mass.*
—620 Sarah,⁷ b. Apr. 10, 1790; d. aged 22 years.
—621 Samuel,⁷ b. Nov. 11, 1791.
—622 William,⁷ b. Oct. 25, 1792.
—623 Lydia,⁷ b. Dec. 10, 1794.
—624 Elizabeth,⁷ b. June 4, 1796; d. in infancy.
—625 Hulda,⁷ b. Feb. 11, 1799.
—626 Lucy,⁷ b. July 4, 1799.
—627 Elijah,⁷ b. Apr. 27, 1801.

279. SAMUEL STRATTON ⁶ (*Samuel*,⁵ *Samuel*,⁴ *Samuel*,³ *John*,² *Samuel* ¹) was born in Natick Dec. 10, 1767 (or Oct. 16, 1768?). Aug. 25, 1797, his father deeded him a piece of land in Natick valued at $500. He married, in Needham, **Hulda Waite** of Rockingham, Vt., Mar. 17, 1798. They lived in Natick until 1802 when they moved to Hancock, Me., where Mr. Stratton died in 1806. In 1808 his widow married Richard Clark, and died Oct. 22, 1845.

Children:—*Born in Natick, Mass.*
+628 John,⁷ b. June 30, 1799.
—629 David,⁷ b. May 13, 1801; d. in childhood.
   Born in Hancock, Me.
+630 Martin,⁷ b. Feb. 28, 1804.
—631 Joseph,⁷ b. 1806; perhaps settled in Machias, Me.

289. SAMUEL STRATTON ⁶ (*Samuel*,⁵ *Enoch*,⁴ *Richard*,³ *Samuel*,² *Samuel* ¹) married, first, **Eleanor Dickinson**, Feb. 1, 1784. She was daughter of *Nathaniel Dickinson* of Berlin. She died

---

* Did this family move from Natick not long after 1801? History of Bangor, Me., mentions an Elijah Stratton, Revolutionary Pensioner, in Hancock Co., Me., in 1832.

Dec. 1, 1784, aged 24 years. He married, second, **Mary Hollister**, July 13, 1786. She was a daughter of *Elijah Hollister*. She died May 9, 1840, aged 75 years.

Children:—*Born in Glastonbury, Conn.*
By first marriage.
—632   Jabez,[7] b. Nov. 13, 1784.
By second marriage.
—633   Mehitable,[7] b. May 1, 1787; m. **Ezra Dayton**; d. at the age of 104 years.
—634   Mary,[7] b. Mar. 1, 1791; m. **James Cogswell**.
—635   Parnelia,[7] b. Feb. 11, 1793; m. **Ashbel Woodbridge**.
—636   Rebecca,[7] b. Jan. 5, 1795; d. aged 2 years.
—637   Electa,[7] b. Feb. 4, 1799; m. **Hames Haskell**.
—638   Dolly,[7] b. Sept. 13, 1800; m. **Alva Morgan** of Salem, Mar. 3, 1822.
—639   Clarissa,[7] b. Sept. 24, 1802; m. **Joseph Stevens**, Jan. 15, 1826.
—640   Betsey Ann,[7] b. Aug. 20, 1804; d. in infancy.
—641   Eliza Ann,[7] b. July 5, 1806; m. **Coddington Smith**.

293.   WILLIAM STRATTON [6] (*Samuel,*[5] *Enoch,*[4] *Samuel,*[3] *Richard,*[2] *Samuel*[1]) was a farmer in Glastonbury. He married **Ruth Goodrich** June 1, 1788. She was daughter of Capt. *Jeremiah* and *Hepzibah (Edwards) Goodrich* of Chatham. He died very suddenly at home of his sister, Mrs. Hubbard, aged 44 years. When his father, who was 82 years old and very frail, was told of his death, he said, "Have William brought home, and I will be buried with him." He died the next morning, and father and son were buried together in the old South Cemetery at Glastonbury. His widow, Ruth, married Noah Goodrich, son of Ephriam Goodrich, and lived in Oswego, N. Y.

Children:—*Born in Glastonbury, Conn.*
—642   Annie,[7] b. Apr. 29, 1789; m. **Ira Hubbard**.
—643   Emily,[7] b. Apr. 24, 1791; m. **Disha Kellogg**, son of Ephraim and Hannah Kellogg, Feb. 7, 1811.
+644   Isaac G.,[7] b. Mar. 5, 1793.
—645   Daniel,[7] b. Nov. 6, 1795; d. in infancy.
—646   Ruth,[7] b. June 25, 1797; m. **Abner Goodrich**.
+647   William,[7] b. Aug. 9, 1799.
—648   George,[7] b. June 28, 1802; m. —— **Woodhull**, and lived for awhile at Hornsdale, Pa.; chn. Cornelia,[8] Sarah,[8] Julia,[8] Frederick George.[8]

298. BENJAMIN STRATTON [6] (Benjamin,[5] Jabez,[4] Samuel,[3] Richard,[2] Samuel [1]) was a Revolutionary soldier. He marched from Brookline at the alarm Apr. 19, 1775, in Capt. Thomas White's Co. Militia, Col. William Heath's Regt.; service 23 days. Also enlisted Jan. 21, 1776, in Capt. Hopestill Hall's Co., Col. Lem Robinson's Regt. In June of the same year he served three days at Nantasket, "driving ships from Boston harbor." He married Sept. 9, 1781 (pub) **Sarah Fillibrown**, daughter of *Edward* and *Susanna Fillibrown*, of Boston. They lived in Brookline until Feb., 1784, when they moved to Fairlee, Vt., where he bought a farm on the banks of the Connecticut, which is still owned by his descendants.

Children:—*Born in Brookline, Mass.*
- —649 Sarah,[7] bapt. Nov. 10, 1782; d. unm. in Fairlee in 1833.
- —650 Susanna,[7] bapt. June 16, 1785; d. unm. in Orford, N. H., in 1847.

Born in Fairlee, Vt.
- —651 Nancy,[7] b. 1787; m. **Steven Palmer**.
- —652 Louisa,[7] b. 1789; m. **Robert Churchill**.
- —653 John,[7] b. 1792; d. in Fairlee in 1815; unm.
- +654 Thomas,[7] b. 1794.
- —655 Abigail,[7] b. 1796; m. **William Howard**; d. Orford, N. H., 1836.

299. JOHN STRATTON [6] (Benjamin,[5] Jabez,[4] Samuel,[3] Richard,[2] Samuel [1]) lived in Brookline and Boston until he was about thirty years old and then went to Hollowell, Me. There he married, Mar. 15, 1796, **Theresa Gilman**. In the same year, Mar. 21, he was transferred from the north parish to the south parish of Hollowell, and made one of the town officers. June 1, 1797, he was appointed one of the jurors of the Supreme Judicial Court. He was the first secretary of the Kennebec Masonic Lodge. Theresa, born Oct. 11, 1776, was daughter of *Elephalet* and *Joanna (Longe) Gilman*, who came to Hollowell in 1785 from Exeter. Elephalet was son of *Jonathan* and *Elizabeth Gilman*, and Joanna was daughter of *John* and *Anna Longe*, all of Exeter. Theresa, wife of John Stratton, died Apr. 27, 1802, aged 36 years. A gravestone stands to her memory in the cemetery at Hollowell on the Gilmore lot. John died Sept. 19 of the same year, aged 35 years. The Boston papers published his death. He died in Hollowell. Benjamin Stratton, Sr., of Fairlee, Vt., was appointed his administrator, but wrote a note to the Judge of

Probate asking that his son Benjamin, Jr., might be appointed in his stead, as it was not convenient for him to come to Hollowell. Benjamin Stratton, Jr., was then appointed.

Children:—*Born in Hollowell, Me.*
—656 Pamelia,[7] b. 1797; m. **Paul Stickney**, son of *Thomas Stickney;* d. in Hollowell May 6, 1826 (gravestone).
—657 William,[7] b. abt. 1799.
+658 John,[7] b. 1800.

William (No. 657) is mentioned in the administration of his father's estate. The author has found no other mention of him. He probably died in childhood.

302. JABEZ STRATTON [6] (*Jabez,*[5] *Jabez,*[4] *Samuel,*[3] *Samuel,*[2] *Samuel*[1]) married **Lydia Knight** in Worcester, Mass., in 1797, who died while her children were young. He lived in Westmoreland, Vt., for a while, and then in Bethlehem, N. H.

Children:—*Born in Bethlehem, N. H.*
—659 Harmon,[7] m. **Elvira Beard**; d. in Pittsfield, Vt., abt. 1850.
—660 Anna,[7] m. **Samuel Fitzgerald**.
—661 Lois,[7] b. Dec. 11, 1805; m. **Charles W. Smith**; res. Burke, Vt.
+662 Josiah,[7] b. Dec. 3, 1807.
—663 Austin,[7] m. —— Spaulding, and lived in Ticonderoga, N. Y.
—664 Jonas,[7] lived in Ohio.

303. SAMUEL STRATTON [6] (*Jabez,*[5] *Jabez,*[4] *Samuel,*[3] *Richard,*[2] *Samuel*[1]) was born July 6, 1765. He was a Revolutionary soldier in 1781, enlisting from Greenwich, where he is described as being "16 years old, 5 feet 1 in., light complexion." He married **Beulah Jones**, daughter of *Joseph Jones*. She died in 1803, aged 35 years. He then married **Tibatha (Simmons?)** who lived to the age of 88 years, dying in 1857. He moved from Greenwich about 1800 to Pawlet, Vt., where he was a farmer, and where he died about 1823.

Children:—*Born in Pawlet, Vt.*
—665 Roxana,[7] m. **Hiram Weeks**.
+666 Issacher.[7]
—667 Samuel.[7]
—668 Seth [7] went West from Vermont while a young man and was lost track of by the family.

THE CHARLES RIVER NEAR WATERTOWN
Pages 182-186. *Vol.* I.

VIEW IN "STRATTON PARK," COLORADO SPRINGS
Page 335.

—669 Curena,⁷ m. **Roswell Chapin.**
—670 Ursula,⁷ m. **Wm. Gibbs;** lived in Marion, N. Y.
—671 Ellathier,⁷ m. **Beulah Chapin,** and moved to York State.
—672 Charles,⁷ lived in Ogdensburg, N. Y.

These names may not be in the correct order.

306. JAMES STRATTON ⁷ (*Josiah,*⁶ *Hezekiah,*⁵ *Samuel,*⁴ *Samuel,*³ *Samuel,*² *Samuel* ¹) married, first, **Abigail Phelps** of Rutland, Nov. 13, 1791; married, second, **Mary Ann Hewett.** He conducted a grocery and produce store in Genoa, N. Y., for several years, then moved to Holden, Mass., where he spent most of his life. He had much trade with the Indians and was a ever popular man with them, who called him the "big white chief." He often visited them in their homes. He died in Holden Oct. 2, 1838.

Children:—B*orn in Holden, Mass.*
By first marriage.
—673 Abigail,⁸ b. Sept. 13, 1792.
+674 Simon Phelps,⁸ b. May 6, 1794.
—675 Mary,⁸ b. Dec. 12, 1795.
—676 Maria,⁸ b. Sept. 10, 1806.
—677 Samuel Austin,⁸ b. May 7, 1809.
By second marriage.
B*orn in Stockbridge, Mass.*
—678 Frances Permelia,⁸ b. Oct. 18, 1816; m. 1st, **Sam'l Adams,** 1835, who lost his life in a steamboat accident near Paducah, Ky., in 1849; m. 2nd, **Jacob Farwell,** who d. in 1867. She d. at the house of her son, John Adams, in Waltham, Dec. 24, 1908.
+679 James M.⁸

307. PAUL STRATTON ⁷ (*Josiah,*⁶ *Hezekiah,*⁵ *Samuel,*⁴ *Samuel,*³ *Samuel,*² *Samuel* ¹) married **Mary Broad,** daughter of *Josiah Broad,* in Holden, Feb. 10, 1794.* They moved to Berlin, Vt., where they remained for two or three years, then returned to Massachusetts. About **1801** they settled in Albion, Me., where they bought a farm. He died **in 1815,** aged **46** years.

---

* Josiah Broad moved with his family from Holden, Mass., to Winslow, Me., making the trip of more than two hundred miles with an ox team.

Children:—*Born in Berlin, Vt.**
+680 Austin,⁸ b. June 3, 1795.
+681 Paul,⁸ Oct. 30, 1796.
       Born in Holden, Mass.
—682 Mary,⁸ b. Oct. 25, 1798.
—683 Eunice,⁸ b. 1800.
       Born in Albion, Me.
—684 Lucinda,⁸ b. 1802; m. **James Parks.**
+685 Frink,⁸ b. Oct. 26, 1804.
—686 Aurelia,⁸ b. 1806.
—687 Sarah,⁸ b. 1809.

308. ISRAEL STRATTON ⁷ (*Joseph,*⁶ *Hezekiah,*⁵ *Samuel,*⁴ *Samuel,*³ *Samuel,*² *Samuel*¹) married, first, **Tabithia Maynard** of Rutland, Nov. 5, 1793. Married, second, **Lucy Bryant,** who died in Holden, May 12, 1856, aged 64 years. He died, Apr. 17, 1862.
Children:—*Born in Holden, Mass.*
       By first marriage.
—688 Hezekiah Moore,⁸ b. July 25, 1794.
—689 Josiah,⁸ b. May 27, 1797.
—690 Tabithia,⁸ b. Sept. 25, 1800; m. **Martin Mayhew,** Nov. 11, 1821.
—691 Mary Wales,⁸ b. Jan. 25, 1805; m. **John P. Earle** of Liechester, Apr. 13, 1824.
—692 Elizabeth Jackson,⁸ b. May 18, 1807; m. **W. J. Barnes** of R. I., Dec. 22, 1831.
—693 Daniel,⁸ b. Sept. 29, 1809.
       By second marriage.
—694 William,⁸ b. Dec. 28, 1817; d. in Holden, aged 28 years.
+695 Harvey,⁸ b. Feb. 1, 1820; m. **Louisa J. Bryant** in Holden, Jan. 1, 1849.
—696 Lucy,⁸ b. Oct. 4, 1824; m. **John Davis.**

In Israel Stratton's will he names only his wife Lucy, sons Daniel and Harvey, and his three daughters Tabithia, Elizabeth and Lucy.

310. JOHN HUBBARD STRATTON ⁷ (*Joseph,*⁶ *Hezekiah,*⁵ *Samuel,*⁴ *Samuel,*³ *Samuel,*² *Samuel*¹) married **Sarah Baxter** in Rutland, June 21, 1804. She was daughter of *Moses* and *Mary (Moore) Baxter* of Sudbury, and was born Sept. 23, 1776. They lived in

---

* The town books at Holden give the births of the two older children, but state that they were born at Berlin, Vt.

Sterling, Mass., where their old home was standing until a few years ago, when it was torn down.

Children:—Born in Sterling, Mass.
- —697 Chloe,[8] b. June 30, 1806; d. unm. in Manchester, Vt., in 1885.
- —698 Sarah,[8] b. 1808; m. Levi Bradford; lived in Vermont.
- —699 John Hubbard,[8] b. Mar. 27, 1810; d. unm. in West Boylston in 1858.
- —700 Samuel Hubbard,[8] b. July 14, 1812; d. in 1813.
- —701 Samuel Hubbard,[8] b. Mar. 6, 1814; d. unm. in West Boylston in 1847.
- +702 Josiah Baxter,[8] b. July 29, 1816.
- —703 Ann Paige,[8] b. 1819; m. 1st, **Mervin W. Chase**, 1839; m. 2nd, **Charles Gates** in 1862; res. Worcester, Mass.
- —704 Harriet Robbins,[8] b. 1822; d. unm. in 1859 in West Boylston.

312. FRINK STRATTON [7] (*Josiah*,[6] *Hezekiah*,[5] *Samuel*,[4] *Samuel*,[3] *Samuel*,[2] *Samuel*[1]) married **Elizabeth Niles**, daughter of *Ebenezer Niles*, Nov. 25, 1802. She was born in Braintree, Jan. 14, 1781. They lived in Boston, where Mr. Stratton died June 1, 1842, and Mrs. Stratton, Aug. 6, 1867. Both are buried in Mt. Auburn.

Children:—Born in Boston, Mass.
- +705 William Frink,[8] b. Aug. 22, 1803.
- +706 Ebenezer Niles,[8] b. Jan. 22, 1805.
- —707 Elizabeth Hunt,[8] b. Feb. 24, 1807; m. **Daniel Burrill, Jr.** (his third wife), May 22, 1850.
- —708 Charles Davis,[8] b. July, 1812; d. June 20, 1812.
- —709 Mary Davis,[8] b. July, 1812; m. **John Quincy Adams Litchfield**.
- —710 Henrietta,[8] b. Jan. 3, 1815; d. aged 10 mos.

316. DANIEL STRATTON [7] (*Daniel*,[6] *Hezekiah*,[5] *Samuel*,[4] *Samuel*,[3] *Samuel*,[2] *Samuel*[1]) married **Jane Stickney**, Feb. 16, 1800, in New Ipswich, N. H. She was daughter of *Joseph* and *Anna* (*Sloss*) *Stickney* and a descendant of *William Stickney*, who came from England to Rowley, Mass., about 1637. About seven years later he moved to Vermont, where he bought a farm about one mile from Newfane. His house, built about 1810, is still standing in very good repair. It was sold by his children in 1871. He died, Oct. 11, 1853.

Children:—*Born in New Ipswich, N. H.*
-711   Anna,⁸ b. 1801; m. —— Kelsey.
-712   Sarah,⁸ b. 1803; m. **John Goodrow.**
+713   Asa,⁸ b. Jan. 29, 1805.
       Born in Newfane, Vt.
-714   Eliza Ann,⁸ b. 1807; m. **Elijah Bartlett**; d. in California.
+715   Joseph Stickney,⁸ b. Sept. 12, 1812.
-716   Jane,⁸ b. Mar., 1810; d. unm., Feb. 8, 1839.
+717   Daniel O.,⁸ b. Nov. 22, 1815.
-718   Lydia L.,⁸ b. June 19, 1819; m. **Plimpton Morse.**

317. John Stratton ⁷ (*Daniel,*⁶ *Hezekiah,*⁵ *Samuel,*⁴ *Samuel,*³ *Samuel,*² *Samuel* ¹) was born in New Ipswich, N. H., Mar. 28, 1775. As a boy he was apprenticed to a dyer and clothier and learned the trade, but later became a wheelwright.* He was Captain of a company of Militia and the sword he wore on "training day" is still preserved. While a young man he emigrated to New York state. About 1808 he married **Charlotte Frink**, then of Pittsfield, N. Y., but of a New England family. She was a daughter of *William* and *Mary (Pendleton) Frink* of Lebanon, Conn.† She was born Apr. 22, 1788. After their marriage they lived for awhile at Binghamton, where he built a mill—one of the first in that section. The settlers brought their grain for twenty miles around to "Stratton's Mill." About 1813 he settled in Oxford, N. Y., building a mill and house about one mile south of the present town of Oxford. The remains of the

---

* Though he never worked at the Clothiers' trade, his knowledge of it stood him in good stead. In the early days at Oxford, Mrs. Stratton spun and wove the cloth for her large family. In coloring the wool her husband was a great help, and his receipts for coloring were kept among his valuable papers. Her flax and wool wheels are still among the treasures at the old homestead.

† Mary Pendleton was a daughter of Benajah Pendleton and a granddaughter of Caleb Pendleton, Jr. The Pendletons came from Connecticut to New York State.

This Stratton-Frink marriage was probably recorded at Pittsfield, a little village near New Berlin, N. Y. The records of that village were burned years ago. A granddaughter still well remembers seeing the marriage record in the old family Bible, in John Stratton's handwriting, and that the name was there spelled "Charlotty Frink." The Bible is still treasured, containing the records of birth of John Stratton, his wife and all his children, but the leaf which contained the marriage record is lost.

old overshot mill wheel may still be seen there.* The house has passed away, only the old chimney remaining to mark its location. He also bought a farm five miles south of Oxford, which is still owned and occupied by his descendants. On this farm he spent the remainder of his life. He was one of the Commissioners in the bridge scheme in 1823.† His sons, as they married, settled on the home farm, or on farms near by, and were among the leading agriculturists of Chenango Co., as are some of his grandsons to-day. He died Jan. 28, 1842. Mrs. Stratton died Mar. 27, 1875.

Children:—*Born in Binghamton, N. Y.*
+719   Albert Galtin,^{8} b. Nov. 17, 1809.
+720   John,^{8} b. Mar. 2, 1812.
       Born in South Oxford.
+721   Ira,^{8} b. Jan. 29, 1815.
+722   William Frink,^{8} b. Jan. 27, 1817.
−723   Charlotte Ambrosia,^{8} b. Feb. 26, 1819; m. **Derrick W. Ten Broeck**, Jan. 11, 1838; her death in Oxford, Sept. 7, 1910, closed a life of singular beauty and she is held in loving memory by a large circle of friends and relatives.
−724   Mary,^{8} b. May 26, 1821; m. **Clark Lewis, Jr.**,‡ Oct.

---

* At this mill, operated for many years by him and his sons, most of the building material used in the lower part of the town of Oxford was sawn by the "up-and-down saw" of that period. An old account book of John Stratton's, still in existence, shows bills of lumber (expressed in £ s. d.) for the years 1811 and 1812, and names many of the old settlers as his customers.
Some records have it that he came first to Oxford, then went to Binghamton about 1809, and returned to Oxford about 1813. Later he built many mill wheels in that section, often being away from home working at this trade. As his sons, John and George, became old enough to help they went with him and so became wheelwrights, learning the trade of their father.

† The inhabitants of the surrounding towns were invited to a "River Bridge Bee" to help in drawing stone and building the bridge across the Chenango River at Oxford. "The day was stormy, Friday, Feb. 28, 1823, but men and teams came from far and near, and each one who assisted in the work was given a ticket marked "Barbecue." Potatoes, bread and beef in large quantities were provided." This was an early "good roads" movement!

‡ Clark Lewis, Sr., of Exeter, R. I., was son of Samuel Lewis, Revolutionary soldier in 1778-9 (see records in office of Sec. of State, Providence), and grandson of George Lewis, whose father, George Lewis, Sr., came from England to Hopkinton, R. I., in 1630.

22, 1839; d. Nov. 21, 1873, at Oxford; a woman of beautiful character, a true wife, a loving and beloved mother.

+725 George,[8] b. Sept. 26, 1823.
+726 Ebenezer Ross,[8] b. Dec. 4, 1825.
—727 Sarah Ann,[8] b. Sept. 26, 1828; d. unm., Dec. 24, 1859.
—728 Caroline Eunice,[8] b. Oct. 29, 1831; d. May 6, 1832.

322. WILLIAM STRATTON [7] (*Daniel,*[6] *Hezekiah,*[5] *Samuel,*[4] *Samuel,*[3] *Samuel,*[2] *Samuel*[1]) was a wheelwright. He went from New Ipswich, N. H., to New York state. Jan. 10, 1815, he married **Esther Rood**, at Plainfield, and settled near Winfield, Herkermer Co., N. Y.

Children:—*Born in Plainfield, N. Y.*
—729 Eliza,[8] b. Oct. 9, 1815; m. **Asa Holmes**, Oct. 20, 1835; d. at West Winfield, July 21, 1882.
+730 William Warren,[8] b. Apr. 21, 1820.

326. JEREMIAH STRATTON [7] (*Daniel,*[6] *Hezekiah,*[5] *Samuel,*[4] *Samuel,*[3] *Samuel,*[2] *Samuel*[1]) married **Abigail Spaulding**, daughter of *Jesse Spaulding* of Chelmsford. She died in Winchenden, Mass., May 10, 1847, aged 49 years, 8 mos. and 3 days. His name appears on the tax list in New Ipswich, N. H., from 1815 to 1827. The family were living in Winchenden from 1835 to 1849.

Children:—*Born in New Ipswich, N. H.*
—731 Charlotte S.,[8] b. in 1822; m. **Aaron Winch**, May 8, 1848, in Winchenden, Mass.
—732 Charles Edwin,[8] b. June 29, 1823.
—733 Eldridge,[8] visited his uncle in Newfane, Vt., in 1853.

A letter written by Jeremiah Stratton in 1835 speaks of his six children. Later records of this family are much desired.

327. SAMUEL STRATTON [7] (*Hezekiah,*[6] *Hezekiah,*[5] *Samuel,*[4] *Samuel,*[3] *Samuel,*[2] *Samuel*[1]) married **Rebecca Broad**, daughter of *Joseph Broad*. He lived in Albion, Maine, and was an influential man in his town and much esteemed.

Children:—*Born in Albion, Me.*
—734 Jane,[8] b. 1802; m. **William Stratton** (No. 338).
—735 Harriet,[8] b. 1803; m. **Israel Owen**.
+736 Wilder,[8] b. Apr. 18, 1805.
—737 Julia,[8] b. 1806; m. **Arna Owen**.

—738 Louisa,[8] b. 1809; m. —— Sinclair, and moved to Minnesota.
—739 Samuel,[8] b. Apr. 19, 1811; m. 1st, **Betsey B. Drake**; 2nd, **Sarah B. Sibley**; children, Eunice A.,[9] Louise F.,[9] Lena D.[9]
+740 Hezekiah,[8] b. Dec. 21, 1817.
—741 Eunice,[8] d. in childhood.

328. WILLIAM STRATTON [7] (*Hezekiah,*[6] *Hezekiah,*[5] *Samuel,*[4] *Samuel,*[3] *Samuel,*[2] *Samuel* [1]) married at Clinton, Me., in 1809, **Abigail May Clark**, who was born in Roxbury, Mass., July 21, 1788. They lived at the home farm at Winslow, first in the little house built by his father on the banks of the Sebasticook (only the cellar walls of this house remain), and in 1810 built near by the house that is still owned and occupied by their descendants. Every stick in the house was hewn out by William Stratton and his father. The blinds and clapboards were added at a later date. They were well known by their neighbors for their honesty and integrity, for their industry and kind neighborliness. Mr. Stratton died Sept. 26, 1849, and Mrs. Stratton, Dec. 27, 1878.

Children:—*Born in Winslow, Maine.*
—742 John Bowman,[8] b. Feb. 27, 1810; m. **Eunice E. Guptill**; d. Mar. 7, 1880; no children.
—743 Eliza,[8] b. Aug. 26, 1811; d. in infancy.
—744 William May,[8] b. Nov. 22, 1812; m. **Mary C. Chandler** in 1839. They had a son and daughter who died in infancy, and a daughter, Delia May,[9] who m. **Edward Austin** in 1859.
—745 Jane,[8] b. June 6, 1815; d. Oct. 2, 1829.
—746 Sibyl,[8] b. Dec. 11, 1816; m. **Edward Paine** in 1848.
—747 Lois,[8] b. Nov. 13, 1818; d. unm. in Augusta, Me., 1883.
 748 Charles Clark,[8] b. Mar. 7, 1820; d. unm. at the homestead, Apr. 4, 1882.
—749 Mary,[8] b. June 20, 1822; m. **Sidney Howard** in 1849.
—750 Charlotte,[8] b. Mar. 11, 1824; m. **Joseph H. Lunt**, June 2, 1863.
—751 George,[8] b. Sept. 18, 1826; d. at the homestead in 1849; unm.
—752 Emily Orissa,[8] b. June 11, 1829; m. **Joseph H. Lunt**, Feb. 7, 1861.
+753 Robert Folger,[8] b. Mar. 22, 1831.

333. EBENEZER STRATTON [7] (*Nehemiah,*[6] *Hezekiah,*[5] *Samuel,*[4] *Samuel,*[3] *Samuel,*[2] *Samuel*[1]) married **Prudelia White**, Dec. 26, 1817. He died in 1876 in Newport, Maine.

Children:—Born in Albion, Me.
- —754 Caroline,[8] b. June 6, 1819; m. **Benjamin R. Lake** in 1850.
- —755 Emmiline,[8] b. Aug. 7, 1821; m. **Hosea B. Rackliffe** in 1852; res. Newport, Me.
- —756 Rosaline,[8] b. May 21, 1823; m. **Rev. Ezekiel T. Fogg**, 1851.
- —757 Henry B.,[8] b. Aug. 10, 1825; m. **Jennie Barrett**, 1856; lived in Boston; children, Martha,[9] Mary P.,[9] Charles,[9] True.[9] Where are they?
- —758 Eliza,[8] b. Dec. 12, 1827; m. **Isaac C. Beckett** in 1865; d. 1866.
- —759 Daniel W.,[8] b. June 1, 1832; m. **Ada R. Murphy**; d. in Albion, May 30, 1872; family moved to Boston; children, Cora,[9] Caroline,[9] Ella.[9]
- —760 Isadore,[8] b. Feb. 25, 1835; m. **James C. Drake**.

335. CHARLES STRATTON [7] (*Nehemiah,*[6] *Hezekiah,*[5] *Samuel,*[4] *Samuel,*[3] *Samuel,*[2] *Samuel*[1]) went from Maine to Kaskaskia, one of the first settlements in Illinois, where he remained until Oct., 1827, when he moved to Pike Co., Ill. "He held several offices, civil and military, and was highly respected. His wife, an accomplished Christian lady, was the only daughter of Capt. John Beard. After moving to Pike Co., Col. Stratton's house became a preaching place on the Atlas circuit, where Cartwright, Akers, Hunter and other noted pioneer ministers preached. This resulted in the prosperous Methodist church at Aker's Chapel, where many were converted and from which so many have gone forth as ministers and missionaries to bless the world."

Children:
- —761 Mary[8] (?), m. **Rev. Edward Troy**.
- —762 Lois,[8] m. **Rev. Wm. J. Rutledge**.
- —763 Harriet,[8] m., Dec. 17, 1846, **Wm. C. Brickley** of Brickley Mills, Va.

Were there other children?

336. JAMES STRATTON [7] (*Nehemiah,*[6] *Hezekiah,*[5] *Samuel,*[4] *Samuel,*[3] *Samuel,*[2] *Samuel*[1]) lived and died in Albion, Me. He married **Rachel Kidder**, daughter of *John Kidder*.

Children:—Born in *Albion, Me.*
+764   James N.,[8] b. Mar. 4, 1829.
—765   Charles,[8] m. **Mary Libby** in 1845. He was a minister; he died in Burnham in 1887; no children.
—766   Lois,[8] m. **Samuel Badger**; d. in Haverhill.
—767   Lucetta,[8] m. **Milton Chalmers**; d. in Albion.
—768   Susan,[8] m. **Richard Williams**; d. in Killery, Me.
+769   Frank K.,[8] b. 1835.

338. WILLIAM STRATTON [7] (*Nehemiah,*[6] *Hezekiah,*[5] *Samuel,*[4] *Samuel,*[3] *Samuel,*[2] *Samuel* [1]) married **Jane Stratton**, daughter of *Samuel Stratton*, who died July 16, 1849. He died Apr. 26, 1851. Both died in Lawrence, Mass. What became of his children?
Children:—Born in *Albion, Me.*
—770   Sprage,[8] m. **Catherine Sibley**.
—771   Lyman.[8]
—772   Gilbert.[8]
—773   Rebecca.[8]
—774   Julia.[8]

340. JONAS STRATTON [7] (*Nehemiah,*[6] *Hezekiah,*[5] *Samuel,*[4] *Samuel,*[3] *Samuel,*[2] *Samuel* [1]) imigrated to Illinois while a young man, and settled on a farm in Adams Co. It was a fine farming country and he became quite well-to-do. He died Jan. 4, 1888. He was a member of the Methodist church. He married four times, first, **Melinda Hull**, who died within the year; second, **Sophia Baxley** in 1832; third, **Elizabeth Harvey** in 1841; fourth, **Mrs. Susan J. Elsworth** in 1853.
Children:—Born in *Adams Co., Ill.*
   By second marriage.
—775   Roxey A.,[8] b. Sept. 25, 1834; m. **William Milner**, Apr. 8, 1853; d. in St. Joseph, Mo., in 1875.
   By third marriage.
+776   Sipio,[8] b. Apr. 1, 1843.
—777   Lois,[8] b. Mar. 9, 1840; d. aged two years.
—778   Charles W.,[8] b. Oct. 8, 1848; a farmer near Tina, Carroll Co., Mo.; m. **Mary Wagy**.
—779   Jane S.,[8] b. Aug. 24, 1851; m. **Robert R. Reed** in 1871; d. New London, Mo., in 1884.
   By fourth marriage.
—780   George W.,[8] a photographer near Plainville, Ill.

—781 David Almon,⁸ b. Dec. 17, 1856; m. **Hattie Hughes**; res. Plainville, Ill.; has one daughter, Anna Katharine.⁹

—782 James G.,⁸ a musician; d. unm. at Lamar, Colo., June, 1893.

—783 Benjamin Franklin,⁸ m. **Joy Cook**, Oct. 10, 1889; d. Oklahoma City, Sept. 18, 1904; chn. Clifford,⁹ Claude,⁹ Albert,⁹ Hazel.⁹

—784 Frances Daisy,⁸ m. **Charles Holcomb**, 1887; res. Davenport, Iowa.

343. Newell Stratton⁷ (*Nehemiah,*⁶ *Hezekiah,*⁵ *Samuel,*⁴ *Samuel,*³ *Samuel,*² *Samuel*¹) married **Abigail Dunham**, Sept. 20, 1834, daughter of *Ebenezer Dunham*. Lived for several years at Bangor, Me. Leaving his family at Bangor, he went to Little Rock, Ark., where he engaged as a mason and contractor for several years, building several large brick houses. In Oct., 1846, he settled with his family in Chicago, where he conducted the Planters' House and the Sanguask Hotel. He died of cholera Aug. 23, 1848. His wife died Mar. 21, 1858.

Children:—*Born in Bangor, Maine.*

—785 Helen Ann,⁸ b. Apr. 28, 1838, living in Chicago in 1909.

—786 Abby Newell,⁸ b. July 29, 1838; m. **William T. Scott**, Sept. 21, 1860, who died Mar. 14, 1898. She died in Chicago, Feb. 7, 1907.

345. Shubael Child Stratton⁷ (*Jonathan,*⁶ *Jonathan,*⁵ *Samuel,*⁴ *Samuel,*³ *Samuel,*² *Samuel*¹) married **Betsey Cook** of New Salem; she died in Crawford Co., Pa. He was a merchant in Phillipston and New Salem, and dealt, too, in real estate, having at his death, Aug. 6, 1816, land in New Salem, Phillipston, Monmouth and Edington. He lived for a few years at Bangor, Me., and did business there, but returned to Phillipston, where he died.*

---

* Among the many papers on the administration of the Estate of Shubael Child Stratton are numerous items of expenses of settlement. The following are here given as showing money values at that time:

   Cash paid Post-rider (for letter).......................$ .12
   Horse hire, 4 times, 12 miles.......................... .48
   Expense money... .07
   Horse hire, 4 miles................................... .16
   For day's time as commissioners (3 men at 50c. per day). 1.50

Sons of Shubael C. Stratton, Sr. *Pages 72, 120, 121.*
Henry   James C.   Ira

Children:—Born in Phillipston, Mass.
- —787 Catherine,[8] b. Oct. 8, 1796; d. July 10, 1800.
- —788 Louisa,[8] b. Oct. 22, 1798; m. **Wisnell Humphrey**, son of Rev. Jas. Humphrey; d. in 1830.

Born in Bangor, Me.
- +789 Franklin,[8] b. July 30, 1801.
- +790 Ira,[8] b. Jan. 6, 1804.
- +791 Henry,[8] b. Oct. 28, 1807.
- +792 George,[8] b. June 16, 1809.
- +793 James, C.,[8] b. Apr. 26, 1812.
- +794 Shubael Child,[8] b. Oct. 28, 1814.

347. BRADDYLL STRATTON [7] (*Jonathan*,[6] *Jonathan*,[5] *Samuel*,[4] *Samuel*,[3] *Samuel*,[2] *Samuel* [1]) married **Hannah Coolidge Harrington** of Lincoln, Dec. 28, 1797. She was a daughter of *Capt. Daniel Harrington*, a Revolutionary soldier at Lexington. She died in Phillipston, Apr. 18, 1800, aged 26 years. Mr. Stratton died Apr. 18, 1826.

Children:—Born in Phillipston, Mass.
- +795 Daniel Harrington,[8] b. Feb. 23, 1799.
- +796 William Coolidge,[8] b. Mar. 23, 1800.

These two boys after the early death of their mother, were brought up by their grandparents—one in Lincoln and the other in Phillipston. In early manhood they drifted apart and lost track of each other. The descendants of each have recently become known to one another through *Vol. I* of *A Book of Strattons*.

350. JONATHAN STRATTON [7] (*Jonathan*,[6] *Jonathan*,[5] *Samuel*,[4] *Samuel*,[3] *Samuel*,[2] *Samuel* [1]) married **Betsey Bowker** in Phillipston, Jan. 29, 1806. She died June 15, 1837, aged 53 years. He died May 24, 1844. Both are buried in the old graveyard near the old Stratton house, one and a half miles from Phillipston on the Petersham road.*

Children:—Born in Phillipston, Mass.
- —797 Harriet Eliza,[8] b. Oct. 3, 1806; m. Apr. 20, 1830, **Phenney Merrill.**

---

* The Stratton lot in this old burial ground is an oblong enclosure with six stone posts, connected by iron rods running through them. In it are six Stratton graves: Jonathan Stratton and wife Sarah, Jonathan Stratton and wife Betsey, Shubael Child Stratton and Susanna Stratton. The latest grave was made more than seventy years ago.

+798   Jonathan Ransom,⁸ b. Apr. 10, 1808.
−799   Susan Bryant,⁸ b. June 19, 1810; d. in Brooklyn, 1893, unm.
+800   Franklin B.,⁸ b. June 12, 1813.
−801   Homer,⁸ b. Feb. 13, 1815; m. **Julia Stratton**, daughter of John Stratton of Swanzy, N. H. (No. 1059). No children.
−802   John Bushrod,⁸ b. July 1, 1817; m. **Clara Cotton**, May 7, 1857; d. in Eureka, Nevada, 1879; no issue.
−803   Hezekiah N.,⁸ b. July 2, 1822; m. **Josephine Curtis Prindle** in 1862; one of the early dentists of Brooklyn, occupying a prominent position.

351.   ISAAC STRATTON ⁷ (*Jonathan,⁶ Jonathan,⁵ Samuel,⁴ Samuel,³ Samuel,² Samuel ¹*) married **Lydia Cook**. He died in New Salem, Apr. 23, 1854.

Children:—*Born in New Salem, Mass.*
−804   Royal Altamont,⁸ m. **Martha Stearns**; chn.:—Charles Cook,⁹ d. unm., and Lydia,⁹ m. **Jabez Trask** of New Salem.
−805   Rosana Relief,⁸ b. 1807; killed by lightning, June 1, 1821, in New Salem.

352.   NATHAN STRATTON ⁷ (*Jonathan,⁶ Jonathan,⁵ Samuel,⁴ Samuel,³ Samuel,² Samuel ¹*) married **Mary Earle** of Gerry, June 26, 1810. She died in 1819, aged 36 years.

Children:—*Born in Phillipston, Mass.*
−806   Mary Alzina,⁸ b. Nov. 10, 1810; m. **Albert Thorpe**.
−807   Charles Dwight,⁸ b. Aug. 16, 1812.
−808   Oscar,⁸ b. Oct. 27, 1814; d. without issue, in Iowa.
−809   Hezekiah,⁸ b. May 2, 1818; d. aged 2 years.

355.   DANIEL STRATTON ⁷ (*Daniel,⁶ Jonathan,⁵ Samuel,⁴ Samuel,³ Samuel,² Samuel ¹*) married **Cally Smith** in Weston, May 23, 1800, daughter of *Capt. Aaron Smith*, a Revolutionary soldier. She was born in Needham, and died in Bolton, Aug. 24, 1857. Mr. Stratton died Apr. 14, 1837. He was a prominent man and held many town offices.

Children:—*Born in Harvard, Mass.*
−810   Martha,⁸ b. 1801; never married.
+811   Rufus,⁸ b. 1802.
−812   Mary,⁸ b. 1804; m. **Samuel Dudley**.

+813 Lorenzo,⁸ b. 1806.
—814 Cynthia,⁸ b. 1808; m. —— Hills.
—815 Caroline,⁸ b. 1810; m. **Albert Randall**, Aug. 17, 1834.
—816 Salinda,⁸ b. 1812.
—817 Harriett,⁸ b. 1815.
Born in Marlboro, Mass.
+818 Daniel,⁸ b. 1817.
—819 Lucy Train,⁸ b. 1819; m. **Charles Burgess**; d. in Hudson, May 3, 1895.
—820 George,⁸ b. 1822; d. aged 4 years.

359. Josiah Stratton ⁷ (*Daniel,*⁶ *Jonathan,*⁵ *Samuel,*⁴ *Samuel,*³ *Samuel,*² *Samuel*¹) married **Sarah Russell**, daughter of *Amos* and *Betsey Russell*, Apr. 19, 1808. She was born in Lexington, Feb. 20, 1783, and died in Woburn, May 27, 1855. Mr. Stratton died June 14, 1865.

Children:—*Born in Woburn.*
—821 Lydia Russell,⁸ b. Feb. 10, 1810; m. 1st, **Albert Richardson**, Apr. 15, 1832; m. 2nd, **Tracy Nichols** in 1838.
—822 Sarah,⁸ b. Apr. 25, 1812; d. aged about 1 year.
+823 Josiah,⁸ b. Apr. 8, 1817.
—824 Calvin,⁸ b. May 8, 1824; d. Dec. 16, 1825.

360. Dana Stratton ⁷ (*Daniel,*⁶ *Jonathan,*⁵ *Samuel,*⁴ *Samuel,*³ *Samuel,*² *Samuel*¹) married **Sarah Townsand**, Feb. 14, 1811, in Malden. He died in Malden, Nov. 19, 1850.

Children:—*Born in Malden, Mass.*
—825 Sarah,⁸ b. June 7, 1811; d. aged about 1 year.
—826 Francis Dana,⁸ b. July 13, 1813; m. **Sarah M. Cutler**, May 31, 1840; chn. Augusta,⁹ Margaret,⁹ Marietta,⁹ George.⁹
—827 Abraham,⁸ b. Aug. 23, 1815; d. Apr. 20, 1816.
—828 Sarah,⁸ b. June 4, 1817; d. in infancy.
—829 Charlotte,⁸ b. June 20, 1819; m. **Franklin Pierce**, Apr. 28, 1839.
—830 Charles,⁸ b. Jan. 13, 1822.

367. Nahum Stratton ⁷ (*Isaac,*⁶ *Jonathan,*⁵ *Samuel,*⁴ *Samuel,*³ *Samuel,*² *Samuel*¹) married, Aug. 13, 1826, **Eliza Read**, daughter of *James* and *Mary Stebbins* (*Brown*) *Read* of Cambridge. He went to Richmond, Va., where he and his family lived for many years. His wife died there in **1837**, and is buried in St. John's churchyard. He died in Richmond during the Civil War.

Children:—*Born in Richmond, Va.*
- —831 Mary Eliza,⁸ educated in Boston; m. Dec. 24, 1855, **John W. Clarke** of Louisville, Ky.
- —832 James Lewis,⁸ in C. S. army; d. in hospital during the Civil War.

369. Henry Stratton ⁷ (*Isaac,⁶ Jonathan,⁵ Samuel,⁴ Samuel,³ Samuel,² Samuel¹*) married **Sylvia Balcom** in Sudbury, May 27, **1819**. He died in Lincoln, Dec. 27, 1874.

Children:—*Born in Weston, Mass.*
- —833 Matilda C.,⁸ b. June 30, 1821; m. **Charles C. P. Harris** in 1847.
- —834 Charles H.,⁸ b. Aug. 26, 1823; m. **Mrs. Annie French**; d. in Lincoln, Mass.; no children.
- —835 Mary Jane,⁸ b. Aug. 27, 1826; m. **John S. Adams**, 1869; res. Lowell, Mass.
- +836 Lewis,⁸ b. Mar. 6, 1830.
- +837 Francis,⁸ b. Nov. 5, 1834.

375. Thomas Stratton ⁷ (*Elisha,⁶ Jonathan,⁵ Samuel,⁴ Samuel,³ Samuel,² Samuel¹*) married **Eunice Smith** of Waltham, Mar. 29, **1812**. Their house was close to the line between Weston and Waltham. He died Nov. 14, 1857. He owned property in Watertown and was taxed there in 1834.

Children:
- —838 Thomas Dexter, b. Mar. 6, 1813; kept a dry goods and general merchandise store for 60 years in Waltham near the Weston line; m. **Ann Sawtell**; d. Jan. 18, 1898. No children.*
- —839 Abigail, b. Oct. 14, 1819; d. unm.

376. Charles Stratton ⁶ (*Elisha,⁵ Jonathan,⁴ Samuel,³ Samuel,² Samuel¹*) lived and died in his native town, where he was an excellent citizen, and one of the active business men of his day. Although he died at the early age of thirty-two, he had

---

* A Waltham man writes: "Thomas D. Stratton was a quaint old landmark. His store was a veritable curiosity shop. Anything could be found at 'Stratton's.' One day a would-be humorist inquired for a second-hand pulpit. 'All out to-day,' said Stratton, 'just sold the last one. Have plenty more in to-morrow.'"

Sons of Shubael C. Stratton, Sr. *Pages* 72, 120, 121.

George   Franklin   Shubael C., Jr.

already been successful in business, and accumulated a considerable property. In addition to other business interests, he was for several years proprietor of the "Stratton Tavern," in Watertown. He married, Oct. 7, 1808, **Elizabeth Hobbs**, daughter of *Nathan* and *Lydia (Child) Hobbs* of Weston, and granddaughter of *Isaac Child* of Waltham. She was born June 8, 1788. Mr. Stratton was captain of the Weston and Medford Light Infantry, Independent Co., First Brigade, Third Division, Mass. Militia. This commission he resigned Apr. 1, 1817.*

Children:—B*orn in Watertown, Mass.*

—840   Martha,[8] b. Dec., 1809; m. **Benjamin Dana**, May 24, 1829; d. in Watertown, Apr. 13, 1865.

—841   Eliza Ann,[8] b. Aug. 22, 1810; a teacher in Boston; d. unm.

+842   Charles Edwin,[8] b. Aug. 12, 1813.

—843   Frances Maria,[8] b. May 1, 1817; m. **Samuel Learnard**, May 17, 1840; d. Mar. 23, 1842.

378. ELISHA STRATTON [7] (*Elisha,*[6] *Jonathan,*[5] *Samuel,*[4] *Samuel,*[3] *Samuel,*[2] *Samuel*[1]) married **Hannah Bond.**[8] For many years he kept the "Stratton Tavern" in Watertown, then moved to Lowell, where he was a shopkeeper and where he died, a widower, Feb. 7, 1854. He is buried in Watertown.†

Child:

—844   Elisha Torry.[8] He was 17 years at the time of his father's death, "only child and sole heir." What became of him?

379. GEORGE STRATTON [6] (*Elisha,*[5] *Jonathan,*[4] *Samuel,*[3] *Samuel,*[2] *Samuel*[1]) was a farmer near Weston. In 1825 he married **Priscella Hurd**, daughter of *David* and *Sybil Hurd*. She died Mar. 22, 1859, aged 60 years. Mr. Stratton died Aug. 29, 1852.

Children:—B*orn in Weston, Mass.*

+845   George Hurd, b. Mar. 22, 1826.

—846   Adaline, b. June, 1834; m. **Josiah Pamenter**; d. in 1892.

---

* In sending in his resignation he says: "The distance from the company under my command is so great that it renders it very inconvenient for me to perform the duties that are encumbent on the Commander of such a company. Also I have had the honor to hold commissions in the Militia of Mass. the full term the law requires. With these reasons I most respectfully request discharge."

† Nov. 25, 1815, he owned "Pew No. 2, Broad aisle, in Watertown Meeting house."

382. ASA STRATTON [7] (*Ebenezer,*[6] *Samuel,*[5] *Samuel,*[4] *Samuel,*[3] *Samuel,*[2] *Samuel*[1]) married in Ashley, Mass., Aug. 4, 1800, **Rhoda Sanders** of Townsend. She died Dec. 17, 1829, and he married, second, Aug. 28, 1804, **Anna Wilker** of Ashburnham, who died in Oct., 1840. He died in Ashley, Aug. 15, 1851. He is called "Captain Stratton" on Ashburnham records.

Children:—*Born in Ashley, Mass.*
+847 Homer,[8] b. Dec. 9, 1800.
—848 Sumner,[8] b. Mar. 6, 1804; died in childhood.

383. JOSIAH STRATTON [7] (*Ebenezer,*[6] *Samuel,*[5] *Samuel,*[4] *Samuel,*[3] *Samuel,*[2] *Samuel*[1]) lived in Jeffrey, N. H. He married **Hepsibah Earl**, Jan. 26, 1808, daughter of *John Earl*. She died Oct. 10, 1853. Mr. Stratton died in Ringe, N. H., Nov. 30, 1856. His will is in the Probate office at Keene.

Children:—*Born in Rindge, N. H.*
—849 John,[8] b. Oct. 18, 1808; d., unm., in Boston, July 20, 1838.
+850 Raymond,[8] b. Feb. 5, 1811.
—851 Grata,[8] b. May 15, 1814; m. **Ephraim W. Lord**, June 4, 1845; res. Westminster, Vt.
—852 Mary J.,[8] b. July 16, 1818; m. **Lucius Streeter**, Oct. 27, 1836.
+853 Josiah,[8] b. June 4, 1821.
—854 Levi,[8] b. July 1, 1824.

386. EBENEZER STRATTON [7] (*Ebenezer,*[6] *Samuel,*[5] *Samuel,*[4] *Samuel,*[3] *Samuel,*[2] *Samuel*[1]) lived in Rindge until 1857, and then moved to Jaffrey. He married, first, **Elizabeth Hildreth** in 1810; second, **Sibyl Adams**, June 1, 1826, daughter of *Israel Adams*. He died June 5, 1864.*

Children:—*Born in Rindge, N. H.*
By first marriage.
—855 Seth Hildreth,[8] b. Feb. 24, 1811.

---

* The author has the following records, but does not know whether they are the children of Ebenezer Stratton by his second marriage, or the children of his brother, Samuel Stratton. Who knows?
  a. Miranda, b. Jan. 13, 1827; d. Dec. 15, 1842.
  b. William, b. Oct. 28, 1829.
  c. Augusta, b. April 27, 1831; d. Oct. 6, 1873.
  d. Samuel A., b. July 9, 1832; lived in Grafton.
  e. Maria Martha, b. Jan. 23, 1835.
Further information is desired.

+856 Stillman,⁸ b. Feb. 17, 1814.
+857 George,⁸ b. Mar. 31, 1818.
—858 Amos,⁸ d. unm.

390. SAMUEL STRATTON ⁷ (*David,⁶ Samuel,⁵ Samuel,⁴ Samuel,³ Samuel,² Samuel¹*) married, first, **Sarah Gilman**, and second, **Abigail Fife**. He was a soldier in the war of 1812. He lived and died in Jaffrey.
Children:—B*orn in Jaffrey, N. H.*
—859 George Washington,⁸ b. 1824.
—860 Samuel Augustus,⁸ b. 1826.
—861 Sarah Ann,⁸ b. 1827.
—862 Mary,⁸ b. 1829.
—863 Martha W.,⁸ b. 1832.
—864 Julias,⁸ twin, 1839.
—865 Julia,⁸ twin, 1839.

391. ISAAC STRATTON ⁷ (*David,⁶ Samuel,⁵ Samuel,⁴ Samuel,³ Samuel,² Samuel¹*) married **Elizabeth Bailey**, daughter of *Isaac Bailey*. She died in 1873 and he in 1877. They lived and died in Jaffrey.
Children:—B*orn in Jaffrey, N. H.*
—866 Jonathan Wheelock,⁸ b. Mar. 3, 1814; m. **Edna J. Parker**; no children.
—867 Mary Elizabeth,⁸ b. May 25, 1816; m. **Wm. Stevens** in 1856.
—868 Elvira,⁸ b. Aug. 8, 1818; m. **Dea. Richard Spaulding,** 1851.
—869 Charles,⁸ b. Aug. 3, 1821.
—870 Lucinda,⁸ b. Aug. 14, 1823; m. **Benjamin Pierce,** 1846; d. June 17, 1888.
—871 James Bailey,⁸ b. Apr. 14, 1828; drowned in the Yuba River, California, Jan. 4, 1853; unm.

395. JOHN STRATTON ⁷ (*Samuel,⁶ Samuel,⁵ Samuel,⁴ Samuel,³ Samuel,² Samuel¹*) lived in Princeton; married **Agnes Manford** in 1823; died Aug. 11, 1870.
Children:—B*orn in Princeton, Mass.*
+872 Samuel,⁸ b. 1824.
+873 Moses B.,⁸ b. 1826.
+874 Danforth D.,⁸ b. 1828.

403. Samuel Stratton [7] (*Samuel*,[6] *Samuel*,[5] *Samuel*,[4] *Samuel*,[3] *Samuel*,[2] *Samuel*[1]) was a blacksmith by trade, and lived in Holden, where he owned considerable real estate. He married **Hannah Hubbard.** She was a daughter of *Joseph* and *Milla Hubbard.* She died in Holden, Nov. 2, 1868, aged 72 years. He went to Indiana, leaving his family in Holden, and died there Mar. 5, 1881.

Children:—*Born in Holden, Mass.*
- —875 Alphonso,[8] b. June 22, 1825; m. **Perris Wyman**; their only child, Henry Alphonso,[9] d. in infancy.
- —876 Frederick Augustus,[8] b. May 23, 1825; m. **Harriet Tenny**; only child, Mary,[9] d. aged 21 years.
- —877 Martha Jane,[8] b. May 15, 1827; d. aged 29 years.
- —878 Julian,[8] b. Sept. 20, 1829; res. Worcester.
- —879 Elizabeth,[8] b. Mar. 24, 1832; m. **Jasper Howe** of Chilton, June 5, 1858.
- —880 Mary Chenery,[8] b. May 14, 1834; d. aged 12 years.
- —881 Hannah Maria,[8] b. Oct. 24, 1836; m. **Abner Perry Greenwood**, Feb. 11, 1859.
- —882 Eleanor,[8] b. 1839; d. 1857.

409. Alpheus Stratton [7] (*Alpheus*,[6] *Samuel*,[5] *Samuel*,[4] *Samuel*,[3] *Samuel*,[2] *Samuel*[1]) married, Dec. 16, 1815, **Sarah Ellis**, daughter of *James* and *Sarah (Stone) Ellis* of Princeton.* She was born Mar. 10, 1796. They lived in Rutland, Paxton, and Holden. Mr. Stratton died in Worcester, July 10, 1853. They were both of Sterling at the time of their marriage.

Children:
- —883 William Jefferson,[8] served in the Civil War.
- —884 Martha Bush,[8] m. **Jacob Jones.**
- +885 Cyprian Kies.[8]
- —886 Francis James.[8]
- +887 Thomas Walter,[8] b. in Holden, Apr. 11, 1829.
- —888 Hiram Horatio.[8]
- —889 Willard Snow,[8] married in Syracuse, N. Y., and went west soon after the Civil War and was not again heard from by his relations. Information regarding him is desired.

---

*James Ellis was a man of some wealth in Princeton—a manufacturer of door latches. He came from England, "leaving a rich father and uncle and discipline, to try his fortune in the new world."

—890 Tryphose Emerite,[8] m. 1st, **Theodore Muzzy**; 2nd, **John L. Bishop**; res. Worcester, Mass.
—891 Sarah Ellis,[8] d. in Rutland, aged 2 years, 6 mos.

410. CRYPRIAN STRATTON [7] (*Alpheus,*[6] *Samuel,*[5] *Samuel,*[4] *Samuel,*[3] *Samuel,*[2] *Samuel* [1]) married, first, **Susanna Child**. They lived in Rutland, where she died, July 4, 1831. He married, second, **Mary Keep** of N. Brookfield, Oct. 1, 1831 (int.). He died May 22, 1854. He was a farmer.
Children:—*Born in Rutland, Mass.*
By first marriage.
—892 Hiram Horatio,[8] b. Oct. 3, 1814; d. aged 4 years.
—893 Lavinia Temple,[8] b. Aug. 11, 1820; m. **Billings F. Richardson**, Apr. 8, 1840.
—894 Mabel Izabel,[8] b. Oct. 13, 1825.
—895 Susan Emeline,[8] b. July 24, 1831.
By second marriage.
—896 Martha Jane,[8] b. Sept. 9, 1838; m. **Solomon Richardson, Jr.**, Oct. 2, 1845.
—897 Charles Henry,[8] b. July 26, 1840.

There were two other children who died in infancy or childhood between 1828 and 1832. Some of above dates may be dates of baptism instead of birth.

411. SAMUEL STRATTON [7] (*Alpheus,*[6] *Samuel,*[5] *Samuel,*[4] *Samuel,*[3] *Samuel,*[2] *Samuel* [1]) lived in Rutland, where he married, Apr. 21, 1814, **Sarah Hubbard**, who died in 1832. He was a farmer.
Children:—*Born in Rutland, Mass.*
—898 Horace Hubbard,[8] b. Oct. 28, 1814; m. **Harriet Willis** in Spencer, July 3, 1843, both of Paxton.
—899 Vasleti Howe,[8] b. Feb. 6, 1815; m. **John Smith**.
+900 Nathaniel Hapgood,[8] b. Feb. 12, 1818.
—901 James McFarland,[8] b. July 3, 1823; m. **Mary Edson**; lived in Greenwich; d. Oct. 30, 1841; no children.
—902 Ebenezer,[8] d. in infancy.

429. CALEB ALLEN STRATTON [7] (*Ebenezer,*[6] *Hezekiah,*[5] *Samuel,*[4] *Samuel,*[3] *Samuel,*[2] *Samuel* [1]) married, first, **Maria Smith**, Jan. 9, 1826. She died the following month. May 7, 1828, he married **Emily Edson** of Brookfield, Vt. She died Apr. 8, 1868, aged 68 years. He married, third, **Mrs. Laura A. Edson**. She

died July, 1879. He lived and died in the house built by his father in Brookfield. The house is still standing in good repair. He was a farmer and a member of the Congregational church. He died Jan. 12, 1882.

Children:—*Born in Brookfield, Vt.*
By first marriage.
—903 Emily M.,⁸ b. Nov. 13, 1830; m. 1st, **Nelson D. Graves**; moved to Walseka, Ill.; m. 2nd, **John Kea** of Primghar, Ill.; d. Jan. 10, 1910.
—904 Cornelius A.,⁸ b. Jan. 9, 1830; m. **Addie Ackley** of San Francisco, Cal. She died Nov., 1894. He died Feb. 3, 1894. They had three daughters, Carrie,⁹ Lucia,⁹ Addie.⁹
—905 Martha,⁸ b. Aug. 25, 1836; m. **Dr. E. L. Holt**, dentist.
—906 Harriet,⁸ b. Oct. 22, 1838; m., in 1898, **G. H. Cook**, his second wife; res. Primghar, Iowa.
—907 Lucia,⁸ b. Aug. 30, 1840; m. **E. F. Hoadley**, 1868, of Swanton, Vt. She died July 31, 1895.
+908 Carlos Edson,⁸ b. June 12, 1844.

436. CALEB STRONG STRATTON ⁷ (*Caleb,⁶ Eleazer,⁵ Hezekiah,⁴ Samuel,³ Samuel,² Samuel¹*) married **Elvira Smith** in 1826 and moved to Lake Co., Ohio, where he bought a farm. He died in 1842.

Children:—*Born in Madison, Ohio.*
—909 Charles S.,⁸ b. 1832; d. aged 4 years.
—910 Eliza,⁸ b. 1834; d. 1854.
+911 Asa Strong,⁸ b. 1836.
—912 Lydia E.,⁸ b. 1838.
—913 Emily,⁸ b. 1842; d. in infancy.

441. ROSWELL STRATTON ⁷ (*Asa,⁶ Eleazer,⁵ Hezekiah,⁴ Samuel,³ Samuel,² Samuel¹*) married, Jan. 26, 1815, **Rhoda Wright**, who died Aug. 28, 1857, aged 74 years. He died Feb. 22, 1842.

Children:—*Born in Northfield, Mass.*
—914 Chester,⁸ b. Mar. 19, 1816. A dentist in Amherst; m. **Charlotte ——**; left no children.
—915 Roswell,⁸ b. Sept. 20, 1818; d. Sept. 20, 1819.
—916 Roswell,⁸ b. Sept. 28, 1819; m. **Mary Belknap**, Nov. 20, 1850; d. Mar. 5, 1898; two children, Willis,⁹ d. in infancy, and Meda E.,⁹ m. **Arnold H. Holton** of Northfield.

+917 George,⁸ b. July 2, 1823.
—918 Augusta Amelia,⁸ b. Jan. 6, 1823; a noted teacher in Ind.; lived at Lafayette; d. Sept. 24, 1899.

442. ASA STRATTON⁷ (*Asa*,⁶ *Eleazer*,⁵ *Hezekiah*,⁴ *Samuel*,³ *Samuel*,² *Samuel*¹) was a farmer on the homestead of his father until 1854, when he sold his part of the estate and moved to Greenfield, where he died Apr. 3, 1869. He married, Dec. 15, 1814, **Sophia Holton**, who was born in Northfield in 1794, a woman of marked ability and brightness, which she retained to the close of her long life of 96 years. She was a daughter of *Samuel Holton*.

Children:—Born in Northfield, Mass.
—919 Sarah S.,⁸ b. Mar. 4, 1816; d. in childhood.
—920 Frederick Spooner,⁸ b. Jan. 31, 1817; a dentist in Keene, N. H.; d. in Greenwich Sept. 20, 1897.
+921 Edwin Alexander,⁸ b. Sept. 15, 1819.
—922 Charles M.,⁸ b. 1823; a business man of Greenfield; m. **Emma E. Mann**, Oct. 30, 1873; d. Aug., 1893; no children.
—923 Sarah A.,⁸ b. Feb. 6, 1827; m. **Cabel Ruffane** of Keene, N. H.
—924 Franklin Asa,⁸ b. Nov. 30, 1829. Col. in 11th Penn. Cavalry; twice wounded in battle; breveted Brigadier-General for gallant and meritorious service. Later civil engineer in government employ at Washington, D. C., and Mare Island, Cal.; m. **Georgeanna Kealing**; d. in Philadelphia in 1895; no children.
—925 Oscar Granville,⁸ b. Aug. 19, 1832; res. Greenville, Mass.; unm.

444. SETH STRATTON⁷ (*Asa*,⁶ *Eleazer*,⁵ *Hezekiah*,⁴ *Samuel*,³ *Samuel*,² *Samuel*¹) married **Freedom Holton (or Holden)** about 1828, and moved to New Ipswich, where he was a wheelwright. Mrs. Stratton died here Jan. 13, 1890, aged 93 years.

Children:
—926 Edward,⁸ m. and lived at Nashua, N. H., and Lowell, Mass. Had a son, Charles,⁹ and perhaps other children.
—927 Sarah Elizabeth,⁸ m. Nov. 11, 1873, **Allen Ripley**; removed to California.

446. ALONZO STRATTON [7] (*Asa*,[6] *Eleazer*,[5] *Hezekiah*,[4] *Samuel*,[3] *Samuel*,[2] *Samuel*[1]) married **Mary Wood**, daughter of *Samuel Wood*. They lived in Athol, where he met his death in a fire in 1871.

Children:—*Born in Athol, Mass.**
- —928   Samuel W.,[8] b. 1827; a sailor; killed by a whale.
- —929   Marshall,[8] b. 1829; settled in Maine?
- —930   Francis E.,[8] b. 1832; m. **Eliza** (or **Elizabeth**) **Putman**.
- —931   Mary J.,[8] b. 1834; m. 1st, **Amos B. Fulsom**; 2nd, **Thomas J. Barnes**; moved to California.
- —932   Lucy M.,[8] b. 1836; m. **Joseph Lord** of Athol.
- —933   Ella,[8] d. aged 9 years.

447. ALBERT STRATTON [7] (*Asa*,[6] *Eleazer*,[5] *Hezekiah*,[4] *Samuel*,[3] *Samuel*,[2] *Samuel*[1]), after receiving the education afforded by the district school at Northfield, acquired first the trade of shoemaker, and then mason, which he followed for some time. Later he purchased a mill which he operated for several years, and then bought a farm upon which he lived for about thirty years. He died at the home of his son at the age of seventy years. He married **Lucy Simpson**, daughter of *Charles Simpson*. She died Mar. 8, 1874, aged 73 years.

Children:—B*orn in Northfield, Mass.*
- +934   Albert S.,[8] b. Nov. 10, 1823.
- —935   Lucy A.,[8] b. 1830; d. aged 16 years.

451. ELEAZER STRATTON [7] (*Eleazer*,[6] *Eleazer*,[5] *Hezekiah*,[4] *Samuel*,[3] *Samuel*,[2] *Samuel*[1]) was a blacksmith by trade. He must have spent his youth in Vermont, and perhaps married there. But later he lived in Massachusetts. He died in Colerain Sept. 23, 1864. He married **Zylpha White**.

Children:—B*orn in Adairsvill, Mass.*
- +936   Leonard White,[8] b. Apr. 28, 1828.
- —937   Sarah Helen,[8] b. Dec. 9, 1832; m. **Miles C. Smith**, Oct. 15, 1855; d. July 20, 1881.

452. ALVIN STRATTON [7] (*Eleazer*,[6] *Eleazer*,[5] *Hezekiah*,[4] *Samuel*,[3] *Samuel*,[2] *Samuel*[1]) married **Loantha Sherman**, daughter of *Jonathan* and *Thankful* (*Smith*) *Sherman*, who was born May 6,

---

* So says *History of Northfield*. The compiler found no records of this family at Athol.

1807, in Barre, Vt. They lived in Barre, Hardwick and Elmore, Vt., and in 1841 they moved to Colerain, Mass., making the journey of more than 125 miles on a one-horse sled. He bought a farm in Colerain, and spent the rest of his life there, a respected, prosperous farmer.

Children:—*Born in Vermont.*
- —938 Philo,[8] b. Nov. 5, 1826. Soldier in the Civil War; Col. in 49th Kentucky Volunteers; married a Kentucky lady, and lived and died in Lexington; buried in Odd Fellows cemetery at Owenton, Ky. No children.
- —939 Clark,[8] b. abt. 1832. Soldier in Federal army; went west after the war. Was at Chicago for awhile, and when last heard from at Marquette, Mich. It is understood that he married but had no children.

Born at Elmore, Vt.
- —940 Tryphene,[8] b. Aug. 28, 1827; m. **Wm. Herrick.**
- —941 Chloe,[8] b. Oct. 23, 1831; m. **Jonathan Peterson,** son of *Sylvanus* and *Lavina (Call) Peterson,* July 3, 1851; d. in Heath, Mass., Feb. 25, 1892.*
- —942 Lydia,[8] b. July 22, 1835; m. **George V. York.**
- —943 Eleazer,[8] b. Dec. 19, 1836; d. aged about 4 years in Colerain.

Born in Colerain, Mass.
- —944 George Franklin,[8] b. June 5, 1842; enlisted June 21, 1861, in Co. H, 10th Mass. Inf.; wounded May 31, 1862, at Fair Oaks, Va.; died 12 days after at David's Island Hospital.
- —945 Solomon,[8] b. July 28, 1848; d. in childhood.

456. SAMUEL STRATTON [7] (*Rufus,*[6] *Hezekiah,*[5] *Hezekiah,*[4] *Samuel,*[3] *Samuel,*[2] *Samuel*[1]) married **Olivia Rawson** in Erving, Mar. 25, 1807. She was born in Uxbridge, Mass., Mar. 14, 1787. They settled in Gill, where he became a prosperous farmer. They were members of the Congregational church. He died at his home in Gill, Oct. 17, 1851. Mrs. Stratton died July 7, 1863, at the home of her daughter, Mrs. Pratt, in Montague, Mass.

---

*Their son, Bion Nelson Peterson, m. Cornelia A. Reynolds, and their children are France A., Alice Stratton, Guy Jonathan and Marion C.

Jonathan Peterson was a man of the strong religious convictions of his *Mayflower* ancestry, greatly respected and trusted by his fellow townsmen, who elected him again and again to offices requiring strict honesty and good, sound judgment.

Children:—*Born in Gill, Mass.*
- —946 Asentha Field,⁸ b. July 10, 1810; m. **Dwight Morgan,** June 1, 1829. Drowned in Conn. River at Gill.
- —947 Sarah Batchelor,⁸ b. Jan. 26, 1814; m. **Prentice Slate,** Apr. 27, 1837; d. Oct. 5, 1857.
- —948 Mary Twing,⁸ b. July 23, 1816; m. July 16, 1844, **Ransom Nutting**; d. in Decatur, Mich.
- —949 Lucy Livia,⁸ b. Aug. 19, 1820; m. **Samuel Pratt,** June 17, 1842; lived in Montague, Mass.
- +950 Samuel Pinkney,⁸ b. Nov. 16, 1822.
- —951 Martha Ann,⁸ b. Mar. 21, 1825; m. **Horace Patridge,** June 17, 1847; res. Cambridge, Mass.
- +952 Alfred Morrell,⁸ b. Feb. 26, 1827.
- —953 Benjamin Franklin,⁸ b. Oct. 29, 1835; m. **Lucy L. Warner** at Salem, Mass.; a Federal soldier in Co. A, 50th Mass. Infantry; d. in hospital at Baton Rouge, La., May 1, 1863. Only child, Mary A.,⁹ b. July 30, 1861, in Boston; m. **John Schühle**; res. Highland, N. Y.
- —954 William Henry,⁸ b. Dec. 29, 1808; d. aged 2 years.
- —955 Elizabeth J.,⁸ b. July 7, 1829; d. in infancy.

457. ELIHU STRATTON ⁷ (*Rufus,*⁶ *Hezekiah,*⁵ *Hezekiah,*⁴ *Samuel,*³ *Samuel,*² *Samuel* ¹) married **Electa Holton,** May 9, 1810, a daughter of *Elisha Holton.* In 1832 he was selectman. He owned a good farm, and was ever interested in agricultural pursuits. In 1813 he introduced into Northfield broom corn as a field crop, and in 1855 there were manufactured in Northfield 155,000 brooms, valued at $27,000.* He died in 1871. Both Mr. and Mrs. Stratton are buried in the beautiful cemetery at Northfield Farms.

Children:—*Born in Northfield, Mass.*
- +956 Elijah,⁸ b. 1811.
- —957 Elihu,⁸ b. 1812; d. aged 21 years.
- +958 Edwin,⁸ b. Sept. 17, 1815.
- —959 Elisha,⁸ b. 1818; m. **Lucy Sawyer**; their only son, Everett,⁹ d. in early manhood.

459. RUFUS STRATTON ⁷ (*Rufus,*⁶ *Hezekiah,*⁵ *Hezekiah,*⁴ *Samuel,*³ *Samuel,*² *Samuel* ¹) married, Dec. 29, 1819, **Henrietta Rug-**

---

*The first brooms made were clumsy affairs and it was a long time before the women could be induced to use them in the place of the Indian or peeled wood brooms to which they had been accustomed.

gles. They lived in Northfield where he was selectman in 1823-24. He died Dec. 21, 1879.

Children:—*Born in Northfield, Mass.*
+960 Edward Ruggles,[8] b. July 1, 1820.
−961 Abigail Field,[8] b. Jan. 17, 1822; d. 1840.
−962 Silas Augustus,[8] b. Sept. 18, 1824; d. in Boston, unm., aged 26 years.
+963 Rufus William,[8] b. Jan. 23, 1827.
−964 Elizabeth Grant,[8] m. **George Cole**.
−965 Stephen Bachelor,[8] b. 1831; d. Mar. 8, 1857.
−966 Martha Butler,[8] twin, b. 1831; m. **Henry Merrick**.
−967 Calista G.,[8] b. Aug. 8, 1833; m. **George Bunker** in 1862; res. Northfield Farms, Mass.
−968 Augusta Maria,[8] b. May 23, 1836; d. 1849.
−969 Abby Sarah,[8] b. Oct. 12, 1840; m. **Charles Bassett**, 1864.

463. LORENZO STRATTON [7] (*Rufus,*[6] *Hezekiah,*[5] *Hezekiah,*[4] *Samuel,*[3] *Samuel,*[2] *Samuel* [1]) married **Adelade Merriman**, Feb. 26, 1821, daughter of *Levi Merriman.* He died July 14, 1828, in Northfield. His widow married Simeon A. Field.

Child:—*Born in Northfield, Mass.*
+969a William H.,[8] b. Dec. 27, 1827.

464. CHARLES STRATTON [7] (*Hezekiah,*[6] *Hezekiah,*[5] *Hezekiah,*[4] *Samuel,*[3] *Samuel,*[2] *Samuel* [1]) was a farmer in Northfield, Mass., where he married, June 1, 1814, **Mary Merriman**, who died Sept. 25, 1835, aged 41. He died Jan. 22, 1839.

Children:—*Born in Northfield, Mass.*
−970 Almira,[8] b. Oct. 20, 1815; m. **Asa F. Richards**.
−971 Horatio,[8] b. Feb. 26, 1817; m. 1st, **Electa Field**, who d. in 1843; m. 2nd, —— **Hildreth**; lived in Swanzy, N. H.; had two daughters, Julia,[9] Mary.[9]
−972 Charles,[8] b. Oct. 4, 1819; went to California.

465. HARRIS STRATTON [7] (*Hezekiah,*[6] *Hezekiah,*[5] *Hezekiah,*[4] *Samuel,*[3] *Samuel,*[2] *Samuel* [1]) lives in Northfield, where he was a selectman in 1834-1837 and 1848. In 1840 he was a representative to the General Court. He married **Sophia Ruggles** in 1810. He died in 1872.

Children:
−973 Erastus,[8] b. July 30, 1811; d. in childhood.

—974 Sarah Starr,[8] b. Dec. 24, 1812; m. **Franklin Lord.**
—975 Erastus W.,[8] b. Dec. 27, 1815; went West; per. to Kansas.
—976 George W.,[8] b. Sept. 30, 1817; m. **Delia Rice** of Deerfield.
—977 Henry,[8] b. 1819; d. in infancy.
—978 Nelson,[8] b. June 23, 1820; m. —— **Shepherd**; went to London, Eng., to live.
—979 Wright,[8] b. Mar. 3, 1822; was representative to General Court in 1857; m. 1st, Apr. 10, 1845, **Martha Cook**, d. of *Robert G. Cook*. She d. Apr. 26, 1858, aged 35 years; he m. 2nd, **Mrs. Lois Cook**; lived in Northfield; had son, Wentworth,[9] who d. in 1860, aged 9 years.
—980 Sumner,[8] b. July 15, 1824; m. **Maria Johnson.**
—981 Sophia M.,[8] b. July 22, 1826; m. **H. E. Parsons.**
—982 Harris,[8] b. Sept. 22, 1828; went West.

466. ARAD STRATTON [7] (*Hezekiah,[6] Hezekiah,[5] Hezekiah,[4] Samuel,[3] Samuel,[2] Samuel[1]*) married, Oct. 6, 1814, **Electa Wells**, and lived in Northfield, where he died Nov. 30, 1845.
Children:
+983 Chester, b. 1815.
—984 Eunice W., b. 1818; m. **Dr. Owen Liele**, Dec. 25, 1838; d. Oct. 16, 1854, in Calawissa, Pa.
—985 Henry,[8] b. Aug. 20, 1820; d. May 9, 1891, in New Berlin, N. Y.; unm.
—986 Mary W.,[8] b. 1822; m. **Hon. S. C. Wells**, 1852; d. 1854.
—987 Fanny S.,[8] b. 1824; d. in childhood.
—988 Hannah G.,[8] b. 1827; m. **Harrison F. Root**; d. in Montague, Mass.
—989 Arad,[8] b. Aug. 29, 1829; m. **Nancy Brown**, Apr. 11, 1855.*
—990 Electa,[8] b. 1835; d. in infancy.
+991 Lemuel,[8] b. 1837.

468. HEZEKIAH STRATTON [7] (*Hezekiah,[6] Hezekiah,[5] Hezekiah,[4] Samuel,[3] Samuel,[2] Samuel[1]*) was a Northfield farmer. He married **Mercy Orric**, May 28, 1827. He died in Winchester, N. H., Mar., 1884, at the home of his son, H. O. Stratton.

---

* The writer understands that Arad Stratton left several children, but has not been able to find them.

Children:—Born in *Northfield, Mass.*
+992   Hezekiah O.,⁸ b. 1828.
+993   Marcellus D.,⁸ b. 1834.

489. ISAAC JOHNSON STRATTON ⁷ (*Daniel,*⁶ *Richard,*⁵ *Ichabod,*⁴ *Richard,*³ *Samuel,*² *Samuel* ¹) married, Sept. 11, 1803, **Rachel Punderson,** daughter of *John* and *Rhoda (Alger) Punderson,* and moved to Smithville, N. Y., and later settled in Oxford, Chenango Co., where he died Feb. 1, 1873.
Children:
+994   Charles,⁸ b. Jan. 8, 1806, in Tyner, N. Y.
—995   Lydia,⁸ b. 1808; m. Dr. Edward York in 1825.

497. EBENEZER STRATTON ⁷ (*Ebenezer,*⁶ *Richard,*⁵ *Ichabod,*⁴ *Richard,*³ *Samuel,*² *Samuel* ¹) married **Alma Harrison,** Jan. 30, 1806. He died Feb. 1, 1813, aged only 30 years.
Children:—Born in *Williamstown, Mass.*
+996   Ebenezer Harrison,⁸ b. Oct. 29, 1806.
—997   Mary Ann,⁸ m. —— Pillsbury.

509. FRANCIS STRATTON ⁷ (*John,*⁶ *Francis,*⁵ *Ichabod,*⁴ *Richard,*³ *Samuel,*² *Samuel* ¹) married, in 1807, **Asenette Jackson,** brother of Joel Jackson. He died in New York state in 1834 and she in Columbus, Wis., in 1840.*
Children:—Born in *Trenton, N. Y.*
— 998   Asenette,⁸ b. 1807; m. **Jedediah** L. Plumb in 1827; d. in Oswego, N. Y.
— 999   Sarah Ann,⁸ b. 1810; d. in Berlin, Wis., 1890; m. 1st, Lucius Warner in 1831; m. 2nd, Daniel Starks in 1870.
—1000   Lydia,⁸ b. 1813; d. 1897; m. Elbert Guyant, 1835.
Born in *Oswego, N. Y.*
+1001   Francis Joel,⁸ b. 1819.
—1002   Roxey Lavinia,⁸ b. 18—; m. **Seth** H. Warner, 1847; res. Berlin, Wis.
—1003   Cornelia,⁸ d. in childhood.

512. RICHARD STRATTON ⁷ (*John,*⁶ *Francis,*⁵ *Ichabod,*⁴ *Richard,*³ *Samuel,*² *Samuel* ¹) married, first, **Lurinda Fitch,** Mar. 29,

---

* His descendants have in their possession a large copy of the New Testament, on the fly-leaf of which is written in beautiful old script: "Francis Stratton, son of John, his book, given him by his grandfather in 1795."

1820. She died Oct. 28, 1828. He married, second, **Mary Jackson**, Apr. 27, 1829. She was a sister of his brother Francis' wife. He died in Columbus, Wis., Nov. 7, 1864.

Children:—*Born in Bridgewater, N. Y.*
By first marriage.

—1004 Ann,[8] b. 1823; m. **John Chase** in 1846; d. in 1850; lived in Belleville, N. Y.
—1005 Lydia,[8] b. 1825; m. **Albert Wright** in 1844; d. in 1891; lived in Richland, N. Y.

Born in Orleans, N. Y.
By second marriage.

+1006 John Jackson,[8] b. abt. 1827.
—1007 Emily,[8] m. **David Rosenkrans**, 1853; res. Columbus, Wis.

516. ASA STRATTON [7] (*Asa*,[6] *Ichabod*,[5] *Ichabod*,[4] *Richard*,[3] *Samuel*,[2] *Samuel* [1]) was born in Massachusetts in 1787, and when about eight years old removed with his parents to Vermont. As a young man he learned the tanners' trade. Nov. 19, 1809, he married **Dorothy Parker** in Cavendish. In this town he bought land in 1810, 1811 and 1814. In 1813 his wife died, and in 1814 he married her sister, **Salone Parker**, who died the following year. In 1818 he went South and settled at Variety Mills, Nelson Co., Va., taking with him his two little sons. Here in 1833, he married **Elizabeth Whitehead**, and here he died Apr. 27, 1842. He was a ruling Elder in the Presbyterian Church. He was called "Capt. Stratton."

Children:—*Born in Cavendish, Vt.*
By first marriage.

+1008 George Washington,[8] b. May 4, 1811.
+1009 Ebenezer Parker,[8] b. Aug. 14, 1812.
By second marriage.
—1009a Stephen,[8] d. in infancy.

Born in Nelson Co., Va.
By third marriage.

—1009b Elizabeth Dorothy,[8] b. Feb. 8, 1834.
+1010 Robert Burcher,[8] b. Nov. 4, 1835.
+1011 Alexander Brown,[8] b. Aug. 12, 1837.
+1012 Floyd Whitehead.[8]
—1013 John Adams,[8] d. in infancy.

531. SHELDON STRATTON [7] (*Joel*,[6] *Ichabod*,[5] *Ichabod*,[4] *Richard*,[3] *Samuel*,[2] *Samuel* [1]) married **Hannah Ayers**, and lived in

Bennington, then in Cambridge, Vt., where he died Apr. 29, 1856.
Children:—*Born in Bennington, Vt.*
—1014 Norman,[8] b. July 16, 1806; m. **Jane Osburn**; d. in Kent, Ohio, Feb. 7, 1883.
—1015 Phœbe,[8] b. July 18, 1808; m. **Edwin Barney**.
—1016 William A.,[8] b. July 10, 1810; m. **Susan Hunt**; d. at Big Bend, Wis.
—1017 Rhoda Harrington,[8] b. Jan. 15, 1813; m. **Hubbard Beeman**, grandson of *Joseph Beeman*, Feb. 9, 1830; d. Dec. 18, 1889. They celebrated their "golden wedding" Feb. 9, 1880.*
—1018 Beriah,[8] b. Apr. 29, 1815; lived at Derby, Vt.; d. in Andersonville prison; left a family.
—1019 Joel,[8] b. Aug. 30, 1816; m. and lived at Crystal Lake, Wis.
—1020 Elhanan,[8] b. 1824; lived at Dell Rapids, So. Dakota.
—1021 Sheldon,[8] b. May 20, 1827; m. **Harriet Austin**; lived at Cambridge, Vt.

534. ELHANAN STRATTON [7] (*Joel,*[6] *Ichabod,*[5] *Ichabod,*[4] *Richard,*[3] *Samuel,*[2] *Samuel*[1]) married **Eunice Wellman**, and lived in Bennington, where he died in 1863.
Children:—*Born in Bennington, Vt.*
—1022 Charlotte,[8] b. 1835.
—1023 Rhoda.[8]
—1024 Green Blackmer,[8] m. **Martha Hathaway**; res. Bennington, Vt.; chn.: Emma,[9] Ella,[9] Morton.[9]
—1025 Eunice,[8] m. **Aaron Denis**.
—1026 Martha,[8] m. **Hiram Denis**.
—1027 Milo,[8] m. **Ann E. Blackmer**; res. Bennington; no children.
—1028 Elhanan,[8] d. in young manhood.

535. JOSEPH B. STRATTON [7] (*Joel,*[6] *Ichabod,*[5] *Ichabod,*[4] *Richard,*[3] *Samuel,*[2] *Samuel*[1]) married **Ruth Olin**, daughter of *Ezra* and *Ruth (Green) Olin*. Two years after their marriage he moved from Bennington, Vt., to Perry, N. Y., making the trip with his own horses, and a wagon which were loaded with a few household effects and his little family. Here he bought an eighty-acre farm. Ten years later they moved to Portage Co.,

---

* Rev. L. L. Beeman[6] of Warren, Mass., is their son. His paternal ancestry is Hubbard,[5] Jedediah,[4] Joseph,[3] Thomas,[2] Simon.[1]

Ohio, settling on a farm of 130 acres, and from time to time purchased adjoining lands until he owned about four hundred acres. Late in life, after most of his children were married he sold this land and moved to Kent, in Portage Co. He was a man of sterling honesty and excellent business judgment. In May, 1874, Mr. and Mrs. Stratton celebrated their golden wedding, and on this occasion, ten of their eleven living children were present. As a memorial of the event, he presented each of his children with the sum of one thousand dollars. Mrs. Stratton died Apr. 23, 1878, and Mr. Stratton married, second, **Mrs. Martha A. Munsee,** whose death occurred a few months before his own. He died July 14, 1887.

Children:—Born in Bennington, Vt.

—1029 Almira,[8] b. Feb. 15, 1825; m. 1st, **Rev. Buel Whitney,** Oct. 8, 1843. He d. Nov. 7, 1875, and she m. 2nd, **George Bradley** in 1878.

—1030 Mary,[8] b. Aug. 12, 1826; m. Sept. 17, 1844, **Dr. Ezra C. Adams** of Erie Co., N. Y. Settled in Kalamazoo Co., Mich.

Born in Wyoming Co., N. Y.

+1031 Asa,[8] b. Feb. 24, 1828.
+1032 Lucas,[8] b. Nov. 8, 1829.
+1033 Samuel,[8] b. Aug. 19, 1831.
+1034 Freeman,[8] b. June 26, 1833.
—1035 Joel,[8] b. 1835; d. in childhood.

Born in Portage Co., Ohio.

+1036 Jonathan N.,[8] b. May 16, 1837.
—1037 Melissa E.,[8] b. May 28, 1839; m. Apr. 26, 1857, **Orvin J. Woodward** of Kalamazoo Co., Mich.
—1038 Susan,[8] b. Dec. 30, 1840; m. May 24, 1863, **Selah W. Burt.** (His first wife was Sarah A. Stone.)
+1039 Joseph W. B.,[8] b. Oct. 22, 1842.
—1040 Clarissa C.,[8] b. July 2, 1848; m. Oct. 3, 1866, **Levi Reed;** d. at Otsego, Mich., 1909.

536. FREEMAN STRATTON [7] (*Joel,*[6] *Ichabod,*[5] *Ichabod,*[4] *Richard,*[3] *Samuel,*[2] *Samuel*[1]) was a farmer and lived and died in his native town. He married **Thankful Harrington,** Mar. 25, 1821, daughter of *Abraham* and *Electra (Galusha) Harrington.* He died in 1884.

Children:—Born in Bennington, Vt.

—1041 Ruth,[8] b. Feb. 11, 1822; d. aged about 2 years.

+1042 Rufus,⁸ b. Feb., 1824.
—1043 Rhoda,⁸ b. Jan. 24, 1828; m. **LaFayette Lyons,** Dec. 7, 1845.
—1044 Susan,⁸ b. Dec. 9, 1829; m. **Barber Chase;** d. in Bennington, Nov. 12, 1888.
—1045 Ruth,⁸ b. Dec. 9, 1833; m. Sept. 24, 1858, **Heman Rockwood;** d. in Bennington May 2, 1912.
—1046 Ruby,⁸ b. Dec. 9, 1833 (twin); m. **Soloman Howard.**
—1047 Philena,⁸ b. Mar. 8, 1836; d. in Shaftsbury, Vt., July 21, 1891; m. **Alonzo Barrett.**
—1048 Lois,⁸ b. Oct. 31, 1840; m. **Jared Howard,** Aug. 16, 1860.
—1049 Edwin,⁸ b. Sept. 9, 1846; m. **Adelaide Bugbee;** served seven months in Civil War; d. in Bennington May 18, 1915; no children.
+1050 Elmer Barber,⁸ b. Oct. 25, 1851.

538. JOHN STRATTON ⁷ (*Richard,*⁶ *John,*⁵ *John,*⁴ *John,*³ *John,*² *Samuel*¹) was born, lived and died in West Swanzy, N. H. He inherited much of his father's estate, and at one time owned nearly one-half of the town of Swanzy. He was a manufacturer of cloth and dealer in lumber, and an extensive farmer. He married, first, Jan. 29, 1807, **Susannah Whitcomb,** who died Aug. 1, 1857. She was daughter of *Jonathan Whitcomb,* and was born July 15, 1788. He married, second, **Nancy Pease** of Hartford, Conn. He died June 16, 1871, aged 83 years. His will is recorded in Keene. Before his death he gave the homestead, the "Old Mansion," to his daughter, Mrs. Frink, and built the house immediately east of it. He also built houses for his other children, and several of these are still standing.

Children:—*Born in Swanzy, N. H.*
By first marriage.
+1051 Isaac,⁸ b. May 25, 1807.
+1052 William,⁸ b. Dec. 21, 1808.
—1053 Alfred,⁸ b. Dec. 3, 1810; m. **Julia Snow;** d. in 1871.
—1054 Lovilla,⁸ b. Nov. 3, 1812; m. **Amos F. Fish.**
—1055 Susannah,⁸ b. Mar. 9, 1815; m. **J. W. Capin.**
—1056 Mariam,⁸ b. June 9, 1817; m. **Philoman W. Foster.**
—1057 Harriet,⁸ b. Apr. 5, 1819; m. **Geo. W. Alexander.**
+1058 John,⁸ b. Mar. 20, 1821.
—1059 Julia Ann,⁸ b. June 10, 1823; m. 1st, **J. W. Frink;** 2nd, **Homer Stratton** (No. 801).

—1060 Jane A.,[8] b. Nov. 27, 1824; m. **John S. Thayer.**
—1061 George,[8] b. Jan. 9, 1827; d. in infancy.
—1062 Eleanor,[8] b. Sept. 27, 1827; m. 1st, **Elliot W. Lane;** 2nd, **Charles Wardner;** res. Clear Creek, Minn.
+1063 Oscar,[8] b. Apr. 24, 1833.

540. Richard Stratton[7] (*Richard,[6] John,[5] John,[4] John,[3] John,[2] Samuel[1]*) married **Clarissa Sumner,** about 1828, who died at Swanzy Apr. 3, 1853. She was a daughter of *Clement A. Sumner.* Mr. Stratton died July 7, 1847, and is buried near his father in the old cemetery at Swanzy.

Children:—*Born at Swanzy, N. H.*
—1064 Andrew J.,[8] d. in California Dec. 28, 1853, aged 24 years.
—1065 Lovena,[8] d. in childhood.
—1066 Leverna,[8] d. Jan. 28, 1841; aged 9 mos.

541. Abijah Stratton[7] (*Abijah,[6] Abijah,[5] Jabez,[4] John,[3] John,[2] Samuel[1]*) married, first, **Hannah Bacon,** Jan. 29, 1797, and second, **Mrs. Hannah (Fuller) Kimball,** who died Apr. 13, 1856. They lived on the old homestead on the road from Sherborn to Natick. His will was made May 31, 1828, and proved Oct. 30, 1838. In it he names his three sons and two daughters.

Children:—*Born in Natick, Mass.*
By first marriage.
+1067 John,[8] b. Nov. 4, 1798.
+1068 Moses,[8] b. Mar. 6, 1805.
+1069 Aaron,[8] b. Jan. 26, 1811.
—1070 Mary,[8] d. unm.
—1071 Sarah,[8] m. **Caleb Foskett,** Mar. 23, 1834.

545. Jonathan Stratton[7] (*Daniel,[6] Abijah,[5] Jabez,[4] John,[3] John,[2] Samuel[1]*) went to Dover, and then to Dorchester, where he married, first, July 29, 1798, **Lydia Tolman,** who died Oct. 1, 1799. She was daughter of *Thomas* and *Mary (Houghton) Tolman,* and was born Dec. 21, 1773. He married, second, **Waitstill Tolman,** July 21, 1800. May 13, 1805, Jonathan Stratton of Roxbury and his wife Waitstill sold land in Dorchester, "his wife in her own right." He died in Roxbury Sept. 26, 1805.*

---

* May 10, 1802, "Ebenezer Withington of Dorchester was appointed Guardian unto Tolman Stratton, son of Jonathan Stratton, under 14 yrs. of age. Sureties: Thomas Savin of Natick, gent., and Jonathan Stratton of Dorchester." This guardianship was probably to inherit property from the Tolman family.

Children:—Born in Dorchester, Mass.
+1072   Tolman.[8]
−1073   Jonathan,[8] m. and lived in Cincinnati; left children, of whom information is desired.

550. JOHN STRATTON [7] (Daniel,[6] Abijah,[5] Jabez,[4] John,[3] John,[2] Samuel [1]) married —— Arnold, of Marlboro. She died soon, and he married, second, her sister Lucinda Arnold.
Children:—Born in Sharon, Mass.
−1074   Adeliza, m. Howard Ames.
−1075   Jane, m. Otis Pratt.
−1076   John. Did he die young?
        By second marriage.
+1077   Joel A.,[8] b. Oct. 20, 1828.
        Born in Sherborn, Mass.
−1078   Lucinda,[8] b. 1832; m. 1st, Ellis Scott; 2nd, Charles Adams of Waltham, Mass.
−1079   William,[8] d. in California.
−1080   Horatio,[8] lived in Helena, Mont.
−1081   George H.,[8] res. "Oak Bluffs," Mass.

552. WILLIAM STRATTON [7] (Daniel,[6] Abijah,[5] Jabez,[4] John,[3] John,[2] Samuel [1]) married Mrs. Sarah Clark, daughter of John and Mary (Whitney) Ballard, and widow of Martin Clark.
Children:—Born in Sherborn, Mass.
−1082   John Ballard,[8] b. Apr. 20, 1820; m. Jane Stevens; lived in Boston and Sherborn; a photographer; d. Oct. 21, 1861.
−1083   Mary Whitney,[8] d. unm.
−1084   Eliza Maria,[8] b. Apr. 6, 1829; m. Andrew Beacher, Oct. 2, 1849; d. in Natick Jan. 6, 1906.

561. JOHN STRATTON [7] (Nathan,[6] Nathan,[5] Jabez,[4] John,[3] John,[2] Samuel [1]) lived in Leominster. He married, first, Lydia Hyde, Jan. 12, 1826; second, Elizabeth Wood, in 1843. She died Sept. 20, 1878. Mr. Stratton died June 23, 1850.
Children:—Born in Leominster, Mass.
        By first marriage.
−1085   George,[8] b. Mar. 2, 1827; removed to Plainview, Minn., in 1861.
−1086   John Crosby,[8] b. Mar. 22, 1830; d. unm. at Plainview, Minn.

—1087 Lydia Caroline,⁸ b. Mar. 22, 1830 (twin); d. aged 4 years.
—1088 Milton Fletcher,⁸ d. in childhood.
By second marriage.
—1089 Charles Wilnot,⁸ b. Oct. 8, 1847; m. **Isabella Adams**, in 1879; res. Leominster; no children.

564. ALBERT STRATTON⁷ (*Nathan,⁶ Nathan,⁵ Jabez,⁴ John,³ John,² Samuel¹*) married **Hannah Mead Whitney**, Jan. 18, 1832. She was born in Harvard, Mass., in 1813, and died in 1880 in Leominster. He died in Leominster Jan. 2, 1881. He learned the blacksmiths' trade, but later became a progressive farmer, and was the first man to take milk into Boston on the cars.
Children:—*Born in Leominster, Mass.*
+1090 Martin Whitcomb,⁸ b. Nov. 13, 1833.
+1091 Joel Augustus,⁸ b. Mar. 9, 1837.
+1092 Albert Osmon,⁸ b. Apr. 19, 1839.
—1093 Charlotte Amelia,⁸ b. Oct. 13, 1841; m. **John H. Willis** in 1896.
—1094 Wilber Fletcher,⁸ b. 1844; d. aged 3 years.
—1095 Ellen Augustus,⁸ b. 1848; d. aged 3 years.
—1096 Adeliza Hannah,⁸ b. 1851; m. **Warren J. Lewis**.
+1097 Porter Raymond,⁸ b. 1855.
—1098 Leslie Aurelia,⁸ b. 1857; d. 1864.

565. WALTER STRATTON⁷ (*Ebenezer,⁶ Elias,⁵ Jabez,⁴ John,³ John,² Samuel¹*) married, Aug. 22, 1815, **Lucy Dudley** of Petersham. They lived in Athol, where he died in 1851, and she seven years later, June 28, 1858, aged 67 years.
Children:—*Born in Athol, Mass.*
—1099 Joel Dudley,⁸ b. Aug., 1816; m. **Susan Day** in 1846; d. in Worcester, Nov. 4, 1860.*
—1100 Lurenda Whipple,⁸ b. Jan., 1820; m. in 1842, **Daniel Davis** of Royalston.
+1101 Austin Chandler,⁸ b. May, 1818.
—1102 James,⁸ b. Dec., 1821; m. **Caroline Hill** in 1848; d. in Athol, 1892. Only child, Carrie Frances,⁹ m. Francis R. Thomas, 1876; res. Athol.
—1103 Emory Fay,⁸ b. Oct., 1823. A soldier in the Civil

---

* Joel Dudley Stratton is the man who took John B. Gough out of the gutter and started him on his temperance work (see *Life of Gough*).

War; d. unm. in soldiers' home in Leavenworth, Kan.
—1104 Hiram Walter,[8] b. June, 1825; d. in Worcester in 1901; m. 1st, **Annette Gilman**; 2nd, **Ella Snow**.
—1105 Lucy Ann,[8] b. Oct., 1827; m. **Merrill Fuller**, 1848.
+1106 Charles Temple,[8] b. Sept. 14, 1829.
—1107 Ann Eliza,[8] b. Apr., 1835; m. **Jeremiah Nichols**.
+1108 Francis Alvin,[8] b. Nov. 28, 1831.

571. EBENEZER STRATTON [7] (*Ebenezer,*[6] *Elias,*[5] *Jabez,*[4] *John,*[3] *John,*[2] *Samuel*[1]) married **Harriet Littlefield**, Nov. 21, 1832. He died in Athol May 9, 1857.
Children:—*Born in Athol, Mass.*
—1109 Sumner Willis,[8] b. Aug. 22, 1850; m. **Evelyn Eugenia Smith**, Dec. 26, 1872; res. Rochester, N. Y.; ch. Edgar W.[9]
—1110 Harriet Angeline,[8] b. Aug. 27, 1836; d. Feb. 15, 1865.
—1111 George Lewis,[8] b. June, 1839.
—1112 Alfred Osmon,[8] b. Aug. 12, 1840; d. aged 12 years.

574. WILDER STRATTON [7] (*Ebenezer,*[6] *Elias,*[5] *Jabez,*[4] *John,*[3] *John,*[2] *Samuel*[1]) married **Harriet L. Beeman**. They lived at Athol, where he was a farmer, and where he died in Jan., 1865.
Child:—*Born in Athol, Mass.*
+1113 Albert W.[8]

575. ELISHA STRATTON [7] (*Elias,*[6] *Elias,*[5] *Jabez,*[4] *John,*[3] *John,*[2] *Samuel*[1]) married **Calista West**, Jan. 28, 1826, and removed to Gill, Mass. He was a farmer. He died Feb. 11, 1836.
Children:—*Born in Gill, Mass.*
+1114 Elber Elisha,[8] b. Sept. 3, 1828.
—1115 George Hinchley,[8] b. May 8, 1833; m. **Amelia Rice** in 1855; lived in Westfield, Mass. Only child, Annie W.,[9] res. Westfield.
—1116 Priscella West,[8] b. Nov. 17, 1826; d. 1938.

576. SAMUEL STRATTON [7] (*Elias,*[6] *Elias,*[5] *Jabez,*[4] *John,*[3] *John,*[2] *Samuel*[1]) lived in Guilford, Vt., and Gill, Mass. He married, first, Jan. 29, 1815, **Mehitable H. Rogers**, who died Jan. 8, 1833, aged 43 years. He married, second, **Mrs. Mary Sears**; married, third, **Mrs. Sarah Brooks**.
Children:—By first marriage.
—1117 Lydia Rogers,[8] b. Nov. 28, 1815; d. in childhood.

—1118 Sarah Young,⁸ b. Feb. 18, 1817; d. in childhood.
—1119 Samuel,⁸ b. July 11, 1818; went to California; married and left children. What became of them?*
—1120 Charles,⁸ b. Feb. 9, 1820; d. in infancy.
+1121 Horace Hubbard,⁸ b. Sept. 24, 1821.
—1122 Mehitable H.,⁸ b. Nov. 16, 1822; d., unm., Jan. 19, 1881.
—1123 Lydia Rogers,⁸ b. June 22, 1828; m. **George H. Taft**.
—1124 Jane W.,⁸ b. June 10, 1830; d. in infancy.
—1125 Augusta,⁸ b. Apr. 10, 1831; d. in infancy.
—1126 Augustine,⁸ b. Apr. 10, 1831, twin; d. in childhood.

581. JOEL STRATTON ⁷ (*Joseph,⁶ Elias,⁵ Jabez,⁴ John,³ John,² Samuel¹*) was a farmer of Athol. He married **Sarah Sprague**, Feb. 24, 1822. She was born Oct. 19, 1798. Mr. Stratton died Feb. 6, 1837, in the South, where he had gone for his health.
Children:—*Born in Athol, Mass.*
—1127 Augustus Joel,⁸ b. Aug. 26, 1824.
—1128 Joshua Sumner,⁸ b. June 30, 1827; d. in Manchester, Eng., in 1850, unm.
—1129 Sarah Maria,⁸ b. Dec. 5, 1830; m. **Levi C. Fessenden**, Oct. 22, 1849.
—1130 Joseph Lincoln,⁸ b. Sept. 15, 1835.

582. JONATHAN STRATTON ⁷ (*Joseph,⁶ Elias,⁵ Jabez,⁴ John,³ John,² Samuel¹*) married, first, **Esther Ward**, Nov. 8, 1821. She died in 1843 and he married, second, **Mrs. Mary Baker**, Apr. 14, 1850, who died June 2, 1886. They lived in Athol, where he was a farmer. He died Feb. 22, 1852.
Children:—*Born in Athol, Mass.*
By first marriage.
—1131 Eleanor,⁸ b. Dec. 5, 1822; m. **Amos Stratton** (Chart H-123), in Athol, Jan. 3, 1849; d. Apr. 2, 1904.
—1132 Lucena,⁸ b. May 11, 1825; d., unm., Oct. 28, 1853.
+1133 Jonathan Winsor,⁸ b. May 18, 1827.

---

* A Samuel Stratton (whom the compiler has not placed) d. in Oconomowac, Wis., in 1852, leaving several children. His son, Samuel Stratton, Jr., b. at Brattleboro, Vt., d. at Spring Valley, Wis., Feb. 5, 1877. He m. **Mary Mason**. Their son, David Richard Stratton, lives at Shell Lake, Wis. Their daughter Mary m. **John A. Martin** of Spring Valley. She d. Jan. 6, 1915. Her son, Harry Stratton Martin, is a missionary in China. Perhaps some one can place this branch and give more complete data?

—1134   Josiah Henry,[8] b. May 18, 1829; m. Lucy Reynolds; d. Jan. 11, 1906.
—1135   Joseph Otis,[8] b Nov. 15. 1831; m. **Rose A. Harvey** of California; d. in San José, Feb. 15, 1897; no children.
—1136   Jacob Milton,[8] b. Jan. 20, 1835; m. **Sarah O. Haskins**, Aug. 24, 1860; d. in Orange, Mass., July 5, 1894; child, Jesse R.[10]

583.   JOSEPH STRATTON [7] (*Joseph*,[6] *Elias*,[5] *Jabez*,[4] *John*,[3] *John*,[2] *Samuel*[1]) was a farmer at Athol. He married, first, **Martha West** of Templeton, Nov. 8, 1826. She died Aug. 17, 1841, aged 36 years, and he married, second, **Alice W. Mann**, daughter of *Thomas Mann*.

Children:—B*orn in Athol, Mass.*
   By first marriage.
—1137   Mary,[8] b. Sept. 2, 1827; m. 1st, **Gilbert Harris**, Aug. 20, 1849; m. 2nd, **Philetus Miles**; d. Nov. 16, 1890, at Fredonia, N. Y.
—1138   Martha,[8] b. June 2, 1829; m. **George Meacham** of Athol, Aug. 15, 1848.
+1139   Joseph Alonzo,[8] b. Oct. 16, 1831.
—1140   Charles West,[8] b. Dec. 3, 1833; m. **Rosette Alzina Adams**, Nov. 20, 1855; res. Greenwood, Ill.; no children.
+1141   Joel W.,[8] b. Jan. 8, 1838.
—1142   Henry Harrison,[8] b. Nov. 16, 1840; m. **Emily Holman**; d. in Worcester, Nov. 9, 1885. Two daughters, Ella H.[9] and Marion.[9]
   By second marriage.
+1143   Horace Minott,[8] b. May 12, 1843.
—1144   Clark M., b. Nov. 3, 1845; d. in infancy.
+1145   Frederick Eugene,[8] b. July 5, 1847.
—1146   Francis Albert,[8] b. June 2, 1849; d. in infancy.

591.   LYMAN STRATTON [7] (*Jabez*,[6] *Elias*,[5] *Jabez*,[4] *John*,[3] *John*,[2] *Samuel*[1]) married **Harriet Beeman**, June 14, 1842. They lived in Petersham and Boston. He died in Athol, Mar. 19, 1892.

Children:—B*orn in Petersham, Mass.*
—1147   Charles,[8] lived in Athol. Did he leave children?
—1148   Leander Beeman,[8] d. in Boston, Mar. 18, 1851, aged 7 years 5 mos.

—1149 Albert Eugene,[8] d. in Boston, Mar. 30, 1851, aged 5 years 5 mos.
—1150 Isabella Anna,[8] d. in Boston, 1851, aged 3 years.
—1151 Eliza,[8] d. in Petersham, Feb. 13, 1850, an infant.

599. LEMUEL PAGE STRATTON[7] (*Lemuel,*[6] *Jonathan,*[5] *Jonathan,*[4] *Joseph,*[3] *John,*[2] *Samuel*[1]) married **Sarah Bowen Johnson** at Salem, Mass., Aug. 8, 1831, and removed to Brighton, Illinois, where they bought a farm. "They were devoted to church, Sunday school and mission work, and their pleasant home was always open to the poor and needy, and to ministers and students, whom they often helped." About 1859 he left the farm and opened a bank in Brighton. His wife died July 2, 1865; several years later he married a **Mrs. Thompson,** who died before he did. He died June 19, 1884, in Brighton.

Children:—*Born in Brighton, Ill.*
—1152 Sarah Eliza,[8] b. May 15, 1832; m. **Rev. Henry Dutton Platt,** Congregational minister; d. in Topeka, Oct. 1, 1908; an inestimable helper in all her husband's church work.*
+1153 Edward Bliss,[8] b. Mar. 5, 1834.
+1154 Nathan Johnson,[8] b. Mar. 20, 1837.
—1155 Anna Maria,[8] b. May 29, 1841; m. **Rev. Frank M. Ellis,** a Baptist minister, Sept. 3, 1863; d. at Lawrence, Kan., Aug. 17, 1870.
+1156 William Page,[8] b. Mar. 24, 1843.

600. STEPHEN JACKSON STRATTON[7] (*Lemuel,*[6] *Jonathan,*[5] *Jonathan,*[4] *Joseph,*[3] *John,*[2] *Samuel*[1]) as a young man went on a whaling voyage and followed the sea for several years. In 1840 he married **Eunice Winslow** and settled at New Bedford, where he died in 1881.

Children:—*Born in New Bedford, Mass.*
—1157 Ellen,[8] b. May 8, 1841; m. Bradford L. **Church;** d. Feb. 9, 1886.
—1158 Martha Tucker,[8] d. in New Bedford in 1861.
—1159 Ann,[8] d. in 1846, aged 1 year.
—1160 Clara Jane,[8] resides in New Bedford.
+1161 Charles Stephen,[8] b. Nov. 26, 1849.

* Their son, Edwin H. Platt, resides at Franklin, Neb. Their daughter, Lucy Stratton Platt, m. Wm. Asbury Harshbarger, head of Dept. of Mathematics at Washburn College. The compiler is indebted to her for much help on this line of Strattons.

602. LEVI WOODBURY STRATTON [7] (*Lemuel*,[6] *Jonathan*,[5] *Jonathan*,[4] *Joseph*,[3] *John*,[2] *Samuel*[1]) left home at the age of twenty-one and went to Marine, Minn., where he made a land claim and worked at his trade of millwright. Later he went to Illinois and at Brighton he married **Perneicy Pellam**, June 28, 1842. In 1852 they moved to St. Anthony (now E. Minneapolis), making the trip by steamboat. Here he was the pioneer stationer and book dealer, in connection with a general store known as the "Farmer's Exchange," of which it was said, "If you cannot find what you want at the *Exchange* you will have to go outside of the territory for it." Minnesota was admitted as a state in 1858. For some years he was a member of the school board. In 1871 he removed to Excelsior, Minn., where he had a vineyard and made a specialty of raising grapes and grape-vines for sale. He died Aug. 9, 1881, his wife having died the previous March. He was a man of slender build and very tall, being six feet four inches in height. A student of books and of nature, it was from him that his children learned to know and love the trees, wild flowers and birds in the region of their home.

Children:

—1162 Lucy M.,[8] m. **Charles R. Beal**, Sept., 1866; res. Fullerton, Cal.

—1163 Carrie V.,[8] res. Minneapolis.

—1164 Emma L.,[8] m. **Will G. Wheeler**, Sept., 1866; d. in Portland, Oregon, in 1910.

—1165 Thomas M.,[8] d. in Vermont in 1877.

—1166 John P.,[8] d. in Mobile, Ala., in 1903.

—1167 Ella M.,[8] has been a teacher for thirty years in the public schools of Excelsior, Minn., and has had charge of the Primary Dept. of Excelsior Congregational Sunday school for about the same time.

—1168 Jannette,[8] m .**C. H. Molter**, Apr. 2, 1882; res. Excelsior, Minn.

—1169 Charles E.,[8] m. **Mrs. Frances Carter**. They reside in Victoria, B. C., where he is a printer.

612. JONAH BRIGHAM STRATTON [7] (*Winsor*,[6] *Samuel*,[5] *Jonathan*,[4] *Joseph*,[3] *John*,[2] *Samuel*[1]) married **Zeruiah Howe**. He died a widower in Cambridge, Feb. 24, 1856.

Children:

—1170 Sarah Ann,[8] b. Mar. 30, 1817; d. aged 4 years.

—1171 Richard Savage,[8] b. May 19, 1819. Was in San Francisco in 1865. Information concerning him desired.
—1172 Mary Ann,[8] b. July 13, 1821; d. aged 17 years.
—1173 Edward Briggs,[8] b. Sept. 26, 1825; enlisted in Co. F, 3rd Regt. Mass. Cavalry, in Sept., 1862, as a private; mustered out as a hospital surgeon in May, 1865; died at Sherborn, May 3, 1885; buried at Northboro.

617. WILLIAM STRATTON [7] (*Winsor,*[6] *Samuel,*[5] *Jonathan,*[4] *Joseph,*[3] *John,*[2] *Samuel*[1]) married, Jan. 18, 1844, Susan H. Rice, who was born June 23, 1814, and died Sept. 18, 1878. They lived in Northboro, where he was a farmer. He died Apr. 16, 1875. His will is recorded at Worcester.

Children:—*Born in Northboro, Mass.*
+1174 George D.,[8] b. Aug. 14, 1845.
—1175 Ellen M.,[8] b. Dec. 10, 1850; d. in childhood.
—1176 Maria S.,[8] b. Aug. 28, 1853; m. George Rice, Jan. 21, 1880.
—1177 William Emerson,[8] b. Aug. 28, 1853; d. Dec. 2, 1902.

628. JOHN STRATTON [7] (*Samuel,*[6] *Samuel,*[5] *Samuel,*[4] *Samuel,*[3] *John,*[2] *Samuel*[1]) was about three years old when his parents moved from Natick, Mass., to Hancock, Me., in 1802. He married Elizabeth Grant. He was a carpenter and builder.

Children:—*Born in Hancock, Maine.*
—1178 Henry,[8] b. June 25, 1826. Master Mariner at Hancock, Me.; sons: Windfield Scott,[9] John R.,[9] Sylvanus L.[9]
—1179 Temperance, b. June 5, 1828; m. Frank Wrann; res. Salem, Mass.
—1180 Warren,[8] b. Mar. 15, 1830; chn. Gertrude,[9] Milton W.,[9] architect at Bar Harbor, Me.
—1181 Leonard, b. Aug. 6, 1832; d. Aug. 20, 1853, unm.
—1182 Letitia, b. June 30, 1834; m. Charles Bunker; d. July 4, 1901, in Salem, Mass.
—1183 Maria, b. Aug. 8, 1836; m. W. J. Nichols; d. Mar. 10, 1876.
—1184 Ellen, b. Jan. 18, 1838; m. Stephen Stratton, son of Samuel Stratton; lived in Sullivan, Me.; d. Nov. 7, 1872.
—1185 George, b. July 8, 1841.

630. MARTIN STRATTON [7] (*Samuel*,[6] *Samuel*,[5] *Samuel*,[4] *Samuel*,[3] *John*,[2] *Samuel* [1]) married **Abigail Gillison**, Mar. 4, 1840. She was born in Harrington, Me., Nov. 16, 1808, daughter of *Winslow Gillison* (or *Gallison*). They lived in Hancock, Me., where he was a ship builder. They were members of the Baptist church. She died Jan. 24, 1853, and the following year he married **Ruth Ann Hodgkins**, who died Nov. 4, 1858. He died Dec. 29, 1893.

Children:—B*orn in Hancock, Me.*
By first marriage.
- —1186 Erastus W.,[8] b. Jan., 1842; d., unm., in California, Apr., 1876.
- —1187 Mirrian E.,[8] b. Apr. 8, 1843; m. **James H. Whitaker** in 1869; res. Brookline, Mass.
- —1188 Howard M.,[8] b. July 18, 1844; killed in battle June 18, 1864; unm.
- —1189 Aubine V.,[8] b. Aug. 19, 1845; m. **Eben P. Wooster** of Waltham, Mass.
- —1190 Flora A.,[8] b. Nov. 20, 1847; d. June 5, 1868.
- —1191 Martin C.,[8] b. Apr. 9, 1850; d. in infancy.
- +1192 Purbot Hill,[8] b. Sept. 26, 1851.

By second marriage.
- —1193 Clifton M.,[8] b. Feb. 18, 1855.
- —1194 Addie W.,[8] b. Feb. 6, 1856; res. Pasadena, Cal.
- —1195 Marion A.,[8] b. Apr. 21, 1857; m. **Coleman Hodkins**; res. Marlboro, Me.
- —1196 Alonzo,[8] b. Nov. 4, 1858; d. in infancy.
- —1197 Phœbe,[8] b. Nov. 4, 1858; twin, d. in infancy.

644. ISAAC G. STRATTON [7] (*William*,[6] *Samuel*,[5] *Enoch*,[4] *Samuel*,[3] *Richard*,[2] *Samuel* [1]) married **Phœbe Congar** some time before 1820. They settled in New Hartford, Oneiga Co., N. Y., where he died in June, 1838. His wife died ten years later. She was daughter of *Jonathan* and *Sarah* (*Meeker*) *Congar*. Her brother Samuel had an estate in Union township, Sussex Co., N. J., a share of which she inherited.

Children:—B*orn in New Hartford, N. Y.*
- +1198 William.[8]
- —1199 Henry,[8] d. in infancy.
- —1200 George,[8] d. in infancy.
- —1201 James,[8] b. 1827; d. in Towanda, Pa., Feb. 15, 1902; left no descendants.

—1202 Mary,⁸ b. 1829; m. **Samuel H. Sackett** in 1853; d. in Honolulu, 1903.
—1203 Sarah,⁸ m. **Patrick Lynch**; lived in Syracuse, N. Y.
+1204 Edward I.,⁸ b. 1838.

647. WILLIAM STRATTON ⁷ (*William,⁶ Samuel,⁵ Enoch,⁴ Samuel,³ Richard,² Samuel¹*) married **Alice Miller,** Apr. 15, 1824, and settled in Newfield, Tompkins Co., N. Y., where he engaged in agriculture. He died Mar. 20, 1872. As a young man he learned the fuller's trade and came to Newfield intending to erect a mill, but bought a farm instead.

Children:—*Born in Newfield, N. Y.*

+1205 David,⁸ b. May 14, 1826.
—1206 Ruth,⁸ b. Oct. 20, 1828; m. **Dr. Charles Woodward,** May 21, 1851; d. in Elmira, Apr. 25, 1852.
—1207 Nancy,⁸ m. **Andrew J. Vankirk,** Jan. 18, 1854; d. in New York four months after celebrating their golden wedding.
—1208 George,⁸ b. Oct. 4, 1834; m., in Rochester, **Emily Barker**; lived in Fairmount, Neb.; a soldier, 1861-1862.
—1209 William⁸ and Henry,⁸ twins, b. Dec. 10, 1836; d. in infancy.
—1210 Edwin,⁸ b. Sept. 22, 1838; m. **Emily M. Gorman**; res. Oswego, N. Y.; ch. Donala.⁹
—1211 Lucy Augusta,⁸ b. Jan. 15, 1841; m. **Percival Dudley,** Dec. 23, 1868; res. St. Louis.
—1212 Wilber Fish,⁸ b. Apr. 26, 1845; m. **Ellen Dudley** in 1874; res. Ovid Center, Seneca Co., N. Y.

654. THOMAS STRATTON ⁷ (*Benjamin,⁶ Benjamin,⁵ Jabez,⁴ Samuel,³ Richard,² Samuel¹*) inherited his father's farm at Fairlee and lived in the homestead. He married **Elizabeth Sturtevant.**

Children:—*Born in Fairlee, Vt.*

—1213 John,⁸ m. **Louisa G. Osborn,** Dec. 2, 1852; d. in Fairlee, Sept. 11, 1882.
—1214 Charles C.,⁸ b. Aug., 1828; m. **Maria S. Pulman**; lived in Fitchburg, Mass.; d. in Fairlee, while on a visit there in 1900. Left one daughter, Louise.⁹
—1215 Mary,⁸ b. Aug., 1830; d. aged 13 years.
—1216 Louisa J.,⁸ b. Aug., 1835; d. Apr., 1860.

—1217 George,[8] b. Aug., 1836; d. 1849.
—1218 Benjamin A.,[8] b. Oct., 1843; soldier in Civil War at 18 years; died in Virginia, 1862.
—1219 Mary,[8] b. Jan., 1853; m. **Hiram Rice**, 1870; d. in Fairlee.

658. JOHN STRATTON [7] (*John*,[6] *Benjamin*,[5] *Jabez*,[4] *Samuel*,[3] *Richard*,[2] *Samuel*[1]) was about two years old when his parents died in Hallowell, Me., in 1802. After his marriage he lived in Charlestown, and later in Boston, at No. 22 Common St., and did business as a merchant at No. 50 Central St., and owned property in Charlestown and Somerville, some of which is still owned by his heirs. He married **Lucy Eveleth** of Stow, who died in Boston, June 8, 1894. Mr. Stratton died in 1871, and is buried in Mount Auburn cemetery.

Children:
—1220 George,[8] m. Laura ——; d. in Boston, 1870.
—1221 John Henry,[8] drowned in Moosehead Lake, aged 16 years.
+1222 Francis John.[8]

662. JOSIAH STRATTON [7] (*Jabez*,[6] *Jabez*,[5] *Jabez*,[4] *Samuel*,[3] *Richard*,[2] *Samuel*[1]) married **Susan Hutchens**, Nov. 25, 1838. He was a furniture maker. He was a member of the Methodist church, superintendent of the Sunday school, and earnest Christian, a good citizen, and had many friends. He moved from Bethlehem, N. H., to Derby, Vt., in 1850, and later lived in Lancaster, N. H., where he died Mar. 16, 1881.

Children:—*Born in Bethlehem, N. H.*
—1223 Cynthia Aurilla.[8]
—1224 Willard Oscar,[8] m. **Helda Maria Smith**; res. Danville, Vt.; mem. Masonic order.
+1225 Edmond Burt.[8]
Born in Derby Center, Vt.
—1226 Lucy Emeline,[8] res. Nashua, N. H.

666. ISSACHER STRATTON [7] (*Samuel*,[6] *Jabez*,[5] *Jabez*,[4] *Samuel*,[3] *Richard*,[2] *Samuel*[1]) in his youth learned the trade of cloth dresser. In Jan., 1825, he married **Amanda Gibbs**. In 1826 he moved to Wayne Co., N. Y., where he bought a farm. His wife died Oct. 11, 1847. He moved to Berlin, Wis., in 1854; died in Newton, Wis., Oct. 21, 1865.

Children:—*Born in Pawlet, Vt.*

—1227 Almira,[8] b. Sept. 10, 1825; m. **Slocum Negus** in 1843; res. Spencer, Iowa.

Born in Wayne Co., N. Y.

—1228 Jacob S.,[8] b. Dec. 22, 1827; m. **Clarrisa Budd**; d. leaving no children.

—1229 Benjamin Franklin,[8] engineer on the Toledo; lost in Lake Michigan; unm.

—1230 George W.,[8] b. June 25, 1832; m. **Mary Hallock** in 1860; lived in Marion, N. Y. Chn. Jennie,[9] Benjamin,[9] George Allen,[9] m. **Hattie D. Hutchinson**, 1888; res. Newark, N. Y.; chn. Belle M.,[10] Rose,[10] Carlyle G.[10]

—1231 Atta A.,[8] b. Aug. 8, 1834; m. **T. S. Bassett**, 1858; res. Berlin, Wis.

—1232 Lucius,[8] b. Jan. 31, 1837; m. —— **Smith**, 1863; d. Oct. 3, 1888; lived in Lucene, Wis.; chn. Herbert,[9] Charles D.,[9] George A.[9]

—1233 Louman,[8] b. Jan. 31, 1837 (twin); d. 1865; unm.

—1234 Jennie,[8] b. Jan. 19, 1839; m. **Robt. Tempany**, 1875; res. Los Angeles, Cal.

—1235 Allen M.,[8] b. July 8, 1843; m. **Justina D. Buck** in 1865; res. Los Angeles.

—1236 Emma A.,[8] b. Sept. 20, 1845; m. **S. F. Buck**; res. Footville, Wis.

674. SIMON PHELPS STRATTON [8] (*James,*[7] *Josiah,*[6] *Hezekiah,*[5] *Samuel,*[4] *Samuel,*[3] *Samuel,*[2] *Samuel* [1]) was born May 6, 1794. May 12, 1825, he married **Julia Townsend** of Rutland. A young man of energy and enterprise, he soon found plenty to do. For some years he was proprietor of the "Stratton Tavern," in Waltham (see picture).* He was also "expressman" for several

---

* For this picture, from a Sepia painting made in 1884, the author is indebted to Mr. John Adams of Waltham, son of Mrs. Parmelia (Stratton) Adams.

This was a popular tavern for many years, at the corner of Stow and Weston streets. It was owned and occupied by Isaac Bemis in 1798, and was kept by him for a long time. John Ball is supposed to have occupied the stand previous to him. Simon Stratton followed Bemis, and was its last landlord. It was then owned by Dr. Spring. The building stood for many years, though not occupied as a public house, a well-known landmark, an object of interest and curiosity, a fair example of the ancient Inn. It was burned to the ground Feb. 11, 1893.

		Born
1	*John Stratton*	1775
2	*John Stratton*	1773
3	*Richard Stratton*	1712
4	*Mary Stratton*	
5	*Ebenezer Stratton*	1745
6	*Daniel Stratton*	1743
7	*David Stratton*	1759
8	*John Stratton*	1735
9	*Daniel Stratton*	1814

REFERENCES

1. Page 66. 2. Page 286, Vol. I. 3-7. Page 26. 8. Page 28 (above date should be 1732, not 1735). 9. Page 243.

large woolen mills, a business in which he employed many teams. When the Boston & Worcester R. R. was built a branch road was run to the mills, and this ended Simon's express enterprise. However, he had saved up considerable money, and in 1843 he gave up the hotel business and removed to Evanston, Ill., where he bought 500 acres of land and engaged in farming. His removal was characteristic of the man, and his way of doing things. He left Waltham for his new home with his family and household goods in several wagons each drawn by four fine horses.

Children:—*Born in Holden and Waltham, Mass.*
- —1237 John Lowell, b. Oct. 6, 1830; lived in Libertyville, Ill.
- —1238 Henry Hill,[9] b. Nov. 16, 1832. What became of him?
- —1239 Charles Cullen,[9] b. Dec. 25, 1836; m. —— Judson; lived in Evanston, Ill., and in Denver; d. June 13, 1907.
- —1240 Schuyler,[9] b. Aug. 5, 1839; moved to California.
- —1241 Edwin C.[9]
- —1242 Harrison Wilder,[9] m. **Carrie Emma Hawks**; lived in Odebold, Iowa. Served in Civil War, in 47th Mass. Vols.

More complete records of this family are desired.

679. JAMES M. STRATTON[8] (*James,*[7] *Josiah,*[6] *Hezekiah,*[5] *Samuel,*[4] *Samuel,*[3] *Samuel,*[2] *Samuel*[1]) was born in Paxton, Mass., Sept. 4, 1828, and lived for awhile at Waterloo, N. Y., and in 1866 moved to Libertyville, Ill., and in 1877 to Odebolt, Iowa, where he was a farmer and carpenter. He married **Maria Rogers** in 1852. He died July 6, 1908.

Children:—B*orn in Mass.*
- —1243 Otis J.,[9] m. **Jane Ellinger**; res. Odebolt, Iowa; chn. Blanch,[10] Earl,[10] Lewis.[10]

  Born in Waterloo, N. Y.
- —1244 Edson H.,[9] m. **Augusta Smith**; res. Kenosha, Wis.
- —1245 Erwin D.,[9] m. **Mamie H. Riggs**; res. Odebolt.
- —1246 Nellie,[9] m. **James Ellinger**; res. Odebolt.

680. AUSTIN STRATTON[8] (*Paul,*[7] *Josiah,*[6] *Hezekiah,*[5] *Samuel,*[4] *Samuel,*[3] *Samuel,*[2] *Samuel*[1]) married **Harriet J. Wilberforce** of St. Johns, N. B., in 1823. They lived at St. Johns, in Bangor and Albion. He died in Albion, Me., in 1887.

Children:
- —1247 Harriet J.,[9] b. 1825; m. **Elijah S. Dudgin** in 1850.

—1248 George W.,⁹ b. Mar. 6, 1827; m. **Helen Page** in 1852. Their only child, Adah B.,⁹ m. a **Mr. Chandler** and lives in Bangor.

—1249 Hubbard B.,⁹ b. Dec. 20, 1833; m. **Mary L. Moulton** of Laconia, N. H.; ch. Earnest L.¹⁰

681. PAUL STRATTON⁸ (*Paul,⁷ Josiah,⁶ Hezekiah,⁵ Samuel,⁴ Samuel,³ Samuel,² Samuel¹*) married, in 1818, Sarah Ann Frazier of St. Johns, N. B., who belonged to an old Scotch family. As early as 1820 he was proprietor of a hotel, "The Golden Bee," in St. Johns. Seven years later he went to Chester, Me., where he was one of the early settlers, going into an unbroken forest and making a large farm there. In 1851 he built a hotel in Winn, Me., which he sold in 1864, and retired from business. Later he returned to Chester where he died Sept. 29, 1883. He was in the war of 1812 and drew a pension for many years. His sons became prosperous men and his daughters married into some of the best families in that part of the state. His old homestead in Chester is still standing. He is described by one who remembers him as a "fine, noble looking old man, honest and upright, fearing no one except his God. He read his Bible every day, and went quietly to sleep of old age."

Children:—*Born in St. Johns, N. B.*

—1250 Mary Ann,⁹ b. Nov. 15, 1820; m. **George Robertson** of St. Johns; d. in Bangor June, 1882.

—1251 Eliza,⁹ b. May 12, 1825; m. **Josiah Snow** of Winn.

+1252 Archie Williamson,⁹ b. Sept. 5, 1827.

Born in Albion, Me.

+1253 Lewis Frazier,⁹ b. Oct. 1, 1830.

Born in Chester, Me.

—1254 Jane,⁹ b. Dec. 12, 1832; m. **James Snow** of Mattaamkeag, Me.

—1255 Eunice,⁹ b. June 6, 1835; m. **James Crowell**.

+1256 George Hubbard,⁹ b. Mar. 12, 1837.

—1257 Ellen,⁹ b. Mar. 18, 1839; m. **Otis T. Hooper**.

—1258 Martha,⁹ b. May 26, 1841; m. **Wm. Jewell** of Gorham, N. H.

+1259 Gilford Dudley,⁹ b. Nov. 22, 1843.

685. FRINK STRATTON⁸ (*Paul,⁷ Josiah,⁶ Hezekiah,⁵ Samuel,⁴ Samuel,³ Samuel,² Samuel¹*) was but about 10 years old when his father died. When about 21 he went to work for a lumberman

in the forest on the Penobscot River. Not being able to get money for his work, he took a lot of wild land, near the present town of Chester, Me. On this he made a clearing and built a house, then returned to his native town and married Lydia L. **Coombs**. Together they made themselves a home in the almost unbroken forest, on the banks of the grand old Penobscot, enduring toil and privations and hardships. There were few settlers between their home and Bangor, a distance of 60 miles, and supplies were brought up the river in a bateau. In March, 1846, the freshet known as "the great ice freshet" destroyed much property along the river, and took away their house and barn. The family escaped in a boat. With indomitable courage they made another start, selecting higher ground for a building spot. Loved and respected by all, they lived to see the wild land converted into farms and settlements, and villages grew up around them, the steamboat running daily on the river and railroad trains passing in sight of their home.

Children:—*Born in Chester, Me.*
- —1260   Hannah H.,[9] b. June 1, 1831; d. 1849.
- —1261   Almira C.,[9] b. Mar., 1832; d. Dec. 2, 1848.
- —1262   Aurilla,[9] b. July 22, 1833; m. **Charles J. Thompson.**
- —1263   Harriet B.,[9] b. Jan. 3, 1835; m. **John W. Combs.**
- —1264   Lydia Ann,[9] b. Jan. 2, 1836; d. Apr., 1850.
- —1265   Mary B.,[9] b. Feb. 27, 1838; d. June 12, 1851.
- —1266   Ira F.,[9] b. Oct. 3, 1839; lost his life in the Civil War Sept., 1861; unm.
- —1267   Charles H.,[9] b. Dec. 26, 1842; d. Sept. 12, 1867, at his father's house from wounds received in Civil War; unm.
- —1268   Wilber R.,[9] b. May 8, 1845; d. June 2, 1898; m. **Emma Hatch,** Sept., 1869; machinist; lived in Norcross and Chester, Me. Their three children, Harriet,[10] Wilber [10] and Emma M.,[10] all died in childhood.
- +1269   Daniel W.,[9] b. May 8, 1846.
- —1270   Isabella,[9] b. Oct. 31, 1849; d. in infancy.
- —1271   Clarica C.,[9] b. May 17, 1841; m. **George Falconer;** d. Apr. 5, 1893, in Winn, Me.

695.   Harvey Stratton [8] (*Israel,*[7] *Josiah,*[6] *Hezekiah,*[5] *Samuel,*[4] *Samuel,*[3] *Samuel,*[2] *Samuel* [1]) married Louisa J. Bryant of Holden. They lived a few years in Holden, and then moved to Plainfield, Ill.

Children:—*Born in Holden, Mass.*
—1272 William Harvey, b. Nov. 26, 1851; m. Lillie **L. Waldo**; res. in Illinois.
—1273 Fanny Louise,[9] b. Oct. 24, 1854.
—1274 Ella Jane,[9] b. June 20, 1856.

702. JOSIAH BAXTER STRATTON [8] (*John H.,*[7] *Josiah,*[6] *Hezekiah,*[5] *Samuel,*[4] *Samuel,*[3] *Samuel,*[2] *Samuel*[1]) married **Caroline A. Hurd**, July 21, 1844, and lived in Holden, Millsbury, and W. Boylston, where he was foreman in mills for carding, spinning and weaving. He died July 25, 1882, aged 66 years. As a young man, being out of health, his physician advised a sea voyage, so he shipped aboard a whaling vessel, making two voyages, one of them three years, the other two years.

Children:—*Born in Boylston, Mass.*
—1275 Emma C.,[9] b. 1846; m. **Albert Franklin Gates**, 1868.
—1276 Henry Josiah Wilber,[9] b. Oct. 4, 1849; m. **Ellen Howard** in 1877; res. Holyoke; chn. Henry G.,[10] Bertha M.,[10] Hattie E.,[10] Edith H.[10]
—1277 Albert Gardner,[9] m. **Mary Sullivan**, July 17, 1878; res. Jefferson, Mass.; chn. Nellie A.,[10] Grace E.[10]
Born in Millbury, Mass.
—1278 Fremont Sherman,[9] b. Mar. 1, 1857; m. **Emma N. Turner**, Oct. 30, 1880; res. Holyoke; chn. Vera L.,[10] Leon F.[10]
—1279 Hattie R.,[9] d. Apr. 22, 1873, aged 11 years, 5 months.
Born in Holden, Mass.
—1280 Frank Baxter,[9] m. **Alberta L. Butler**, Nov. 25, 1883; res. Providence, R. I.; chn. Frank E.,[10] m. **Emma E. Taylor**, June 22, 1914; Merle J.,[10] m. **Laura A. Bishop**, July 6, 1914; Lillian E.,[10] Harold H.[10]

705. WILLIAM FRINK STRATTON [8] (*Frink,*[7] *Josiah,*[6] *Hezekiah,*[5] *Samuel,*[4] *Samuel,*[3] *Samuel,*[2] *Samuel*[1]) was a designer, engraver and draftsman for many years with Dennison Manufacturing Co. in Boston. Later in life he spent much time in painting, and left many large oil paintings, some of which were sold after his death.* He married, first, **Martha H. Child**, Nov. 22, 1825. She was daughter of *Josiah* and *Beulah (Fay) Child.* Married,

---

* His office and studio was at the corner of Winter and Washington streets, with the sign "Stratton, engraver," over the door.

second, **Lucy Sessions,** daughter of *Chester Sessions.* He died Aug. 6, 1846, and is buried in Trinity church yard, Boston. (See his portrait.)*

Children:—B*orn in Boston.*
- —1281 Martha Child,[9] b. Sept. 20, 1826; m. **Samuel Miles;** d. Dorchester, Mass., 1892.
- —1282 William Davis,[9] b. (per. in Cambridge) Nov. 10, 1828; m. **Sarah** ——; d. in 1892 at Highlands, Mass.; no issue.
- —1283 Caroline,[9] b. Oct. 7, 1830; d. in Boston Apr. 21, 1898; m. **Luther L. Jenkins,** June 16, 1853, son of Isaiah and Abigail (Allen) Jenkins, and grandson of Elijah Allen, a Revolutionary soldier.

706. EBENEZER NILES STRATTON [8] (*Frink,*[7] *Josiah,*[6] *Hezekiah,*[5] *Samuel,*[4] *Samuel,*[3] *Samuel,*[2] *Samuel*[1]) married **Sophia A. Pearson,** Nov. 8, 1827, daughter of *John* and *Mary Pearson.* They both died in San Francisco, Cal. She Jan. 30, 1871, and he Nov. 5, 1882.

Children:—B*orn in Boston.*
- —1284 Henrietta Newland,[9] b. Sept. 21, 1828; d. Sept. 13, 1859.
- —1285 Sophia Henrietta,[9] b. Jan. 24, 1831; d. Jan. 7, 1876.

B*orn in Baltimore, Md.*
- —1286 Mary Elizabeth,[9] b. June 24, 1838.

713. ASA STRATTON [8] (*Daniel,*[7] *Daniel,*[6] *Hezekiah,*[5] *Samuel,*[4] *Samuel,*[3] *Samuel,*[2] *Samuel*[1]) was a farmer in Newfane, Vt., on the farm which his father bought in 1807. He married **Mary Morse** in 1828. The house that he built about the time of his marriage is still standing.

Children:—B*orn in Newfane, Vt.*
- —1287 Albert O.,[9] b. 1831; d. aged seven years.
- +1288 Ebenezer M.,[9] b. Jan. 19, 1833.
- +1289 John S.,[9] b. Oct. 13, 1835.
- +1290 Asa H.,[9] b. Mar. 29, 1839.
- —1291 Mary E.,[9] b. May 9, 1841; d. Aug. 14, 1859.
- —1292 Frances E.,[9] b. Aug. 9, 1843; d. in infancy.
- —1293 Charles M.,[9] b. Dec. 27, 1845; res. Newfane, Vt.

---

*This portrait is from a painting in colors on porcelain, and was sent the compiler by Mrs. Ella C. Brown of Arlington, N. J., daughter of Luther J. and Caroline (Stratton) Jenkins.

—1294 Ella R.,⁹ b. Jan. 25, 1849; m. **John H. Merrifield**, Feb. 24, 1886; res. Williamsville, Vt.
—1295 Sarah J.,⁹ b. Mar. 18, 1851; m. **Wm. A. Brooks**, Nov. 24, 1881; d. May 19, 1892, in Newfane.

715. Joseph Stickney Stratton ⁸ (*Daniel,⁷ Daniel,⁶ Hezekiah,⁵ Samuel,⁴ Samuel,³ Samuel,² Samuel¹*) was a farmer at Marlboro, Vt. He married **Dollie P. Gipson**, Feb. 13, 1834, in Ashburnham. She was born in Rindge Oct. 20, 1815, and died in Newfane Jan. 19, 1900. He died Oct. 29, 1867.

Children:—*Born in North Rindge.*
—1296 Henry O.,⁹ b. Feb. 13, 1835.
—1297 Ann M.,⁹ b. Sept. 16, 1836; m. **Sumner Shepherd**, Jan. 19, 1860.

Born in Marlboro, Vt.
—1298 Orlando M.,⁹ b. May 6, 1839.
—1299 George S.,⁹ b. Sept. 8, 1845.
—1300 Emma J.,⁹ b. Jan. 11, 1847; m. **S. G. Shepherd**.
+1301 Alonzo V.,⁹ b. July 6, 1849.

717. Daniel O. Stratton ⁸ (*Daniel,⁷ Daniel,⁶ Hezekiah,⁵ Samuel,⁴ Samuel,³ Samuel,² Samuel¹*) was a farmer at Newfane. He married **Julia Adams**, Mar. 10, 1842. He died Sept. 22, 1895.

Children:—*Born in Newfane, Vt.*
—1302 Albert A.,⁹ b. Oct. 10, 1843; d. Sept. 11, 1851.
—1303 Marcia H.,⁹ b. Apr. 8, 1848; d. Mar. 15, 1879; m. **Wm. A. Brooks**, Jan. 20, 1868.
—1304 Stella J.,⁹ b. Jan. 24, 1851; d. July 28, 1859.
—1305 Alice A.,⁹ b. Feb. 21, 1858; d. July 12, 1893; m. **Eugene C. Bailey**, Sept. 11, 1885.

719. Albert Galtin Stratton ⁸ (*John,⁷ Daniel,⁶ Hezekiah,⁵ Samuel,⁴ Samuel,³ Samuel,² Samuel¹*) spent his boyhood and youth on his father's farm at South Oxford. The eldest of a large family, he early assumed home responsibilities, and while yet a boy often had charge of the farm for weeks at a time while his father was away working at his trade as a wheelwright. In manhood he became one of the prosperous, well-to-do farmers of that section. Nov. 12, 1835, he married **Caroline Wilcox**, who was a true helpmate during their long lives together, and whose memory is treasured by her children. Her parents, *Harrington* and *Charity Wilcox*, were among the very early settlers

of Chenango Co. About 1847, Mr. Stratton built the farmhouse now owned and occupied by his youngest son, a homestead around which cling many loving memories. Here Mrs. Stratton died in January, 1883, aged 67 years, and Mr. Stratton July 15, 1890, leaving behind an honored name and the record of a good life.

Children:—B*orn in South Oxford, N. Y.*
- —1306 Adelaide Charity,⁹ b. Nov. 19, 1836; d. in Mexico City Dec. 2, 1907; m. 1st, **Isaac Bronson**, in 1855; m. 2nd, his brother **Edward D. Bronson**, in Nov., 1867.
- —1307 John Avery,⁹ b. Aug. 26, 1836; d. Apr. 13, 1841.
- —1308 Mary Clarinda,⁹ b. Jan. 29, 1840; d. Apr. 8, 1841.
- —1309 Mary Louise,⁹ b. Apr. 14, 1842; d. July 3, 1858.
- +1310 Charles Juliand,⁹ b. Feb. 12, 1844.
- —1311 Sarah DeFrances,⁹ b. Oct. 28, 1845; m. **Henry Marvin Juliand**, Sept. 15, 1869; res. Greene, N. Y.*
- —1312 Tracy,⁹ b. July 19, 1848; d. Feb. 16, 1850.
- —1313 Rosella Hart,⁹ b. Sept. 8, 1850; m. **Rector W. Willoughby**, Sept. 23, 1874; resided in Howard, Col., where her death occurred Mar. 11, 1916.
- +1314 Melville Bronson,⁹ b. Sept. 14, 1856.

720. JOHN STRATTON ⁸ (*John*,⁷ *Daniel*,⁶ *Hezekiah*,⁵ *Samuel*,⁴ *Samuel*,³ *Samuel*,² *Samuel* ¹) learned the millwright trade from his father and as a young man worked at his trade with his father and his brother George. Later he became a prosperous, progressive farmer, owning a farm joining that of his brother Albert, the two houses in the beautiful Chenango Valley being within calling distance of each other, while the home of their brother George was three quarters of a mile below.† Jan. 5, 1844,

---

* Of their twin sons, Charles Stratton Juliand resides in Greene, N. Y. Albert Stratton Juliand died Sept. 12, 1898, after a bright and happy life of twenty years,—a noble, Christian young man.

Mr. Juliand is descended from Joseph Juliand, sea-captain, who was born in Lyons, France, in 1749 and settled in Green, N. Y., which was first a settlement of French Huguenots.

† An old gentleman who remembers this part of Chenango County forty-five years ago writes the author: "It was a delight to an observing man to pass through the Stratton neighborhood, to see the well kept farms, buildings and yards, the signs of industry and thrift on every hand. They were exemplary men, sturdy in a high degree, physically, mentally, morally."

he married **Hannah Duncan Wilcox,** a sister of his brother Albert's wife. She was born Jan. 19, 1821, and died Jan. 4, 1904. Mr. Stratton died Jan. 2, 1886. Genial, pleasant and helpful, he was a great favorite, especially with the children of the family.

Children:—*Born in So. Oxford, N. Y.*

+1315   Eli Burton,[9] b. Sept. 26, 1845.

—1316   Ella Louise,[9] b. July 9, 1847; m. **Dr. C. C. Miller,** Feb. 15, 1871, of Detroit. His sister married D. M. Ferry, the Detroit seedsman.

+1317   Latson William,[9] b. July 3, 1849.

—1318   Emma Charlotte,[9] b. July 15, 1853; m. **Chester Willoughby;** res. Sidney, N. Y.

—1319   Gilbert John,[9] b. July 15, 1855; m. **Jennie V. Hodge,** Nov. 18, 1896; d. in Oxford Mar. 29, 1906; chn. Chester H.,[10] John N.[10]

—1320   Clark Lewis,[9] b. May 3, 1858; m. **Bertha L. Berry,** Oct. 26, 1887; she d. at Oxford Dec. 6, 1909; ch. Percy F.[10]

721.   IRA STRATTON [8] (*John,*[7] *Daniel,*[6] *Hezekiah,*[5] *Samuel,*[4] *Samuel,*[3] *Samuel,*[2] *Samuel* [1]) was born in South Oxford Jan. 29, 1815. He married, May 6, 1838, **Ann Eliza Dent,** a woman of noble character. She was born Aug. 16, 1819, and died Oct. 7, 1884. He died Sept. 22, 1883, respected by all who knew him. He was deprived of many of the pleasures of life by disease affecting his eyes from which he suffered many years.

Children:—*Born in Oxford, N. Y.*

—1321   William Henry,[9] b. Sept. 25, 1838; m. **Hester Jane Waterman,** who died Nov. 7, 1903. He d. at East Pharsalia, N. Y., Sept. 20, 1910. No children.

+1322   George Wesley,[9] b. Jan. 10, 1840.

—1323   John Alfred,[9] b. Apr. 28, 1842; m. **Frances Cole;** d. May 4, 1906. No children.

Born in Southville, N. Y.

+1324   James Darwin,[9] b. Nov. 14, 1844.

—1325   Frederick Albert,[9] b. 1846; d. 1852.

—1326   Mary Elizabeth,[9] b. Mar. 8, 1849; m. 1st, **Daniel Webster Hull;** 2nd, **Harvey D. Breed,** Oct. 27, 1844.

—1327   Alice Adelia,[9] b. Apr. 27, 1851; m. **Frank C. Wessels,** Oct. 18, 1871.

722. William Frink Stratton [8] (*John,*[7] *Daniel,*[6] *Hezekiah,*[5] *Samuel,*[4] *Samuel,*[3] *Samuel,*[2] *Samuel* [1]) was born in So. Oxford Jan. 27, 1817, and died in his native town Oct. 31, 1847. He was a mechanic by trade, a good Christian man, loved and respected by all his acquaintances. He married, Jan. 11, 1840, **Maria Symonds**. She was born Jan. 11, 1820, and died July 30, 1890.*

Children:—B*orn in So. Oxford, N. Y.*
+1328 Whitman,[9] b. Sept. 7, 1840.
−1329 Charlotte,[9] b. Mar. 31, 1842; res. Norwich, N. Y.
−1330 Avery,[9] b. Mar. 31, 1844; m. **Louisa A. Wood**, Aug. 27, 1864. Served in Navy, 1862-3, on U. S. Frigate *Potomac,* and other vessels at Pensacola and Arkansas Pass, and took part in battle of Galveston; discharged on account of health, Aug. 26, 1863; d. Sept. 3, 1865.
−1331 Garrett Smith,[9] b. Aug. 24, 1846; d. Mar. 18, 1848.

725. George Stratton [8] (*John,*[7] *Daniel,*[6] *Hezekiah,*[5] *Samuel,*[4] *Samuel,*[3] *Samuel,*[2] *Samuel* [1]) married, first, **Mariette Robinson**, Jan. 8, 1845. She died Apr. 6, 1865. He married, second, **Maria Robinson**. He was a farmer in Oxford, owning a fine, well cultivated farm near the old homestead. For several years he was Supervisor of the town. He was a man greatly beloved and respected, a good musician, playing on several different instruments, and at one time leader of the Oxford band. With his fine voice, he was a leader of the church choir. He died Sept. 1, 1910.

Children:—B*orn in South Oxford, N. Y.*
    By first marriage.
−1332 William Avery,[9] b. Mar. 23, 1845; res. Oxford.
+1333 Edward L.,[9] b. Dec. 8, 1847.

---

*"She was a noble Christian woman, who fought life's trials bravely for herself and her family, and was always ready to lend a helping hand to any in sickness or need. She was a daughter of Deacon John and Lucia (Cheesbrough) Symonds, who were among the very early settlers in the Chenango Valley. They traveled by ox-team from Connecticut, bringing all their worldly goods in a large red chest which served them for some time as a table. He was a deeply religious man, and because of his strict Presbyterian training refused to travel on the Sabbath Day, and so he and his family were left behind by the rest of the party, arriving two days later, but in a better condition to begin the new life in the wilderness after the long, tiresome journey."

+1334   Harvey J.,⁹ b. Jan. 24, 1850.
−1335   Luke A.,⁹ b. Mar. 5, 1853; d. Mar. 2, 1862.
−1336   Tracy Frink,⁹ b. June 9, 1858; m. **Minnie Miller,** May 4, 1887; res. Oxford, N. Y.; only child, Ethel.¹⁰
−1337   Alice Robinson,⁹ b. Feb. 6, 1864; m. **Ira B. McFarland,** Oct. 21, 1885; res. Indian Springs, Nev.

726. EBENEZER ROSS STRATTON ⁸ (*John,*⁷ *Daniel,*⁶ *Hezekiah,*⁵ *Samuel,*⁴ *Samuel,*³ *Samuel,*² *Samuel*¹) was a mechanic by trade, and one of the best of his day and section. Married **Hannah A. Symonds,** Oct. 18, 1846. She was born Oct. 20, 1828, and died July 21, 1889. Not being strong enough to continuously work at his trade (in which he was considered a genius) in later life he spent much of his time on the farm. He had decided musical talent and was a fine violinist. He and his beloved wife are lovingly remembered for their real worth and kind hospitality. He died Aug. 16, 1889.

Children:—*Born in Oxford, N. Y.*
−1338   Harriet,⁹ b. Sept. 20, 1847; m. **Charles O. Wilcox,** June 2, 1869; d. Apr. 22, 1906.
−1339   Curtis,⁹ b. June 20, 1850; m. **Jennie Copeland,** July 3, 1879; only child, Earl,¹⁰ d. young.
−1340   Clara,⁹ b. Oct. 11, 1852; m. **Alexis Wheeler,** Sept. 3, 1872; res. Mt. Upton, N. Y.
−1341   Albert,⁹ b. Mar. 30, 1855; m. **Lettie Tiffany,** Dec. 26, 1877; d. July, 1889, in Robinsonville, Miss.; only child, Esther.¹⁰
−1342   George,⁹ b. June 14, 1857; m. **Addie Eaton,** Sept. 22, 1881; res. Buffalo, N. Y.
−1343   Marietta,⁹ b. June 20, 1862; d. aged 2 years.
+1344   Luverne,⁹ b. Aug. 4, 1864.

730. WILLIAM WARNER STRATTON ⁸ (*William,*⁷ *Daniel,*⁶ *Hezekiah,*⁵ *Samuel,*⁴ *Samuel,*³ *Samuel,*² *Samuel*¹) married **Amy Permelia Fuller,** June 30, 1844. He died at Unadilla Forks, Osage Co., N. Y., Oct. 21, 1849, aged 30 years. His widow died in Simeon, Neb., Dec. 21, 1895, aged 71 years.

Children:—*Born in Hartford, Courtland Co., N. Y.*
+1345   William Henry,⁹ b. Aug. 13. 1845.
−1346   Mary Elizabeth,⁹ d. Oct. 21, 1849, aged 1 year.
−1347   Amy Marietta,⁹ d. May 3, 1850, aged 1 month.

1. George Stratton. 2. Ebenezer R. Stratton.
3. Charlotte (Stratton) Ten Broeck.
4. John Stratton. 5. Mary (Stratton) Lewis.
Pages 67-68. *Also,* 113-116.

736. WILDER STRATTON[8] (*Samuel,*[7] *Hezekiah,*[6] *Hezekiah,*[5] *Samuel,*[4] *Samuel,*[3] *Samuel,*[2] *Samuel*[1]) was born in Albion, Me., Apr. 18, 1805. While a young man he went to Northern Maine, and did an extensive lumber business along the St. John's River and its branches, and at Aroostook, where he lived for some time. He was one of the first settlers of Washburn, "taking up" one of the best farms there. He married, at Woodstock, N. B., **Nancy Bull**, a descendant of the Tory general of that name. She died about 1850, and he married her sister, **Martha Bull**. He died at Presque Isle in 1884.*

Children:—B*orn in Washburn, Me.*

By first marriage.
- —1348 Samuel Wesley,[9] b. Aug. 20, 1841; m. **Jannette Hall**, about 1870; served five years in the Civil War, in 15th Me. Vols.; ch. Grace.[10]
- +1349 Albion Wilder,[9] b. May 10, 1843.
- +1350 George Frank,[9] b. May 9, 1849.

By second marriage.
- —1351 Helen M.[9]
- —1352 Wilber,[9] d. in childhood.
- —1353 Julia O.,[9] m. **Alvah Merrill**; res. Turner Center, Me.

740. HEZEKIAH STRATTON[8] (*Samuel,*[7] *Hezekiah,*[6] *Hezekiah,*[5] *Samuel,*[4] *Samuel,*[3] *Samuel,*[2] *Samuel*[1]) was a merchant and trader in Albion, where he was highly esteemed. In 1857 he married **Arabella Farnham**, daughter of *Enoch Farnham*, a lawyer of Albion. She was born Aug. 30, 1833, and died July 21, 1878. He died Mar. 10, 1873.

Children:—B*orn in Albion, Me.*
- —1354 Flora Belle,[9] d. Oct. 17, 1880, aged 20 years.
- —1355 Ada Farnham,[9] m. **Simon Bradstreet**, Dec. 31, 1886; res. So. Freedom, Me.
- —1356 Emma Jane,[9] m. **Charles F. Bythers**, Oct. 25, 1888, of Albion.
- —1357 Nettie Frances,[9] d. Oct. 4, 1896.
- —1358 Enoch Farnham,[9] m. **Grace Varney**, Mar., 1895; res. Clinton, Me.; ch. Seth V.[10]
- —1359 Clara Mae,[9] d. Aug. 8, 1896.

---

* It is understood in the family that he was named for his mother's brother, Wilder Broad, whose mother (or grandmother?) was a Wilder of the Hingham line—from Edward Wilder.[1]

753. ROBERT FOLGER STRATTON [8] (*William,*[7] *Hezekiah,*[6] *Hezekiah,*[5] *Samuel,*[4] *Samuel,*[3] *Samuel,*[2] *Samuel*[1]) graduated from Waterville (Me.) College in 1853; from Harvard Medical College in 1859. Surgeon in 11th Illinois Regt., 1861-1861; served in Army of Tenn.; was at battles of Shiloh, Corinth and many similar battles. He married **Caroline Jane Langley** in 1859; res. St. Joseph, Mich.

Children:
—1360 Robert May.[9]
—1361 Kate Langley.[9]
—1362 Charles William,[9] grad. University of Mich., 1896; lawyer at St. Joseph, Mich.

764. JAMES N. STRATTON [8] (*James,*[7] *Nehemiah,*[6] *Hezekiah,*[5] *Samuel,*[4] *Samuel,*[3] *Samuel,*[2] *Samuel*[1]) married, in 1863, **Sarah B. Taylor,** daughter of *Jesse Taylor,* and granddaughter of *Capt. Edward Taylor.* They lived in Albion, Me., where his widow still lives.

Children:—*Born in Albion, Me.*
—1363 Ella B.,[9] m. **R. H. Black,** Sept. 15, 1883.
—1364 Adelbert M.,[9] m. **Alice Meader,** Sept. 29, 1891. They live in Albion, and have one daughter, Louise J.[10]

769. FRANK K. STRATTON [8] (*James,*[7] *Nehemiah,*[6] *Hezekiah,*[5] *Samuel,*[4] *Samuel,*[3] *Samuel,*[2] *Samuel*[1]) is a Methodist minister, educated at Boston University. He was Chaplain in the 11th Vols., Civil War. He has held pastorates in Boston, Springfield, Haverhill, and other cities. He married, first, **Annie M. Cox;** second, Louie Ricker; third, **Mrs. Eliza A. Crawford.** Dr. Stratton is now in his 80th year, with a voice as firm and clear as ever, the beloved pastor of Hillside Peoples M. E. Church at Melrose, Mass.

Children:—*Born in Springfield, Mass.*
  By first marriage.
—1365 Frank W., d. Sept. 5, 1872, aged 11 mos.
  By second marriage.
—1366 Annie Florence.[9]
—1367 Ralph Ricker,[9] physician at Melrose; m. **Ethel Blake;** ch. Frank B.[10]
  Born in Norwich, Conn.
—1368 Grace Marion,[9] m. **Geo. Raymond Bancroft.**

776. SEPIO STRATTON [8] (*Jonas*,[7] *Nehemiah*,[6] *Hezekiah*,[5] *Samuel*,[4] *Samuel*,[3] *Samuel*,[2] *Samuel*[1]) married, first, **Mary F. Love**, Sept. 1, 1866. She died in Quincy, Ill., in 1876. Two years later, Mar. 10, 1878, he married **Mary E. Lynch**. He was a soldier in the Civil War—in 118th Illinois, 1862-3, in 50th Illinois, under Sherman, Feb., 1864, to close of war. He is a pattern maker by trade. Has lived in Kansas, Missouri, and San Francisco, but most of his life in Pike Co., Ill. Now he resides in Beloit, Wis.

Children:—B*orn in Kansas.*
By first marriage.
—1369 Lois E.,[9] d. Dec. 25, 1883, aged 13 years.
—1370 Jonas A.,[9] d. Sept. 27, 1877, aged 1 year.
By second marriage.
—1371 Clara M.,[9] d. in infancy.
—1372 Bessie May,[9] d. aged 7 years.
—1373 Irma B.,[9] d. in infancy.
—1374 Grace M.,[9] res. Beloit, Wis.
—1375 Joseph W.,[9] d. in infancy.

789. FRANKLIN STRATTON [8] (*Shubael C.*,[7] *Jonathan*,[6] *Jonathan*,[5] *Samuel*,[4] *Samuel*,[3] *Samuel*,[2] *Samuel*[1]) went from Franklin Co., Mass., to Crawford Co., Pa., in 1820, and became one of the early settlers of that section. July 12, 1829, he married **Caroline Hotchkiss**. Their home was at Evansburg, now Conneaut Lake, and later at Meadville in the same county, where he died Sept. 30, 1846. He was a man of ability and influence, and accumulated a considerable fortune. His business integrity, good judgment and fidelity to duty gave him a high standing in his community. At the time of his death he had many business interests.

Children:—B*orn in Evansburg, Pa.*
—1376 Louisa Maria,[9] b. 1830; d. aged 4 years.
—1377 Charles,[9] b. May 19, 1833; d. unm. June 21, 1909; a man of the highest personal character, and strictest business integrity; at 16 accepted the responsibility of the care of his mother and young brothers and sisters, and of his father's business interests, entering a business career in which he was actively engaged for nearly half a century, winning the respect and confidence of all with whom he had dealings.
—1378 Henry,[9] b. Mar. 19, 1838; d. aged 2 years.

—1379 Adelaide,⁹ b. May 10, 1840; d. in Meadville, Pa., July 8, 1914.
+1380 Henry,⁹ b. Oct. 18, 1841.
—1381 Frances Ann,⁹ b. Sept. 12, 1843; d. Feb. 7, 1880, in Meadville.

B*orn in Meadville, Pa.*

—1382 Franklin,⁹ b. Oct. 3, 1846; m. **Jennie A. Rouse,** Jan. 26, 1882; m. 2nd, **Katherine Connely,** March 3, 1886; res. Franklin, Pa. Chn. Jane Ann,¹⁰ Franklin,¹⁰ d. in infancy.

790. IRA STRATTON ⁸ (*Shubael C.,⁷ Jonathan,⁶ Jonathan,⁵ Samuel,⁴ Samuel,³ Samuel,² Samuel¹*) married, Nov. 6, 1835, **Martha Ann Coolidge,** and settled in Cambridge, where he became one of the business men of the town, and where he died in Aug., 1873, highly esteemed by all who knew him.

Children:—B*orn in Cambridge, Mass.*

—1383 Flavel Coolidge,⁹ b. Feb. 14, 1840; d. unm. July 23, 1906; a prominent citizen of Cambridge, a man of admirable traits, of noted purity of character, a generous contributor to every call for financial aid in any good cause, greatly beloved by his friends and held in high esteem by all his acquaintances.
—1384 Martha,⁹ m. **Dwight W. Ensign** of Cambridge, son of Seymour and Diantha (Holmes) Ensign, grandson of Otis Ensign, Rev. soldier; gt.-grandson of Eliphalet Ensign, who was killed at the Wyoming Massacre. He d. July 6, 1915.
—1385 Anna Maria,⁹ d. Sept. 23, 1850, aged 2 years.

791. HENRY STRATTON ⁸ (*Shubael C.,⁷ Jonathan,⁶ Jonathan,⁵ Samuel,⁴ Sameul,³ Sameul,² Samuel¹*) went to Crawford Co., Pa., while a young man, where he became a clerk in the store of his brother Franklin at Conneaut Lake, and later engaged in other business affairs in the vicinity. He married **Emiline Bradley** of Cassewago, Nov. 3, 1831. He died Apr. 13, 1836, after a brief illness.

Children:—B*orn at Conneaut Lake, Pa.*

—1386 Ella,⁹ b. Dec. 25, 1832; d. Aug. 29, 1850.
+1387 Royal Altamont,⁹ b. Mar. 9, 1834.
—1388 Henrietta,⁹ b. Nov. 17, 1835; d. Dec. 17, 1910.

792. GEORGE STRATTON [8] (*Shubael C.,*[7] *Jonathan,*[6] *Jonathan,*[5] *Samuel,*[4] *Samuel,*[3] *Samuel,*[2] *Samuel*[1]) married **Lucinda Bailey**, Oct. 30, 1833. She was a daughter of *Amherst* and *Lydia Bailey* of Berlin, Mass. She died Feb. 17, 1890. Mr. Stratton died April 5, 1877.

Children:—*Born in Lancaster, Mass.*
- —1389 Henry Oscar,[9] b. Jan. 5, 1838; m. **Helen P. Brace** in 1862; d. in Winthrope, 1895; chn. Edith Louise,[10] and Mabel Stewart.[10]
- +1390 George Lyman,[9] b. Nov. 13, 1839.
- —1391 Jennie R.,[9] b. Jan. 4, 1841; res. Worcester, Mass.
- —1392 Lewis Franklin,[9] b. Jan. 5, 1845; m. **Harriet Valentine**; no children.
- —1393 Lydia Ann,[9] b. Mar. 4, 1848; d. in infancy.
- —1394 Ella Louise,[9] b. Apr. 2, 1852; d. 1899, at Clinton; m. **Walter F. Howard**, 1882.

793. JAMES COOK STRATTON [8] (*Shubael C.,*[7] *Jonathan,*[6] *Jonathan,*[5] *Samuel,*[4] *Samuel,*[3] *Samuel,*[2] *Samuel*[1]) went from Massachusetts to Crawford Co., Pennsylvania, while a young man, and engaged in mercantile business with his brother Franklin, and later was in business by himself. June 5, 1865, he married **Lovilla Jennings** in Conneaut Lake. She was daughter of *Ira* and *Hulda (Mallory) Jennings* of Buckland, Mass., and Pierpont, Ohio. He married, second, **Caroline (Hotchkiss) Stratton**, widow of his brother Franklin. He died Mar. 10, 1854.

Children:—*Born at Conneaut Lake, Pa.*
- —1395 Lydia,[9] b. Feb. 19, 1837; m. **Allen Kinne**, Aug. 27, 1857; d. in Pierpoint, Ohio.
- —1396 Cynthia,[9] b. July 11, 1838; m. **Robert Miller**, Feb. 14, 1861; res. Decorah, Iowa. They have a son Fred Stratton Miller, and a grandson Stratton Miller.
- —1397 Adelbert,[9] b. 1840; d. in infancy.
- —1398 Emma,[9] b. Sept. 21, 1843; m. **Edward C. Caine**, Aug. 29, 1867; res. Decorah, Iowa.
- —1399 Clara,[9] b. Mar. 14, 1846; d. 1892; m. **Russell M. Webb** in 1868; they have a daughter Grace Stratton Webb.

794. SHUBAEL CHILD STRATTON [8] (*Shubael C.,*[7] *Jonathan,*[6] *Jonathan,*[5] *Samuel,*[4] *Samuel,*[3] *Samuel,*[2] *Samuel*[1]) moved at the age of 17 with his mother and brothers, Henry and James, to

Evansburg (Conneaut Lake), Pennsylvania. As a boy he had to work out by the day, and at twenty was in business for himself. When he retired from business after a long career of honor and integrity he had amassed, measured by his home town standards, a large fortune. Devoted to his business, he was yet a lover of home, and a public-spirited man. Loyal to his Christian faith, his home church and the parsonage were largely built through his activity and contributions, and he gave for their perpetual maintenance a valuable rental property. In the name of his wife he endowed a scholarship in St. Lawrence University. He died at his home in Lineville, Pa., Sept. 23, 1906. He married, first, **Melvina Strong**, in Lineville; second, **Almira Van Winkle** in 1846. She was daughter of *Thomas* and *Nancy (Miller) Van Winkle*, who moved at an early date to Western Pennsylvania from New Jersey.

Children:—*Born in Lineville, Pa.*

By first marriage.

—1400 Walter,[9] b. 1842; d. aged 2 years.

By second marriage.

—1401 Ira,[9] b. 1847; m. **Marriette Taylor**; res. Lineville; one child, Blanch Edith.[10]

—1402 George,[9] clerk of Universalist church; Supt. of Sunday school; m. **Martha Bunday**; no children.

—-403 Thomas,[9] b. 1849; Universalist minister; graduate of Theological Dept. St. Lawrence University, Canton, N. Y., 1888; held pastorates at Plymouth, Potsdam, and Hightown, N. Y., Rockland, Me., and Rutland, Vt. In 1907 was elected Secretary and State Supt. of University work in Vermont and Quebec; m. **Bertha Brackman**; only child, Mabel R.,[10] grad. of St. Lawrence University.

—1404 Isaac,[9] b. 1852; m. **Ida M. Shattuck**; res. Lineville, Pa.; ch. Shubael Child.[10]

795. DANIEL HARRINGTON STRATTON [8] (*Braddyll*,[7] *Jonathan*,[6] *Jonathan*,[5] *Samuel*,[4] *Samuel*,[3] *Samuel*,[2] *Samuel* [1]) was born in Phillipston, Mass. He was not yet two years old when his mother died. He was brought up by his mother's parents in Lincoln. July 5, 1824, he married **Sarah Perry**. He was killed by lightning in Lincoln, June 11, 1838, while sitting at an open window watching a storm.

Children:—*Born in Lincoln, Mass.*
—1405 Daniel Coolidge,[9] b. Jan. 19, 1826.
+1406 Thomas Sullivan,[9] b. Dec. 10, 1827.
Two other children died in infancy.

796. WILLIAM COOLIDGE STRATTON [8] (*Braddyll,*[7] *Jonathan,*[6] *Jonathan,*[5] *Samuel,*[4] *Samuel,*[3] *Samuel,*[2] *Samuel*[1]) spent his boyhood in Phillipston, Mass. In 1826 he was in Farmingham, and joined the Masonic lodge there. Two years later he took the money left him by his grandfather Harrington and went west. Later he returned to New England and died in Hartford, Conn., in 1878. He married **Clarissa House** in 1830. She died Nov. 16, 1900.
Children:—B*orn in* B*ristol, Conn.*
+1407 William Dwight,[9] b. 1831.
—1408 Louise Maria Harrington,[9] b. 1833; m. Edward B. Barnes in 1872; res. Wethersfield, Conn.

798. JONATHAN RANSOM STRATTON [8] (*Jonathan,*[7] *Jonathan,*[6] *Jonathan,*[5] *Samuel,*[4] *Samuel,*[3] *Samuel,*[2] *Samuel*[1]) married **Lucy Moar Potter**, Jan. 22, 1835. He died in Vermont (?), May 15, 1855.
Children:
—1409 Rosaline Susan,[9] b. 1837; m. **Jonathan Eldred**.
—1410 Byron,[9] b. Oct. 2, 1835; m. in 1862, **Emma R. Minnis**. They had one son, Byron Phillips,[10] who married and died in Brooklyn without issue.
—1411 Harriet E. L.,[9] b. July 6, 1841; m. J. **Marshall Clapp**.
—1412 Lucy Moar,[9] b. Nov. 3, 1842; m. **Mortimer Gavitt**.

800. FRANKLIN B. STRATTON [8] (*Jonathan,*[7] *Jonathan,*[6] *Jonathan,*[5] *Samuel,*[4] *Samuel,*[3] *Samuel,*[2] *Samuel*[1]) married, first, **Isabella Miller** in 1836, who died in Phillipston in 1841, aged 36 years. Sept. 18, 1849, he married, second, **Harriet F. Marsh**, who died three years later. In 1858 he married, third, **Louisa Caldwell**. He was a merchant; a member of the Presbyterian church. He died in Brooklyn, N. Y., Sept., 1865.
Children:—*Born in Phillipston, Mass.*
—1413 Betsey Bowker,[9] m. **Samuel R. St. John** of Brooklyn; d. July 6, 1903.
Born in Southold, L. I.
—1414 Rudolph Marsh,[9] graduate of Philadelphia College of

Dentistry; 15 years' service in Pa. National Guard; m. **Caroline A. Hyatt**; res. Scranton, Pa.

811. RUFUS STRATTON [8] (*Daniel*,[7] *Daniel*,[6] *Jonathan*,[5] *Daniel*,[4] *Samuel*,[3] *Samuel*,[2] *Samuel*[1]) was administrator of his father's estate in Hudson, Mass., in 1837. In 1834 he married **Clarinda Gibson**. About 1860 he moved with his family to Illinois. He died June 30, 1887, in Chicago.

Children:—*Born in Marlboro, Mass.*

—1414a Daniel,[9] b. 1836; d. unm. in Iowa, in 1860.
—1415 George F.,[9] b. Jan. 30, 1840. Capt. in Ill. Regt. in Civil War. Lived for awhile in New Orleans; mem. Dr. Palmer's church; d. 1906 in Chicago; unm.
—1416 Frank Rufus,[9] b. Nov. 29, 1842; went to Sherman, Texas; m. Ida Marsh; d. 1907; only child, Daniel,[10] d. aged 22 yrs.
—1417 Clara Eldora,[9] b. May 7, 1845; m. Jerome B. Hall, who d. in 1904; res. Chicago.

813. LORENZO STRATTON [8] (*Daniel*,[7] *Daniel*,[6] *Jonathan*,[5] *Samuel*,[4] *Samuel*,[3] *Samuel*,[2] *Samuel*[1]) married **Mary E. Parks** of Stow, Mass., in 1830, and lived in that part of Hudson which was a part of Feltonville (earlier Marlboro), where he was connected with the boot and shoe business and farming. He died in Hudson, Mass., Apr. 8, 1865.

Children:—Born in Marlboro, Mass.

—1418 George,[9] b. Feb. 22, 1831; m. **Mary Chamberlain** in 1851; had one son, Edwin C.,[10] who died unm.
—1419 Rufus,[9] b. Oct. 21, 1832; m. Lovina L. **Tyler**; d. in Hudson, June 22, 1890; chn. Effie L.,[10] d. in infancy; Nellie G.,[10] d. in childhood; Blanch M.,[10] d. in infancy; Grace W.[10]
+1420 Lorenzo,[9] b. Jan. 5, 1835.
+1421 Joseph,[9] b. Apr. 22, 1841.
—1422 John,[9] b. Feb. 8, 1847; d. in Marlboro, Oct. 8, 1864.
—1423 Sarah,[9] m. **Henry B. Crossett**, Sept. 19, 1863, who was born in Bemington, Vt., and was a teacher in Williamstown, Mass. She died in Brooklyn, Feb. 23, 1885.

818. DANIEL STRATTON [8] (*Daniel*,[7] *Daniel*,[6] *Jonathan*,[5] *Samuel*,[4] *Samuel*,[3] *Samuel*,[2] *Samuel*[1]) married **Tryphena Rice Hol-**

man in Sterling, Dec. 31, 1839. She was daughter of *Elijah* and *Lucy (Tucker) Holman.* He died in Hudson, Jan. 1, 1890, the day after celebrating his golden wedding anniversary. He was a progressive and prosperous farmer on the farm where he lived as a boy, and where he erected new buildings and made many improvements. He built one of the first silos in the country. He was active in town affairs, holding several town offices. He was also a great church worker, and helped to establish the Hudson Methodist church.

Children:—*Born in Bolton, Mass.*

—1424   Mary,[9] b. Nov. 21, 1840; m. **James Pike** of Danvers, Mass.; a popular teacher until her marriage.

—1425   Ellen,[9] b. July 7, 1842; m. 1st, **Joseph Hale**; 2nd, **Earnest Albertin.**

—1426   Albert S.,[9] b. 1846; d. aged 4 mos.

+1427   Daniel Wilber,[9] b. Apr. 22, 1848.

+1428   Theodore,[9] b. Feb. 3, 1851.

+1429   Herbert,[9] b. Oct. 17, 1857.

823.   Josiah Stratton[8] (*Josiah,*[7] *Daniel,*[6] *Jonathan,*[5] *Samuel,*[4] *Samuel,*[3] *Samuel,*[2] *Samuel*[1]) was a pianoforte maker in Winchester, Mass. He married **Abigail Richerson**, July 8, 1847. Enlisted in 1861 as sergeant in Co. F., 22nd Mass. Regt.; killed, June 27, 1862, in seven days' battle before Richmond, under Gen. McClellan; was in command at the time of his death, the captain having been previously killed.

Children:—*Born in Winchester, Mass.*

—1430   George Gardener,[9] b. Jan. 16, 1849; m. **Florence Lelia Carter**, Dec. 20, 1876, who died in Boston, Oct. 2, 1877. He belongs to the Ancient and Honorable Artillery Co. chartered in 1638, to Society of Colonial Wars, Sons of American Revolution, Commandry Knights Templars and to all Masonic orders; res. Winchester, Mass.; only child, Roscoe Carter,[10] d. July 14, 1878, aged 1 year 2 mos.

—1431   Josiah James,[9] res. in Winchester; unm.

836.   Lewis Stratton[8] (*Henry,*[7] *Isaac,*[6] *Jonathan,*[5] *Samuel,*[4] *Samuel,*[3] *Samuel,*[2] *Samuel*[1]) married **Emogene W. Harris** in 1855. He died in Lawrence, Nov. 1, 1889.

Children:—*Born in Lawrence, Mass.*

—1432   Fannie H.,[9] b. Sept. 26, 1856.

—1433   Mary B.,⁹ m. **John J. Cate** in 1883, lives in Lawrence.
+1434   Charles L.⁹

837. Francis Stratton ⁸ (*Henry,*⁷ *Isaac,*⁶ *Jonathan,*⁵ *Samuel,*⁴ *Samuel,*³ *Samuel,*² *Samuel* ¹) settled in Harrisonville, N. H., about 1854, where he died June 14, 1905. He married, first, Emily M. Holt, Dec. 30, 1860; second, **Rosa M. Aldrich,** Sept. 1, 1880.

Children:—Born in Harrisonville, N. H.
+1435   Henry F.,⁹ b. Dec. 18, 1861.
—1436   Frederick Adams,⁹ lived in Harrisonville, where he died Oct. 8, 1908; m. three times, left no children.
—1437   Edgar Holt,⁹ b. 1871; d. in infancy.

842. Charles Edwin Stratton ⁸ (*Charles,*⁷ *Elisha,*⁶ *Jonathan,*⁵ *Samuel,*⁴ *Samuel,*³ *Samuel,*² *Samuel* ¹) was only four years old when his father died. At seventeen he went to Boston and was soon engaged in business there. He became a steel and iron merchant, and a man of more than usual business ability. At forty he had accumulated what he regarded as a sufficient fortune and retired from business. Dec. 23, 1841, he married **Sarah Hollis Piper,** daughter of *Solomon Piper,* a merchant and banker of Boston. She died Mar. 10, 1897. Mr. Stratton died Dec. 5, 1871.

Children:—Born in Boston.
  1437a   Frances Maria,⁹ m. **John James French**; res. Boston.
—1438   Susan Elizabeth,⁹ m. **Nathaniel Wales**; d. Feb. 2, 1901.
—1439   Charles Edwin,⁹ graduate of Harvard, Clerk of his class, has degrees A.B., L.L.B., A.M.; 12 years Chairman Boston Board of Park Commissioners; mem. of Society of Colonial Wars; res. Boston.
—1440   Solomon Piper,⁹ m. **Annie Flagg Wales**; of the firm of Jones, McDuffee & Stratton, Boston, among the largest importers of China in the United States; their daughter, Katherine Wales,¹⁰ m. Niels Christensen of Beaufort, S. C.

845. George Hurd Stratton ⁸ (*George,*⁷ *Elisha,*⁶ *Jonathan,*⁵ *Samuel,*⁴ *Samuel,*³ *Samuel,*² *Samuel* ¹) married **Susan H. Clark** in 1856.

Children:—Born in *Weston, Mass.*
+1441 Irwin C.,⁹ b. 1858.
−1442 Nellie A.,⁹ m. **Warren Caldwell**, 1883.
−1443 Florence S.,⁹ m. **William Baker**, 1887.
−1444 Edith P.,⁹ m., 1898, **Albert H. Plumb, Jr.**, a Congregational minister.

847. HOMER STRATTON⁸ (*Asa,*⁷ *Ebenezer,*⁶ *Samuel,*⁵ *Samuel,*⁴ *Samuel,*³ *Samuel,*² *Samuel*¹) married **Susan Damon**, Jan. 16, 1875. She was daughter of *John* and *Hepsibath (Flint) Damon*, and was born in Reading and died in Lexington, Jan. 29, 1893, aged 89 years.
Children:—Born in *Ashley, Mass.*
−1445 Sumner,⁹ b. Feb. 1, 1829; d. in infancy.
−1446 Asa S.,⁹ b. May 17, 1832; d. in childhood.
−1447 Delia A.,⁹ b. Mar. 25, 1840; m., Nov. 25, 1875, **George Stratton** (857), son of Ebenezer Stratton.

850. RAYMOND STRATTON⁸ (*Josiah,*⁷ *Ebenezer,*⁶ *Samuel,*⁵ *Samuel,*⁴ *Samuel,*³ *Samuel,*² *Samuel*¹) married **Mary Tyler**, June 5, 1811, of Barnet, Vt. They moved to Harmon, Ohio, where he died in 1868.
Children:—Born in *Ringe, Mass.*
−1448 Mary Elizabeth,⁹ b. Apr. 22, 1839; m. **M. G. Knox** of Harmon, Ohio.
Born in *Fitzwilliams, N. H.*
−1449 Esther T.,⁹ b. Mar. 6, 1841; m. —— **Birdsall**; moved to California.

853. JOSIAH STRATTON⁸ (*Josiah,*⁷ *Ebenezer,*⁶ *Samuel,*⁵ *Samuel,*⁴ *Samuel,*³ *Samuel,*² *Samuel*¹) married, Nov. 26, 1846, **Mary J. Burnett**, daughter of *Capt. James Burnett*. They lived on the home farm until 1871, and then moved to Fitchburg, where he was selectman for many years.
Children:—Born in *Ringe, Mass.*
−1450 Emerancy H.,⁹ b. July 28, 1848; d. Apr., 1876.
+1451 Rodney J.,⁹ b. June 10, 1852.
−1452 Jennie M.,⁹ d. in infancy.

856. STILLMAN STRATTON⁸ (*Ebenezer,*⁷ *Ebenezer,*⁶ *Samuel,*⁵ *Samuel,*⁴ *Samuel,*³ *Samuel,*² *Samuel*¹) married, Dec. 28, 1837, **Maria Keyes**, daughter of *Capt. Amos* and *Eunice (Spofford) Keyes* of Ringe. They lived for some years in Winchester, and

about 1839 moved to New Ipswich and settled on a farm near the Mason town line. He died and his widow married, second, Dea. Harvey Wyman.

Children:—*Born in New Ipswich, N. H.*
- —1453 Susan Jane,^{9} b. Nov. 2, 1839; d. Oct. 19, 1898; m., Apr. 16, 1861, William L. Woodcock of Winchester, Mass.
- —1454 James Stillman,^{9} b. Jan. 4, 1841, served in Civil War in 21st Mass. Regt. and was killed at Antietum.
- —1455 Etta Elizabeth,^{9} b. Oct. 9, 1844; m. **George W. Eddy,** a merchant of Ashburnham.
- —1456 Charles Henry,^{9} b. Dec. 17, 1846; m. **Caroline E. Groves,** daughter of *James* and *Asenath* (*Worry*) *Groves* of Portland, Me. Enlisted in 25th Mass. Regt., and was wounded at Roanoke Landing, but served through the war in the veteran reserve corps; lived in Portland, Me., and Malden, Mass.
- —1457 Emma Frances,^{9} b. Feb. 18, 1853; m., Dec. 21, 1882, **Frederick Lord,** son of Emory and Rebecca L. (Spear) Lord of Orange, Mass.

857. GEORGE STRATTON ^{8} (*Ebenezer,*^{7} *Ebenezer,*^{6} *Samuel,*^{5} *Samuel,*^{4} *Samuel,*^{3} *Samuel,*^{2} *Samuel*^{1}) married, Apr. 8, 1841, Sarah J. Holton, who was born Oct. 28, 1817. They settled in New Ipswich on a farm, where they lived for many years. She died Aug. 9, 1870, and he married, second, **Delia Stratton,** daughter of Homer Stratton (847). He married, third, **Annie Whitehead.** He died in 1897.

Children:—*Born in New Ipswich, N. H.*
By first marriage.
- —1458 George Frederick,^{9} m. **Martha Moore,** Apr. 13, 1869, who died in 1873. He married again and lived in Peterboro, N. H.
- —1459 Emogene A.,^{9} b. Nov. 28, 1849; d. Aug. 9, 1870.

872. SAMUEL STRATTON ^{8} (*John,*^{7} *Samuel,*^{6} *Samuel,*^{5} *Samuel,*^{4} *Samuel,*^{3} *Samuel,*^{2} *Samuel*^{1}) married **Isabella Brunhall** in 1846. He was a merchant in Worcester, where he died in 1905.
Children:
- —1460 Ida,^{9} b. 1854; m. **William J. Wheeler;** res. Worcester.
- —1461 Frank,^{9} b. 1866.
- —1462 Samuel,^{9} b. 1869.

873. MOSES B. STRATTON [8] (*John,*[7] *Samuel,*[6] *Samuel,*[5] *Samuel,*[4] *Samuel,*[3] *Samuel,*[2] *Samuel*[1]) went to sea while a young man, worked his way up until he became captain of his own ship; after retiring he lived in Worcester, Mass. He married, first, **Mary Small**; second, **Abbie Talbot**; third, **Katherine Goodyear**. Died Apr. 17, 1915, in Worcester, where his widow now resides.

Children:—B*orn in West Newton, Mass.*
By first marriage.
1462a Florence Elizabeth; d. in Worcester.
—1463 Charles A.,[9] res. Chicago; m. **Rose Wilhelmina Baehr**.
By third marriage.
—1464 Maude G.[9]
—1465 Henry T.[9]

874. DANFORTH D. STRATTON [8] (*John,*[7] *Samuel,*[6] *Samuel,*[5] *Samuel,*[4] *Samuel,*[3] *Samuel,*[2] *Samuel*[1]) is a merchant broker in Boston. He married **Frances Small**. Died in Melrose, Nov. 12, 1911.

Children:
—1466 Nellie,[9] a student at Mt. Holyoke; m. **Rev. George Allchin**. They are missionaries in Japan.
—1467 Elizabeth,[9] m. **James W. Savage**; res. Lynn, Mass.

885. CYPRIAN KIES STRATTON [8] (*Alpheus,*[7] *Alpheus,*[6] *Samuel,*[5] *Samuel,*[4] *Samuel,*[3] *Samuel,*[2] *Samuel*[1]) was born in Paxton, Mass. He married **Rosina C. Miller**. Enlisted in Co. "C," 25th Mass. Vols. Inft., Sept., 1861. Re-enlisted "for the war" Dec., 1863. Participated in many battles, among them Roanoke Landing, Newburg, Cold Harbor, and Petersburg. Honorably discharged June 21, 1865. He died in Portsmouth, N. H., in 1900.

Children:—B*orn in Worcester, Mass.*
—1468 Ellen O.[9]
—1469 Emma E.,[9] d. aged 6 mos.
—1470 Florence H.,[9] m. **Charles Churchill**; res. Portsmouth, N. H.
+1471 Edwin A.[9]

887. THOMAS WALTER STRATTON [8] (*Alpheus,*[7] *Alpheus,*[6] *Samuel,*[5] *Samuel,*[4] *Samuel,*[3] *Samuel,*[2] *Samuel*[1]) married, first, Feb. 3, 1848, **Mary Pierce Cutting**, whose mother was *Polly* (*Wilder*) *Cutting;* second, **Maria J. McLaughlin**, Oct. 3, 1891. He resides in Worcester.

Children:—*Born in Spencer, Mass.*
>By first marriage.

—1472 Alpheus Wilder,⁹ b. Jan. 21, 1849; d., unm., in early manhood.

—1473 Martha Jane,⁹ m. **Charles Abbott**; res. Monson, Mass.

>*Born in Rutland, Mass.*

—1474 Frank Walter,⁹ b. Sept. 30, 1858; d., unm., in early manhood.

—1475 Richard Vallangidham,⁹ b. Feb. 15, 1861; m. **Mary D. Pierce**; an engineer; res. East Brookfield, Mass. They have one child, Elsie Mary,¹⁰ m. **George Andrew Putney**, Sept. 9, 1909.

>*Born in Pellam, Mass.*

—1476 William Thomas,⁹ m. **Florence Hodge**; res. Spencer, Mass.

—1477 Mary Ellis,⁹ m. **Rufus Aldrich**; d. in Fishkill, N. Y.

900. NATHANIEL HAPGOOD STRATTON⁸ (*Samuel,⁷ Alpheus,⁶ Samuel,⁵ Samuel,⁴ Samuel,³ Samuel,² Samuel¹*) was a silver plater, and lived in Greenwich, Mass., until 1855; then moved to Montpelier. He married **Susan H. Legge**, Sept. 25, 1839. He was a lieutenant in the Federal Army. He died Oct. 10, 1883, in Montpelier. Mrs. Stratton died in Oct., 1906.

Children:—*Born in Greenwich, Mass.*

—1478 Emma,⁹ m. **Henry Barnes**, May 23, 1866, and resides in Elliott, Iowa.

—1479 Isadore F.,⁹ b. July 1, 1846; d. May 14, 1849.

+1480 George Oren.⁹

908. CARLOS EDSON STRATTON⁸ (*Caleb A.,⁷ Ebenezer,⁶ Hezekiah,⁵ Samuel,⁴ Samuel,³ Samuel,² Samuel¹*) married, Sept. 5, 1866, **Annie Brown** of Norwich, N. H. He was a farmer; a member of the Congregational church; served in the Civil War in Company "C," 15th Vermont Regt. He died Feb. 14, 1890, in Brookfield.

Children:—*Born in Brookfield, Vt.*

—1481 Jerome Brown,⁹ m. **Grace E. Parker**, Aug. 19, 1904; res. Nashua, N. H.; chn. Mildred Gladys,¹⁰ Carl Parker.¹⁰

—1482 Mercy Emily,⁹ d. May 17, 1901, aged 21 years.

Mrs. Louisa (Stratton) Russell, born 1786. Mother of the Russell brothers who founded the large manufacturing plant at Massillon, Ohio. *Page* 42. *Also* 210, *Vol.* I.

911. Asa Strong Stratton [8] (*Caleb S.,*[7] *Caleb,*[6] *Eleazer,*[5] *Hezekiah,*[4] *Samuel,*[3] *Samuel,*[2] *Samuel*[1]) was educated at Oberlin, Ohio. He married **Sarah Glezen** in 1866. Now president of the bank of Madison in which for many years he was cashier. A man of sterling worth and strictest business integrity.

Children:—*Born in Madison, Ohio.*

—1483 Philip G.,[9] m. **Mabel Kelley** in 1905; res. Superior, Wis. They have three little daughters: Faith,[10] Mabel,[10] and Sarah.[10]

—1484 Stella,[9] b. 1871; d. 1904.

—1485 Samuel,[9] b. 1875; d. in infancy.

917. George Stratton [8] (*Roswell,*[7] *Asa,*[6] *Eleazer,*[5] *Hezekiah,*[4] *Samuel,*[3] *Samuel,*[2] *Samuel*[1]) married, first, **Roxana P. Quint** in 1848. She died in 1849 and in 1863 he married **Sarah Ann Bates.** He was a cabinet maker, and lived in Millbury, where he died Nov. 19, 1889. He was a soldier in the Federal army; a prominent member of the Unitarian church.

Children:—*Born in Millbury.*

By first marriage.

—1486 George Roswell,[9] b. 1849; d. in infancy.

By second marriage.

—1487 Ida Frances,[9] m. **Orrin A. McIntire** in 1873; res. Fall River, Mass.

—1488 Anna Augusta,[9] m. **Henry C. Thompson,** 1880; d. in Millbury, July 26, 1893.

—1489 Charlotte Sarah,[9] m. **Charles H. Hakes,** 1882; res. Millbury.

—1490 Mary Florence,[9] m. **Walter N. Walling,** 1890; res. Auburndale, Mass.

—1491 Maud Louise,[9] a teacher at Millbury.

921. Edwin Alexander Stratton [8] (*Asa,*[7] *Asa,*[6] *Eleazer,*[5] *Hezekiah,*[4] *Samuel,*[3] *Samuel,*[2] *Samuel*[1]) resides in Greenfield, Mass. He married, first, in 1851, **Almira Purple,** daughter of *Roswell Purple.* She died Oct. 9, 1854, and he married, second, May 7, 1857, **Ellen Sawyer,** daughter of *Asahel Sawyer.* A carpenter by trade and becoming a contractor he built many houses in Greenfield and vicinity. From 1862 to 1865 he was employed by the U. S. Government in the Springfield Armory. In 1869 he and his brother established a local manufactory in Greenfield which has grown to an extensive business, manufacturing wooden and metal levels. He is a member of the Unitarian church.

Children:—*Born in Greenfield, Mass.*
  By first marriage.
—1492 Almira,⁹ m. **Fred Chase**; res. Keene, N. H.
  By second marriage.
—1493 Edith A.,⁹ m. **Raymond O. Stetson**, June 20, 1901.
—1494 Lena L.,⁹ grad. Smith College, 1892; res. Greenfield.

934. ALBERT S. STRATTON⁸ (*Albert,⁷ Asa,⁶ Eleazer,⁵ Hezekiah,⁴ Samuel,³ Samuel,² Samuel¹*) is a business man of Northfield, owning valuable real estate in this vicinity and in other states. He married, in 1850, **Nancy D. Drake**, daughter of *Tisdale* and *Ruth (Davis) Drake* of Maine.

Children:—Born in Northfield, Mass.
—1495 Ella, m. **Eugene Brown** of Winchester.
—1496 Carrie, m. **Dwight Preston** of So. Vernon, Vt.
—1497 Earnest E., m. **Dora Stearns**; a jeweler in Hinsdale.

936. LEONARD WHITE STRATTON⁸ (*Eleazer,⁷ Eleazer,⁶ Eleazer,⁵ Hezekiah,⁴ Samuel,³ Samuel,² Samuel¹*) lived in Adamsville and Colrain City. At the latter place he owned and managed a blacksmith shop, and later bought a farm where he lived for many years. Sept. 8, 1853, he married **Rowena Clark**, who was born in 1829 and died in 1906. Mr. Stratton died the same year.

Children:
+1498 George Leonard,⁹ b. Nov. 26, 1856.
—1499 Charles William,⁹ m. **Ella Clark**, Aug. 28, 1881; no children.
—1500 Lizzie Ella,⁹ for 13 years taught in the school sof Colrain; m. **Alvah Eldridge**, Feb. 28, 1898. They have a son, Dean Stratton Eldridge.

950. SAMUEL PINKNEY STRATTON⁸ (*Samuel,⁷ Rufus,⁶ Hezekiah,⁵ Hezekiah,⁴ Samuel,³ Samuel,² Samuel¹*) married, Nov. 5, 1846, **Fannie Amanda Pratt** of Montague. They resided in Gill, where he was a progressive and prosperous farmer. He held the office of town treasurer for several years and was chairman of the board of selectmen for 21 years. Mrs. Stratton died Nov. 13, 1901. Mr. Stratton died Mar. 8, 1909, in Neenah, Wis.,

while on a visit in the home of his daughter. Both are buried in Gill.

Children:—B*orn in Gill, Mass.*
—1501 Donna F.,[9] m. **Alpheus F. S.** Lyons, May 14, 1878; res. Neenah, Wis.; they have a son, Harold Stratton Lyons.
—1502 Arthur S.,[9] m. **Mary E. Purple**; res. Gill; no children.
—1503 Lyman F.,[9] b. 1885; m. **Mary D. Ellenwood**; d. in Orange, Mass., in 1896; ch. Samuel Ray,[10] res. Greenfield, Mass.

952. ALFRED MORRELL STRATTON [8] (*Samuel,*[7] *Rufus,*[6] *Hezekiah,*[5] *Samuel,*[4] *Samuel,*[3] *Samuel,*[2] *Samuel*[1]) married **Adeline Doolittle**. Resides in Barnardston, Mass.

Children:—Born in Gill, Mass.
—1504 Willis A.,[9] m. 1st **Ella Sanderson**; 2nd **Ida E. Hunter**; res. Bernardston; ch. Sumner,[10] m. Carrie E. Stratton.
—1505 Adella,[9] m. **Adelbert Mann**.
—1506 Everett,[9] m. **May Wyatt**; their only child died young; res. Bernardston, Mass.

956. ELIJAH STRATTON [8] (*Elihu,*[7] *Rufus,*[6] *Hezekiah,*[5] *Samuel,*[4] *Samuel,*[3] *Samuel,*[2] *Samuel*[1]) married **Mary Turner Bruce**, Aug. 17, 1835, and was for many years an active physician in Northfield. He died July 14, 1870. Mrs. Stratton died in 1809.

Children:—B*orn in Northfield, Mass.*
—1507 Robert Bruce,[9] b. Aug. 8, 1836; d. aged 3 years.
—1508 Mary Turner,[9] b. Mar. 16, 1838.
—1509 Thomas Bruce,[9] b. June 1, 1840; m. **Elnora Pratt**, May 26, 1867, daughter of *Samuel* and *Lucy (Stratton) Pratt* (No. 949); ch. Henry Pratt,[10] res. Miller's Falls, Mass.
—1510 Virginia S.,[9] m. **George Hastings** in 1861.
—1511 John Donsman,[9] m. **Nellie Bemis**, Oct. 22, 1877; d. at Morrisville, Vt.; chn. Florence,[10] Harold B.[10]

958. EDWIN STRATTON [8] (*Elihu,*[7] *Rufus,*[6] *Hezekiah,*[5] *Hezekiah,*[4] *Samuel,*[3] *Samuel,*[2] *Samuel*[1]) was a surveyor and civil engineer. He was chief engineer during the construction of the Troy & Greenfield railroad, the Cape Cod Central, and the Worcester and Gardner, and helped to survey the Massachusetts Central. In 1855 he went west, where he helped to survey the

Manitowoc and Menasha and the Logansport and Peoria railroads. Returning to Massachusetts, he assisted in the survey of the Hoosac Tunnel line, and was the first man to pass through the tunnel when the ends were connected in 1874. In 1880 he was elected register of deeds for Franklin Co., and held the office until 1897, when he retired from active business. May 16, 1854, Mr. Stratton married **Jane Smith Fuller**, a daughter of *Farnum Fuller* of North Adams. In politics he was a Republican. He was a member of the Unitarian church, of which he was a regular attendant. He was a member of the Masonic fraternity for 53 years and an Odd Fellow for 61 years. He enjoyed perfect health up to the last years of his life. In his 94th year he declined a gold-headed cane offered him by a Boston newspaper for being the oldest man in town, saying that he had "never used a cane, and did not need one." He died at his pleasant home in Greenfield, Dec. 31, 1910, aged 95 years.

Children:—*Born in North Adams, Mass.*
—1512 Jennie R.,^{9} m. **George E. Heath** of Fitchburg.
Born in Shelburne Falls, Mass.
—1513 Charlotte E.,^{9} Asst. Reg. of Deeds at Greenfield.
—1514 Edwin F.,^{9} official in Northampton Savings Bank.

960. EDWARD RUGGLES STRATTON ^{8} (*Rufus,^{7} Rufus,^{6} Hezekiah,^{5} Hezekiah,^{4} Samuel,^{3} Samuel,^{2} Samuel^1*) married **Charlotte E. Allison** in 1845. He died in Boston Mar. 24, 1867.

Children:—*Born in Boston.*
—1515 Eugene Edward,^{9} res. Washington, D. C.
+1516 Earnest A.^{9}

963. RUFUS WILLIAM STRATTON ^{8} (*Rufus,^{7} Hezekiah,^{6} Hezekiah,^{5} Samuel,^{4} Samuel,^{3} Samuel,^{2} Samuel^1*) married **Jane E. Clapp** of Montague in 1850. He lived in Amherst, where he conducted a shoe store for many years, and was in the insurance business for 12 years. He was one of the organizers of Grace Episcopal Church at Amherst, and one of its wardens. He was a staunch Republican, casting his first vote for Freemont in 1856. He died Jan. 20, 1914.

Children:—*Born in Amherst, Mass.*
—1517 Jennie Elizabeth,^{9} m. **Geo. W. Foster**.
—1518 Edward J.,^{9} b. 1854; d. 1889; unm.
—1519 Lillian,^{9} d. in infancy.
—1520 Gertrude Ellsworth,^{9} res. Amherst.

969a. WILLIAM H. STRATTON [8] (*Lorenzo,*[7] *Rufus,*[6] *Hezekiah,*[5] *Samuel,*[4] *Samuel,*[3] *Samuel,*[2] *Samuel*[1]) married **Martha G. Gage** in 1846. He was a farmer in Northfield, where he died Apr. 21, 1901.
Children:—B*orn in Northfield, Mass.*
—1521 Ella F.,[9] d. Sept. 14, 1905.
—1522 Mary L.,[9] m. Louis R. **Taft**; d. Nov. 15, 1907.
—1523 Clarence W.,[9] m. Margaret H. **Rose**, Mar. 9, 1903; res. Northfield.

983. CHESTER STRATTON [8] (*Arad,*[7] *Hezekiah,*[6] *Hezekiah,*[5] *Hezekiah,*[4] *Samuel,*[3] *Samuel,*[2] *Samuel*[1]) married **Martha Willette,** Oct. 21, 1845, and moved to Ripley, Ohio. He died July 16, 1879.
Children:
—1524 Wellington,[9] lived in Hillsboro, Ohio.
—1525 Angelius,[9] m. —— **Kirkpatrick** and resided at Mt. Sterling, Ky.
—1526 Eugenia,[9] Zanesville, Ohio.
—1527 Arthur,[9] d. young.
—1528 Mary,[9] d. young.
—1529 Willis,[9] lived in Warren, Ohio.
—1530 Amelia,[9] m. **Charles Chappelear,** Zanesville, Ohio.

991. LEMUEL STRATTON [8] (*Arad,*[7] *Hezekiah,*[6] *Hezekiah,*[5] *Hezekiah,*[4] *Samuel,*[3] *Samuel,*[2] *Samuel*[1]) married **Martha Wells,** Sept. 3, 1859, and lived for awhile at Gill, Mass., and then removed to Elmira, N. Y. He died in New Berlin, N. Y., Nov. 24, 1889.
Children:—*Born in Gill, Mass.*
—1531 Emma, m. Ansel **Burr,** 1883.
Born in Norwich, N. Y.
+1532 Herbert.[9]
—1533 Chester,[9] m. Libbie B. **Whitman** in 1887; res. Berlin; ch. Ernest,[10] Pearl,[10] Mason.[10]
+1534 Henry.[9]
Born in New Berlin, N. Y.
—1535 Jennie,[9] m. Floyd **Hayes,** 1897.

992. HEZEKIAH O. STRATTON [8] (*Hezekiah,*[7] *Hezekiah,*[6] *Hezekiah,*[5] *Hezekiah,*[4] *Samuel,*[3] *Samuel,*[2] *Samuel*[1]) married **Abbie F. Burt,** daughter of Rufus Burt, in 1852, and lived in Winchester, Mass., and Keene, N. H., where he was a farmer. He died in 1898.

Children:—*Born in Winchester.*
—1536 Talline Osborn,⁹ d. Feb. 19, 1857, aged 4 years.
—1537 Mary Abbie,⁹ d. Feb. 4, 1857, aged 2 years.
—1538 Frank Rufus,⁹ a bookkeeper in Fitsburg, Mass., m. **Lillian M. Graham**, Apr. 18, 1898. They have a daughter, Mildred Graham.¹⁰
—1539 Julia Abbie,⁹ d. Dec. 7, 1863, aged 3 years.
—1540 Hattie Mercy,⁹ m. **Carlon N. Stowell**, d. Dec. 4, 1901; res. Orange, N. J.

993. MARCELLUS D. STRATTON ⁸ (*Hezekiah,⁷ Hezekiah,⁶ Hezekiah,⁵ Hezekiah,⁴ Samuel,³ Samuel,² Samuel¹*) married **Henrietta Capen** in 1858, and lives in Greenfield, Mass.
Children:
—1541 George M.,⁹ m. **Florence Cowdry** and lives in Montague, Mass.
—1542 Carrie E.,⁹ m. **Sumner Stratton** of Barnardston, Mass. He is a son of Willis Stratton (1504) of Gill; res. Greenfield.

994. CHARLES STRATTON ⁸ (*Isaac J.,⁷ Daniel,⁶ Richard,⁵ Ichabod,⁴ Richard,³ Samuel,² Samuel¹*) married **Lovenia Loomis**, Feb. 7, 1827, and lived in Tyner and Oxford, N. Y. He was drowned in Chenango River, Aug. 22, 1839. Mrs. Stratton died Jan. 3, 1870.
Children:
—1543 Lydia,⁹ m. **Samuel Williams**.
—1544 Louise,⁹ m. **J. W. Hamilton**; d. in Oxford, Dec. 2, 1892.
—1545 Diana,⁹ m. **Horace Wood**; d. 1878.
—1546 Isaac J.,⁹ m. **Margaret Bartle**; d., 1903, in Portland, Or.
+1547 Charles E.,⁹ b. Sept. 2, 1836.

996. EBENEZER HARRISON STRATTON ⁸ (*Ebenezer,⁷ Ebenezer,⁶ Richard,⁵ Ichabod,⁴ Richard,³ Samuel,² Samuel¹*) graduated from Williams College in 1828 and of Auburn Theological Seminary in 1831 and was a faithful and beloved pastor of various Presbyterian churches in New York State for forty-six years. He was three times married, first, to **Olivia Minervia Bennett**, Mar. 11,

1833; second, to **Charlotte Lewis**, at Orangeville, N. Y., Dec. 10, 1854; third, to **Frances Bush**, Dec. 10, 1874. At the time of his death, Jan. 27, 1899, at the age of 93 years, he was the oldest minister in the General Assembly of the Presbyterian church and the oldest graduate of Williams College.

Children:
> By first marriage.

—1548   Mary Ann,[9] b. Dec. 24, 1833, m. **Patrick Lane.**
—1549   Sarah Amelia,[9] d. Mar., 1905, in Newton, Mass.
—1550   Frances Elizabeth,[9] m. **Albert Greenleaf**; d. in Rochester, Oct. 19, 1898.
—1551   Martha Amelia,[9] b. Nov. 4, 1840.
—1552   Olivia Alma,[9] m. **Wm. Douglas**, Jan. 15, 1872.
—1553   Alice Mancy,[9] m. **Filman Deal.**
—1554   Charles Bennett,[9] d. in Auburn, N. Y., Dec. 13, 1869, aged 22 years.

> By second marriage.

—1555   Laura,[9] m., May 13, 1890, **Rev. Henry Bradley Sayre**, a Presbyterian minister at Branchport, N. Y.; res. Geneva, N. Y.

1001. FRANCIS JOEL STRATTON [8] (*Francis*,[7] *John*,[6] *Francis*,[5] *Ichabod*,[4] *Richard*,[3] *Samuel*,[2] *Samuel*[1]) married, first, **Asenath Hawkes**; second, **Mercy Ann Warner**; third, **Hester A. Donnelson**, daughter of *Nelson Donnelson*. He was a physician and when the war broke out he joined the Federal army and died in Washington, D. C., in 1863.

Children:—B*orn in Rochester, N. Y.*
> By first marriage.

—1556   Julia,[9] m. **Norman Putnam**; d. in Washington (State) in 1900.

> By second marriage.

—1557   Lucius,[9] m. **Adell Moon**; d. in Rochester, N. Y.; ch. Mabel,[10] m. **John Quinn**; res. Rochester.
—1558   Adelaide,[9] m. **H. E. Walker**, Nov., 1886; res. Buffalo, N. Y.

> By third marriage.

+1559   Frank Nelson,[9] b. 1860.

1006. JOHN JACKSON STRATTON [8] (*Richard*,[7] *John*,[6] *Francis*,[5] *Ichabod*,[4] *Richard*,[3] *Samuel*,[2] *Samuel*[1]) went to Wisconsin about 1848; married **Rachel Ann May**, June 21, 1854. Moved to

Nebraska in 1885; died in Suburb, N. C., Sept. 25, 1900. Mrs. Stratton died in Nebraska July 14, 1896.

Children:—*Born in Columbus, Wis.*
—1560   Mary Jane.⁹
—1561   John Martin,⁹ living in Holt Co., Neb.

1008. GEORGE WASHINGTON STRATTON⁸ (*Asa,⁷ Asa,⁶ Ichabod,⁵ Ichabod,⁴ Richard,³ Samuel,² Samuel¹*) lived and died in Nelson Co., Va. Nov. 23, 1831, he married **Frances E. Loving**. It is understood that he has descendants still living in Nelson Co.

1009. EBENEZER PARKER STRATTON⁸ (*Asa,⁷ Asa,⁶ Ichabod,⁵ Ichabod,⁴ Richard,³ Samuel,² Samuel¹*) was born in Vermont in 1812 and while a boy went with his father to Virginia. While a young man he went from Virginia to Mississippi and for many years he was engaged in mercantile pursuits in several towns of that state. Always interested in public affairs he was elected mayor of every town in which he lived after reaching manhood. He was a Presbyterian of strong convictions; a Sunday school superintendent for more than forty years. In 1838 he married a Miss Wilson in Granada, Miss. She died in 1844. Two years later he married **Harriet Washburn** who survived him several years. He died in 1880 in Magnolia, Miss.

Children:
      By first marriage.
—1562   Margaret,⁹ m. **Herbert E. Poindexter**.
—1563   Della,⁹ m. **B. C. Quin**.
      By second marriage.
—1564   Luna,⁹ d. in girlhood.
—1565   Edward,⁹ m. **Addie Aldritch**; their only son, Henry,¹⁰ lives at Meriden (?), La.

1010. ROBERT BURCHER STRATTON⁸ (*Asa,⁷ Asa,⁶ Ichabod,⁵ Ichabod,⁴ Richard,³ Samuel,² Samuel¹*) married, first, **Mary Elizabeth Peyton**, June 8, 1870; second, **Mary Elizabeth Bruce**, Aug. 8, 1883. He lives in Lynchburg, and was for many years engaged in the drygoods business, from which he retired on account of failing eyesight. He has been blind for nearly twenty years. He is an Elder in the Presbyterian Church.

Children:
—1566   Margaret Sibyl.⁹
—1567   Robert,⁹ d. aged 12 yrs.

—1568   Alexander.⁹
—1569   Elizabeth.⁹
—1570   Lavinia.⁹

1011. ALEXANDER BROWN STRATTON ⁸ (*Asa,⁷ Asa,⁶ Ichabod,⁵ Ichabod,⁴ Richard,³ Samuel,² Samuel¹*), born in 1837; started in business early in life in Amherst Co., Va., and about 1858 moved to Lynchburg, where he became a successful leading drygoods merchant, and was prominent in the business, political and religious interests of the town. May 12, 1863, he married **Alice V. Roberts.**
Children:
—1571   Charles Massee,⁹ d. in Eddy, N. Mexico, at the age of 29 years; buried at Abilene, Texas.
—1572   Elizabeth Lindsay,⁹ res. Lynchburg.
—1573   Alexander Brown,⁹ res. Lynchburg.
—1574   Alice,⁹ d. aged 7 years.

1012. FLOYD WHITEHEAD STRATTON ⁸ (*Asa,⁷ Asa,⁶ Ichabod,⁵ Ichabod,⁴ Richard,³ Samuel,² Samuel¹*) was born at Variety Mills, Va. While still a boy he went to Liberty, Miss., where his brother, E. P. Stratton, had previously settled. When the Civil War broke out he joined the Confederate army. He married, Apr. 5, 1866, **Judith Elizabeth Quin.** He was a business man at Liberty, and postmaster there for some time; for many years a ruling elder in the Presbyterian Church. He died June 5, 1904.
Children:—*Born at Liberty, Miss.*
—1575   Asa Graham, editor and proprietor of the *Southern Herald* at Liberty.
—1576   Sibyl Quin.
—1577   Floyd Bayard.
—1578   Ethel Wayne.

1031. ASA STRATTON ⁸ (*Joseph B.,⁷ Joel,⁶ Ichabod,⁵ Ichabod,⁴ Richard,³ Samuel,² Samuel¹*) moved with his parents from Wyoming Co., N. Y., to Portage Co., Ohio, when he was 8 years old, and here, with his brothers, he helped to clear up and cultivate the new farm. At seventeen his father hired him out to a neighboring farmer, at twelve dollars a month. From this time until he began for himself he was either helping on the farm or working out, his father receiving his wages. Three months before he was of age his father gave him his time and "made him a present of an axe and a pair of sheep shears with which he started out to cut his own way through the world." How well he succeeded is proven by the pleasant home which he built in Richland, Mich., where he settled in the fall of 1851,—the beautiful, well cultivated farm and the large, comfortable dwelling house, and especially by the good home training, education and substantial help which he gave his children. May 4, 1851, he married **Eliza B. Foster**, daughter of *Samuel, Jr.*, and *Sarah (Foote) Foster* of Franklin, O. She lived to see all of her children, except the two youngest, settled in homes of their own. Some time after her death he married **Sara Parmalee**.

Children:—*Born in Richland, Mich.*

By first marriage.

—1579 Sarah R.,[9] b. Aug. 18, 1852; m. **Clarence Harvey**, Nov. 23, 1870; res. Allegan, Mich.

—1580 Freeman S.[9] (twin), b. Feb. 10, 1854; m. **Emma J. Travis**, Oct. 27, 1880; a farmer near Richland; ch. Nellie M.[10]

—1581 Herman J.[9] (twin), m. **Kattie May Friend**; res. Cooper, Mich.; portrait painter, ch. Mabel Lillian.[10]

—1582 Electa May,[9] b. July 2, 1857; m. **Joseph E. Young**, Feb. 7, 1877; res. Allegan, Mich.

—1583 Luther A.,[9] b. June 15, 1859; m. **Maggie McPherson**, Nov. 11, 1879; res. Bedford, Mich.; ch. Fred.[10]

—1584 George L.,[9] b. Apr. 23, 1861; m. **Melissa Shryer**; res. Hazelton, Dak.; chn. Foster A.,[10] Howard.[10]

—1585 Frank E.,[9] b. June 27, 1863; m. **Helen A. Ford**, Dec. 28, 1881; res. Berry, Mich.; ch. J. Ford.[10]

—1586 Burt E.,[9] b. June 16, 1866; d. in infancy.

—1587 Charles O.,[9] b. Mar., 1868; m. **Cora J. Vosburg**, May 28, 1890; res. Richland, Mich.; chn. Emil H.,[10] Edwin,[10] Freeman.[10]

—1588 Frederick W.,[9] b. Oct. 29, 1869.

—1589 Grace E.,[9] b. Dec. 1, 1872.

1032. LUCAS STRATTON [8] (*Joseph B.*,[7] *Joel*,[6] *Ichabod*,[5] *Ichabod*,[4] *Richard*,[3] *Samuel*,[2] *Samuel* [1]) spent his youth on his father's farm in Franklin Township, O., which furnished him with plenty of employment. He had few school advantages, but plenty of instruction in the practical lessons of life. Sept. 11, 1853, he married **Clarinda Frazier,** who was born Nov. 15, 1834, in Portage Co., Ohio. For nearly thirty years he was engaged in farming and dairying in Ohio, Indiana and Michigan. In 1882 he sold his farm in Allegan Co., Mich., for $14,500, and, after a trip through the farming regions of several western states, returned to Michigan and bought a 140-acre farm near Galesburg where he now resides.

Children:—*Born in Franklin, O.*
- —1590 Mary C.,^{9} b. Oct. 9, 1854; d. in infancy.
- —1591 Ella L.,^{9} b. Mar. 12, 1857; m. **Christopher H. West;** res. Omaha, Neb.
- —1592 Carrie D.,^{9} b. Sept. 22, 1859; d. aged 11 years.
- —1593 Will B.,^{9} b. July 20, 1862; m. Dec. 28, 1887, **Edith E. Chapman** of Earlville, O.; res. Galesburg, Mich. They have one daughter, Independence C.^{10}
- —1593a Ina D.,^{9} b. Nov. 12, 1865; m. Oct. 27, 1886, **George E. Walker;** res. Richland, Mich.

1033. SAMUEL STRATTON ^{8} (*Joseph B.,*^{7} *Joel,*^{6} *Ichabod,*^{5} *Ichabod,*^{4} *Richard,*^{3} *Samuel,*^{2} *Samuel*^{1}) remained on his father's farm in Franklin Township, Ohio, until he was 22 years old. Feb. 19, 1854, he married **Mary Thompson,** who was born May 21, 1833, in Delkeith, Scotland, and came to America with her parents when a year old, settling in Sheetsboro, Ohio. He has engaged in farming and kindred pursuits in Ohio, Indiana and Illinois and now resides in Ashland, Neb., where he is engaged in farming and stock raising.

Children:—*Born in Lenox, Ohio.*
- +1594 Charles E.,^{9} b. Mar., 1855.

  Born in Paxton, Ill.
- —1595 Delia,^{9} b. Mar. 4, 1864; graduate of Neb. State University; a teacher.

1034. FREEMAN STRATTON ^{8} (*Joseph B.,*^{7} *Joel,*^{6} *Ichabod,*^{5} *Ichabod,*^{4} *Richard,*^{3} *Samuel,*^{2} *Samuel*^{1}) married, May 5, 1857, **Emelia Willard,** daughter of *Frederic Willard,* one of the early settlers of Portage Co., Ohio. She was a woman of much ability, a teacher in early life, and her death, in 1888, left a long felt vacancy among a large circle of friends. He has been a farmer in Portage Co. all his life. In 1879 he purchased the old Willard homestead, which has ever since been his home.

Children:—*Born in Franklin Township, Ohio.*
—1596 Maggie,⁹ b. Sept. 10, 1866; d. aged 2 years.
—1597 Georgiana.⁹
—1598 Harry J.,⁹ m. **Mertie Rhodes**; res. Kent, Ohio.
—1599 Franklin S.,⁹ m. **Florence Clark**; res. Cleveland, Ohio.

1036. JONATHAN N. STRATTON ⁸ (*Joseph B.,*⁷ *Joel,*⁶ *Ichabod,*⁵ *Ichabod,*⁴ *Richard,*³ *Samuel,*² *Samuel* ¹) married **Harriet F. Dewey**, Oct. 29, 1862. They resided first at the old Dewey homestead, north of Kent, O., and, after six years, built a new house nearby which has been the home of the family ever since. He engaged for about eight years in the mercantile business in Kent, and later devoted himself to farming. He died in 1891.

Children:—*Born in Franklin, Ohio.*
—1600 Addie M.,⁹ m. Dec. 20, 1888, **John Lemmermen**; res. Franklin, O.
—1601 Fidelia F.⁹

1039. JOSEPH W. B. STRATTON ⁸ (*Joseph B.,*⁷ *Joel,*⁶ *Ichabod,*⁵ *Ichabod,*⁴ *Richard,*³ *Samuel,*² *Samuel* ¹) married, Feb. 26, 1865, **Euphemia A. Thompson**. In the autumn of the same year they moved to Richland, Mich., where he bought a farm of 53 acres. In 1871 he sold this farm and moved to Missouri. Seven years later he sold his farm in Missouri and returned to Otsego, Allegan Co., Mich., purchasing the 50-acre farm upon which he lived the remainder of his life; he died Aug. 28, 1909.

Children:—*Born in Richland, Mich.*
—1602 Albert T.,⁹ m. **Nellie Mason**; res. Otsego, Mich.
—1603 Harry S.,⁹ b. Feb. 7, 1870; d. in 1890.
—1604 Jessie May,⁹ m. **Fred Horton**, Mar. 26, 1903.
—1605 Ruth Hazel.⁹

1042. RUFUS STRATTON ⁸ (*Freemen,*⁷ *Joel,*⁶ *Ichabod,*⁵ *Ichabod,*⁴ *Richard,*³ *Samuel,*² *Samuel* ¹) married **Charlotte Galusha**, and moved to Hazzardville, Conn., where he died Mar. 4, 1891. He was a machinist in the powder manufactory.

Children:—*Born in Bennington, Vt.*
—1606 Ruth,⁹ d. aged 14 years.
—1607 Polina,⁹ m. **Wm. Kerr**.
—1608 Barber,⁹ m. **Maggie Tooms**; killed by an explosion in the powder mill at Hazzardville.
—1609 Ida,⁹ res. Hazzardville.

Born in *Hazzardville, Conn.*
—1610 Rufus,[9] m. **Phœbe McLaughlin**; res. Hazzardville.
—1611 George,[9] m. **Maggie Turner**; res. Hazzardville.

1050. ELMER BARBER STRATTON [8] (*Freeman,*[7] *Joel,*[6] *Ichabod,*[5] *Ichabod,*[4] *Richard,*[3] *Samuel,*[2] *Samuel*[1]) married Laura E. Ayres, Feb. 11, 1874. She was a teacher, daughter of *Joseph* and *Elizabeth (Van Buskirk) Ayres*. Her father was born in Colerain, Mass., Jan. 11, 1816, and her mother in Hoosic Falls, N. Y., Mar. 16, 1825. The following year, 1875, they moved to Hebron, Ill., where he was a farmer and mechanic. In Nov., 1906, they moved to Kenosha, Wis., where for several years he was connected with the American Brass Co., and where they still reside.

Children:—Born at *Hebron, Ill.*
—1612 Susan Chase,[9] d. of diphtheria Feb. 11, 1881, at Hebron, aged 6 yrs.
—1613 Elizabeth Thankful,[9] m. **Charles L. Steadman**, Oct. 28, 1896; res. Alden, Ill.
—1614 Edwin Freeman,[9] machinist; m. **Glennie Stone**, Sept. 17, 1902; res. Woodstock, Ill.; chn. Joseph Ayres,[10] Dorothy.[10]
—1615 Helen Rowe,[9] m. **Sanford Watkins**, Jan. 15, 1902; m. 2nd, **Frank C. Slavin**, Feb. 10, 1913.
—1616 Carrie Joanna,[9] m. **George Arthur Parker**, Nov. 20, 1907; they have three sons one of whom is John Stratton Parker.
—1617 Elmer Barber,[9] d. July 18, 1896; aged 12 years.
—1618 John Ayres,[9] shipping clerk in Am. Brass Co., at Kenosha; m. Oct. 10, 1914, **Ellen Waldo**, d. *Charles* and *Eva Waldo*.
—1619 Annie Laura,[9] res. Kenosha, Wis.

1051. Hon. ISAAC STRATTON [8] (*John,*[7] *Richard,*[6] *John,*[5] *John,*[4] *John,*[3] *John,*[2] *Samuel*[1]) married, first, Mar. 31, 1831, Elizabeth Wright, daughter of *Calvin Wright*. She was born in 1812, and died Dec. 28, 1862. July 2, 1883, Mr. Stratton married Mrs. Lucy E. Frink, who was born Jan. 8, 1837. He was a prominent man in West Swanzey and Keene, N. H., active in temperance and educational work. He died Apr. 11, 1893.

Children:—Born in *West Swanzey, N. H.*
—1620 Menzies E.,[9] b. Jan. 28, 1832; m. 1st, **Clarena E. Whitcomb**; 2nd, **Rexaville Green**. He was a

jeweler at Springfield, chn. Mabel,[10] Wallace E.,[10] d. in Keene July 31, 1910.

—1621 Edwin W.,[9] b. Dec. 20, 1833; m. May 5, 1870, at Titusville, Pa., **Emily E. Roberts** of Edinburgh, Scotland, who died in 1873. He died in 1871. Ch. Edwin Isaac William,[10] b. July 27, 1871; adopted by a family named Mitchell and took their name.

—1622 Isaac Edgar,[9] b. 1836; d. in infancy.

—1623 Josephine,[9] b. Nov. 7, 1839; m. Lloyd **D. Richardson.**

—1624 Emory W.,[9] b. Nov. 22, 1843; m. Nov. 24, 1872, **Charlotte E. Kendall**; d. May 19, 1887; ch. Bessie,[10] lives in Springfield, Mass.

1052. WILLIAM STRATTON [8] (*John,[7] Richard,[6] John,[5] John,[4] John,[3] John,[2] Samuel* [1]) married, first, **Mary F. Lombard**, who died Feb. 24, 1837, aged 33 years. Married, second, **Adeline Johnson**, of Lowell, Mass. He died in 1873.

Children:—*Born in West Swanzey, N. H.*

—1625 Judith,[9] b. 1828.

+1626 George W.,[9] b. 1830.

—1627 John F.,[9] b. Sept. 14, 1832; went to Leipsic, Ger., in 1866, and engaged in the manufacture of musical instruments; dealer in musical instruments in New York City for many years; d. Oct. 23, 1912, in Brooklyn, where his widow still resides.

—1628 Addis H.,[9] b. 1834; d. in childhood.

By second marriage.

—1629 Edward S.,[9] res. Manchester, N. H.

—1630 William, Jr.[9]

1058. JOHN STRATTON [8] (*John,[7] Richard,[6] John,[5] John,[4] John,[3] John,[2] Samuel* [1]) was proprietor of the Central House, a Boston hotel, where he died in 1870, aged 49 years. He is buried in West Swanzey. He married **Lora Dodge** at Keene, N. H.

Children:—*Born in West Swanzey, N. H.*

—1631 Loretta,[9] b. 1843; m. **M. E. Ward**; d. Jan. 5, 1866.

—1632 Abbie,[9] b. 1844.

—1633 Florence Louise,[9] b. 1850; m. **H. S. Martin**; res. Keene.

—1634 John C.,[9] b. 1853; merchant in New York City.

—1635 Byron F.,[9] b. 1854; d. Nov. 6, 1898; m.; left no children.

1063. OSCAR STRATTON [8] (*John,*[7] *Richard,*[6] *John,*[5] *John,*[4] *John,*[3] *John,*[2] *Samuel*[1]) married **Ellen Amelia Esterbrook**, June 21, 1854, in Princeton, N. J., daughter of *Capt. Washington* and *Lydia (Watson) Esterbrook*. By trade he was a "finisher of leather." Lived in West Swanzey, N. H., Sterling and Grafton, Mass., and then went to Denver, Colo., where he died Jan. 28, 1898.

Children:—B*orn in West Swanzey, N. H.*

+1636   Melville Oscar,[9] b. Sept. 14, 1857.
−1637   Lizzie Allen,[9] b. Apr. 2, 1861; d. aged 6 years.
−1638   Chester Esterbrook,[9] m. **Jennie Frances Walters** of Washington, Ind., Jan. 10, 1895. Manager of the Tri-State Telephone Co., at El Paso, Texas. They have one daughter, Helen E.[10]

1067. JOHN STRATTON [8] (*Abijah,*[7] *Abijah,*[6] *Abijah,*[5] *Jabez,*[4] *John,*[3] *John,*[2] *Samuel*[1]) inherited the old homestead at Natick. He was executor of his grandfather's will in 1830, and of his father's will in 1838. He married **Betsey Kimball**, Mar. 23, 1820.

Children:—B*orn in Natick, Mass.*

−1639   Catherine D.,[9] b. 1820; d. 1825.
−1640   Elizabeth A.,[9] d. in infancy.
−1641   Harriet Ann,[9] d. in infancy.
−1642   Hannah,[9] b. 1824; d. 1885; m. **George Morse**, Nov. 27, 1845.
−1643   Catherine D.,[9] b. 1827; d. 1852.
−1644   Abijah E.,[9] b. 1830; d. in childhood.
+1645   John H.,[9] b. Nov. 22, 1832.
−1646   Martha I.,[9] b. 1835; d. in Natick, unm., June 15, 1903.
−1647   George W.,[9] b. 1837; m. **Georgiana Mann**, Apr. 23, 1869. They had three daughters, Nellie M.,[10] Emma A.,[10] and Susan E.[10]

1068. MOSES STRATTON [8] (*Abijah,*[7] *Abijah,*[6] *Abijah,*[5] *Jabez,*[4] *John,*[3] *John,*[2] *Samuel*[1]) married, first, **Mary Whitney**, daughter of *Aaron Whitney*, who died Dec. 31, 1832; second, **Martha Whitney**, daughter of *Col. Isaac Whitney* of Sherborn.

Children:—B*orn in Natick, Mass.*

−1648   Mary W.,[9] b. Dec. 31, 1832.
−1649   Charles.
−1650   Francis, b. Mar. 1, 1836.
−1651   Mariam C., b. Oct. 2, 1842; m. **Frederick Valentine**.

1069. AARON STRATTON [8] (*Abijah*,[7] *Abijah*,[6] *Abijah*,[5] *Jabez*,[4] *John*,[3] *John*,[2] *Samuel* [1]) married **Susanna Russell**, daughter of *Jonathan* and *Sarah Russell*. She was born in 1813.

Children:—*Born in Sherborn, Mass.*

—1652 John Edward,[9] m. Mary E. Ward in Sherborn in 1864, d. of *Nathan* and *Lucy A. Ward*.

—1653 Horace J.,[9] m. Rosabell Taylor, Jan. 1, 1868; lived in Sherborn; d. May 19, 1892; chn. Lizzie Ann,[10] Joel Horace,[10] m. Edith A. Hunt, Nov. 9, 1894; chn. Nellie M.,[11] Gladys C.[11]

1072. TOLMAN STRATTON [8] (*Jonathan*,[7] *Daniel*,[6] *Abijah*,[5] *Jabez*,[4] *John*,[3] *John*,[2] *Samuel* [1]) left Massachusetts while a young man, and settled in Kentucky, where he married **Sarah Richards** about 1822. In 1832 he sold a lot of land in Surry, N. H., to William Stratton of Sherburne. He died in Greenup Co. in 1837. In early life he followed the sea for several years as a sailor boy. As there were Tolmans in Greenup County he may have gone there with his mother's people.

Children:—*Born in Greenup Co., Ky.*

—1654 Zacharias,[9] b. July 12, 1826; d. in 1847.
—1655 Polly,[9] b. Apr., 1827; d. in infancy.
+1656 Jonathan,[9] b. Nov. 11, 1829.
—1657 John Tolman,[9] b. Apr., 1831. Drowned in Little Sandy River, aged 13 years.
—1658 Martha Ann [9] (twin), b. Apr., 1831; d. in childhood.
—1659 William,[9] b. Nov., 1832; killed in Civil War in 1865.

1077. JOEL A. STRATTON [8] (*John*,[7] *Daniel*,[6] *Abijah*,[5] *Jabez*,[4] *John*,[3] *John*,[2] *Samuel* [1]) passed his boyhood on his father's farm at Sherborn. As a young man he followed the sea for several years; was first officer of a merchant ship, then mate on the ship *Kingfisher,* and during the Civil War enlisted in the Navy, serving fourteen months. He married **Charlotte Godfrey Coffin**, June 2, 1852, daughter of *Albert* and *Sarah O. (Earle) Coffin* of Nantucket. After leaving the sea he, for many years, did a good work for the sailors, going from place to place among them. He engaged in the mercantile business at New London, Bridgeport and other places. He died in East Providence, R. I., Jan. 1, 1908.

Child:

—1660 Wallace C. Stratton,[9] a physician of San Francisco.

1090. Martin Whitcomb Stratton [8] (*Albert,*[7] *Nathan,*[6] *Nathan,*[5] *Jabez,*[4] *John,*[3] *John,*[2] *Samuel*[1]) engaged with his brother Joel in the grain, feed and lumber business in Leominster, Mass., from 1864 to 1879 as "Stratton Brothers," and then removed to Reading, Kan., and purchased land on the Indian Reservation, and is now in the real estate business in Kansas City, under the firm name of "Silver & Stratton." He married, first, **Mary A. Litchfield**, June 14, 1857; second, **Mrs. Martha Gale**, Nov., 1876, and third, **Kate Rhodes**, Dec. 30, 1896.

Children:—*Born in Leominster, Mass.*
- —1661 Lillian Marilla,[9] d. 1899; unm.
- —1662 Albert James,[9] b. Mar. 5, 1860; m. in Kansas, Nov., 1894, **Florence Lidzy**, d. of *Rev. Thos.* and *Elizabeth (Fellows) Lidzy.*
- +1663 Javius Litchfield.[9]
- —1664 Ellen Adelia.[9]
- —1665 Mary Alice.[9]

Born in Reading, Kan.
- —1666 Edwin L.[9]

Born in Kansas City, Kan.
- —1667 James L.[9]

1091. Joel Augustus Stratton [8] (*Albert,*[7] *Nathan,*[6] *Nathan,*[5] *Jabez,*[4] *John,*[3] *John,*[2] *Samuel*[1]) remained on his father's farm until Sept., 1862, when he enlisted as chaplain in Co. C, 53rd Mass. Vols.; was assigned to Dept. of Gulf, and participated in the battle of Fort Bisland and Fort Hudson, La., May 27, 1863, and the second battle of Fort Hudson Jan. 14, 1863, where he was severely wounded. Just before entering the battle he was promoted to the command of Major. Oct. 4, 1865, he married **Hannah W. Corney**, and in 1879 removed from Leominster, Mass., to Reading, Kan., where he now resides. He was member of Massachusetts Legislature in 1864; has continually held some public office,—selectman, justice of the peace, police judge, notary public. He was trustee of the M. E. Church at Leominster, also in Reading.

Children:—*Born in Leominster.*
- —1668 Joel Alfred,[9] d. in Leominster.
- —1669 Isabella Corney,[9] m. **D. A. Simkins**, 1895.
- —1670 Stanley H.,[9] res. Kansas City, Kan.
- —1671 Arthur,[9] d. in Leominster.
- —1672 Ethel May,[9] m. **Alonzo C. Nickel**, Feb., 1896.

1092. ALBERT OSMON STRATTON [8] (*Albert,*[7] *Nathan,*[6] *Nathan,*[5] *Jabez,*[4] *John,*[3] *John,*[2] *Samuel*[1]) married **Mrs. Jennie L. Stone**; served three years in the Civil War in 37th Mass. Vols. In 19 battles and skirmishes. He is a farmer in Cheshire, Conn.

Children:—*Born in Lauensburg, Mass.*
- —1673   Jared Osman,[9] m. **Della Cook**; res. Hartford, Conn.
- —1674   William Arnold,[9] m. **Cora Long**; res. Hartford, Conn.
- —1675   Frank Wilber,[9] m. **Katherine Grassier**.
- —1676   Fred S.,[9] m. **Amelia Krum**.
- —1677   George O.[9]

1097. PORTER RAYMOND STRATTON [8] (*Albert,*[7] *Nathan,*[6] *Nathan,*[5] *Jabez,*[4] *John,*[3] *John,*[2] *Samuel*[1]) is a Methodist minister, joining the New England conference in 1885. Has been pastor of the church in Ashburnham, Enfield, North Brookfield, Oxford, and other Massachusetts towns; also preached four years in the East Maine conference. He married **Annie M. Jewett**, Mar. 15, 1880, daughter of *Dea. Charles Jewett* of Leominster. She died in Denver, Colo., Nov. 25, 1893. In 1899 he married **Maria J. Howe**.

Children:
  By first marriage.
- —1678   Edith Jewett,[9] d. in 1898, aged 8 years.
- —1679   Leslie Whitney.[9]

1101. AUSTIN CHANDLER STRATTON [8] (*Walter,*[7] *Ebenezer,*[6] *Elias,*[5] *Jabez,*[4] *John,*[3] *John,*[2] *Samuel*[1]) lived in Athol, Templeton and Harvard. He was a farmer. He was married three times, first, to **Sophia H. Sibley**, Jan. 17, 1843; second, to **Mary Haskins**, Nov. 24, 1858; third, to **Laura Haskill**, Aug. 9, 1877. He died in Harvard, Mass., Dec. 30, 1905.

Children:—*Born in Templeton, Mass.*
  By first marriage.
- —1680   Josephine S.,[9] d. Sept. 14, 1892.
- —1681   Orin P.,[9] d. Nov. 5, 1847, aged 1 year, 7 mos.
- —1682   Israel Sibley,[9] d. Sept. 23, 1850.
  By second marriage.
- —1683   George Austin,[9] d. Oct. 30, 1861.
- —1684   Jesse Frank,[9] d. Nov. 11, 1861.
  By third marriage.
- —1685   Ethel Elizabeth,[9] d. Mar. 4, 1880.
- —1686   Stella Gertrude,[9] m. **Herbert Downing**, Sept. 16, 1908. Res. Ayer, Mass.

1106. CHARLES TEMPLE STRATTON [8] (*Walter*,[7] *Ebenezer*,[6] *Elias*,[5] *Jabez*,[4] *John*,[3] *John*,[2] *Samuel* [1]) married **Jane M. Griffin,** Oct. 19, 1854. He was a machinist by trade, and lived in Athol and Worcester, Mass. He died in Worcester July 19, 1907.

Children:—*Born in Worcester, Mass.*
- —1687 Isabelle Curtis,[9] m. 1st, **John P. K. Otis,** Oct. 19, 1874; m. 2nd, **Edward P. King,** Aug. 20, 1907.
- —1688 Charles Griffin,[9] Pres. of Curtis Mfg. Co., makers of woolens, Worcester.
- —1689 Albert Curtis,[9] d. Feb. 6, 1862.

1108. FRANCIS ALVIN STRATTON [8] (*Walter*,[7] *Ebenezer*,[6] *Elias*,[5] *Jabez*,[4] *John*,[3] *John*,[2] *Samuel* [1]) went to Iowa in 1858; married **Belle Ritter Trime,** June 10, 1874. He became a successful farmer and retired in 1901.

Children:—*Born in Iowa City.*
- —1690 Blanch,[9] m. **Irvin V. Cozine;** res. Iowa City.
- —1691 Frances E.[9]
- —1692 Maude.[9]
- —1693 Fred.[9]

1113. ALBERT W. STRATTON [8] (*Wilder*,[7] *Ebenezer*,[6] *Elias*,[5] *Jabez*,[4] *John*,[3] *John*,[2] *Samuel* [1]) moved from Athol to Fitchburg, Mass., in 1868, and from there to Gardner in 1898. By trade he was a sash and door maker, and later was engaged in the provision business. Nov. 21, 1864, he married **Eliza Ellen Watson,** who was born in Acton, Me., May 17, 1844, and died in Gardner Apr. 26, 1909. She was a member of the St. Paul's Episcopal Church.

Child:
- —1694 Albert Loren,[9] Dept. Commissioner Mass. Department Fisheries and Game; Knight Templar; mem. Episcopal Church; res. Gardner, Mass.

1114. ELBER ELISHA STRATTON [8] (*Elisha*,[7] *Elias*,[6] *Elias*,[5] *Jabez*,[4] *John*,[3] *John*,[2] *Samuel* [1]) was a carpenter and later a farmer. He went from Gill, Mass., to Buckland. He married **Electa Trombridge,** June 6, 1867.

Child:—*Born in Buckland, Mass.*
- —1695 George Eber,[9] connected with the U. S. Geological Survey, Washington, D. C.

1121. HORACE HUBBARD STRATTON[8] (*Samuel,*[7] *Elias,*[6] *Elias,*[5] *Jabez,*[4] *John,*[3] *John,*[2] *Samuel*[1]) married, May 29, 1860, **Catherine L. Brewster,** daughter of *Nathan C. Brewster* of Montague. He died Mar. 10, 1901.

Children:—B*orn in Gill, Mass.*
—1696 Herbert Rogers,[9] res. Gill; unm.
—1697 Clesson Horace,[9] m. Dec. 10, 1890, **Nettie Louise Hale**; res. Barnardston, Mass. They have two daughters, Florence Susan,[10] Blanche Gertrude.[10]

1133. JONATHAN WINSOR STRATTON[8] (*Jonathan,*[7] *Joseph,*[6] *Elias,*[5] *Jabez,*[4] *John,*[3] *John,*[2] *Samuel*[1]) married **Laura Nelson,** Apr. 29, 1851. He died in Athol Nov. 3, 1871.

Children:—B*orn in Petersham, Mass.*
—1698 Herbert S.,[9] m. **Addie Jennings**; res. Orange, Mass.
—1699 Cora L.,[9] res. Petersham.
—1700 Carrie,[9] d. 1876, aged 16 years.
—1701 William Henry,[9] m. **Maud Robins**; res. Munsonville, N. Y.

1139. JOSEPH ALONZO STRATTON[8] (*Joseph,*[7] *Joseph,*[6] *Elias,*[5] *Jabez,*[4] *John,*[3] *John,*[2] *Samuel*[1]), born in Athol, Mass., Oct. 16, 1831; married **Harriet L. Adams** of Athol; lived in Kennedy, N. Y., Greenwood and Woodstock, Ill. He died July 15, 1899.

Children:
—1702 Emmerson, A.[9]
—1703 Edgar L.[9]
—1704 Edith M.[9]
—1705 Edna E.[9]
—1706 Francis A.[9]

1141. JOEL W. STRATTON[8] (*Joseph,*[7] *Joseph,*[6] *Elias,*[5] *Jabez,*[4] *John,*[3] *John,*[2] *Samuel*[1]), born in Athol, Mass., Jan. 8, 1838; married **Victoria Harris** in 1860; res. Spartenburg, Pa.

Children:—B*orn in Centerville, Pa.*
—1707 Frank E.[9]
—1708 Lucella A.,[9] m. **Omar C. Martin.**
—1709 Louie M.[9]

1143. HORACE MINOT STRATTON[8] (*Joseph,*[7] *Joseph,*[6] *Elias,*[5] *Jabez,*[4] *John,*[3] *John,*[2] *Samuel*[1]) married **Helen Mann,** daughter of *Thomas Mann,* and lives in Greenfield, Mass.

STRATTONS: 1. David; *Page* 198. 2. Jonas; *Page* 203. 3. Amos T.; *Page* 208. 4. Cyrus W.; *Page* 211. 5. Henry D., one of the founders of the Stratton & Bryant Business Colleges; *Page* 217.

Children:—*Born in Greenfield.*
—1710 Stella May.[9]
—1711 Earle Minot.[9]
—1712 Horace Frederick.[9]
—1713 Rolland Aubrey.[9]

1145. FREDERICK EUGENE STRATTON [8] (*Joseph,*[7] *Joseph,*[6] *Elias,*[5] *Jabez,*[4] *John,*[3] *John,*[2] *Samuel*[1]) graduated from Williams College in 1871. Mar. 14, 1874, he married **Trephena Goddard** of Davenport, Iowa. In 1883 they moved from Massachusetts to Davenport, where he was principal of the High School, and in 1892 moved to Northfield, Minn., where he became Professor of Greek in Carlton College, which position he held for fourteen years. In 1906 he was elected Dean of Fargo College and Professor of Greek, which position he still holds. A faithful, conscientious teacher for more than forty years, he is loved and respected by the many of this generation who have come under his care as an instructor and advisor, and through them his influence for good will go down through the ages.

Child:
—1714 Alice Bell,[9] grad. Wellesley, 1903; a teacher for several years. Aug. 26, 1908, m. **Rev. Dr. Harry E. Stocker.** They reside at So. Bethlehem, Pa., where he is pastor of the First Moravian church.

1153. EDWARD BLISS STRATTON [8] (*Lemuel P.,*[7] *Lemuel,*[6] *Jonathan,*[5] *Jonathan,*[4] *Joseph,*[3] *John,*[2] *Samuel*[1]) married **Jane Ann Stewart**, Sept. 5, 1855. He was for many years a deacon in the Congregational church of which his father was one of the founders in Brighton. About 1882 he moved to Lebanon, Mo., where he bought a farm, where he lived the remainder of his life. He died Aug. 31, 1914, greatly respected for his honest, helpful, sincere, Christian life. Mrs. Stratton died Sept. 10, 1894.

Children:—*Born in Brighton, Ill.*
—1714a Edward Page,[9] m. 1st, Jan. 2, 1878, **Jane Bayless**; chn. Margaret Alice,[10] James Edward,[10] res. St. Louis; m. 2nd, Nov., 1893, **Alice Turner**; chn. John Hilary,[10] George Bliss[10]; d. at Phillipsburg, Mo., Feb. 7, 1915.
—1714b Robert Stewart,[9] a successful farmer of Lebanon, Mo.; m. **Nettie L. Courser**, Oct. 2, 1884; chn. Grace Louisa,[10] Robert Charles,[10] Hattie Louisa.[10]

—1714c Annetta Jane,[9] m. **John Marion Spiller**, July 15, 1914; res. Lebanon, Mo.; a teacher before her marriage.

1154. NATHAN JOHNSON STRATTON [8] (*Lemuel P.,*[7] *Lemuel,*[6] *Jonathan,*[5] *Jonathan,*[4] *Joseph,*[3] *John,*[2] *Samuel*[1]) married **Clarissa Rebecca Rice**, Apr. 19, 1858. He has been for many years a grain dealer, having had large interests in this business in Brighton, Chicago, Quincy, Marysville, and other towns in Illinois, Missouri, Kansas and Nebraska. He is now residing at Edna, Kansas, in his eightieth year. Energetic, helpful and public spirited, he has often been chosen to public offices of trust and responsibility. In every town in which he has lived, he and Mrs. Stratton have been closely connected with the Presbyterian or Congregational church in which they have been faithful, loyal and untiring workers, giving liberally of their time and means to church and mission work.

Child:—*Born in Brighton, Ill.*

—1714d Edwin Luther,[9] m. **Mary L. Andrews**, June 14, 1883; educated at Jacksonville, Ill., and Oberlin College, Ohio; connected with a business firm at Pueblo, Colo., where he now resides and where he is an elder in the Presbyterian church.

1156. WILLIAM PAGE STRATTON [8] (*Lemuel P.,*[7] *Lemuel,*[6] *Jonathan,*[5] *Jonathan,*[4] *Joseph,*[3] *John,*[2] *Samuel*[1]) married **Rebecca Vanneman**, Nov. 2, 1869. He served in the Civil War in Co. O, 122nd Ill. Vol. Inf. While in the service he received an injury in the knee which caused trouble which finally resulted in his death at the age of fifty-six years. He was a member of the G. A. R. He died in Bloomington, Neb., Oct. 16, 1899.

Children:—*Born at Oldman, Ill.*

—1714e Annie M.,[9] m. **John R. Ess**, Feb. 25, 1894; res. Bloomington.

—1714f Charley Page,[9] m. **Olah Mae Smith**, Feb. 20, 1902; res. Mexico, Mo. Chn. Floyd Francis,[10] d. Apr. 3, 1905; Carl Smith,[10] Lemuel Page.[10]

1161. CHARLES STEPHEN STRATTON [8] (*Stephen J.,*[7] *Lemuel,*[6] *Jonathan,*[5] *Jonathan,*[4] *Joseph,*[3] *John,*[2] *Samuel*[1]) married **Mary E. Gifford**, Jan., 1876, daughter of *Christopher* and *Susan Gifford*. She died in 1911. He is a master mechanic at the Quissett Mills, in New Bedford.

Children:—*Born in New Bedford, Mass.*
—1714g Edward Winslow,[9] m. **Sylvia Fontone**, March, 1910; superintendent of the Golden Boulder Mining Company at Fairview, Nevada.
—1714h George Wendell [9] (twin), m. **Lena Hammett**, June 6, 1908; a machinist at Quissett Mills; ch. Florence Hammett.[10]
—1714i John Paul [9] (twin), m. **Maria Hammett**, Oct. 19, 1899; machinist at the Beacon Blanket Mills, New Bedford.
—1714j Caroline Eunice.[9]

1174. GEORGE D. STRATTON [8] (*William,*[7] *Winsor,*[6] *Samuel,*[5] *Jonathan,*[4] *Joseph,*[3] *John,*[2] *Samuel* [1]) was a farmer of Northboro; a member of the Unitarian church. June 11, 1879, he married **Ellen Maria Ballou**, who died Aug. 27, 1889. Mr. Stratton died Feb. 22, 1886.

Children:—*Born in Northboro, Mass.*
—1715 Walter Stanley,[9] m. **Priscilla Spooner**; res. New Bedford, Mass.
—1716 Frank Henry,[9] m. Jan. 28, 1911, **Lillian Elmira Ballou**; res. Braintree, Mass.

1192. PURBOT HILL STRATTON [8] (*Martin,*[7] *Samuel,*[6] *Samuel,*[5] *Samuel,*[4] *Samuel,*[3] *John,*[2] *Samuel* [1]) married, July 30, 1874, **Julia S. Hutchins**, daughter of *John* and *Julia* (*Wentworth*) *Hutchins* and granddaughter of *Eastman* and *Betsey* (*Atherton*) *Hutchins*. They live in Cambridge, Mass., where he is a contractor and builder.

Children:—*Born in Hancock, Me.*
—1717 Carl L.,[9] m. **Alice Hubley** in 1905.
—1718 Harry C.,[9] m. **Annie J. Longly** in 1879.
Born in Bar Harbor, Me.
—1719 Daisy M.,[9] b. Aug. 5, 1882; d. Feb. 4, 1899.
Born in Ellsworth, Me.
—1720 Vivian H.[9]
—1721 Earle P.[9]

1198. WILLIAM STRATTON [8] (*Isaac G.,*[7] *William,*[6] *Samuel,*[5] *Enoch,*[4] *Samuel,*[3] *Richard,*[2] *Samuel* [1]) was a farmer in New Hartford. He married **Electa Rice**. He died in 1870.

Children:—*Born in New Hartford, N. Y.*
—1722 Isaac G.,[9] served three years in Co. D., N. Y. heavy

artillery; married **Catherine Hendricks** in **1861**; res. Chadwick, N. Y. Chn. Elida,[10] Cora B.,[10] Mary E.[10]
—1723 William.[9]
—1724 Cornelia,[9] m. **Arthur G. Cunningham.**
—1725 James.[9]
—1726 Eliza,[9] m. **Geo. Horrocks.**
—1727 Edward,[9] m. **Nettie Stevens.**
—1728 Lewis.[9]

1204. EDWARD I. STRATTON[8] (*Isaac,[7] William,[6] Samuel,[5] Enoch,[4] Samuel,[3] Richard,[2] Samuel[1]*) resides now in Newark Valley, N. Y. He served three years in the Federal Army in 52nd Regt., Penn. Infantry. Was in many battles. Oct. 19, 1869, he married **Amanda Crain.** She died June 15, 1898, in Union Center, N. Y.

Children:—*Born in Burlington, Pa.*
—1729 Samuel S.,[9] m. **Carrie Grover**, May, 1897; chn. Maude,[10] Ruth,[10] Ward.[10]
—1730 Harry C.,[9] m. **Vella Miller**, Jan., 1900; ch. Dayton W.[10]

1205. DAVID STRATTON[8] (*William,[7] William,[6] Samuel,[5] Enoch,[4] Samuel,[3] Richard,[2] Samuel[1]*) was a practical farmer in Tompkins Co., N. Y. He married **Lucretia H. Buck**, Jan. 20, 1864. They were members of the Methodist church. He died in Elmira, N. Y., Dec. 23, 1887.

Children:—*Born in Newfield, N. Y.*
—1731 William Buck,[9] grad. Cornell University, 1888. Served in Spanish-American war; architect, "Stratton & Baldwin," in Detroit, Mich.; mem. Congregational church.
—1732 Roscoe Wood,[9] engaged in agriculture; res. Elmira, N. Y.

1222. FRANCIS JOHN STRATTON[8] (*John,[7] John,[6] Benjamin,[5] Jabez,[4] Samuel,[3] Richard,[2] Samuel[1]*) married **Mrs. Grace Middleton (Metcalfe) Johnson** in San Francisco. He died in Boston, Mar. 9, 1888. Buried at Mount Auburn Cemetery.

Children:—*Born in San Francisco, Cal.*
—1733 Frank Herbert,[9] d. in Chicago, aged about 3 years.
—1734 Grace Lillian.[9]

Born in Boston.
—1735 Beatrice Caroline,[9] m. **Robert Moss** Lockwood in New York City, Jan. 3, 1893.

1225. EDMOND BURT STRATTON [8] (*Josiah,*[7] *Jabez,*[6] *Jabez,*[5] *Jabez,*[4] *Samuel,*[3] *Samuel,*[2] *Samuel* [1]) married **Sarah Adelia Goodwin**, Dec. 25, 1872. He was a furniture maker. Resided in Putman, Conn., where he recently died.
Children:—Born in Lancaster, N. H.
—1736 Carrie Elsie,[9] m. **Charles E. Briggs**, Nov. 3, 1898; res. Arlington, Conn.
—1737 Harry Ernest,[9] m. **Mabel Evans**, Apr. 18, 1903; ch. Gladys Isabell.[10]

1252. ARCHIE WILLIAMSON STRATTON [9] (*Paul,*[8] *Paul,*[7] *Josiah,*[6] *Hezekiah,*[5] *Samuel,*[4] *Samuel,*[3] *Samuel,*[2] *Samuel* [1]) moved with his parents from St. Johns, N. B., to Chester, Me., when about 8 years old. Oct. 5, 1851, he married **Julia A. Snow**. Her father and grandfather were both sea captains, sailing from Bangor to the West Indies. After their marriage they lived for awhile in Winn, Me., and in 1862 settled in Chester, where he died Nov. 8, 1885.
Children:—Born in Winn, Me.
—1738 Ida May,[10] d. 1875.
+1739 Henry Herbert.[10]
+1740 Paul.[10]
—1741 Everett Burnside,[10] m. **Melissa Stewart** in 1891; res. Richmond, Me.
—1742 Fred William,[10] d. June 10, 1907, unm.
+1743 Charles Albert.[10]
—1744 Sadie A.,[10] m. **Frank Lint**, Sept. 5, 1893; res. Richmond, Me.

1253. LEWIS FRAZIER STRATTON [9] (*Paul,*[8] *Paul,*[7] *Josiah,*[6] *Hezekiah,*[5] *Samuel,*[4] *Samuel,*[3] *Samuel,*[2] *Samuel* [1]) was a successful lumber dealer of Bangor, Me. Lived for awhile at Mattawamkeag, was sheriff of Penobscot Co. In 1854 he married **Sarah Brown**. He died in 1891. Their son, Albert Olando,[10] married **Jane Chadbourne** in 1875 and died in 1899, leaving one child, Ethel.[11]

1256. GEORGE HUBBARD STRATTON [9] (*Paul,*[8] *Paul,*[7] *Josiah,*[6] *Hezekiah,*[5] *Samuel,*[4] *Samuel,*[3] *Samuel,*[2] *Samuel* [1]) was for some time a lumber dealer in Maine. In 1860 he enlisted in the 11th

Maine Regt. and was Lieutenant of his Company. Removed to Ballard, Wash., where he was U. S. Oil Inspector and Chief of Police. March 2, 1861, he married **Susan Estes**.

Children:—*Born in Winn, Me.*
- —1745 Willard George,[10] b. 1865; d. in Ballard, Wash., in 1903; m. **Gertrude Killworth** in 1898.
- —1746 Guy,[10] d. in childhood.
- —1747 Dorothy.[10]

1259. GILFORD DUDLEY STRATTON[9] (*Paul,*[8] *Paul,*[7] *Josiah,*[6] *Hezekiah,*[5] *Samuel,*[4] *Samuel,*[3] *Samuel,*[2] *Samuel*[1]) has been a hotel proprietor for many years. At 25 he built a large hotel in Winn, Me. Four years later he bought the Mattawamkeag House, of which he was proprietor for nine years. Later he bought the Gorham House, and was proprietor of the Alpine House in Gorham, N. H., for twenty-three years, and of the Umbagog House at Errol, N. H., for several years. He was the organizer of the Berlin, N. H., water company, and with his brother-in-law established the *Lewiston Daily Sun*. After retiring from the hotel business he moved to Laconia, N. H. Oct. 21, 1873, he married **Eva Louise Wing**, who was born in Watertown, Me., Dec. 29, 1851. She was daughter of *Henry E.* and *Hannah* (*Smith*) *Wing*.

Children:—*Born in Mattawamkeag.*
- —1748 Alice May,[10] m. **Alpha Haven Harriman, M. D.**, Oct. 4, 1904; res. Laconia.
- —1749 Rose Belle,[10] m. **Nathaniel Winslow Shaw**, June 12, 1906; res. Portland, Me.
- —1750 Roy Hubbard.[10]
- —1751 Annie Louise,[10] grad. of Wellesley, 1903; m. **Clifton A. Towle**, June 20, 1908, Prof. of Biology and Physiography, Worcester Academy, Worcester, Mass.

1269. DANIEL W. STRATTON[9] (*Frink,*[8] *Paul,*[7] *Josiah,*[6] *Hezekiah,*[5] *Samuel,*[4] *Samuel,*[3] *Samuel,*[2] *Samuel*[1]) married **Hattie W. Phillips**, Mar. 22, 1868, and resided in Winn, where he died Sept. 3, 1893.

Children:—*Born in Winn, Me.*
- —1752 Wilmot,[10] b. 1868; d. aged 2 years.
- —1753 Mila Frances,[10] m. **John W. Barlow**.
- —1754 Gracie L.,[10] b. 1877; d. aged 3 years.
- +1755 Ora Earnest.[10]

1288. EBENEZER M. STRATTON [9] (*Asa*,[8] *Daniel*,[7] *Daniel*,[6] *Hezekiah*,[5] *Samuel*,[4] *Samuel*,[3] *Samuel*,[2] *Samuel*[1]) married **May Ann King**, June 9, 1853. Deacon in Baptist church for more than 30 years. Resides in South Newfane.

Children:—*Born in Newfane, Vt.*
- —1756 Clara A.,[10] m. **Charles Brown**, July 18, 1878.
- —1757 Amelia J.,[10] d. July 17, 1877, aged 19 years.
- —1758 Abbie N.,[10] m. **Lennie Bailey**, Mar. 8, 1888; lives in Suffield, Conn.
- —1759 Willie J.,[10] d. Mar. 9, 1879, aged 11 years.
- —1760 Nellie R.,[10] m. **Edward Morse**, June 5, 1900; res. Battleboro, Vt.
- —1761 Frank A.,[10] d. Mar. 9, 1879, aged 3 years.

1289. JOHN S. STRATTON [9] (*Asa*,[8] *Daniel*,[7] *Daniel*,[6] *Hezekiah*,[5] *Samuel*,[4] *Samuel*,[3] *Samuel*,[2] *Samuel*[1]) is a farmer of So. Newfane, Vt. Jan. 19, 1860, he married **Adelia Powers**.

Children:—*Born in Dummerston, Vt.*
- —1762 Ida M.,[10] d. June 29, 1877, aged 17 years.
- —1763 Ella J.,[10]
- —1764 John M.,[10] m. **Tena L. Allen**, Oct. 23, 1901; res. Williamsville, Vt.; chn. Harold G.,[11] Dorothy M.[11]

1290. ASA H. STRATTON [9] (*Asa*,[8] *Daniel*,[7] *Daniel*,[6] *Hezekiah*,[5] *Samuel*,[4] *Samuel*,[3] *Samuel*,[2] *Samuel*[1]) served two years in the Civil War, 1862-1864. In 1865 he married **Ellen Powers**; resides in West Brattleboro, Vt.

Children:
- —1765 Dana Albert,[10] m. **Elvira M. Taylor**, Mar. 19, 1896; res. Guilford, Vt.; ch. Dana Paul.[11]
- +1766 Leslie Elbridge.[10]
- —1767 Herbert Powers,[10] res. Springfield, Mass.
- —1768 Mary Ellen,[10] res. Williamsville.

1301. ALONZO V. STRATTON [9] (*Joseph*,[8] *Daniel*,[7] *Daniel*,[6] *Hezekiah*,[5] *Samuel*,[4] *Samuel*,[3] *Samuel*,[2] *Samuel*[1]) is a farmer of South Newfane. He married in 1870 **Louise A. Charter**, daughter of *King D.* and *Esther* (*Bartlett*) *Charter* of Marlboro. She was born Feb. 16, 1852, and died May 27, 1914, leaving many friends to mourn their loss in the home, the Sunday school and church, where she had long been a faithful and efficient worker. Mr. Stratton died just four months earlier.

Children:—*Born in Newfane, Vt.*
—1769   George Perley,[10] res. Springfield, Mass.
—1770   Walter L.,[10] res. Springfield, Mass.
—1771   Cecil C.[10]

1310.   CHARLES JULIAND STRATTON [9] (*Albert G.,*[8] *John,*[7] *Daniel,*[6] *Hezekiah,*[5] *Samuel,*[4] *Samuel,*[3] *Samuel,*[2] *Samuel*[1]) married **Mary Kinney,** May 1, 1865. They lived in So. Oxford, Hamptonburg, and Amsterdam, N. Y., and in 1881 moved to Chicago, where he died, Jan. 14, 1899.

Children:—*Born in So. Oxford.*
—1772   DeForest Albert,[10] m. **Alice A. Brecher** in Nov., 1889; lived in Grand Rapids for several years, now president of the D. A. Stratton Lumber Co. at Atlantic Mine, Mich.; only child, Gladys Mary,[11] b. in Alba, Mich.
—1773   Adalaide Bronson,[10] m. **S. Edward Thompson,** Feb. 15, 1899; res. Bedford, Iowa.

1314.   MILVILLE BRONSON STRATTON [9] (*Albert G.,*[8] *John,*[7] *Daniel,*[6] *Hezekiah,*[5] *Samuel,*[4] *Samuel,*[3] *Samuel,*[2] *Samuel*[1]) married **Harriet McFarland,** Oct. 24, 1877. She was born in Oxford, July 9, 1857. He is a farmer, owning and occupying the old Stratton homestead on the farm owned by his grandfather a full century ago.

Child:—*Born in So. Oxford, N. Y.*
—1774   Julian Arthur,[10] grad. Cornell University in 1904, with degree of M.E.E.E., and now in the employ of Western Electric Co. of Chicago.

1315.   ELI BURTON STRATTON [9] (*John,*[8] *John,*[7] *Daniel,*[6] *Hezekiah,*[5] *Samuel,*[4] *Samuel,*[3] *Samuel,*[2] *Samuel*[1]) married, May 23, 1869, **Annie Abigail Race**; res. Greene, N. Y.

Children:—*Born in Greene.*
—1775   Milton John,[10] m. **Nellie Daniels,** Mar. 28, 1901; res. Creso, Pa.

Born in Smithville, N. Y.
—1776   Callie Louina,[10] b. Sept. 23, 1876; d. Oct. 14, 1882.
—1777   Jessie Louise,[10] m. 1st, **Earle F. Race,** Nov. 3, 1904; 2nd, **Henry W. Walsh,** Nov. 29, 1911.

1317.   LATSON WILLIAM STRATTON [9] (*John,*[8] *John,*[7] *Daniel,*[6] *Hezekiah,*[5] *Samuel,*[4] *Samuel,*[3] *Samuel,*[2] *Samuel*[1]) married **Ella McNeil** in Amsterdam, N. Y., June 21, 1883; res. Chicago.

Children:
-1778 Jeanette May,[10] m. **Samuel Sutherland Chambers** in 1890.
-1779 Ethel Hannah,[10]
-1780 Laurence J.[10]
-1781 Harold.[10]

1322. GEORGE WESLEY STRATTON[9] (*Ira,[8] John,[7] Daniel,[6] Hezekiah,[5] Samuel,[4] Samuel,[3] Samuel,[2] Samuel[1]*) married **Mary Jane Webb** of Smithville, N. Y., July 3, 1862, and lived in Oxford, Smithville and McDonough, N. Y. He died Aug. 9, 1906.

Children:
+1782 Arthur Wesley.[10]
-1783 Ella E.,[10] m. **Adelbert Holmes**, Jan. 29, 1884.
-1784 Frederick Arial,[10] m. **Arvilla Wedge**, June, 1893.
-1785 Sabra H.,[10] d. Dec. 16, 1885, aged 15 years.
-1786 Ernestine J.,[10] d. Dec. 5, 1888, aged 17 years.
-1787 Carrie L.,[10] m. **Davilla Woodard**, Aug. 12, 1895.
-1788 Della May,[10] m. **Frank Marshall**, Dec. 23, 1900.
-1789 Minnie B.,[10] m. **Orlin Richmond**, Dec. 10, 1895.
-1790 Rosella E.,[10] m. **Julian Simmons**, Oct. 12, 1898.
-1791 Anna Belle.[10]
-1792 George Albert,[10] m. **Carrie D. Kimble**, June 14, 1913; res. Norwich, N. Y.
-1793 Everett Lewis,[10] m. **Elizabeth Sherwood**, Apr. 14, 1909; res. Norwich; chn. Keneth L.,[11] Karl E.,[11] Lyle W.[11]

1324. JAMES DARWIN STRATTON[9] (*Ira,[8] John,[7] Daniel,[6] Hezekiah,[5] Samuel,[4] Samuel,[3] Samuel,[2] Samuel[1]*) married, June 8, 1871, **Helen Maria Holladay**, who was born Sept. 10, 1845; res. Binghamton, N. Y.

Children:
-1794 Ethel May,[10] m. **Arthur Vance**, Oct. 18, 1894.
-1795 Grace Elma,[10] m. **Albert Barnes**.
-1796 Florence Hyde.[10]
-1797 Lewis Darwin.[10]
-1798 Edna Harriet,[10] m. **A. L. Bonell**.
-1799 Helen Anna.[10]

1328. WHITMAN STRATTON[9] (*William F.,[8] John,[7] Daniel,[6] Hezekiah,[5] Samuel,[4] Samuel,[3] Samuel,[2] Samuel[1]*) served three years in the Federal army. Enlisted Sept. 16, 1861; as private in Co. E, 89th New York Volunteers, discharged as Sergeant, Oct. 6, 1864, at Bermuda Hundred, Va. He took part in more than twenty battles and skirmishes, among them Antietam, Fredricksburg, Cold Harbor, Petersburg. He married **Margaret Sheffer**, Apr. 30, 1867. Res. Norwich.

Children:—*Born in Norwich, N. Y.*
- +1800 William Frink.[10]
- —1801 Alica May,[10] m. **Gregory Wick**, Jan. 29, 1890. He d. Nov. 13, 1902.
- —1802 Howard Grant,[10] m. **Maud Clinton**, Aug. 27, 1903. Res. Norwich, N. Y.; chn. Margery,[11] Jay.[11]
- —1803 Maria Louise,[10] m. **Raymond W. Vickers**, Sept. 7, 1904.

1333. EDWARD L. STRATTON [9] (*George*,[8] *John*,[7] *Daniel*,[6] *Hezekiah*,[5] *Samuel*,[4] *Samuel*,[3] *Samuel*,[2] *Samuel*[1]) married **Mary G. Mason**, Oct. 7, 1875; res. Oxford. He now owns and occupies the "George Stratton Homestead," with its fine farm and buildings.

Children:—*Born in Oxford, N. Y.*
- —1804 Henry Mason.[10]
- —1805 Frederick L.,[10] d. Nov. 3, 1902, aged 20 years.

Born in Smithville, N. Y.
- —1806 Emmett A.,[10] m. **Gertrude Mary Frost**, Oct. 11, 1911; res. Oxford; ch. Frederick Lynn.[11]

1334. HARVY J. STRATTON [9] (*George*,[8] *John*,[7] *Daniel*,[6] *Hezekiah*,[5] *Samuel*,[4] *Samuel*,[3] *Samuel*,[2] *Samuel*[1]) married **Fannie Jane Copeland**, Aug. 20, 1876; res. Oxford.

Children:—*Born in Greene, N. Y.*
- —1807 Rachel Mae,[10] m. **Herbert A. Ireland**, Oct. 16, 1902.
- —1808 George Robinson,[10] m. **Leona Hill**, June 1, 1910; res. Oxford.

1344. LUVERNE STRATTON [9] (*Ross*,[8] *John*,[7] *Daniel*,[6] *Hezekiah*,[5] *Samuel*,[4] *Samuel*,[3] *Samuel*,[2] *Samuel*[1]) married **Cora Church**, Dec. 5, 1888; died at Oxford, Nov. 8, 1910.

Children:
- —1809 Claude C.,[10] d. May 28, 1912, aged 21 years.
- —1810 Clara A.[10]
- —1811 Erwin Ross.[10]
- —1812 Albert L.[10]

1345. WILLIAM HENRY STRATTON [9] (*William W.*,[8] *William,*[7] *Daniel,*[6] *Hezekiah,*[5] *Samuel,*[4] *Samuel,*[3] *Samuel,*[2] *Samuel*[1]) married, Dec. 9, 1878, at Bainbridge (now Huntley), Neb., Julia Ann Dodd. He is a merchant at Valentine, Neb.

Children:—B*orn at Huntley, Neb.*
—1813 William Warner,[10] a stockman at Simeon, Neb.; unm.
—1814 Essie Pearl,[10] m. Herbert Clinton Houser, Oct. 18, 1903; res. Hastings, Neb.
—1815 Ray Dodd,[10] m., Dec. 23, 1912, Mabel M. Thompson; res. Superior, Neb., where he is engaged with "Stratton's Poster Adv. Service."

B*orn in Malcome, Iowa.*
—1816 Addie Foote,[10] m. Benjamin Franklin Chesterman, Feb. 7, 1905; res. Rexford, Kan.
—1817 Calvin Riggs,[10] res. Oasis, Neb.

B*orn in Arabia, Neb.*
—1818 Hazel Thornton,[10] m. Leota M. Nine, Apr. 5, 1913; res. Oasis, Neb.

B*orn in Oasis, Neb.*
—1819 Sarah Ann,[10] res. Simeon, Neb.
—1820 Amy Permelia,[10] res. Valentine, Neb.
—1821 Floyd Elmer.[10]
—1822 Alice Elizabeth.[10]
—1823 Grace May.[10]

1349. ALBION WILDER STRATTON [9] (*Wilder,*[8] *Samuel,*[7] *Hezekiah,*[6] *Hezekiah,*[5] *Samuel,*[4] *Samuel,*[3] *Samuel,*[2] *Samuel*[1]) was a soldier in the Civil War; enlisted at nineteen years of age in the 16th Regt. Me. Vols. and served until the end of the war. Was at Fredericksburg, Gettysburg, Hatcher's Run, and other engagements, and was wounded three times. At Gettysburg, the "Fighting Sixteenth" was ordered "to hold that position at any cost until we get the guns placed." They did it, but when roll call came but about forty men answered to it. Mr. Stratton was wounded and left in the church at Gettysburg when the place was evacuated by the Confederates. In 1867 he married Ella Hines, to whom the compiler is indebted for many records of New England Strattons. They lived at the old home farm at Washburn until 1891, then removed to Massachusetts, living at Medway, then Holliston, then Hopkinton.

Children:
—1824 Edward Melville.[10]

—1825   Harold Wilber.[10]
—1826   Hadley Fairfield.[10]
—1827   Ray Hollingsworth.[10]
—1828   Jeanneth Marcella.[10]
—1829   Josephine Winslow.[10]
—1830   Ruth Hall.[10]

1350. GEORGE FRANK STRATTON [9] (*Wilder,*[8] *Samuel,*[7] *Hezekiah,*[6] *Hezekiah,*[5] *Samuel,*[4] *Samuel,*[3] *Samuel,*[2] *Samuel*[1]) was a merchant at Mattawamkeag, Me. Mar. 14, 1875, he married **Elmira Martin**. Since his death his business has been carried on by his children under the name of the "G. F. Stratton Co."

Children:—*Born in Mattawamkeag, Me.*
—1831   Mae S.,[10] res. Bridgeport, Conn.
—1832   George Lester,[10] m. **Mary A. Keeley**, Nov. 5, 1906; chn. Wesley,[11] George,[11] Albion.[11]
—1833   William A.,[10] m. **Jessie Lyons**, Oct. 25, 1904; ch: William A., Jr.[11]
—1834   Martin G.[10]
—1835   Wesley A.,[10] res. Mattawamkeag; ch: Almon H.[11]
—1836   Amy E.[10]
—1837   Lena E.,[10] res. Bangor, Me.

1380. HENRY STRATTON [9] (*Franklin,*[8] *Shubael C.,*[7] *Jonathan,*[6] *Jonathan,*[5] *Samuel,*[4] *Samuel,*[3] *Samuel,*[2] *Samuel*[1]) is a business man of Erie, Pa., with "Stratton Manufacturing Co." July 28, 1864, he married **Jane M. Shattock**.

Children:—B*orn at Evansburg, Pa.*
+1838   Charles E.[10]
—1839   Helena,[10] m. **Wm. R. Rhum**, 1890.
—1840   Edith Louisa,[10] m. **Joseph Paul Smith**, 1898.
Born at Erie, Pa.
—1841   Earle C.,[10] m. **Mary S. Young** in 1908; ch. Henry Hodges,[11] b. Richmond, Cal.

1387. ROYAL ALTAMONT STRATTON [9] (*Henry,*[8] *Shubael C.,*[7] *Jonathan,*[6] *Jonathan,*[5] *Samuel,*[4] *Samuel,*[3] *Samuel,*[2] *Samuel*[1]) resides at Conneaut Lake, where he was a prominent business man and where he was postmaster for several years. He died Feb. 14, 1915. Aug. 5, 1856, he married **Samantha A. Clarke**.

Children:—B*orn at Conneaut Lake, Pa.*
—1842   Ellen Cora,[10] m. **Rev. J. D. Sands**, Sept. 10, 1878.

—1843   Harry James,[10] b. 1863; d. in infancy.
—1844   Blanche,[10] to whom the compiler is indebted for the portrait of her grandfather, Henry Stratton.
—1845   Grace.[10]
+1846   Henry Clarke.[10]
—1847   Alta,[10] m. 1st, **John R. Barker**, Aug. 25, 1891; m. 2nd, Oct. 27, 1915, James D. Lyle of Cleveland. She has a son Altamont Stratton Barker.
—1848   Arthur James,[10] now in Oklahoma.

1390. GEORGE LYMAN STRATTON [9] (*George,*[8] *Shubael C.,*[7] *Jonathan,*[6] *Jonathan,*[5] *Samuel,*[4] *Samuel,*[3] *Samuel,*[2] *Samuel*[1]) married, Nov. 16, 1865, **Annie Maria Bridge**, daughter of *Samuel* and *Hannah M.* (*Wellington*) *Bridge;* lived in Lexington and in Concord, N. H.; one of the incorporators of the Lexington Savings Bank.
Children:—B*orn in Lexington, Mass.*
—1849   Florence Gardner,[10] m. **Dr. Josiah O. Tilton**, Oct. 31, 1894.
—1850   George Bridge,[10] m. **Betty Morrison Carlton**, June 29, 1904; chn. Ann,[11] George L.,[11] Frances.[11]

1406. THOMAS SULLIVAN STRATTON [9] (*Daniel H.,*[8] *Braddyll,*[7] *Jonathan,*[6] *Jonathan,*[5] *Samuel,*[4] *Samuel,*[3] *Samuel,*[2] *Samuel*[1]) married in Waltham, Mass., **Jennie Fisher Owen** of Dedham, Oct. 4, 1852. Settled in Baltimore in 1872 and became a successful business man of that city.
Children:
—1851   Harry Coolidge,[10] m. **Flora White** in 1880; res. Baltimore.
—1852   William E.,[10] a physician; res. Brooklyn, N. Y.

1407. WILLIAM DWIGHT STRATTON [9] (*William C.,*[8] *Braddyll,*[7] *Jonathan,*[6] *Jonathan,*[5] *Samuel,*[4] *Samuel,*[3] *Samuel,*[2] *Samuel*[1]) married **Clara Hubbard** in 1856; d. about 1868.
Children:—B*orn in Hartford, Conn.*
—1853   Frances Maria,[10] m. **Frank Kingman**, 1875.
—1854   Charles Rollin,[10] b. 1859; d. 1898; unm.
—1855   Eugene Coolidge,[10] m. **Mary Amanda Strong** in 1882; res. Sheffield, Conn.
—1856   Albert Minor,[10] m. **Lizzie A. Parker**, 1887; res. Hartford; chn. Edna L.,[11] Frank P.,[11] Hattie M.,[11] Emma L[11]

1420. LORENZO STRATTON [9] (*Lorenzo*,[8] *Daniel*,[7] *Daniel*,[6] *Jonathan*,[5] *Samuel*,[4] *Samuel*,[3] *Samuel*,[2] *Samuel*[1]) married **Lucy L. Crosby**, Nov. 27, 1856, who died in 1885. They lived in Hudson, where he died Aug. 18, 1910.

Children:—*Born in Marlboro, Mass.*
—1857 Walter Lorenzo,[10] res. Hundon.
—1858 Laura Geneva,[10] m. **Herbert Whitcomb Monroe**, Oct. 29, 1882.
    Born in Hudson, Mass.
—1859 Elliott Revere.[10]

1421. JOSEPH STRATTON [9] (*Lorenzo*,[8] *Daniel*,[7] *Daniel*,[6] *Jonathan*,[5] *Samuel*,[4] *Samuel*,[3] *Samuel*,[2] *Samuel*[1]) married, first, **Martha C. Burgess** of New Ipswich, Nov. 30, 1862; second, **Sarah (Babcock) Shattuck**, June 8, 1879, daughter of *Albert Babcock* and widow of Geo. Marshall Shattuck.

Children:—*Born in Boston, Mass.*
    By first marriage.
—1860 Wilbert E.,[10] m. **Grace Huntley**, 1889.
    Born in Wayland.
    By second marriage.
—1861 Albert Lorenzo,[10] m. **Helen Mabel Hutchings**, Oct. 9, 1912; cashier in Worcester bank; ch. Albert Lorenzo, Jr.[11]
    Born in Natick.
—1862 May Gertrude.[10]

1427. DANIEL WILBER STRATTON [9] (*Daniel*,[8] *Daniel*,[7] *Daniel*,[6] *Jonathan*,[5] *Samuel*,[4] *Samuel*,[3] *Samuel*,[2] *Samuel*[1]) was active in town affairs at Hudson. Town clerk for many years. Treasurer of Hudson Savings Bank and superintendent of town waterworks. June 9, 1880, he married **Annie Scott Webster**. He died Jan. 8, 1909.

Children:—Born in Hudson, Mass.
—1863 Mary Edith.[10]
—1864 Walter Daniel,[10] grad. from Harvard, 1908. Shoe manufacturer at Hudson, m. **Ruth Evelyn Fosgate**, Oct. 8, 1912.
—1865 Helen Inez,[10] m. **Harold A. Bond**, Sept. 6, 1909; d. June 8, 1910.

1428. THEODORE STRATTON [9] (*Daniel*,[8] *Daniel*,[7] *Daniel*,[6] *Jonathan*,[5] *Samuel*,[4] *Samuel*,[3] *Samuel*,[2] *Samuel*[1]) is a farmer and

EIGHTH GENERATION: 1. Rufus Stratton. 2. Daniel Stratton, Jr. 3. The Daniel Stratton, Sr. farm. 4. Lorenzo Stratton house, blown up to stop the spread of the flames during the great fire at Hudson, Mass. 5. Lorenzo Stratton. *Pages* 124, 165.

business man of Hudson, where he married **Nellie A. Ingraham,** June 25, 1878.

Children:—B*orn in Hudson, Mass.*
—1866 Nellie Maud,[10] b. Aug. 21, 1879; d. in East Boston.
—1867 Mary Ellen,[10] d. aged 18 years.
—1868 George Ingraham.[10]

1429. HERBERT STRATTON [9] (*Daniel,*[8] *Daniel,*[7] *Daniel,*[6] *Jonathan,*[5] *Samuel,*[4] *Samuel,*[3] *Samuel,*[2] *Samuel*[1]) is a farmer on the old Stratton place, near Hudson, where a part of the old red house built by his great-grandfather is still standing, but used only as a store house. In 1884 he married **Viola E. Folsom.**

Children:—B*orn in Hudson, Mass.*
—1869 Eleanor Fay,[10] m. **Willis Greeley,** Oct. 26, 1911.
—1870 Marion Folsom,[10] m. **George S. Miller,** Aug. 14, 1913.
—1871 Olive,[10] a teacher.
—1871a Pauline.[10]

1434. CHARLES L. STRATTON [9] (*Lewis,*[8] *Henry,*[7] *Isaac,*[6] *Jonathan,*[5] *Samuel,*[4] *Samuel,*[3] *Samuel,*[2] *Samuel*[1]) married, first, **Fostina C. Somes,** Apr. 25, 1883; second, **Elizabeth Reuddock,** Dec. 17, 1903.

Children:
    By first marriage.
—1872 Emogene Frances,[10] m., Feb. 10, 1909, **Willis Peter Shumway,** Melrose.
    By second marriage.
—1873 Justine.[10]
—1874 Frank.[10]

1435. HENRY FRANCIS STRATTON [9] (*Francis,*[8] *Henry,*[7] *Isaac,*[6] *Jonathan,*[5] *Samuel,*[4] *Samuel,*[3] *Samuel,*[2] *Samuel*[1]) was a locomotive engineer for fifteen years, then in the livery and stage business for many years. Lived in Harrisville and Bellows Falls; now resides in Auburn, Me. Married **Ida Louisa Clark,** Oct. 10, 1897.

Children:—B*orn at Bellows Falls, Vt.*
—1875 Carl Henry.[10]
—1876 Beatrice Emma.[10]

1441. IRVIN C. STRATTON [9] (*George H.,*[8] *George,*[7] *Elisha,*[6] *Jonathan,*[5] *Samuel,*[4] *Samuel,*[3] *Samuel,*[2] *Samuel*[1]) married, first, **Adella Ingrain** in 1881; second, **Mary Davis,** 1893.

Children:—*Born in Weston, Mass.*
—1876½ Everett I.
    Born in Hartland, Conn.
—1877 Dexter A.[10]
—1878 Byron C.[10]
—1879 Susan A.[10]
—1880 George A.[10]
—1881 Beatrice E.[10]
—1882 Warren W.[10]
—1883 Irwin H.[10]

1451. RODNEY J. STRATTON [9] (*Josiah,*[8] *Josiah,*[7] *Ebenezer,*[6] *Samuel,*[5] *Samuel,*[4] *Samuel,*[3] *Samuel,*[2] *Samuel*[1]) resides in North Adams, Mass. June 12, 1878, he married **Annie A. Farnum** of Waltham. She died Aug. 25, 1881, and July 1, 1884, he married **Anna J. Davis**.
Children:
    By first marriage.
—1884 Emerancy F.[10]
    By second marriage.
—1885 Rodney Wilson.[10]

1471. EDWIN A. STRATTON [9] (*Cyprian K.,*[8] *Alpheus,*[7] *Alpheus,*[6] *Samuel,*[5] *Samuel,*[4] *Samuel,*[3] *Samuel,*[2] *Samuel*[1]) married **Margaret Egan** and lives in Worcester.
Children:—*Born in Worcester, Mass.*
—1886 Frederick C.,[10] m. **Clara T. Pellegrine**, July 10, 1901; res. Worcester.
—1887 George E.,[10] m. **Mary E. Fenton**, Nov. 25, 1908.
—1888 Walter A.[10]
—1889 Florence H.[10]

1480. GEORGE OREN STRATTON [9] (*Nathaniel H.,*[8] *Samuel,*[7] *Alpheus,*[6] *Samuel,*[5] *Samuel,*[4] *Samuel,*[3] *Samuel,*[2] *Samuel*[1]) was born June 4, 1851. He married **Marion E. Baker**, Sept. 25, 1873. He is a prominent business man of Montpelier and represented his city in the Legislature in 1906. He is president of the Vermont Mutual Fire Insurance Company.
Children:—*Born in Montpelier, Vt.*
—1890 Arthur Nathaniel,[10] m. **Addie M. Spear**, Jan. 7, 1899; a farmer at E. Montpelier; chn. George Robert,[11] Ruth,[11] Raymond.[11]
—1891 Bertha Louise,[10] m. **Jos. Vian**, Sept. 7, 1899.
—1892 William Brigham,[10] m. **Charlotte K. Nutting**, June 4, 1907; res. Montpelier.

1498. GEORGE LEONARD STRATTON [9] (*Leonard W.,*[8] *Eleazer,*[7] *Eleazer,*[6] *Eleazer,*[5] *Hezekiah,*[4] *Samuel,*[3] *Samuel,*[2] *Samuel*[1]) married **Ida C. Bruce,** June 12, 1877. He is a shoe merchant.

Children:
- —1893   Alice,[10] d. aged 25 years.
- —1894   Belle,[10] d. aged 17 years.
- —1895   Erwin.[10]
- —1896   Leon.[10]
- —1897   Ruby.[10]
- —1898   Arthur.[10]
- —1899   Clarence.[10]

1516. EARNEST A. STRATTON [9] (*Edward R.,*[8] *Rufus,*[7] *Rufus,*[6] *Hezekiah,*[5] *Hezekiah,*[4] *Samuel,*[3] *Samuel,*[2] *Samuel*[1]) was a bookkeeper and cashier in Brooklyn, N. Y., where he died in 1901. He married **Ida E. Chute** in 1872. At the time of his death he was deacon and clerk in the Baptist church.

Children:—Born in New York.
- —1900   Eugene B.,[10] m. **Anna L. Walker,** Nov. 28, 1894.
- —1901   Mabel Evelyn,[10] a trained nurse.
- —1902   Helen Edna,[10] m. **Henry C. Bloom,** June 17, 1897.
- —1903   Earnest Dean Robert,[10] d. in Phila., Feb. 7, 1908; buried in Maple Grove Cemetery, Brooklyn.

1532. ROBERT STRATTON [9] (*Lemuel,*[8] *Arad,*[7] *Hezekiah,*[6] *Hezekiah,*[5] *Hezekiah,*[4] *Samuel,*[3] *Samuel,*[2] *Samuel*[1]) married **Lucy Cole** in 1885 and lived in Berlin, N. Y.

Children:
- —1904   Emma V.[10]
- —1905   Florence A.[10]
- —1906   William H.[10]
- —1907   Robert C.[10]

1534. HENRY STRATTON [9] (*Lemuel,*[8] *Arad,*[7] *Hezekiah,*[6] *Hezekiah,*[5] *Hezekiah,*[4] *Samuel,*[3] *Samuel,*[2] *Samuel*[1]) married **Frances Cole** in 1888.

Children:
- —1908   Bertha M.[10]
- —1909   Lyman L.[10]
- —1910   Agnes M.[10]
- —1911   Onita W.[10]

1547. CHARLES E. STRATTON [9] (*Charles*,[8] *Isaac J.*,[7] *Daniel*,[6] *Richard*,[5] *Ichabod*,[4] *Richard*,[3] *Samuel*,[2] *Samuel* [1]) married **Marion L. Buckly.** Lived in Oxford, N. Y.

Children:
—1912 Flora L.,[10] m. **Edwin L. Haynes.**
—1913 Herbert C.,[10] m. **Florence Lewis.**
—1914 Robert B.,[10] m. **Minnie B. Brown.**
—1915 Vernon D.,[10] m. **Lottie McFarland;** grad. LL.B., Cornell, 1893; res. Oxford.
—1916 Carroll I.,[10] m. **Genevieve Carpenter;** a lawyer at Oxford.

1559. FRANK NELSON STRATTON [9] (*Francis J.*,[8] *Francis*,[7] *John*,[6] *Francis*,[5] *Ichabod*,[4] *Richard*,[3] *Samuel*,[2] *Samuel* [1]) was a prominent attorney of Kokomo, Ind. For several years he was a regular contributor to a number of the leading magazines. The stories of western life from his versatile pen are delightfully written, for he was a sympathetic observer who saw the best in every situation, as well as the more humorous, and knew how to give interest and action to the scenes which he depicted. Several of his stories are of the pathetic sort which makes the reader kinder and better for the reading of them. His first stories are written under the name of "Frank Nelson." In 1888 he married **Otellie Shellsmith.** He died Feb. 15, 1905. He was a prominent member of the Red Men, Odd Fellows, Woodmen, Pathfinders, and Ben Hur lodges, and was very popular among all classes in his own city. These organizations had more than 800 men in procession at his funeral.

Children:—*Born in Kokomo, Ind.*
—1917 Frank H.[10]
—1918 Frederick N.[10]
—1919 Ferdinand P.[10]

1594. CHARLES E. STRATTON [9] (*Samuel*,[8] *Joseph B.*,[7] *Joel*,[6] *Ichabod*,[5] *Ichabod*,[4] *Richard*,[3] *Samuel*,[2] *Samuel* [1]) is a graduate of Nebraska State University. He engaged in the real estate and loan business in Omaha and later in Denver, Col., where he now lives. June 26, 1885, he married **Minnie Codding.**

Children.
—1920 Veda.[10]
—1921 Charles R.[10]

1626. GEORGE WILLIAM STRATTON [9] (*William*,[8] *John*,[7] *Richard*,[6] *John*,[5] *John*,[4] *John*,[3] *John*,[2] *Samuel*[1]) was born in West Swanzey, Aug. 1, 1830. From a child he showed great musical ability, and at nine years of age played the clarionet at concerts in several New England towns. At twenty-one he was a teacher of music—on several different instruments. In 1860 he opened a store in Boston for the sale of musical instruments. About this time he composed and published the operetta "Laila," which was received with great favor all over the country, and which all through his life brought in a very good revenue, his widow still receiving something every year from the sale of the books. This was followed by other musical compositions, all of which were popular for a time. In 1862 he married **Lucy Ladd**, daughter of *Hiram* and *Aurelia (Palmer) Ladd*, of a well known New Hampshire family. In 1871, taking his wife and household goods, he went to Leipsic, Saxony, to assist his brother, John F. Stratton, who had there established a musical instrument factory. Keeping his store in Boston, and his interest in the business in Leipsic, importing all kinds of musical instruments from foreign manufactories, Mr. Stratton crossed the ocean thirty-five times. About 1895, his health failing, he sold out his business and spent most of his time abroad. He died, suddenly, in Berlin, Germany, October 14, 1901.* Ambitious, studious, and passionately fond of music, even as a boy, he longed for opportunities for study which his native town did not afford, and he was heard to say that if ever he was able to give West Swanzey a library he would do it, that other boys might have advantages which were denied him. In 1880 he began making plans to carry out this long-cherished project. In 1885 the finished library building, well stocked with books and pictures, was given to the town—"Stratton Free Library and Art Gallery."

1636. MELVILLE OSCAR STRATTON [9] (*Oscar*,[8] *John*,[7] *Richard*,[6] *John*,[5] *John*,[4] *John*,[3] *John*,[2] *Samuel*[1]) married **Clara Gertrude Narcross**, Jan. 30, 1883, daughter of *Daniel Webster* and *Delia Augusta Narcross* of Grafton, Mass. They moved from Grafton

---

*In his pocket was found a diary giving date of each time he had crossed the ocean and name of ship in which he had embarked. By written directions, carried in his pocket for years, his wife caused his body to be cremated at Hamburg, brought home the ashes in an urn, and, as per his will, deposited it in a niche prepared for it, in the Library, where, "after an anxious, hard working life, they rest in peace."

to Denver, Col., where he became a prominent business man. He died Jan. 22, 1914.

Children:—*Born in Denver, Col.*

—1922 Melville Narcross,[10] m. **Helen Elizabeth Hickey**, June 24, 1908, daughter of *Martin* and *Elizabeth Hickey* of Grafton. They reside in Springfield, Mass.

Chn. Eleanor N.,[11] Elizabeth G.,[11] Geraldine F.[11]

—1923 Grenville Webster,[10] m. **Mrs. Cora Laura (Beck) Updike**, Sept. 5, 1913; res. Chicago, Ill.

—1924 Bruce Ellsworth,[10] m., July 23, 1914, **Katherine Knight Kirkland**, daughter of *Samuel M.* and *Nancy Kirkland;* res. Denver, Col.; ch. Adrienne Kirkland.[11]

—1925 Rosamond Field,[10] m. **Joseph Lincoln Sebring** of Colorado Springs, Jan. 15, 1914; res. Denver.

—1926 Madelyn Gertrude.[10]

1645. JOHN H. STRATTON [9] (*John,*[8] *Abijah,*[7] *Abijah,*[6] *Abijah,*[5] *Jabez,*[4] *John,*[3] *John,*[2] *Samuel*[1]) married **Carrie M. Greenwood**, Dec. 13, 1860. They lived in Natick, Mass., and in Trenton and Vineland, N. J.

Children:

—1927 Albert E.[10]
—1928 George H.[10]
—1929 John W.[10]
—1930 Charles.[10]
—1931 Florence.[10]

1656. JONATHAN STRATTON [9] (*Tolman,*[8] *Jonathan,*[7] *Daniel,*[6] *Abijah,*[5] *Jabez,*[4] *John,*[3] *John,*[2] *Samuel*[1]) married **Sarah Jane Lansdowne** in Greenup Co., Ky., Dec. 12, 1850, where he was a farmer. In 1865 he moved with his family to Iowa. In that state he lived eight years, then removed to Lawrence, Kan., and eleven years later to California and is living at Bonsall, San Diego Co. Mrs. Stratton died Mar. 20, 1897.

Children:—*Born in Greenup Co., Ky.*

—1932 Nancy Ellen,[10] b. 1852; m. 1st, **Wm. Dusing;** 2nd, **S. A. Jones.**

+1933 William Abiod,[10] b. July 23, 1854.

Born in Flemming Co., Ky.

+1934 Hiram Vincent,[10] b. Aug. 17, 1856.

—1935 Malvina C.,[10] m. **John Ballagh**, Feb. 26, 1880; res. Parsons, Kas.
—1936 Samuel Morton,[10] b. Feb. 23, 1862; m. **Tabitha Wooten**, Sept. 17, 1884. He is a carpenter and builder in Los Angeles, Cal. Chn. Maude Ethel,[11] Myrtle Ivy.[11]
—1937 James Madison,[10] b. July 2, 1864; m. **Lucy Conn**, May 1, 1887; d. Sept. 1, 1891. Their three children died in infancy.

Born in Muscatine Co., Iowa.
+1938 John J.,[10] Dec. 23, 1866.
+1939 Ulysses Grant,[10] Feb. 5, 1869.

1663. JAVIUS LITCHFIELD STRATTON [9] (*Martin W.*,[8] *Albert*,[7] *Nathan*,[6] *Nathan*,[5] *Jabez*,[4] *John*,[3] *John*,[2] *Samuel*[1]) married, at Reading, Kan., Dec. 25, 1884, **Martha Jane Hultz**, daughter of *Isaac* and *Catherine* (*Bower*) *Hultz*. She was born at Mt. Lebanon. They reside in Reading, Kan.

Children:
—1940 Clifton Javius.[10]
—1941 Clyde Roe.[10]
—1942 Jay Webster.[10]
—1943 Kate Carter.[10]
—1944 Bert Hultz.[10]

1739. HENRY HERBERT STRATTON [10] (*Archie W.*,[9] *Paul*,[8] *Paul*,[7] *Josiah*,[6] *Hezekiah*,[5] *Samuel*,[4] *Samuel*,[3] *Samuel*,[2] *Samuel*[1]) is a farmer, lumberman and ferry proprietor at Winn, Me. Sept. 8, 1888, he married **Abbie E. Lyon**.

Children:—*Born in Winn, Me.*
—1945 Archie Lee,[11] d. in infancy.
—1946 Vaughn Henry.[11]
—1947 Robert Earl.[11]
—1948 Edith Elizabeth.[11]
—1949 Clara Augusta.[11]
—1950 Everett Albert,[11] d. in infancy.
—1951 Ida Emily.[11]

1740. PAUL STRATTON [10] (*Archie W.*,[9] *Paul*,[8] *Paul*,[7] *Josiah*,[6] *Hezekiah*,[5] *Samuel*,[4] *Samuel*,[3] *Samuel*,[2] *Samuel*[1]) married **Susan Harriman** in 1888 and now resides in Gray, Me.

Children:—*Born in Richmond, Me.*
—1952 Archie William.[11]
Born in Randolph, Me.
—1953 Lewis Lee.[11]
Born in Bemis, Me.
—1954 Bemis Jotham.[11]
—1955 Hortence Allen.[11]

1743. CHARLES ALBERT STRATTON [10] (*Archie W.,*[9] *Paul,*[8] *Paul,*[7] *Josiah,*[6] *Hezekiah,*[5] *Samuel,*[4] *Samuel,*[3] *Samuel,*[2] *Samuel* [1]) married **Mae Lint**, May 6, 1890. Resides in Randolph, Me.
Children:
—1956 Sarah D.[11]
—1957 Olive J.[11]
—1958 Walter M.[11]

1755. ORA EARNEST STRATTON [10] (*Daniel W.,*[9] *Frink,*[8] *Paul,*[7] *Josiah,*[6] *Hezekiah,*[5] *Samuel,*[4] *Samuel,*[3] *Samuel,*[2] *Samuel* [1]) married **Edith I. Hunt** in 1895. Resides in Winn.
Children:—*Born in Winn, Me.*
—1959 Daniel W.[11]
—1960 Wilber R.[11]
—1961 Eugene.[11]
—1962 Frances Charlotte.[11]

1766. LESLIE ELBRIDGE STRATTON [10] *Asa H.,*[9] *Asa,*[8] *Daniel,*[7] *Josiah,*[6] *Hezekiah,*[5] *Samuel,*[4] *Samuel,*[3] *Samuel* [2] *Samuel* [1]) married **Nellie Adams**, daughter of *Francis C. Adams*, and lives in Williamsville, Vt.
Children:
—1963 Frank L.[11]
—1964 Grace N.[11]

1782. ARTHUR WESLEY STRATTON [10] (*George W.,*[9] *Ira,*[8] *John,*[7] *Daniel,*[6] *Hezekiah,*[5] *Samuel,*[4] *Samuel,*[3] *Samuel,*[2] *Samuel* [1]), born in Oxford, N. Y., Oct. 11, 1863; married **Carrie M. Webster**, June 10, 1885. Res. Olmsville, Tioga Co., N. Y.
Children:—*Born in Wellsboro, Pa.*
—1965 Lena May,[11] m. **Benjamin Griffin**, Nov. 9, 1912; res. Norwich, N. Y.
+1966 Minor Alvin.[11]

Born in Niles Valley.
—1967 Florance Minnie,[11] m. William Townsend, May 8, 1915.
—1968 Lewis Arthur.[11]
Born in Wellsboro.
—1969 Ralph Eber.[11]
—1970 Helen Edith.[11]
—1971 Harvey Webster.[11]

1800. WILLIAM FRINK STRATTON [10] (*Whitman,*[9] *William F.,*[8] *John,*[7] *Daniel,*[6] *Hezekiah,*[5] *Samuel,*[4] *Samuel,*[3] *Samuel,*[2] *Samuel*[1]) married **Mary Hull**, Oct. 19, 1893. Resided in Norwich, N. Y., where he died Jan. 8, 1915.
Children:—*Born in Norwich, N. Y.*
—1972 William Frink,[11] d. Aug. 30, 1895, aged 9 mos.
—1973 Frank Hull.[11]

1838. CHARLES E. STRATTON [10] (*Henry,*[9] *Franklin,*[8] *Shubael C.,*[7] *Jonathan,*[6] *Jonathan,*[5] *Samuel,*[4] *Samuel,*[3] *Samuel,*[2] *Samuel*[1]) is connected with the "Stratton Manufacturing Co." at Erie, Pa. He married **Rebecca Judson Dickinson**, Feb. 4, 1886.
Children:—*Born in Erie, Pa.*
—1974 Charles Edwin,[11] d. Oct. 6, 1906.
—1975 Dorothy Ellen.[11]

1846. HENRY CLARKE STRATTON [10] (*Royal A.,*[9] *Henry,*[8] *Shubael C.,*[7] *Jonathan,*[6] *Jonathan,*[5] *Samuel,*[4] *Samuel,*[3] *Samuel,*[2] *Samuel*[1]) married **Ida Woods**, Aug. 27, 1890; now resides in Meadville, Pa.
Children:—*Born at Conneaut Lake, Pa.*
—1976 Marjory Henrietta.[11]
—1977 Helen Josephine.[11]
—1978 Jessie Adell.[11]
—1979 Ethel Clarke.[11]
—1980 Martha Samantha.[11]
—1981 Marian Adelaide.[11]
—1982 Dorothy Irene.[11]
—1982a Bernice Louise.[11]

1933. WILLIAM ABIOD STRATTON [10] (*Jonathan,*[9] *Tolman,*[8] *Jonathan,*[7] *Daniel,*[6] *Abijah,*[5] *Jabez,*[4] *John,*[3] *John,*[2] *Samuel*[1]) moved with his parents from Kentucky to Iowa when he was eleven years old; from Iowa to Kansas in 1871; and to California in 1881; married **Minnie E. Tolman**, daughter of *Rufus J. Tolman*, Dec. 5, 1882. He was a building superintendent at Los Angeles several years. Now lives in Pasadena.

Children:—*Born in Los Angeles, Cal.*
- —1983 Mabel Sarah.[11]
- —1984 Frank Rufus,[11] m. **Maud Fisher**, Dec. 24, 1904; res. Los Angeles.
- —1985 Charles,[11] a carpenter at Pomona, Cal.
- —1986 Grace Ethel,[11] m. **Ralph McAlpine**, Oct. 23, 1907; res. Los Angeles.
- —1987 Lily Violet.[11]

1934. HIRAM VINCENT STRATTON[10] (*Jonathan,*[9] *Tolman,*[8] *Jonathan,*[7] *Daniel,*[6] *Abijah,*[5] *Jabez,*[4] *John,*[3] *John,*[2] *Samuel*[1]) married, first, **Tryphena Jane Dressler**, Apr. 5, 1877, who died Feb. 25, 1878. He married, second, **Mary Jane Keefoner**. He moved from Kansas to Los Angeles, California.

Children:—*Born in Williamstown, Kan.*
  By first marriage.
- —1988 Enoch V.,[11] res. Los Angeles.
  By second marriage.
- —1989 Herbert Earl,[11] photographer at Los Angeles; m. **Iva Scott**, July 7, 1909.
  Born in Waterville, Kan.
- —1990 Arthur R.,[11] m. **Nina Hall**; ch. Bertha D.[12]
  Born in Los Angeles.
- —1991 Daisy D.[11]
- —1992 Clifford C.[11]

1938. JOHN J. STRATTON[10] (*Jonathan,*[9] *Tolman,*[8] *Jonathan,*[7] *Daniel,*[6] *Abijah,*[5] *Jabez,*[4] *John,*[3] *John,*[2] *Samuel*[1]) lives in Pomona, Cal., where he is a carpenter and builder. Dec. 23, 1902, he married **Katie Thomas**. They are members of the Methodist church.

Children:—*Born in Los Angeles, Cal.*
- —1993 John J., Jr.[11]
- —1994 Wesley Lincoln.[11]
  Born in Pomona, Cal.
- —1995 Leonard Thomas.[11]
- —1996 Marjorie May.[11]

1939. ULYSSES GRANT STRATTON [10] (*Jonathan,[9] Tolman,[8] Jonathan,[7] Daniel,[6] Abijah,[5] Jabez,[4] John,[3] John,[2] Samuel[1]*) is an engineer, living in Los Angeles. He married, first, **Annie G. Arnaelsteen,** who died Dec. 23, 1897. Nov. 1, 1905, he married **Ursie Swift.**

Children:—Born in Los Angeles, Cal.
    By first marriage.
—1997 Edward John.[11]
    By second marriage.
—1998 Howard Harvey.[11]

1966. MINOR ALVIN STRATTON [11] (*Arthur W.,[10] George W.,[9] Ira,[8] John,[7] Daniel,[6] Hezekiah,[5] Samuel,[4] Samuel,[3] Samuel,[2] Samuel[1]*) is a farmer of Wellsboro, Pa. He married **Ella M. Orr,** Mar. 23, 1910.

Children:
—1999 Katherine Mae.[12]
—2000 Tracy Minor.[12]

CALEB STRATTON OF BOSTON

(*Chart B, Vol. I*)

"'Tis sweet to remember. I would not forego
The charm which the past o'er the present can throw."
CLARK.

IN the early days of the Revolution the whale fisheries along the Atlantic were broken up by the English Marines. About 1783 a considerable number of the inhabitants of Nantucket determined to leave the island and makes a settlement somewhere upon the Hudson. An association was formed by those concerned in whaling and navigation. Many of these were Quakers. Among them were several Nantucket Strattons.* They were joined by Friends from Providence and other points. The largest settlements were made at Hudson and Nine Partners. The

---

* It will be remembered that Caleb Stratton of Nantucket had eight sons (see Vol. I, p. 95-96), all of whom grew to manhood in their island home. At least five of these sons had children, yet no Strattons were living in Nantucket a generation later. The census of 1810 gives but one person by the name of Stratton. This was Abigal, widow of Christopher Stratton. The children had all left their native island and only a few have been definitely located elsewhere.

Since Vol. I was published it has been found that Philip Stratton (No. 23, Chart B) died in Providence, R. L., in 1791. The published index to wills at Providence says that he left a will, Docket A. 1364. The will itself the compiler has been unable to find. His widow, Lucretia, married Francis Gardner in Providence, May 14, 1800. Perhaps the Phœbe Stratton who married **Merrick Chamberlain** in Providence, January 14, 1787, was his daughter.

Although Folgar, the Nantucket historian, says that Anthony, Caleb and Philip left no descendants, this may not be true of any of them. Folgar based his opinion mainly upon Friends' Records. As several of the Strattons had been "disowned" for marrying outside of the society, or had withdrawn from the Friends' Society, the births of their children would not be found on the Friends' Records.

At Darmouth, Mass., the compiler found the records of the birth of these two children of Odar Stratton:
Judith, b. July 1757.
Lois, b. Aug. 1763.

latter was on a grant given to nine men long before the Revolution.

FIFTH GENERATION

28. BENJAMIN STRATTON [5] (*Benjamin,*[4] *Caleb,*[3] *William,*[2] *Caleb*[1]) was born in Nantucket August 8, 1764. He was but eleven years old when his father removed to New Partners, N. Y. By his father's will he was given lands in Nantucket, but he never returned there to live. Before 1800 he married **Anne**—and lived for awhile in New York, then removed to Philadelphia, where he died July 7th, 1820.* He is probably the Benjamin Stratton, block maker, whose name appears in the Philadelphia Directory for 1806 to 1820.†

Children:
+36 William,[6] b. 1800; d. about 1857.
—37 Enos Alley,[6] b. Sept. 27, 1802; d. July 21, 1803.

Also at the same place are the following records:

Hannah, d. of the late Wm. Stratton, married Aug. 28, 1740, Joshua **Sherman,** son of *Timothy and Deborah Sherman.*

William Stratton of Sherborn married Deborah **Sherman** of Darmouth, Dec. 22, 1790.

There was a John Stratton, Jr., of Warwick and Exeter, R. I., who served in the War of 1812—was Lieut. in 1819, Capt. in 1821, Colonel in 1822. He m. 1st **Phœbe Clemmons** in 1816, and 2nd Eunice (**Lewis**) Arnold in 1822. After 1827 he settled in New York State. He had by 1st marriage George Alford, b. May 28, 1819, who m. a Miss White and moved to Wisconsin; John Clemmons, who m. Elizabeth Matterson. By 2nd marriage, Wm. Dexter, b. July 8, 1824, who m. Almira Wilcox and has a son, Arthur Yale Stratton, living at Tyner (or Oxford, R. F. D.), N. Y.; Thomas Jones, b. June 4, 1827, m. **Ruth I. Moore,** and their daughter, Sarah De Etta Stratton, m. Bert E. **Pudney** and lives at Sidney, N. Y. Information leading to the ancestry of these Strattons is very much desired.

* His removal, with his wife and five children, is recorded on the "Monthly Meeting Records" at New York, Nov. 1, 1815.

† A Block Maker was one who made one or more pulleys mounted in a shell of wood called a block. It is a hoisting tackle, and when Nantucket was a whaling port the making of "Blocks" for use on ship board was an important and lucrative trade. The best blocks were made of oak, the wheels of Lignum Vitæ. To-day many blocks are made of steel.

The Philadelphia Directories from 1804 to about 1816 give Joseph Stratton, Robert Stratton, George Stratton, and John Stratton, whom the compiler has not yet been able to place satisfactorily. These last two were ship masters, and lived in that part of the city known as Northern Liberties.

—38   Samuel W.⁶
—39   Joseph.⁶
—40   Eliza Ann,⁶ m. —— **Gager**.
—41   Benjamin.⁶ Perhaps this is the Benjamin Stratton who died in Philadelphia Aug. 8, 1882, aged 77 years.*

31. LATHAM STRATTON ⁵ (*Benj.,*⁴ *Caleb,*³ *William,*² *Caleb* ¹) was born in Nantucket June 29, 1775. The following November his parents moved to Nine Partners, N. Y. At the age of 19, he went with his father to New York City and for some time they were located at Crane Wharf, as coopers. October 27th, 1797, he married **Phœbe Mead**, daughter of *Nathaniel* and *Hannah Mead*, of Dutchess Co.

In 1818 his name appears as foreman of a fire company in New York. Later in the same year he removed to Troy, and became a foundryman, conducting the "Stratton Foundry" there. The family story is that he cast the first plowshare and the first air-tight stove cast in this country. Latham and Phœbe were life long members of the Society of Friends. Phœbe was born Nov. 1, 1780, and died Dec. 31, 1829. A year later Latham married **Eunice Hanks**, of Washington Co., N. Y. He died in Troy March 4th, 1849,—a man of sterling integrity, and greatly respected.†

Children:—*Born in New York City.*

—42   Lydia,⁶ b. July 5, 1798; m. **Alexander J. Coffin**, of Athens, N. Y.; d. in Poughkeepsie, March 23, 1832.
—43   Hannah,⁶ b. June 19, 1800; d. unmarried in 1820.
+44   Robert Macy,⁶ b. 1803; d. 1874.
+45   Nathaniel Mead,⁶ b. 1807; d. 1860.
—46   Cynthia,⁶ b. Oct. 12, 1809; m. **William Plumb**, Apr. 11, 1827.

---

* The author would be greatly pleased to get into communication with any one having further knowledge of the family of Benjamin Stratton⁵.

† Hidden away in a closet in the old Quaker church in New York, 144 East 20th Street, was recently found a record of the names of the members of the Preparative meeting of New York for five of six years beginning with 1801. On this list are thirteen Strattons—Benjamin Stratton and his daughter Elizabeth, his sons Benjamin and Latham, and their children.

For this list, giving the correct list of births, as well as for the portrait and autograph of Latham Stratton, the Author is indebted to Robert Macy Stratton of New York, who has in his possession the old family Bible of Latham Stratton.

1. Latham Stratton, from an old oil painting. 2. Robert Macy Stratton. 3. Nathaniel Mead Stratton; *Pages* 178-180.

+47   Alexander Moores,⁶ b. 1813; d. 1854.
—48   Phœbe Ann,⁶ b. Jan. 4, 1817; d. unmarried in Troy, N. Y., Nov. 13, 1831.

All the above children were named in the will of their aunt Elizabeth Stratton (No. 27, *Chart B*).

36. WILLIAM STRATTON⁶ (*Benjamin,⁵ Benjamin,⁴ Caleb,³ William,² Caleb* ¹) was born "21 day of 12 m. 1800." In 1807 his parents removed from New York to Philadelphia. In 1856 he was living in Frankfort, a suburb of Philadelphia, where he kept a boot and shoe store. At that time he owned a watch, formerly his father's, on the dial of which were the twelve letters Benj. Stratton instead of figures to indicate the hours. He died about 1857 or '58.

Child:
—49   William,⁷ m. **Eliza**—and soon after his father's death removed from Philadelphia to Washington, D. C., where he opened a school for young ladies. Later information concerning him is desired.

If William Stratton ⁶ had other children the compiler would be glad to learn of them.

44. ROBERT MACY STRATTON ⁶ (*Latham,⁵ Benjamin,⁴ Caleb,³ William,² Caleb* ¹) was born in New York City May 23, 1803. For many years he was the financial partner of a large iron foundry and machine shops, "The Novelty Iron Works," builders of steam engines and other machinery, perhaps the largest works of its kind in the country at that time. They employed many men. The foundry, machine shops and wharfs covered five acres at the foot of 12th Street on East River. He was a birthright Quaker, was disowned for marrying outside the Society, but later rejoined the Friends and became a recommended minister of the Friends' Society in which position he remained until his death.

June 23, he married **Jane Wilson**. She was born Apr. 13, 1805, and died Aug. 11, 1856. Oct. 6, 1859, he married **Louise C. Macy** of Nantucket. He died Apr. 10, 1874, in New York.*

---

* He was an expert accountant. From 1843 to the time of his death he was a Trustee of the Bowery Savings Bank, and from 1850 to 1861 Vice President of the same bank. He was a member of the Society of Mechanics and Tradesmen, and of the American Institute, and from

Children:—*Born in New York City.*

—50 Mary Lois,⁷ b. Jan. 5, 1825; d. June 30, 1829.
—51 James Wilson,⁷ b. 1829; d. 1876.
—52 Frances Jane,⁷ b. Aug. 4, 1834: m. **Jerome Walker**; d. 1874.
—53 Cornelia G.,⁷ b. Sept. 22, 1841; m. **Henry J. Campbell** of New York.
—54 Robert Macy,⁷ b. Feb. 13, 1844; graduate of Bryant & Stratton's Business College; granted certificate by the University of State of New York to practice as Public Accountant; member of the Religious Society of Friends; member of the N. Y. S. Society of Public Accountants; the American Institute, the People's Choral Union of N. Y. City, and the New York State Society of Sons of the American Revolution. Res. New York City.

45. NATHANIEL MEAD STRATTON⁶ (*Latham,⁵ Benjamin,⁴ Caleb,³ William,² Caleb¹*) was born Feb. 20, 1807. He was a foundryman in New York City. With his brother, Robert Macy Stratton, he was long connected with the Novelty Iron Works. As foreman of the factory he was greatly loved by the 200 or 300 men working under him. Kind hearted and generous, he was always looking out for their welfare, caring for them in sickness, and visiting them in their trouble. Hence they were strongly attached to him, responding promptly and cheerfully to any order from him. When some piece of work was a "hurry job," he had but to give the word and the men responded quickly, doing their very best for him. He was a birth-right Friend, but in early manhood, being very fond of music, he learned to play the flute, which was against the principles of the Friends' meetings. He was waited upon by a committee and given his choice of giving up the flute or being "read out of meeting." He chose the latter. Later he became an Episcopalian, and was a Vestryman for twenty-one consecutive years in All Saints Church on Henry Street, New York. He married **Mary Oatman** in Troy, Oct. 6, 1830. She was a daughter of *Daniel* and *Parmelia Oat-*

1851 to 1855 a member of the Chamber of Commerce. Like his father, he was for years a volunteer fireman of the New York Fire Department, resigning from Eagle Engine Co. No. 13 in 1837 because disabled for fire duty.

man. She was born in Arlington, Vt., Feb. 19, 1811, and died May 30, 1862. He died in New York City Nov. 17, 1860.*

Children:—B*orn in Troy, N. Y.*

—55   Mary Esther,[7] b. July 19, 1831; d., unm., June 9, 1849.
—56   Phœbe Jane,[7] b. Oct. 6, 1834; d. Sept. 6, 1912.
—57   Robert J.,[7] b. Mar. 25, 1836; d. in childhood.

B*orn in New York City.*

+58   Alfred Henry,[7] b. 1839.
—59   Amelia Anna,[7] b. Apr. 13, 1845; d. in childhood.
—60   Hannah Juliet,[7] b. Sept. 26, 1847; m. T. C. Buckmaster, Newburg, N. Y.

47. ALEXANDER MOORES STRATTON [6] (*Latham,*[5] *Benjamin,*[4] *Caleb,*[3] *William,*[2] *Caleb* [1]) was born Jan. 30, 1813, in New York City. Five years later his father moved to Troy, where as a boy Alexander worked in the "Stratton Foundry," early learning the trade of his father and elder brother. As a young man he was connected for several years with the Novelty Iron Works, in New York City, as Superintendent. For about five years prior to his death he was purser on the Collins Line Steamer *Pacific*, running between New York and Liverpool. He resigned this position just before the *Pacific* made its last voyage. The steamer was lost and all on board. He married, Oct. 23, 1833, **Angeline M. Prescott**, daughter of *Charles B.* and *Henrietta (Blekkingh) Prescott*, of Troy. She was born in Troy, Feb. 21, 1818, and died in Morrisania, Mar. 31, 1861. Her mother was a native of Amsterdam, Holland. Alexander M. Stratton was a consistent member of the Friends' Society all his life. He died in his home in Morrisania Dec. 15, 1854, aged only 41 years.

Children:—B*orn in Troy, N. Y.*

—61   Henrietta M.,[7] b. Oct. 11, 1834; d. Oct. 30, 1856.
—62   Jane Eliza,[7] b. Apr. 16, 1839; d. Oct. 10, 1873.
—63   Mary Lois,[7] b. Feb. 4, 1837; m. **William Adams**, 1855, born in Poughkeepsie, N. Y.

---

*"At the breaking out of the California gold fever in 1849 several of the men left the foundry to try their fortunes in the gold fields. They remembered their kind employer by sending several beautiful nuggets of gold; one with the wish that he might have a ring made from it and wear in remembrance of them. When he left the foundry in 1859 the men presented him with a gold watch and chain, with an appropriate inscription, as a tribute of their esteem. I am wearing the ring and watch to-day." *A. H. Stratton.*

—64   Angeline Prescott,[7] b. Aug. 4, 1841; d. aged 10 years.
     Born in Morrisania, N. Y.
+65   Prescott Blekkingh,[7] b. March 13, 1851.

51. JAMES WILSON STRATTON [7] (*Robert M.,*[6] *Latham,*[5] *Benjamin,*[4] *Caleb,*[3] *William,*[2] *Caleb* [1]) was born July 25, 1829, and married **Josephine A. Trotter**, of Brooklyn, May 13, 1851. He was confidential clerk in the Novelty Iron Works and later became a partner in the firm of William Wright & Co., Newburg, N. Y., builders of steam engines. He was a member of the Reformed Episcopal Church, and a member of the American Institute. He died at his home in Newburg Mar. 17, 1876. Five years after his death his family moved to Riverside, California, where their pleasant, hospitable home was known as "The Anchorage."

Children:—*Born in New York City.*
—66   Charles Harrison,[8] d. Nov. 22, 1856.
—67   Frances,[8] b. Dec. 15, 1858; d. at Riverside.
—68   Josephine,[8] d. Feb. 2, 1883, at Riverside.
—69   Emily Baily,[8] d. Mar. 1, 1877, at Newburg.
—70   Marie Louise,[8] m. **Gerald Wm. Barton**, June 8, 1891; d. Mar. 23, 1892.
     Born in Newburg, N. Y.
+71   George Draper,[8] b. 1870; d. 1905.
—72   Wilson Eugene,[8] b. 1862; d. aged 2 years.
—73   Cornelia Gilbert,[8] d. in infancy.
—74   Robert M.,[8] d. Dec. 22, 1866.

38. ALFRED HENRY [7] (*Nathaniel M.,*[6] *Lathem,*[5] *Benjamin,*[4] *Caleb,*[3] *Wm.,*[2] *Caleb* [1]) was born Nov. 25, 1839. He was educated at Trinity School, New York City, which is under the control of old Trinity Church. He studied architecture but did not follow that profession. He has been connected with the Custom House, New York, for over 50 years. He is a member of the Empire State Society of Sons of the American Revolution. His home is in Little Falls, N. J. He married first **Elizabeth Henrietta Pearson**, Sept. 2, 1867, who died in Arlington, Aug. 20, 1889, leaving two children. She was a daughter of *Sidney* and *Sarah Pearson.* Sept. 7, 1892, he married **Julia A. Noyes**. She died Nov. 15, 1896.

Children:—*Born in Brooklyn.*
—75   Sidney Pearson.[8]
—76   Lillian.[8]

65. PRESCOTT BLEKKINGH STRATTON [7] (*Alexander M.*,[6] *Latham*,[5] *Benjamin*,[4] *Caleb*,[3] *William*,[2] *Caleb* [1]) lives in Milwaukee, Wis. At the age of 18 he went from Morrisania, N. Y., to Walworth Co., Wis., where he worked on a farm for five years. In 1878 he became connected with the Chicago, Milwaukee & St. Paul R. R., with office in Milwaukee. In 1904 he entered the grain, flour and feed business in Milwaukee and is now of the firm of "Donehue and Stratton." Oct. 7, 1877, he married **Martha Elizabeth Lull.** His home is in West Alles, a suburb of Milwaukee.

Children:—*Born in Troy Center, Wis.*
+77 Harold Mead.[8]
—78 Genevieve.[8]
+79 Frederick Alexander.[8]

71. GEORGE DRAPER STRATTON [8] (*James W.*,[7] *Robert M.*,[6] *Latham*,[5] *Benjamin*,[4] *Caleb*,[3] *William*,[2] *Caleb* [1]) was born in Newburg, N. Y., June 5, 1870, and died in Oakland, California, Oct. 21, 1905. He married, Jan. 17, 1899, **Jeannie Gift,** youngest daughter of *Capt. George W.* and *Ellen Gift.* She was born in Memphis, Tenn.

Child:—*Born in Oakland, California.*
—80 Marian Trotter.[9]

77. HAROLD M. STRATTON [8] (*Prescott B.*,[7] *Alexander M.*,[6] *Latham*,[5] *Benjamin*,[4] *Caleb*,[3] *William*,[2] *Caleb* [1]), after finishing school at the Milwaukee Business College, entered the grain business in 1893. He is now a partner in the firm of "Donehue and Stratton," receivers and shippers of grain, flour and feed in Milwaukee. Oct. 20, 1903, he married **Bessie Adele Frantz.**

Children:—*Born in Milwaukee, Wis.*
—81 John Frantz.[9]
—81a Elizabeth Mary.[9]
—81b Frederick Frantz.[9]

79. FREDERICK ALEXANDER STRATTON [8] (*Prescott B.*,[7] *Alexander M.*,[6] *Latham*,[5] *Benjamin*,[4] *Caleb*,[3] *William*,[2] *Caleb* [1]) graduated from the Wisconsin College of Physicians and Surgeons in Milwaukee in 1903, and became connected with the "National Home of Disabled Volunteers," in Milwaukee, as Assistant Surgeon. In 1906 he opened an office in Milwaukee and is now a practicing physician in that city. Oct. 30, 1907, he married

Marie Louise Berthelet, daughter of *Joseph R.* and *Louise Berthelet.* She died June 10, 1914. He married second **Fannie Berthelet**, Aug. 15, 1915.

Children:—*Born in Milwaukee.*

By first marriage.

—82 Jane Elizabeth Louise.⁹

—82a Susan Mary.⁹

[83.] SETH STRATTON ⁵ (———,⁴ *Caleb,*³ *William,*² *Caleb* ¹) was born in Nantucket, Feb. 11, 1772. He was a grandson of Caleb Stratton ³ (*William,*² *Caleb* ¹). He left his native island while a youth and went to New York state. July 24, 1794, he married **Rebecca Gardner**, at Hudson, N. Y. She also was a native of Nantucket, born April 19, 1778.* They were Quakers and lived and died in that faith. For about twelve years after their marriage they lived in Hudson, and then moved to Oxford, N. Y., where he bought a farm. Rebecca died Feb. 1, 1832, and Seth married **Betsey Suley**, Feb. 24, 1833, who survived him. He died in May, 1856. A tombstone stands to his memory in the burial ground at Oxford.

Children:—*Born in Hudson, N. Y.*

By first marriage.

—84 William H.,⁶ b. Aug. 13, 1795; m. Jan. 1, 1817, **Eliza Jacobs**.

—85 Phœbe A.,⁶ b. July 17, 1798; m. **Thomas Jacobs** of Oxford Oct. 6, 1817; d. Feb. 1883.

—86 Frederick G.,⁶ b. June 16, 1800.

—87 Edward,⁶ b. Apr. 25, 1802; d. Oct. 4, 1803.

—88 Eliza A.,⁶ b. May 9, 1804; m. Nov. 20, 1825, **Thomas C. Healy**, who was born at Hudson, Dec. 26, 1794.

Born in Oxford, N. Y.

—89 Edward W.,⁶ b. May 18, 1807.

+90 Gardner,⁶ b. 1808, d. 1900.

—91 George M.,⁶ b. Dec. 3, 1812; d. May 18, 1834; unm.

—92 Sally M.,⁶ b. Feb. 3, 1814; d. unm.

—93 Charles A.,⁶ b. July 9, 1816; married and lived near

---

* These dates are from the old family Bible of Seth Stratton, which is now in possession of one of his descendants. The compiler has found no clew as to which of the sons of Caleb Stratton was the father of Seth. Rebecca was probably the daughter of Capt. Elisha, and Ruth Gardner, who moved to Oxford from Hudson, where he died Feb. 18, 1825, aged 80 years. There is a tombstone at his grave in Oxford.

Rev. William Obediah Stratton
Page 187.

Buffalo; was a sailor on the lakes. He is said to have left a family. Where are they?

—94 Mary A., [6] b. Feb. 7, 1820.

—95 Lydia M., [6] b. May, 1826; d. Oct. 3, 1827.

By second marriage.

—96 James O., [6] b. Dec. 4, 1833; was a cabinet maker at Coventry, N. Y.; d. Feb. 9, 1865. Left no descendants.

90. GARDNER STRATTON [6] (*Seth*, [5] ———, [4] *Caleb*, [3] *William*, [2] *Caleb* [1]) was born in Oxford, Chanango Co., N. Y., Feb. 3, 1809. He learned the hatters trade, and had a shop in Oxford and later in Addison, N. Y. Lived for a while at Bath, N. Y. Oct. 3, 1832, he married Clarissa Bemis, from Connecticut. He had become acquainted with her while she was on a visit to Oxford, and they were married at the home of her parents, *Amariah* and *Sally (Shumway) Bemis*, of Stratford, Conn. In 1849 they moved to Wantoma, Wisconsin, a new town, of which he became the first Town Clerk. He bought a tract of land there and spent the rest of his life as a farmer. He was a Universalist. Of him a granddaughter writes: "He was a strong advocate of temperance, a total abstainer, never used tobacco in any form, was very dignified and though rather peculiar in his ways was greatly respected." Both Mr. and Mrs. Stratton lived to be over 90 years of age, retaining to a remarkable degree the full possession of memory, intellect, and physical powers to the end of their long lives.

Children:—*Born in Oxford, N. Y.*

—97 Helen, [7] b. Mar. 5, 1834; m. Denison Hoxie, Aug. 1, 1855.

—98 Agnes, [7] b. June 14, 1836; m. Edward Smith, Jan. 1, 1856.

—99 Mary, [7] b. Feb. 1, 1839; m. Pheneas Weeks, Nov. 5, 1856.

Born in Addison N. Y.

+100 George O., b. 1841.

—101 Ida, b. May 11, 1848; m. Fred Berray, Nov. 5, 1868.

+102 Albert Amariah, b. 1849.

Born in Wantoma, Wis.

+103 Gardner.

100. GEORGE O. STRATTON [7] (*Gardner*, [6] *Seth*, [5] ———, [4] *Caleb*, [3] *William*, [2] *Caleb* [1]) was born in Addison, N. Y., Feb. 12, 1841,

and died in the army at Vicksburg, Va., Nov. 18, 1864. In Feb., 1864, he married **Ann Eagan.**

Child:

—104 George I.,[8] res., Duluth, Minn. He has a son Clarence.[9]

102. ALBERT AMARIAH STRATTON [7] (*Gardner*,[6] *Seth*,[5] ——,[4] *Caleb*,[3] *William*,[2] *Caleb* [1]) was born Nov. 18, 1849, in Addison, N. Y. As a youth he learned the blacksmith's trade. June 26, 1872, he married **Florence Wright**, daughter of *James Wright*. He died in Plainfield, Wis., Dec. 4, 1904.

Children:—*Born in Wantoma, Wis.*

+105 Otis James.[8]
—106 Archie Ransom,[8] d., unm., July 30, 1898.
—107 Ruby,[8] res. Wantoma, Wis.
—108 Claude L.,[8] b. in Richford, Wis.

103. GARDNER STRATTON [7] (*Gardner*,[6] *Seth*,[5] ——,[4] *Caleb*,[3] *William*,[2] *Caleb* [1]) is a farmer and lives in his native town, Wantoma, Wis. Apr. 21, 1875, he married **Ida Porter** of Berlin, Wis.

Children:—*Born in Wantoma, Wis.*

—109 Allie P.,[8] m. **Eliza Davis**, Oct. 2, 1900; a farmer at Wantoma; has two daughters, Leona Maude,[9] Ida Alline.[9]
—110 Clara M.,[8] m. **Clyde H. Gustin** Feb. 22, 1896.
—111 Murrell E.,[8] m. **Frank W. Darling**, Oct. 18, 1898.
—112 Maud E.,[8] m. **Annon J. Holt** June 3, 1903; d., Wantoma, Aug. 7, 1903.
—113 Henry B.,[8] deceased.
—114 George O.,[8] m. **Frances Walker** Nov. 10, 1911; res. Wantoma; one child, Margaret.[9]
—115 Ella L.,[8] m. **Roy Austin** Nov. 28, 1910; res. Stevens Point, Wis.
—116 Anna,[8] d. 1891.
—117 Lucele E.[8]
—118 Charles P.[8]

105. OTIS JAMES STRATTON [8] (*Albert A.*,[7] *Gardner*,[6] *Seth*,[5] ——,[4] *Caleb*,[3] *William*,[2] *Caleb* [1]) was born in Wantoma, Wis., and married **Florence Cronkite** Sept. 30, 1869, daughter of *Riley* and *Alice Cronkite*. He is an engraver; res. Grand Rapids, Wis.

Children:

—119 Neva Irene.[9]
—120 Rollis Archie.[9]

106. CLAUDE L. STRATTON [8] (*Albert A.,*[7] *Gardner,*[6] *Seth,*[5] ———,[4] *Caleb,*[3] *William,*[2] *Caleb* [1]) married **Anna Lamb** June 8, 1897. He is a carpenter and lives in Wilsonville, Neb.
Children:
—121 Robert LeRoy.[9]
—122 Lillian Lorenda.[9]

[123.] WILLIAM STRATTON [5] (———,[4] *Caleb,*[3] *William,*[2] *Caleb* [1]) was a Quaker sea captain who traded between the United States and the West Indies. According to the town records of Baltimore, Md., he married in that city, Feb. 21, 1796, **Mary Ann Howard**. The *Baltimore Directories* show that from 1796 to 1801 he was living at No. 34 Wolf street, Fells Point, Baltimore, where he was styled a "Ship Master." He died on board his vessel at sea in 1802-3, leaving his wife and "only son" in Baltimore. Some time after his death his widow married a *Mr. Wilson*, who died early and left her with two little daughters. She did not remain long in Baltimore but went with her three children to Hudson, N. Y., where, it will be remembered, several Nantucket Strattons had settled. In 1838 she was with her son in Canfield, Ohio. She died in New York about 1852.*
Child:—*Born in Baltimore.*
+124 William Obediah,[6] b. Nov. 19, 1798.

124. WILLIAM OBEDIAH STRATTON [6] (*William,*[5] ———,[4] *Caleb,*[3] *William,*[2] *Caleb* [1]) was born in Baltimore but passed his youth in New York state and became a Presbyterian minister. He received his theological training at Princeton, and at the age of twenty-six was licensed to preach by the Presbytery of New York. Aug. 23, 1828, he was called to Canfield, Ohio, and in October of the same year, was ordained and installed as pastor of the Presbyterian church there. In 1844 he moved to Deerfield, Ohio, and was pastor of the church there for twenty years, when he retired from active service after forty years of arduous, faith-

---

* That William Stratton, the Quaker sea-captain, was of the Nantucket line there can be no doubt. Undoubtedly he was a grandson of Caleb Stratton[3]. Although *actual proof* of this has not been found, the compiler assumes this to have been his ancestry.
It is now known that James Latham Stratton (Vol I, p. 233, footnote) was William's nephew. Robert Stratton, who died in Baltimore in 1836, was probably another nephew—or possibly a younger brother.
Was this the Robert Stratton of Baltimore who left five children, Charlotte m. a Mr. Moore, Mary Ann, Robert, Jr., Thomas and Edward? What became of these three sons?

ful duties as a pastor, during which time he had preached nearly 5,000 times. In 1866 he moved to Warren, Ohio. Though he retired from active service, he continued to preach occasionally to within a few weeks of his death, which occurred at Warren, Jan. 27, 1884. He was a splendid example of a "self-educated man." His father died when he was only four years old and, as the son of a widow (left a widow a second time when he was still a boy), he had his own way to make in the world, helping at the same time to support his mother. He early evinced a love of study and determined to get an education. He succeeded so well, mainly through his own efforts, that for years he was considered the best linguist in the Presbytery with which he was connected. He was a profound Latin, Greek and Hebrew scholar, an indefatigable student. He studied French after he was sixty years old and read books in that language with ease and pleasure. He considered himself deficient in mathematics, of which he was not fond, but continued his study in this branch of learning to his last illness. His last work, the solving of some difficult problems in geometry, was found in his room after his death, having been performed Wednesday evening, and he passed away Sunday evening. His death came as the result of a cold contracted during a long sleigh ride to the home of a former parishioner. In Canfield, in 1832, he married **Anna M. Whittlesey,** daughter of *Hon. Elisha Whittlesey,* associated with so many public affairs, and Comptroller of the U. S. Treasury from 1849 to his death in 1860.

Mr. and Mrs. Stratton celebrated their golden wedding in Warren in 1882. She was born Nov. 7, 1812, and died Aug. 13, 1897.

Children:—*Born in Canfield, O.*
+125 Howard Whittlesey,[7] b. 1833; d. 1895.
—126 Lucy Jane,[7] b. Apr. 19, 1835; m. **Elisha Whittlesey Collins** in 1857; res. Chicago.
+127 Henry Grenville,[7] b. 1837.
—128 Mary Amelia,[7] b. Mar. 11, 1840; m. **Homer C. Reid;** res. Warren, O.
—129 Harriet,[7] b. Dec., 1843; d. young.
Born in Deerfield, O.
—130 Alice Virginia,[7] b. Jan. 9, 1848; m. **George M. Hall** of Spokane, Wash.
—131 Julia M.,[7] b. Feb. 10, 1855; m. **George Harrison Brescoe,** of Cleveland, O.

125. HOWARD WHITTLESEY STRATTON [7] (*William O.*,[6] *William*,[5] ———,[4] *Caleb*,[3] *William*,[2] *Caleb* [1]) was born in Canfield, O., and like his father became a Presbyterian minister. He held pastorates in North Benton, Huntsburg and Cadiz, O.; in Kansas and in Seattle and Spokane, Wash., and for several years was Synodical Missionary in Oregon. He moved from Ohio to Kansas in 1870, and from Kansas to Oregon in 1875. At Spokane he secured property from the government which is now known as the "Stratton Addition." In Pittsburg, Pa., June 20, 1854, he married **Mary White**, daughter of *Thomas* and *Mary* (*Shaw*) *White*. He died in Spokane Aug. 23, 1895.

Children:—*Born in North Benton, O.*
—132 Anna Whittlesey,[8] m. **J. J. Brown**, June 16, 1874.
+133 Charles Henry.[8]
+134 Alfred Ritzel.[8]
+135 Howard Clarence.[8]

127. HENRY GRENVILLE STRATTON [7] (*William O.*,[6] *William*,[5] ———,[4] *Caleb*,[3] *William*,[2] *Caleb* [1]) was born Mar. 1, 1837, in Canfield, O. He was Lieutenant of the 19th Ohio Regiment at the beginning of the Civil War, and Colonel of the same regiment at the close of the war, having served the entire time. He was at the battles of Rich Mountain, Pittsburg Landing, Chickamauga, Missionary Ridge, campaign and capture of Atlanta and other noted engagements. He married **Susie McClain**, Oct. 14, 1868; res. Waitsburg, Washington.

Child:
—136 Florence.[8]

133. CHARLES HENRY STRATTON [8] (*Howard W.*,[7] *William O.*,[6] *William*,[5] ———,[4] *Caleb*,[3] *William*,[2] *Caleb* [1]) was born in North Benton, Ohio, and resides in Spokane, Wash. He married **Laura B. Jay**, Apr. 21, 1881.

Child:—*Born in Spokane.*
—137 Leah Evaline,[9] m. **Theron G. Posten**, of Berkeley, Cal.

134. ALFRED RITZEL STRATTON [8] (*Howard*,[7] *William O.*,[6] *William*,[5] ———,[4] *Caleb*,[3] *William*,[2] *Caleb* [1]) is a farmer living near Spokane, Wash. He married **Libbie Gould**, Sept. 26, 1886.
—138 Ethel May,[9] twin,
—139 Elma May,[9] twin.

—140   Howard Browne.[9]
—141   Roland.[9]

135.   HOWARD CLARENCE STRATTON [8] (*Howard W.*,[7] *William O.*,[6] *William*,[5] ——,[4] *Caleb*,[3] *William*,[2] *Caleb* [1]) was born in Cadiz, O., and moved with his parents to Kansas when he was about eight years old, and five years later to Portland, Oregon. At sixteen he began earning his own living, first in a printing office, then in the railroad service, until the completion of the Northern and Union Pacific railroads. Then he resigned to accept a position in a Portland bank, of which he was elected Cashier at the age of twenty-three. In 1900 he moved to San Francisco and has ever since been identified with the business interests of that city. Apr. 12, 1882, he married Cora Alice Cox, daughter of *Leander M.* and *Annie Olivia Cox,* who was born in Sheldon, N. Y.

Children:—*Born in Portland, Oregon.*
—142   Vivian,[9] m. George Fiske Charleston, of Portland.
—143   Clarence Melville.[9]

1. *Thomas Stratton* — Born 1670

2. *James Stratton* — 1729

3. *Zebulun Stratton* — 1753

4. *James Stratton* — 1786

5. *Lorenzo Stratton* — 1816

6. *Stephen Stratton* — 1743

7. *Peleg Stratton* — 1748

8. *A. E Stratton* — 1798

9. *Latham Stratton* — 1775

REFERENCES

1. Page 191. 2. Page 192, Vol. I. 3. Page 192. 4. Pages 194, 204. 5. Page 219. 6. Page 194, Vol. I. 7. Page 195, Vol. I. 8. Page 199. 9. Page 178.

JOHN STRATTON OF WATERTOWN

(*Chart H, Vol. I*)

"*Honor thy father and thy mother.*" EXODUS xx, 12.

RECENT research has brought to light, from the Cambridge court files, two papers which will be of much interest to all descendants of Thomas Stratton [2] (*John* [1]) of Watertown and Waltham (see *Vol. I*, p. 185). The first of these is dated Charlestown, Apr. 15, 1690, and reads as follows:

"To the Hon County Court
sitting in Camb.

We whose names are underwritten Listed in the service of the country against the French, being ordered down to Charlestown by our Commander Capt. Nathaniel Wade do testify, that being denyed Quarters elsewhere in said Town this last night, the Widow Mary Peachie did readily Entertain us with very good usage, and with great care that no disorders might be committed.

We therefore Humbly pray that the Hon Court will please to grant her Liberty to renew her License for the year ensuing, & that you will confirm the same to her, wherein you will greatly oblige,

Yo's & the countryes Humble Servts."

To this is attached the signatures of twenty men of the Company, and among them is that of Thomas Stratton.*

---

* The other signatures to this petition are Nathaniel Barsham, Lieut. William Devenport, Sergeant Samuel Barnard, Corporal Richard Mellins, John Applin, John Fish, Peter Munsell, John Smith, John Stratin (Stratton?), Henry Spring, John Fay, Thomas Wilson, Nathaniel Wood, Solomon Roy, Corp. Stevens, John Frary, Josiah Jones, Joseph Garfield, James Ball,—and all are autographs, some in old "court hand," and some "chancery script," and some in plain "running hand." The petition itself is written in the beautiful "copper plate" penmanship of Capt. Lawrence Hammond, Recorder at Charlestown.

The widow Peachie was Mary Robinson when she married Thomas

The second paper, dated Sept. 28, 1738, is as follows:

"Thomas Stratton of Waltham, Husbandman, for divers good causes me moving and £3 sold to my son James at a place called Pequoid all rights the General Court may grant for the expedition of 1690, I being a soldier in the aforesaid expedition in a company that was under Major Waldo's command."*

Here is satisfying proof of the colonial war service of Thomas Stratton.[2] It will be remembered that James Stratton,[3] son of Thomas,[2] settled in Pequoid (later Athol) in 1736, on one of the sixty lots granted the proprietors (*Vol. I*, p. 189).

As no record of the death of Thomas, or his wife Dorcas, is found in Watertown (or Waltham) it is quite probable that they followed their elder son James to Athol and died there. The records of the first fifteen years of that town were destroyed by fire.

FIFTH GENERATION

42. ZEBULON STRATTON [5] (*James*,[4] *James*,[3] *Thomas*,[2] *John* [1]) was born May 15, 1753, in Athol, Mass. In boyhood he received only the education afforded by a few winter terms in the district school, served an apprenticeship to a shoemaker, and at the age of nineteen entered the boot and shoe business.

His youth was spent in those stirring days just before the Revolution, and he lacked none of the patriotic spirit which actuated so many young men of his native town. On the morning of April 19, 1775, with other "minute men," he responded to the call of his country and marched to Lexington in Col. Doolittle's Reg't, serving five days. At the end of this service he enlisted in the company just organized by Capt. Ichabod Dexter in Col. Woodbridge's Regt., and served three months and fourteen days. Aug. 21, 1777, he again enlisted, this time in Capt. Thomas Lord's

---

Peachie of Charleston in 1665. He died in 1683. His widow kept a house of entertainment from the year of his death until she died, ten months after this petition was signed.

*This was the expedition against Canada from which so many never returned. Two of the transports carrying soldiers back from Quebec were lost, many men were killed and many more died of wounds. The general court passed an order that the wives and heirs might draw the pay due these soldiers without administration of their estates. Thus many of the estates fail to show in the probate court files, and doubtless many "disappearances" about this time are due to this expedition and the above order.

Company, Col. Nathan Sparhawk's Regt., and in five days' march reached Bennington, 96 miles away. In 1778 he served in Capt. Josiah Wilder's Co. at Rutland Barracks under command of Maj. Daniel Clapp.

Jan. 9, 1780, he married in Winchenden, **Jerusha Bradish**, daughter of *Jonas* and *Jerusha* (*Morton*) B*radish*. She was born July 20, 1759.* Their home on "The Street," in Athol was a part of the original Stratton Grant. Here they lived for nearly thirty years.

In 1815, Mr. Stratton visited his son in Western New York, making the trip alone on horseback, part of the way along an Indian trail, and covering the distance of more than three hundred miles in seven days. Returning to Athol, he disposed of his farm and business there, and with his wife and daughter Meribah moved to Concord, N. Y., where they lived for six years. The remainder of their lives was spent in the home of their son James in Little Valley, N. Y. Here Mrs. Stratton died Dec. 27, 1840. Her husband survived her nearly two years, dying Aug. 18, 1842. Both are buried in the Annis graveyard, where stones stand to their memory.

Mr. Stratton was a man a little below medium height, with a noticeably high, broad forehead and pleasant blue eyes. He possessed a genial, cheerful disposition, which he retained to the end of his long life of 89 years. In later life he spent much time reading. Among his favorite books were those of a religious nature, and he was a diligent Bible student, his well thumbed Bible being yet in the hands of his descendants.

Mrs. Stratton was a woman of strong convictions, of more than ordinary intelligence and strength of character.† Their home

---

* Jonas Bradish, born in Marlboro Aug. 7, 1724, was son of James and Damaris (Rice) Bradish, grandson of Joseph and Mary Bradish, who were in Cambridge as early as 1631. Jerusha Morton was a daughter of Samuel and Lydia Morton (see Vol. I, p, 192).

† A granddaughter who remembered her at the time of her removal from Concord in her sixty-fourth year describes her as she rode to her new home on horseback, as a "stately erect lady in a scarlet riding habit." The story is told of how, when a young woman of but eighteen years, the news having reached her that her brother had been wounded at Lexington, she went alone on horseback from New Salem, riding thirty-six hours with only four hours' rest. Arriving at Lexington, she was told that her brother was in the hospital, to which she would not be admitted since "it was no place for a woman." After several hours of argument, going from one official to another, she finally gained admission, procured medical aid for her brother, who was supposed to be fatally wounded, and after

was ever a favorite stopping place for pioneer ministers, who always found a warm welcome, and who were fond of drawing the old gentleman into a discussion (in which his wife usually joined), often receiving help from his original thoughts on the religious questions of the day.

Children:—*Born in Athol, Mass.*
- — 97 Meribah,[6] b. July 20, 1781; d. unm. in Little Valley Center, N. Y., in 1845, at the home of her brother James.
- — 98 Achsah,[6] b. Jan. 7, 1785; m. **Nehemiah Fay**, in Athol; moved to Concord, N. Y., about 1814; d. in Great Valley in 1872.
- + 99 James,[6] b. Aug. 5, 1786; d. 1874.
- —100 Zebulon,[6] d. in childhood.
- —101 Jerusha,[6] d. in childhood.*

44. Thomas Stratton[5] (*James,*[4] *James,*[3] *Thomas,*[2] *John*[1]) was born Oct. 3, 1758, and married **Thankful Rich**, Aug. 5, 1784. He was town clerk from 1788 to 1797; selectman, 1792-96, and town treasurer in 1797 and '98. His carefully kept records and fine penmanship are shown by the old town records of Athol. About 1812 he sold his possessions in Athol and moved to Fitzwilliam, N. H., where the records show that on Oct. 16, 1818, he was killed by the falling of a tree.

Child:—*Born in Athol, Mass.*
102 Austice,[6] b. Dec. 14, 1784; m. **Levi Tower**.

47. James Stratton[5] (*William,*[4] *James,*[3] *Thomas,*[2] *John*[1]) was born Dec. 11, 1780; married **Susannah Ward** in 1827, and lived in Athol, where he died Aug. 25, 1851.

Child:—*Born in Athol.*
203 Sarah W.[6]

---

several weeks of nursing brought him home with her. Later he married and has descendants living in New York State.

*These two children died of scarlet fever. On stones in the old cemetery at Athol are these peculiar inscriptions, showing the curious use of titles at that particular period:

In memory of	In memory of
Mr. Zebulon Stratton, son of Mr. Zebulon and Mrs. Jerusha Stratton, who died June 13, 1775, aged 7 yrs. and 2 mo's.	Miss Jerusha Stratton, daughter of Mr. Zebulon and Mrs. Jerusha Stratton, who died June 19, 1795, aged 1 yr. and 9 mo's.

JAMES AND ELIZABETH (WHEELER) STRATTON
Page 204.

A PICTURESQUE GLIMPSE OF ATHOL
Pages 192-193.

49. ASA STRATTON [5] (*William*,[4] *James*,[3] *Thomas*,[2] *John*[1]), born Nov. 25, 1785; married **Susannah Giles** in 1807, and died in Athol July 15, 1835. His will, dated May 26, 1835, is recorded in Worcester. His widow died Oct. 12, 1842, aged 56 years.

Children:—*Born in Athol, Mass.*
- —104 Lemira D.,[6] b. 1807; m. **Prescott Giles** in 1829; d. 1844.
- —105 William M.,[6] b. 1809; d. 1876.
- —106 Asa A.,[6] b. 1811.
- —107 Susan G.,[6] b. 1815; m. —— Larabee.
- —108 Nancy,[6] b. 1817; m. **George Ward**; d. 1852.

56. NATHANIEL STRATTON [5] (*Stephen*,[4] *James*,[3] *Thomas*,[2] *John*[1]) was born in Athol Jan. 30, 1770. He married **Esther Richardson**, daughter of *Samuel Richardson*, at Brookfield Apr. 8, 1792. About 1805 he settled in Northfield. After his death, which occurred before 1831, his widow married Asa Robins.

Children:—*Born in Athol, Mass.**
- +109 Harvey,[6] b. 1793.
- +110 Warren,[6] b. 1800; d. 1883.
- +111 Willard,[6] d. 1867.

Born in Northfield, Mass.
- —112 Stephen,[6] b. Aug. 30, 1805.
- —113 Melinda,[6] b. Feb. 9, 1807; d. Nov. 6, 1828.
- —114 Norris,[6] b. 1810, d. 1876; m. **Nancy B. Piper**; lived in Northfield and Leydou; ch. Estella Hope; d. aged 8 yrs.

57. LEVI STRATTON [5] (*Stephen*,[4] *James*,[3] *Thomas*,[2] *John*[1]), born May 12, 1772; married **Lois Hunphry** in Apr., 1795, and lived and died in his native town where a stone stands to his memory in the old cemetery, near the graves of his father and mother. He died Apr. 7, 1821.

Children:—*Born in Athol, Mass.*
- —115 Lydia,[6] b. 1796.

---

*There may have been other children in this family. An aged granddaughter of Nathaniel Stratton remembers an "Uncle Nathan" and an "Aunt Tammason," whom she thinks were her grandfather Stratton's children. She believes that Nathaniel's Bible with family records is in possession of some one of his grandchildren. The compiler has not been able to find it.

—116   Lucy,⁶ b. Nov. 12, 1801; m. **Enos Twitchell,** and lived in Buffalo, N. Y.
—117   Lavina,⁶ b. Oct. 30, 1806; d. Nov. 21, 1814.
—118   Lois,⁶ b. Mar. 7, 1812; m. **Samuel Twitchell.**
—119   Levi,⁶ b. 1819.

59.   ABNER STRATTON⁵ (*Stephen,⁴ James,³ Thomas,² John¹*) was a farmer of Athol, Mass., where he was born May 3, 1776. He married **Abigail Stone,** Jan. 1, 1806, and died in his native town May 2, 1850.

Children:—*Born in Athol, Mass.*
—120   Mary Tufts,⁶ b. Sept. 3, 1807; m. **Sumner K. Morse,** his second wife; d. Mar. 2, 1880.
—121   Nancy,⁶ b. Aug. 16, 1810; m. **Sumner K. Morse;** d. Apr. 19, 1848.
—122   Abigail,⁶ b. May 9, 1814; m. **Asa Twitchell,** Nov. 24, 1842; m. 2nd, **Elias Bassett;** d. in New Salem Sept. 19, 1893.
+123   Amos T.,⁶ b. 1818; d. 1898.
+124   Abner Graves,⁶ b. 1820; d. 1882.

61.   EZRA STRATTON⁵ (*Stephen,⁴ James,³ Thomas,² John¹*) was born Apr. 26, 1781, married **Abigail** ——, and moved to Vermont some time in 1817.

Children:—*Born in Athol, Mass.*
—125   Melanda,⁶ b. Oct. 17, 1807.
—126   Aaron Smith,⁶ b. Mar. 25, 1809.
—127   Leander Graves,⁶ b. July 28, 1812.
—128   Stephen Austin,⁶ b. Jan. 22, 1815.
—129   Clarissa,⁶ b. Apr. 4, 1817.

Further knowledge of this family is desired. One of the sons is supposed to have settled in Albany.

63.   HARVEY STRATTON⁵ (*Stephen,⁴ James,³ Thomas,² John¹*) was born in Athol in 1784. He may have married **Olive Evans.** History of Northfield says he settled in that town. The compiler has found nothing to confirm this. His nephew, Harvey Stratton,⁶ son of Nathaniel,⁵ is known to have settled in Northfield (see No. 109). Further information is desired.

67.   ABEL STRATTON⁵ (*Peleg,⁴ James,³ Thomas,² John¹*) was born in Athol Apr. 16, 1775. Feb. 11, 1829, he married **Betsey Bachelor** and lived in Petersham, where he was a farmer and

where he died in 1829. He is buried in Athol in the cemetery on Pleasant Street. After his death his family lived in Athol where his widow died Feb. 24, 1857, aged 75 years.

Children:—*Born in Petersham, Mass.*
+130 Reuben,[6] b. 1802; d. 1876.
—131 Hannah,[6] b. Sept. 3, 1807; m. Charles Crawford of Petersham, Apr. 12, 1837.
+132 Abel,[6] b. 1808; d. 1844.
—133 Charles,[6] m. Hannah Harrington, in Grafton, Nov. 1, 1834; d. in Rutland, 1850; ch. Charles Harrington,[7] res. Three Rivers, Mass.
—134 Henry,[6] d. unm. in South Carolina.
—135 Laura,[6] m. George Like; lived and died in Wisconsin.

69. PELEG STRATTON[5] (*Peleg,*[4] *James,*[3] *Thomas,*[2] *John*[1]) was born in Athol Feb. 10, 1781. He married **Lois Batchelor**, Nov. 7, 1810. She was a daughter of *Stephen* and *Meribah Bachelor* of Royalston, was born Dec. 19, 1788, and died in Templeton, aged 55 years. Soon after his marriage he settled at Templeton where he bought a farm. Like his father he was noted among his neighbors for his readiness in repartee, his courageous cheerfulness under all circumstances, and his kind helpfulness to all with whom he came in contact. Hard work on his small rocky farm hardly sufficed to supply the needs of his growing family, and during the long cold winter months he made trips to Boston with sled loads of shingles cut from his woodland. Once when asked by a Boston friend of what crop his farm was most productive his laconic reply was "children." He was a member and regular attendant of the Methodist church. He died at the age of seventy-nine years.

Children:—*Born in Templeton, Mass.*
—136 Benjamin Franklin,[6] b. Jan. 17, 1812; d. Nov. 14, 1839.
—137 David Parks,[6] b. Mar., 1814; d. Sept., 1816.
—138 David Parks,[6] b. Feb., 1816; d. Nov., 1819.
—139 Thomas,[6] b. Sept. 15, 1818; d. unm. Aug. 25, 1848.
—140 Frederick Alonzo,[6] b. Sept. 1, 1821; d. in Templeton Sept. 2, 1898. Never married.
—141 Addison Dwight,[6] b. Jan. 30, 1823; d. Jan. 28, 1848; unm.
—142 Sarah Louisa,[6] b. Apr. 25, 1825; d. Dec. 9, 1835.
—143 Mary Elizabeth,[6] b. Aug. 7, 1827; m. **Joseph B. Garfield**; d. in Ashburnham, Mass., Mar. 8, 1908.

+144   James Batchelor,⁶ b. 1829; d. 1904.
−145   Philip Dodridge,⁶ b. Dec. 22, 1833; m. **Mrs. Joseph Wood.**

71. DAVID STRATTON ⁵ (*Peleg,*⁴ *James,*³ *Thomas,*² *John* ¹) was born June 20, 1786, in Athol. By trade he was a shoemaker. June 5, 1810, he married **Sarah Wadsword** of Grafton, and after her death, in 1824, he married **Rachel Dyke** of Athol. He lived in Grafton and Athol. He died in Grafton July 1, 1853, where a gravestone stands to his memory. "He was a consistent church member, eloquent in prayer, a lifelong Christian," writes a grandson. While another in writing of him says: "He was witty, fond of a joke, a lover of children, a genial companion, and a staunch friend. Like some other Strattons, a little bit odd, but a man of large heart and broad sympathies, and we all loved him."

Children:—*Born in Athol, Mass.*
  By first marriage.
−146   Sarah Maria,⁶ b. Mar. 25, 1811; m. **Otis Newton** of Westboro, Sept. 10, 1831.
+147   Jesse Kendall,⁶ b. 1813.
−148   Lucy Brooks,⁶ b. Feb. 17, 1815; m. **Seth Jones Axtell,** Nov. 18, 1832; d. in Grafton, aged 93 years.
+149   Cyrus Wadsworth,⁶ b. Aug., 1817.
+150   Asa Scott,⁶ b. 1818.
−151   Marietta,⁶ m. **Albert Bradish** of Grafton.
  By second marriage.
−152   George D.,⁶ b. July 6, 1826; d. in Worcester Dec. 6, 1852.
−153   Mary Young,⁶ m. **Thomas Axtell Leland.**
−154   Laura,⁶ d. unm. in Athol Mar. 30, 1855.
−155   Susan Elizabeth,⁶ m. —— **Sutton.**

72. JESSE STRATTON ⁵ (*Peleg,*⁴ *James,*³ *Thomas,*² *John* ¹) was born in Athol Jan. 1, 1789. He was educated in Cambridge and became a Presbyterian minister. In 1830 he went to Hillsboro, Ga., where three of his brothers were engaged in business. In 1839 he removed to Panola Co., Miss., where he had charge of several churches and was much beloved. He died just at the close of the Civil War. Late in life he married **Mrs. Mendenthall.** He left no children.

73. ANDREW STRATTON⁵ (*Peleg,⁴ James,³ Thomas,² John¹*), born in Athol, Mass., Nov. 15, 1791; married **Lois Kendall Ward** in 1817 and lived for ten years in Petersham, Mass., where he was a boot and shoe manufacturer. Here his wife died in 1827. The following year, leaving his three small children with his parents in Athol, he took a stock of boots and shoes to Hillsboro, Ga., where his brothers, James and Asa E., were already engaged in mercantile business. In 1838 he removed to Panola Co., Miss., but later returned to Georgia and died in Dalton in 1848.

Children:—*Born in Petersham, Mass.*
+156 Charles Lorenzo,⁶ b. 1818.
+157 James Evans,⁶ b. 1819.
−158 Elizabeth Kendall,⁶ b. 1821; m. **John E. Morse** in 1845, at the home of her uncle, A. E. Stratton, in Panola Co., Miss., by Rev. Jesse Stratton.
−159 Lois Ward,⁶ b. in 1827; d. in infancy, the same day as her mother's death.

75. ASA EVANS STRATTON⁵ (*Peleg,⁴ James,³ Thomas,² John¹*) was born in Athol, Mass., June 13, 1798. His early educational advantages were such as the common schools of his native town afforded. At the age of twenty-one he emigrated to Hillsboro, Jasper Co., Ga., where he resided for sixteen years as a merchant, dealing largely in boots and shoes.* In 1836 he removed to Panola Co., Miss., where he purchased large and valuable tracts of land, and was one of the early settlers of that section of the state.† For more than twenty years he was a prosperous planter, identified with the building up and improvement of North Mississippi. He was one of the originators of the Mississippi & Tennessee Railroad, and one of its first directors. In 1859 he moved to Texas, lived for one year in Bastrop Co., and then purchased a plantation in Brazoria Co., near Cedar Lake, where he was extensively engaged in the cultivation of sugar and cotton. A man of unconquerable energy, he often said he would rather wear out than rust out, and, although in his eightieth year, he still maintained his mental and physical activity to an unusual degree,

---

* His goods were shipped from Boston to Savannah and then hauled overland by team to Hillsboro, a distance of one hundred and fifty miles.

† He had then received a commission from the U. S. Government to furnish beef for the Indians who were being moved from the Southeastern States and settled in Indian Territory.

and up to within a few weeks of his death was actively engaged in the management of his plantation and general business affairs. In early life he made a profession of religion and became a member of the church. Although retaining to the last many of his strong New England characteristics, he became identified with the South, and gave to her, in prosperity and adversity, a uniform support. He was a Major in the Confederate army. Mr. Stratton was married four times, and was fortunate and happy in his marital relations, and fortunate in seeing the kindly and fraternal relations existing between the children of his four marriages.

In March, 1824, he married **Mary Graves Alexander** of Jasper Co., Ga. She died two years after their removal to Mississippi. Feb. 26, 1843, he married **Amanda Ann (Gibbons) Wood** of Marshall Co., Miss. She died June 9, 1847. He married, third, **Mrs. Caroline Ann (Steger) Pearson**, who died in 1854. In 1856 he married **Mary Jane Chisholm**, who died in Texas in 1872. Major Stratton died on Sabbath morning, July 22, 1877, at his home in Luling, Texas.

Children:—*Born in Jasper Co., Ga.*
  By first marriage.
—160 Dorcas Elizabeth,[6] b. 1824; d. 1826.
—161 Jane Alexander,[6] b. 1827; m. **Thomas J. Hill**, Mar. 25, 1846; lived in Bastrop Co., Texas, where they have children and grandchildren now living.
—162 Mary Elizabeth,[6] b. 1830; m. **James E. Stratton** (No. 157).
—163 George Henry,[6] b. 1833; d. unm. in 1861.
—164 James Marshall,[6] b. 1835; d. 1837.
  Born in Panola Co., Miss.
—165 Cassandra Victoria,[6] b. 1838; d. 1844.
  By second marriage.
+166 Asa Evans,[6] b. 1844.
—167 Sarah Emily,[6] b. 1847; m. **Samuel Irvin Bryan** in 1866; living in Brazoria Co., Texas.
  By third marriage.
+168 James Thomas,[6] b. 1849.
  By fourth marriage.
+169 Jesse David Tait,[6] b. 1857.
—170 Edward Everett,[6] b. 1858; d. 1858.
—171 George,[6] b. 1861; d. 1863.
  Born in Brazoria Co., Texas.

—172 Amanda Ann,⁶ b. 1863; m. **Dr. W. V. Ezell** of Angleton, Texas, in 1887.

81. ISAAC STRATTON ⁵ (*David,*⁴ *David,*³ *Thomas,*² *John* ¹) was born in Boston, Sept. 2, 1782. He became a minister in the Methodist Episcopal church, and held pastorates in several towns in his native state. Jan. 19, 1810, he married **Mary Goodale** in Marlboro.

Children:—*Born in Boston.*
+173 Nahum,⁶ b. 1811; d. 1901.
—174 Mary,⁶ b. 1812; m. **Lewis Harlow**.
—175 Isaac,⁶ b. 1814; d. in childhood.
—176 Dolly,⁶ b. 1817; d. unm.
+177 David,⁶ b. 1819; d. 1907.
—178 James,⁶ b. 1820; m. **Augusta** ——; moved to Berkley, Cal.; ch. Ida ⁷ m. a **Mr. Cody**.
—179 Lydia,⁶ b. 1822; d. in Springfield Mar. 31, 1848, unm.
—180 Lucy Thurston,⁶ b. 1824; m. **Robert Bloomer** in 1850; lived in Proctor, Vt.
—181 Henry Goodale,⁶ b. 1826; d. unm.

87. LEWIS STRATTON ⁵ (*Jonas,*⁴ *David,*³ *Thomas,*² *John* ¹) was born in Stow, Mass., Feb. 17, 1773. The eldest son of a large family, at the death of his father he was appointed guardian for several of his younger brothers and sisters. Sept. 23, 1797, he married **Sarah Hartshorne**, daughter of *James* and *Tabetha* (*Pratt*) *Hartshorne* of Amherst, N. H. After their marriage they lived in Waltham for a few years and then settled on a farm near the town of Milford.

Children:—*Born in Waltham, Mass.*
—182 Charles, b. Mar. 17, 1799; d. July 3, 1801.
Born in Milford, Mass.
—183 Sarah,⁶ b. July, 1802; d. Oct. 28, 1892; m. **Joseph Winn**, son of Joseph and Sarah (Boutwell) Winn, Nov. 9, 1824.
—184 Abigail,⁶ b. Sept. 11, 1804; m. **Horatio G. Brown** of Ipswick, Sept. 23, 1830; d. in Reading Feb. 10, 1895.
—185 Ann,⁶ b. Sept. 26, 1807; m. **Etson Damon**, son of David Damon of Reading, Oct. 26, 1829; d. Aug. 25, 1893.*

---

* Their daughter married Rev. George A. Stratton.

—186   Charles,⁶ b. 1809; d. 1854; m. **Lydia Ball,** Oct. 26, 1831; ch: Adelia A.,⁷ an artist in New York City, m. 1st, **Mr. Lawson;** 2nd, **Bentley T. Hassell.**
—187   Sophia,⁶ b. Jan. 30, 1812; d. Oct. 13, 1831.
—188   Mary E.,⁶ b. Dec. 24, 1815; d. Dec. 14, 1842; m. Jan. 7, 1836, **Henry M. Pratt,** son of David and Anna (Pratt) Pratt.

88. SEWELL STRATTON⁵ (*Jonas,*⁴ *David,*³ *Thomas,*² *John*¹) was born in Stow, Mass., Mar. 22, 1775, and received his education in the public schools of his native town, going to school winters and working on his father's farm during the summer. Feb. 5, 1800, he married **Velana Cutting,** daughter of *Nathan Cutting* of Royalston, Mass. She is remembered as a woman of strong individuality, with a high sense of Christian honor. She was the mother of eleven children, the youngest but ten years old when she was left a widow. She ever strove to instill into their young minds the principles of integrity and industry. A grandson who was often in her house in his boyhood days writes, "The things that I remember most distinctly about these visits are my grandmother's delicious cookies, and the motto which always hung upon her wall, 'Death before Dishonor.'"

After their marriage Mr. and Mrs. Stratton lived in Amherst, Milford and Royalston for about twenty years and then moved to Bedford where he died Jan. 29, 1830. Mrs. Stratton died Apr. 11, 1855, aged 77 years.

Children:—*Born in Amherst, N. H.**
—189   Maria,⁶ b. Dec. 22, 1800; m. **Nathaniel Manning;** d. May 8, 1873.
Born in Royalston, Mass.
+190   Jonas,⁶ b. 1802; d. 1867.
—191   Leonard,⁶ b. Aug. 31, 1804; m. **Mary Brown;** lived in Manchester and Goffstown, N. H. No children.
Born in Milford, N. H.
—192   Nathan W.,⁶ b. Sept. 22, 1806; m. late in life a widow with two children; d. in Charlestown, Mass., 1863. No issue.
—193   Lucy,⁶ b. Sept. 29, 1808; m. **Hugh M. Campbell.**

---

* Part of these births are recorded at Amherst, and part at Millford. They were probably all born in the same place, but the line between the two towns was changed about 1810. The dates of birth given here are taken from Sewell Stratton's old family Bible.

—194 Sewell,⁶ b. Dec. 1, 1810; m. **Belinda Farmer**; lived and died on his farm near Bedford; no children.
+195 Asa Bachelder,⁶ b. 1813; d. 1876.
—196 Sarah B.,⁶ b. Mar. 24, 1815; m. Sept. 17, 1842, David Monroe Howe; d. Mar. 30, 1820.
—197 Lydia Velana,⁶ b. Mar. 5, 1817; m. **George W. George**; d. Dec. 27, 1841.
—198 Rodney,⁶ b. Apr. 29, 1819; d. unm. Jan. 10, 1840.

Born in Bedford, N. H.

+199 Willard Parker,⁶ b. 1821; d. 1881.

90. JOHN STRATTON⁵ (*Jonas,⁴ David,³ Thomas,² John¹*) was born in Stow, Mass., July 12, 1782. In 1799 he was living in Amherst, N. H., and William Fisher was his guardian. Further data concerning him is desired.

93. JONAS STRATTON⁵ (*Jonas,⁴ David,³ Thomas,² John¹*) was born in Stow, Mass., Oct. 10, 1791. He was but six years old when his father died. As one of a large family of children, he was early forced to shift for himself. He lived for awhile with his older brother Lewis in Amherst, N. H., and here he learned the cabinet makers' trade. While still little more than a boy he emigrated to the "wilds of Ohio" where several of his Amherst neighbors had settled and named the little settlement Amherst, after their New Hampshire home. He worked at his trade and presently bought a farm and built a house. Mar. 31, 1822, he married **Lucy Smith**, and their hospitable home became the center of many happy recollections.

In this home they lived to a good old age. Mr. Stratton died Sept. 26, 1878. They were both members of the Congregationalist church.

Children:—*Born in Amherst, O.*

—200 Amanda E.,⁶ b. Dec. 29, 1822; m. **Alonzo Gaston**, Oct. 13, 1844; d. in Russia, O., Feb. 14, 1885.
+201 Henry Dwight,⁶ b. 1824; d. 1867.
—202 Sewel Barnard,⁶ b. Feb. 4, 1830; d. aged 5 years.
—203 Lucy Ann,⁶ b. Dec. 23, 1823; m. **Henry Beadman Bryant**, May 29, 1854. This was a double wedding, as her brother, Henry D. Stratton, married Henry B. Bryant's sister same date and place. Dr. Finney of Oberlin officiated. These young people had all been Oberlin College students. She died in Chicago Feb. 11, 1870.

94. David Stratton[5] (*Jonas,*[4] *David,*[3] *Thomas,*[2] *John*[1]) was born May 13, 1794. About 1829 he married **Mary Mann** of Exeter, who was born Sept. 4, 1796, and died June 19, 1888. He died in Townshead, Mass., in 1870. He lived for awhile in Hollis and Amherst, N. H., and in Reading, Mass. About 1835 he moved to Boston where he was in the employ of the city for twenty-five years.

Children:—*Born in Amherst, N. H.*
+204   Charles Mann,[6] b. 1831.
—205   Mary Etta,[6] b. Dec. 28, 1834; m. **Ira W. Clifford**, Oct. 21, 1851; d. in Leominster, Mass., 1898.

Born in Boston.
—206   Harriet Elizabeth,[6] b. Nov. 30, 1837; m. **Charles F. Wright**, Dec. 27, 1868.

95. Bernard Stratton[5] (*Jonas,*[4] *David,*[3] *Thomas,*[2] *John*[1]) was married and lived for awhile in Amherst, N. H.

Children:
—207   Levi.[6]
—208   Martha.[6]

Further information concerning this family is wanted. There may have been other children.

99. James Stratton[6] (*Zebulon,*[5] *James,*[4] *James,*[3] *Thomas,*[2] *John*[1]) married **Elizabeth Wheeler**, Feb. 20, 1811. She was born May 5, 1788, and was the oldest daughter of *Joshua* and *Mary (Pulsifer) Wheeler* of New Salem. Her grandparents were *Joshua, Sr.,* and *Mehitible (Hadley) Wheeler* and *Edmund* and *Mary (Day) Pulsifer* of Cape Cod.*

Many of the younger men of Massachusetts were looking toward "the West" and James Stratton, industrious and enterprising, and innately a pioneer, caught the "western fever." He made a trip on horseback to Erie (then Niagara) County, N. Y., a distance of nearly four hundred miles, much of the way through an unbroken forest, along an Indian trail or bridlepath. At Concord (twenty-five miles from Buffalo), where a small

---

*Joshua and Mehitible Wheeler were among the very early settlers of New Salem. Their son Joshua was born Oct. 20, 1751. The early records of New Salem were burned.

Joshua Wheeler and Edmond Pulsifer were both Revolutionary soldiers, as shown by records in the military archives in Boston.

Mary Day was a descendant of Anthony Day of Cape Cod.

frontier settlement had just been made, he bought a piece of land, made a small clearing, built a log house with a bark roof and returned to Massachusetts.* In the following spring (1812), with his wife and little son, with all their household goods packed in two covered wagons drawn by oxen, they made their way to this new home in the wilderness. Several Athol and New Salem families came with them. The journey covered 30 days. Sometimes hewing their way through the forest, and again delayed by swollen streams, across which there were no bridges, they arrived in Concord the third week in May.† The next winter Mr. Stratton built the first frame barn in that region, and a year later a frame house. In May, 1819, he sold this farm to his brother-in-law, Nehemiah Fay, and moved to a better farming section, in a long, narrow valley (later known as Little Valley Center), twenty-five miles south of Concord, settling on a tract of 300 acres of woodland which he had bought the previous year.

Here again a log house was built and a small "girdling" made—the nucleus of the farm still known as the "Stratton Place." In 1829 the house, still standing, was built.

The woods along the Allegheny River, two miles away, were full of Indians with whom Mr. Stratton had much dealing. They always regarded him as their friend, were often in his house, and he and his family showed them many a kindness. The nearest point at which dry goods and groceries could be obtained was Buffalo, 40 miles away, and during the long winter months trips were made with sled loads of farm produce, skins and alkali to exchange for such things as were needed for the family and implements for farming.‡ The opening of the Erie Canal in 1825 hastened western immigration, and in time the New York & Erie

---

* Buffalo was then a little village of about 125 inhabitants. The following year it was burned to the ground by the British and Indians. Only three houses were left standing. Between forty and fifty people were killed and scalped by the Canadian Indians.

† War was declared with England the following month, June 1812, and for the next six years the frontier was in constant danger of attack by the Indians from across the Canadian border. Yet there seems to have been no thought of leaving these new homes. Such was the dauntless courage of our pioneer ancestors in the face of danger and peril.

‡ Mink, otter and beaver were in abundance along the streams, while the woods abounded in fox, wolves, bear and deer. The sale of furs and skins was a source of considerable revenue. Also the skins of these animals formed a good share of the dress of the early pioneers. Alkali made from the ashes of beach and maple and other hardwood trees was another source of profit.

R. R. was built through the valley.* Always highly esteemed by his townsmen, Mr. Stratton was elected to several town offices. In politics he was a Whig and a Republican. Though quiet and unassuming in manner, in conversation he was quick at repartee and with dry original jokes. Mrs. Stratton was of a more serious disposition, possessing a marked dignity of manner; a devoted wife and mother, an earnest, lifelong Christian.† During the last years of his life he received a pension for services in the war of 1812. He died Aug. 16, 1874, and Mrs. Stratton five years later, Jan. 5, 1879.

Children:—*Born in Athol, Mass.*

+209   Leander, b. Jan. 27, 1812; d. 1898.

Born in Concord, N. Y.

+210   Lorenzo,[7] b. Aug. 3, 1816; d. 1884.

−211   Luana,[7] b. May 18, 1818; m., Apr. 13, 1850. **Nathan C. Brown,** son of Hosea and Hester (Smith) Brown; ‡ d. in Grassy Cove, Tenn., Mar. 29, 1905.
A woman of strong original personality, a teacher before her marriage, a lifelong Christian.§

−212   Achsah,[7] b. June 5, 1820; d., unm., Mar. 20, 1845; for five years a faithful, beloved teacher of Cattaraugus County.

Born in Little Valley Center, N. Y.

−213   Louisa,[7] b. Mar. 10, 1822; m. **Chester Foster,** son of Jonathan and Parney (Chase) Foster; d. in Grand View, Tenn., May 26, 1901. Both were members

---

*The canal project was discussed as early as 1797. The subject was brought before Congress by DeWitt Clinton in 1810, and work was begun in 1817. Much of the route lay through an uninhabited wilderness. Its completion brought great prosperity to the state.

† Of a quiet, deeply religious nature, she impressed upon her children a veneration for the Christian religion—not so much by her words, which were few, as by her quiet, consistent life. None of them were ever heard to speak lightly of any sacred subject.

‡ Hosea Brown, son of a Revolutionary soldier, was born in Westmoreland, N. H., in 1791. In 1896 he was one of the six survivors of the War of 1812, and the oldest man drawing a pension in the United States. He died the following year at the extreme age of one hundred and six years, having voted for United States Presidents nineteen times, the last time being carried to the poles on the shoulders of four young men and enjoying as much as they the circuitous route through the town and the playing of the band which accompanied them.

§ Both Mr. and Mrs. Brown are buried in the burial ground near the Baptist Church in Grassy Cove.

1. Leander Stratton; 2. Lorenzo Stratton at thirty years of age; 3. Zebulon Stratton; 4. Luana (Stratton) Brown, aged eighty-seven years; 5. Louisa (Stratton) Foster. *Pages* 206, 218-221.

of the Grand View Presbyterian church, which they helped to organize, and in whose cemetery they are buried.

+214 Zebulon,[7] b. Oct. 16, 1826; d. 1889.

109. HARVEY STRATTON [6] (*Nathaniel*,[5] *Stephen*,[4] *James*,[3] *Thomas*,[2] *John* [1]) was born in Athol, Mass., May 23, 1793, and in 1816 married **Hannah Foster**, who was born Sept. 21, 1794. They lived in Northfield, where he died June 8, 1844.

Children:—*Born in Northfield, Mass.*
—215 Susan F.,[7] b. Sept. 23, 1817; m., June 3, 1835, **Joseph Foster**, son of Stephen and Lydia (Nicholas) Foster of Sullivan, N. H.*
—216 Mary F.,[7] b. Dec. 12, 1818.
—217 James H.,[7] b. Oct. —, 1821.
—218 Stephen W.,[7] b. Oct. 14, 1824.
—219 Lucinda H.,[7] b. July 24, 1827; d. Apr. 10, 1831.
—220 Dudley B.,[7] b. Oct. 7, 1829.

The compiler would be glad to get further information of the above sons.

110. WARREN STRATTON [6] (*Nathaniel*,[5] *Stephen*,[4] *James*,[3] *Thomas*,[2] *John* [1]), born Aug. 6, 1800. Married, first, **Cynthia Piper**, daughter of *Amos Piper;* second, **Lucy Bruce**; third, **Mrs. Elizabeth C. (Croft) Learned**, in Sept., 1863. He died in Northfield, July 17, 1883.

Children:—*Born in Northfield, Mass.*
By first marriage.
—221 Maria,[7] m. **Henry Sheldon**.
—222 Henry.[7]
—223 Jason.[7]
—224 Amherst.[7]
—225 Melinda,[7] m. 1st, **Adolphus Hosly**, 2nd, **Henry Willey**.
—226 Susan Jennie,[7] adopted in infancy, after her mother's death, by her uncle Norris Stratton (No. 114).
By second marriage.
—227 Stephen.[7]

Further knowledge of this family is desired.

---
*Their daughter, Susan Augusta Foster, married John H. Loomis of Chicago, son of Osmyn and Jane M. (Cadwell) Loomis of N. Granville, N. Y., and Lowell, Mich.

111. WILLARD STRATTON [6] (*Nathaniel*,[5] *Stephen*,[4] *James*,[3] *Thomas*,[2] *John*[1]) married **Euphema Larvis**, March 27, 1819. They settled in Saratoga Springs, N. Y., where some of their descendants still live.

Children:—*Born in Saratoga Springs.*
- —228 Nathan R.,[7] b. Feb. 28, 1820; settled in Louisiana, where he died in 1900.
- —229 Nelson F.,[7] b. 1821; d. 1880.
- —230 William H.,[7] b. Jan. 4, 1824; m., Aug. 5, 1843, **Mary A. Cushing**; d. Mar. 27, 1889. Left no children.
- —231 James Harvey,[7] b. Sept. 9, 1826; m., July 11, 1847, **Emily Stevens**; d. Aug. 14, 1889.
- —232 Emily Ann,[7] b. Sept. 1, 1829; d. in infancy.
- —233 Mary Jane,[7] b. Jan. 7, 1832; m. **Russell Bixby**, Oct. 11, 1858; d. Feb. 21, 1907.
- —234 Sarah Emily,[7] b. Nov. 14, 1837; m. **Joseph Bigham**, Nov. 17, 1854.

What became of the above sons?

123. AMOS T. STRATTON [6] (*Abner*,[5] *Stephen*,[4] *James*,[3] *Thomas*,[2] *John*[1]) was born in Athol, July 31, 1818. He married **Eleanor Stratton** (No. 1131, Chart G), June 3, 1849. He spent his entire life in his native town with whose best interests he was always closely connected. He died June 19, 1898. Mrs. Stratton survived him six years, dying Apr. 25, 1904. The following obituary notices are from an Athol paper:

"In the death of Amos Stratton, Athol loses one of her oldest and most respected citizens. Mr. Stratton was born at the old Stratton homestead on the South Athol road, and would in about six weeks have reached his 80th birthday. At this farm four generations of Strattons have been born, and five generations have made it their home. He was for many years engaged in farming and the lumbering business. Mr. Stratton was a quiet citizen of honorable character and kindly nature, an excellent man in every respect."

"Mrs. Stratton had been a lifelong resident of Athol. For many years she had been an invalid, during the past three years unable to leave her bed, and yet she bore her sufferings in a patient, Christian-like manner, never uttering complaint, and always greeting her visitors with a cheery smile and pleasant word. Mrs. Stratton has many friends in Athol who will sincerely mourn her death. Her example of fortitude under great trial was like a benediction to all who witnessed it. In her early days she taught school. She leaves two daughters and one son, all of Athol. Her daughters have cared for her with noble loving devotion through her long years of suffering."

Children:—Born in Athol, Mass.
- —235 Myron T.,[7] m. Emma I. Ball in 1878; ch. Mabel A.,[8] m. Clarence E. Deane, 1898; d. Oct. 11, 1905.
- —236 Mary A.,[7] res. Athol, Mass.
- —237 Myra A.,[7] res. Athol, Mass.
- —238 Abby S.,[7] d. Oct. 20, 1956, aged 4 mos.

124. ABNER GRAVES STRATTON[6] (Abner,[5] Stephen,[4] James,[3] Thomas,[2] John[1]) was born Feb. 8, 1820. He married, first, **Ophelia Barton**, July 7, 1842, and second, **Mrs. Fannie Thompson**. He was an active, energetic man and engaged in several lines of business at Athol, among them the manufacture of palm-leaf hats and the boot and shoe business. The esteem and trust with which he was regarded by his fellow townsmen is shown by the fact that for more than a third of a century he held one or more town offices. He was active in the organization of the Worcester Agricultural and Mechanic Society. His keen wit and "yankee genius" are well remembered by the older people of his native town who tell many amusing incidents of his public life. He died March 27, 1882.

Children:—Born in Athol, Mass.
- —239 Frederick Abner,[7] b. 1845; m. Sophia Berry, Sept. 22, 1866; ch: Arlington F.,[8] d. Aug. 31, 1906.
- —240 Solon H.,[7] moved to Chicago in 1885.

130. REUBEN STRATTON[6] (Abel,[5] Peleg,[4] James,[3] Thomas,[2] John[1]), born July 19, 1802, lived in Athol, where he was a manufacturer of packing boxes. Since his death, Dec. 31, 1876, his sons have carried on his business under the name of "Stratton Brothers," having added much to their planing mills and lumber yard. He married **Hannah Stratton** (Chart G), in 1835.

Children:—Born in Athol, Mass.
- +241 Henry W.,[7] b. 1836; d. 1899.
- —242 Sarah Rebecca,[7] b. 1838; m. Austin Farnworth Ellenwood in 1869; d. Apr. 15, 1870.
- —243 Francis Reuben,[7] m. Eliza Rice; one of the firm of "Stratton Bros." at Athol. Chn. Adella Frances,[8] d. Jan. 9, 1889, aged 7 years; Rebecca Farnsworth.[8]

—244   Cyrus W.,[7] d. Feb. 24, 1849, aged 3 years 7 mos.
—245   Laura Mann,[7] b. 1843.

132. ABEL STRATTON[6] (*Abel*,[5] *Peleg*,[4] *James*,[3] *Thomas*,[2] *John*[1]) was born in Petersham, Oct. 1, 1808. He married **Susan Page**. By trade he was a shoemaker. He died of consumption in Athol at the age of 44 years, 3 mos. and 17 days.

Children:—*Born in Athol, Mass.*

—246   Edward Page,[7] b. 1839; m. **Mary L. Mansfield**, Aug. 16, 1861; a soldier in Co. K, 6th Regt. N. H. V.; d. in camp at Annapolis, Md., in 1862. Ch. Lucy Page,[8] m. **John Withington**, Mar. 13, 1862.
—247   Eliza Augusta,[7] after the death of her father, lived with the Shakers in E. Canterbury, N. H., for many years. Res. Concord, N. H.
—248   Susan,[7] d. May 12, 1844, aged five months.

144. JAMES BATCHELOR STRATTON[6] (*Peleg*,[5] *Peleg*,[4] *James*,[3] *Thomas*,[2] *John*[1]) was born in Templeton, Mass., Aug. 25, 1829. While a boy he lived much of the time with his uncle, Dr. James Batchelor in Royalston, where he attended school. His mother died when he was six years old. In 1851 he went to California, making the four months' trip in a sailing vessel. In 1853 he returned to Massachusetts and, Nov. 22, 1855, married **Helen L. Marks** of Chicopee and settled in Grafton, where for twenty years he was engaged in the shoe business. In 1877 he removed to Williamsett, where they occupied the old Griswold homestead, the family house of Mrs. Stratton, the remainder of their lives.

They were members of the Baptist church, in which Mr. Stratton was a faithful worker and a deacon for eighteen years. Personally Mr. Stratton was an interesting man. "When with him one never lost sight of the fact that he was a New Englander with all the sturdy, positive traits of character that go with them. Friendly, straightforward and frank, he made many friends and kept them." He passed away Oct. 26, 1904.

Children:—*Born in Grafton.*

—249   Helen L.,[7] d. in infancy.
—250   Homer J.,[7] m. **Louise Smith**.
—251   Fannie Elizabeth,[7] m. **Moses Seward Chapin**.

147. JESSE KENDALL STRATTON[6] (*David*,[5] *Peleg*,[4] *James*,[3] *Thomas*,[2] *John*[1]) was baptized in Athol, March 21, 1813. While a young man he went to Savannah, Ga. When the Mexican war broke out he joined the army. After the war he returned to Massachusetts and was with his father at the time of his death. Later he married and settled at Como, Miss., where he died.

Children:—*Born in Mississippi.*
—252   Leona.[7]
—253   Jesse Kendall, Jr.[7]

149.   CYRUS W. STRATTON [6] (*David,*[5] *Peleg,*[4] *James,*[3] *Thomas,*[2] *John*[1]), born in Athol, Aug., 1817, married, first, **Eliza A. Bosworth**, daughter of *Stacy* and *Eliza Bosworth*, in Grafton, Apr. 4, 1843; second, **Almira Brown**; third, **Elizabeth Sargent**. He lived in Worcester, Westboro, Grafton and Gardner. Died in Gardner in 1889. In Grafton, where he spent most of his life, he was a boot and shoe manufacturer. He was a member of the Baptist church, and always a highly respected citizen.

Children:—By first marriage.
+254   George Kendall,[7] b. 1846.
+255   Herbert Stacy,[7] b. 1850.
+256   Asa Evans,[7] b. 1854.
         By second marriage.
—257   Eliza J.,[7] d. in infancy.
—258   Charles L.,[7] d. in infancy.

150.   ASA SCOTT STRATTON [6] (*David,*[5] *Peleg,*[4] *James,*[3] *Thomas,*[2] *John*[1]) was born in 1818. He studied medicine and went when a young man to Panola, Miss. Afterwards settled in Collinsville, Tenn., where he was a practicing physician. He married **Mary Elizabeth Chamberlain**. They left no children.

156.   CHARLES LORENZO STRATTON [6] (*Andrew,*[5] *Peleg,*[4] *James,*[3] *Thomas,*[2] *John*[1]) was born Jan. 14, 1818, in Petersham, Mass. His mother died when he was nine years old and for three years he lived with his grandparents in Petersham. When twelve years old he joined his father in Hillsboro, Ga., and there learned the shoemaker's trade and worked in his father's store. Later he went to New York state, lived for awhile in Herkimer Co., and then settled in Chautauqua Co. on a farm near Kennedy. He married, first, **Caroline E. Miller** of Kennedy in 1844; second, **Mrs. Jennie (Haskins) Fairbanks** in 1873. He died March 9, 1882.

Children:—*Born in Poland, N. Y.*
By first marriage.
—259 Charles Evans,[7] m. **Rose A. Taylor** of Randolph, N. Y.; ch. Caroline A.,[8] m. Marvin L. Case, 2nd J. Delevan Curtiss.
Born in Chautauqua Co., N. Y.
By second marriage.
—260 Earl.[7]
—261 Kendall.[7]

157. JAMES EVANS STRATTON[6] (*Andrew*,[5] *Peleg*,[4] *James*,[3] *Thomas*,[2] *John*[1]) was born in Petersham, Mass., June 18, 1819. He spent his boyhood in Athol. While a young man he went South, first to Hillsboro, Ga., and then to Mississippi. From 1842 to 1858 he was a merchant and farmer at Panola, Miss. In 1859 he settled in Texas. He married **Mary E. Stratton** (No. 162) in Mississippi, Dec. 1, 1847. He died in DeWitt Co., Texas, Oct. 8, 1864. Mrs. Stratton survived him many years, dying at the age of 78.

Children:—*Born in Panola Co., Miss.*
—262 Charles Andrew,[7] b. Dec. 7, 1848; m. **Charlotte M. Wheeler**; d. Oct. 8, 1890.
+263 Henry Ward,[7] b. 1852.
—264 Anna Jane,[7] d. 8 mos.
—265 Mary Jeanette,[7] d. 1 year.
Born in Bishop Co., Texas.
—266 James Evans,[7] b. in 1860; m. **Tennessee U. Friar** in DeWitt Co., Texas.
—267 Emily Douglas,[7] d. in 1864, aged 11 mos.

166. ASA EVANS STRATTON, JR.,[6] (*Asa E.*,[5] *Peleg*,[4] *James*,[3] *Thomas*,[2] *John*[1]) was born in Panola Co., Miss., January 13, 1844.

He married twice, first, **Louisa Henrietta Waldmann** in Matagorda, Texas, Feb. 7, 1867. She died in Montgomery, Ala., Nov. 24, 1895. His second wife was **Mrs. Ina Lee Smith**, whom he married Sept. 27, 1904. He was educated in Semple-Broadus College, Desoto County, Miss., and Soule University, Washington County, Texas. He belonged to Bates Legion of Texas troops, Confederate States army, was transferred to Co. "G," Brown's Regt. (13th Regiment) of Texas cavalry, C. S. Army, served in the Trans-Mississippi department nearly four years, was orderly

Lorenzo Stratton Home. *Page 220.*

STRATTON PLACE, NEAR ELKDALE, LITTLE VALLEY CENTER, N. Y.
James Stratton homestead built 1829. *Page 204.*

sergeant of his company and sergeant major of the regiment. Later he was judge of the County Court of Brazoria County, Texas; County Attorney of the county; State Senator in the Legislature of Texas from the 10th District; United States Attorney for Eastern District of Texas, appointed by President Arthur. In 1887 he moved to Alabama and was Presidential Elector 6th Alabama District in 1888; Chief Deputy collector Internal Revenue of District of Alabama; United States Commissioner; Supervisor of the 12th census, 1900, for 3rd District of Alabama; Republican candidate for Governor of Alabama in 1906, and later was appointed Referee in Bankruptcy at Montgomery, Ala.

Children:—*Born in Matagorda, Texas.*

By first marriage.

—268 Charles Waldmann,[7] b. 1868; d. aged 2 years.
—269 Emily Bryan,[7] m. **Walter Herbert Stevens**; res. Beaumont, Texas.
—270 Louisa Waldmann.[7]
—271 Bertha Amanda,[7] d., 1902, in Montgomery, Ala., aged 27 years.
—272 Florence.[7]

168. JAMES THOMAS STRATTON [6] (*Asa E.,*[5] *Peleg,*[4] *James,*[3] *Thomas,*[2] *John*[1]) was born in Panola Co., Miss., Oct. 8, 1849, and moved with his parents to Texas in the summer of 1859. He married, first, **Lavinia Perry Bryan**, daughter of *William Joel Bryan*, Feb. 18, 1873. After her death he married **Minnie C. Dewey** in 1883. She is the daughter of *Major E. C. Dewey.* He died at his home in Velasco, Texas, July 2, 1910. He was long closely connected with the best interests of the region in which he lived, and was several times elected to offices of trust in his county. He was an elder in the Presbyterian church and an earnest, faithful Christian worker. Of a very friendly, genial nature, he had many friends among all classes. He will long be remembered by those among whom he worked—those whom he has helped materially and encouraged by his kindly smile and hearty handclasp.

Children:—*Born in Brazoria Co., Texas.*

By first marriage.

+273 Joel Bryan.[7]
—274 Caroline Austin,[7] m. Fred A. Brock, Nov. 24, 1897.

—275 James Thomas, Jr.,[7] m. **Bert Johnson**, Oct. 18, 1904; res. Houston, Tex.; ch. Cleo.[8]
—276 Samuel Irwin,[7] m. **Rosa Hill**, Dec. 7, 1901; res. Durango, Texas; chn. Samuel I., Jr.,[8] Louannie.[8]

By second marriage.

—277 Minnie Claire,[7] d. Jan. 8, 1889.
—278 Cleve.[7]
—279 Merle Dewey.[7]
—280 Dewey.[7]

169. JESSE DAVID TAIT STRATTON [6] (*Asa E.,*[5] *Peleg,*[4] *James,*[3] *Thomas,*[2] *John* [1]) was born in Como, Panola Co., Miss., Apr. 30, 1857. He moved with his parents to Texas when he was two years old. After receiving instruction in the public and private schools near home he attended the Texas Military College at Austin, spent twelve years in mercantile business, about ten years in the dairy business and the raising of Jersey cattle, and is now engaged in general farming at Angleton, Texas. He is a member of the Methodist church, of which he is one of the stewards and is secretary of the Sunday school. He married **Sarah Ruble Kirkland**, Sept. 8, 1886. She is a daughter of *Jesse Ruble* and *Sarah Lucinda (Penn) Kirkland* and is a graduate of Brandon Female College.*

Children:—*Born in Alvin, Texas.*

—281 Asa Kirkland,[7] educated in public schools and Massey Business College.

Born in Brazoria Co., Texas.

—282 Thomas Tait,[7] graduate of public school, student of Southwestern University, Texas. As the subject for graduating oration he took the Stratton motto, "Tento Surgere."

173. NAHUM STRATTON [6] (*Isaac,*[5] *David,*[4] *David,*[3] *Thomas,*[2] *John* [1]), born in Boston, Mass., in 1811, married, first, **Elizabeth** ——, and, second, **Mary Stevens** of Stow, in 1843. He died in Bolton, aged 90 years.

Children:—*Born in Bolton, Mass.*

By first marriage.

—283 Elizabeth,[7] b. 1833.

---

* Her grandparents were Obed and Mary (Wynn) Kirkland of Covington, La., and Abraham and Delphine (Laurens) Penn. Abraham Penn was from Patrick Co., Va., and tradition says descended from a brother of Wm. Penn.

—284 Dolly,⁷ b. 1885; m. George Brown, 1838.
—285 Mary Ann,⁷ b. 1838.
By second marriage.
—286 Hannah,⁷ b. 1844.
—287 Isaac Chase,⁷ b. 1846.
—288 Nahum,⁷ 1847.

177. DAVID STRATTON⁶ (*Isaac,⁵ David,⁴ David,³ Thomas,² John¹*), born in Bolton, Jan. 23, 1819, married **Mary Ann Butler**. He lived in Holyoke and died there Jan. 1, 1907. The following notice appeared in a paper of his town: "David Stratton, widely known throughout the state as the oldest of the old-time school masters of western Massachusetts, died in his home here to-day, aged 88 years. For fifty years he was connected with the North Chestnut Street school, being principal for twenty-five years. Although a strict disciplinarian, he retained the affection of the pupils, and had the faculty of arousing in them an enthusiasm for study. Many of Holyoke's leading citizens began their education under the direction of this beloved school master, and many there are who attribute to Mr. Stratton's teaching the foundation of their own character and success."

Children:—*Born in Holyoke, Mass.*
—289 Edwin.⁷
—290 Myra,⁷ m. **M. W. Condit**.
—291 Elizabeth,⁷ d. in childhood.

190. JONAS STRATTON⁶ (*Sewell,⁵ Jonas,⁴ David,³ Thomas,² John¹*), born Sept. 12, 1802. Lived in Andover, Lawrence, and Boston. Married **Mary Dunkle**, who was born Sept. 1, 1805, and died in 1849. He was captain of the Night Watch in Boston for many years, and was considered the strongest man in the county and very faithful and efficient in his office. He died in Andover, Feb. 12, 1867.

Children:—B*orn in Cambridge, Mass.*
+292 Henry Campbell,⁷ b. 1826.
Born in Boston.
—293 Theodore Wilson,⁷ b. Mar. 29, 1829; m. but left no children; d. about 1875.
—294 Rebecca V.,⁷ b. Mar. 12, 1831; m. **Deacon David Abbott** of Stoneham; d. in 1905.
—295 Daniel Edward,⁷ b. Feb. 27, 1835; d. aged 7 months.
—296 Jonas Lane,⁷ b. June 22, 1846; d. aged 4 months.

195. ASA BACHELDER STRATTON[6] (*Sewell*,[5] *Jonas*,[4] *David*,[3] *Thomas*,[2] *John*[1]) was born in Milford, N. H., Feb. 1, 1813. His early life was spent upon the farm of his parents. His education was simply that which he received in the district school of Milford and Bedford. At the age of 21 he went to Lowell, where he worked with a jeweler. Nov. 29, 1842, he married **Martha H. Everton**, daughter of *James Everton* of Londonderry, and soon after their marriage they removed to New York City, where he worked at his trade. Mrs. Stratton died Feb. 24, 1865. He married, second, **Laura Bowen** of Manchester, N. H., who also died in New York. Sept. 24, 1872, Mr. Stratton married **Mrs. Eliza Gooden**. Shortly after his third marriage he sold his property in New York and settled in Manchester, N. H., where he purchased a residence and business block, afterwards known as the "Stratton Block." A strict Baptist he endeavored to bring up his children in the love and fear of God. He died in Manchester in 1876.

Children:—*Born in New York City.*
    By first marriage.
—297 James Everton,[7] b. 1845; d. aged 11 years and 9 months, an unusually bright lad, being at this early age fitted for the Academy.
+298 George Asa,[7] b. 1847.
    By second marriage.
—299 Edwin A.,[7] m. **Lillian Rollins**, lives in Manchester; a jeweller of the firm of "Lovejoy & Stratton."
—300 Cora Belle,[7] m. **Charles Harvey**.

199. WILLARD PARKER STRATTON[6] (*Sewell*,[5] *Jonas*,[4] *David*,[3] *Thomas*,[2] *John*[1]), born June 24, 1821, married **Emorency C. Annis**, Nov. 16, 1840. They lived in Manchester, where he kept a hardware store, dealing extensively in hydraulic rams. By trade he was a tinsmith and a metal worker. An active, earnest Christian, he was an ordained minister in the Second-day Advent church. Though never holding a pastorate, he often went out to the country churches to teach and preach. In stature he was a very small man, as was his brother Sewell Stratton, Jr., being but five feet two inches in height and never weighing over 105 pounds. He died in Manchester, March 17, 1881, much esteemed by his many friends.

LORENZO STRATTON
Page 219.

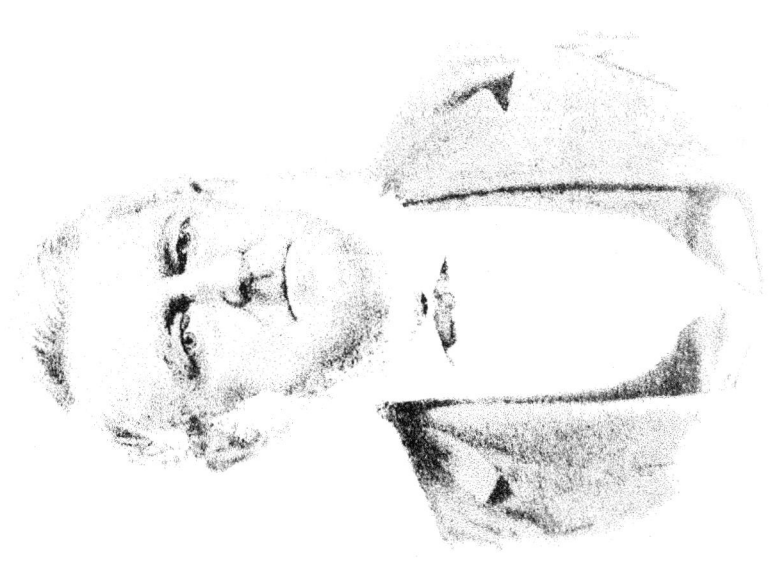

ASA EVANS STRATTON
Page 199.

Children:—*Born in Manchester, N. H.*
—301 Hervey, b. Nov. 14, 1849; m. Louisa Davis; dealer in hardware in Manchester. No children.
—302 Christina, b. Oct. 24, 1853; m. George L. Robinson, Nov. 17, 1878.
—303 Lucretia, b. Sept. 23, 1855 m. George F. Battles, Mar. 13, 1875.

201. HENRY DWIGHT STRATTON [6] (*Jonas,*[5] *Jonas,*[4] *David,*[3] *Thomas,*[2] *John*[1]) was born in Amherst, O., Aug. 24, 1824, and died in New York City, Feb. 20, 1867. He was educated in the public schools of Amherst and in Oberlin College. He married **Parmela C. Bryant**, May 29, 1854. A man of fine attainments, of attractive manners, deeply interested in educational progress, he became a benefactor to many young people. With his brother-in-law, Henry B. Bryant, he established the "Bryant and Stratton Colleges," which at the time of his death numbered more than fifty, located in the principal cities of the United States and Canada.

Children:—Born in Amherst, O.
—304 Henry Dwight, Jr.,[7] b. Mar. 29, 1855; d. in Colorado, where he had gone for his health, Dec. 27, 1877.
—305 Sewell Bryant,[7] b. May 28, 1861; d. aged 4 mos.
—306 Edith P.,[7] b. May 25, 1866; m. Frederick A. Saville, June 6, 1889; res. Buffalo, N. Y.

204. CHARLES MANN STRATTON [6] (*David,*[5] *Jonas,*[4] *David,*[3] *Thomas,*[2] *John*[1]), born Aug. 14, 1831. Was in the banking business in early life in Cambridge, and later was a farmer near Hollis, N. H. Mr. Stratton was married three times as follows: first, to **Fannie E. Whitney**, Apr. 12, 1857; second, **Mary Ann Ober**, daughter of *Joseph* and *Rhoda* (*Colburn*) *Ober*, June 28, 1865; third, **Jennie Hartwell**, Jan. 29, 1871, daughter of *Joseph* and *Hannah* (*Hodgman*) *Hartwell*.

Children:—*Born in Cambridge.*
By second marriage.
—307 Nettie L., b. Apr. 5, 1866; d. Aug. 5, 1867.
—308 M. Louise, res. Hollis, N. H.
By third marriage.
—309 Lyman, res. Indianola, Miss.
—310 Edwin Hartwell.
Born in Hollis.
—311 Jennie Frances.

209. LEANDER STRATTON [8] (*James*,[7] *Zebulon*,[6] *James*,[5] *James*,[4] *James*,[3] *Thomas*,[2] *John* [1]) moved with his parents from Athol, Mass., to Concord, N. Y., in 1812, and seven years later to Cattaraugus Co., N. Y. Here, on the farm, his youth and early manhood was spent. In 1835 he married **Lucy Foster**, only daughter of *Jonathan, Jr.*, and *Pharney (Chase) Foster*, and settled on a farm adjoining his father's in Little Valley Center.* He was chosen to fill various town offices, and for several years was Town Clerk. In 1872 Mrs. Stratton died after many months of painful illness borne with patient Christian fortitude. She was a quiet, unpretending woman, devoted to her family and never tiring in her work for them. Three years later Mr. Stratton moved to the mountains of East Tennessee and settled in Grand View, Rhea County, where the more genial climate did much to restore his then failing health. Just before moving south he married **Mrs. Mary (Wheeler) Fellows**, daughter of *Pliney* and *Martha (King) Wheeler*.

In the quiet, peacefulness of his mountain home he spent many hours in reading and writing. During the last twenty-five years of his life he was a regular contributor to the *Forest & Stream*, furnishing articles largely reminiscent of the early days and fraught with an intimate knowledge of natural history, gained by a long life spent "near to Nature's heart." Many of his articles were written after he was 75 years old, and up to a few months before his death. That all his life he had been a close student of the "Book of Nature" is very evident from those little sketches.† He died on Thanksgiving Day, Nov. 30, 1899, respected and loved by all who knew him. His widow died Aug. 26, 1914. Both were members of the Presbyterian church and are buried in the Presbyterian cemetery at Grand View.

Children:—*Born in Little Valley Center, N. Y.*

+312 Alonzo,[8] b. Feb. 22, 1836.

—313 Alzina Pharney,[8] b. July 25, 1839; m. **Amenzo Sibley**, son of Charles and Sarah Sibley, Mar. 10, 1858; d. in Napoli, N. Y., June 21, 1917.

---

* Pharney Chase was daughter of David (son of Abner and Hannah Chase) and Lucy Chase, who came from Petersham, Mass., and settled in Little Valley, N. Y., in 1817, one of the three first families to settle in that section, then an almost unbroken forest.

† He wrote over the pen name of "Antler" (and sometimes E. L. Stratton). His contributions to the *Forest and Stream* have been collected and re-published with a biographical sketch. They are well worth preserving as an addition to historic and natural history literature.

—314 Alzora Betsey,[8] b. Aug. 14, 1843; m. **George C. Waterman,*** only son of Dwight and Julia M. (Whitmore) Waterman of Napoli, Apr. 8, 1866; d. in Grand View, Tenn., Dec. 17, 1912. Mr. Waterman m. 2nd, Blanche (Foster) Franklin, widow of John Franklin.

—315 Albert Lorenzo,[8] b. Dec. 16, 1850; d. aged 7 mos.

—316 Alzada Ella,[8] m., Oct. 4, 1879, **Leonard Lafayette Barton,**† son of Leonard and Eveline (Fargo) Barton; res. Grand View, Tenn.

210. LORENZO STRATTON [7] (*James*,[6] *Zebulon*,[5] *James*,[4] *James*,[3] *Thomas*,[2] *John* [1]) was born in Concord, Erie Co., N. Y., Aug. 3, 1816. When he was three years old his parents moved to Little Valley Center, Cattaraugus Co. His early education, as far as schools are concerned, consisted of four winter terms in the district school of that newly settled country. At other seasons the boy's services were needed on the farm. Encouraged by his mother to study at home, he early developed a taste for reading and eagerly read the few books in his own home and all that he could borrow in the neighborhood. He soon showed an aptitude for business, and at sixteen was given a position in a store in Little Valley. At eighteen he was sent to Buffalo to buy the fall stock of goods for the store. Two years later he went west, and for the next four years was engaged in business in Rockford, Ill., and Beloit, Wis. This was before any railroad was built in Illinois, and while Chicago was but a small hamlet. Goods were bought in Buffalo and sent by way of the lakes, and Mr. Stratton made many trips through the lakes from Chicago to Milwaukee. He built the first brick store in Beloit. During 1841 he had charge of a book store in Akron, Ohio, and then for three years engaged in mercantile business in Buffalo at 212 Main Street. In 1844 he went to Cincinnati, and for eight years was actively engaged in the book business, having a retail and wholesale book store and publishing house at 131 Main Street—at that time the largest book store in the city.‡ Oct. 21, 1846, he married **Sophia Joanna Hill**, youngest

---

* Grandson of Daniel and Chloe (Wilcox) Whitmore, and Ambros and Hulda (Sanford) Waterman, of Barnstable, Mass.

† Grandson of Samuel and Elizabeth Fargo, and James and Dorcas (Akerley) Barton of Cattaraugus Co., N. Y.

‡ He was the publisher of a good many books, and for several years published a periodical, *The Flag of Our Country*, in which appeared

daughter of *Hon. Henry, Jr.,* and *Lucy M. (Russell) Hill.* She was born in Brazil, S. A., Jan. 2, 1826, where her father was United States Consul to the port of Bahia.* In 1852, his health failing, he sold his business in Cincinnati and returned to Little Valley, where he bought the home farm, building a new house near the old homestead. Here he had an opportunity for putting into practice theories which he had long entertained concerning the domesticating of certain wild animals. His ideas on the subject were far in advance of his time and only recently have been promoted by the American Bison Society and other associations for the preservation and domestication of some of the native denizens of our primeval forests. His experiments with the American elk, and several kinds of fur-bearing animals were quite successful and were watched by naturalists all over the country—many of whom came to see the animals in his parks and pens, and he had an extensive correspondence with Spencer F. Baird, Prof. Joseph Henry, Dr. Charles Gurley, and many others of this stamp.† Then, hoping to extend his experiments in a more genial climate, and to give more attention to general agriculture, he moved with his family to Grassy Cove, Tennessee, in the Cumberland Mountains, where he had bought a plantation of 1,800 acres known as the "Old Greer Stand." The Devon cattle which he brought to this farm attracted the attention of farmers throughout East Tennessee, and descendants of this herd are found on many farms to-day. He also experimented to some extent with Angora goats, and at one time had a flock of more than one hundred of them.‡ Before the opportunity came for more extended experiments his health again failed. He died June 30, 1884.§ Two years after

---

the first poems of Alice and Phœbe Cary, whose father was his intimate friend.

*This was Henry Hill[6] (Henry,[5] Henry,[4] Hon. Samuel,[3] John,[2] John,[1] who settled in Guilford, Conn. in 1654, from Northamptonshire, Eng.)

Lucy Munson Russell was eldest daughter of Hon. Samuel Russell[4] (Rev. William,[3] Rev. Noadiah,[2] William,[1] born in Hertfordshire, Eng., 1612; died in New Haven, Conn., 1664).

† See Reports of the New York State Agricultural Society, and Smithsonian Reports for accounts of his experiments. Elkdale, N. Y., was named for the elk in his park.

‡ As a student of Nature, he became interested in the Botany and Geology of this interesting region, and many men interested in kindred subjects found their way to his Grassy Cove home.

§ The *Cattaraugus Republican* contained this notice of his death:
"The older residents of Little Valley will be pained to learn of the death of a former well known and highly esteemed citizen of this town,

A Summer Morning at Cactus Cottage
Mrs. Sophia J. Stratton (aged 80 years) making lace as she learned to make it when a child in South America. *Pages* 220, 221.

his death his family moved to Chattanooga. Mrs. Stratton survived her husband many years, and was the center of a devoted home circle, where her long, cheerful, Christian life was a benediction to many. She died June 28, 1813, beloved by all who knew her. Both Mr. and Mrs. Stratton were members of the Presbyterian Church. They are buried in Forest Hill Cemetery, Chattanooga.

Children:—*Born in Cincinnati, Ohio.*
+317   Charles Lorenzo.[8]
Born in Little Valley, N. Y.
+318   Francis Augustus.[8]
—319   Henry Hill,[8] publisher, dealer in articles for the army and navy, Chattanooga.
—320   Harriet Russell,[8] teacher, compiler of "A Book of Strattons."
—321   Nettie Maria,[8] stenographer, Chattanooga.
—322   Cora Sophia,[8] artist, studio in Chattanooga.

214. ZEBULON STRATTON [7] (*James,*[6] *Zebulon,*[5] *James,*[4] *James,*[3] *Thomas,*[2] *John*[1]) spent his entire life in his native county, first at the old Stratton homestead where he was born, and after April, 1865, on a farm of his own on Whig Street, a few miles from the homestead. In 1854 he married **Martha Foy,** daughter of *Daniel* and *Harriet (Morton) Foy* of Napoli, N. Y., and granddaughter of *Samuel* and *Sarah Foy* of Vermont. She was born May 14, 1831. Educated in the county schools of three quarters of a century ago, an invalid during much of his life, and living always on a farm, Mr. Stratton was a lover of Nature, a great reader, familiar with many of the best authors, and well

---

who for many years occupied a prominent place among our people for enterprise and uprightness of character. Mr. Lorenzo Stratton died at his home in Grassy Cove, Tennessee, on the 30th of June last.

"While a resident here he owned and greatly improved the "home farm" located at Little Valley Center, introducing many novel features thereon, the most notable of which was the raising of American Elk, which he prosecuted with considerable success. Among his sales of these animals was a pair to the king of Italy, Victor Emanuel, who sent an agent from his realms to make the purchase. The elks were safely transported to Italy, where at latest accounts they continued to thrive. Mr. S. was a good business man, always manifesting a lively zeal in agriculture and its kindred interests. For a number of years he was intimately identified with our county Agricultural Society, of which he was vice-president. He removed to his southern home several years ago, but has always retained a love for Cattaraugus."

posted on current events. Of a genial, friendly disposition, he always had many friends. In his pleasant home his parents spent the last years of their lives. He died Aug. 16, 1889. Mrs. Stratton died nine years later, Aug. 14, 1898. Of a quiet, domestic nature, devoted to her family, thoughtfully kind to her neighbors and friends, she was greatly loved.

Children:
- —323 Emma Martha,[8] b. 1857; d. aged five years.
- —324 Edward Ara,[8] m. **Rose Greeley.** For many years closely connected with the educational interests of Cattaraugus Co. as teacher and school commissioner; res. Randolph, N. Y.
- —325 Adelbert L.,[8] m. **Bina Winship**, May 11, 1889, daughter of *Truman* and *Cadace Winship*; chn. Marjorie Bell,[9] Mabel May;[9] res. Little Valley, N. Y.

241. HENRY W. STRATTON [7] (*Reuben,*[6] *Abel,*[5] *Peleg,*[4] *James,*[3] *Thomas,*[2] *John*[1]), born in 1836, in Athol, Mass., was a lifelong resident of his native town, highly respected for his upright character, a worthy and useful citizen, a leading member of the Advent church. He died May 14, 1899. He early became identified with his father in the box manufacturing business, on the Petersham road, in what was then known as the "Stockwell neighborhood," and after his father's death, established, with his brother, the successful lumber and manufacturing business of "Stratton Brothers," near the Athol depot. He married **Fannie M. Kendall** in 1861.

Children:—*Born in Athol.*
- —326 Fannie T.,[8] m. **C. E. Marsh**, Dec. 25, 1890.
- —327 Luna Kendall,[8] bookkeeper for the firm of Stratton Bros.

254. GEORGE KENDALL STRATTON [7] (*Cyrus,*[6] *David,*[5] *Peleg,*[4] *James,*[3] *Thomas,*[2] *John*[1]), born in Westboro, Mass., Jan. 6, 1846, married **Mary J. Hastings** of Westboro, Feb. 9, 1870. She died Aug. 3, 1883, and Oct. 28, 1885, he married **Fannie F. Goodridge** of Newton, N. H. Aug. 10, 1864, enlisted for three years in 1st Mass. Battalion Heavy Artillery; mustered out Jan. 24, 1865; res. Grafton.

Children:—*Born in Grafton, Mass.*
    By first marriage.
- —328 Eva Gertrude,[8] d. Nov. 9, 1888, aged 18 years.

—329 Herbert E.,[8] m. **Pearl Twinning**, Sept. 6, 1896; res. Arlington, Mass.; salesman.
—330 Robert H., m. **Lena Mae Twinning** in 1904; res. Ashland, Mass.; chn. Robt. H., Jr.,[9] Barbara.[9]
By second marriage.
—331 Fred L.[8]
—332 Harriet G.[8]
—333 Stanley C.[8]
—334 Raymond W.,[8] b. Sept. 25, 1895; d. Mar. 13, 1903.

255. HERBERT STACY STRATTON [7] (*Cyrus W.*,[6] *David*,[5] *Peleg*,[4] *James*,[3] *Thomas*,[2] *John* [1]), born Jan. 28, 1850, married **Mary Whitney Heywood** in 1876, daughter of *Charles* and *Fannie (Green) Heywood*, born 1856, died 1899. Lived in Gardner, Mass., where he was one of the best known business men of the place; represented his district in the House in 1888. Moved to Springfield in 1898. Manufacturer and dealer in pictures, frames and art novelties, Broomfield Street, Boston, first under firm name "H. S. Stratton & Co.," and then "H. S. Stratton & Son." He died in Springfield, Jan. 2, 1914.

Children:—*Born in Grafton, Mass.*
—335 Charles Heywood,[8] grad. from Mass. Inst. Tech. in architecture in 1900. 1901-1909 Inspector, Dept. Bldgs & Grounds U. S. Naval Academy, Annapolis, Md.; now Supt. Construction, U. S. Public Bldgs, Field Force, of Supervising Archt. Office, Treas. Dept.; add. Washington, D. C. Married, Sept. 29, 1904, **Marion M. Woolley**, daughter *Lucius L.* and *Ellen Electa (Moseley) Woolley* of Medford, Mass.
—336 George Cyrus,[8] educated high school and business college; with Taber-Prang Art Co.; then in picture and art trade in New York City; in 1908 became a partner in his father's business in Boston; since 1914 is carrying on the business alone; m., 1906, **Jean L. Ritchie**; chn. Leonard,[9] Mary Heywood.[9]
—337 Fanny Eliza,[8] m. **Willis Edmond Blodgett**, 1907; res. Agawam, Mass.
—338 Ralph H.,[8] b. May, 1885; d. Nov., 1899.

256. ASA EVANS STRATTON [7] (*Cyrus W.*,[6] *David*,[5] *Peleg*,[4] *James*,[3] *Thomas*,[2] *John* [1]), born in Grafton, Mass.; graduate of

Brown University; lawyer; member Delta Phi Fraternity and of Phi Beta Kappa; in 1906 City Editor of *Fitchburg Daily Sentinel*. April 10, 1878, married **Eda F. Biglow**, a graduate of Dr. Gannett's school, Boston.

Child:—*Born in Fitchburg, Mass.*

—339   Helen Florence,[8] graduate Smith College; teacher English Literature, Fitchburg high school.

263.   Henry Ward Stratton [7] (*James E.*,[6] *Andrew*,[5] *Peleg*,[4] *James*,[3] *Thomas*,[2] *John* [1]), born in Panola Co., Miss., attended Concrete College, DeWitt Co., Texas, and Burgiss Commercial College, Galveston; a farmer of Brown Co., Texas, on a farm which he bought in 1877, while the county yet abounded in buffalo, deer, antelope and wild turkey, of which Mr. Stratton can tell many delightful stories. He married **Margarett Taylor** in 1882.

Children:—*Born in Brown Co., Texas.*

—340   William,[8] m. **Margaret Dennis**.
—341   Louella,[8] m. **Leonard W. Baker**.
—342   Charles Ward.[8]
—343   Henry Andrew.[8]
—344   John Evans.[8]
—345   Thomas Alexander,[8] b. 1892; d. aged 7 years.
—346   Samuel.[8]
—347   Margarett A.[8]
—348   Mary Elizabeth.[8]
—349   Edward Luther.[8]
—350   Austin Bryan.[8]
—351   Myrtle Gilliam,[8] b. 1908.

273.   Joel Bryan Stratton [7] (*James*,[6] *Asa E.*,[5] *Peleg*,[4] *James*,[3] *Thomas*,[2] *John* [1]) married, Aug. 20, 1860, **Maude Biggs**, daughter of *John O.* and *Mary J. Biggs*.

Children:—*Born in Dickens, Texas.*

—352   Joel Bryan, Jr.[8]

Born in Deming, New Mexico.

—353   LeRoy Biggs.[8]

292.   Henry Campbell Stratton [7] (*Jonas*,[6] *Sewell*,[5] *Jonas*,[4] *David*,[3] *Thomas*,[2] *John* [1]), born in Cambridge, Nov. 19, 1826; married **Esther Boyden White**, Dec., 1854; died at Neponsett, Mass., Jan. 30, 1875. Lived in Boston, where he was a member

The "Old Grocer Stand"   The STRATTON HOME, CHATTANOOGA   "Stratton's," Grassy Cove
See pages 220-221.

of the Unitarian church; constable in municipality for many years; Knights Templar, Boston Commandery. Mr. Stratton was a handsome man, tall and strong, black hair and blue eyes, generous to a fault, hospitable in entertaining relatives and friends, a delightful talker and letter writer.

Children:—*Born in Boston.*
- −354 Winella White,[8] m. Cyril H. Burdett, Feb. 21, 1888; res. Branchville, Conn.
- −355 Esther Rebecca,[8] m. Willis J. Banks, Dec. 21, 1886; res. Evanston, Ill.
- −356 Jonas Mason,[8] m. Margaret Shoals, Nov. 24, 1885; res. Worcester, Mass.
- −357 Henry Wilson,[8] m. Bessie Newton, Oct. 27, 1897; res. Boston, Mass.
- −358 Edith Louise,[8] d. unm., Nov., 1907.
- −359 Gertrude Whitney,[8] m. Ernest Blasius, Sept. 25, 1895; d. Jan. 27, 1900.
- −360 Andrew Dwight,[8] m. Carrie Gill, July 4, 1891.
- −361 Ralph Hemans,[8] d. in Roxbury, 1870.
- −362 Guy Bascom,[8] d. in Neponsett, 1872.

298. REV. GEORGE ASA STRATTON [7] (*Asa B.*,[6] *Sewell*,[5] *Jonas*,[4] *David*,[3] *Thomas*,[2] *John* [1]) was born in New York City, Dec. 20, 1847, attended public schools of the city, the free Academy, and Columbia Law School. Was admitted to the bar at New York in 1866. Licensed to preach the Gospel in 1888 by the First Baptist church of Reading, Mass. Held pastorates at West Newberry and Marrimacport, Mass., and in Dorchester, N. H. Failing health has obliged him to retire from the ministry. Resides at Reading, Mass. He married **Mary Ann Wakefield Damon**, daughter of *Etson* and *Ann* (*Stratton*) *Damon* (see No. 185).

Children:—*Born in Reading, Mass.*
- −363 Marietta, m. 1st, John Wetmore of Lynn, 2nd, Charles W. Marshall.
- +364 George Albert.
  Born in Marblehead.
- −365 Charles Etson.

312. ALONZO STRATTON [8] (*Leander*,[7] *James*,[6] *Zebulon*,[5] *James*,[4] *James*,[3] *Thomas*,[2] *John* [1]) married **Frances Kilburn**, Aug. 16, 1862. She was daughter of *George* and *Betsey* (*Wright*) *Kilburn*, who settled in Little Valley from Rhode Island. He was a farmer, first in Little Valley and then in Salamanca, N. Y., where he died in 1909.

Children:—*Born in Little Valley, N. Y.*
—366　Ella Celia,[8] m. **Watson Brown Eddy,** son of Jas. and Elvira Eddy; res. Portland, O.

Born in Salamanca, N. Y.
—367　Allan Adelbert,[8] m. **Inez Akres**; res. Salamanca; ch. Frances M.[9]
—368　Charles Albert,[8] m. **Mabel Leggett**; res. Salamanca; ch. George.[9]

317.　Charles Lorenzo Stratton[8] (*Lorenzo*,[7] *James*,[6] *Zebulon*,[5] *James*,[4] *James*,[3] *Thomas*,[2] *John*[1]) was born in Cincinnati, Ohio, and spent his boyhood on the old Stratton homestead in Little Valley, N. Y. Attended school at Randolph Academy and East Tenn. University. Has been engaged in the lumber business in Tennessee and adjoining states since **1885**, except two years when he was editor of the *Southern Farm Journal*. Nov. 19, **1889**, he married **Carrie L. Crews**, daughter of *Josiah* and *Ann* (*Boseman*) *Crews* and granddaughter of *Jesse* and *Nancy* (*Carter*) *Crews* and *Judge Luke* and *Nancy* (*Cross*) *Boseman* of Illinois. Res. Chattanooga.

Children:—*Born in Chattanooga, Tenn.*
—369　Carolyn Lucy,[9] m. July 11, 1916, **Ladd Mills Sumner,** son of Frank Alexander and Florence (Turner) Sumner of Asheville, N. C. Ch. Ladd Mills, Jr.
—370　Helen Russell,[9] d. Aug. 30, 1910, a beautiful girl of 14 years.
—371　Charles Lorenzo Crews.[9]

318.　Francis Augustus Stratton[8] (*Lorenzo*,[7] *James*,[6] *Zebulon*,[5] *James*,[4] *James*,[3] *Thomas*,[2] *John*[1]) spent his boyhood and youth on his father's farm, first in Little Valley, N. Y., and then in Grassy Cove, Tenn. From here he went to Chattanooga, where he received an appointment as Assistant Commissioner for the state of Tennessee, to the Centennial Exposition at Philadelphia. At the close of the exposition he was employed as clerk in the Chattanooga postoffice and was soon promoted to the position of assistant postmaster. Resigning this position he engaged in the lumber business in East Tennessee, and later had large dealings in coal and timber lands in Tenn., N. Car., Vir., and Ky., during which time he removed to Johnson City, Tenn., where he helped to organize and establish the state bank, the electric street railroad and electric lighting plant. In 1899 he removed to New York City and a year later to Mount Vernon, N. Y., where he is president and chairman of the Board of Directors of the Westchester Lighting Company. Also, president of the Peekskill Lighting and Railroad Company and of the Quaker Ridge Improvement Company; also a director of the Westchester Chamber of Commerce and the Mount Vernon Trust Company. He is a member of the Republican Club of New York, The Lawyer's, Transportation, and Lotos Clubs of New York, the Huguenot Club, Wykagl Country Club and Yacht Club of New Rochelle.

Feb. 28, 1882, he married **Annie Wilder**, daughter of *Gen. John Thomas* and *Martha (Stuart) Wilder*, and a descendant of *Edward Wilder*[1] of Hingham, Mass., in 1632.* Their summer home "Menigawum" is on an island at the mouth of the Damariscotta river, Maine.

Child:—*Born in Chattanooga, Tenn.*
—372 Wilder Lorenzo,[9] treas. and gen. mgr. Hudson R. and Eastern Traction Co.; mem. Princeton, N. Y. Republican, and other clubs; commissioned Ensign in U. S. Naval Reserve Force March 20, called to active duty Apr. 14, 1917.

364. GEORGE ALBERT STRATTON[8] (*George*,[7] *Asa B.*,[6] *Sewell*,[5] *Jonas*,[4] *David*,[3] *Thomas*,[2] *John*[1]), born in Reading, Mass., married **Lula Conway**, Sept. 12, 1891, daughter of *James* and *Marie (Desing) Conway*.

Children:
—373 Martha A.[9]
—374 George Albert, Jr.[9]
—375 James Edward.[9]

365. CHARLES ETSON STRATTON[8] (*George A.*,[7] *Asa B.*,[6] *Sewell*,[5] *Jonas*,[4] *David*,[3] *Thomas*,[2] *John*[1]), born in Marblehead, Mass., resides in Reading. Married **Carrie A. Sias**, Feb. 15, 1891.

Children:—*Born in Reading, Mass.*
—376 Charles Pettingill.[9]
—377 Florence May,[5] d. 1902, aged 2 years.
—378 Willard Evlin.[9]
—379 Elmer Baxter.[9]

---

*Thus: John T. Wilder[7] (Reuben,[6] Seth,[5] Seth,[4] Ephraim,[3] John,[2] Edward[1]).

—380 Maybelle Gertrude.[9]
—381 Arthur Damon.[9]

JOSEPH STRATTON OF WALTHAM

(Chart J, Vol I)

It has been suggested that Joseph Stratton of Waltham who married **Sarah Hager** in 1717 (*Vol. I*, p. 197) was a son of John Stratton [2] (*John* [1]) by his first wife **Mary Butters** (p. 184, Vol. I) and the compiler is inclined to believe that this is the solution to this problem which has long puzzled researchers.*

The compiler has found but little more about his descendants. Joseph Stratton (No. 13, p. 200) settled in Roxbury, where he was a "housewright." June 21, 1801, he married **Sarah Hayward**, daughter of *Samuel Hayward* of Situate. He was a deacon in the church at Roxbury and was living there as late as 1837. Births of only two children are found, Susanna, b. July 9, 1802, and Elizabeth, b. July, 1805; d. Apr. 4, 1809.

John Stratton (No. 14, p. 200, *Vol. I*) seems to have been living in Newton in 1796, when he received $450 from his father's estate. After this the compiler has found no record of him. When *Vol. I* was issued it was thought that this was the John Stratton who died in Hallowell, Me., in 1801, aged 26 years. It has since been proven that this man belonged to another line of Strattons, as shown on another page of this volume.

---

* This suggestion was first made by Mr. Edward L. Smith of Boston, to whom the compiler is indebted for many helpful notes on the Strattons of that vicinity, especially on Jonathan Stratton of Weston.

Wm. Butters settled in Woburn before 1666. He was in King Philip's War. His wife's name was Mary. They were probably married across the water. He died in 1692. The History of Woburn states that "Widow Butters" d. in Watertown in 1701. The only child of record is William, born (g. s. rec.) in 1665. There can be hardly any doubt, however, that they had a daughter Mary who married John Stratton [2] in 1691. She died in 1695 and it is reasonable to suppose that her son Joseph lived with his grandmother Butters after his mother's death.

REV. DANIEL STRATTON
Page 243.

STRATTONS OF LONG ISLAND
RICHARD STRATTON OF EASTHAMPTON

(Chart C, Vol. I)

"There is a moral and philosophical respect for our ancestors which elevates the character and improves the mind."

DANIEL WEBSTER.

ABOUT 1720 a tract of land (about 700 acres) was set off in what is now South Foxboro, Mass., to be sold for the benefit of the schools of Dorchester—the first land set apart for the use of public schools in this country. The farm bought by Richard Stratton[4] was a part of this land. The picture of the house built by him about 1750 is from a photograph taken for the compiler only a few months before the house was destroyed by fire in 1908. It had long been a landmark in this section, and an attraction for lovers of the antique. Near it is the old burial ground with its quaint epitaphs.

FIFTH GENERATION

52. JAMES STRATTON[5] (*Richard,[4] Richard,[3] Richard,[2] Richard[1]*) was born Sept. 27, 1751. He was the oldest son and by his father's will was left in charge of the estate, which he was to divide among his brothers and sisters. In 1773 he married **Lydia Tower**. They lived on the old Stratton farm just out of South Foxboro, Mass., in the house built by his father. James Stratton was born, lived and died in this house and here his children were born. He died Jan. 27, 1809; his wife died Sept. 1, 1835.

Children:—*Born in Foxboro, Mass.*
+81   John,[6] b. 1774; d. 1852.
−82   Waitstill,[6] b. May 17, 1777; m. **Oliver Morse,** July 23, 1797.
+83   Welcome,[6] b. 1779.
−84   Mary,[6] b. Oct. 23, 1782; m. May 5, 1864, **Joseph Shepherd** (his second wife).

—85 Sarah,⁶ b. Sept. 19, 1786; m. **James Payson**, Apr. 26, 1808.

—86 Anna⁶ (or Any), b. Sept. 18, 1789; m. **James Plympton**.

55. GEORGE STRATTON⁵ (*Richard,⁴ Richard,³ Richard,² Richard¹*) was born Sept. 24, 1756. He was married Jan. 27, 1782, to Caroline Freeman, by Rev. Roland Green. They lived in Foxboro. He was a privateer in the Revolution, and saved considerable money. He was known as "Capt. Stratton." In 1781, with Uriah Atherton, Jos. Hewes, and John Knapp, he built a foundry on Mill street, where the Foxboro Foundry now stands, Capt. Stratton furnishing one-half the capital. They made cannons and cannon balls at first, and later hollow ware. In 1813 he sold his interest in this 10-acre plant to Gen. Shephard Leach. A foundry has been in operation on this plant to this day. Mr. Stratton died July 14, 1817; Mrs. Stratton, Mar. 3, 1830.

Children:—*Born in Foxboro, Mass.*

—87 Milton,⁶ b. May 6, 1782; m. **Nancy Comee**, Feb. 5, 1805. She was born Apr. 8, 1787, and d. July 20, 1811; he died Mar. 12, 1812. Did they leave any children?

—88 Tyler,⁶ b. May 1, 1785; m. May 23, 1809, **Sarah Bird**, who d. Mar. 10, 1810, aged 22 years. What became of him?

—89 Nancy,⁶ b. Feb. 27, 1787; m. **Beriah Mann** Mar. 14, 1805.

—90 Hannah,⁶ b. May 3, 1790; m. **Jedediah Carpenter** May 23, 1809.

—91 George, Jr.,⁶ b. Mar. 31, 1792; d. Apr. 14, 1814.

57. LEMUEL STRATTON⁵ (*Richard,⁴ Richard,³ Richard,² Richard¹*), born May 23, 1761; m. **Abigail Sternes**, daughter of *Capt. John Sternes* of Attleboro. She was born in 1760, and died Mar. 15, 1848. Lemuel Stratton died in 1816. His estate was administered by Jabez Newell.

Children:—*Born in Attleboro, Mass.*

—92 Mary,⁶ b. Oct. 7, 1783; m. **Adonijah Lewis**.

—93 Lemuel,⁶ b. Jan. 30, 1791; d., unm., Mar. 4, 1858. Gravestones to him and his mother in cemetery at South Attleboro.

59. ROBERT STRATTON⁵ (*Richard,⁴ Richard,³ Richard,² Richard¹*) was born July 9, 1765. He married **Elizabeth Shepherd** Sept. 22, 1797. He was a farmer, owning land in Foxboro, where

he died Feb. 28, 1842. His widow died May 10, 1857, aged 80 years. His farm was a part of the old Stratton estate—once known as the "School Farm."
Children:—*Born in Foxboro, Mass.*
+94 Richard S.,[6] b. 1798; d. 1876.
—95 Schuyler,[6] b. Sept. 26, 1801; d. Sept. 14, 1835, unm.
+96 Chandler,[6] b. 1814; d. 1875.
    Adaline Shepherd Stratton,[6] an adopted daughter, m. Ezekill C. Grant, of Billingham, Mass.

61. DAVID STRATTON [5] (*Richard,[4] Richard,[3] Richard,[2] Richard[1]*) was born March, 1768. He settled in Sandisfield, Mass., where he was a farmer, and where he died Oct. 3, 1841. He married **Eliza Morton**.
Children:—*Born in Sandisfield.*
+97 Milo,[6] b. 1797.
—98 Cynthia,[6] b. May 4, 1800.
—99 Eunice,[6] b. Oct. 31, 1802.
+100 Edward A.,[6] b. 1804; d. 1888.

62. JOSEPH STRATTON [5] (*Richard,[4] Richard,[3] Richard,[2] Richard[1]*) lived and died in Foxboro. He was born in 1769 and died Dec. 31, 1806. Dec. 13, 1795, he married **Elizabeth Pettee**, Rev. T. Kendall officiating. A tombstone to his memory stands in the old Foxboro burial ground. His widow married Beriah Billings.
Children:—*Born in Foxboro.*
—101 Cynthia,[6] b. Dec. 1, 1796; d. aged 16 years.
—102 Lucy Nason,[6] b. May 8, 1798; m. **John Farwell** Feb. 13, 1823.
—103 Nabby,[6] b. Aug. 21, 1799.
—104 Elvira,[6] b. Jan. 21, 1801; d., single, in Foxboro 1846.
—105 Eliza,[6] b. Sept. 20, 1802; m. —— Paine.
—106 Caroline,[6] b. Apr. 24, 1804; d. aged 5 years.
—107 Joseph Pettee,[6] b. Sept. 15, 1805.
—108 Sophrona,[6] b. Aug. 25, 1806.

68. JAMES STRATTON [5] (*Benjamin,[4] Benjamin,[3] Benjamin,[2] Richard[1]*) was born Aug. 20, 1755. He was but four years old when his father died. Of his early life and education we are not informed. He studied medicine under Dr. Benjamin Harris, of Salem Co., N. J. Upon the breaking out of the war of 1776 he gave his services to his country's cause. After the war he graduated (M.D.) from the University of Pennsylvania and became a successful and distinguished physician, President of the New Jersey Medical Society, and a man of influence in civic and political affairs. Quoting from an obituary published at the time of his death: "Dr. Stratton was of that description of man who are justly styled the 'pillars of society,' active, intelligent, sensible, dignified, a Christian and a patriot."

He early joined the Protestant Episcopal Church, of which he was an efficient member, though he always retained a preference for the Puritan faith of his forefathers, and on Sunday afternoons was accustomed to assemble his family to instruct them in the Westminster Catechism. Although his medical practice was large, extending over a circuit of 30 miles, he so timed his engagements, that he was seldom absent from his place in church, always leading the singing with his fine bass voice. He was handsome and commanding in appearance, kindly pleasant in his manner, entertaining in conversation and was greatly loved and respected. He accumulated considerable property and left a large landed estate, the value of which, however, was much reduced by the fall in prices after the war of 1812. Dr. Stratton was twice married, first, Feb. 15, 1779, to **Anna Harris**, the daughter of his early preceptor. She died Feb. 19, 1783, and Jan. 1, 1787, he married **Mary Creighton**, daughter of *Hugh* and *Mary (McCullough-French) Creighton*, of Haddonfield, N. J. She was born Dec. 9, 1762, and died April 30, 1847. Soon after his first marriage he bought the historic old Hatton House in Swedesboro, and lived there for several years.* In 1794 he built the large brick house on the North side of Raccoon Creek, near Swedesboro, known as "Stratton Hall" (see *picture, Vol. I, opposite p. 114*). This house was long famous for its genial hospitality, and remained in the possession and occupancy of the family until the death of his son, Governor Stratton, in 1859. The

---

* The Hatton House of Swedesboro was built long before the Revolution by John Hatton of Canterbury, Eng., who was at that time Tax Collector of West Jersey, and who made this his home until the beginning of the war, when he became a fugitive and joined the army of the King. According to the law passed Dec. 11, 1778, the owner being a fugitive, the property was confiscated and ordered sold. Dr. James Stratton was the purchaser, paying, according to the old deed, thirteen hundred and twenty pounds for the house and fifteen acres of land—in what kind of money this high price was paid the deed does not say.

tombstone placed to Dr. Stratton's memory in Trinity churchyard, Swedesboro, bear these words:

"Sacred to the memory of
Dr. James Stratton
who departed this life Mar. 29, 1812, in the 57th year of his age. With a mind strong and well cultivated, he was uncommonly useful as a citizen, and as a christian his piety and virtue will long be held in remembrance."

Children:—Born in Swedesboro, N. J.
By first marriage.
—109   Benjamin Harris,[6] b. Apr. 18, 1780; d. aged 15 years.
—110   Sarah Harris,[6] b. Sept. 30, 1781; d. Feb. 12, 1852; m. Sept. 5, 1799, Edward Carpenter, son of Thomas Carpenter, of Carpenter's Landing, Pa.
—111   Anna Harris,[6] b. Dec. 12, 1782; d. May 15, 1810; m. **John L. Stratton** (*No. 72, Chart C*).
By second marriage.
—112   Maria,[6] b. Nov. 17, 1789; d. Apr. 12, 1857; m. 1st, May 9, 1812, **Dr. Erkurius Fithian**, son of Joel and Elizabeth (Beatty) Fithian; 2d **Daniel P. Stratton** (*No. 70, Chart C*).
—113   James Creighton,[6] b. Nov. 16, 1792; d. aged 8 mos.
+114   Samuel C.,[6] b. 1794; d. 1860.
+115   Charles C.,[6] b. 1796; d. 1859.
—116   Harriet,[6] b. Jan. 4, 1798; in Woodbury, N. J., May 9, 1850; m. Nov. 12, 1817, **Dr. Joseph** Fithian, son of Amos and Rachel (Leake) Fithian.
—117   Isabella,[6] b. July 10, 1799; d. July 1, 1847; m. Feb. 20, 1817, **Benjamin Matlack**, son of Isaac Howey and Abigail Matlack.
—118   Frances,[6] b. Mar. 24, 1802; d., unm., Feb. 2, 1890, in Phila.
—119   Abigail,[6] b. Jan. 5, 1805; d. aged 4 mos.

70. DANIEL POWELL STRATTON [5] (*Levi,*[4] *Benjamin,*[3] *Benjaman,*[2] *Richard*[1]) was born in 1784. His mother died the year following his birth, and his father seven years later. Of his early life we know but little. Financially he had a good start in life. He inherited some property from his father and was one of the next of kin to James Harris who died in 1803, leaving no children and leaving personal property appraised at $45,000—

at that time and in that place esteemed a large amount. March 30, 1808, Mr. Stratton married **Ruth Seeley Buck**. She died Feb. 29, 1816, at the age of 26 years. In Jan., 1818, he married **Mrs. Maria (Stratton) Fithian**, widow of Erkurius Fithian and daughter of *Dr. James Stratton (No. 112, Chart C)*.

About this time he moved to Bridgeton, N. J., and engaged in business there, first as one of the mercantile firm of "Buck & Stratton"—John Buck and Nathan L. Stratton being the other members of the firm—and later he became quite a large dealer in real estate. He purchased the house on the corner of Commerce and Atlantic streets, where he resided the remainder of his life. He was an excellent man, earnest in promoting every good cause and was held in high esteem by his acquaintances. Early in life he united with the Presbyterian Church, and for many years was a ruling elder. He died June 6, 1840.

Children:—*Born in Fairfield, N. J.*
      By first marriage.
—120   Edward,^{6} b. Mar. 19, 1809; d. aged 6 mos.
+121   James,^{6} b. 1810.
—122   Robert,^{6} b. Nov. 1, 1812; d. in infancy.
    Born in Bridgeton, N. J.
      By second marriage.
+123   Daniel,^{6} b. 1814; d. 1866.
—124   Edward,^{6} b. 1818; d. in infancy.
—125   Sarah,^{6} b. 1820; d. in infancy.
—126   Harriet,^{6} b. Mar. 23, 1822; d. Aug. 1, 1873, at her home in Bridgeton, esteemed by an entire community, where she had rendered earnest service in the Presbyterian Church, in night schools, Christian mission work, and other social and religious enterprises.
—127   Maria Creighton,^{6} b. Aug. 7, 1824; d., unm., Oct. 11, 1859.
—128   Hannah Giles,^{6} b. 1826; d. in infancy.
—129   Frances,^{6} b. Aug. 16, 1828; d. aged 20 years.

72. JOHN LEAKE STRATTON ^{5} (*John,*^{4} *Benjamin,*^{3} *Benjamin,*^{2} *Richard* ^{1}) was born Feb. 23, 1778. His boyhood was spent on his father's farm. Attending school winters he obtained a common school education. At nineteen he began studying medicine with his cousin Dr. James Stratton. In 1800 he graduated from the University of Pennsylvania, and at once began the practice of medicine and surgery at Mount Holly, N. J.

"Dr. John L. Stratton was a fine specimen of manhood, affable, amiable and affectionate, he sympathized earnestly with his patients of all classes and conditions, and after a life of self-sacrifice and devoted usefulness to his profession and his patients, he died as he had lived—an honored Christian gentleman"—Aug. 17, 1845.

Dr. Stratton married first **Anna Stratton** (*No. 111, Chart C*) in 1804. She died May 15, 1810, and Dec. 26, 1816, he married **Ann Newbold**, who died Apr. 18, 1888. About the time of his first marriage he came into possession of the brick house on Mill street, in Mount Holly, which is now owned and occupied by his granddaughter (see *picture opposite page 114, Vol. I*). This house was built before 1776, and was occupied by soldiers at one time during the Revolution, while the Hessians were quartered in the tavern near by. Dr. Stratton added to the house in 1822, building on to the front part as shown in the picture. He also bought a part of the historic old Woolman property, out on Mill street, at the edge of Mount Holly, rebuilt the house and spent the greater part of his married life there. This property passed out of the Stratton family at the death of his son, Dr. B. H. Stratton.*

Children:—*Born in Mt. Holly, N. J.*
    By first marriage.
+130 Benjamin H.,[6] b. 1804; d. 1875.
—131 James,[6] d. in infancy.
    By second marriage.
+132 John Leake Newbold,[6] b. 1817; d. 1889.

74. NATHAN LEAKE STRATTON [5] (*John,*[4] *Benjamin,*[3] *Benjamin,*[2] *Richard*[1]) was born Jan. 31, 1786. In 1814 he went to Bridgeton and entered into partnership with Daniel P. Stratton and Joseph Buck in the mercantile business. The fol-

---

* The old carpenter shop of John Woolman (the celebrated Quaker preacher), which the New Jersey legislature is considering buying, stands on another property.

The compiler has records, from an old family Bible, of a John L. Stratton who was born in Camden Co., N. J., Aug. 11, 1788. It is understood by his descendants that he was son of a Revolutionary soldier, and they have in their possession a pistol which was carried by him during service in the Colonial army. They have always understood, also, that he was a near relative of Gov. Charles Stratton. He married Clara Holden, who was born in Matthew Co., Va., July 4, 1792. They lived for a while in Baltimore. They had children, Clara, Phœbe and James Holden, named for his mother's brother. James Holden Strat-

lowing year, Mar. 7, 1815, he married **Hannah Buck**, daughter of *Joseph* and *Ruth (Seeley) Buck*.* Two years later he built the large brick house on Commerce street, which remained in possession of the family for ninety years. For more than a quarter of a century Mr. Stratton was one of the active business men of Bridgeton, having charge of the general merchandise department of the firm, and the business became the largest transacted in the county. Mrs. Stratton died in 1854, aged 63 years, and Mr. Stratton in 1862.

Children:—*Born in Bridgeton, N. J.*
+133   Joseph Buck,⁶ b. 1815; d. 1903.
—134   Alexander,⁶ b. Dec. 17, 1817; a merchant and ship owner for many years in Bridgeton, where he died, unm., Jan. 3, 1873.
—135   Eleanor Leake,⁶ lived at the old homestead in Bridgeton, where she died Nov. 20, 1903.
—136   Nathan,⁶ b. Apr. 23, 1822; d. in childhood.
—137   George,⁶ b. Jan. 11, 1824; d., unm., in Bridgeton in 1884.
—138   John,⁶ b. Feb. 13, 1826; d. May 20, 1855.
+139   Charles Preston,⁶ b. 1828; d. 1884.
—140   Anna Ruth,⁶ b. May 12, 1830; d. in Bridgeton, aged 22 years.
—141   Edgar, Robert ⁶ (142), and Henry (143), d. in infancy.
—144   Sophia Hill,⁶ m. **Dr. Charles Elton Buck**, who died in Wilmington, Del., Sept. 2, 1891. She died in Baltimore, Feb. 23, 1905. Both are buried at Laurel Hill, Phila.

75. LEVI STRATTON ⁵ (*John,⁴ Benjamin,³ Benjamin,² Richard ¹*) was born in Deerfield, N. J., May 29, 1791. He married in 1826 **Sarah Stratton Buck**, daughter of *Reuben* and *Sarah (Stratton) Buck (No. 69, Chart C, Vol. I)*. They lived for awhile at Bridgeton, and then removed to a farm near Deerfield, where Mr. Stratton died in 1838.

---

ton, born in Baltimore April 16, 1813, married Amanda M. (Tyrrell) Haines March 14, 1845, and died Oct. 31, 1884, in Charleston, S. C. Their son, John Paul Stratton, lives in Augusta, Ga. He married, Jan. 24, 1883, Hattie M. Dowell, d. of Samuel L. and Louise H. (Girard) Dowell. Their children are Helen M., Harriet M., Pauline E., Dorothy, John P., Jr., Agnes.

* Joseph Buck was a Revolutionary patriot, present at the execution of Major Andrie in 1780, and at Johnstown in 1781. Original member of the Society of Cincinnati.

NATHAN LEAKE STRATTON    REV. JOSEPH B. STRATTON, D.D.

Children:—*Born in Bridgeton, N. J.*
+145 Nathan Leake,⁶ b. Nov. 11, 1828.
Born in Deerfield.
—146 Jonathan Freeman,⁶ b. Feb. 18, 1831. Settled in Frankford, Ind., where he was a merchant, and where he died about 1870.
—147 Levi,⁶ b. Aug. 26, 1833. Went West, engaged in business at Noodle, Texas, where he was tax assessor and collector; d., unm., Oct. 2, 1870.

76. WILLIAM STRATTON⁵ (*William,⁴ William,³ Benjamin,² Richard¹*) was born in Deerfield, N. J. He was a blacksmith by trade. He married **Jemima Davis**, in Cumberland Co., N. J., Nov. 9, 1796, and settled in Philadelphia some time after 1805, and died there in 1815.

Children:—*Born in Deerfield, N. J.*
—148 Rebecca.⁶
+149 William,⁶ b. 1805.
—150 Nancy.⁶
—151 Emily,⁶ m. —— Shaw.

There may have been other children. The Compiler would like to know more of this family.*

---

*But little has been learned concerning the descendants of William.³ Referring to Vol. I, p. 110, it will be seen that three of his sons are unaccounted for—Jonathan,⁴ Ephriam⁴ and Aaron,⁴ and we know but little of William.⁴ One of these sons was the father of Lot Stratton who married **Elizabeth Duff** Jan. 21, 1773. She died at Deerfield in 1776, and he went to Pennsylvania.

Ephraim⁴ had a son Fithian (called "Fithian, Jr."), b. about 1770, d. 1820, who had two daughters, Judith and Sarah, and perhaps other children. William⁴ is believed to have had several children, though we have records of only one son, William,⁵ above.

It is probably to this branch of Strattons that belongs Noah Stratton of Deerfield township, who married **Rhoda Loder** Oct. 21, 1772, and had several children, among them Charles, b. 1773, and John, who is probably the man who married **Phœbe Bateman** April 10, 1798. Sarah Stratton, who married **Daniel Loder** of Deerfield Nov. 17, 1775, and Abigail Stratton, who married **Reuben Loder** Aug. 25, 1774, doubtless belong to this same family. Perhaps some one who reads this footnote may be able to supply the compiler with the data desired to complete these records.

In Brown Co., Ohio, are Strattons who have the following family records: William Stratton married **Katherine Keethler** and had children—Lot, Aaron, Lewis, John, Anderson, Sanford, Christopher, Nancy, Lucinda, Mary, Levina, America and Susan. The son Lot settled in Ohio from Pennsylvania, married **Mary Davison**, and had children—Louisa,

78. BENJAMIN STRATTON [5] (*Benjamin*,[4] *Jonathan*,[3] *Benjamin*,[2] *Richard*[1]) was born in Easthampton about 1765, and settled in Stillwater, Saratoga Co., N. Y., where he married **Elizabeth Comstock**, and where he spent the remainder of his life.

Children:—*Born in Saratoga Co., N. Y.*

+152 Stephen.[6]
—153 John,[6] d. unmarried.
+154 Charles B.[6]
—155 Henry.[6]
—156 James.[6]
—157 Norman,[6] m. **Rebecca Marvin**; civil eng. in U. S. Navy yard in Brooklyn in 1878; d. about 1882. Buried in Troy, N. Y.
—158 William,[6] m. **Sarah Haskens**.
—159 Mary.[6]
—160 Elizabeth,[6] m. —— **Bingham**.
—161 Eliza.[6]

More complete records of this family are desired. The compiler has some doubt about the correctness of some of the above names.

80. JONATHAN STRATTON [5] (*Benjamin*,[4] *Jonathan*,[3] *Benjamin*,[2] *Richard*[1]), baptized in Easthampton, Feb. 19, 1769; died there Nov. 26, 1833. A gravestone stands to his memory in the old cemetery. From 1802 to the year of his death his name constantly appears in the list of town officers, and at various times he was Overseer of the Poor, Commissioner of Highways, Fence Viewer, pounder, trustee and tithing man. He married, Feb. 9, 1840, **Mary Dayton**, daughter of *Samuel Dayton*, a prominent man of Easthampton. They lived in the old Stratton house (see *p. 116, Vol. I*). This house is believed to have been built

---

Napolian B., Francis M., Nancy, Martin V., Susan, Albina, Thomas B. and Lucinda.

The compiler believes that they are descended from William Stratton [3] of Deerfield, and would be glad to get further records of them.

From Mrs. Cranford of Philadelphia the compiler has also the following records: William Stratton of New Jersey m. **Rebecca Hubbard** and died leaving two sons: Samuel Torrance, m. **Susan Lawrence,** who had son Samuel Torrance, Jr.; George Washington, b. in Phila. 1814, m. **Frances J. Elliot**; d. 1851; had two sons, Charles Elliot, d. unm., Henry Clay, m. **Cora Atkinson** Dec. 9, 1875. Children: Frances Josephine (m. **Dr. Edgar Dewitt Cranford**), Henry Clay, Jr. (d. in infancy), Anna Thomas, Elliot Gwynn.

about 1730. Mr. Stratton died Nov. 26, 1833; Mrs. Stratton, Feb. 9, 1840.

Children:—*Born in Easthampton, L. I.*

+162   Henry Dayton,[6] b. 1803.
+163   George Newton.[6]
—164   Jonathan C.,[6] m. Jane Hand, daughter of *Mulford Hand.*
—165   Mary,[6] b. 1807; d. 1829.

81. JOHN STRATTON [6] (*James,*[5] *Richard,*[4] *Richard,*[3] *Richard,*[2] *Richard* [1]), born Nov. 27, 1774, was married by Rev. T. Kendall to Lucy Nason, in Foxboro, Mar. 27, 1799. She died Aug. 14, 1836. He died Oct. 1, 1852. In the town records he is called "Capt. John Stratton."

Children:—*Born in Foxboro, Mass.*

—166   Fanny,[7] b. Sept. 1, 1799; m. George Groover in Mansfield Jan. 12, 1882.
—167   James,[7] b. Dec. 10, 1800; d. July 5, 1882; m. Eliza Payne; one child, Adaline Augusta.[8]
—168   Merritt,[7] b. Nov. 22, 1802; d., unm., aged 87 years.
+169   Harrison,[7] b. 1805.
—170   Adaline,[7] b. Dec. 6, 1807; m. Ezekiel C. Grant, Sept. 27, 1828.
—171   Elbridge Gerry,[7] b. Apr. 3, 1810; d. Sept. 3, 1832.
—172   Charlotte Nason,[7] b. Oct. 24, 1812; m. Albert Tales, of Foxboro, Nov. 9, 1834.

83. WELCOME STRATTON [6] (*James,*[5] *Richard,*[4] *Richard,*[3] *Richard,*[2] *Richard* [1]) was born Nov. 20, 1779. He married first Rebecca Smith, Nov. 22, 1807. She died Dec. 4, 1814. She was a daughter of *Stephen Smith,* of Mansfield, Mass. He married second Peddy (or Experience) Robinson, Oct. 20, 1817. He died in Mansfield, Jan. 26, 1868.

Children:—*Births recorded in Foxboro, Mass.*

By first marriage.

—173   Charles,[7] b. Feb. 8, 1809; m. Eleanor Dixon, of Foxboro, Nov. 26, 1840. He died in Mansfield, Jan. 2, 1865.
—174   Lydia Ann,[7] b. 1810; d. 1813.
—175   Emeline,[7] b. Aug. 1, 1814.

By second marriage.

—176   Milton Warren,[7] b. Feb. 8, 1821; d. Aug. 16, 1824.
+177   Henry Edward,[7] b. Jan. 16, 1825.

94. RICHARD SHEPHERD STRATTON [6] (*Robert*,[5] *Richard*,[4] *Richard*,[3] *Richard*,[2] *Richard* [1]) was born Feb. 18, 1798. Jan. 9, 1833, he married **Ann Eliza Sweetland**, daughter of *Rufus* and *Clarissa (Bell) Sweetland*. She was of Norton at the time of her marriage, but was born in Attleboro in 1805. About the time of his marriage Mr. Stratton built the Stratton House, which is still standing in Foxboro.* He died Sept. 1, 1876.

Children:—*Born in Foxboro, Mass.*

—178 Clarissa Elizabeth,[7] b. Sept. 9, 1834; m. **George T. Cook**, Jan. 1, 1858. Resides in Foxboro.

—179 Nancy Ann,[7] born Oct. 23, 1836; d. aged 19 years.

—180 David,[7] b. July 15, 1839; m. **Susan H. Shepherd**, daughter of *Elijah* and *Susan Shepherd* of Mansfield, Feb. 10, 1869. No children.

—181 Milo,[7] b. Nov. 15, 1848; d., unm., Mar. 26, 1886.

96. CHANDLER STRATTON [6] (*Robert*,[5] *Richard*,[4] *Richard*,[3] *Richard*,[2] *Richard* [1]), born Aug. 18, 1814, was married Apr. 25, 1836, by Rev. Mr. Pierce, to **Cynthia A. White**, daughter of *Warner* and *Cynthia (Hardon) White* of Mansfield. Mr. Stratton died in South Foxboro, June 7, 1875, and Mrs. Stratton, Apr. 12, 1877.

Children:—*Born in South Foxboro, Mass.*

+182 Schuyler,[7] b. 1837.

—183 Emily,[7] b. June 23, 1844; m. **William Reed**, son of Simeon and Prudence (Ford) Reed of Penbroke. She died Sept. 28, 1913.

—184 Charles Henry,[7] b. Jan. 26, 1851; d., unm., in Boston, Feb. 25, 1893.

97. MILO STRATTON [6] (*David*,[5] *Richard*,[4] *Richard*,[3] *Richard*,[2] *Richard* [1]) was born Oct. 27, 1797, and settled in Sandisfield, Mass., where he died Aug. 2, 1884. He married **Calista Rice**, Oct. 21, 1823. She died March 21, 1893.

Children:—*Born in Sandisfield, Mass.*

—185 Theodore A.,[7] b. Sept. 27, 1827.

—186 Edward W.,[7] b. Oct. 29, 1829.

—187 Chandler,[7] b. Sept. 9, 1830; d. Aug. 31, 1889.

—188 Mary A.,[7] b. May 9, 1833; d. Aug. 28, 1870.

---

* This photograph, and that of the old Richard Stratton house which was recently destroyed by fire, was furnished by Mrs. Clarissa Stratton Cook, who has kindly given the writer much help on this line.

—189 Augusta,⁷ b. Dec. 25, 1839; m. **James Clark**, July 5, 1838.

—190 David,⁷ b. Aug. 1, 1844.

More complete records of the Sandisfield Strattons are desired.

100. EDWARD A. STRATTON ⁶ (*David,⁵ Richard,⁴ Richard,³ Richard,² Richard* ¹) was born Dec. 4, 1804, and lived in Sandisfield, where he died April 17, 1888.

Children:—*Born in Sandisfield, Mass.*

—191 Jane E.,⁷ b. Nov. 14, 1833; m. **Olcott W. Case**.

—192 Nelson,⁷ b. Dec. 7, 1835; d. aged three years.

—193 Helen,⁷ b. June 30, 1841; m. **Henry Stedman**, Nov. 24, 1858.

—194 James,⁷ b. Apr. 10, 1837.

—195 Gordon,⁷ b. Jan. 6, 1844; m. **Mary Hubbard**, Nov. 15, 1866.

—196 Wilber,⁷ b. Nov. 24, 1853; d. Sept. 6, 1872.

114. SAMUEL CREIGHTON STRATTON ⁶ (*James,⁵ Benjamin,⁴ Benjamin,³ Benjamin,² Richard* ¹) was born in Swedesboro, May 10, 1794. Nov. 17, 1825, he married **Margaret Shepherd Kerr**, daughter of *George* and *Sarah Kerr* of Sylvan Retreat, Eastern Shore, Virginia. She died Jan. 10, 1832, and two years later he married **Elizabeth Hood** of Philadelphia. He died Oct. 28, 1860, and is buried in Trinity Churchyard, Swedesboro. He was carefully educated at Rutgers College, and for forty-three years was a faithful minister of the Protestant Episcopal Church. He held pastorates in several states, his first charge being at Snow Hill, Maryland. For several years he was at Newtown, Conn., where his first wife is buried, and where, after his death, a memorial window was placed to his memory in the church, showing the love and esteem in which he was held by his parishoners.

Children:

—197 Mary,⁷ b. Apr. 8, 1825; d. Oct. 5, 1886.

—198 James,⁷ m. **Sarah B. Almy**, at Fall River, Mass., June 17, 1869. They lived at Bordentown. They had no children.

115. CHARLES CREIGHTON STRATTON ⁶ (*James,⁵ Benjamin,⁴ Benjamin,³ Benjamin,² Richard* ¹), born at Stratton Hall, Swedesboro, N. J., Mar. 6, 1796 (see *picture, Vol. I, opposite p. 114*).

Was a graduate of Rutgers College, New Brunswick. Soon after his graduation he was sent to the state Legislature, of which he remained a member for several terms. For many years he was connected with the political interests of his native state. He was twice a member of Congress, and was Governor of New Jersey from 1844 to 1848. He filled these positions with faithfulness and integrity, these traits being prominent features of his character. His name was a pledge of straightforward honesty to all who knew him. Feb. 1, 1854, Gov. Stratton married **Sarah Taggart**, daughter of *Joseph* and *Sarah Taggart* of Philadelphia. The last years of his life were devoted to agricultural pursuits at his farm near Swedesboro, where he died Mar. 30, 1859. He is buried in the yard of Trinity Church, Swedesboro, of which he was an earnest, consistent member and regular attendant. He left no descendants.

121. JAMES STRATTON [6] (*Daniel P.,*[5] *Levi,*[4] *Benjamin,*[3] *Benjamin,*[2] *Richard*[1]) was born Aug. 10, 1810. His boyhood was spent at Bridgeton, where he attended the public schools. In 1830 he graduated from the College of New Jersey and studied Theology at Princeton and at Union Seminary, Va. In 1836 he was ordained a Presbyterian minister. He held pastorates in Georgia, N. Carolina, Alabama, Mississippi and Louisiana. His last charge was at Jackson, La., where he was greatly loved and respected. In 1838 he married at Eufala, Ala., **Elizabeth Floyd**, daughter of *Rev. Laurence* and *Mary (Wilson) Floyd* of Charlestown, S. C.

Children:

—199 Wallace Howard,[7] b. Apr. 26, 1839, at Eufala, Ala., graduated at Oakland College, Miss., and became a Presbyterian minister, receiving his theological training at Columbia, S. C. At the time of his death, Aug. 21, 1873, he was Pastor of the Presbyterian Church at Baton Rouge, La. He left no descendants.

—200 Eugene Floyd,[7] b. 1843, lost his life in the Confederate army in 1863, dying from a wound by a cannon ball during the siege of Vicksburg.

—201 William McLain,[7] b. at Portsmouth, 1845, received his college education at Columbia, S. C., and Union Seminary, Va. Held charges at Baton Rouge, La., and Pattonville, Mo.; d. Apr. 13, 1878.

+202 James,[7] b. 1849; d. 1905.

CHARLES C. STRATTON
Governor of New Jersey in 1844.
Page 241.

MYRON STRATTON; *Page* 325.
Father of Winfield Scott Stratton
Page 335.

−203　Henry V.,[7] b. Washington, N. C., in **1851**; educated at Centenary College, La.; d. unm.

Three other children, Charles C., Mary and Theresa, died in infancy.

123. DANIEL STRATTON [6] (*Daniel P.*,[5] *Levi*,[4] *Benjamin*,[3] *Benjamin*,[2] *Richard* [1]) was born at Bridgeton, N. J., Sept. 28, 1814. He became a member of the Presbyterian Church at the age of thirteen, and early devoted himself to the ministry. He graduated at Princeton in 1833, and received his theological training at Princeton and at Union Seminary, Va. His first charge was at New Bern, N. C., at which place he remained for fifteen years, leaving behind him the reverence and love of the entire community. The remainder of his life was passed at Salem, N. J. The present Presbyterian building at Salem was erected during his ministry. On the right of the pulpit in this church is a tablet inscribed as follows:

OUR PASTOR.

To the
Rev. Daniel Stratton,
for fourteen years
the faithful and beloved
Pastor of this church
this memorial is erected
by his bereaved
congregation.
Born Sept. 28, 1814.
Died Aug. 24, 1866.
He being dead yet speaketh.

In 1836 Mr. Stratton married **Eleanor C. Hancock**, daughter of Morris and Sarah Hancock, of Salem.

Children:—*Born in New Bern, N. C.*

+204　Morris Hancock,[7] b. July 18, 1838.

Born in Salem, N. J.

+205　Daniel Powell,[7] b. 1839.

−206　Henry,[7] b. July 12, 1843; d. aged 1 year.

−207　Eleanor Yorke,[7] b. Aug. 17, 1854; d. Aug. 7, 1855.

−208　John Quinton,[7] b. Feb. 10, 1858; d. in infancy.

130. BENJAMIN HARRIS STRATTON [6] (*John L.*,[5] *John*,[4] *Benjamin*,[3] *Benjamin*,[2] *Richard* [1]) was born at Mount Holly, Feb. 6,

1804. He graduated at Princeton College in 1823 and commenced the study of medicine with his father. In 1829 he graduated from the medical department of the University of Penn., and at once entered into partnership with his father—a partnership which continued until the infirmities of old age caused his father to withdraw from active practice. Dr. Stratton continued his professional labors at Mount Holly for half a century—how conscientiously and successfully his work was done was shown by the love, veneration and respect of the community he so long served. He was one of the founders of the Burlington County Medical Society, of which he was elected President several times, and served as Treasurer for many years. In 1838 he was elected President of the New Jersey State Medical Society. May 11, 1829, he married **Emeline Whithall**, daughter of *Samuel* and *Lydia (Newbold) Whithall*, who survived him. He died Dec. 31, 1875.

Children:—*Born in Mount Holly.*
- —209 Anna H.,[7] m. **Dr. C. A. Kingsbury**, Sept. 29, 1853. Res. Phila., Pa.
- —210 Mary Virginia, m. **A. Mario**.

132. JOHN LEAKE NEWBOLD STRATTON [6] (*John L.,[5] John,[4] Benjamin,[3] Benjamin,[2] Richard [1]*) was born in the Stratton House at Mount Holly, N. J., Nov. 27, 1817. He married Caroline Elizabeth Newbold, Sept. 14, 1842. She died at Mount Holly, Nov. 6, 1897. Mr. Stratton studied law and was admitted to the Bar in 1839. He was a graduate of Princeton; was twice elected to Congress; was President of the Farmer's Bank of New Jersey at Salem; was member of the vestry at St. Andrews Church at Mount Holly; in politics he was a Whig,—later a Republican.

Children:—*Born in Mt. Holly, N. J.*
- —211 James,[7] b. Aug. 26, 1845; graduate of Princeton, a lawyer; Major of the 4th New Jersey regiment in 1864; d. Dec. 3, 1886, unm.
- —212 Louisa,[7] b. Nov. 1, 1849; m. 1st **William Delany Wetherill** of Philadelphia, m. 2nd **Amos Gibbs** of Mt. Holly. She is now living in the old Stratton house, the birthplace of her father (see *picture, opposite p. 114, Vol. I*).

133. JOSEPH BUCK STRATTON [6] (*Nathan L.,[5] John,[4] Benjamin,[3] Benjamin,[2] Richard [1]*) was born Dec. 24, 1815. After a

preparatory training at Laurenceville Academy he entered Princeton College in 1833. He studied law in Philadelphia and was admitted to the Bar in 1837. After practicing law for three years he commenced preparation for the Christian ministry. Finishing the theological course at Princeton in the spring of 1843, he received a call to the Presbyterian church at Natchez, Miss., and was ordained and installed as pastor there in December of the same year. Gentle and refined in manner, with an earnest and sincere simplicity in all that he did and said, Dr. Stratton won the confidence, love and admiration of his fellows. In 1880 he was a delegate from the Southwestern Presbyterian Church to Philadelphia, and presided at one of its sessions. In 1884 he was the Commissioner appointed by the General Assembly of the Southern Church to bear to the General Assembly of the Northern Church, which met at Saratoga, N. Y., the ratification of the fraternal relations which had been established between the two bodies. He contributed largely to the religious periodicals, and published several works of a devotional and historical character. A small volume of "Prayers for the use of families" has had a large circulation in the South. In 1889 he published his last work, *A Pastor's Valedictory*.

For full fifty years Dr. Stratton remained the beloved pastor of the church at Natchez, resigning his charge over it in April, 1894. His Presbytery, at the request of his congregation, conferred upon him the title of "Pastor Emeritus." He died April 14, 1903, after only a few hours of sickness, though in frail health for several years.

He remained with his people in Natchez during the terrible epidemics of 1853, 1855, 1858, and 1871, when the yellow scourge stalked through the fair city, striking down its victims among the high and low. His presence during these periods was a benediction in many a home of sorrow, for he never faltered in his work of ministering to the sick, comforting the dying and consoling the sorrowing among the rich and poor alike. He staid with his people during the Civil War, sharing patiently with them the rigors and privations of those troublous times, thoughtful always of their welfare, never of his own personal convenience and comfort. It is no wonder they loved and reverenced him. A memorial Sunday school building in connection with the church was dedicated three years before his death as "Stratton Chapel." We quote from a Natchez daily paper:

"All Natchez joined to-day in the sweet and beautiful tribute of respect to the memory of their beloved and faithful friend, Dr. Joseph Buck Stratton. Around the bier in Stratton Chapel gathered people of all denominations, old and young, rich and poor, white and colored—in life he was their friend and brother. He knew no rank or station, or dividing line. He loved his work, and consecrated his life to its full performance. How well and how faithful the service he rendered was amply attested when the people of Natchez laid all else aside to pay feeling tribute to his memory. The public schools closed at noon, and during the funeral service, by common consent, and without an interchange of thought, the business men, moved by a single thought—respect for their beloved dead—closed their doors. There was no exception."

Oct. 8, 1844, Dr. Stratton married **Mary Vanuxem Smith**, daughter of *Nathan* and *Louisa (Vanuxem) Smith*, of Philadelphia, who, in the four short years of her life as a pastor's wife in Natchez, won the love and esteem of the strangers among whom she had come to dwell. She died Dec. 22, 1848, and is buried in Laurel Hill, Philadelphia. Four years later, Nov. 16, 1852, Dr. Stratton married **Caroline Matilda Routh**, daughter of *Austin* and *Caroline M. Routh*, of Natchez.

Children:—Born in Natchez, Miss.

By first marriage.
—213   Sidney Vanuxem,[7] b. Aug. 8, 1845; res. Natchez.
—214   Mary Louisa,[7] b. Apr. 25, 1847; d. Oct. 7, 1863.

By second marriage.
+215   Joseph Buck,[7] b. 1853; d. 1888.

139. CHARLES PRESTON STRATTON [6] (*Nathan L.,*[5] *John,*[4] *Benjamin,*[3] *Benjamin,*[2] *Richard*[1]) was born June 18, 1828. He graduated at Princeton, admitted to the Bar in 1852, and opened a law office in Camden, where he became one of New Jersey's most prominent lawyers, acquiring a lucrative practice. In 1872 he was elected Judge of Camden County for a term of five years. As a member of the City Counsel he was instrumental in securing several important municipal reforms. He took a warm interest in politics, voted the Republican ticket, was Director of Camden & Philadelphia Ferry Co., the Bridgeton National Bank, West Jersey Railroad Co., and several other corporations. Dec. 18, 1856, he married **Clara Cooper**, daughter of *Benjamin* and *Abigail (Pride) Cooper*. He died July 30, 1884.

Children:—*Born in Camden, N. J.*
- —216 Clara Cooper,[7] m. **Thomas L. Perot**, of Phila., Jan. 18, 1887.
- +217 Charles Preston, Jr.[7]
- —218 Anna Ruth,[7] m. **L. Hoffman Livingston** of Camden, July 26, 1910.
- —219 Richard Cooper,[7] m. **Marion Eleanor Macgill**, Aug. 19, 1912; res. Redwood, Cal.

145. NATHAN LEAKE STRATTON [6] (*Levi*,[5] *John*,[4] *Benjamin*,[3] *Benjamin*,[2] *Richard* [1]) was born in Bridgeton, N. J., Nov. 11, 1828. His father dying when he was but ten years old, and his mother soon after, Nathan was brought up in the hospitable home of his uncle, Dr. John Leake Stratton, at Mount Holly (see *picture, opposite p. 114, Vol. I*). Ambitious, enterprising and resolute, he left New Jersey while a young man to make a place for himself in the West, settling in the western part of Texas in 1853—at a period when it took courage and determination to build a home in that wild, unsettled country. Here he became an active business man, closely identified with the history of that section of the state in which he lived. He was a member of Capt. Black's company of minute men, was a Government contractor for many years, and in 1870 was sent to the city of Mexico to establish a precedent in the execution of criminals between the United States and the Republic of Mexico, under the extradition treaty then existing between the two countries.

Jan. 27, 1863, Mr. Stratton married **Melverda Gillian MacKinney**. In faith a Presbyterian, but living where there was no church of his denomination, Mr. Stratton went with his family to the Episcopal church to worship, and his children naturally became Episcopalians. A Republican in politics, his sons have all adhered to his political faith. In 1901 the family moved from Texas to Safford, Arizona, where they now reside.

Children:—*Born in San Antonio, Texas.*
- +220 Lee Nathan.[7]
- —221 Lulu May,[7] m. **Jule Maurel**; d. Nov. 3, 1907.
- —222 Nora Jane,[7] m. **William Henry Clark**.
  B*orn in Uvaldo, Texas.*
- —223 Charles,[7] d. in infancy.
- +224 John Newton.[7]
- —225 Joseph Buck,[7] an electrical engineer at Stafford; m. Feb. 15, 1908, **Margaret Elizabeth Webber**, daughter

of *John* and *Katherine (Horigan) Webber;* one child, Margaret M.³

149. WILLIAM STRATTON⁶ (*William*,⁵ *William*,⁴ *William*,³ *Benjamin*,² *Richard*¹) was born in Deerfield, N. J., Feb. 2, 1805. He lived in Philadelphia where he was engaged in the shoe trade. He married **Mary Nutt Ashman** in 1829. She was born in Philadelphia in Oct., 1808, and died in Camden, Dec. 23, 1878. Mr. Stratton died Aug. 1, 1861.

Children:—*Born in Philadelphia.*
—226 Elizabeth,⁷ b. 1831; d. unm.
—227 Edward,⁷ b. 1833; m. **Margaret White**, 1855. He was Presbyterian minister, at one time pastor in Middletown, Conn. Did he leave children?
—228 Rebecca,⁷ b. 1836; m. **Rev. Charles Holloway**; resided in Philadelphia.
+229 James Patterson,⁷ b. 1839.
—230 Mary,⁷ m. **Joseph Sherman.**
—231 William,⁷ b. 1844; missing after the battle of Chancellorsville, Va.
—232 Henry,⁷ b. 1848; d. 1855 at Greenport, L. I.

152. STEPHEN STRATTON⁶ (*Jonathan*,⁵ *Benjamin*,⁴ *Jonathan*,³ *Benjamin*,² *Richard*¹) married **Elizabeth** Ford of Albany, N. Y., and lived in Saratoga Co., where he died Oct. 13, 1833. His widow married a Mr. Beckman before 1835.

Children:
—230 Charles,⁷ m. and moved west—probably to Minnesota.
—233 Louisa.⁷
—234 Franklin.⁷
—235 Anna,⁷ m. **Edward Hanna.**

Further data is desired of this family.

154. CHARLES BINGLEY STRATTON⁶ (*Benjamin*,⁵ *Benjamin*,⁴ *Jonathan*,³ *Benjamin*,² *Richard*¹) married **Eliza Briggs**, in Schaghticoke, N. Y.

Children:
+236 Amos Briggs.⁷
—237 Caroline Elizabeth,⁷ m. **Julius Butts**, Brooklyn, N. Y.
—238 Emma Augusta,⁷ m. **Thomas Christie**, Brooklyn, N. Y.
—239 Stella Ambrosia,⁷ d. unm.

See pages 348, 169, 245, 492, 278, 229. No. 6 is Stratton Mountain, Vt. *See page* 9, *Vol.* I.

−240 Charles Edgar,[7] d. in Andersonville prison, 1865, aged 19 years.
−241 Anna Briggs,[7] m. **George Dolen**, New York City.

162. HENRY DAYTON STRATTON [6] (*Jonathan,*[5] *Benjamin,*[4] *Jonathan,*[3] *Benjamin,*[2] *Richard*[1]) was born at Easthampton, L. I., in 1803. He was one of the substantial citizens of his native town, was elected to various town offices, and was a Trustee of the town for many years. He married **Helen Miller,** daughter of *Jeremiah Miller* of Easthampton. She died in 1900, aged 90 years. Mr. Stratton died in 1890.

Children:—*Born in Easthampton.*
+242 Samuel Dayton,[7] b. 1832.
−243 Katherine,[7] b. 1837; m. **Wesley Grindle,** in 1856.
−244 Theodore Miller,[7] b. 1842; m. **Dora L. Bahr,** no children.

163. GEORGE NEWTON STRATTON [6] (*Jonathan,*[5] *Benjamin,*[4] *Jonathan,*[3] *Benjamin,*[2] *Richard*[1]) married first, June 15, 1837, **Mary Hand,** daughter of *Mulford Hand.* She died in 1840. Married second, Oct. 5, 1847, **Nancy Edwards.** He was Postmaster at Easthampton in 1851. He then lived on a farm at Amagansett, L. I. In July, 1853, he moved to DeKalb Co., Illinois, where he died Jan. 2, 1888, aged 77 years. He and his family were Presbyterians.

Children:—*Born in Amagansett, L. I.*
 By first marriage.
+245 Jonathan Mulford,[7] b. Apr. 4, 1839.
 Born in Victor, DeKalb Co., Ill.
 By second marriage.
+246 Samuel Edwards.[7]

169. HARRISON STRATTON [7] (*John,*[6] *James,*[5] *Richard,*[4] *Richard,*[3] *Richard,*[2] *Richard*[1]), born Sept. 11, 1805, married, Dec. 31, 1832, **Hannah Talbot.** She was a daughter of *Enoch* and *Hannah Talbot* and was born in Sharon in 1810 and died in Boston Oct. 2?, 1878. Mr. Stratton died in 1880.

Children:—*Born in Foxboro, Mass.*
−247 Eliza J.,[8] b. Jan. 29, 1834; m., Nov. 23, 1864, **Samuel W. Whittmore,** son of Joshua and Eunice Whittmore.
 Born in Sharon, Mass.
−248 William H.,[8] born Feb. 1, 1870; m., July 3, 1861, **Cor-**

delia F. Forest, daughter of *Martin Forest*, res. Foxboro. They have one child, Emma F.,[9] m. **John F. Rancliffe.**

177. HENRY EDWARD STRATTON [7] (*Welcome*,[6] *James*,[5] *Richard*,[4] *Richard*,[3] *Richard*,[2] *Richard*[1]), born in Foxboro, June 8, 1825; married first **Eliza Leonard**, daughter of *Ellis* and *Luce Leonard*, Jan. 17, 1847, who died Nov. 5, 1851; married second **Amanda M. ——**. She died Feb. 28, 1908. Mr. Stratton died July 19, 1894, in Mansfield.

Children:—*Born in Mansfield, Mass.*
—249 Martha Maria,[8] b. 1848; m. **Thomas W. D. Deane**, son of Elijah Deane, Jan. 14, 1871.
—250 Alice E.,[8] b. 1851; d. May 14, 1868.
—250a Edward C.,[8] b. 1855; m., Sept. 26, 1885, **Lucy P. Petequin**, daughter of *Ephrain* and *Mary Ann Petequin*, who died May 20, 1894; one child, Hattie Winnifred.[9]

182. SCHUYLER STRATTON [7] (*Chandler*,[6] *Robert*,[5] *Richard*,[4] *Richard*,[3] *Richard*,[2] *Richard*[1]) was born June 13, 1837. He died Feb. 17, 1903, at Cloverdale, Cal. He was a butcher in Foxboro and later an engineer. He was four times married: first, May 1, 1859, to **Nancy M. Monroe**, born Sept. 24, 1835, at Plainfield, Conn.; second, June 18, 1872, at Aurora, Ind., to **Elizabeth Ione Shockley**, of Milan, Ind.; third, Apr. 15, 1879, at St. Louis., Mo., to **Annie F. Strome**, daughter of *Jacob* and *Theresa (Rapeseloer) Strome*, of Cincinnati; fourth, Dec. 2, 1891, at Santa Rosa, Cal., to **Jemima Ferguson**, daughter of *Henry* and *Janet (Sudden) Ferguson*. She was born at San Francisco, Sept. 30, 1874. After Mr. Stratton's death she married Peter Johnson at Cloverdale, Cal.

Children:—*Born in Centerville, Conn.*
By first marriage.
—251 William Munroe,[8] m. Jan. 25, 1891, **Emma C. Leonard**, daughter of *Addison* C. and *Sarah (Webster) Leonard;* farmer and live stock dealer; res. Burlington, Wis.
Born in Cleremont, Iowa.
+252 Edward Earnest.[8]
Born in South Foxboro, Mass.
By second marriage.
—253 George Louis,[8] an engineer; m. June 1, 1898, **Amanda**

Rons, daughter of *Hans* and *Charlotte* (*Varmeyer*) *Rons*, res. St. Louis, Mo.
Born in St. Louis.
—254 Emily Shockley,[8] m., June 20, 1900, **Charles Jay Franklin**, son of *Jeremy* and *Sophia Jane* (*Trembly*) *Franklin*.
Born in Oak Grove, Mo.
By third marriage.
—255 William Joseph,[8] a carpenter; unm., res. San Francisco.
Born in Troy, Mo.
—256 Charles Jacob,[8] d. in San Francisco, Aug. 7, 1891, aged 9 years.
—257 Roy Lessley,[8] bookkeeper, res. San Francisco.
Born in San Francisco.
By fourth marriage.
—258 Schuyler,[8] res. Cloverdale, Cal.

202. JAMES STRATTON [7] (*James*,[6] *Daniel P.*,[5] *Levi*,[4] *Benjamin*,[3] *Benjamin*,[2] *Richard* [1]) was born in Washington, D. C., Jan. 16, 1849; married in Jackson, La., Apr. 16, 1874, **Ida McClelland**, daughter of *George* and *Virginia* (*Flournoy*) *McClelland*. Mr. McClelland was a lawyer of Jackson, but a native of New York. Mr. Stratton died in New Orleans, May 30, 1905, and is buried in Jackson.
Children:—*Born in Jackson, La.*
—259 Ida McClelland.[8]
—260 William McClelland.[8]
—261 Jennie,[8] m. **Joe A. Wax**; res. Brockton, Miss.
—262 Mary,[8] m. **Charles Canfield**.
—263 Lillian.[8]
—264 Eugene James.[8]
—265 Hazel,[8] b. Jackson, Oct. 25, 1890, aged 3 years.

204. MORRIS HANCOCK STRATTON [7] (*Daniel*,[6] *Daniel P.*,[5] *Levi*,[4] *Benjamin*,[3] *Benjamin*,[2] *Richard* [1]) graduated from Princeton University in 1858, studied law in Troy, N. Y., was admitted to the New Jersey Bar in 1877 and became a prominent attorney and business man at Salem, where he spent the remainder of his life. He served in the Civil War, being Captain of the Second New Jersey Cavalry. He died Jan. 12, 1914, leaving an honorable name and a good record. He was a strong man intellectu-

ally, of wide learning, and long filled a prominent place in his community. A democrat in politics, he always took an interest in political affairs. He was a devoted Presbyterian, for many years a ruling elder and superintendent of the Sunday school, and several times was honored by being sent as a delegate to the General Assembly. He was a Trustee of Princeton Theological Seminary, secretary of the Salem County Bible Society, and for twenty years had charge of the Salem Public Library. In June, 1876, he married **Ellen C. Smith,** daughter of *Horace Smith* of Salem. She died July 14, 1877.

Child:—*Born in Salem, N. J.*
—266 Morris Hancock, Jr.,[8] m. Jan. 19, 1905, **Elsie Harris,** daughter of *John* and *Melissa Harris* of Salem.

205. DANIEL POWELL STRATTON [7] (*Daniel,*[6] *Daniel,*[5] *Levi,*[4] *Benjamin,*[3] *Benjamin,*[2] *Richard* [1]) was born in Salem, N. J., Sept. 19, 1839. He studied law in Albany, N. Y. He was admitted to the Bar and opened an office at Salem. Nov. 28, 1866, he married **Arabella Barnes,** daughter of *Joseph* and *Phœbe Ann (High) Barnes.* She was born in Woodstown, N. J., Feb. 12, 1846. In the fall of 1867 they removed to Stockton, Mo., where Judge Stratton became one of the most prominent lawyers in Southwestern Missouri, and widely known throughout the entire state. In 1882 they moved to Nevada, Mo., where in 1886 he was elected Circuit Judge by the Democratic party, re-elected in 1892, and served twelve years on the bench.

"As a Judge he was fair, conscientious and able. He possessed a rare knowledge of law, both in theory and practice, was a close student and one of the best informed men in his section of the state." He died in Eldorado Springs, Mo., Jan., 1901. Mrs. Stratton died Sept. 2, 1905, at Neosho, Mo.*

Children:—*Born in Salem, N. J.*
—267 Eleanor Hancock,[8] m. **Cassius M. Shartel,** Oct. 3, 1889; res. Neosho, Nev.

---

* A will of Levi Stratton,[4] dated Feb. 14, 1792 (the day before his death), has recently been found among unrecorded and unindexed papers of Cumberland County. It shows that he was married the second time. It names "My wife Elizabeth, my wife's daughter Jemima, my son Daniel Powell, and daughter Sarah." A belief has been current among some of his descendants that Abigail Powell was a widow when Levi Stratton [4] married her. This may be an error, arising from the fact that his second wife was a widow.

Born in Stockton, Mo.
- —268 Rebecca Barnes,[8] m. **James Frank Barr**, June, 1898; res. Nevada, Mo.
- —269 Arabella,[8] b. 1875; d. in infancy.
- —270 Daniel S.,[8] graduated 1889, A.B., Westminster College, Fulton, Mo., L.L.B., University of Michigan; m., Dec. 18, 1907, **Jessie Josephine Graves**; res. Neosho, Mo.
- —271 Henrietta Gibbon,[8] graduated A.B. University of Michigan; A.M. University of Pennsylvania; Prof. of History in Western College, Oxford, Ohio, 1906-1907; m. **William Alderman Jaquette**, June 14, 1907; res. Salem, N. J.
- —272 Joseph Barnes,[8] res. Seattle, Wash.

215. JOSEPH BUCK STRATTON [7] (*Joseph B.*,[6] *Nathan L.*,[5] *John*,[4] *Benjamin*,[3] *Benjamin*,[2] *Richard* [1]) was born in Natchez, Miss., Oct. 15, 1853. He married, Apr. 18, 1883, **Ruth Audley Britton**, daughter of *Audley* C. and *Eliza* (*Macrery*) *Britton*. He died Sept. 16, 1888. His widow married Wm. A. S. Wheeler, of New Orleans.

Children:—*Born in Natchez, Miss.*
- —273 Eliza Macrery Britton,[8] m., Nov. 9, 1908, **Alfred Vidal Davis**, Jr. They have a daughter, Carolyn Stratton.[9]
- —274 Sidney Vanuxem, Jr.,[8] res. Natchez.
- —275 Carolyn Josephine.[8]

217. CHARLES PRESTON STRATTON [7] (*Charles P.*,[6] *Nathan L.*,[5] *John*,[4] *Benjamin*,[3] *Benjamin*,[2] *Richard* [1]) is an architect at Chester, Pa., where he settled in 1890. He married, Nov. 20, 1889, **Rose Eleanor McLaughlin**, daughter of *Edward Joseph* and *Rose Ellen* (*Grant*) *McLaughlin*.

Children:—*Born in Chester, Pa.*
- —276 Charles Francis.[8]
- —277 Richard.[8]

220. LEE NATHAN STRATTON [7] (*Nathan L.*,[6] *Levi*,[5] *John*,[4] *Benjamin*,[3] *Benjamin*,[2] *Richard* [1]), educated in San Antonio, Texas, studied law, admitted to the Bar in 1894; elected County Attorney of Uvalde Co. in 1896; moved to Arizona and elected District Attorney there in 1900 and again in 1906. Appointed by Gov. Richard E. Sloan a member of the Territorial Board of

Equalization in 1909. A prominent member of Masonic Order. June 29, 1910, he married **Gillie Archer,** daughter of *Eugene* and *Elizabeth (Taylor) Arche*r.

Child:—*Born in Safford, Ariz.*
—278   Lee Nathan.[8]

124.   JOHN NEWTON STRATTON [7] (*Nathan L.,*[6] *Levi,*[5] *John,*[4] *Benjamin,*[3] *Benjamin,*[2] *Richard* [1]) studied medicine at the Southwestern Medical College, Dallas, Texas, and is a practicing physician and surgeon at Safford, Arizona. April 25, 1908, he married **Katherine Hunter,** daughter of *Thomas T.* and *Ollie (Gallaspy) Hunter.*

Children:—*Born in Safford, Arizona.*
—279   Newton Hunter.[8]
—280   Robert Anderson.[8]

229.   JAMES PATERSON STRATTON [7] (*William,*[6] *William,*[5] *William,*[4] *William,*[3] *Benjamin,*[2] *Richard* [1]) was born in Philadelphia, Apr. 24, 1839. He is a Presbyterian minister. In 1867 he married **Catherine Landy.**

Children:
—281   William Henry, b. in Philadelphia; grad. Cornell University; a civil engineer; m. **Catherine Hayne,** Jan. 22, 1892; res. Montclair, N. J.
—282   Milton Greene, b. Malden, N. J.; electrical engineer; m. **Anna M. Walters,** Nov. 30, 1898.
—283   James Landy., d. in 1877, aged 4 years.
—284   Henry Frost, b. in Crawfordsville, Ind.; mechanical engineer; grad. of Cornell; m. **Marion Cromwell Prentiss,** Jan. 20, 1905.

236.   AMOS BRIGGS STRATTON [7] (*Charles B.,*[6] *Benjamin,*[5] *Benjamin,*[4] *Jonathan,*[3] *Benjamin,*[2] *Richard* [1]) was born in Schaghticoke, N. Y. He married **Rose Anna Thompson,** Aug. 8, 1860. He was a flour merchant of the firm of Warren & Stratton in New York City, member of the Produce Exchange for 30 years. A lifelong member of the Madison Ave. Presbyterian Church, of which he was an elder and treasurer for many years. He died Sept. 30, 1902.

Children:—*Born in New York City.*
—285   Clara Eliza,[8] m. 1st, **Freeman Warren,** 2nd, **Donald McGregor,** 3rd, **Henry R. Burk;** res. Laurence Park, Bronxville, N. Y.

—286 George.[8]
—287 Harry Lincoln,[8] joined Seventh Regiment Home Guards, 1897, promoted to Lieutenant and then to Captain in the Eleventh Regiment. Resigned from service June, 1913; m. **Mary Harral Rowland**, Aug. 22, 1910; res. Bronxville, N. Y.

242. SAMUEL DAYTON STRATTON [7] (*Henry D.*,[6] *Jonathan*,[5] *Benjamin*,[4] *Jonathan*,[3] *Benjamin*,[2] *Richard* [1]), born in 1832. He married **Lucia Miller** of East Hampton, L. I.; moved to Illinois. Children:
—288 George Miller,[8] b. 1854; d. 1855.
+289 George Dayton,[8] b. 1857.
—290 Henry and Charles,[8] twins, d. in infancy.
—291 Mary Lucia,[8] b. 1876; m. 1st **William A. Hedges**, m. 2nd **Nathan H. Dayton**.

245. JONATHAN MULFORD STRATTON [7] (*George N.*,[6] *Jonathan*,[5] *Benjamin*,[4] *Jonathan*,[3] *Benjamin*,[2] *Richard* [1]) went to Illinois, July 2, 1853, with his parents. He became a farmer, residing at Ross Grove, Ill. He married **Christina J. Wesson**. She died Dec. 1, 1878, aged 33 years and 9 months. Mr. Stratton died Aug. 26, 1882.
Children:—B*orn in Illinois.*
—292 Blanch,[8] d. Feb. 1, 1888; aged 15 years.
—292a Eva,[8] m. —— **Griffeth**.

246. SAMUEL EDWARDS STRATTON [7] (*George N.*,[6] *Jonathan*,[5] *Benjamin*,[4] *Jonathan*,[3] *Benjamin*,[2] *Richard* [1]) married **Mary J. Challand**, Dec. 19, 1877. They lived in Victor, Ill., until the spring of 1891, then moved to Sandwich, Ill., where he is a farmer. They are Presbyterians.
Children:—B*orn in Victor, Ill.*
+293 George Henry.[8]
—294 Lila J.,[8] m. **Roy W. Cook**, a lawyer, June 28, 1911; res. Aurora, Il.
—295 Mary Mabel,[8] a teacher in Sandwich, Ill.

252. EDWARD EARNEST STRATTON [8] (*Schuyler*,[7] *Chandler*,[6] *Robert*,[5] *Richard*,[4] *Richard*,[3] *Richard*,[2] *Richard* [1]) is a farmer in Burlington, Wis. He was born in Clearmont, Iowa, March 7, 1864. He married, Nov. 30, 1890, at Waterford, Wis., **Anna**

Bendickson, daughter of *Halvor* and *Anna (Anderson) Bendickson.*
  Children:—*Born in Burlington, Wis.*
  —296 Ella B.⁹
  —297 Fern B.⁹
  —298 Edward C.⁹
  —299 Florence M.⁹

289. GEORGE DAYTON STRATTON⁸ (*Samuel D.,⁷ Henry D.,⁶ Jonathan,⁵ Benjamin,⁴ Jonathan,³ Benjamin,² Richard¹*), born in Illinois, Apr. 22, 1857. Married **Mrs. Lizzie E. Glessner** in 1897. He is a carpenter and resides in Sandwich, Ill.
  Children:—*Born in Sandwich, Ill.*
  —300 Henry Samuel.⁹
  —301 Helen Lucia.⁹

293. GEORGE HENRY STRATTON⁸ (*Samuel E.,⁷ George N.,⁶ Jonathan,⁵ Benjamin,⁴ Jonathan,³ Benjamin,² Richard¹*) is a farmer at Victor, Ill. He married **Margaret M'cMaster,** Nov. 28, 1901.
  Children:—*Born in Sandwich, Ill.*
  —302 George Newton.⁹
       Born in Victor, Ill.
  —303 Gertrude Nancy.⁹
  —304 Samuel Edwards.⁹
  —305 James LeRoy.⁹
  —306 William Raymond.⁹

DAVID STRATTON OF MILLVILLE

[307.] DAVID STRATTON lived in Cumberland Co., N. J.* He married **Sarah** —— about **1772**, and settled at Millville at an

---

* A great deal of time and study has been given to research regarding this David Stratton. He has many descendants. His sons became men of prominence and influence, occupying positions of trust and importance, but concerning their father no written record has been found. In the possession of a descendant is an old family Bible giving his children's names, but his own name does not appear, nor that of his wife.
  Among his descendants it is very generally understood that their ancestor came to New Jersey from Easthampton. If he is descended from Benjamin Stratton² who settled in New Jersey in 1715 (P. 106), he must be of the fourth generation, and for convenience in tracing he is so considered in this volume, leaving it to future research to solve the problem of the missing links—a problem that has long baffled the

early date, probably about the time of his marriage.* He died in Millville.

Children:—*Born in Millville, N. J.*

+308   Preston,⁵ b. 1773; d. 1840.
—309   Sarah,⁵ b. 1774; m. **Enos Woodruff**, who died July 4, 1827, son of John Woodruff. She died Dec. 27, 1849.†
—310   Lydia,⁵ m. 1st **Ephriam Gaston**, Jan. 12, 1796, 2nd **William Ostler**. She died June 2, 1867, aged 91 years.
+311   Jeremiah,⁵ b. 1779; d. 1851.
+312   Israel,⁵ b. 1783; d. 1860.

308. PRESTON STRATTON ⁵ (*David* ⁴) was born Dec. 16, 1773. He was a prominent citizen of Millville for nearly fifty years, a member of the Presbyterian church, and a successful business man. June 2, 1798, he married **Sarah Bateman**. She was born July 16, 1778, and died in Millville, Oct. 22, 1842. He died Apr. 19, 1840.

---

compiler. That the connection will some time be found the writer doubts not, and only hopes that the facts given here may serve to help some one else to find what she has failed to discover. Some deed, will, gravestone, church or court record must hold the data so much desired. It will be remembered that Isaac³ and David³ very likely left children, though no record of them has yet been found (p. 107, *Vol. I*).

Unsuccessful search has been made for his burial place. Port Elizabeth, six miles from Millville, was then a much more important place than Millville, and it is believed that he and his wife were buried there in the old grave yard containing many unmarked graves. Perhaps some Stratton who reads this may know of some facts which may throw light on the subject.

* Some of her descendants believe that her name was Sarah Preston. Roger Preston, b. 1614, came to America with wife Martha in the *Elizabeth and Ann* in 1635. He was of Ipswich and Salem, Mass. He had seven children—Thomas, Samuel, John, Jacob, Levi b. 1662, Elizabeth and Mary. Levi (and perhaps others) settled in Cumberland Co., N. J. His children were Levi, Jr., b. 1697, Martha, John b. 1701, Mary, Abigail (m. Benjamin Stratton³), Isaac b. 1707, and Freelove. It is quite likely that somewhere in this family may be found a Sarah of suitable age for the wife of David Stratton, and perhaps some Preston will, or administration, may furnish the clew needed.

† She was named for her mother, and she named her son for her father, David Stratton. He was born in 1805, and the name David Stratton Woodruff has come down through four generations and been repeated in several branches of her descendants.

Children:—*Born in Millville, N. J.*
- −313 David,⁶ b. Apr. 6, 1799; died aged 1 year.
- +314 Jeremiah,⁶ b. 1801.
- +315 John,⁶ b. 1803.
- −316 Levi Preston,⁶ b. June 9, 1804; d. Sept. 10, 1820.
- −317 Rachel,⁶ b. Apr. 4, 1806; d. 1819.
- −318 Lorenzo Dow,⁶ b. Feb. 24, 1808; d., unm., July 16, 1835.
- −319 Sarah,⁶ b. Oct. 7, 1811; d. 1820.
- +320 Israel,⁶ b. Jan. 1, 1815.
- +321 Isaac Watts,⁶ b. 1816; d. 1865.
- +322 Enos Woodruff,⁶ b. 1818; d. 1902.
- −323 Mary,⁶ b. Aug. 19, 1819; m. **Avery Messick**, Jan. 6, 1838.

There were other children who died in infancy. These dates are from the Bible of Preston Stratton.

311. JEREMIAH STRATTON⁵ (*David*⁴) was born Sept. 1, 1779 (see his picture). He married, first, **Zerviah Bateman**, Nov. 8, 1800. She died Apr. 24, 1836, aged 62 years and 7 days, and he married, second, **Mrs. Margaret Busby**, who died in 1865, aged 65 years. He lived all his life in his native town, where he was a highly esteemed citizen, and for upwards of forty years was in public life, filling various offices of trust and honor. He was a Justice of the Peace for many years, Judge of the County Court, and several times a member of the state legislature. As a testimonial of the esteem in which he was held, all the places of business in the town were closed on the day of his funeral. Quoting from a newspaper clipping dated May, 1851: "Judge Stratton was one of the oldest and most useful citizens of Millville. But much as he will be missed by his fellow citizens, the church has sustained a loss which cannot soon be replaced. She mourns one of her ablest and most willing supporters. For forty five years he has held the office of ruling elder in the Presbyterian church with fidelity and acceptance." He died May 26, 1851, and is buried in Mt. Pleasant cemetery.

Children:—*Born in Millville, N. J.*
      By first marriage.
- −324 David,⁶ b. Sept. 7, 1801; d. Oct. 11, 1823.
- +325 William,⁶ b. 1803; d. 1843.
- −320 Rachel,⁶ b. Oct. 20, 1804; d. June 12, 1881; unm.
- −327 Thomas B.,⁶ b. Oct. 11, 1806; studied medicine and

went west to practice his profession; died in Madison, Ill., in 1845; unm.
—328 Hannah,⁶ b. July 18, 1808; d. Sept. 14, 1826.
+329 Preston,⁶ b. 1810; d. 1850.
+330 Nathaniel,⁶ b. 1812; d. 1897.

312. ISRAEL STRATTON ⁵ (*David* ⁴) was born Oct. 9, 1783. He married **Hannah Loper** Mar. 23, 1807, and settled in Port Elizabeth, N. J., where for fifty years he was a prominent citizen. He was a member of the State Assembly in 1825; State Legislature 1833 and 1837; Judge of Common Pleas Court for several years, and Trustee of the Peace for many years. He carried on a shoe-making business at Port Elizabeth. He was a soldier in the Mexican War. He died May 16, 1860. His wife, who was born Nov. 5, 1788, died Feb. 24, 1877, "a fine old lady," says a prominent citizen of Port Elizabeth who used to "eat many of her good cookies," when a boy.

Children:—*Born in Port Elizabeth, N. J.*
—331 George,⁶ m. and lived in Cape May Co., N. J. Information concerning him desired.
—332 Eliza,⁶ b. May 17, 1812; unm. Nov. 8, 1875.
—333 Sarah,⁶ m. **Charles Townsend**.
—334 Bernard,⁶ d. Sept. 21, 1837, aged 23 years.

In the Methodist Episcopal cemetery at Port Elizabeth are stones to the memory of Judge Stratton and his wife Hannah and their two children Eliza and Bernard. His will, made in 1858, mentions only his wife, his daughter Eliza and nephew Nathaniel.

314. JEREMIAH STRATTON ⁶ (*Preston*,⁵ *David* ⁴), born Apr. 3, 1801, married **Barbara Hampton** Dec. 19, 1826.
Children:
—335 Deborah,⁷ m. —— Carlisle.
—336 Sarah,⁷ m. —— Eldridge of Philadelphia.
—337 Henry,⁷ m. **Sarah Fisher**, of Philadelphia, and left children of whom information is desired.

315. JOHN STRATTON ⁶ (*Preston*,⁵ *David* ⁴) was born June 19, 1803, and spent his youth in Millville. After his marriage he lived for awhile in Gloucester Co., N. J., and then returned to his native town, where he died June 4, 1864. He married, first,

Caroline Connor, May 31, 1831, and, second, Catherine Vail.
Children:—*Born in Millville, N. J.*
- −338 Mary Ann,[7] b. May 31, 1832; d. 1884; m. Joseph Carson.

Born in Gloucester Co., N. J.
- +339 Jeremiah B.,[7] b. 1834.
- −340 Rachel,[7] b. Apr. 2, 1836; m. Henry Westcott; res. Carlton, Ill.
- −341 Frances E.,[7] b. Aug. 12, 1838; Franklin F. Elmer; d. Oct. 3, 1889.

Born in Fairfield, N. J.
- −342 John,[7] b. Apr. 4, 1841; m. in Bridgeton, N. J., Mary Welch, Jan. 23, 1864; d. in Camden, N. J., Jan. 27, 1890; no children.

Born in Millville.
- −343 Rebecca,[7] b. July 24, 1843; m. Jacob Rocap, Aug., 1863.
- −344 Caroline,[7] b. June 12, 1847.
- −345 Catherine,[7] b. Aug. 29, 1849.
- −346 Edith D.,[7] b. Aug. 31, 1850; m. John Stevens.

320. ISRAEL STRATTON[6] (*Preston,*[5] *David*[4]), born Jan. 1, 1815, married Elizabeth Speakman Ogden, Nov. 11, 1839, and lived in Philadelphia.

Children:
- −347 Josephine,[7] m. George Adams of Philadelphia.
- −348 Elizabeth,[7] m. —— Halleburton.

321. ISAAC WATTS STRATTON[6] (*Preston,*[5] *David*[4]) was born Apr. 4, 1816, and died in Washington, D. C., June 23, 1865. He married Hannah Carson in 1838.

Children:—*Born in Millville, N. J.*
- −349 Catherine Amanda,[7] b. 1839; d. 1865.
- −350 Elizabeth Ogden,[7] b. 1841; m. John McKeage; res. Philadelphia.
- −351 Anna Williams,[7] b. 1843; m. Samuel Thomas.
- −352 Mary Jane,[7] b. 1845; m. John Van Fossen.

Born in Philadelphia.
- −353 Charles Murphy, b. 1848; d. 1901; m. Elizabeth Lambert; no children.
- −354 Isaac Watts, Jr., b. 1851; d. 1872, in Philadelphia; unm.
- −355 Emma Virginia, b. 1854; d. 1903; m. John Dallas.

322. Enos Woodruff Stratton [6] (*Preston*,[5] *David* [4]) was born May 17, 1818. He was twice married, first, to **Frances Burnsides**, May 5, 1835; second, to **Mrs. Ellen (Kincard) Hann**, Aug. 12, 1869.

Children:
By first marriage.
—356 Enos Woodruff,[7] m. **Rachel Hill**.
By second marriage.
—357 Preston.[7]
—358 Samuel.[7]
—359 Howard.[7]
—360 Charles.[7]

325. William Stratton [6] (*Jeremiah*,[5] *David* [4]) was born in Millville Mar. 25, 1803, and died there June 4, 1853. He married **Rachel L. Hover**, who was born Oct. 4, 1798, and died May 14, 1869.

Children:—*Born in Millville, N. J.*
—361 Caroline,[7] b. Aug. 4, 1824; d. July 25, 1894; m. Aug. 5, 1845, **Isaac Brandiff**, b. May 17, 1820.
—362 Justina S.,[7] b. Oct. 10, 1825; d. Dec. 9, 1850.
—363 Zerva,[7] b. Dec. 13, 1826; d. aged 10 yrs.
—364 Hannah,[7] b. Feb. 10, 1827; m. **John Bate**; lived and died in Brooklyn, N. Y.
—365 Frances D.,[7] b. July 19, 1829; d. aged 6 yrs.
—366 Charles P.,[7] b. Sept. 31, 1831; d. aged 4 yrs.
—367 William,[7] b. Mar. 14, 1834; m. **Annie Gole** of Cederville, N. J.; lived in Boston.
—368 Charles F.,[7] b. Mar. 22, 1836; d. aged 2 yrs.
—369 Joseph H.,[7] b. July 26, 1838; d. in Boston and left children there.
+370 Frederick A.,[7] b. Apr. 28, 1840.

The will of William Stratton,[6] made the April before his death, mentions his wife, his nephew Nathaniel, and his five children, the only ones living at that date.

329. Preston Stratton [6] (*Jeremiah*,[5] *David* [4]) was born in Millville Aug. 30, 1810, and lived all his life in his native town, where he was a useful and esteemed citizen. He was a ruling elder in the Presbyterian church, as was his father before him. He married **Hannah A. Wilson**, Mar. 30, 1834. She was a daughter of *Stacy Wilson*, and was born Dec. 22, 1818; died Sept. 27, 1875. Mr. Stratton died Sept. 17, 1850.

Children:—*Born in Millville, N. J.*

—371 Amanda Fithian,⁷ b. Jan. 21, 1835; d. 1873; m. **John Hood** of Camden.
+372 Jeremiah,⁷ b. 1836.
+373 Benjamin F.,⁷ b. 1838.
—374 Sarah Wilson,⁷ b. Feb. 7, 1840; m. **Hosea Sithens** (?) of Philadelphia; d. July 2, 1907.
—375 Rebecca,⁷ d. in infancy.
+376 Thomas B.,⁷ b. 1843.
—377 Charles T.,⁷ b. Sept. 3, 1845; d. at Greenwich, N. J., in 1894; m. **Mary E. Tyler**; had one daughter, Etta Tyler,⁸ who married **Wm. Stewart**, and died in 1904, aged 23 years.
—378 Elizabeth Powell,⁷ b. July 4, 1847; m. **Geo. H. Foster,** Mar. 21, 1866. Their son, Walter, m. **Eliza R. Stratton** in 1899.
—379 Margaret,⁷ b. 1849; d. aged 1 year.
+380 Preston,⁷ b. 1851.

330. NATHANIEL STRATTON ⁶ (*Jeremiah*,⁵ *David* ⁴), born July 9, 1812, married **Mary B. Mulford**, Apr. 6, 1838, and lived and died in Millville where he was a prominent merchant. Prominent in politics; a democrat; sheriff on the Temperance ticket. He served several terms in the legislature, and in 1859 was elected state senator. For a number of years was Judge in the court of Common Pleas. He died Dec. 25, 1897.

Children:—*Born in Millville, N. J.*

—381 Zerviah Bateman,⁷ m. **Dr. Charles E. Thomas** of Woodbury, N. J.
—382 Rachel Mulford,⁷ b. Mar. 5, 1841; d. May 11, 1875.
—383 Louis Mulford,⁷ b. Feb. 15, 1842; d. aged 3 years.
—384 Emma H.,⁷ d. in infancy.
—385 Edward West,⁷ b. 1845; d. 1846.
—386 David Bateman,⁷ b. 1847; d. 1849.
—387 Rebecca Davidson,⁷ b. 1849; d. Oct. 28, 1860.
—388 Anna Murdock,⁷ b. May 11, 1851; d. Feb. 21, 1852.
—389 Nathaniel Frances,⁷ b. May 28, 1853; m. **Anna Bellis** of Philadelphia; no children; res. Millville.
—390 Mary T.,⁷ b. May 7, 1855; d. June 21, 1856.
—391 Furman Mulford,⁷ d. in infancy.

—392 Mary Grace,[7] b. Nov. 17, 1858. Living in the old homestead at Millville.
—393 Beulah,[7] b. Oct. 21, 1860; d. Jan. 5, 1862.
—394 William,[7] b. Feb. 9, 1862; d. in infancy.

339. JEREMIAH B. STRATTON[7] (*John*,[6] *Preston*,[4] *David* [5]) was born Apr. 27, 1834. Resides in Bridgeton, N. J. Married **Theodosia Hogben.** She was born May 21, 1835, and died Apr. 19, 1904.
Children:
—395 George, m. **Georgia Sherman**; res. Sedalia, Mo.
—396 Addie T., m. **David Marts**; res. Bridgeton, N. J.
—397 Thomas D., m. **Kelsie Moore**; res. Trenton, N. J.
—398 Jennie M., m. **Roscoe Kennedy**; res. Philadelphia, Pa.
—399 Daisy C., m. **George Golder**; res. Bridgeton. N, J.

370. FREDERICK A. STRATTON [7] (*William*,[6] *Jeremiah*,[5] *David* [4]) married **Rhoda Ann Wills,** and lived in New York City.
Children:
—400 James Will,[8] b. Feb. 23, 1867; d. Dec. 11, 1890.
—401 Mary Bayless,[8] b. Apr. 25, 1872; d. Mar. 3, 1890.
—402 Frederick S.,[8] b. Aug., 1876.
—403 John Bate,[8] b. Nov. 12, 1878.
—404 Jessie B.,[8] b. Nov. 11, 1881.

372. JEREMIAH STRATTON [7] (*Preston*,[6] *Jeremiah*,[5] *David* [4]), born Aug. 8, 1836, married **Kate McCornick** Feb. 17, 1859. He died in Philadelphia Sept. 14, 1892. At the time of his death he was Assistant Superintendent of the Prudential Life Insurance Co. with office in Camden. He is buried in Mt. Pleasant cemetery, Millville.
Children:—*Born in Millville, N. J.*
—405 Thomas B.[8]
—406 George B. McClellen,[8] res. Philadelphia.
—407 Lillian,[8] m. **Wallace Carson**; res. Philadelphia.
Born in Cape May.
—408 Preston,[8] res. Philadelphia; unm.

373. BENJAMIN FRANKLIN STRATTON [7] (*Preston*,[6] *Jeremiah*,[5] *David* [4]), born Feb. 3, 1838. Married **Mary Ann Felton,** daughter of *Lewis* and *Martha Felton,* Jan. 20, 1860.

Children:
- —409 Lewis Felton,[8] b. Dec. 27, 1860; d. aged 1 year.
- —410 Joseph Felton,[8] b. Oct. 15, 1862; d. Apr. 2, 1864.
- —411 William Hood,[8] res. Philadelphia.
- —412 Mattie May,[8] died in childhood.
- —413 Edwin Bell,[8] b. Sept. 9, 1870; d. May 31, 1871.
- —414 Herbert,[8] m. **Lillian May O'Brian**, Oct. 21, 1899. They have a daughter Ethel May.[9]

376. THOMAS BATEMAN STRATTON [7] (*Preston*,[6] *Jeremiah*,[5] *David*[4]) resides in Trenton, N. J. He was born Aug. 23, 1843, and was but seven years old when his father died. At the age of sixteen he went to work in the store of his uncle, Judge Nathaniel Stratton. From 1875 to 1890 he was connected with an wholesale drygoods house in Philadelphia and since has been employed with a firm in Trenton. At the age of 35 he was elected ruling elder of the Presbyterian Church in Millville—the same church in which his father and his grandfather had served in the same office. Upon his removal to Trenton he was elected elder in the third Presbyterian Church there, and has continued in that office ever since. He was Commissioner to the General Assembly in 1885, and was again elected to represent his Presbytery in General Assembly in 1910. He married **Ann Elizabeth Carson**, Mar. 29, 1865, daughter of *Thomas* and *Hannah Carson*. -CORSON

Children:—*Born in Millville, N. J.*
- —415 Nellie,[8] d. Mar. 15, 1867, aged 7 mos.
- —416 Justina[8] was a teacher in State Normal School; drowned while on a steamboat excursion on the Delaware, Aug. 28, 1901.
- —417 Hannah C.,[8] Principal of one of the largest public schools of Trenton.
- —418 Martha Felton,[8] m. **John Y. Parke**, 1901; d. Nov. 12, 1902.
- —419 Nathaniel,[8] m. Feb. 16, 1909, **Florence Fine**, d. of *Stacy* and *Mary Fine*.
- —420 Paul,[8] grad. Princeton; pastor Day Spring Presbyterian Church, Yonkers, N. Y.; m. Jan. 7, 1909, **Ethel Green Russell**, d. of *Geo. Isaac* and *Pauline E. (Underhill) Russell*.
- —421 Edwin Carson,[8] m. Apr. 29, 1902, **Clara Meyers**, d. of *Milton* and *Lena Meyers*.

—422 Henry Mayers,[8] m. June 4, 1908, **Matilda Bronkhurst Fulkert**, d. of *Charles* and *Louisa Fulkert*.
—423 Benjamin Frank,[8] m. Oct. 5, 1910, **Rose Coyle**, d. of *Wm.* and *Mary M. Coyle*. They have a little daughter, Jeane.[9]

380. PRESTON STRATTON [7] (*Preston*,[6] *Jeremiah*,[5] *David* [4]) was born in Millville, N. J., Feb. 27, 1851. He lived for awhile in Philadelphia. Since 1878 has lived in Bridgeport, N. J., where he is a substantial business man—a member of the Presbyterian Church. He married **Fannie Fern Wells** in 1873.
Children:—*Born in Philadelphia, Pa.*
+424 Joseph McKnight.[8]
—425 Leta Minnie,[8] m. **Ross Dale Gilmore** of Ridley Park, Pa.; d. June 13, 1908, at the home of his father in Bridgeton.
—426 Rebecca May.[8]

411. WILLIAM HOOD STRATTON [8] (*Benjamin F.*,[7] *Preston*,[6] *Jeremiah*,[4] *David* [5]) married **Mary Peters** of Philadelphia.
Children:
—427 William Harold.[9]
—428 Norman Peters.[9]
—429 Ronald Rice.[9]
—430 Paul.[9]

424. JOSEPH McKNIGHT STRATTON [8] (*Preston*,[7] *Preston*,[6] *Jeremiah*,[5] *David* [4]) is an active, successful young business man of Bridgeport, N. J., where he is engaged in the grocery business. He was born in Philadelphia, June 17, 1874. He married **Harriet Jepson**.
Children:—*Born in Bridgeton, N. J.*
—431 Fannie.[9]
—432 Preston.[9]

JONATHAN STRATTON OF PHILADELPHIA

[433.] JONATHAN STRATTON, with wife **Elizabeth**, was living in Philadelphia in 1780, where they were members of the Second Presbyterian Church. He died five years later. The record of his burial (Nov. 21, 1785) on the church books says that he was 31 years old. (He may have been in his 31st year.) The baptisms of his children are also recorded on the books of the second church.*

Children:—*Born in Philadelphia.*
+434 Benjamin,⁶ bapt. 1781.
—435 An infant child buried May 14, 1782.
—436 Mary,⁶ bapt. Aug. 20, 1785; m. **Uriah Gilman**, Mar. 24, 1812.

434. BENJAMIN STRATTON⁶ (*Jonathan⁵*) was born Feb. 25, 1780, and baptised Mar. 12, 1781, by Rev. J. Sproat, in the Third Presbyterian Church of Philadelphia. This apparently is the Benjamin Stratton whose name first appears in the Philadelphia City Directory in 1804 as a block and pump-maker. He married, first, **Elizabeth Parker**, Oct. 10, 1801. She was a daughter of *Elisha* and *Mary Parker* of Philadelphia.† She died about 1812, and he married, second, **Grizelda Hazlet**, May 10, 1816.‡ They were married by Rev. Ezra Stileseby, of the third church. She died Apr. 24, 1863, aged 73 years, as shown by her gravestone at Laurel Hill. His will was made Dec. 28, 1818, and probated Jan. 25, 1819.

Children:—*Born in Philadelphia.*
By first marriage.§
+437 Henry,⁷ b. Dec. 24, 1802; bapt. Aug. 16, 1807.
—438 Jonathan,⁷ b. Sept. 25, 1804; bapt. Aug. 16, 1807.

---

* Long and faithful research has failed to positively establish the parentage of this Jonathan Stratton.

It seems quite probable that he was Jonathan⁵ (64) who was born in Fairfield, N. J., about 1755 (see Vol I, p. 113). It is now known that Jonathan⁴ (30) died in 1759 of that terrible epidemic (now believed to have been black measles) which carried away in one year so many people in that part of New Jersey, among whom were five members of the family of Benjamin Stratton³ (17).

This would have left Jonathan⁵ (64) an orphan at the age of about five years, as his mother died in 1756. Assuming this to be the parentage of this Jonathan Stratton of Philadelphia, the author designates him as of the fifth generation in this record of his descendants.

† Elisha Parker died in Philadelphia in 1816, and his wife in 1818. They came to Philadelphia from Gloucester Co., N. J.

‡ This marriage is recorded as above on the books of the Third Church, Philadelphia. She had a sister, Margaret Hazlet, who married John Stevenson of Philadelphia, and whose descendants live in that city to-day.

§ The births and baptisms of these four children are given above just as they appear on the books of the Third Church. In each case the record reads: "Son (or daughter) of Benjamin and Elizabeth Stratton."

—439 Benjamin,⁷ b. Aug. 26, 1806; bapt. Aug. 16, 1807.*
—440 Elizabeth,⁷ b. Aug. 10, 1811; bapt. Nov. 26, 1811.
By second marriage.
—441 James,⁷ b. Sept. 25, 1816. (This may be the James Stratton who married, in Philadelphia Sept. 20, 1835, Harriet Schreinen. What became of him?)
—442 Mary,⁷ bapt. Oct. 31, 1818; m. Charles T. Wilson, Oct. 20, 1847; d. Feb. 1858; buried in Laurel Hill. She has descendants living in Philadelphia.

ABSTRACT OF WILL OF BENJAMIN STRATTON

Will of Benjamin Stratton of Philadelphia, Block and Pump Maker. Sick and weak in body but of sound mind, memory and understanding. Payment of just debts and funeral charges.

My four children, Henry, Jonathan, Benjamin and Elizabeth, all under age, the sum of $50.00 each as they become of age, the boys at 21 years, the girls at 18. As they severally become entitled to the same, and before receiving it, they are to resign to my executor all claim they may be entitled to on account of the sum of $160.00 I received from the estate of their grandfather Elisha Parker.

All the rest of the estate to wife Grizelda Stratton, her heirs, etc., the better to help her to educate the said Elizabeth and

---

Now, on the same books are these records:

"Mary, born Mar. 1, 1808; bapst. June 8, 1808; daughter of Benjamin and Elizabeth Stratton.

"Benjamin Thackary, b. Oct. 18, 1809; bapst. Jan. 31, 1810; son of Benjamin and Elizabeth Stratton.

"Sarah, bapst. May 4, 1814 (no date of birth); daughter Benjamin and Elizabeth Stratton."

The compiler is at a loss to know how to place these. Were there two Benjamin Strattons with wife Elizabeth in Philadelphia? Or were our Benjamin and Elizabeth the parents of seven children, three of whom died before the making of the will which names only four children of Benjamin and Elizabeth Stratton? It is left for some future student of this particular line of Strattons to solve the problem over which the compiler of this volume has spent many hours of study and research (see footnote, Vol. I, p. 110).

*Is this the Benjamin Stratton who with wife Elizabeth is buried at Laurel Hill? The inscription on their gravestones reads as follows:
"Benjamin Stratton, Died August 8, 1882, aged 77 yrs. Elizabeth Stratton, his wife, Died May 7, 1856, aged 52 yrs."

our two children James and Mary during their minority. Wife sole executrix.

 29th of December, 1818.   Benjamin Stratton (Seal).
 Witnesses;—T. Mitchell & Sophia Cerah.
 Probated January 25th, 1819.
         Philadelphia Wills Liber 6 folio 630.

 437. HENRY STRATTON [7] (*Benjamin*,[6] *Jonathan* [5]) lived in Philadelphia where he was born in 1802. He died while his children were still young. In 1823 he was living at No. 15 Relief Street as shown by the City Directory of that date. Soon after this he was engaged in the mercantile business with Mr. Wilson at Nos. 13 and 14 Water Street. Later he went to South America on a merchant ship and never returned. It is supposed he was killed in an earthquake near Caracus.*

 Children:—*Born in Philadelphia.*
—443 Ellen M.,[8] d. unm. Nov. 23, 1849, aged 27 years; buried in Laurel Hill Cemetery.
—444 Margaret,[8] b. Jan. 12, 1823; d. May 2, 1827.
+445 Henry,[8] b. 1826; d. 1875.
—446 James,[8] m. Annie ——; d. abt. 1864, leaving two daughters in Philadelphia. He was a soldier in the Civil War.

 445. HENRY STRATTON [8] (*Henry*,[7] *Benjamin*,[6] *Jonathan* [5]) was born May 24, 1826. On the records of the communicants of St. Paul Church, Philadelphia, is a notice of his removal to Richmond, Va., Apr. 18, 1843. Although then but seventeen years of age, he at once became engaged in the book and stationary business in Richmond. Later he removed to Petersburg, Va., where for many years he successfully engaged in the mercantile business, and where he owned considerable property, and where he was most highly esteemed and respected. June 6, 1853, he married **Mary Lavinia Whyte**, a daughter of *Henry* and

---

*The record of his marriage has not yet been found. One family tradition has it that he married the widow of Dr. Napeer of Philadelphia, that she died early and that the children, left orphans while quite young, were brought up by their grandmother, Grizelda (Hazlet) Stratton. Others believe that the name of the wife of Henry Stratton was Grizelda Hazlet, the same as that of his stepmother, and perhaps she was his stepmother's niece. Any one having exact knowledge of this generation of Strattons will confer a favor by writing the compiler.

Eliza Ann (Tafts) Whyte.* She was born in Petersburg June 27, 1831.

In 1859 Mr. Stratton, with a military company from Petersburg, took part in the capture of John Brown at Harper's Ferry. When the Civil War broke out he espoused the cause of his adopted home, and joined the Confederate army, serving first under the command of Capt. C. F. Fisher, and then under Capt. Robt. D. McLlwaine in Petersburg Cavalry of Volunteers. Later as a staff officer under Major-General George Edward Pickett, of Gettysburg fame, and continued in service until the close of the war. He died Feb. 20, 1875, at his home in Petersburg.

Children:—*Born in Petersburg, Va.*
—447 Mary Hazlett.[9]
—448 Lavinia Whyte,[9] d. Oct. 11, 1864, aged 8 years.
—449 Eliza Whyte.[9]
—450 Henry Pickett,[9] d. Aug. 16, 1864, aged 5 years.
—451 Thomas Beauregard,[9] d. Nov. 15, 1864, aged 3 years.
—452 Ellen Madeline,[9] d. June 28, 1908.
+453 Harry Pickett.[9]
—454 Albert Sydney,[9] d. Apr. 18, 1867, aged 4 months.
—455 Bessie Posey.[9]
—456 Francis Gerard,[9] m. **Lillian Prentis**, Jan. 25, 1899, and resides in Petersburg.

453. HENRY PICKETT STRATTON [9] (*Henry,*[8] *Henry,*[7] *Benjamin,*[6] *Jonathan*[5]) resides in Petersburg, Va., and is one of the live business men of that city. He is President of the Stratton & Bragg Co. and is connected with several other large and important industries. June 3, 1896, he married **Ella Louise (Lawrence) Romaine**, widow of Charles Nichols Romaine.

Children:—*Born in Petersburg.*
—457 Florence Traver.
—458 Ella Louise.

BENJAMIN STRATTON OF PITTSGROVE

[459.] BENJAMIN STRATTON lived in Pittsgrove township, near Woodstown, N. J., where he was a farmer. He married

---

* Henry Whyte was born in Dublin, Ireland, Dec. 24, 1798, and died in Petersburg, Va., March 20, 1842. Eliza Ann Tafts was born in New York City Jan. 9, 1802, and died in Petersburg Feb. 26, 1880.

Sarah Poulson. After his death his widow married Samuel Layman and died leaving two small children by her second marriage, a son and daughter.*

Children:—*Born near Woodstown, N. J.*
+460 William.
—461 Ann, m. James Hutchinson.

460. WILLIAM STRATTON [6] (*Benjamin* [5]) was only two years old when his father died. He was adopted by his uncle and aunt Jeremiah and Rachel Poulson, and brought up by them. He married **Hannah Banks** about 1829 and lived on a farm near Woodstown, N. J. He is remembered as a large, noble looking man of great strength and activity, commonly called the "giant constable," feared by criminals and loved by the honest. He was tax collector for several years. He was highly esteemed for his integrity and good judgment. He died June 24, 1868, aged 58 years, 3 months and 14 days.

Children:—*Born in Salem Co., N. J.*
—462 Jeremiah Poulson,[7] b. 1831; d. aged 8 years.
+463 John B.,[7] b. 1833.
—464 Elizabeth P.,[7] b. 1835; m. **Aaron Brandith**; d. 1860.
+465 Benjamin,[7] b. 1837.
—466 Samuel,[7] b. 1839; d. aged 25 years.
—467 Levi L.,[7] b. 1841; m. **Mary A. Anderson**; children John B.[8] and Essie.[8]
+468 David B.,[7] b. 1843.
+469 William B.,[7] b. 1845.
—470 Sarah,[7] b. 1847; m. **Elias Brown**; d. aged 25 years.

463. JOHN BANKS STRATTON[7] (*William,*[6] *Benjamin* [5]) was born Aug. 20, 1833, and died Feb. 4, 1876. He was a farmer of

---

* There can be no doubt about this Benjamin Stratton being a descendant of Benjamin Stratton [2] who settled in New Jersey in 1715 (Vol I, p. 106). Whether of the fifth or sixth generation has not yet been determined. Until research, which is yet being made, brings to light something more definite, he is here regarded as of the fifth generation. He has many descendants in New Jersey. May not some of them find the "connecting link"—in some old family record, on some gravestone, in some will or administration? His son William inherited some property from the Poulson estate. Some clew might be found there.

In the old Christ church cemetery, below Fairton, N. J., is a stone bearing this inscription: "In memory of Benjamin, son of Benjamin and Sarah Stratton, who departed this life Oct. 2, 1750, aged 17 years." Who was he?

Salem Co., N. J. He married **Annie Moslander,** Jan. 21, 1855. She was born in Cape May Co., Jan. 7, 1832.

Children:—*Born in Salem Co., N. J.*

—471 Hannah A.,[8] m. **George D. Maul,** Jan. 26, 1876; d. May 19, 1876.

—472 Eva M.,[8] m. **James H. Austin,** Apr. 5, 1876; d. Apr. 1, 1878.

—473 William M.,[8] m. **Sallie L. J. Mills,** Mar. 31, 1886.

—474 Henry M.[8] and Frank, d. July 28 and 29, 1864.

+475 Gervas H.[8]

465. BENJAMIN STRATTON [7] (*William,*[6] *Benjamin*[5]) was born in Salem, N. J., in 1837, and has lived all his life in his native town where he is a manufacturer of cements, dealer in lime, sand, etc. He married first, in 1859, **Margaret Fowler,** daughter of *Asa* and *Sarah (Robinson) Fowler;* second, **Mary Halter,** daughter of *John* and *Mary (Biddle) Halter;* res. Salem, N. J.*

Children:—*Born in Salem, N. J.*

By first marriage.

—476 Charles, d. Sept., 1884, aged 24 years.

—477 Elizabeth, d. aged 2 years.

—478 Harriet, d. aged 6 months.

—479 Edward, Superintendent Mitchell & Van Meter's Foundries, Reading, Pa.; m. **Louisa Whitney,** daughter of *Daniel* and *Elizabeth Whitney.*

—480 Henry W., m. **Esther Livingston;** res. Philadelphia, Pa.

—481 Benjamin, m. **Frances Miller;** res. Salem, N. J.

—482 Bessie Davis, m. **William R. Brown,** son of William and Hannah Brown.

—483 John Preston, m. Jan. 16, 1908, **Emma Hogan,** daughter of *George* and *Mary A. Hogan.* They have a little daughter, Hilda H.; res. Philadelphia, Pa.

By second marriage.

—484 Ruloff Van Cleve Lawrence, enlisted in the U. S. Navy at 18. Honorably discharged in 1906. Clerk in Dept. of Commerce and Labor at Washington. Grad. Nat. Univ. of Law, Wash.; m. **Anderena**

---

* This Mr. Stratton was given, by his father, a pair of gold cuff links marked "B. S." and was told that they had been handed down through the Benjamins of the family for generations, and that he was to give them to his son Benjamin.

Southland, Aug. 13, 1906, daughter of *Charles C.* and *Laura E. (Pettit) Southland.*
—485 Earnest Kenneth.

468. DAVID B. STRATTON [7] (*William*,[6] *Benjamin*[5]) was born in 1843; married **Sarah Daniels.** Died in 1878.
Children:—*Born in Salem, N. J.*
—486 Samuel R., m. **Mary E. Bolles,** Oct. 1, 1901—a Baptist minister; res. Pleasantville, N. J.
—487 Ida P., m. **William Kragler,** Jan. 1, 1895; d. in Camden, N. J., May 30, 1902.

469. WILLIAM BROADWAY STRATTON [7] (*William*,[6] *Benjamin*[5]) married **Isabella G. Anderson;** res. Glassboro, N. J.; wholesale milk dealer.
Children:
—488 Edwin Grant,[8] m. **Mattie W. Rhodes;** they have one child, Helen.[9]
—489 William B., Jr.,[8] m. **Carrie F. Young;** one child, Harold Belford.[9]

475. GERVAS H. STRATTON [8] (*John B.*,[7] *William*,[6] *Benjamin*[5]) married **Pluma I. Burlew,** Nov. 25, 1891, and lives in Vineland, N. J.
Children:—*Born in Salem.*
—490 Anne M.[9]
—491 Gervas H., Jr.[9]
—492 Elsie P.[9]
—493 James Albert.[9]

JOHN STRATTON OF EASTHAMPTON ·

(Chart D, Vol. I)

"One generation shall praise thy works to another." PSALMS cxlv, 3.

FROM 1649 for more than an hundred years the name of John Stratton appears continually on church and town records at Easthampton, and many times it is impossible to tell to which John Stratton the record refers. The dates of baptism on the church records there are not always to be relied upon. They seem sometimes to have been made from memory at the end of the year, or later. In several places the baptism of the same child is recorded twice under different dates. On one page is the record "Baptised the 4 children of Jon. Stratton, John, Henry, Selvanus and Frederick," while on other pages these baptisms are recorded under different dates.

Recently a most careful and thoughtful study has been made of all these records and the following conclusions are submitted:

First, that John Stratton's son baptised July 8, 1760 (name not given in record of baptism, see p. 132, Vol. I), was Samuel, who was born in 1759, and who was drowned at Sag Harbor in 1789, leaving three children, Mary, Samuel and Sidney.

Second, that the history of Easthampton and other authorities (including Vol. I of *A Book of Strattons*) are in error concerning the two John Strattons, Nos. 21 and 26 of Chart D, Vol. I. The compiler now believes that it was John[4] (*John,*[3] *Stephen,*[2] *John*[1]) who died leaving five daughters, Ruth, Sarah, Mary, Hannah and Anna.* While it was John[4] (*John,*[3] *John,*[2] *John*[1]) whose sons John, Henry, Frederick, Selvanus and Samuel were baptised in Easthampton by Rev. Samuel Buell.

Among other things which have led to this conclusion are these:

---

*These names are said to have been taken from the will of a John Stratton which mentions "my daughters, Ruth Hedges, Sarah Jessup, Mary Conklin, Hannah Chatfield, Anna Hildreth." The compiler has never been able to find this will.

John Stratton [2] (*John* [1]) was a prominent man in the community, and, as eldest son, inherited the greater part of his father's property, was highly esteemed, married the daughter of the pastor, Rev. Thomas James, and lived to the good old age of 90 years. His property was inherited by his only son, John,[3] who died in Sept., 1721, at the age of 22 years, and whose son, John,[4] was born the following October. He (John [4]) inherited the property of his father and grandfather, married the daughter of the well-known Lion Gardiner and continued to live in Easthampton, where some of his descendants still reside. The estate was probably divided up among the sons of John.[4] John,[5] the eldest son (perhaps receiving a double portion), settled in Clinton Co., N. Y., while Samuel [5] remained in Easthampton and his great-grandson is living there to-day.

Now the Clinton County Strattons still have in their possession a fine old copy of the Genevan Version of the Bible, printed in London in 1610, which has been passed down from father to son for many generations. It is well understood by them that it has passed down through a *John Stratton* in each generation. They have no knowledge or tradition of a *Stephen* in their ancestry.*

---

* This Bible, a rare old book, is owned by Mr. A. T. Stratton,[8] now of Columbia, S. C., to whom it was given by his father, John T. Stratton,[7] who received it from his uncle, John Stratton,[6] who died without issue. It was brought to Clinton Co., N. Y., by John Stratton [5] (No. 61). The only family record in it is the following, written in beautiful large script:

> John Stratton April 1.
> John Stratton, his heir
> April 1st Anno
> Dominie 1762.

The book was rebound some time before 1790—probably at Easthampton (?). The original fly leaves are pasted down to the covers—who can tell what invaluable records, now indecipherable, may have been written on them? On the title page is the following:

> Imprinted at
> London by Robert Barker
> Printer to the King's most
> Excellent Majesty
> 1610.

It is the "Black Letter Edition" of the version translated in 1560 by English refugees who were staying with Calvin in Geneva, and was the authorized version of the Bible in England from 1560 until superseded by the King James Version, the first edition of which was printed by Robert Barker in 1611.

If, then, the reader of this will make the following corrections in his copy of Vol. I of *A Book of Strattons* he will have what the compiler is now convinced is the true record:

On page 131 draw a pencil through the lines, "There are no records of children on the church books of Easthampton. A family record says that this John Stratton died leaving the following" and in place of the names "Ruth, Sarah, Mary, Hannah and Anna" write John, Henry, Frederick, Selvanus and Samuel.

On page 132 draw a pencil through "but he seems to have been living in his native town as late as 1759, when he is mentioned in his father's will." Also through "Baptised at Easthampton" and in place of the names "John, Henry, Frederick, Selvanus and a son," write Ruth, Sarah, Mary, Hannah and Anna. Make these same changes in names on Chart D. Then John⁵ will be No. 54 instead of No. 61, and Samuel⁵ will be No. 58 instead of No. 65.*

FIFTH GENERATION

54 (61 in Vol. I). JOHN STRATTON⁵ (*John,*⁴ *John,*³ *John,*² *John*¹) was born in 1745. He married **Esther Talmage**, who was born May 5, 1745. She was daughter of *Nathaniel* and *Mary (Fithian) Talmage* of Easthampton. (See *Easthampton records.*) After their marriage they lived for some time at Smithtown, L. I., and may have lived for a while at Newburgh.† About 1790 they settled at Plattsburg, Clinton Co., N. Y., where he bought a tract of land, covered with virgin forest, on the shore of Lake Champlain. On the list of the first eighteen members of the First Presbyterian Church at Plattsburg, appears the

---

* Easthampton records contain these entries:
Mr. Jon Stratton died May 30, 1766.
John Stratton's wife died Jan. 1793.
The compiler believes the first to be John⁴ (*John,*³ *John*²) whose wife, Mary Gardiner Stratton, died in 1759, and the last to be the wife of John⁴ (*John,*³ *Stephen*²), whose husband probably died later, leaving the will giving the names of his five daughters.
A more complete research than the compiler has been able to make, of deeds and land transfers, might throw some further light on these John Strattons.

† Closely connected with John Stratton at Smithtown and at Plattsburg was Judge Thomas Treadwell, of honored memory. They bought adjoining farms on Lake Champlain, and the families were close friends.

names of John and Esther Stratton.* Esther died Apr. 12, 1819, aged 74 years. Both are buried in the old burial ground in Beekmantown (once a part of Plattsburg) on what was then the David Parsons farm, where tombstones stand to their memory. On John's stone is this inscription: "In memory of John Stratton, Esq., who died April 26, 1821, aged 76 years.

> My flesh shall slumber in the ground,
> Till the last trumpet's joyful sound,
> Then burst the chains with sweet surprise,
> And in my Saviour's image rise."

John's will, made in 1817, and Esther's, made the same year, are recorded in Plattsburg.†

Children:—*Probably born in Smithtown, L. I.*

- —106 John,[6] d. unm. Apr. 8, 1844, aged 69 years; made his will in 1841; tombstone at Beekmantown.
- +107 Henry,[6] b. 1776; d. 1864.
- —108 Mary,[6] m. **Thomas Treadwell, Jr.**, before 1817.
- —109 Joel,[6] d. unm.‡
- —110 Hannah,[6] unm. in 1817; later married and moved west; d. before 1841.

---

* The other names on the list are Ezekiel Hubbard, Abner Pomroy, William and Mrs. Badlam, Moses Corbin, Elizabeth Adams, Catherine Hagerman, Catherine Marsh, Lucretia Miller, Phebe Platt, Mary Adams, Stephen and Mrs. Mix, Martha Coe, William Platt and John Culner. Another early settler in Plattsburg was Elias Woodruff.

† One of the executors of these wills was Nathan Miller. Several Millers from Easthampton settled in Clinton Co.

‡ Joel was killed by a falling tree; his tombstone is in the old burial ground on the farm formerly owned by the Hon. Thomas Treadwell. It bears this inscription:

"In memory of Joel Stratton, son of John and Esther Stratton, who died Dec. 28, 1798, aged 19 years.

> The rising morning can't assure
> That we shall end the day,
> For death stands ready every hour
> To snatch our lives away."

Many helpful notes on this family of Plattsburg Strattons have been furnished the compiler by Mr. James A. Stratton, born in Canada of English and Scotch ancestry, son of James and Jane (Orr) Stratton. He settled in Plattsburg in 1884, and is a well-known business man there, having been city chamberlain and loan commissioner, civil service commissioner, Master Mason of Clinton Lodge, and for nine years member of Board of Health.

58 (65 in Vol. I). SAMUEL STRATTON [5] (*John,*[4] *John,*[3] *John,*[2] *John* [1]) was born in 1759, and at the age of 17 was on the muster roll of Col. Joshua Smith's Regt. in 1776. (*Easthampton Records.*) He owned a home and land in Easthampton and by trade was a tailor. He married **Sarah** —— about 1783. Feb. 20, 1784, "Samuel Stratton and Sallie his consort" were received into the church at Easthampton by Rev. Samuel Buell. On that stormy night of Oct. 5, 1789, returning from a day's work at his trade, crossing between Sag Harbor and Shelton Island, the boat capsized and Samuel was drowned. With him was Sidney Havens, who was also drowned.

Children:—*Born in Easthampton.*
- —111 Mary,[6] bapt. Jan. 18, 1784; m. **Samuel Dayton**.
- +112 Samuel,[6] b. 1786.
- +113 Sidney,[6] bapt. Jan. 30, 1790. The record says, "The widow Stratton's son."

66. SAMUEL STRATTON [5] (*Samuel,*[4] *John,*[3] *Stephen,*[2] *John* [1]) has not been farther traced. Information concerning him is desired. The Samuel who died Sept. 3, 1784, was 13 years old (see *Easthampton Records*) and so may have been son of Mathew (29).

68. JOHN STRATTON [5] (*Mathew,*[4] *John,*[3] *Stephen,*[2] *John* [1]) inherited the home of his father in Easthampton. He married **Abigail Davis** Nov. 20, 1803. She died Apr. 16, 1840. This is probably the John Stratton who died Feb. 1, 1848, aged 84 years. He was chosen "Fence viewer" by the town meeting April, 1814, and Assessor of Taxes in 1818. There may have been other children than those named here.

Children:—*Born in Easthampton.*
- —114 Phoebe,[6] b. Nov. 9, 1804; d. unm. 1879.
- —115 Mary,[6] Oct. 2, 1814; m. **George W. Huntting**; d. 1875.

73. JONATHAN STRATTON [5] (*Joseph,*[4] *Joseph,*[3] *Cornelius,*[2] *John* [1]) was born in Huntington, L. I., in 1748. He was a weaver by trade. He married **Mary Godfrey** at Westport, Conn., Aug. 30, 1770. They were married by Rev. Hezekiah Ripley. They were admitted into West Farms Church, Fairfield, Feb. 24, 1771. She died Oct. 13, 1833; he died three years later, July 3, 1837.*

---

*There is a tradition current among his descendants, as there is in several other branches of Strattons, that Staten Island once belonged to the Strattons. The writer has found nothing to account for this tradition.

Child:—*Born in Fairfield Township, Conn.*
+116   Jonathan,⁶ 1775.

74.   JOSEPH STRATTON ⁵ (*John*,⁴ *Joseph*,³ *Cornelius*,² *John* ¹) was born July, 1751, in Fairfield, Conn. He was a Revolutionary soldier, a Corporal in the 7th Regt., enlisting at Fairfield with his father and his brother Stephen. He was at Fairfield when the town was burned by the British.* In 1778 he married **Eunice Berry**. About 1792 he settled in Roxbury, Delaware Co., N. Y., where he and his brother Samuel were among the very first settlers. Here he became a successful farmer. His farm was two miles below the present village of Roxbury. The beautiful "Stratton Falls," on a small branch of the Delaware, are on this farm, which was then an unbroken wilderness, reached by these sturdy first settlers by cutting the brush and logs before them, and carrying their household goods on an ox sled. Near the falls is the old burial ground, known as the "Old School Baptist Church Cemetery," where many Strattons are buried. Joseph died in 1827, and Eunice, his widow, in 1842, aged 88 years. Tombstones stand in their memory.

Children:—*Born in Fairfield, Conn.*
+117   David,⁶ b. 1779; d. 1850.
+118   Eli,⁶ b. 1780; d. 1869.
+119   Walter,⁶ b. 1784; d. 1866.
−120   Clarity,⁶ b. 1788; m. —— **Squire**.
+121   Lewis,⁶ b. 1791; d. 1849.
       Born in Roxbury, N. Y.
−122   Sarah,⁶ m. **James Allaben**.
−123   Joseph,⁶ d. Mar. 25, 1812, aged 12 years.
−124   Ezra W.,⁶ b. 1799; m. **Mary** ——; bought land at Monmouth, N. J., in 1870; d. at Red Bank, N. J., Oct. 24, 1876. His wife died earlier. Left no descendants.

---

*Connecticut colonial records show that John Stratton⁴ and his sons, Joseph and Stephen, enlisted in the 7th Regiment July 19, 1775, at Fairfield, Conn. The regiment was ordered by Gen. Washington to Boston camps Sept. 14, 1775, and was there assigned to Gen. Sullivan's brigade at Winter Hill, on the left of the besieging line. It remained there until the city was evacuated by the British. The regiment then returned to Connecticut, where it served as minute men along the sound, and was called out on various alarms during the war. John Stratton⁴ served nine years as a soldier and was discharged at Fishkill, N. Y., Oct. 5, 1786. He and his sons received "bounty land" in New York State.

75. STEPHEN STRATTON [5] (*John*,[4] *Joseph*,[3] *Cornelius*,[2] *John*[1]) was born Jan. 23, 1754. Dec. 25, 1777, he married **Sarah Darrow** of Fairfield, Conn. He was a Revolutionary soldier, enlisting in the 7th Regt. at Fairfield. On list of enlisted men he is called first Corporal, and then Sergeant, in Capt. Dimon's Company. (See footnote under Joseph No. 74.) In 1814 he settled in Thompsonville, Sullivan Co., N. Y., where he was a pioneer farmer, clearing a farm from the forest of the new country to which he and his large family had come. He died Jan. 26, 1842. His wife died one year earlier, Feb. 17, 1841.

Children:—*Born in Fairfield.*
- —125 John,[6] b. 1778; d. in infancy.
- —126 John,[6] b. Sept. 22, 1780.
- —127 William,[6] b. Sept. 2, 1782.
- +128 Elphalet,[6] b. 1784; d. 1858.
- —129 Stephen,[6] b. Sept. 19, 1786.
- +130 Alby,[6] b. 1789; d. 1854.
- +131 Jonathan,[6] b. 1791; d. 1863.
- —132 Uriah,[6] b. Aug. 26, 1793.
- —133 Sarah,[6] b. 1796; d. 1862; m. —— **Starr**.
- +134 Thomas,[6] b. 1797; d. 1859.
- —135 Elizabeth,[6] b. 1799; d. 1878; m. —— **Bradley**.
- —136 Laura,[6] b. 1802; d. 1883; m. 1st, —— **Starr**.

Information concerning John, William, Stephen and Uriah is desired. Some of them may have remained in Connecticut and married there.

76. SAMUEL STRATTON [5] (*John*,[4] *Joseph*,[3] *Cornelius*,[2] *John*[1]) was born in Fairfield, Conn., in 1755, and was living there when he enlisted in 1776, under Capt. Ebenezer Hill, in Col. Jonathan Dimon's Regt. and marched to New York City. He remained with his company until after the British had taken New York, when he was discharged near Kingsbridge. In March, 1777, he enlisted to serve during the war in the same regiment under Capt. Elphalet Thorp. He was in the battles of Ridgefield, Fairfield and Norwalk, and was in service when Fairfield was burned. He was also a soldier in the war of 1812. March 30, 1779, he married **Grace Darrow**, and about 1790 they settled in Roxbury, N. Y., where he bought land and cleared a farm and also engaged in the manufacture of woolen goods, and built a

large mill just below Stratton Falls. He died Oct. 3, 1838.* In 1832 he was granted a pension.

Children:—*Born in Fairfield, Conn.*
—137 Nabby⁶ (or Abigail), m. **Daniel Squires.**
+138 Jesse,⁶ b. 1779; d. 1837.
+139 Jonathan,⁶ b. 1781; d. 1851.
       Born in Roxbury, N. Y.
—140 Anna,⁶ m. **Enos Carroll,** 1823; d. in Roxbury, 1893.
—141 Mary,⁶ m. **James Ballard.**

86. Hull Stratton⁵ (*Cornelius,⁴ Joseph,³ Cornelius,² John¹*) married **Lydia** ——. The church record at West Farms says, "Hull Stratton and wife admitted to the church Mar. 16, 1800." "Lydia, wife of Hull Stratton admitted to full communion in church Mar. 7, 1810." Possibly Lydia was his second wife?

Children:—*Baptism recorded in West Farms Church.*
—142 Gold,⁶ bapt. Mar. 16, 1800.
—143 Philander,⁶ bapt. Feb. 14, 1801; d. same day.
—144 Philander,⁶ bapt. Nov. 14, 1802; d. Feb. 11, 1804, aged 11 mos.
—145 Anna Comstock,⁶ bapt. Feb. 17, 1805.
—146 Lucretia,⁶ bapt. May 24, 1807.

87. Eliphalet Stratton⁵ (*Cornelius,⁴ Joseph,³ Cornelius,² John¹*) was baptised Apr. 18, 1779. Aug. 3, 1806, he married **Sarah Moorhouse,** daughter of *Solomon Moorhouse* of Westport and Fairfield, a captain in the Revolution.

Children:—*Born in Westport, Fairfield Co., Conn.*
+147 Ezra M.,⁶ b. 1809; d. 1883.
—148 Anson,⁶ d. at Green Farms, Conn. Records of him and his family are wanted.
—149 Sarah Ann,⁶ m. 1st, **Brazela Banks** of Bridgeport, 2nd, —— **Hoosear.**
—150 Caroline.⁶
+151 Eliphalet.⁶

95. Abraham Stratton⁵ (*Abraham,⁴ Eliphalet,³ Cornelius,² John¹*) was born July 19, 1760. He married Mary Brown,

---

* Stratton Falls are on Mill Creek, which runs into the East Branch of the Delaware near Roxbury. The Stratton burial ground is just below the falls. Roxbury is the native town of John Burroughs, and here at "Woodchuck Lodge" he still spends his summers.

Nov. 15, 1780. She was born June 27, 1759, and died Jan. 23, 1806. The year of their marriage they settled in Montgomery Co., N. Y., where he bought land and was a farmer. Sept. 11, 1797, he was drowned in Schorarie Creek.

Children:—*Born in Glenn, Montgomery Co., N. Y.*

+152 Eliphalet,[6] b. 1781; d. 1842.
+153 Abraham,[6] b. 1784; d. 1845.
—154 James B.,[6] b. June 15, 1786; d. Dec. 11, 1841; married and had a son, Nathan,[7] and probably other children of whom records are desired.
—155 Fithian,[6] b. Feb. 2, 1789; d. aged about 1 year.
—156 Samuel,[6] b. Aug. 3, 1791; m. and lived in Albany. Had children among whom were William[7] and Abram.[7] Further information desired.
+157 Oliver,[6] b. 1794.
—158 Silas Cooper,[6] b. Apr. 14, 1798. Further records desired.

96. ELIPHALET STRATTON[5] (*Abraham*,[4] *Eliphalet*,[3] *Cornelius*,[2] *John*[1]) has not yet been located. When Vol. I of *A Book of Strattons* was issued it was supposed that records of him had been found in New York state. Further research shows that these records are of Eliphalet,[6] nephew of Eliphalet[5] (No. 151), of this line. Data concerning Eliphalet[5] (96) are greatly desired.

104. PLATT STRATTON[5] (*Eliphalet*,[4] *Samuel*,[3] *Cornelius*,[2] *John*[1]) was born at Huntington, L. I., May 9, 1787, and removed with his parents to Flushing, N. Y. (now College Point), while a boy. He early turned his attention to business, and later was of the firm of "Stratton and Winthrop," cotton and shipping merchants. They owned and operated the ships *Selma* and *Tuscalusa*, chiefly between New York and the ports of Mexico and London. He inherited from his father the Stratton homestead (see picture in Vol. I) and the estate of 350 acres, which embraced nearly the entire water front of Flushing Bay, Queens Co. He married **Elizabeth Hewlett Jones**, Apr. 27, 1836. She was a daughter of *William H. Jones* of Woodbury, Queens Co. She was born Aug. 12, 1813, and died Dec. 8, 1893. Mr. Stratton died Sept. 8, 1854. His four children inherited in equal portions his real and personal estate.

Children:—*Born in Flushing, N. Y.*

—159 Mary Victoria,[6] b. Mar. 6, 1837; d. Mar. 11, 1890.

+160   William H.,⁶ 1838.
−161   Elizabeth Jane,⁶ b. Mar. 20, 1842; m. **Captain John Graham**, of College Point.
+162   Eliphalet Platt,⁶ b. 1844.

107. HENRY STRATTON ⁶ (*John,⁵ John,⁴ John,³ John,² John ¹*) was born in 1775, and came with his parents to Plattsburg, N. Y., when he was 14 years old. He was a successful farmer of Clinton Co. In politics a staunch Democrat, as were all his sons. He married **Dorcas Hackett** in 1808. Their home was in West Chazy, where the house built by them is still standing. Henry died Oct. 16, 1849, intestate. Dorcas died Sept. 21, 1869, aged 78 years.

Children:—*Born in West Chazy, N. Y.*
−163   Mary,⁷ b. Mar. 29, 1809; d., unm., in West Chazy, July 3, 1881.
−164   Joel,⁷ b. Apr. 4, 1812; d. aged 3 years.
−165   Sidney,⁷ b. Aug. 23, 1813; d. aged 11 mos.
−166   Eleanor,⁷ b. Aug. 8, 1815; m. **Stephen T. Sweet**; d. at Moores, N. Y., Aug. 5, 1882.
−167   Edward,⁷ b. Aug. 18, 1817; m. **Rosina Clark**; d. West Chazy, Oct. 8, 1897; no issue.
+168   Walter,⁷ b. 1819; d. 1864.
+169   Jonas,⁷ b. 1821; d. 1901.
−170   Henry,⁷ b. Sept. 8, 1823; d. Sept. 6, 1864; lived in Beckmantown; m. Mary Mutter, Apr. 9, 1860. Had one child who died in infancy.
+171   John Talmage,⁷ b. 1826; d. 1885.
−172   Cyrenius,⁷ b. Dec. 19, 1827; m. **Eliza J. Ober**, March 31, 1859; d. May 5, 1906; no issue.
+173   Philander,⁷ b. 1830; d. 1898.
−174   Caroline,⁷ b. Mar. 6, 1832; m. **Elihu Hall**; d. in Ellenburg, N. Y., Nov. 29, 1892.

112. SAMUEL STRATTON ⁶ (*Samuel,⁵ John,⁴ John,³ John,² John ¹*) was born Oct. 4, 1786, and bapt. in November of the same year. He resided in Easthampton, where he married **Mary Osborn**, Aug. 15, 1807. She was born Oct. 18, 1786, daughter of *Jonathan Osborn* of Easthampton. Samuel died July 13, 1845. His wife died 18 years later—Nov. 17, 1863.

Children:—*Born in Easthampton.*
−175   Anna Case,⁷ b. Mar. 28, 1875; m. **Wm. Parsons**, Nov. 9, 1849; d. Apr. 28, 1875.

—176 Selvanus,[7] b. Mar. 27, 1810; d. Oct. 26, 1819.
—177 Sidney Havens,[7] b. Dec. 12, 1812; d., unm., at Montauk, Apr. 19, 1878.
—178 Sarah B.,[7] b. June 12, 1816; m. Jeremiah J. Mulford, Mar. 11, 1841; d. June 13, 1886.
—179 Esther Talmage,[7] b. Apr., 1819; m. Austin Goldsmith; d. June 21, 1878.
—180 Mary Osborn,[7] b. Apr. 25, 1822; m. Edmond Conklin; d. Sept. 14, 1892.
+181 Samuel Thomas,[7] b. 1824; d. 1894.
—182 Caroline C.,[7] b. Feb. 19, 1827; m. George H. Miller, Oct. 22, 1851; d. Oct. 14, 1906.

113. SIDNEY STRATTON [6] (*Samuel,*[5] *John,*[4] *John,*[3] *John,*[2] *John* [1]) lived in Easthampton, in Salem, N. Y., in Wilton, Conn., and in Brooklyn, N. Y. He died in Brooklyn. He married, first, **Edith Webb**; second, —— **Smith**.

Children:—*By first marriage.*
—183 Sarah,[7] m. Gilson Willette; d. in Brooklyn.
—184 Maria,[7] b. Salem, N. Y., in 1822. At the age of seven, at the death of her mother, she went to live with her uncle, Samuel Dayton, of Easthampton. She married **Charles Jackson Jennings,** of Wilton, Conn.; died in Norwalk, Conn., Feb. 23, 1911.
—185 Ruth,[7] m. **John Davis**; resided in Brooklyn.
—186 Wallace,[7] probably died in childhood.

116. JONATHAN STRATTON [6] (*Jonathan,*[5] *Joseph,*[4] *Joseph,*[3] *Cornelius,*[2] *John* [1]) was born Mar. 17, 1775. Of his father he learned the weavers trade. Apr. 16, 1803, he was married to **Elizabeth Totten,** at South Huntington, by Rev. Lyman Beecher. They were admitted into the church there Sept. 28, 1805. In 1811 they removed to New York state. A record written by Jonathan [6] reads: "July 28, 1811, we set out on our journey, and Aug. 6 we reached Union Center (now called Vestal), Broome Co., N. Y." In 1841 they moved from Vestal to Barton, Tioga Co., N. Y., where she died Jan. 28, 1848, and he, Mar. 11, 1859.

Children:—*Born on Long Island.*
+187 Cornelius,[7] b. 1804; d. 1875.

—188 Rachel,⁷ b. Mar. 4, 1806; m. **Lewis Munday,** Sept. 2, 1822.*
—189 Mary Godfrey,⁷ b. Nov. 22, 1808; m. **Jonah Kellum.**
—190 Jacob,⁷ b. June 1, 1811; d. aged 1 year.
Born in Union Center, N. Y.
—191 Elizabeth,⁷ b. Apr. 19, 1813.
+192 John,⁷ b. 1816.
—193 Martha,⁷ b. Sept. 25, 1820; m. **Wm. Dilts.**
+194 Richard,⁷ b. 1825; d. 1905.

117. David Stratton ⁶ (*Joseph,⁵ John,⁴ Joseph,³ Cornelius,² John¹*) was born Apr. 20, 1779, at Fairfield, Conn., and came to Roxbury when about 14 years of age. He was in the war of 1812, and was stationed for some time at Staten Island. He was a weaver by trade. He had an excellent and well-trained voice and in his home town was noted as a teacher of singing. He married **Cleressa Patchen,** who was born Dec. 8, 1786, and died Nov. 9, 1859. David died Oct. 22, 1850.

Children:—*Born in Roxbury, N. Y.*
—195 Harriet Hubbell,⁷ m. 1st —— **Roach,** 2nd, **Hiram Darling;** d. 1875 in Windham, N. Y.
—196 Julia A.,⁷ m. **Warren Preston.**
—197 Charity Squire,⁷ b. 1817; d. at Harpersfield, N. Y., Feb. 5, 1890; m. **Samuel Adee Scutt,** Oct. 25, 1814.†
+198 John Hunt.⁷
—199 Eunice Middlebrook,⁷ b. 1820; d. July 11, 1899; m. **Dr. Horace Scutt;** resided at Griffin Corners, N. Y.

118. Eli Stratton ⁶ (*Joseph,⁵ John,⁴ Joseph,³ Cornelius,² John¹*) was born Dec. 2, 1780. Married in Roxbury Oct. 17, 1805, **Joanna Dewey,** who was born Apr. 23, 1788. In 1813 they removed to Richmond Dale, Ross Co., O., where he was a farmer for many years. He was a staunch Democrat, as were most of the Strattons of this branch. A man greatly respected and liked

---

* In the old Bible given Rachel by her grandfather is this record: "Baptised in the first year of her age by Rev. Luther Gleason, pastor of the Presbyterian church at New Babylon, L. I."

† He was son of Jonathan and Ann (Adee) Scutt, and grandson of Samuel Scutt who came to Dutchess Co. prior to the Revolution. He was of German descent, the name formerly spelled Schutt. Mr. Stratton Scutt of Ethelwin farm, Harpersfield, N. Y., is a son of Charity and Samuel A. Scutt.

by all who knew him. He died Dec. 10, 1860. His wife, Joanna, died twenty years earlier, Aug. 6, 1840.

Children:—*Born in Roxbury, N. Y.*

—200 Amanda,[7] b. July 8, 1807; m. **Hiram Philley**, Oct. 25, 1823; lived in Fort Wayne, Ind.

—201 Aurilla,[7] b. Oct. 9, 1808; m. **Thomas Griffith**; d. Mar. 15, 1823; lived in Fort Wayne, Ind.

—202 Squire D.,[7] b. 1810;[13] m. **Electa Miner**, June 18, 1831; two children: Emily,[8] Adelia.*

+203 Lewis T.,[7] b. 1811; d. 1851.

—204 Sarah S.,[7] d. in infancy.

Born in Richmond Dale, Ohio.

+205 Joseph,[7] b. 1815; d. 1882.

—206 Elenor T.,[7] b. Mar. 23, 1817; d. aged 3 years.

—207 Jerial R.,[7] b. Dec. 30, 1818; lived at Carthage, near Cincinnati; was in poor health and decided to move west, hoping to regain his health; started with his family to journey overland, died on the way. The family never returned. Information concerning them is desired.

+208 Morgan W.,[7] b. 1821; d. 1859.

+209 Heman Dewey,[7] b. 1822; d. 1901.

+210 Adam King,[7] b. 1824; d. 1903.

—211 Milton M.,[7] b. Feb. 12, 1826; d., unm., Aug. 16, 1866.

+212 Morrison W.,[7] b. 1828; d. 1903.

—213 Julia Black,[7] b. July 2, 1829; m. **Charles Rush**, of Lexington, Ky.; d. in Lexington Mar., 1905.

—214 Jason,[7] b. 1831; d. aged 2 years.

+215 Jason Gould,[7] b. 1833; d. 1903.†

119. Walter Stratton[6] (*Joseph,*[5] *John,*[4] *Joseph,*[3] *Cornelius,*[2] *John*[1]) was born in Fairfield, Conn., Dec. 4, 1784. Oct. 16, 1808, he married **Esther Allaben**, youngest daughter of *Jonathan* and *Mercy (Bonton) Allaben.* She was born in Freeport, L. I., Apr.

---

* The Squire family of America originated from the Squire or Squier family of Peterboro, Eng. Sergeant Thomas Squire, b. 1643, was an early settler in Fairfield, Conn., where he died in 1690. The Squires of Roxbury came from Fairfield about the same date that the Strattons, Goulds, and Burroughs settled there.

† The Goulds lived near the Strattons in Roxbury, and the families were intimate friends there, as their grand-parents had been in Connecticut. Jay Gould's father always called his son "Jason." The beautiful new church and library was given to Roxbury by Miss Helen Gould.

7, 1787. Mr. Stratton was one of the prosperous farmers of Roxbury, highly esteemed by his fellow townsmen, member of the Presbyterian church, a staunch Democrat. He served in the war of 1812. His house, built of stone in 1827, is still standing. His wife, a devoted Christian, beloved by all who knew her, died Oct. 4, 1847.

Children:—*Born in Roxbury.*
- —216 Malinda,⁷ b. 1810; m. **Cyrenus Pallam**, 1830; d. in Iowa.
- +217 Alanson W.,⁷ b. 1811; d. 1902.
- —218 Lucinda,⁷ b. 1814; d. 1864; m. **Reuben Bassett**, 1845.
- +219 David Williams,⁷ b. 1816; d. 1902.
- —220 Mary,⁷ b. 1818; d. 1884; m. **Richard Osterhoudt**.
- —221 Electa,⁷ b. 1822; m. **Dyer Todd**.
- —222 Adaline,⁷ b. 1824; m. **Benjamin Scudder**, 1873.
- +223 Jason W.,⁷ b. 1831; d. 1891.

121. Lewis Stratton⁶ (*Joseph,*⁵ *John,*⁴ *Joseph,*³ *Cornelius,*² *John*¹), born June 3, 1791; married **Sarah Lee** in 1816. He moved from Roxbury to Richmond Dale, Ohio, and from there to Waverly, O., where he died in 1849.

Children:—*Born in Richmond Dale, O.*
- +224 Calistus Lee,⁷ b. 1822; d. 1898.
- —225 Calista Ann,⁷ b. Mar. 20, 1820; d. 1886; m. **Horace Puffer**.
- —226 Elizabeth Lorenza,⁷ b. Nov. 17, 1823; m. **James C. McGowan**.
- —227 Lorenzo,⁷ b. Nov. 2, 1826; d. 1857, unm.

128. Eliphalet Stratton⁶ (*Stephen,*⁵ *John,*⁴ *Joseph,*³ *Cornelius,*² *John*¹) was born Sept. 5, 1784. He married in Connecticut, Mar. 11, 1808, **Rachel Lawson**, who was born Jan. 20, 1793, and died May 23, 1888. In 1813 they settled at Thompsonville, Sullivan Co., N. Y., where they spent the remainder of their lives on a farm, building first a log house, and then a substantial farm house. He was in the war of 1812, and at various times was chosen to fill several different town offices. He died Nov. 12, 1858.

Children:—*Born in Connecticut.*
- +228 William B.,⁷ b. 1810; d. 1887.
- —229 Sarah Emiline,⁷ b. Sept. 12, 1812; m. **Shelden Atwell**, died in March, 1840.

Born in *Thomsonville, N. Y.*

—230 Nancy Maria,⁷ b. Dec. 12, 1814; m. **Henry Fairchild** in 1844.
+231 Levi L.,⁷ b. 1816; d. 1859.
—232 Eliza Ann,⁷ b. Aug. 12, 1819; m. **Richard Haight.**
—233 John Edgar,⁷ b. Aug. 12, 1821; m. **Laura Warren.** Killed in the battle of Gettysburg.
—234 Abraham Nelson,⁷ b. Jan. 30, 1826. Went South while a young man and was last heard of in Virginia. Information concerning him is much desired.
—235 Samuel Edward,⁷ b. Dec. 14, 1828; d. aged 2 years.
—236 Marietta,⁷ b. Feb. 24, 1830; m. **John Palmer.**
—237 Henrietta,⁷ b. Feb. 24, 1830 (twin); m. **James Stilson.**
+238 Leonard B.,⁷ b. 1832.
+239 Henry W.,⁷ b. 1836.
—240 George Sheldon,⁷ b. Mar. 30, 1838; m. **Maggie E. Quackenbush**, 1870, had but one child, a daughter, Lena May,⁸ who died at the age of twenty.

130. ALBY STRATTON ⁶ (*Stephen,⁵ John,⁴ Joseph,³ Cornelius,² John ¹*), born in Fairfield, Conn., Mar. 24, 1789. Came to New York state about 1814. He married and lived for awhile in Chenango Co, then moved to the western part of the state and joined the army (War of 1812) and was killed in battle near Buffalo. It is believed that one or more of his brothers was killed at the same time.

Child:

+240ª Alby,⁷ b. May 25, 1811.

131. JONATHAN STRATTON ⁶ (*Stephen,⁵ John,⁴ Joseph,³ Cornelius,² John ¹*) was born Aug. 24, 1791. He went from Connecticut to Steuben Co., N. Y., in 1811. In 1813 he enlisted in the war of 1812 and with his company was stationed on the Niagara frontier under Gen. Scott. In 1816 he went to Thompsonville, Sullivan Co., where his father then resided. Here he engaged in merchandising and in the manufacture of leather and lumber. He represented his county in the state Legislature several terms, and was colonel of the local regiment of the New York State Militia. July 8, 1829, Col. Stratton married **Cornelia A. Thompson.** She was daughter of *Judge Wm. A.* and *Amy (Knapp) Thompson.** She was born Jan. 4, 1800, and died in

---

* Judge Thompson was a prominent early jurist in New York. In 1795 he purchased large tracts of land in the western part of Ulster Co.,

Thompsonville, N. Y., Jan. 10, 1887. Mr. Stratton died in 1863.
Children:—*Born in Thompsonville, N. Y.*
+241   James T.,[7] b. 1830.
−242   Adaline A.,[7] m. **Noah M. Brown,** resides in the old homestead in Thompsonville.
−243   Catherine E.,[7] d., unm., Jan., 1894.
−244   Frances C.,[7] m. **Robert Thompson**; d. 1910, aged 64 years.
−245   William A.,[7] b. Oct. 15, 1836; went to California while a young man; m. 1st, **Hannah M. Styles,** at Stockton, Cal., Oct. 27, 1860; m. 2nd, **Elizabeth S. Williams**; a nurseryman and florist, editor and writer on horticultural matters for more than fifty years; res. in Petaluma, Cal.

134. Thomas Stratton [6] (*Stephen,*[5] *John,*[4] *Joseph,*[3] *Cornelius,*[2] *John* [1]) was born Nov. 8, 1798, and came to New York state with his parents about 1814. He married **Clarrissa Smith,** Mar. 23, 1820, and settled in Fallsburgh, Sullivan Co., which was then an almost unbroken wilderness, built a first log house and cleared up a large productive farm, which is still in possession of some of his descendants. He died Mar. 2, 1857. His widow died Nov. 29, 1887, aged 88 years.

Children:—*Born in Fallsburgh, N. Y.*
−246   Eliza Jane,[7] b. Aug. 20, 1821; m. **Walter Denneston,** Jan. 3, 1841.
+247   William D.,[7] b. 1823; d. 1888.
−248   Mary Ann,[7] b. 1825; m. **Ira Wells,** Aug. 6, 1851; d. in New York City, Feb. 10, 1876.
−249   Sarah Frances,[7] b. Oct. 2, 1827; m. **Reuben R. Hall,** Dec., 1848; d. in Santa Paula, Cal.
−250   Walter J.,[7] b. Dec. 13, 1831; went to California in Dec., 1852, where he married and has a family. Information concerning him is desired.
−251   Laura E.,[7] b. Jan. 25, 1833; m. **Ronald Katcham** in 1856; d. in San Leandro, Cal.
−252   Oscar B.,[7] b. 1834; m. **Mary E. Tuttle,** Nov. 22, 1859; res. Addison, N. Y.

---

afterwards set off as Sullivan Co. He was a frequent contributor on geological subjects to the scientific journals of the day, and a member of the Royal Geological Society of France. A fine, old oil painting of him was recently presented to Sullivan County by his granddaughter, Mrs. Adaline Stratton Brown, and hangs in the Court House there.

—253 Orson,[7] b. 1834 (twin); m. **Helen Seaman**; res. at the old homestead; child, Fred J., m. **Clara Stratton**.
+254 George W.,[7] b. 1840.

138. JESSE STRATTON[6] (*Samuel*,[5] *John*,[4] *Joseph*,[3] *Cornelius*,[2] *John*[1]) was born June 9, 1779. He married, Jan. 10, 1805, **Sarah Patchen**, who died in Roxbury, Dec. 10, 1854. He died May 25, 1837. He was a well-to-do farmer. He and his wife, son and daughters are buried in the cemetery of the Old School Baptist church in Roxbury, where tombstones stand to their memory. He donated the land upon which this church was built. Several generations of Strattons have worshipped here, also the ancestors of Jay Gould and of John Burrough. His will is recorded at Delhi, N. Y.

Children:—*Born in Roxbury, N. Y.*
—255 Eliza Marietta,[7] b. Apr. 2, 1812; d. Sept. 11, 1835; she was a teacher greatly loved and highly esteemed.
—256 Elizabeth,[7] m. **Abram Van Blarcum**; d. Nov. 6, 1881; settled in Mich.
—257 Minerva,[7] d. Aug. 13, 1845.
—258 Eli,[7] drowned when 11 years old, June 20, 1827.
+259 Daniel S.,[7] b. July 4, 1821.

139. JONATHAN STRATTON[6] (*Samuel*,[5] *John*,[4] *Joseph*,[3] *Cornelius*,[2] *John*[1]) was born May 11, 1781, and came with his father to Roxbury, N. Y. He married **Mary Silliman**, who was born Jan. 12, 1781, and died Aug. 18, 1847. He died Mar. 14, 1851. Both are buried in the Baptist church cemetery, with tombstones to their memory.

Children:—*Born in Roxbury, N. Y.*
—260 Caroline,[7] m. **Levi Sanford**.
—261 Elizabeth,[7] m. **Levi Sanford** (his second wife).
—262 Sarah,[7] m. **George Winship**.
—263 Clarinda,[7] m. **Elder Cyrus Fuller**, a Baptist minister, son of John and Lucena (Crosby) Fuller, who came from New Haven to Roxbury.

147. EZRA MOORHOUSE STRATTON[6] (*Eliphalet*,[5] *Cornelius*,[4] *Joseph*,[3] *Cornelius*,[2] *John*[1]) married **Angeline Keys** about 1833, who died in 1907 in her 90th year. He was a carriage builder in New York City; publisher of New York *Coach Maker's Magazine* from 1859 to 1875; author of "The World on Wheels." He died Nov. 21, 1888.

Children:
- —264 Elvira,[7] m. **James Fitzgerald.**
- —265 Ezra Washington,[7] a carriage maker; res. Brooklyn, N. Y.
- —266 Lavinia Jane,[7] m. **Edward Him.**

151. ELIPHALET STRATTON[6] (*Eliphalet*,[5] *Cornelius*,[4] *Joseph*,[3] *Cornelius*,[2] *John*[1]) lived in Bridgeport and Brooklyn; married Catherine **Valentine** in 1832. He died in Brooklyn, N. Y., Sept. 14, 1896.

Children:—*Born in Westport, Conn.*
- —267 Valentine,[7] m. **Angeline** ——.
- —268 Anson,[7] m. **Catherine L. Smith.**
- —269 Eliphalet William,[7] b. May 28, 1836; m. 1st, **Emma J. Smith**; 2nd, **Elizabeth Durhan.** He d. in Brooklyn, Aug. 29, 1906. Was Lieutenant in Seventh New York Regiment during Civil War; mem. G. A. R. Chn. Katherine,[8] m. Frank H. Hyatt; Florence M.,[8] m. Bridgeman Smith; Walter Francis.[8]
- —270 Hannah,[7] m. **Richard T. Ludlam.**
- —271 Jennie,[7] m. **Silas Gregory.**
- —271a George,[7] m. **Florence** ——.

152. ELIPHALET STRATTON[6] (*Abraham*,[5] *Abraham*,[4] *Eliphalet*,[3] *Cornelius*,[2] *John*[1]) was born Sept. 9, 1781. He married Eliza **Smith.** He was appointed administrator of the estate of his mother, Mary Brown Stratton, in Montgomery Co., Mar. 1, 1806. Later he removed to Clyde, Wayne Co., N. Y., where he bought a farm, and where he died Jan. 27, 1842.

Children:—*Born in Clyde, N. Y.*
- +272 Oliver,[7] b. 1818.
- +273 John Smith,[7] b. 1822.
- —274 Mary,[7] b. 1825.
- +275 Abram Wooley,[7] b. 1827.
- —276 James,[7] b. Oct. 24, 1830; d., unm., Jan. 23, 1865. He was carried into the Salmon River, Idaho, by a snow slide and his body was never recovered.
- +277 Edwin,[7] b. 1833.

153. ABRAHAM STRATTON[6] (*Abraham*,[5] *Abraham*,[4] *Eliphalet*,[3] *Cornelius*,[2] *John*[1]) was born June 18, 1784. He married Eunice **Wooley**, and moved to Wayne Co. where he was a farmer, and where he died May 15, 1815.

Children:—*Born in Clyde, N. Y.*
+278 Abram,[7] b. 1805; d. 1877.
−279 Nathan,[7] went to New Orleans, and later was lost at sea.

157. OLIVER STRATTON [6] (*Abraham,*[5] *Abraham,*[4] *Eliphalet,*[3] *Cornelius,*[2] *John*[1]) was born Sept. 15, 1794. He was a farmer, a member of the Baptist Church. He married **Deanthia Hanchett** in 1818. About 1830 he moved from Glenn, Montgomery Co., to Howard, Steuben Co., N. Y. Here he bought a farm upon which he spent the remainder of his life. He died in 1873.

Children:—*Born in Glenn, N. Y.*
+280 David, 1819.
−281 Ruth Ann, m. **John Martin**, 1847.
−282 Julia, d. unm.
−283 Henry Kimball, b. Nov. 24, 1824; d. unm. Apr. 1, 1858.
−284 Sarah Green, d. unm.
−285 James, b. May 9, 1828; d. aged 3 years.
+286 John V., 1829.
Born in Howard, N. Y.
−287 James B., b. Nov. 16, 1832; d. aged 15 years.
+288 Charles, b. 1834.
−289 Elizabeth, d. unm.

160. WILLIAM HEWHETT STRATTON [6] (*Platt,*[5] *Eliphalet,*[4] *Samuel,*[3] *Cornelius,*[2] *John*[1]) was born Jan. 27, 1838. He was a member of the 7th Regt., N. Y. State Militia, with which he went to the front Apr. 19, 1861. Later he recruited and commanded a company in the 6th Regt., N. Y. State Volunteers. He took part in the campaign of the Army of the Potomac under Gen. Burnside. He married, first, **Ada S. Little** of New York. After her death he removed to Omaha, Neb. He married, second, **Vina White**, who was from Boston. From Omaha he removed to Freeport, Ill., where he now resides.

Children:
 By first marriage.
−290 Elizabeth.[7]
−291 Florence.[7]
 By second marriage.
−292 William Edward.[7]

162. ELIPHALET PLATT STRATTON [6] (*Platt,*[5] *Eliphalet,*[4] *Samuel,*[3] *Cornelius,*[2] *John*[1]) was born June 12, 1844. He resides at

College Point, N. Y. He was educated at Flushing Institute, and Walnut Hill Academy, Geneva, N. Y. He learned mechanical engineering, and shipbuilding at the Morgan Iron Works, N. Y., becoming a recognized authority on engineering and naval architecture. Served the government as inspector and supervising inspector for the port of New York for about twelve years, and later was chief engineer surveyor of the American Bureau of Shipping. Invented the "Stratton Separator," a device for extracting water from steam, which is recognized as the most efficient apparatus of its kind that has ever been produced. Mr. Stratton is also consulting engineer of the Bureau of Marine Underwriters of New York; one of the counsel of the Society of Naval Architects of Great Britain and of the American Society of Mechanical Engineers.

Apr. 27, 1871, he married **Harriet Louise Woodhull**, daughter of *Jeffrey Amherst* and *Anna E. Woodhull* of Huntington, L. I.

Children:—*Born at College Point, N. Y.*
- —293 Jennie Louise,[7] m. Sept. 14, 1910, Rev. **Roy Farrel Duffield**, Canon of St. Paul's Cathedral at College Point, and Archdeacon of Queens and Nassau.
- —294 Harriet Woodhull,[7] m. June 6, 1903, **Henry Hewlett Tredwell** of E. Welleston, L. I.

168. WALTER STRATTON [7] (*Henry*,[6] *John*,[5] *John*,[4] *John*,[3] *John*,[2] *John*[1]) was born May 27, 1819. He married, first, **Betsey Aldridge**, Mar. 3, 1850, who died soon after their marriage. He married, second, **Salome Hooper**, in Dec. 1858. Walter died in the army at David's Island, Sept. 27, 1864. Just before entering the army he made his will which is on record at Plattsburg.

Child:—*By second marriage.*
- +295 Walter Fayette.[8]

169. JONAS STRATTON [7] (*Henry*,[6] *John*,[5] *John*,[4] *John*,[3] *John*,[2] *John*[1]), born July 31, 1821; married **Betsey Ferris**, Sept. 28, 1844. He was a farmer, owning a home and farm in Chazy.

Children:—*Born in Chazy, N. Y.*
- —296 Clinton,[8] d. in the army.
- —297 Julia,[8] d. while attending school at Philadelphia.
- +298 Cyrenius A.[8]
- —299 Eliza J.,[8] m. **William Kivess**; res. Whitehall, N. J.
- —300 Mary,[8] m. **Joseph A. Fay**; res. Newark, N. J.
- —301 Cassie,[8] m. **James Young**; res. Gasner, Iowa.
- —302 Eunice,[8] m. **Stephen Schultz**; res. Plattsburg.

171. JOHN TALMAGE STRATTON [7] (*Henry*,[6] *John*,[5] *John*,[4] *John*,[3] *John*,[2] *John* [1]), born July 23, 1826; a farmer of West Chazy; died in Isle La Motte, Vt., Dec. 4, 1885. He married **Anna Wilson** Oct. 17, 1852. She was born in Peru, N. Y., a daughter of *James Wilson*, who was a native of England.

Children:—*Born in W. Chazy, N. Y.*
+303 Arthur Talmage.[8]
—304 Jennie C.[8]

173. PHILANDER STRATTON (*Henry*,[6] *John*,[5] *John*,[4] *John*,[3] *John*,[2] *John* [1]), born May 6, 1830; married **Elvira M. Denton**, Dec. 11, 1865. He owned the old homestead and acquired considerable property besides owning about 600 well-stocked acres of land in Clinton Co. and was a successful farmer and speculator for many years in West Chazy, where he died Sept. 6, 1898. His will recorded at Plattsburg, Mar., 1895. He was a member of the Methodist Church.

Children:—*Born in West Chazy, N. Y.*
—305 Henry, a farmer, m. **Marian Miller Cox** in 1893; res. Scuylerfalls, N. Y.; no issue.
+306 Herbert W.
—307 Harriet, m. **George Doty** Apr., 1898; res. Ingraham, N. Y.
—308 Lillian M., m. **Frank Slack**, 1905; res. Pawtucket, R. I.

181. SAMUEL THOMAS STRATTON [7] (*Samuel*,[6] *Samuel*,[5] *John*,[4] *John*,[3] *John*,[2] *John* [1]), born July 19, 1824; married May 20, 1851, *Glorianna Conklin*, who was born in Easthampton June 2, 1831. They lived for thirty years at Montauk, where Mr. Stratton had charge of a large tract of land and where he was greatly esteemed by all with whom he came in contact. About 1884 he moved to his home in Easthampton where he lived the remainder of his life. He died Dec. 14, 1894.

Children:—*Born at Easthampton, L. I.*
—309 Isabel H.,[8] m. at Montauk, **Samuel M. Mulford** of Easthampton.
+310 Frank Sidney.[8]
Born at Montauk, L. I.
—311 Glorianna Conklin [8] (twin), m. at Easthampton Nov. 4, 1891, **Edwin Post Maynard**; res. Brooklyn, N. Y.
—312 Samuel Thomas, Jr.,[8] d. at Montauk Apr. 17, 1880, aged 14 years.

187. Cornelius Stratton [7] (*Jonathan*,[6] *Jonathan*,[5] *Joseph*,[4] *Joseph*,[3] *Cornelius*,[2] *John* [1]), born Apr. 15, 1805; married May 24, 1835, Mary Hall, who was born Sept. 7, 1817. He died in Vestal Center, N. Y., Sept. 6, 1875.

Children:—*Born in Vestal Center, N. Y.*
—313 Oliver,[8] b. May 17, 1836; res. Vestal Center; a farmer; unm.
+314 Jonathan,[8] b. 1838.
—315 Howard Edgar,[8] b. Nov. 28, 1841; a soldier in the Civil War, 100th N. Y. Regt. Died in Andersonville prison Oct. 10, 1864; unm.
—316 George,[8] b. June 1, 1844; d. in infancy.
—317 Nancy E.,[8] b. May 10, 1845; m. **Daniel Taylor** Sept. 24, 1869.
—318 Charles,[8] b. 1848; res. Vestal Center; a soldier in the Civil War.
—319 Franklin,[8] b. 1852; m. **Mary Campbell**, July 24, 1876; d. Jan. 10, 1886.
—320 Patience M.,[8] b. May 1, 1856; m. **George Hoyt**, 1871.

192. John Stratton [7] (*Jonathan*,[6] *Jonathan*,[5] *Joseph*,[4] *Joseph*,[3] *Cornelius*,[2] *John* [1]), born June 4, 1816; married, first, **Rachel Grapp Mills**, June 18, 1845. She died Oct. 6, 1845, and he married, second, **Elizabeth Keeler**, June 16, 1849.

Children:
—321 Rachel E.
—322 Camelia, d. Feb. 7, 1872, aged 21 years.
—323 John Frederick.
—324 William Henry.

194. Richard Stratton [7] (*Jonathan*,[6] *Jonathan*,[5] *Joseph*,[4] *Joseph*,[3] *Cornelius*,[2] *John* [1]) was born Apr. 26, 1825. Jan. 23, 1850, at Camden, N. Y., he married **Eliza Ann Russell**, born May 13, 1831. He was a wagon manufacturer in Oswego, N. Y., until 1877; was connected with some silver mines in Nevada for a year, then bought a farm upon which he lived until two years before his death. Died Jan. 13, 1905, at the home of his son James in Oswego.

Children:—*Born in Oswego, N. Y.*
+325 James Herbert.[8]
+326 Richard Totten.

—327 Eliza Cordelia, m. **Randall A. Huntley**, May 15, 1883; d. Apr. 12, 1901.
—328 Georgia A., m. **James A. Houghtaling**, Dec. 5, 1875; res. Moores Mills, N. Y.
—329 Fannie May, d. Oct. 3, 1867, aged 8 years.
—330 Walter Pearl, m. **Beatrix Brown**; res. Danville, Ill.
—331 Martha Elizabeth, m. **Edgar Stratton.**

198. JOHN HUNT STRATTON [7] (*David,*[6] *Joseph,*[5] *John,*[4] *Joseph,*[3] *Cornelius,*[2] *John*[1]) left Roxbury at 16, and went to Marbletown as a school teacher. Later was employed as a purser on a Hudson River steamboat, and then became a steamboat captain. He married **Wyan Hanver.** During Buchanan's administration he was Port Master at Roudout, N. Y.
Children:
—332 Harriet E.,[8] d. 1892; m. **James Cornwell** in 1885.
—333 Emma,[8] m. **Frederick Van Wert**, Highland, N. Y.

203. LEWIS STRATTON [7] (*Eli,*[6] *Joseph,*[5] *John,*[4] *Joseph,*[3] *Cornelius,*[2] *John*[1]) was born Nov. 14, 1811; married **Jane Ann Lockwood** in 1838. She was born July 20, 1821, and died Nov. 1, 1905. He died Jan. 14, 1851. They resided in Roxbury, N. Y.
Children:—*Born in Roxbury, N. Y.*
—334 Katherine N.,[8] b. Nov. 17, 1839; m. **Samuel D. Andrews**, Feb. 22, 1859.
—335 Elizabeth,[8] b. Apr. 27, 1842; m. **James L. Patterson**, Mar. 21, 1866.
—336 Abram Lockwood,[8] b. Aug. 24, 1844; d. Nov. 1, 1888; no issue.
—337 Milton Dewey,[8] b. Aug. 19, 1847; d. May 11, 1899; no issue.
—338 Amanda Joanna,[8] b. Dec. 7, 1850; m. **O. V. B. Taylor**, Sept. 27, 1877.

205. JOSEPH STRATTON [7] (*Eli,*[6] *Joseph,*[5] *John,*[4] *Joseph,*[3] *Cornelius,*[2] *John*[1]), born May 25, 1815. While a young man he went to Richmond Dale, O., where he married **Jane Cordray**. He died near Chillicothe, O., Mar. 10, 1882.
Children:—*Born in Chillicothe, O.*
—339 Dora,[8] m. **Marion Calver.**
—340 Lotta,[8] m. **James D. Blazer.**
+341 William.[8]

—342　Clinton,⁸ lives at Wyoming, Ill.
—343　Elizabeth,⁸ m. **Samuel Butts**.
+344　Douglass.⁸
—345　Harlow,⁸ d. unm.
—346　Clara,⁸ d. young.

208.　Morgan W. Stratton ⁷ (*Eli*,⁶ *Joseph*,⁵ *John*,⁴ *Joseph*,³ *Cornelius*,² *John* ¹), born July 8, 1821; married **Eliza Turk** in 1842. He was a farmer of Ross Co., O. He died in 1859.

Children:—*Born near Richmond Dale, O.*
—347　Eliza,⁸ b. Jan., 1843.
—348　Nancy,⁸ b. Dec. 11, 1844; m. **Marion Hagely**, 1864.
—349　Joanna,⁸ b. Jan. 11, 1846; m. **Presly Jenkins** in 1868; d. in Logan, Ill., 1897.
—350　Morrison W.,⁸ b. Oct. 11, 1848; m. **Frances Houston**, 1881; res. Logan, Ill.
—351　James,⁸ 1850-1872.
—352　Ella,⁸ 1853-1856.

209.　Heman Dewey Stratton ⁷ (*Eli*,⁶ *Joseph*,⁵ *John*,⁴ *Joseph*,³ *Cornelius*,² *John* ¹), born Sept. 10, 1822; married **Susan Hester Penick**, daughter of *Jonathan J.* and *Elizabeth Frances (McGlasson) Penick*. Her father was a farmer of Grant Co., Ky. Their married life of almost fifty years was an exceptionally happy one. She died Jan. 6, 1901. Mr. Stratton was educated in the common schools of his native county, and spent two years at Dick's Collegiate Institute at Brooklyn, N. Y. He was in the Mexican war and was with Gen. Scott's army from Vera Cruz to the City of Mexico. He came to Kentucky in 1850 and resided at Williamsburg. For more than thirty years he was one of the leading educators of Grant and Kenton counties. As teacher and as superintendent of public schools he did much to improve the public school system of that part of Kentucky. He was a devoted and active member of the Christian Church from 1852, and for fifty years was a prominent member of the order of Odd Fellows. In politics he never voted any but the Democratic ticket. In social life he was pleasant and agreeable, and had many friends. He died in Williamstown, Dec. 16, 1896.

Children:—*Born in Williamstown, Ky.*
—353　William Penick,⁸ a merchant in Williamsburg; unm.
—354　Joanna Elizabeth,⁸ m. **James H. Humlong**.
—355　Ruth,⁸ resides in Williamstown.

210. ADAM KING STRATTON [7] (*Eli*,[6] *Joseph*,[5] *John*,[4] *Joseph*,[3] *Cornelius*,[2] *John* [1]), born Mar. 20, 1824; married Elizabeth A. Patterson, Nov. 23, 1850. He died in Roxbury, at the home of his son Edgar, Dec. 16, 1903. Mrs. Stratton died June 19, 1906, aged 76 years.

Children:
—356 Eli,[8] b. July 25, 1851; d. Dec. 10, 1860.
—357 Henry Edgar,[8] resides in Roxbury.
—358 Milton A.[8]

212. MORRISON W. STRATTON [7] (*Eli*,[6] *Joseph*,[5] *John*,[4] *Joseph*,[3] *Cornelius*,[2] *John* [1]) was born Oct. 2, 1828. Feb. 12, 1850, he married Elizabeth Scott, of Fort Wayne. He lived for a short time in Fort Wayne, and then in Ross Co., O., where he was a farmer. He died in Waverly, O., in Aug., 1903.

Children:—*Born in Richmond Dale, O.*
—359 Alice,[8] d. in infancy.
—360 Julia Estelle,[8] m. Edward Bark of Vigo, O.
—361 Mary Edith,[8] d. in infancy.
—362 Kate Irene,[8] m. William Clements of Given, O.
Born in Waverly, O.
—363 Joanna Dewey,[8] a teacher; res. Waverly.
—364 Morgan,[8] d. in infancy.
—365 Edward,[8] d. in infancy.
—366 Flora A.,[8] d. June 15, 1896.
—367 Charles A.,[8] m. Laura Higby, Dec. 25, 1892; res. Milton, N. D.
—368 Walter Scott,[8] m. Lizzie King in 1897; res. Cleveland, O.

215. JASON GOULD STRATTON [7] (*Eli*,[6] *Joseph*,[5] *John*,[4] *Joseph*,[3] *Cornelius*,[2] *John* [1]) was born Sept. 24, 1833. He married Judith Boone of Grant Co., O.

Children:—*Born in Forklick, Grant Co., O.*
—369 Eli,[8] a blacksmith, was twice married.
—370 John,[8] lived and died in Cincinnati, O.
—371 Julia,[8] m. —— Stevens.
—372 Charles,[8] d. in Cincinnati; unm.
—373 William,[8] d. in boyhood in Forklick.
—374 Ada,[8] a professional nurse; res. Cincinnati.
—375 Anna,[8] m. Bert Cochran, 1896.

217. ALANSON WELLS STRATTON⁷ (*Walter,*⁶ *Joseph,*⁵ *John,*⁴ *Joseph,*³ *Cornelius,*² *John*¹) was born Nov. 28, 1811. Jan. 24, 1849, he married **Angeline W. Shout**, daughter of *Henry* and *Elizabeth (Bonton) Shout,* of Roxbury. He lived in his native town all his life of 91 years, and at different times represented his town in various official capacities to the entire satisfaction of his constituents. He was a man noted for his honesty and good judgment, and was highly respected by all who knew him. He died Dec. 15, 1902.

Children:—*Born in Roxbury, N. Y.*
—376   Mary Salina,⁸ d. in **1884.**
—377   Nettie Bonton,⁸ res. Roxbury.
—378   Ida Adele,⁸ m. **William L. Powell,** May 14, 1890; res. Roxbury.

219. DAVID WILLIAMS STRATTON⁷ (*Walter,*⁶ *Joseph,*⁵ *John,*⁴ *Joseph,*³ *Cornelius,*² *John*¹) was born Apr. 14, 1816. He married **Jane Shout,** Oct. 14, 1840. She was born in Roxbury Mar. 14, 1816, and died there Jan. 10, 1842. Dec. 24, 1846, he married **Maria D. Turner,** who was born in Wawarsing, Ulster Co., N. Y., Mar. 19, 1828. He was a teacher for sixty years, teaching his first school in Wawarsing when he was 17 years of age and closing his last school June 24, 1892. At Loccannissing he had a pupil whose father and grandfather had been his pupils, thus teaching three generations. He gave Jay Gould his first lesson in the "A B C's." He was a man beloved by many, and having the respect of all who knew him; a member of the Methodist Church. He died in Napanock, Ulster Co., Feb. 18, 1902.

Children:—*Born in Wawarsing, N. Y.*
   By second marriage.
—379   Alonzo D.,⁸ m. **Sarah Van Gorger,** June 27, 1894; resides in Ellenville, N. Y.
+380   Judson B.⁸

223. JASON W. STRATTON⁷ (*Walter,*⁶ *Joseph,*⁵ *John,*⁴ *Joseph,*³ *Cornelius,*² *John*¹) was born Nov. 20, 1832. He was educated in the district school of Roxbury and the academy at Binghamton, N. Y. He married **Emma Maria Minkler** in 1858; served three years in the Civil War and was captain of home guards previous to enlistment. Politically he was a Democrat. He was a member of the Methodist Church. In 1874 he moved from Roxbury to Bergen, where he conducted a coal business. Associate Judge of Genesee Co. four years, and Justice of the Peace eight years. Died May, 1891.

Children:—*Born in Roxbury.*
+381   Edward E.[8]
−382   Jessie O.,[8] m. Charles Patterson, 1892.
−383   Nellie E.,[8] m. Orvil Partridge in 1902.

224. CALISTUS LEE STRATTON [7] (*Lewis,*[6] *Joseph,*[5] *John,*[4] *Joseph,*[3] *Cornelius,*[2] *John* [1]), born Jan. 14, 1822; died in Elkheart, Ill., 1898; married **Sarah Ann Marshall**, Sept. 9, 1848.

Children:
−384   Oliver Orten,[8] m. 1st, **Sarah Jane Harpool**; m. 2nd, **Laura A. Davis**; ch. by 1st m., Arthur Edgar.[9]
−385   Cecilia Lorenzo,[8] m. **Abraham Eiseminger**.
−386   Minerva Ella,[8] m. **Daniel Altman**, 1880; res. St. Louis, Mo.
−387   William Alexander,[8] d. 1877, aged 13 years.

228. WILLIAM BENJAMIN STRATTON [7] (*Eliphalet,*[6] *Stephen,*[5] *John,*[4] *Joseph,*[3] *Cornelius,*[2] *John* [1]) was born July 28, 1810. He married **Sarah Canfield**, 1843. He died Feb. 11, 1887.

Children:—*Born in Thompsonville, N. Y.*
−388   William D., m. **Mary Katherine O'Neille**; res. Middletown, N. Y.
 389   Eliphalet, m. **Fannie Manette**.
−390   Frank M., d. 1872; unm.
−391   James A., m. **Henrietta Hanna**.
−392   Benjamin Theadore, m. **Edith Avery**; a farmer of South Fallsburg, N. Y.

231. LEVI LUCKY STRATTON [7] (*Eliphalet,*[6] *Stephen,*[5] *John,*[4] *Joseph,*[3] *Cornelius,*[2] *John* [1]) was born Aug. 24, 1816. He married **Eunice Lord Bowers**, July 3, 1842. She was born Mar. 19, 1825. He died in Fallsburg, N. Y.

Children:
−393   Charles G.,[8] b. May 13, 1845; m. **Sarah Caroline Hack**, Apr. 13, 1870; ch. Howard Robinson,[9] m. **Frances J. Tight**, 1901; res. New York City.
−394   James N.,[8] b. 1847; m. **Athena Hasbrook**, Mar. 16, 1868; d. in Toledo, 1891; ch. Georgiana,[9] m. **Edwin C. Keen**.
+395   Edward L.,[8] b. 1852.

—396 Alice Lillian,[8] m. **Robert Kirkpatrick,** July 2, 1874; res. Nobleville, Ind.
—397 Mary Virginia,[8] m. **Howard Hammond,** July 2, 1871; d. Jan. 2, 1881.
—398 Helen Ada,[8] m. **Edwin Thorpe,** Dec. 20, 1882.

238. LEONARD BRIGGS STRATTON [7] (*Eliphalet,*[6] *Stephen,*[5] *John,*[4] *Joseph,*[3] *Cornelius,*[2] *John* [1]) was born in Thompsonville, Aug. 14, 1832, and married there **Claressa A. Manette,** Jan. 27, 1869.
Children:
+399 Rienzie H.[8]
—400 Minnie Lovella,[8] m. **Hurbert Hill,** Dec. 13, 1894.
—401 Jonathan James.[8]
—402 George Vincent.[8]
—403 Otis Lenord.[8]
—404 Robert Manette,[8] m. **Nellie Smith,** Jan. 29, 1902.
—405 Eula Irene.[8]
—406 Helen Rachel.[8]

239. HENRY WASHINGTON STRATTON [7] (*Eliphalet,*[6] *Stephen,*[5] *John,*[4] *Joseph,*[3] *Cornelius,*[2] *John* [1]) was born Jan. 14, 1838. Jan. 2, 1862, he married **Sarah E. O'Neill,** daughter of *Charles O'Neill* and granddaughter of *Stafford O'Neill* of Fallsburg. He resides in Monticello, N. Y., where he is engaged in the furniture business.
Children:—*Born in Thompsonville, N. Y.*
—407 Clara Amanda.[8]
—408 Frederick L.,[8] an engineer and interested in business with his father.
—409 Leah Belle,[8] d. Nov. 10, 1872, aged 3 years.
—410 Henry Blake,[8] Ass't Postmaster at Monticello.

240a. ALBY STRATTON [7] (*Alby,*[6] *Stephen,*[5] *John,*[4] *Joseph,*[3] *Cornelius,*[2] *John* [1]) was about eight years old when his father was killed in battle. Soon after he came to live with his grandfather Stratton, who went to Albion, N. Y., after him. He had one sister who married and moved to Ohio. In 1830 he belonged to the State militia. He married **Mary Jane Howse.** He was a farmer of Thompsonville where he died Aug. 23, 1875.
Children:—*Born in Thompsonville, N. Y.*
—411 Albert E.,[8] b. Mar. 20, 1834; m. **Nancy A. Barnum,** Dec. 25, 1871; resided in Centerville, N. Y.

—412 Cyrus J.,⁸ b. Sept. 10, 1835; m. **Emma Barthey**, Dec. 31, 1860; res. Thompsonville; served in Civil War.
—413 Edward A.,⁸ b. Sept. 27, 1837; d. in Horseheads, N. Y.
—414 Mary M.,⁸ b. Feb. 5, 1840; m. **Wm. D. Stratton**; res. South Fallsburgh, N. Y.
—415 George,⁸ b. Sept. 28, 1841; m. **Caroline Zimmerman** Mar. 14, 1860; chn. Elmer E.,⁹ South Fallsburgh, Laura J.,⁹ Fannie M.⁹
—416 Milton A.,⁸ b. Aug. 4, 1846; m. **Eva Cooper**, Feb., 1870; res. Thompsonville.
—417 Lucinda,⁸ d. July 22, 1856, aged 4 yrs.

241. JAMES T. STRATTON ⁷ (*Jonathan,*⁶ *Stephen,*⁵ *John,*⁴ *Joseph,*³ *Cornelius,*² *John* ¹) was born Oct. 9, 1830, educated in the public schools of his native county and in the grammar school of Columbia College. Began active life at the age of seventeen as civil engineer on the Hudson River Railroad between Sing Sing and Peekskill. Three years later he went to California via Panama, and after three years' experience among the mines took up his profession, adding to it land surveying. Returned east and on Oct. 30, 1854, married **Cornelia A. Smith** in Sing Sing (now Ossining), N. Y., daughter of *Isaac C. Smith,* a noted Hudson River captain and shipbuilder of Hoboken, N. J. Returning to California with his bride, he settled in Oakland, where he resided until his death. He made many of the most important California surveys of that early period and was identified with the surveying of large tracts of land made by the Spanish and Mexican authorities, and so became an acknowledged expert on the titles and surveyed lands of such land grants. He subdivided more of the big land grants than any other surveyor ever in California. In 1873 President Grant appointed him United States Land Surveyor General for California. He died March 15, 1905.

Children:—*Born in Oakland, Cal.*
—418 Carrie,⁸ d. Oct. 24, 1856, aged 1 year.
+419 Frederick S.⁸
+420 Robert T.⁸
—421 George Malcolm,⁸ grad. B.A. from University of California, 1888; grad. M.A. from Yale, 1890; grad. Ph.D. from University of Leipzig, Germany, 1896. Professor of Psychology in University of California and Johns Hopkins University, Baltimore. May 17,

1894, m. **Alice E. Miller,** daughter of *Frederick* and *Wilhelmina Miller* of Oakland.
—422 Edward,[8] d. in infancy.
—423 Jeanne,[8] m. **Walter C. Good,** June 22, 1819; d. Aug. 22, 1900.

247. WILLIAM DEWITT STRATTON [7] (*Thomas,*[6] *Stephen,*[5] *John,*[4] *Joseph,*[3] *Cornelius,*[2] *John* [1]) was born Sept. 3, 1823. He married, first, Caroline E. Fuller, Mar. 1, 1848; married, second, Mary M. Stratton,[8] Nov. 5, 1863. They resided in South Fallsburg. After his death, Sept. 3, 1888, she married **Peter Carney.**
Children:—*Born in Fallsburg, N. Y.*
    By first marriage.
—424 Julia.[8]
—425 Ida.[8]
—426 Walter E.,[8] b. Apr. 19, 1858; m. **Lizzie McMillen;** moved to Michigan in 1879; d. June, 1901.
    By second marriage.
—427 Ida May,[8] m. **Geo. H. Smith,** Oct. 22, 1890.
—428 Gracie,[8] d. Feb. 12, 1871, aged 2 years.
—429 Oscar DeWitt.[8]
—430 Nellie Blanche.[8]

254. GEORGE W. STRATTON [7] (*Thomas,*[6] *Stephen,*[5] *John,*[4] *Joseph,*[3] *Cornelius,*[2] *John* [1]), born May 26, 1840. In May, 1861, he enlisted in Elmira in Co. K, 23rd Regt., N. Y. Volunteers, re-enlisted in 1862 at Monticello, in Co. A, 143rd Regt., N. Y. Volunteers; discharged in 1865 at expiration of the war. Married **Julia A. Thurber** in Lindley, N. Y., Nov. 22, 1871. Settled in Addison, 1873; engaged in the tanning business until 1893 when he sold out to the U. S. Tanning Co. Appointed post master by President McKinley, reappointed by President Roosevelt.
Children:—*Born in Lindley, N. Y.*
—431 Carolyn, m. **Charles F. Park,** Oct. 20, 1898.
    Born in Addison.
—432 Metta, m. **Lewis W. Dorsett,** Sayer, Pa., Oct. 15, 1903.

259. DANIEL SQUIRES STRATTON [7] (*Jesse,*[6] *Samuel,*[5] *John,*[4] *Joseph,*[3] *Cornelius,*[2] *John* [1]) was a prosperous farmer of Roxbury. He inherited his father's farm and added to it by buying that part of the Ezra Stratton farm which included the store and Falls. He married, Oct. 6, 1845, **Lucy Underwood,** who was born Feb.

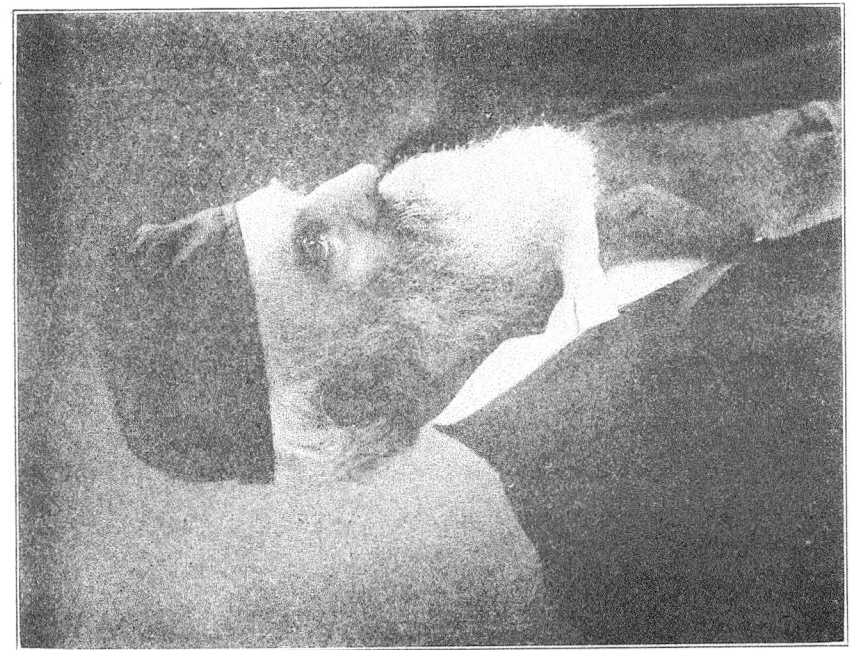

Rev. Charles C. Stratton, D.D.

1, 1822. She is a daughter of *Dr. Oliver* and *Jemima (Parker) Underwood*. Dr. Underwood was one of the pioneer physicians of Roxbury. Mr. Stratton died Sept. 18, 1851.

Children:—*Born in Roxbury, N. Y.*
—433 Ada Addie, m. **James D. Rutherford.**
—434 Emma, m. **Luman Merritt Cole.**

272. OLIVER STRATTON[7] (*Eliphalet,*[6] *Abraham,*[5] *Abraham,*[4] *Eliphalet,*[3] *Cornelius,*[2] *John*[1]) was born Feb. 16, 1818. He was a farmer of Clyde, N. Y., where he married **Sarah Ann Weed** in 1843. He died Sept. 3, 1888.

Children:—*Born in Clyde, N. Y.*
—435 Henry Eliphalet,[8] b. Aug. 5, 1845; m. **Dora Comrike**; lived in Clyde until 1887, then moved to San Francisco, Cal., where he died Mar. 19, 1896.
—436 Theron Abram,[8] b. June 23, 1847; d. in Clyde Dec. 29, 1898; m. 1st, **Cora Beadle**; 2nd, **Anna Shugart.**
—437 Edwin L.,[8] b. Aug. 25, 1849; a produce merchant of Clyde.
+438 Thurlow Weed.[8]
—439 Orr,[8] b. Apr. 14, 1853; res. San Quinton, Cal.
—440 Mary E.,[8] m. **J. M. Mann**, 1907.
—441 Cornelia,[8] m. **A. G. Tompkin.**
—442 James C.,[8] m. **Minnie C. Cummings** in 1902.
—443 Clara.[8]

If any of the above sons have children, the compiler would be glad to receive records of them.

273. JOHN SMITH STRATTON[7] (*Eliphalet,*[6] *Abraham,*[5] *Abraham,*[4] *Eliphalet,*[3] *Cornelius,*[2] *John*[1]) was born June 11, 1822. He married, first, **Cordelia Colvin**, who was born June 1, 1829, and died June 3, 1859. He married, second, **Mrs. Amanda B. Smith**, Sept. 28, 1870. Res. San Rafael, Cal.

Children:
By first marriage.
+444 Emerson O.[8]
—445 Charles Calvin,[8] b. June 1, 1852; d. aged 9 years.
—446 James,[8] b. Aug. 13, 1859; d. aged 2 years.
By second marriage.
—447 Charles Clark,[8] m. **Susie Mae Hardy**, Sept. 28, 1896; res. San Rafael, Cal.; chn. Edna Mae,[9] Ella Frances.[9]

275. ABRAM WOOLEY STRATTON [7] (*Eliphalet*,[6] *Abraham*,[5] *Abraham*,[4] *Eliphalet*,[3] *Cornelius*,[2] *John* [1]) was born Apr. 17, 1827. He was a " '49-er," going to California during the gold excitement, arriving in San Francisco in Oct., 1849. He married **Cornelia Howland Angell**, Nov., 1852. He was a member of the Society of California Pioneers, and of the Vigilance Committees organized to suppress the lawless element in the fifties, and took a deep interest in all movements for the advance of good government. He was a contractor and built the first wharf in the harbor of Eureka, Humbolt Bay, in 1852. He was a member of the Baptist church. He died at the age of 47 years.

Children:—*Born in San Francisco.*
—448   Mary C.,[8] d. July 10, 1874, aged 19 years.
     Born in Clyde, N. Y.
—449   Frank Williams,[8] res. Pataluma, Cal.

277. EDWIN STRATTON [7] (*Eliphalet*,[6] *Abraham*,[5] *Abraham*,[4] *Eliphalet*,[3] *Cornelius*,[2] *John* [1]), born July 12, 1833; married **Lillie Walker**; died in San Francisco.

Child:
—450   George,[8] of whom information is desired.

278. ABRAM STRATTON [7] (*Abraham*,[6] *Abraham*,[5] *Abraham*,[4] *Eliphalet*,[3] *Cornelius*,[2] *John* [1]) was born Feb. 18, 1805. At an early age, prompted by the pioneer spirit of his forefathers, he went to Bureau Co., Ill. He was one of the very early settlers of that region. After deciding to make a home there he returned to York State for tools to till the soil. He was gone one year, walking much of the way. On his return in June, 1831, he bought a yoke of oxen and sled at Dearborn (there were no horses or wagons there) and with these and the farm implements that he brought on the sled he began farming, and became a successful farmer. He married **Sarah Baggs** Sept. 6, 1831. He died Sept. 28, 1877, and is buried at Princeton, Ill.

Children:—*Born in Bureau Co., Ill.*
—451   Eliza,[8] b. Jan. 23, 1833; m. **S. S. Newton**; lives in Wyoming.
+452   Lemuel Nathan,[8] b. 1834.
+453   Samuel Fay,[8] b. 1837 (a twin).
—454   Sylvester Brigham,[8] b. Aug. 27, 1837; d. aged 8 years.
+455   John Leander,[8] b. 1848.
+456   Abram Manny,[8] b. 1856.

280. DAVID STRATTON [7] (*Oliver,*[6] *Abraham,*[5] *Abraham,*[4] *Eliphalet,*[3] *Cornelius,*[2] *John*[1]) was born in Montgomery Co., N. Y., Dec. 16, 1819, and moved with his father to Steuben Co. when eleven years old. He married, first, **Harriet Aber**, and, second, **Hester Emerson**.

Children:—*Born in Howard, Steuben Co., N. Y.*
—457 Nelson,[8] b. Sept. 5, 1841; d. aged 14 years.
—458 Elizabeth.[8]
—459 Charles,[8] b. Jan., 1847; d. Jan., 1863.
+460 George O.[8]

286. JOHN V. STRATTON [7] (*Oliver,*[6] *Abraham,*[5] *Abraham,*[4] *Eliphalet,*[3] *Cornelius,*[2] *John*[1]), born Oct. 3, 1829. He married **Martha Cooper**. He lived in Bath, and at Olean, N. Y.

Children:—*Born in Bath, Steuben Co., N. Y.*
+461 Oliver.
—462 Jennie, m. **Burns T. Carroll**.
—463 George, m. **Nellie A. Penny**, 1898; res. Olean, N. Y.

288. CHARLES STRATTON [7] (*Oliver,*[6] *Abraham,*[5] *Abraham,*[4] *Eliphalet,*[3] *Cornelius,*[2] *John*[1]) was born Dec. 31, 1834. He married **Susan Brundage**, Dec. 29, 1869. Res. Bath, N. Y.

Child:—*Born in Bath.*
—464 James Brundage.[8]

295. WALTER FAYETTE STRATTON [8] (*Walter,*[7] *Henry,*[6] *John,*[5] *John,*[4] *John,*[3] *John,*[2] *John*[1]), a painter by trade; married **Nellie Witherill**, daughter of *Sanforn* and *Abagail Witherill*; res. Chazy.

Children:—*Born in West Chazy, N. Y.*
—465 Maud,[9] m. **David S. Lawson**, Dec. 17, 1909; res. Lyon Mountain, N. Y.
—466 May,[9] m. **William Potter**, Sept., 1909, of Ellenburg, N. Y.
—467 Jennie.[9]
—468 Wendell W.[9]
—469 Wayland W.[9]
—470 Edna E.[9]

298. CYRENIUS A. STRATTON [8] (*Jonas,*[7] *Henry,*[6] *John,*[5] *John,*[4] *John,*[3] *John,*[2] *John*[1]) married **Nellie Stephens**, and moved to Clear Lake, Iowa, where he is engaged in farming.

Children:
—471 Byron.[9]
—472 Bessie.[9]

303. ARTHUR TALMAGE STRATTON [8] (*John T.*,[7] *Henry*,[6] *John*,[5] *John*,[4] *John*,[3] *John*,[2] *John* [1]) married **Emma I. Harvey,** June 25, 1888. For twenty-five years he has been engaged in earnest work in connection with the Young Men's Christian Association, first as Ass't Secretary at Burlington, Vt., then as General Secretary at Middlebury, N. Y., Dover, N. H., Pawtucket, R. I., Fall River, Mass., and then Columbia, S. C., where he is now located.

Children:—*Born in Dover, N. H.*
—473 Philip Harvey.[9]
   Born in Pawtucket, R. I.
—474 Arthur Talmage, Jr.,[9] b. May 21, 1892; d. aged 2 years.
—475 Ruth A.[9]

306. HERBERT W. STRATTON [8] (*Philander*,[7] *Henry*,[6] *John*,[5] *John*,[4] *John*,[3] *John*,[2] *John* [1]) married **Mary O'Neal.** He is a machinist, and lives at Lowell, Mass.

Children:
—476 Herbert.[9]
—477 Harold.[9]

310. FRANK SIDNEY STRATTON [8] (*Samuel T.*,[7] *Samuel*,[6] *Samuel*,[5] *John*,[4] *John*,[3] *John*,[2] *John* [1]) resides at Easthampton. He married **Ellen F. Gordon,** May 8, 1888.

Children:—*Born at Easthampton.*
—478 Ruth Gordon.[9]
—479 Marcia I.[9]

314. JONATHAN STRATTON [8] (*Cornelius*,[7] *Jonathan*,[6] *Jonathan*,[5] *Joseph*,[4] *Joseph*,[3] *Cornelius*,[2] *John* [1]) was a soldier in the Civil War, enlisting in Co. A, 179th Regt., N. Y.; was in the battle of Cold Harbor, taken prisoner at St. Petersburg, June 17, 1864; in Andersonville prison four months; transferred to Malton prison; paroled Nov. 24, 1864; honorably discharged June 24, 1865. He married **Mary A. Adamson,** Apr. 23, 1867.

Children:—*Born in Vestal, N. Y.*
—480 Edgar,[9] m. Martha E. Stratton, Nov. 9, 1889, and resides in Poughkeepsie, N. Y. They have one child, Katherine.[10]
+481 William Cornelius.[9]
—482 Mary Jane,[9] m. Seymour G. Twining, Oct. 6, 1897.
—483 Margaret Belle,[9] m. Earl Neilson, Oct. 24, 1894; d. Mar. 30, 1896.

—484   Fannie May,[9] m. **Alva Deidrick,** Dec. 20, 1898.
—485   Ella Janet,[9] m. **George Willson,** Mar. 17, 1896.
—486   James Oliver.[9]
—487   Jonathan, Jr.[9]
—488   Melvin.[9]
—489   Carrie Alma.[9]

325. JAMES HERBERT STRATTON [8] (*Richard*,[7] *Jonathan*,[6] *Jonathan*,[5] *Joseph*,[4] *Joseph*,[3] *Cornelius*,[2] *John*[1]), a bridge builder; res. Oswego, N. Y. Married, first, **Oda Powell,** May 20, 1874. She died in 1878. He married, second, **Edna Ingersol,** Oct. 10, 1882. Children:—*Born in Oswego, N. Y.*
  By first marriage.
—490   Phœbe,[9] d. aged 2 years.
  By second marriage.
—491   Rupert Earnest,[9] m. **Ida May Raymond,** Nov. 20, 1907.

326. RICHARD TOTEN STRATTON [8] (*Richard*,[7] *Jonathan*,[6] *Jonathan*,[5] *Joseph*,[4] *Joseph*,[3] *Cornelius*,[2] *John*[1]) married **Florence Pierce** in 1888.
Children:—*Born in Morris, Pa.*
—492   Fannie May.[9]
  Born in Oswego.
—493   Archie.[9]
—494   Nina Betsey.[9]

341. WILLIAM STRATTON [8] (*Joseph*,[7] *Eli*,[6] *Joseph*,[5] *John*,[4] *Joseph*,[3] *Cornelius*,[2] *John*[1]) was born in Chillicothe, O., Nov. 9, 1855, and died there Mar. 14, 1883. In 1876 he married **Mrs. Mary Powers.**
Children:
+495   Walter.[9]
—496   Myrtle,[9] m. **Wilson Thompson,** res. Yellow Springs, O.
—497   Morgan,[9] m. **Susie McKinney;** res. Trebeins, O.; child, Grace.[10]
—498   Beamia,[9] m. **Charles Beavers.**

344. DOUGLASS STRATTON [8] (*Joseph*,[7] *Eli*,[6] *Joseph*,[5] *John*,[4] *Joseph*,[3] *Cornelius*,[2] *John*[1]) is a farmer of Bloomingburg, O. Dec. 17, 1887, he married **Emma Blazer,** daughter of *Mortica* and *Abbie Blaze*r of Jasper, O. He lived in Yankeetown, O., for 16 years, and then moved to Bloomington.

Children:—*Born in Yankeetown, O.*
—499 Walter D.⁹
—500 Lucelle Elizabeth.⁹
—501 Clarence Ray.⁹
—502 Florence Mae.⁹

380. JUDSON B. STRATTON ⁸ (*David W.*,⁷ *Walter*,⁶ *Joseph*,⁵ *John*,⁴ *Joseph*,³ *Cornelius*,² *John* ¹) resides in Yorktown Heights, N. Y. Oct. 25, 1876, he married **Mary E. Ritch.**
Children:—*Born at Napanoch, N. Y.*
—503 Barnard R., m. **Grace A. Hull,** Dec. 25, 1904; res. Bridgeport, Conn.
—504 David W., res. Yorktown Heights, N. Y.

381. EDWARD E. STRATTON ⁸ (*Jason W.*,⁷ *Walter*,⁶ *Joseph*,⁵ *John*,⁴ *Joseph*,³ *Cornelius*,² *John* ¹) married **Sadie McCullock** in 1895; resides in Akron, O.
Children:—*Born in Akron, O.*
—505 Albert Edward.⁹
—506 Helen Isabel.⁹
—507 Jason Walter.⁹

395. EDWARD LEVI STRATTON ⁸ (*Levi L.*,⁷ *Eliphalet*,⁶ *Stephen*,⁵ *John*,⁴ *Joseph*,³ *Cornelius*,² *John* ¹) married **Frances Frantz,** June 4, 1884. Resides in Pittsburg, Pa.
Children:—*Born in Pennsylvania.*
—508 William E.,⁹ d. aged 1 year.
—509 Thurman.⁹
—510 Edith Helen.⁹

399. RIENZIE HOLMES STRATTON ⁸ (*Leonard B.*,⁷ *Eliphalet*,⁶ *Stephen*,⁵ *John*,⁴ *Joseph*,³ *Cornelius*,² *John* ¹) resides in Thompsonville, where he married **Margarite Heacock,** Jan. 30, 1898.
Children:—*Born in Thompsonville, N. Y.*
—511 Dorothy.⁹
—512 Earl.⁹

419. FREDERICK SMITH STRATTON ⁸ (*James T.*,⁷ *Jonathan*,⁶ *Stephen*,⁵ *John*,⁴ *Joseph*,³ *Cornelius*,² *John* ¹) graduated from the Law Department of the University of California in 1881; appointed special counsel for the United States in the Alabama Claims Commission cases in 1886; attorney for the State Board of

Harbor Commissioners in San Francisco in 1890-1895. State senator for Oakland, 1896-1900, and for several years was collector of customs at the port of San Francisco. Nov. 13, 1884, he married in Oakland **Alica T. Lee,** daughter of *Henry C.* and *Harriet T. Lee.* She died May 16, 1897. June 6, 1899, he married in New York **Grace Gregory,** daughter of *Silas W.* and *Grace (Hopkins) Gregory.* Resided in Oakland.

Children:—*Born in Oakland, Cal.*
By first marriage.
—512 Cornelia,[9] m. **Wm. S. Parker,** Aug. 15, 1907. Both are graduates of the University of California.
By second marriage.
—513 Annie Gregory.[9]
—514 Frederick Smith, Jr.[9]

420. Robert Thompson Stratton [8] (*James T.,*[7] *Jonathan,*[6] *Stephen,*[5] *John,*[4] *Joseph,*[3] *Cornelius,*[2] *John*[1]) graduated from Jefferson Medical College, Philadelphia, in 1886. He resides in Oakland, where he has won distinction in his profession, especially as a brain specialist, and is surgeon in charge of the Oakland Receiving Hospital. Nov. 20, 1888, he married **Gertrude A. Walker,** daughter of *John* and *Frances (Murry) Walker* of Calistoga, Cal.

Children:—*Born in Oakland, Cal.*
—515 Robert Walker.[9]
—516 Irene Frances.[9]
—517 Bernice.[9]
—518 Evelyn.[9]

438. Thurlow Weed Stratton [8] (*Oliver,*[7] *Eliphalet,*[6] *Abraham,*[5] *Abraham,*[4] *Eliphalet,*[3] *Cornelius,*[2] *John*[1]) was born May 9, 1851. In 1885 he moved from Clyde, N. Y., to Oakdale, Neb., where he was engaged in business, and where he was county assessor for three years. In 1905 he moved to Valparaiso, Neb., where he is now a produce merchant. He married **Kate Margaret Wilson,** June 9, 1892. They are members of the Presbyterian church.

Child:—*Born in Oakdale, Neb.*
—519 Oliver Wilson.[9]

444. Emerson Oliver Stratton [8] (*John S.,*[7] *Eliphalet,*[6] *Abraham,*[5] *Abraham,*[4] *Eliphalet,*[3] *Cornelius,*[2] *John*[1]) was born Nov. 1,

1846. He married **Carrie Croker Ames**, Dec. 15, 1869, daughter of *Simeon L. Ames* of Hyannis, Mass. She was born Nov. 30, 1847. Residence Tuscon, Arizona.

Children:—*Born in Tuscon.*
—520   Mabel,⁹ m. **Thomas Foot Jones.**
—521   Edith Olive,⁹ m. **George F. Kitt.**
—522   John Simeon,⁹ b. July 23, 1881; d. Dec. 4, 1887.
—523   Elmer Willis,⁹ m. **Evylin Evans**, res. Tuscon, Ariz.

452. LEMUEL NATHAN STRATTON ⁸ (*Abram,⁷ Abraham,⁶ Abraham,⁵ Abraham,⁴ Eliphalet,³ Cornelius,² John ¹*) was born in Bureau, Ill., Dec. 28, 1834. He married **Maria Louise Norwood**, July 9, 1862. He is a Congregational minister; has had charge of churches in Syracuse and Pratville, N. Y. Pastor Maplewood church, Chicago, for five years. Residence Lockport, Ill., where he is pastor of the Homer Congregational church.

Children:—*Born in Syracuse, N. Y.*
—524   Owen Lovejoy,⁹ b. Jan. 22, 1866.*
+525   Abram Burton.⁹
         Born in Prattville, N. Y.
+526   Norwood.⁹
         Born in Syracuse, N. Y.
—527   Avis Claribell,⁹ m. **Dr. R. C. Libberton** of Chicago.
—528   Genevive Elizabeth,⁹ prof. nurse, Englewood Hospital, Chicago.

453. SAMUEL FAY STRATTON ⁸ (*Abram,⁷ Abraham,⁶ Abraham,⁵ Abraham,⁴ Eliphalet,³ Cornelius,² John ¹*), born Aug. 27, 1837. Married **Florence Lucy Jones**, Apr. 3, 1878. Died Sept. 20, 1883; buried in Burian, Ill.

Children:—*Born in Lish, Ill.*
+529   Samuel Edwards.⁹
         Born in Downess Grove, Ill.
—530   Florence Genevive,⁹ m. **DeWitt Shufelt**; res. Minooka, Ill.
—531   Lois Mabel.⁹

---

* After a college education and a year at the Oberlin Conservatory of Music, he engaged in business for several years. Then, after three years study and practice in the Moody Bible Institute, he went, in 1895, to China, first as a teacher, then as an agent for an eastern music firm, and later gave himself to mission work at Wuhu, China, where his earnest devotion to his chosen work and consecrated Christian life greatly endeared him to the people among whom he labored, and enabled him to accomplish much good. He died of cholera Aug. 30, 1908.

455. JOHN LEANDER STRATTON [8] (*Abram,*[7] *Abraham,*[6] *Abraham,*[5] *Abraham,*[4] *Eliphalet,*[3] *Cornelius,*[2] *John*[1]) was born Aug. 3, 1848; married **Calista L. Thompson**; res. Ottawa, Kan.
Children
—532 Marian.[9]
—533 Bayard Lucius.[9]

456. ABRAM MANNY STRATTON [8] (*Abram,*[7] *Abraham,*[6] *Abraham,*[5] *Abraham,*[4] *Eliphalet,*[3] *Cornelius,*[2] *John*[1]) was born in Bureau, Ill., Apr. 27, 1856; res. Carlton, Oregon.
Children:—*Born in Ligonier, Ind.*
—534 Abram Leander,[9] res. Reno, Neb.
—535 Edna.[9]

460. GEORGE OLIVER STRATTON [8] (*David,*[7] *Oliver,*[6] *Abraham,*[5] *Abraham,*[4] *Eliphalet,*[3] *Cornelius,*[2] *John*[1]) lives at Rheims, Steuben Co., N. Y.
Children:
—536 Charles D.,[9] lived in Woodstock, Ill.
—537 Abram.[9]

461. OLIVER STRATTON [8] (*John V.,*[7] *Oliver,*[6] *Abraham,*[5] *Abraham,*[4] *Eliphalet,*[3] *Cornelius,*[2] *John*[1]) was born in Bath and now resides in Kanona, N. Y.
Children:
—538 John,[9] b. Sept. 1, 1888; d. aged 8 years.
—539 Fred.[9]
—540 Lizzie.[9]
—541 Archie.[9]

481. WILLIAM CORNELIUS STRATTON [9] (*Jonathan,*[8] *Cornelius,*[7] *Jonathan,*[6] *Jonathan,*[5] *Joseph,*[4] *Joseph,*[3] *Cornelius,*[2] *John*[1]) married **Mary Barnes Hopkins**, July 16, 1893. They reside in Binghamton, N. Y.
Children:—*Born in Binghamton.*
—542 Ethel May.[10]
—543 William.[10]

495. WALTER STRATTON [9] (*William,*[8] *Joseph,*[7] *Eli,*[6] *Joseph,*[5] *John,*[4] *Joseph,*[3] *Cornelius,*[2] *John*[1]) married **Daisy Hoover**, and lives in Mt. Sterling, Ohio.

Children:
—544 Louise.[10]
—545 Russell.[10]
—546 May.[10]

526. ABRAM BURTON STRATTON [9] (*Lemuel N.,*[8] *Abram,*[7] *Abraham,*[6] *Abraham,*[5] *Abraham,*[4] *Eliphalet,*[3] *Cornelius,*[2] *John* [1]) married Carrie May Helmer, May 27, 1891. He lives in Chicago where he is attorney for the Armour Packing Co.
Children:—*Born in Wheaton, Ill.*
—547 Bernice Elizabeth.[10]
—548 Helen Helmer.[10]
       Born in Chicago.
—549 Olive Hazel.[9]

527. NORWOOD STRATTON [9] (*Lemuel N.,*[8] *Abram,*[7] *Abraham,*[6] *Abraham,*[5] *Abraham,*[4] *Eliphalet,*[3] *Cornelius,*[2] *John* [1]) married Ellen Stewart, June 28, 1903. He resides in Chicago and is connected with the Armour Packing Co. He is a member of the Sons of the American Revolution.
Children:—*Born in Chicago.*
—550 Gretchen Avis.[10]
—551 Norwood Stewart.[10]

529. SAMUEL EDWARDS STRATTON [9] (*Samuel F.,*[8] *Abram,*[7] *Abraham,*[6] *Abraham,*[5] *Abraham,*[4] *Eliphalet,*[3] *Cornelius,*[2] *John* [1]) resides in Benton City, Mo., where he has won a reputation as a farmer and stockman—a breeder of fine cattle. He married **Ella May Platt**, Nov. 10, 1892, who died Sept. 27, 1893. Jan. 11, 1899, he married **Hattie C. Campbell.**
Children:—*Born in Massena, Iowa.*
       By second marriage.
—552 Samuel Walter.[10]
—553 Winifred Alveretta.[10]

SAMUEL EDWARDS STRATTON
Worshipful Master of Masonic Lodge.
Page 314.

GEORGE W. STRATTON
Gave "Stratton Free Library" to his native town. *Page* 439.

STRATTONS OF CONNECTICUT
JOHN STRATTON OF WOODBURY

(*Chart K, Vol. I*)

"Genealogy helps to solve many problems in history." W. H. MILLS.

AS John Stratton owned land in Woodbury in 1682 he must have been at least twenty-one years old at that time. He may have been much older. As he received four "lay outs" of land he seems to have been a man of some prominence in the colony. Whether a son of some earlier emigrant or an "after-planter" from England, the most thorough study that the compiler has been able to make has failed to reveal. It is still hoped that future research will discover his parentage, either here or in England.* Recently a few additional items have been found concerning some of his descendants in the third and fourth generation. (See page 226, Vol. I.) They are here given:

4. JOHN STRATTON [3] moved with his family to his father's homestead on Main St. in Stratford, June 11, 1807. The compiler has found no other mention of him or his family. Some think that he settled in Vermont.†

6. THOMAS STRATTON [3] lived in Stratford village, where he died in July, 1787. Did he leave children?

---

*Among his descendants the tradition is current that their English ancestor came first to Long Island, and then to Connecticut—and this seems most probable. The compiler has found nothing to indicate that this branch of Strattons came from Concord.

† A John Barlow Stratton was born in North Stratford, May 2, 1785, and married **Lorenda Couger** in St. Albans, Vt., March 31, 1814. He became a widely known and much loved minister in the Methodist Episcopal Church—was Presiding Elder for many years. He held charges from 1812 to 1863 at St. Albans, Ticonderoga, Plattsburg, Middlebrug, New York City, Saratoga, Troy, Sag Harbor, and Brooklyn. He died in Jonesville, Saratoga Co., N. Y., in March 1863, after only three days' sickness. "He was faithful in every field of labor, true to every interest committed to him." He left no descendants. Whose son was he?

14. DAVID STRATTON⁴ married, first, Dec. 28, 1780, **Mary French** at Trumbull; second, Apr. 7, 1783, **Olive Treadwell.** Nothing more has been found of him in Connecticut, and he too may have settled in Vermont.

15. THOMAS STRATTON⁴ (*Thomas*,³ *Thomas*,² *John*¹) was a Revolutionary soldier, serving in Col. Sam Whiting's regt. Conn. Militia, in campaign at Fishkill.

17. JOHN STRATTON⁴ (*Thomas*,³ *Thomas*,² *John*¹) married, first, **Mary Burrough.** See *Vol. I*, p. 229. Their children were:
—32   John William, b. July, 1806. What became of him?
—33   Elizabeth, m. **Albert Burritt.**
—34   Joseph, b. Mar. 21, 1810; m. **Antoinette Kellogg Nash,** d. of *William* and *Emeline* (*Lockwood*) *Nash*, Sept. 12, 1867, and resided in Stratford.

24. DAVID STRATTON⁴ (*David*,³ *Thomas*,² *John*¹) married **Aurilla Biersley,** and lived in Bridgeport. Information concerning him and his family is wanted.

27. ROBERT CHAPMAN STRATTON⁴ had (in addition to the children given on p. 230, *Vol. I*) a daughter Mary, who married **William Baldwin** in 1834. His daughter Aurilla (Stratton) Reed died in Los Angeles Nov. 2, 1908. She always claimed that she was a relative of Horace Greeley. How related?

FIFTH GENERATION

28. SAMUEL EDWARDS STRATTON⁵ (*Thomas*,⁴ *Thomas*,³ *Thomas*,² *John*¹) was born Mar. 8, 1778, in Trumbull, near Bridgeport, Conn.* For many years he was an iron and steel merchant in Bridgeport of the firm of "Brooks and Stratton," on Water Street. His house is still standing, No. 1044 North Avenue, formerly "Kings High Way," the old road from Boston to New York. Here all his children were born. After his second marriage he moved into a new house on Commerce Street. He was a man of considerable wealth for that time and place.† He

---

* This is the date of birth given in the church records at Trumbull. The same source gives April 18, 1779, as date of his baptism.

† When P. T. Barnum was a manufacturer and dealer in clocks at Bridgeport, Mr. Stratton signed papers for his security for borrowed money to the amount of $10,000.

was head warden in St. John's Episcopal Church until Christ's Church was built when he became a member there. He was Worshipful Master in the Masonic lodge, and was elected to several town offices. He married, first, **Elizabeth Powell,** and second, **Lamira Beers,** about 1846. He died in 1861, and was buried with Masonic honors.

Children:—*Born in Trumbull, Conn.*
    By first marriage.
+49 Samuel Edwards,[6] b. 1815; d. 1859.
—50 Shelton,[6] m. his cousin **Laurena Stratton** (No. 60); d. in 1866. Had one son Shelton B.,[7] who died in youth, and a daughter Catharine F.,[7] who married **George Bostwick.**
—51 Mary, m. **John Beach.**
+52 George Smith, b. 1826.

29. Seth Sherwood Stratton[5] (*Thomas*,[4] *Thomas*,[3] *Thomas*,[2] *John*[1]) was born at Trumbull in 1782. He lived in Bridgeport. He married **Amy Sharp** of Oxford, Conn. She was born in 1783, and died Aug. 6, 1843. He died Oct. 12, 1831. Both are buried near Easton, Conn., where gravestones stand to their memory.

Children:—*Born in Bridgeport, Conn.*
+53 Seth Le Grand,[6] b. 1805.
—54 Lucretia,[6] m. **Alonzo Hayes.**
+55 Sherwood Edwards.[6]
—56 Daniel Sharp,[6] d. Oct., 1813, aged 1 year, 9 mos.
+57 Daniel Sharp,[6] b. 1817.
—58 Henry Thomas,[6] m. **Caroline Mills;** lived in Bridgeport; chn. Nellie,[7] Fred,[7] Emma.[7]
—59 Lossena[6] (twin), m. —— **Peet.**
—60 Laurena[6] (twin), m. her cousin **Shelton Stratton.**

37. Marcus Stratton[5] (*Daniel*,[4] *Thomas*,[3] *Thomas*,[2] *John*[1]) was born in Milford, Conn., Sept. 5, 1811. He married **Mrs. Sarah S. (Curtis) Williams,** Apr. 13, 1834. They lived in Milford, Stratford and New Haven; members of the Methodist Episcopal Church. He died in Milford, Aug. 9, 1898. *New Hav*

Children:—*Born in Milford, Conn.*
—61 Margaret Elizabeth,[6] b. Apr. 17, 1844. Educated in Stratford and New Haven, taught in the public schools in Conn., then in the South for 10 years, doing

pioneer work among the freedmen of Fla. and Va. Graduated Oberlin, O., 1879; made A.M., 1882. Asst. Principal Woman's Dept., Oberlin, 1878-82. Prof. English and Rhetoric, Wellesley, 1883-95. Dean of Wellesley, 1886-98. Dean of Woman's University of Colorado, 1901-1904. Spent the years, 1885, 1892-3, 1899-1900, 1905, 1908-9 in Europe.

—62 Henry Warren, d. in Seymour, Conn., Jan. 26, 1903.
—63 Althia J., m. **Alfred Curtis**; d. in Stratford Jan. 17, 1881.
—64 Frederick, enlisted in volunteer U. S. Army; in service from Aug., 1862, to May, 1865, first as private, then corporal, sergeant, lieutenant.

40. DAVID GOULD STRATTON [5] (*Daniel*,[4] *Thomas*,[3] *Thomas*,[2] *John*[1]) was born in Milford Apr. 9, 1819. He was a contractor and builder. June 30, 1844, he married **Elizabeth Potter Clark**, daughter of *William Holt* and *Susan (Potter) Clark* of New London. She died in 1894. He died May 28, 1906, at the home of his daughter in New York City. For nearly 70 years he was a member and earnest worker in the Methodist Episcopal church, often occupying the pulpit as local preacher.* Both are buried in New London.

Child

—65 Mary Elizabeth, m. **T. L. Dresenberre**; res. New York City.

44. ALLEN STRATTON [5] (*Robert C.*,[4] *David*,[3] *Thomas*,[2] *John*[1]) was born Nov. 9, 1813, and died in Highland, N. Y., June 2, 1895. He married **Eliza N. Buckhout**, daughter of *John A.* and *Temperence (Ellsworth) Buckhout*, May 17, 1848. She died in 1857. They were married in Paltz, N. Y., by Rev. J. B. Stratton. At the time of his marriage he was engaged in the shoe business in Maiden Lane, New York City. His health failing, he bought a farm in Connecticut, where he lived for five or six years, then removed to Lewisburg (now Highlands) where he built a home and became engaged in the shipping business, in which business he remained until he retired in 1885, being master and owner of a sailing vessel. Both Mr. and Mrs. Stratton are buried in Highland cemetery.

---

* His mother (see p. 229, Vol. I) was a daughter of Samuel (Rev. soldier) and Eunice Gould Ware (or Wier) of Melford—a woman of great strength of character, and an ardent Methodist. She was born in 1785.

Children:—*Born in Connecticut.*
—66 John Buckhout,[6] b. Oct. 6, 1849; d. aged 5 mos.
—67 John Jay,[6] b. Poughkeepsie, N. Y.; master and pilot of steamboat plying the waters of New York Harbor, Long Island Sound and Hudson River; m. **Mary J. Colbert**; res. Jersey City. Their only child, Edward Allen,[7] died May 28, 1883, aged 10 mos.
—68 James Emory,[6] b. Ulster Co., N. Y.; m. **Minnie A. J. Baker**, 1902, in N. Y. City; master and pilot of steamboat plying Hudson River, N. Y. Harbor and coastwise. They have two children, Helen[7] and Ruth.[7]

49. SAMUEL EDWARDS STRATTON[6] (*Samuel E.*,[5] *Thomas*,[4] *Thomas*,[3] *Thomas*,[2] *John*[1]) was born in Bridgeport, Conn., in 1815. At the age of 21 he went to Columbia, S. C., where he engaged in the boot and shoe business, and later became a dealer in general merchandise. He married **Martha A. Nutting**, daughter of *George* and *Mary (Campbell) Nutting*. She was born in Columbia May 15, 1815.* In 1849 Mr. Stratton, with others in Columbia, "caught the California fever." Going to New York, they took passage on a sailing vessel, went around Cape Horn, and reached San Francisco after a voyage of 151 days, stopping 8 days on the island of Juan Fernandez. After a few weeks' prospecting for gold in the mountains, Mr. Stratton was taken sick, and advised to return home at once. Arriving in New York, he went to Bridgeport, and remained with his parents for two months before he was able to return to his southern home. He never recovered his health. He died in Jan., 1859, in Columbia.

Children:—B*orn in Columbia, S. C.*
—69 Imogene Elizabeth, b. 1839; d. Apr., 1853.
—70 Samuel Edwards, resides in Columbia, where for about 20 years he was a merchant. For several years served his native city and county as a Trial Justice and for about 35 years has been Notary Public. In politics he is a National Republican; attends the Episcopal church. Served in Co. C, 1st Regt., S. C.

---

* George Nutting was born in Boston, and Mary Campbell in North Carolina. Their daughter, Martha (Nutting) Stratton, inherited a fine old place in Columbia, which became the home of the Strattons there. The house was built in 1792, and until about 1820 was the principal hotel in Columbia, in which Washington and Lafayette had rooms when they visited the city. The house was burned to the ground a few years ago.

Vol. Infantry, Bragg and McGowan's Brigade, under command of Gen. Stonewall Jackson, in Virginia.

—71 Ida S., m. **Jesse Elsrode**, Aug. 17, 1856; res. Hempstead, Md.

—72 Walter Sherwood, res. Columbia; clerk in So. R. R. Co.; served in Co. K, 3rd Regt., S. C. Vol. State troops.

—73 William Stanley, with Union News Co., Columbia.

—74 Issoline M., m. 1st, **James D. Gillman**; 2nd, **Dr. L. K. Philpot**; res. Columbia, S. C.

—75 Evelyn L., b. Dec. 4, 1856; d. Feb. 4, 1857.

52. GEORGE SMITH STRATTON[6] (*Samuel E.,*[5] *Thomas,*[4] *Thomas,*[3] *Thomas,*[2] *John*[1]) was born in Aug., 1826, and died in Bridgeport in 1870. May 5, 1847, he married **Eliza Wooley**, daughter of *Joseph* and *Fannie (Buroughs) Wooley* of Bridgeport.* They lived in the old Stratton homestead on North Avenue, and their children were born there.

Children:—*Born in Bridgeport, Conn.*

—76 Harriet Ann,[7] b. Feb. 1, 1845; m. **Alfred Stockbridge**; res. Philadelphia, Pa.

—77 Charles Sanford,[7] b. 1847; d. unm. in Bridgeport.

—78 William George,[7] d. abt. 1867. No issue.

—79 Frederick Stephen,[7] b. Mar. 10, 1858; m. **Elizabeth Wood** in 1888; res. Hartford, Conn.

—80 Samuel Buroughs,[7] m. **Lizzie Bower**; res. Asbury Park, N. J.

—81 Nathaniel Augustus,[7] res. Melrose, Mass.

—82 Joseph J.,[7] d. in New York City, aged 21 years.

—83 Mary E.,[7] d. 1875, aged 8 years.

—84 Jennie Martha,[7] m. May 18, 1878, **William E. Tucker** of Hartford, a Civil War soldier. Their daughter, Ola May Tucker, m. William Clift of Brooklyn.

53. SETH LEGRAND STRATTON[6] (*Seth S.,*[5] *Thomas,*[4] *Thomas,*[3] *Thomas,*[2] *John*[1]) was born in Bridgeport, Conn., July 21, 1805. He married **Nancy Soule Stelson** in 1828. By trade he was a carpenter. They lived for awhile in Cleveland, N. Y., and then returned to Bridgeport.

Children:

—85 Joan,[7] b. Mar. 8, 1829; d. May 3, 1841.

—86 Jane,[7] b. Aug. 16, 1832; d. June 10, 1845.

---

* Fannie Buroughs was a daughter of Capt. Isaac Bnroughs, of local fame.

- —87 Adaline Frances,⁷ b. Nov. 30, 1833; d. May 7, 1869; m. **George B. Hinman,** Feb. 15, 1852.
- —88 Augusta Gould,⁷ b. Sept. 22, 1835; m. **Charles E. Marks,** Nov. 25, 1855.
- +89 George Smith,⁷ b. 1837.
- +90 Seth LeGrand, Jr.⁷
- —91 Nancy,⁷ d. 1843, aged 1 year.
- +92 John Henry.⁷

55. SHERWOOD EDWARDS STRATTON⁶ (*Seth S.,*⁵ *Thomas,*⁴ *Thomas,*³ *Thomas,*² *John*¹) lived in Bridgeport and West Haven. He married **Cynthia Thompson,** who died in New Haven Mar. 26, 1884, aged 74 years.

Children:—*Born in Bridgeport, Conn.*
- —93 Frances Jane,⁷ m. 1st, **Theodore Hubbell;** 2nd, **Royal Bassett,** of Derby, Mar. 26, 1859.
- —94 Mary Elizabeth,⁷ m. **William H. Bassett.**
- —95 Charles Sherwood,⁷ "Tom Thumb," b. Jan. 4, 1838; m. **Minnie Warren Bump** of Middleborough, Conn., Feb. 10, 1863. He died July 15, 1883. A marble monument, surmounted by a full length statue, marks his burial place in Bridgeport.
- +96 William Edward,⁷ b. 1852.

57. DANIEL SHARP STRATTON⁶ (*Seth S.,*⁵ *Thomas,*⁴ *Thomas,*³ *Thomas,*² *John*¹) was born in 1817. He lived in Bridgeport, and was a tinsmith by trade. He married, first, **Susan Curtis,** May 29, 1839; second, **Mary Hall,** Mar. 19, 1848. He died Dec. 21, 1894.

Children:—*Born in Bridgeport, Conn.*
- —97 Sarah Elizabeth,⁷ b. 1840; m. **Frank Booth.**
- —98 Edward Curtis,⁷ b. Jan. 19, 1847; unm.

By second marriage.
- —99 Clifford Hall,⁷ b. Sept. 18, 1860; m. Sept. 20, 1882, **Catherine E. Kinder.**

89. GEORGE SMITH STRATTON⁷ (*Seth L.,*⁶ *Seth S.,*⁵ *Thomas,*⁴ *Thomas,*³ *Thomas,*² *John*¹) was born June 25, 1837. He married, first, **Cordelia Osborn;** married, second, **Hattie Russell,** May 22, 1860.

Children:

By first marriage.
- —100 Cornet Stetson,⁷ d. aged 10 years.

—101   Jane,⁷ m. **Robert Parmer.**
         By second marriage.
—102   Charles Russell,⁷ m. **Grace M. Burlock**; no children; res. Palm Beach, Fla.

90. SETH LEGRAND STRATTON, JR.⁷ (*Seth L.,⁶ Seth S.,⁵ Thomas,⁴ Thomas,³ Thomas,² John¹*) was born Sept. 8, 1841. He married **Louise Hubbell**, daughter of *Reuben J. Hubbell*, Oct. 12, 1865. He was a carpenter by trade. He died in Bridgeport June 24, 1907.

Children:—*Born in Bridgeport, Conn.*

—103   Elwood Everett,⁸ a printer, of Bridgeport; m. **Isabelle Bloss**, d. of *John J. Bloss*, in 1896; ch. Clifford Bloss.⁹
—104   Earl L.,⁸ m. **Grace Osborne**, 1903; res. Bridgeport; ch: Raymond Osborne.
—105   Arthur C.,⁸ b. 1866; d. in infancy.
—106   Edward,⁸ b. 1869; d. in infancy.
—107   Howard,⁸ b. 1872; d. in infancy.
—108   Walter M.,⁸ b. 1875; d. 1876.
—109   Amy Elizabeth,⁸ b. 1881; d. aged 4 years.

92. JOHN HENRY STRATTON⁷ (*Seth L.,⁶ Seth S.,⁵ Thomas,⁴ Thomas,³ Thomas,² John¹*) was born June 24, 1843. He was a Civil War soldier from Aug. 25, 1861, to Sept. 4, 1864, Co. I, 6th Regt. He married, first, **Mary C. Stafford**, Oct. 12, 1871. She died Feb. 6, 1875. He married, second, **Margaret Green.** He resides in Holyoke, Mass.

Child:
    By first marriage.
110   Mabelle,⁸ m. **Frederic Darwin Thorpe**, Nov. 29, 1890; res. Holyoke.

96. WILLIAM EDWARD STRATTON⁷ (*Sherwood E.,⁶ Seth S.,⁵ Thomas,⁴ Thomas,³ Thomas,² John¹*) was born Sept. 24, 1852, in Bridgeport, Conn. He married **Emily D. Cook**, daughter of *Chauncy M. Cook*, Aug. 20, 1873. He resides in New Haven. He is a prominent member of the Knights of Pythias.

Children:
—111   Levinea Adella, m. **Oliver Frederick Roberts.**
—112   Ida, m. **Frank Peckingham.**
—113   Edward D., m. **Jeneth Lydia Hungerford.**

WILLIAM STRATTON OF WINDSOR

(Chart L, Vol. I)

"The use of arms is closely connected with the study of genealogy."
DALLAWAY, A.D. 1793.

THE little we know of William Stratton of Windsor seems to indicate that he was a man of some standing in his day and time. Windsor, it will be remembered, was one of the settlements made by Massachusetts people—emigrants who objected to the law which refused the right to vote to those not members of the Puritan church, and who desired to form communities where all might have the franchise. For two or more decades there was a constant movement from the older Massachuetts towns to the newer settlements in the fertile Connecticut Valley. In many cases they were joined by the sons of the earliest settlers on Long Island. From either one of these sources William Stratton, or his parents, may have come, for we know of Strattons whose names early disappeared from the records of these older settlements and who have not been definitely located elsewhere. (See pages 71, 92, 104, Vol. I.)

If he was an "after-planter," coming as a young man from England, a research there might discover his ancestry. Some will, administration or court record there might identify him as the William Stratton of this Connecticut colony.*

Of the seven sons of Martin Stratton[3] (*Serajah*,[2] *William*[1]) of Simsbury, Conn. (see p. 233, *Vol. I*) six are known to have left Connecticut soon after the Revolution and settled in Pennsylvania or New York.† It is believed that Martin[3] came also, with his sons, to Bradford Co., Pa., and died there. The compiler

---

* There is a tradition that William Stratton of Windsor belonged to an armigerous line. The compiler has found a coat-of-arms in several families, but has been unable to discover its origin. It seems to have been used by them for several generations.

† Recent research shows that Phineas Stratton[4] (*Martin*,[3] *Seraiah*,[2] *William*[1]) was born May 24, 1786, married **Camilla Taylor**, daughter of Wm. and Abigail (Case) Taylor and granddaughter of David Case, Jr.,

has found no official record of military service of Martin Stratton[3] but family tradition says that he was a "Revolutionary patriot, who bankrupted himself to supply the army with flour." The official Revolutionary records of Connecticut are far from complete. It is very probable that he, like many Connecticut soldiers, received land grants for his service to his country and that he and his sons settled on these grants in Pennsylvania and New York.*

When *Vol. I* was issued only two children of Martin[4] (*Martin*[3]) had been found—Samuel[5] and Martha[5] (p. 234). Recently the compiler has come across six others as follows:

Children of Martin Stratton[4]:—*Born in Bradford Co., Pa.*

+24 Samuel.[5]
—25 Martha.[5]
+25a Hiram.[5]
—25b Nancy Elizabeth,[5] m. **John Bloom** of Burlington, Pa.
—25c Hannah,[5] m. **Anson Simmons** of Ulster, Pa., and moved to Indiana.
—25d Esther[5] (or Hester), m. **Loren Kingsbury.**
—25e Caroline,[5] m. **John Muncy**; lived in Wells, Ind.
—25f Mary,[5] m. **George Simmons**, and moved to Indiana.

FIFTH GENERATION

24. SAMUEL STRATTON[5] (*Martin*,[4] *Martin*,[3] *Serajah*,[2] *William*[1]) was born in North Towanda Feb. 19, 1808. He was a farmer and millwright and lived all his life on the old homestead where he died, aged nearly ninety years. He married **Euphrasia Foster**, Apr. 17, 1846. They were connected with the Methodist Episcopal church. The old homestead, built by Martin[4] about 1798, is now owned by his granddaughter. A modern porch was recently added.

Children:—*Born in North Towanda, Pa.*
+59 Porter,[6] b. 1849; res. North Towanda.
—60 Mary J.,[6] m. **John B. Taylor**, May 31, 1868; their d. Katherine m. **Manford Granger** and resides in N. Towanda.

---

of Simsbury. They settled in Delaware Co., N. Y., where he died Feb. 28, 1875. His will mentions only wife Camilla, and daughter, Helen Stratton.[5]

* The compiler has recently been informed that a tombstone stands to the memory of Martin Stratton[4] and his wife, Rebecca, at "Riverside," Towanda.

TIMOTHY STRATTON, SR. (1772-1853)
Page 235. *Vol.* I.

Copy of original drawing furnished by his great grandson, M. B. Stratton. *Page* 339.

—61 Florence,⁶ m. Marshall B. Wheeler; owns and occupies the old homestead.
—62 Ellen,⁶ m. Daniel Hiney.
—63 Harry,⁶ d. Mar. 23, 1864, aged 2 years.
—64 Eliza Jane,⁶ b. May 11, 1865; m. Charles Chambers, Aug. 16, 1884; res. Coming, N. Y.
—65 William J.,⁶ b. July 28, 1866; d. unm. in Philadelphia June 4, 1906.
—66 Martin Samuel,⁶ b. June 23, 1870; a carpenter; unm.; res. in Towanda.
—67 Annie,⁶ d. Jan. 17, 1872.
—68 John B.,⁶ b. June 5, 1873; m. Nancy Bailey; res. Sayer, Pa.; no children.

25a. HIRAM STRATTON ⁵ (*Martin,⁴ Martin,³ Serajah,² William ¹*) was born in North Towanda in 1804. As a boy he worked in the mill of his father built on Sugar Creek, Bradford Co., Pa. He learned the carpenter's trade and was a good mechanic. Later he engaged in the lumber business along the Susquehanna River. In 1841 he moved to Benton Co., Mo., where he died Dec. 9, 1881. He married **Olive Parmelia Stewart.** She died Mar. 17, 1898. In 1861 they went to Iowa, but returned to Benton Co. in 1867.

Children:—*Born in Bradford Co., Pa.*
—69 Louisa,⁶ never married.
+70 Myron L.,⁶ b. 1837; d. 1872.
+71 Stewart C.,⁶ b. 1836; d. 1906.
+72 George B.⁶
Born in Senaca Co., O.
—73 Emma,⁶ d. unm. in Benton Co., 1903.
Born in Logan Co., O.
—74 Wilson Harvey,⁶ d. unm. in 1906.
—75 Kennie,⁶ m. **Andy J. Stewart**; res. Lincoln, Neb.
—76 Olive Parmelia,⁶ m. **Thomas J. League.**

27. CURTIS PHILANDER STRATTON ⁵ (*Cephas,⁴ Martin,³ Serajah,² William ¹*) was born Dec. 31, 1799, in Ulster, Bradford Co., Pa. He married **Lavinia Fields Fitch** in 1820 in Tiago Co., Pa., where they lived for about fifteen years. He was a millwright and wheelwright. Eighteen hundred and thirty-six and 1837 they spent in Cincinnati, Ohio, and then moved to Jefferson Co., Ind., where they lived another fifteen years. In 1852 Mr.

Stratton and his eldest son went to California, remaining about one year, and then settling in Oregon where they were followed by the rest of the family in 1854. He died in Salem, Oregon, Feb. 26, 1873. He was a devout Methodist.

Children:—*Born in Tiago Co., Pa.*

—77 Riley Evans,⁶ b. June 30, 1821; m. **Sarah Dearborn**; d. in Oregon Dec. 26, 1866; judge of the Supreme Bench. No children.

—78 Brittania,⁶ d. in childhood.

—79 Delia C.,⁶ b. Oct. 8, 1826; m. 1st, **Wm. Van Winkle**, in 1845; m. 2nd, **James Patton**, in 1851; d. July 11, 1910.

—80 Roxana,⁶ d. aged 9 years.

—81 Susan Victoria,⁶ b. 1831; d. 1891; m. **Harvey Gorden** in 1853, who died about 1863; m. 2nd, **Andrew McCasly**.

+82 Charles C.,⁶ b. 1833; d. 1910.

+83 Horace F.,⁶ b. 1835; d. 1906.

Born in Jefferson Co., Ind.

+84 Milton A.,⁶ b. 1838; d. 1895.

—85 Lura Melvina,⁶ b. May 10, 1840; d. in 1886; m. 1st, **Chas. H. Evans**, 1859; m. 2nd, **Arch Simmons**, 1866.

—86 Augusta Josephine,⁶ b. Aug. 20, 1842; m. **Dr. Samuel Whitemore**, Nov. 9, 1864; res. Seattle, Washington.

+87 Julius A.,⁶ b. Oct. 13, 1844.

—88 Irene Haseltine,⁶ b. 1847; m. **Paris L. Willis**; res. Portland, Oregon.

28. ORANGE STRATTON⁵ (*Cephas*,⁴ *Martin*,³ *Serajah*,² *William*¹) was born Sept. 15, 1800, near Blossburg, Bradford Co., Pa. At the age of 21 he went West, stopping in Cummingsville, a suburb of Cincinnati, Ohio. Here he married **Isabella Long**, the daughter of *James* and *Sarah Long*, Sept. 29, 1824. Six years later they removed to Christiansburg, Miami Co., Ohio, where they bought a farm and resided the remainder of their lives. He died Nov. 1, 1876.

Children:—*Born in Cummingsville, Ohio.*

—89 William L.,⁶ b. July 16, 1825; d. Mar. 4, 1831.

+90 Milton S.,⁶ b. 1827; d. 1876.

—91 David Furgerson,⁶ b. Nov. 8, 1829; m. **Sarah J. French**, Jan. 9, 1864; d. in Addison, O., July 18, 1870. Left no children.

Born in Christiansburg, O.
+92 John R.,⁶ b. 1831; d. 1905.
+93 James H.,⁶ b. 1833.
+94 DeWitt C.,⁶ b. 1835.
—95 Elizabeth J.,⁶ b. Nov. 18, 1837; d. Sept. 26, 1843.
—96 Huldah M.,⁶ b. Oct. 31, 1839; m. **John E. Walker**, Dec. 1, 1864; res. Casstown, Ohio.
—97 Sarah D.,⁶ b. Sept. 21, 1841; m. **Josiah N. Wiley**, Sept. 11, 1866; d. Sept. 19, 1868.
—98 Jasper N.,⁶ b. May 19, 1843; d. Mar. 20, 1854.
—99 Martha H.,⁶ b. Feb. 3, 1846; d. July 27, 1905.

31. MARTIN STRATTON⁵ (*Sephas,*⁴ *Martin,*³ *Serajah,*² *William* ¹) was born in 1806. In 1832 he married **Elizabeth Holden**. Children:
—100 Daniel H.,⁶ b. Jan. 1, 1834; m. **May C. Scott**, 1859.
—101 Myron S.,⁶ killed on the railroad, 1893.

There were other children. The compiler would be glad to get into communication with any of the family.

33. MYRON STRATTON⁵ (*Cephas,*⁴ *Martin,*³ *Serajah,*² *William* ¹) was born in North Towanda, Bradford Co., Pa., in 1812. When six years old his father removed with his family to Cummingsville, O. About 1835 he settled in Jeffersonville, Ind., where for over half a century he was an active business man, a prominent and highly respected citizen, and for forty-six years a devoted member of the Christian Church. Oct. 30, 1838, he married **Mary Anna Halstead**, Bishop Nathan Field officiating. She was born Apr. 19, 1820, and died in Jeffersonville Nov. 26, 1865, when her youngest child was but three years old. "A dear companion, a devoted, self-denying mother, an affectionate sister, a true friend and a devout Christian." Mr. Stratton was a member of the old boat-building firm of "Logan & Stratton," which built many of the swift cruisers which navigated the waters of the Ohio and Mississippi prior to 1860. Retiring early from active business with what was then considered a very comfortable fortune, he settled down to private life. His energy and popularity, however, would not long permit him to remain in obscurity, and he was elected to represent his party in the City Council. Here his untiring zeal and interest in the welfare of

the city made him one of the most important members. He was elected and re-elected until he had served twenty-one years in that body. He was a member of the Jeffersonville Lodge of Odd Fellows and a Mason, and after retiring from business gave a good deal of time to these societies. Oct. 3, 1869, he married, second, **Helen T. Cline,** who died in Louisville in 1876. He died in Jeffersonville Nov. 10, 1885, of a stroke of paralysis, and his estate was divided equally among the four children then living.*

Children:—*Born in Jeffersonville, Ind.*

By first marriage.

- —102 Diantha Jane,⁶ b. 1839; d. Mar. 10, 1865; unm.
- —103 Harriett Newell,⁶ b. May 9, 1841; d. June 16, 1901; m. **Alfred Warner Hamblin.**
- —104 James Augustus,⁶ d. in infancy.
- —105 William Riley,⁶ d. in infancy.
- —106 Anna Augusta,⁶ b. Nov., 1846; d. Aug. 24, 1894; m. **George W. Chamberlin.** The compiler is indebted to their daughter, Miss Pearle Chamberlin, for the portrait of Myron Stratton.
- +107 Winfield Scott.⁶
- —108 Mary Anne,⁶ b. Sept. 22, 1851; d. unm. Oct. 26, 1877.
- —109 Hannah Virginia,⁶ b. Oct. 29, 1853; m. **Harry Henderson Cobb,** May 13, 1873, at Jeffersonville, Ind.; res. San José, Cal. Their daughter, Lillian, who gave the compiler much help on this line, m. Gentry Shelton.
- —110 Luella,⁶ d. at the age of 6 years, Dec. 28, 1860.
- —111 Jesse Eliza,⁶ d. at the age of 3 years, Dec. 31, 1860.
- —112 Ada Carman,⁶ d. at the age of 1 year, Jan. 13, 1861.
- —113 Frank Myron,⁶ b. May 24, 1862; d. aged 4 years.

37. Stephen Curry Stratton⁵ (*Timothy,*⁴ *Martin,*³ *Serajah,*² *William*¹) was born in Bradford Co., Pa., Feb. 10, 1800, and died Nov. 29, 1836. He married **Harriet Holcomb.** He moved

---

* The records of the City of Jeffersonville show that Myron Stratton served his city as follows:

Councilman from 5th Ward, 1848-1852.

Councilman from 4th Ward, 1853-1854, 1857-1873.

School Trustee, 1854-1861.

A monument was erected to his memory on the Stratton lot in Eastern Cemetery, Jeffersonville, and the trustees were given $500, the interest to be used in keeping up the lot.

from Ohio to Illinois. He is believed to have left children, information of whom is desired.*

38. TIMOTHY STRATTON [5] (*Timothy*,[4] *Martin*,[3] *Serajah*,[2] *William*[1]) was born in Bradford Co., Pa., Mar. 4, 1802, and moved with his parents to Springfield, Ohio, when he was 14 years of age. He married **Elizabeth Lane** in 1828. In 1838 they settled in Joy Co., Ind., obtaining land there through the Government office at Fort Wayne. This farm is still in possession of the Strattons. The old house built in 1839 has been torn down, but the barn 40x60 feet is still standing, the first barn built in that section of the country.

Children:—*Born in Clark Co., Ohio.*
+114   Stephen A.,[6] b. 1830.
—115   Robert L.,[6] d. in Nebraska City, 1856.
—116   Elizabeth Ellen,[6] b. Nov. 28, 1835; d. aged 11 years.
Born in Joy Co., Ind.
+117   Isaac N.,[6] b. 1839.
+118   Lewis F.,[6] b. 1841.
+119   Cyrus M.,[6] b. 1847.
—120   Casper B.,[6] b. Nov. 16, 1849; d. May 21, 1850.
—121   Mary J.,[6] b. Nov. 26, 1852; d. Oct. 24, 1858.

40. WILLIAM STRATTON [5] (*Timothy*,[4] *Martin*,[3] *Serajah*,[2] *William*[1]) was born May 29, 1807. He married and lived for awhile at Yellow Springs, Ohio, and then moved to Joy Co., Ind., where he was a farmer.

Children:
—122   Charlotte, m. **Joseph LaFollette**; res. Portland, Ind.
—123   Isaac, a soldier in the Civil War, from Joy Co. His children resided at Redkey, Ind.
—124   George.
—125   Henry.

---

* A letter from Stephen Curry Stratton, written to his father from Fulton Co., Ill., dated June 22, 1827, tells of the fine crops they have on their newly cleared land, and their "market in three ways." One way was to St. Louis, about two hundred miles, where they could get all family necessities; another to the lead mines, about two hundred miles to the north, and then "our market to Chicaugoe, about two hundred and fifty miles, is going to be our best market. A great many cattle are drove there now. They have erected a slanter-house there where they pack porke and beef and ship to New York."

41. HENRY SPADDEN STRATTON [5] (*Timothy,*[4] *Martin,*[3] *Sarajah,*[2] *William*[1]), born May 11, 1809; died Apr. 7, 1905; married **Rebecca Hendricks**.

Children:—*Born in Clark Co., O.*
- —126 David Fredrick,[6] b. Apr. 15, 1837.
- —127 Timothy Lewis,[6] b. June 1, 1838.

  Born in Joy Co., Ind.
- —128 William Henry,[6] b. Nov. 29, 1839; d. at Memphis Mar. 1, 1863; a Federal soldier.
- —129 Euphema Moody,[6] b. June 11, 1841.
- —130 Solon Curtis,[6] b. Dec. 24, 1842; d. at Holly Springs, Dec. 2, 1862; a Federal soldier.
- —131 John Hawkins,[6] b. Feb. 13, 1844.
- —132 Finley Robert,[6] b. Nov. 9, 1845.
- —133 Laura Louise,[6] b. May 22, 1847.
- —134 Milton Lycurgus,[6] b. Oct. 21, 1848; d. Jan. 2, 1884.
- —135 Rebecca Jane,[6] b. Oct. 15, 1850; d. Apr. 22, 1885.
- —136 Florine Leon,[6] b. July 12, 1854; d. July 5, 1861.
- —137 Emma Fola,[6] b. May 30, 1859; d. Nov. 10, 1863.

42. CALVIN STRATTON [5] (*Timothy,*[4] *Martin,*[3] *Serajah,*[2] *William*[1]) was born July 3, 1811, in Bradford Co., Pa., and was five years old when his parents removed to Springfield, Ohio. He married **Elizabeth Curtice** in 1844, and in 1868 removed to Wapella, Ill., and later to Atlanta, Ill., where he died.

Children:
- —138 Solon, m. **Frances Stewart**; res. Atlanta, Ill.
- —139 Sophia, m. **W. H. Hover**.
- —140 Calvin C.
- +141 John Curtice.
- —142 Henry.
- —143 Alice, m. Prof. **Albert M. Ellis** of Wapella, Sept. 20, 1880.
- —144 Carrie, m. **Jacob R. Bell**, Aug. 1, 1891; res. Wapella.

44. ISAAC HORTON STRATTON [5] (*Timothy,*[4] *Martin,*[3] *Serajah,*[2] *William*[1]) was born in Springfield, Ohio, May 4, 1817, and died there Oct. 16, 1904. He married **Sarah Leffel**, Feb. 28, 1845.

Children:—*Born in Springfield, O.*
- —145 Leslie C., b. Dec. 23, 1845; m. **Emma J. Hinkle**, Feb. 28, 1879; res. Springfield, Ohio.

—146 Calista Ann, b. Apr. 2, 1847; m. **Thomas M. Hess,** Jan. 11, 1870.

 —147 Mary Jane, b. Jan. 14, 1852; m. **John R. Hinkle,** Dec. 23, 1875; res. Springfield.

51. CALVIN STRATTON⁵ (*Calvin,⁴ Martin,³ Serajah,² William¹*). When *Vol. I* was issued it was thought that the Strattons of DeWitt Co., Ill., were the children of Calvin Stratton.⁵ This has been found to be a mistake. His descendants are yet unknown to the compiler.*

53. JULIUS STRATTON⁵ (*Harvey,⁴ John,³ William,² William¹*) was born about 1812 and lived for several years at East Granby.
Children:—*Born in E. Granby, Conn.*

 —148 Aurelia,⁶ d. unm.

 +149 Chauncey J.,⁶ b. 1826.

57. MORGAN STRATTON⁵ (*Harvey,⁴ John,³ William,² William¹*) was born in Simsbury, Conn., July 13, 1815. He married **Amelia Cook,** Dec. 31, 1838, at Windsor, where he lived for about twelve years after his marriage, and then moved to Hartford, where he had charge of the outdoor work of the Colt's Manufacturing Co. for thirty years, a faithful, upright man. In 1889 he gave up this work and bought a home in Bloomfield, where he spent the remainder of his life.†

Children:—*Born in Windsor, Conn.*

 —150 Harvey M.,⁶ b. June 1, 1840; d. in infancy.

 —151 Orleana,⁶ b. Oct. 14, 1842; m. **Charles L. Clark,** Jan. 27, 1861; d. in Hartford Jan. 24, 1863.

 —152 Morgan E.,⁶ b. June 15, 1847; d. in infancy.

 —153 Wilber W.,⁶ b. Sept. 21, 1848; d. in infancy.

 —154 Gabrella S.,⁶ b. Mar. 16, 1850; m. **Charles E. Burr,** son of Emerson Burr, in 1872; d. Jan. 28, 1890, at Avon, Conn.

 —155 Isadora,⁶ b. Mar. 16, 1850; m. **William Burr,** May 1, 1873.

---

* There is some doubt as to the correctness of the list of children (46 to 52 on page 236, Vol. I). More correct information concerning Calvin⁴ (No. 16), son of Martin,³ is desired.

† The name of the second wife of Harvey Stratton⁴ was Mrs. Lucy (Pettebone) Adams. He married her in 1816. She died in Bloomfield, Conn., Sept. 13, 1871. She was the mother of his four younger children (see Vol. I).

—156 Albert L.,⁶ b. June 2, 1852; d. in infancy.
—157 Adelbert W.,⁶ b. June 2, 1852; d. in infancy.

59. PORTER STRATTON ⁶ (*Samuel M.,*⁵ *Martin,*⁴ *Martin,*³ *Serajah,*² *William* ¹) was born in North Towanda, Pa., Aug. 30, 1849. He married **Anna (Fairchild) Hess,** and lives in his native town.

Children:—*Born in North Towanda, Pa.*
—158 Lelia Anna, m. **Paul E. Warner,** Sept. 13, 1902; res. North Towanda.
—159 Mary Euprasia, m. **Walter A. Stowell,** Oct. 21, 1908; res. in N. Towanda.
—160 Willis Roger.

70. MYRON LUTHER STRATTON ⁶ (*Hiram,*⁵ *Martin,*⁴ *Martin,*³ *Serajah,*² *William* ¹) was born in 1837 and died in Benton Co., Mo., in 1872. Sept. 21, 1857, he married **Mary Rank,** daughter of *John* and *Catherine Rank,* who moved from Pennsylvania to Missouri in 1837. He lived on a farm near Warsaw, Mo., farming summers and teaching school winters. In 1866 he was elected circuit court clerk and recorder of deeds, which office he held until his death. He served several years in the state militia.

Children:—*Born in Benton Co., Mo.*
—161 Sarah C., m. **Robert Menter,** Nov. 23, 1878; lives in Lincoln, Neb.; unm.
—162 Julia A.
—163 Mary M., m. **George W. Skipton,** July 3, 1889; res. Rushville, Ind.
+164 Myron L.
+165 Frank B.

71. STEWART CHARLES STRATTON ⁶ (*Hiram,*⁵ *Martin,*⁴ *Martin,*³ *Serajah,*² *William* ¹), born Jan. 31, 1836, and married, first, **Christina Orr,** 1862; second, **Nancy Orr,** in 1868. Lived on a farm in Benton Co., Mo. Was school commissioner two years and clerk of the county for eight years. From early manhood he was a licensed preacher in the Methodist Episcopal church and, although he never took a regular pastorate, was always an earnest church worker. He died Mar. 8, 1906.

Children:—*Born in Benton Co., Mo.*
  By first marriage.
—166 Minnie Bell,⁷ m. **William Feaster,** 1884.

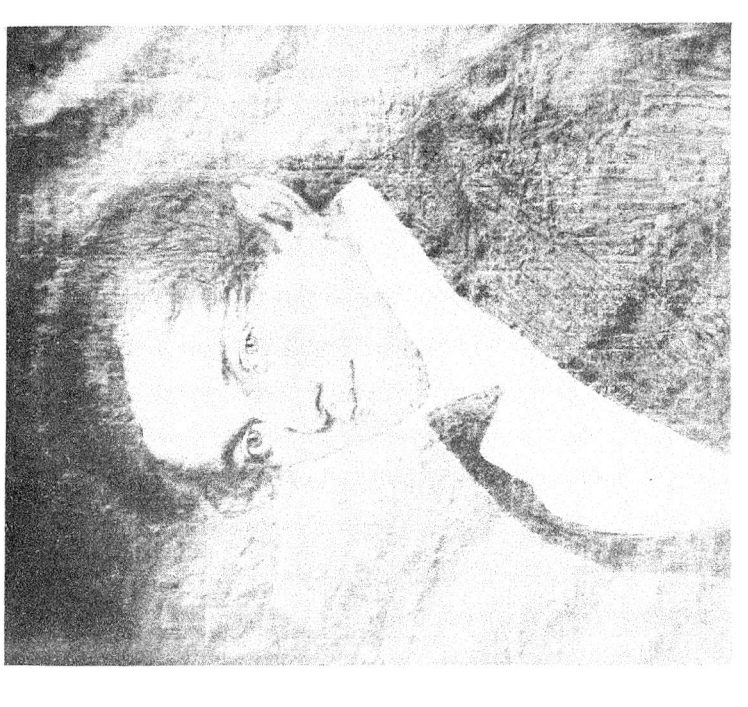

Asa Evans Stratton, Sr., at the age of 28. From a painting made in 1826 at Dalton, Ga. *Page* 199.

Catherine (Stratton) Snow; *Page* 374. Mother of C. A. Snow. From painting in possession of her granddaughter, Mrs. Nina (Snow) Foust.

—167 George Wilson [7] (M.D.), attended Medical College at St. Louis; m. **Ella Hughes** in 1892; res. Marysville, Cal.

By second marriage.

+168 Charles Stewart.[7]
—169 Samuel Oliver,[7] m. **Mary Dillon**, 1901; a physician; res. Edmondson, Mo.
—170 Edward Bernum,[7] m. **Jestie Neal**, May, 1909.
—171 Lucy May,[7] m. **William Arnold**, 1896.

72. GEORGE BINGHAM STRATTON [6] (*Hiram*,[5] *Martin*,[4] *Martin*,[3] *Serajah*,[2] *William* [1]) is a retired farmer in Mena, Ark. He married **Ruth Ellen League**, Feb. 4, 1869. He enlisted in the 33rd reg't and served three years in the Civil War. Was wounded in Battle of Jenken's Ferry, Ark., and taken prisoner; in prison ten months at Tyler, Texas. Paroled just before close of war. Mustered out of service and returned to Missouri in 1865; taught school for a few years, then settled on a farm where he lived for 38 years, and where his youngest daughter now lives.

Children:—*Born in Missouri.*

—172 Almeda League, unm.; keeps house for her father at Mena, Ark.
—173 Myron Allen, m. **Lida Kelly**, 1902; student at State University; taught school three terms. Dep't County Clerk for 8 years. Now in real estate business in Mena, Ark.
—174 William James, m. **Margaret Ford**, 1902. Hardware dealer, Henry Co., Mo.
—175 Myrtle Elizabeth, m. **Leslie B. Gray**, 1900.

82. CHARLES CARREL STRATTON [6] (*Curtis P.*,[5] *Cephas*,[4] *Martin*,[3] *Serajah*,[2] *William* [1]) was born in Mansfield, Pa., Jan. 4, 1833. When he was three years old his parents moved to Indiana, and in 1854 he crossed the plains and settled with his father's family at Salem, Oregon. From early boyhood he was drawn towards the ministry, and, upon his arrival in Oregon, entered Willamette University and became a Methodist minister. After passing his examination at Willamette, he was elected to the chair of Natural Science in that institution. In 1872 he was elected a delegate to the General Conference, which met in Brooklyn, N. Y. The following autumn he was appointed to a pastorate at Salt Lake City. In 1877 was elected President of the University of the

Pacific at San José, Cal., and filled that position for ten years, increasing the roll of students from 150 to 500 and greatly improving the financial condition of the university. During this time he usually preached at two services each Sabbath, in the churches of Oakland, San Francisco and elsewhere. Under these manifold labors his health failed, compelling his resignation from the presidency. The degree of Doctor of Divinity was conferred on him by the University of Evanston, Ill. His alma mater honored him in like manner. In 1891 he was elected Chancellor of Willamette University, resigning the following year to accept the presidency of Portland University. Earnest, scholarly, cheerful, Dr. Stratton went his helpful way among men, his persuasive eloquence as a preacher and sympathetic helpfulness as a teacher greatly endearing him to those with whom he came in contact, and winning many to the Master for whose glory he so earnestly labored. He died in Salem, Oregon, April 4, 1910. In 1858, Dr. Stratton married **Julia E. Walker**, daughter of *Rev. Alvin F. Walker*, one of the early Methodist missionaries, who arrived in Oregon about 1840.

Children:—*Born in Rosebury, Oregon.*
—176   Mary Elepha.[7]

Born in Olympia, Wash.
—177   Harvey Gordon,[7] m. **Grace B. Stiles**, June 10, 1907, d. of J. A. and *Antonette Stiles* of Portland; res. Spokane, Wash.

83.   HORACE FITCH STRATTON [6] (*Curtis P.*,[5] *Cephas*,[4] *Martin*,[3] *Serajah*,[2] *William* [1]) was born in Blossburg, Pa., May 31, 1835, and died in Seattle, Wash., Oct. 6, 1906. July 14, 1869, he married **Marilda F. Dunn**. He was asst. quartermaster in the Indian war in Oregon, in 1855-56. He was early interested in mining, an enthusiastic student of geology and mineralogy in the mountains of Oregon and Washington, and was one of the first to go to the mines of Alaska and Cook's Inlet. He was a merchant in Eugene, Oregon, from 1864 to 1879. A member of the legislature from Salem in 1878. Moved to Seattle, Wash., in 1879 where he lived the remainder of his life. In 1881 he was a member of the legislature of the State of Washington. He is buried in Mt. Pleasant Cemetery, Seattle.

Children:—*Born in Eugene, Oregon.*
—178   Curtis Dunn.[7]
—179   Gertrude Lavinia,[7] m. 1914, **James Funchion.**

—180 Dwight Fitch,[7] m. **Gladys E. Melvin,** 1905.
—181 Helen Irene,[7] d. in Seattle in 1902, aged 23 years.

84. MILTON ADAMS STRATTON [6] (*Curtis P.,*[5] *Cephas,*[4] *Martin,*[3] *Serajah,*[2] *William* [1]), born at Big Creek, Ind., Jan. 10, 1838. Died in Portland, Oregon, Feb. 24, 1895. Nov. 9, 1870, he married **Helen Laraine Williams,** in Salem, Oregon. She was born in Finlay, O., daughter of *Elijah* and *Lucia (Biglow) Williams,* and granddaughter of *Rev. Henry Williams,* Congregational minister, graduate of Yale in 1802, who lived in Middletown, Vt. Mr. and Mrs. Stratton located in Oregon City, where for twenty years he was secretary of the Oregon City woolen mills. They then moved to Portland, where he was elected President of the First National Bank, which office he held until his death. He was regarded as a fine business man, quiet, thoughtful, and with a heart filled with love for his fellow men; unassuming in manners, much beloved and esteemed by his many friends. His family still reside in Portland, where his sons are in business.

Children:—*Born in Oregon City, Oregon.*
—182 Creed Williams,[7] Juneau, Alaska.
—183 Carroll Biglow,[7] Portland, Or.
—184 Milton Adams, Jr.,[7] a dentist of Portland; m. **Jessie Lee Wood,** b. in Tennessee. They have one daughter, Helen Loraine.[8]
—185 Floyd Loraine,[7] res. Portland.

87. JULIUS AUGUSTINE STRATTON [6] (*Curtis P.,*[5] *Cephas,*[4] *Martin,*[3] *Serajah,*[2] *William* [1]) is an attorney at Seattle. He was born Oct. 23, 1844. Educated in Williamette University, Salem, Oregon; settled in Seattle about 1887; Judge of Superior Court. Married, in 1884, **Martha L. Powell,** who died in Apr., 1895. In Aug., 1900, he married **Laura M. Adams,** daughter of J. R. and *Minerva Tabor (Woodman) Adams.*

Child:—*Born in Seattle, Wash.*
By second marriage.
—186 Julius Adams, Jr.[7]

90. MILTON LAFAYETTE STRATTON [6] (*Orange,*[5] *Cephas,*[4] *Martin,*[3] *Serajah,*[2] *William* [1]) was born in 1827. He learned the carpenter's trade in his youth; taught school for several years. He married **Anna LaRue Douglas,** May 5, 1851, and lived in Addison, O. In May, 1871, they moved to Dayton, O., where he

died Jan. 15, 1875. He served three years in the army, enlisting at St. Paris in 1862 to the close of the war.

Children:—*Born in Addison, Ohio.*
—187 Ella Douglas, m. **Winfield S. Kline**, Apr. 22, 1872.
—188 Irene Candace, m. **Jacob E. Moore**.
+189 Norval Orange.
—190 Fannie B., m. **Sidney Herbert Stebbins**, June, 1894; res. Paunee City, Neb.

92. JOHN R. STRATTON [6] (*Orange*,[5] *Cephas*,[4] *Martin*,[3] *Serajah*,[2] *William* [1]), born Nov. 27, 1831. Married **Jane Ann Walker** of Shelby Co., O., Dec. 13, 1866. They lived on a farm near Addison, O., until 1903, when they retired from farming and moved to Troy, Ohio, where he died, Feb. 29, 1905.

Children:—*Born near Addison, O.*
—191 Eugene Clifford,[7] m. **Alma Pearl Green**.
—192 Curtis Walker,[7] m. **Erma Maude Atkinson**; res. Troy, O.
—193 Sue Viola,[7] res. Troy, O.

93. JAMES H. STRATTON [6] (*Orange*,[5] *Cephas*,[4] *Martin*,[3] *Serajah*,[2] *William* [1]), born in Miami Co., O., Sept. 11, 1833, married **Laura C. Rapp**, daughter of *Barnett* and *Mary Rapp*, June 21, 1859. Settled in Indiana in 1861; res. Marion, Ind.

Children:—*Born in Mexico, Ind.*
—194 Luella Alice,[7] d. 1863.
—195 Edith Vernon,[7] d. 1882, aged 16 years.
—196 Charles Orange,[7] res. New York City.
—197 Harry Everett,[7] d. 1880, aged 8 years.
—198 Pearl Hartley,[7] res. Marion, Ind.
—199 Edna Irene,[7] m. **Elbert S. Kline**, 1894.
+200 Orville Guy.[7]
—201 Lora Glee,[7] m. **Thomas A. Kinerk**, 1900.

94. DEWITT C. STRATTON [6] (*Orange*,[5] *Cephas*,[4] *Martin*,[3] *Serajah*,[2] *William* [1]) was born Sept. 21, 1836. He married **Sarah J. Leggett**, daughter of *James* and *Eliza* (*Spalar*) *Leggett*, Oct. 21, 1863. In 1870 he moved from Ohio to Pawnee City, Neb., where he was engaged in the grocery business for about fifteen years and then retired to his farm. He has been an elder in the Presbyterian Church for 21 years.

Child:

—202 Florence Eva, educated in Pawnee public schools, Pine State Normal, and Bellevue Presbyterian College; m. **John S. Lowe**, June 1, 1898.

107. WINFIELD SCOTT STRATTON [6] (*Myron*,[5] *Cephas*,[4] *Martin*,[3] *Serajah*,[2] *William*[1]) was born in Jeffersonville, Ind., July 22, 1848. Working as a boy in his father's boat building plant, he later learned the carpenter's trade, and at the age of twenty went west. In Colorado he worked for awhile at his trade, and then became interested in mining. Having a taste for geology and mineralogy, he procured books on the subject and carefully studied them in connection with the natural features of the country. Possessed of intelligence, energy and any amount of pluck and patience, he worked for several years as a prospector under the most discouraging conditions, and was finally rewarded by striking a vein of ore as rich as any in the country, and opened the world-famous "Independence Gold Mine" in Cripple Creek, Colorado, so-called because his discovery was made on the 4th of July. He soon had large interests in other mines and other extensive business enterprises and a beautiful estate in Colorado Springs. Mr. Stratton died Sept. 14, 1902, a multimillionaire, in the town in which a few years before he had worked as a carpenter. A local paper a short time before his death describes him as a "modest, slender, frail-looking man, quiet, unassuming, unassertive in manner, and wholly inconspicuous in appearance except for his clear piercing gray eyes." By his will his wealth of more than eleven millions, after a few legacies to relatives and friends, was left to build an institution in Colorado Springs, to be known as the "Myron Stratton Home" in memory of his father,—an institution "for the unfortunate honest and worthy of Colorado, incapacitated for self-support by illness or accident, where they may come for rest, medical attendance and recuperation, and where they may be so cared for that they may forget they are objects of charity." This institution on a one-thousand acre tract of land is being developed by its trustees into an industrial school—a model home for homeless boys and girls as well as a home for the aged and sick. Connected with it is the beautiful Stratton Park, also a gift from Mr. Stratton to Colorado Springs.

Mr. Stratton married Zura **V. Stewart** in June, 1876.

Child:—*Born in Danville, Ill.*
—203   Izaak Harrison,[7] m. **Josephine A. Larabee** in Oshkosh, Wis.; res. Pasadena, Cal.

114. STEPHEN A. STRATTON [6] (*Timothy,*[5] *Martin,*[4] *Martin,*[3] *Serajah,*[2] *William*[1]) was born Mar. 4, 1830. Oct. 10, 1852, he married **Martha Jane Montgomery**, daughter of *William* and *Mary Montgomery* of Fountain Co., Ind. He enlisted in the 89th Reg. Volunteers; died in hospital at Memphis, Tenn., Aug. 8, 1863. His widow married Mordica Phillips in 1867.

Children:—*Born in Portland, Ind.*
—204   Robert Lane,[7] b. Mar. 23, 1857; m. 1st, **Alice Rudd Varger**; 2nd, **Mary M. Boyd**, Nov. 29, 1899; res. Portland, Ind.
—205   Lewis L.,[7] b. Oct. 7, 1860; a farmer at Dewey, Indian Territory; m. **Ruth Ross**, Jan. 3, 1905.
+206   Stephen W.,[7] b. 1863.

117. ISAAC N. STRATTON [6] (*Timothy,*[5] *Timothy,*[4] *Martin,*[3] *Serajah,*[2] *William*[1]), born Feb. 12, 1839. He married **Emily Hiatt**, Feb. 14, 1867. Was Captain of Co. I, Indiana Volunteers, Infantry; resides at Ridgeville, Ind., a retired farmer.

Children:—*Born in Joy Co., Ind.*
—207   Nellie Grant,[7] m. **I. N. Reitenour**, 1892; res. Union City, Ind.
—208   Alice Cary,[7] m. **O. M. Fowler**, 1890.
+209   Melvin B.[7]
  Born in Ridgedale, Ind.
—210   Ruth Winona,[7] m. **Charles S. Ewing**, 1897; res. Indianapolis, Ind.
—211   Edith Mabel,[7] m. **Hallie Wolverton**.
—212   Kate Mildred,[7] m. **Wm. Stegall**; res. Ridgedale, Ind.

118. LEWIS F. STRATTON [6] (*Timothy,*[5] *Timothy,*[4] *Martin,*[3] *Serajah,*[2] *William*[1]) was a farmer in Joy Co., Ind.; a member of the Christian church; married **Julia A. Starr**, Sept. 17, 1865; soldier in Co. F, 140th Reg. Ind. Volunteers, 1864 and 1865. Died in Joy Co., Aug. 24, 1902. His widow died Mar. 3, 1908.

Children:—*Born in Joy Co., Ind.*
+213   Charles N.[7]
+214   Silas S.[7]
—215   Jennie,[7] m. **A. W. Masters**, 1893.

—216 Addie,[7] m. Frank **Hummer**, 1898.
—217 Lodema,[7] m. Will W. **Murry**, 1898; res. Mt. Calm, Mich.

119. CYRUS M. STRATTON [6] (*Timothy*,[5] *Timothy*,[4] *Martin*,[3] *Serajah*,[2] *William* [1]) is living on a farm near New Mt. Pleasant, five miles east of Redkey, Ind. He married **Lusetta Nixon**, Oct. 6, 1872, and began housekeeping on the farm on which they have lived ever since. He was born Dec. 24, 1847. They are members of the Christian Church.

Children:—*Born near New Mt. Pleasant, Ind.*
+218 John C.[7]
—219 Nellie Blanche,[7] m. Frank **Martin**, 1901.
—220 Montana,[7] m. Julia **Brunsworth**, Oct. 19, 1908; res. Portland, Ind.
—221 Nevada May,[7] m. Oscar **Beckner**, Feb. 14, 1909.
+222 William Timothy.[7]

141. JOHN CURTICE STRATTON [6] (*Calvin*,[5] *Timothy*,[4] *Martin*,[3] *Serajah*,[2] *William* [1]) married **Laura Losetta Steele**. They lived in Henderson Co., Ill.; moved to Oxford, Kansas, in 1834.
Children:
—223 Estella Lily.[7]
—224 Calvin Allison.[7]
—225 Lewis Elmer.[7]
—226 Frank.[7]
—227 Charles Erwin,[7]
—228 Bert.[7]
—229 Grace Pearl.[7]
—230 Shirley Smith.[7]
—231 Nona.[7]

149. CHAUNCEY J. STRATTON [6] (*Julius*,[5] *Harvey*,[4] *John*,[3] *William*,[2] *William* [1]), born in 1826; died in Suffield, Conn., in 1902. He married **Susan M. Pease** in 1864.
Children:
+232 Edwin E.[7]
—233 Herman C.,[7] b. Jan. 29, 1873; d., unm., Nov. 27, 1901.

164. MYRON L. STRATTON [7] (*Myron L.*,[6] *Hiram*,[5] *Martin*,[4] *Martin*,[3] *Serajah*,[2] *William* [1]) married **Mary Dillon** and resides at Edmonson, Mo.
Children:—*Born in Edmonson, Mo.*
—234 Gertrude.[8]
—235 Carl.[8]

—236 Elsie.[8]
—237 Paul.[8]
—238 Mary.[8]

165. FRANK B. STRATTON [7] (*Myron L.*,[6] *Hiram*,[5] *Martin*,[4] *Martin*,[3] *Serajah*,[2] *William* [1]) married **Gertrude Allison** and lives in Anderson, Ind., where he is city electrician and manager of Indiana Electrical Company.
Children:
—239 Harold.[8]
—240 B. Allison.[8]
—241 Gertrude Alice.[8]
—242 Ralph.[8]

168. CHARLES STUART STRATTON [7] (*Stuart*,[6] *Hiram*,[5] *Martin*,[4] *Martin*,[3] *Serajah*,[2] *William* [1]) married, June 6, 1908, **Sophia Lee Donovan**, daughter of *James Guinn* and *Virginia Donovan*; graduated from the St. Louis Medical College in 1899; resides at Roscoe, Mo., where he is a practicing physician.
Child:—*Born in Roscoe, Mo.*
—243 Charles Stuart, Jr.[8]

189. NORVAL ORANGE STRATTON [7] (*Milton L.*,[6] *Orange*,[5] *Cephas*,[4] *Martin*,[3] *Serajah*,[2] *William* [1]) married **Catherine Olophant**, Mar. 6, 1889, and now resides in Piqua, Ohio.
Children:—*Born in Dayton, Ohio.*
—244 Harley La Rue.[8]
—245 Forest Herbert,[8] d. in infancy.

200. ORVILLE GUY STRATTON [7] (*James H.*,[6] *Orange*,[5] *Cephas*,[4] *Martin*,[3] *Serajah*,[2] *William* [1]) was born in Mexico, Ind. Married **Rosa Smith** and resides in Niles, O.
Children:
—246 Gael Hillis,[8] deceased.
—247 Roy Kenneth.[8]
—248 Norman Charles.[8]

206. STEPHEN W. STRATTON [7] (*Stephen A.*,[6] *Timothy*,[5] *Martin*,[4] *Martin*,[3] *Serajah*,[2] *William* [1] resides at Blufton, Ohio. He married **Eva J. Smith**, Oct. 20, 1889, in Portland, Ind., and resided there until June, 1891; then in Coldwater, Ohio, for six years, then in Albany, Ind., until 1902, and since that date in

Blufton. All the time in the employ of the Lake Erie and Western R. R. Co., each move being a promotion.
Children:—*Born in Portland, Ind.*
—249   Paul Revere.[8]
—250   Russell Smith,[8] b. in Blufton.

209. MELVIN BROWN STRATTON [7] (*Isaac N.,*[6] *Timothy,*[5] *Timothy,*[4] *Martin,*[3] *Serajah,*[2] *William* [1]) married **Hetty E. Champ** in 1896; resides in Indianapolis, a prominent business man, president of "Stratton Broom Co."
Child:—*Born in Indianapolis, Ind.*
—251   Allen Hiatt.[8]

213. CHARLES N. STRATTON [7] (*Lewis F.,*[6] *Timothy,*[5] *Timothy,*[4] *Martin,*[3] *Serajah,*[2] *William* [1]) is a farmer, living in Portland. He married, first, **Sarah E. Lake,** Sept. 1, 1889; second, **Jessie M. Wood,** May 30, 1908.
Children:—*Born in Portland, Ind.*
   By first marriage.
—252   Fay.[8]
—253   Ray.[8]

214. SILAS S. STRATTON [7] (*Lewis F.,*[6] *Timothy,*[5] *Timothy,*[4] *Martin,*[3] *Serajah,*[2] *William* [1]) married **Mabel M. McFarland,** Nov. 26, 1896, and lives in Portland, where he is engaged in insurance and real estate business.
Children:—*Born in Portland, Ind.*
—254   Lucile M.[8]
—255   Erma W.[8]

218. JOHN CLARENCE STRATTON [7] (*Cyrus M.,*[6] *Timothy,*[5] *Timothy,*[4] *Martin,*[3] *Serajah,*[2] *William* [1]) is professor of mathematics in Evansville high school. He married **Allie Van Skyock,** Sept. 29, 1898. She is a daughter of *Elias* and *Mary A. Van Skyock.*
Children:—*Born at Mt. Pleasant, Ind.*
—256   Herman J.[8]
   Born in Evansville, Ind.
—257   Mary Lusetta.[8]

222. WILLIAM TIMOTHY STRATTON [7] (*Cyrus M.,*[6] *Timothy,*[5] *Timothy,*[4] *Martin,*[3] *Serajah,*[2] *William* [1]) graduated from Indiana University, and has been teaching eight years. He is now prin-

cipal of McCray-Dewey Academy at Troy, Ill. Aug. 25, 1905, he married **Daisy Thomas**, daughter of *Charles W. Thomas, Jr.*, of Corydon, Ind., and a descendant of *Wm. Marsh,* captain in the American Revolution. They are members of the Christian Church.

Children:—*Born in Red Key, Ind.*
—258 Charles William.[8]
Born in Troy, Ill.
—259 Carol Lusetta.[8]

232. Edwin E. Stratton [7] (*Chauncey,*[6] *Julius,*[5] *Harvey,*[4] *John,*[3] *William,*[2] *William* [1]) married **Ellen C. Palmer.** Lives at Southwick, Conn.
Children:
—260 Morgan Chauncey.[8]
—261 Edith May.[8]
—262 Lucy Alice.[8]
—263 Myrtle Irene.[8]
—264 Viola Maude.[8]
—265 Merton Oliver.[8]

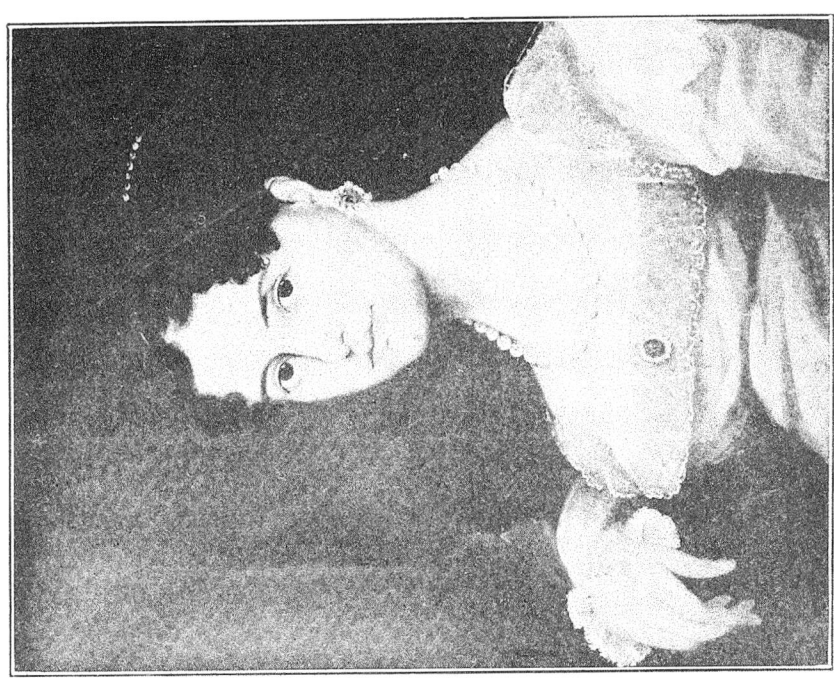

Senator John Stratton of Virginia and His Beautiful Daughter, Anne Gertrude

STRATTONS OF VIRGINIA
THOMAS STRATTON OF THE EASTERN SHORE

(*Chart E, Vol. I*)

*"For praise, that's due, doth give no more
To worth than what it had before."*
DEAN SWIFT.

AT Portsmouth, Va., are the oldest records of Norfolk County, going back to 1640. The first mention of a Stratton there is Jan. 14, 1669, when Henry Stratton, planter of Linhaven, sold to Edward Atwood 200 acres of land for 3,000 lbs. of tobacco. This to include "all houses, buildings, orchards, gardens, woods, pastures and everything whatsoever belonging to, or in any way appertaining to, said land."

The next record is on March 15, 1669, and this time Henry Stratton sells to Thomas Goodacre a tract of land in Linhaven, County of Lower Norfolk in "consideration of valuable satisfaction to me in hand paid." This land is described as "a piece of land formerly given by William East (?) to my brother John Stratton." The deed is signed "Henry ✕ Stratton his mark."

The Stratton name was not found again on the books at Norfolk for more than one hundred years, when in 1786 John Stratton, Sr., of Northampton bought land in the Borough of Norfolk, which in 1793 he deeded to his daughter Sarah Nivison.

In 1792, 1795 and 1797 are recorded deeds of land in the Borough of Norfolk bought and sold by John Stratton and wife Peggy.

And then comes this document which shows that a John Stratton was more than a half century ahead of Lincoln:

"Know all men by these presents, that I John Stratton of the Borrough of Norfolk and State of Virg[a] from full persuation that freedom is the Natural right of all Men, do hereby Manumit and absolutely set free a negro man belonging unto me named

Peter Wakefield, about twenty five years of age, so that hencefourth the above mentioned Negro shall be deemed adjudged and taken as and for a free person, to be at liberty to act for himself without let hindrance or molestation of me or any person or persons claiming or to claim, by, from or under me forever. In testimony hereof I do hereunto set my hand & affix my Seal this the 15th day of August 1795.

JOHN STRATTON.

At Hastings Court held the 28th day of Sept. 1795 this Deed of Emansipation from John Stratton to his negro Peter Wakefield and acknowledged by the said Stratton and ordered to be recorded.

Test. ALEX MOSELY.
C. N. C.

Which of the John Strattons of that period made this early "Deed of Emancipation" the compiler is not informed.

It will be seen that the records of the East Shore Strattons are yet very far from complete, and several sons are unaccounted for.* It is not unlikely some of them followed the trend of emigration toward "the west," and are the ancestors of untraced Strattons in Western Virginia, Kentucky and Tennessee.

FIFTH GENERATION

13. BENJAMIN STRATTON [5] (*John,[4] Benjamin,[3] Thomas,[2] Thomas [1]*) was born in Northampton Co., Va., Oct. 18, 1721.† He married **Elizabeth Stewart**, Sept. 12, 1746. They lived in Stratton Manor (*see Vol. I, pp. 142, 145*), where Elizabeth died Sept. 15, 1773, "aged 49 years less seven months," and Benjamin, Feb. 15, 1784. He owned several plantations besides the Manor plantation, and his will shows him to have been a man of considerable wealth for that period. The title of "Mr." prefixed to his name in the county records indicates the esteem and respect in which he was held. He remodled Stratton Manor about 1795,

---

* Perhaps the time will come when some Stratton of this line, who is in a position to make an exhaustive research in Virginia and in England, may complete these records and so add interesting data to the slowly accumulating store of Virginia genealogy.

† It should be noted that John Stratton [4] had also a daughter Anne, who married a Mr. Jacob. (See his will, p. 151, Vol. I.)

and his name may be seen to-day carved in one of the stones of the chimney. (*See picture, Vol. I*).

Children:—*Born in Stratton Manor, Va.*

—20 John,⁶ b. Oct. 16, 1748; d. aged 5 years.
—21 Ada,⁶ b. Mar. 29, 1751; d. Feb. 2, 1775; m. William Stoakley.*
—22 Susanna,⁶ b. Nov. 6, 1753; d. Dec. 3, 1753.
—23 Thomas,⁶ b. Jan. 3, 1756; d. Sept. 11, 1773.
+24 William,⁶ b. 1759; d. 1815.
+25 Benjamin,⁶ b. 1762; d. 1817.
—26 Elizabeth,⁶ b. Apr. 12, 1767.

ABSTRACT OF WILL OF BENJAMIN STRATTON⁵
OF STRATTON MANOR †

I Benjamin Stratton Sen, of Northumberland Co. Va. last will and testament.

To son William Stratton Plantation I now live on 585 acres, including 80 acres I bought of John Shaw, except 15 acres I purchased of John Wilkins, and his wife, which I give to my son Benjamin Stratton.

To son William Stratton a Pair of large Looking Glasses, horse saddle & bridle, My Still its head and worm, ½ doz. table spoons marked B.E., desk, chest, drawers, yoke of oxen, & steers.

To Son William Stratton negro, named Pleasant, providing he pays 20 pounds to my son Benjamin Stratton, and 20 pounds to my grand son Thomas S. Stokeley when 21 years of age.

Son William Stratton is pay daughter Betsy Stratton 240 pounds and if he refuses so to do my daughter Betsy shall have the land I bought of John Shaw.

---

*They had a son, Thomas Stratton Stoakley, whose son Thomas Stratton Stoakley, Jr., m. Sarah A. Scott, daughter of Thomas G. Scott and his wife Elizabeth (Nichols), daughter of John Nichols of the Eastern Shore. Their son, Dr. William Stratton Stoakley, of Cheriton, Va., furnished the compiler with the photograph of Stratton Manor and with much valuable information concerning this line.

The Stoakleys are an early East Shore family. The records show that Francis Stoakley (or Stockly) with wife Jane were there in 1634. They had a son, John Stoakley, born about 1657, who died leaving a widow Elizabeth, who married, second, a John Stratton, whose parentage the writer has not been able to trace.

† All the wills given of this line are from Northampton Co., recorded at Eastville.

To son Benjamin Stratton my Plantation on the sea side 284 acres, and negro called Luke, ½ doz. table spoons marked B.E. walnut desk, chest of drawers, gun, saddle and bridle, crops at sea side 2 yoke of oxen, steer one pair of Hand Mill Stones, and 40 pounds cash.

To daughter Betsey Stratton 4 negroes Priscilla, Joe, Stephen, and Lyhia, with 40 pounds cash, drawers, small trunk, chest, horse, riding chair, 1 doz. silver spoons, tongs, bed & furniture when 18 years of age.

The remainder of negroes be equally divided between sons William, and Benjamin Stratton, and grand son Thomas S. Stokeley, provided that such negroes as have made their escape to the British or other wise should return, in that case my desire is that such negroes shall be equally divided as above.

Personal estate not other wise disposed of to sons William, and Benjamin, and daughter Betsy, and grand son Thomas S. Stokeley, and son Benjamin is to keep daughter Betsey untill she is of age.

Appoints brother John Stratton, and son William Stratton executors dated 25. Sept. 1783.

BENJAMIN STRATTON, seal.

Witneses, William Stals,
John Hughes,
Littleton Jones,   Probated 13. April 1784.
Patience Stripe.

15. JOHN STRATTON [5] (*John*,[4] B*enjamin*,[3] *Thomas*,[2] *Thomas* [1]) was born in 1726 at Old Castle in the Parish of Hungers Creek, Northampton, Va. (see picture, Vol. I, p. 148). He inherited the homestead and lived there all this life. He owned several plantations, one of which, of 498 acres, was at Maggotty Bay. He was held in high respect and esteem by his fellow citizens. In 1743 he was a member of the House of Delegates for Northampton, and in 1774 his name appears on a committee of Safety for the same county. Feb. 15, 1754, he married **Gertrude Tazewell**, daughter of *William* and *Sophia Tazewell*. As early as 1786 he bought land in Norfolk, which in 1793 he deeded to his daughter, Sarah Nivison, and her son Wm. Tazewell Nivison, in consideration of the "love and affection he beerest unto them." He died in March 28, 1795.

Children:—*Born in Old Castle, Northampton Co., Va.*

—27   Sarah,[6] b. 1756; m. **Col. John Nivison;** their daughter

Anne Nivison married Hon. Littleton Walter Tazewell, member of Congress, and Governor of Virginia.*
—28 Annie,⁶ m. Griffin Stith of Northampton, married in June and died the following November.
+29 John⁶ b. 1769; d. 1804.

WILL OF JOHN STRATTON ⁵

I John Stratton, Sen. of county of Northampton in the Parish of Hungars Creek, make my last will and testament. I give to my son John Stratton the Reversion which I purchased of Col. Isaac Aery of the tract late the property of Hillary Sturgeon, and late I purchased of Henry Guy, called Town Field, providing he shall convey the Plantation in Maggotty Bay containing 498 acres which I conveyed to my son by deed unto my daughter Sarah Nivison, and my son in-law John Nivison for their lives, thereafter to my grand son William Tazewell Nivison. If he be dead then to my grand daughter Sarah Stratton Nivison, in default of my son conveying the said 498 acres I give the land before deeded to him to my daughter and son in-law.

I give to my daughter Sarah Nivison a small lot I purchased of John Goffigan, Jr. I give my son John Stratton all my other lands in the county.

I give to my grand daughter Anne Stratton Nivison, grand son William Tazewell Nivison, and grand daughter Sarah Stratton Nivison, the following slaves, Andrew, Babel, Jack, Zeck, Joe, Rose, and her children Joe, and Adah, and Tamer. I give my two grand daughters Anne Stratton Nivison, and Sarah Nivison the debts due from estate of Donild Campbell and my nephew John Stratton upwards of 1000 pounds. I give to my daughter Sarah Nivison the amount of Fletcher and Orpways note of 100 pounds, the debt due from Thomas Parson and Bennet Thompkins by bond out of which I desire my son in-law John Nivison shall purchase her a Chariot. I give my daughter and son in-law Sarah and John Nivison a new dressing table.

I give my son all my stock debts money not heretofore given to my son John Stratton.

I give to my daughter Lucy Stratton a Gold watch, to the value of 50 pounds and direct that my son John shall purchase it for her.

---

*The family records say that Sarah Stratton and Col. John Nivison were cousins, but do not explain how this relationship existed.

Appoints son John Stratton, and son in-law John Nivison executors. Dated 20th. of March **1795**.

Witnesses, Sally Diggs,   JOHN STRATTON, seal.
William Willis,   Probated 14th April **1795**.

17. NATHANIEL STRATTON [5] (*John,*[4] *Benjamin,*[3] *Thomas,*[2] *Thomas* [1]) was not yet of age when his father died in **1751**, and he chose his brother John Stratton as his guardian. He married **Elicia Hunt** about **1760**. They lived in Northampton Co. He died before **1769**, and his brother John was his Executor. His widow, Elicia, died in Dec., **1780**. She left a will in which she gives her estate in equal parts to her four children; also personal gifts to each,—to John, feather bed and furniture; to Molley, mahogany desk; to Nathaniel, feather bed, saddle and bridle; to Anne, riding chair, the white mare and furniture. In **1789** the estate had not yet been settled, and the three younger children brought suit against the older son John, who with William Jervis, Robert Bill, and Wm. Simpkins, made division of the negroes as follows: To Mary—Elisha, Big Peter and Patience. To Anne—Rose, Little Peter and Frances; to Nathaniel—Stephen, Tab, and Sarah; to John—Henry, Esther, and Luke. No land is mentioned.

Children:—*Born in Northampton Co., Va.*
+30   John.[6]
−31   Nathaniel,[6] was living in **1789**, after which the Compiler has failed to find any record of him.
−32   Anne.[6]
−33   Mary,[6] was living in Norfolk, Va., Jan. 14, **1817**, unm.

24. WILLIAM STRATTON [6] (*Benjamin,*[5] *John,*[4] *Benjamin,*[3] *Thomas,*[2] *Thomas* [1]) was born May 21, **1759**, in Northampton Co., and lived and died there. He married, first, **Esther Guy**, May 1, **1787**. She lived but six years after their marriage, and, Dec. 7, **1795**, he married **Elizabeth Robins**. He died Aug. 29, **1815**, leaving a will dated Aug. 12 of the same year.

Children:—*Born in Stratton Manor, Va.*
    By first marriage.
−34   John Grey,[6] b. Sept. 1, **1788**; d., unm., Sept. 15, **1815**, just one month after date of his father's will, and only 17 days after the death of his father.
−35   William,[6] b. **1793**; d. **1794**.

Top row (left to right).—Old Elm tree, Albert Stratton home; *Page* 113. Stratton homestead at Thompsonville; *Pages* 279, 288. Samuel Stratton house, built 1806, Craftsbury, Va.; *Page* 32.

Bottom row (left to right).—Church built on land donated by Jesse Stratton, abt. 1830; *Page* 289. Franklin Stratton home; *Page* 119. Aaron Stratton home; *Page* 417.

ABSTRACT OF WILL OF WILLIAM STRATTON [6]

I William Stratton of Northampton Co. Va. last will. Wills 900 acres of land to son John G. Stratton, but should he die without issue then to my nephew William D. Stratton son of my brother Benjamin Stratton, should William D. Stratton die without issue, then to his sisters Anne and Sarah Stratton, and if William D. Stratton my nephew should died with out issue before my son John G. Stratton, without issue then I give the aforesaid to my brother Benjamin.

To my wife as full set of morning, as she may choose, my Gig called Gallant, with horse and furniture.

To William D. Stratton son of Benjamin Stratton all wearing apparel.

Residue of estate to son John G. Stratton, and my wife. Appoints wife and son John G. Stratton and friend William Satchel executors.

Dated 12. Aug. 1815.

Witnesses, Polly Bancroft,   WM. STRATTON, seal.
   William Wingate,
   John Lumkins.   Probated 9th. Oct. 1815.

25. BENJAMIN STRATTON [6] (*Benjamin*,[5] *John*,[4] *Benjamin*,[3] *Thomas*,[2] *Thomas* [1]) was born Apr. 22, 1762. By his father's will he came into possession of a plantation of 284 acres "on the seaside." This was probably the Stratton estate known as "Old Plantation," upon a part of which the town of Cape Charles now stands.* The estate passed out of the hands of the Strattons many years ago—probably at his death. He was married three times, first, to **Susannah Henry**, June 6, 1789. She died in 1792 and two years later he married **Margaret Mapp Harmanson**, who lived only a year. Sept. 4, 1799, he married, third, **Esther Parsons**, daughter of *Thomas* and *Anna* (*Wise*) *Parsons*.† She died in 1815. Mr. Stratton died two years later, on Easter morning, Apr. 6, 1817.

Children:—*Born at "Old Plantation," Eastern Shore, Va.*
 By second marriage.
—36 William Harmanson,[6] b. Mar. 19, 1795; d. Sept. 10, 1806.
 By third marriage.

---

* It joined the Stratton Manor plantation at one time.

† Thomas Parsons was second cousin to Daniel P. Curtis of Arlington, first husband of Martha Dandridge, later the wife of George Washington.

—37 Benjamin Stewart,⁶ b. June 1, 1800; d. in infancy.

—38 Anne Wise,⁶ b. July 18, 1801; m., Mar. 26, 1827, **William Kennard**, formerly of Philadelphia, Rev. Stephen G. Gunter officiating. She was then of "Kings Creek, Eastern Shore, Va."*

—39 William Douglass,⁶ b. 1804; d., unm., in 1832. Came into possession of Stratton Manor upon the death of his cousin John G. Stratton (see will of William,⁶ No. 24).

—40 Sarah,⁶ b. 1806; d. 1827.

29. JOHN STRATTON ⁶ (*John,⁵ John,⁴ Benjamin,³ Thomas,² Thomas ¹*) was born Aug. 19, 1769, "being on a Saturday at about 2 o'clock P. M."† He was a lawyer and a young man of more than usual ability. At the age of 32 he was a member of Congress from Virginia, re-elected in 1803.‡ About 1790 he built "Elkington," which still belongs to his descendants, a home so long noted for its genial hospitality.§ He died very suddenly of apoplexy, May 10, 1804, while on a visit to his daughter, Mrs. Nivison, in Norfolk, and is buried in the yard of the historic old St. Paul's Church, where his grave may be seen, not far from the church, covered with a stone slab, about 3 by 6 feet, bearing an inscription to his memory. His death at the early age of thirty-six was greatly regretted, not only

---

*Upon the death of her brother, William D. Stratton, she became the owner of Stratton Manor, which remained in the possession of her family until about the time of the civil war, when it was sold by her daughter, Mrs. John E. Nottingham—though the part of the estate north of the Bayside road had been sold earlier.

† In the Stratton Manor Register (see p. 146, Vol. I) the records are all given in this quaint old style.

‡ A letter of his written in 1803 contains this: "Life in Washington is very dull. We have to go to Alexandria for amusement, and something good to eat."

§ See picture in Vol. I, p. 148, from a photo furnished by a descendant, Mrs. Thomas C. Walston, of Williamsburg, daughter of Dr. G. L. Upshur, who thus writes of it: "This view of Elkington was taken from the southeast, and gives no idea of the grounds, which are extensive and beautiful, containing many large and unusually handsome trees of many varieties, and which are bordered on the north and west by a pretty inlet from Hunger's Creek. Just north of the house is the family burial ground, where are graves of five generations. The outside doors have bright brass locks, 12 by 7 inches, which were imported from England when the house was built, about 1790.

by his family and personal friends, but by the people whom he had represented in various public positions. The *Norfolk Herald* of May 12, 1804, contains a long article on Hon. John Stratton, from which the following is taken: "Selected for the discharge of public duties by those who best knew his worth, in the execution of all these trusts he so conducted himself, so faithfully performed his part, as to show that their confidence had not been misplaced, and on his retirement from various public affairs, he always carried with him the grateful and willing acknowledgments of those whom he had served." See p. 148 Vol. I.

June 3, 1793, he married at Yorktown, Va., **Lucy Digges**, daughter of *Hon. Dudley* and *Elizabeth (Wormeley) Digges*, of the Eastern Shore. She was born Oct. 13, 1771, and is buried in the family burial ground at Elkington.* See "Elkington," Vol. I.

Children:—B*orn at Old Castle, Eastern Shore, Va.*

—41 John Henry,[7] b. Nov. 21, 1793; d. Sept. 13, 1794.
—42 Anna Gertrude,[7] b. Feb. 2, 1795; m., Feb. 6, 1811, **Dr. Jacob G. Parker**; d. May 28, 1883; buried at Elkington.†

Born at Elkington.

—43 Eliza,[7] b. Nov. 9, 1796; d. aged 6 months.
—44 John Nivison,[7] b. Dec. 21, 1797; a brilliant young lawyer; represented Northampton county in the state Legislature before he was of age; became a Mason at 21; was admitted to the bar at 22; d., unm., before he was 30.

---

* Dudley Digges was a member of the Council of Virginia under Patrick Henry, and a member of the Committee of Safety. He was a descendant of Sir Dudley Digges, who braved the Duke of Buckingham, and was committed to the Tower by King Charles I. He was twice married, his first wife being Martha, daughter of Henry and Martha (Burwell) Armistead.

† Many are the words of praise and admiration written of Anne Gertrude (Stratton) Parker—of her rare personality, her fine literary tastes and attainments, her exulted Christian character, her devotion to her church, and her many acts of benevolence. "Tender and gentle and loving always, she had her reward in the love and veneration not only of her own family but of the entire community," writes a descendant. (See her portrait which was furnished the compiler by her granddaughters, who still have the pearls worn when this portrait was painted.) Of her children, John Stratton Parker m. Anne Elizabeth Floyd; Sarah Parker m. Dr. George Littleton Upshur, who gave his life for others in the terrible yellow fever epidemic in Richmond in 1855; Anne Parker m. Alexander Thom of Norfolk.

—45 Edward,[7] b. Apr. 13, 1799; m. **Mary Ann Frances Wilson** of Woodland, Oct. 13, 1819. Their two children died in infancy.

—46 Sarah,[7] b. Mar. 9, 1801; m. **John T. Wilson**; d. in Baltimore, Mar. 13, 1875.

30. JOHN STRATTON [6] (*Nathaniel,*[5] *John,*[4] *Benjamin,*[3] *Thomas,*[2] *Thomas* [1]) lived in Norfolk where he bought land of Wm. Cooper in 1792 for £400, a part of which he sold to Samuel Pyron in 1795 for £100. In 1800 John Stratton and Abner Cox bought land in the Borough of Norfolk of Cuddy Dunn. In the same year John Stratton, Richard Green, with others, trustees, bought land for the Methodist Episcopal Church, and in 1801 the same trustees sold a part of this church property to Wm. Atkinson. He married (perhaps 2nd marriage) **Peggy Wilkins**.

In 1805 John Stratton of Norfolk paid to Mary Stratton $820, for which he stood indebted to her, "being her portion of the estate of Elicia Stratton (deceased)." The witnesses to this are Thomas Stratton and Littleton Kendall. About this date he seems to have parted with all the land he had owned in the Borough of Norfolk. His wife, Peggy Stratton, signing the several deeds with him, and in May of this year he sold at public auction various articles of household furniture. He seems then to be preparing to leave Norfolk and the compiler has failed to find again his name on the records there.*

Children:

—47 John,[7] b. 1780.
—48 Nathaniel,[7] b. 1781.
—49 Thomas, b. 1782.
—50 John, b. 1783.
—51 Robert,[7] b. 1791.
—52 Nathaniel W.,[7] b. 1798.
—53 William,[7] b. 1801.
—54 James,[7] b. 1802.
—55 Benjamin,[7] b. 1806.

---

* The births of his children are from an old Bible in possession of Miss Virginia Gordon (perhaps a granddaughter of Thomas Stratton, No. 49 [2]), and the writer understands that they are entered in the Bible as children of "John and Peggy Stratton." The compiler has failed to find anything more about them in Norfolk.

STRATTONS: 1. Samuel T.; *Page* 293. 2. Henry; *Page* 268. 3. William; *Page* 270. 4. Jeremiah; *Page* 258. 5. Nethaniel; *Page* 262. 6. Rev. James; *Page* 242. 7. Robert G.; *Page* 383. 8 and 9. Elizabeth and John, founders of Strattonville, Pa.; *Vol.* I.; *Page* 286.

THOMAS STRATTON OF PITTSYLVANIA COUNTY

Dec. 1, 1764, a Thomas Stratton received a patent for 400 acres of land on South Branch of Sandy Creek in Pittsylvania Co., Virginia. Three years later 292 acres were surveyed to him on North Branch of Sandy Creek.* In 1778 he sold to Jeremiah White for £50 current money, and in 1783 he sold 12 acres to Robert Williams. There is nothing on the county books to show what became of the rest of the land, nor does Thomas Stratton's name again appear on the records. His name appears as a revolutionary soldier in a recently printed report of the Virginia state library. In 1771 a John Stratton was witness to prove a will of John King of Pittsylvania Co. He came from a distance and received pay for four days' attendance according to law. He is not mentioned again. In 1780, Benjamin Stratton and William Stratton owned land on Sandy Creek, and they bought and sold land in the county for about thirty years as shown by the deed books.

In 1804, Oct. 6th, Benjamin Stratton, William Stratton and Armistead Stratton gave to Triphena Stratton and Elizabeth Stratton for $200 a deed to a parcel of land on the waters of Sandy Creek, containing 100 acres. And on the same date William, Armistead, Elizabeth and Tryphena Stratton, for $200, made a deed to Benjamin Stratton for 98 acres on Sandy Creek.

Sept. 9, 1805, Elizabeth and Tryphena Stratton of Pittsylvania Co., Va., and Owen Stratton of Davidson Co., Tenn., sold to John White for £107, 10s. 100 acres on Sandy Creek.

From the above we gather that Benjamin, William, Owen,

---

*This land was surveyed by John Donehue, who a few years later was appointed by government to settle Indian difficulties along the frontier. He became so charmed with the beautiful country, "beyond the mountains," that he came home and persuaded hundreds of families to go with him to Tennessee. He was widely known and it was not difficult to persuade many to follow him. From 1778 to about 1810 emigration turned toward Middle Tennessee, many families stopping in Kentucky, and we have seen that among these pioneers were many Virginia Strattons.

Pittsylvania was formed from Halifax County in June 1767; Halifax from Brunswick in 1752; Henry County was formed from Pittsylvania in 1776, and Patrick County from Henry a few years later. This division of counties adds to the difficulty and expense of genealogical work, for to do thorough work it becomes necessary to search the records of each county for wills, deeds, marriage licenses, etc.

Armistead, Elizabeth and Tryphena were brothers and sisters, and that Thomas was their father.*

Of Tryphena nothing more is known. Elizabeth married **Thomas Chambers** in 1806 and settled in Robertson Co., Tenn. Owen seems to have gone from Davidson Co., Tenn., to Buckingham Co., N. C., and was living there in 1808, when he sold to Wm. Wimbush 97 acres of land on Sandy Creek. His name does not appear again in Pittsylvania Co.

Armistead continued to live in Pittsylvania Co., where he owned quite a large estate. He died about 1840. Royall King was the administrator of his estate. The books show nothing as to how it was distributed, or what became of it.†

Assuming this to be Thomas Stratton of the East Shore line (No. 14, p. 148, *Vol. I*), he is designated as Thomas [5] in the following records of the descendants of his sons Benjamin and William. He probably lived in King and Queen Co. for a while after leaving the Eastern Shore.

[56.] BENJAMIN STRATTON [6] (*Thomas* [5]) was living in Pittsylvania Co. and owned land there from 1780 to 1808. The Revo-

---

* In the following pages the compiler assumes this to be the relationship, and it seems altogether probable that this is the Thomas Stratton [5] of the Eastern Shore, who was born in 1722 and whose name was not found on East Shore records after 1758. At that date he was in Northampton Co. and witnessed a deed there, though he may have moved from there a few years earlier (see pp. 148 and 149, Vol. I). Notice, also, that this Thomas of the Eastern Shore had two brothers, Benjamin and William, after whom, perhaps, he named his sons.

† The compiler has a record of a William Stratton who may belong to this family. He was born Sept. 1, 1801, in Virginia, married, first, **Mary Snow**; second, **Deliah Baldwin**, Jan. 10, 1825, a daughter of John Baldwin. He was drowned in Buck River, Tenn., in 1842. He is said to have had a brother Thomas, who married **Winnie** ——— and had a son, Wm. Brock Stratton, who went west. He had children as follows:

Williamson, b. Nov. 14, 1825. Left home soon after his father's death and was never again heard from by the family.

Ansel, b. March 3, 1826; d. in Green Co., Mo., Sept. 25, 1882. Has a son, J. T. Stratton, living in Bettena, Okla.

Armistead, b. Oct. 4, 1829; m. **Ann Brown**; received a legacy from Virginia after his marriage.

Mary Ann, m. **Henderson Bass**; resided in Bassville, Mo.

Thomas, b. Dec. 26, 1832.

Louisa, m. **Daniel Womback**; resided in Caddo, Mo.

Jamima, m. **A. G. Smith**.

William A., b. May 1831; m. **Sophronia Brown**; resided in Fair Grove, Mo.

lutionary records of Virginia contain this statement: "Benjamin Stratton, b. 1750 in King and Queen Co., raised in Pittsylvania Co., enlisted in Col. Stevens' Regt. for 9 mos., lived in Henry Co. when application was made for pension in 1831." The record refers to Armistead Stratton as a living witness; pension paid to 1833. He married **Eleanor** ———, whose name appears with his on a deed of 97 acres of land which he sold on Sandy Creek. Soon after this he bought a farm in Henry Co., where he died and where he has descendants still living.

Children:
+58 John.[7]
+59 Benjamin.[7]
And perhaps others.

[57.] WILLIAM STRATTON [6] (*Thomas* [5]) married **Edith Adams**. Her name appears with his on several deeds to land which he sold in Pittsylvania Co. The last of these deeds was in 1804, when they sold to Jacob Meadows, for $1,000, a farm of 300 acres lying on both sides of Sweetings Fork of Sandy Creek. They moved with their family to Logan Co., Ky., where they bought a farm, which is still in possession of their descendants. They were there as early at least as 1805, and were among the very first settlers of that county, which was then an almost unbroken forest with plenty of Indians about. The beautiful spring on this farm, famous throughout that region for its abundant supply of clear cold water, had been a favorite camping place for the Indians for untold years. Here Mr. and Mrs. Stratton lived to a good old age. Mr. Stratton died at the age of 92 years. Both are buried in the "Stratton Burial Ground" on this farm. His name appears on the pension report of the Secretary of War in 1835.

Children:—*Born in Virginia.*
+60 Benjamin,[7] b. about 1789.
−61 Annie.[7]
+62 William,[7] b. 1795.
−63 John,[7] of whom information is desired.

There may have been other children in this family.

58. JOHN STRATTON [7] (*Benjamin*,[6] *Thomas* [5]) was a farmer living not far from Martinsville, Va.

Children:—*Born in Henry Co., Va.*
+64 William Jackson.[8]

—65 Minerva,[8] m. **Thomas McGouldrick** and moved first to Bean Station, Tenn., and then to Maconpin Co., Ill.
+66 Marshall Henry.[8]
—67 Nancy.[8]

59. BENJAMIN STRATTON[7] (*Benjamin,*[6] *Thomas*[5]) died in early manhood, leaving a wife and little son who moved to Logan Co., Ky., where his uncle, William Stratton, had already settled.
Child:—*Born in Henry Co., Va.*
+68 Robertson.[8]

60. BENJAMIN STRATTON[7] (*William,*[6] *Thomas*[5]) came from Virginia to Logan Co., Ky., with his parents. In Nov., 1812, he married **Nancy Jolley**, who was born Mar. 12, 1793. She was the daughter of *John* and *Mary (Campbell) Jolley*. She lived to the age of 87 years, dying June 28, 1880. Mr. Stratton died in Sept., 1835.
Children:—*Born in Logan Co., Ky.*
—69 Lucy.[8]
—70 William.[8]
+71 John,[8] b. 1820.
—72 Elizabeth.[8]
—73 Louis.[8]
—74 Edith.[8]
—75 James,[8] served 3 years in C. S. army.
—76 Mary.[8]
—77 Jane,[8] m. —— Watson.

62. WILLIAM STRATTON[7] (*William,*[6] *Thomas*[5]) was born in Virginia in 1795. Came to Logan Co., Ky., about 1805, where on a farm he spent the rest of his long life. He died in 1886 aged 91 years. He married **Willie Williams**.
Children:—*Born in Logan Co., Ky.*
—78 Nancy,[8] 1824; m. **John Ellis**. Her daughter, Mary Ellis,[4] m. James Stratton (see *No. 95*).
—79 Susan,[8] b. 1830.
—80 Harrison,[8] b. 1832; d. in Illinois; left children. Where are they?
—81 Jackson,[8] d. unm.

64. WILLIAM JACKSON STRATTON[8] (*John,*[7] *Benjamin,*[6] *Thomas*[5]) was born in Henry Co., Illinois, in 1805. He lived and died in his native county where he was a farmer, and owned considerable real estate. He married **Arminda** ——, who was his widow in 1876.

Children:

—82   Dowell T., d. in 1865; unm.
—83   Henry Marshall, m. **Matilda Davis**; moved to Tennessee, near Bristol.
—84   Melissa, m. **Henry D. Handley**, of Axton, Va.

66. MARSHALL HENRY STRATTON[8] (*John,*[7] *Benjamin,*[6] *Thomas*[5]) was born Jan. 24, 1813, near Martinsville. His mother died while he was a small boy, and he spent the most of his boyhood in his grandfather's home. At 18 years of age he went tto live with his sister, Mrs. Gouldrick, at Bean Station, Tenn. In 1833 he went to Maconpin Co., Illinois. In 1840 he married **Rebecca Blackburn**. They rented a farm on Spanish Needle Prairie, afterwards purchasing the same, which is a part of the old Stratton homestead, which comprises a portion of the eleven hundred acres of Maconpin county real estate accumulated by them, "commencing with a capital of only stout hearts, willing hands, pluck and energy, and a determination to succeed." In 1870 they retired from farm life and moved into Carlinville, Ill. Here Mrs. Stratton died in 1875, and Mr. Stratton Jan. 13, 1898, "A citizen of the most exemplary character, a man of determined convictions and stout will, having many friends, and believing strongly in the principle, 'Do unto others as ye would have them do unto you.'"

Child:—*Born in Maconpin Co., Ill.*

—85   Mary J., b. 1841; m. **H. C. Anderson**; res. Carlinville.

68. ROBERTSON STRATTON[8] (*Benjamin,*[7] *Benjamin,*[6] *Thomas*[5]) was born in Henry Co., Va., and removed while young to Logan Co., Ky. From early boyhood he was the support of his mother. He owned a farm not far from Russellville. He married **Nancy Miles**, sister of Alexander Miles. He died in 1836.* Soon after his death his widow, with her five small children, moved to Maconpin Co., Ill., settling near Brighton, where several of her relatives had previously settled.†

---

* The compiler understands that the house which he built, and where his children were born, is still standing near Keysburg, Logan Co., Ky.

† Miles Station, in Maconpin Co., Ill., is named for them and there are many of this name in that region, and in Henry Co., Va.

Children:—*Born in Logan Co., Ky.*
- —86 Wesley,[9] d. in infancy.
- —87 Sarah Elizabeth,[9] m. **Henry Kendall**; d. in Pierce City, Mo.
- +88 Thomas.[9]
- —89 Eliza,[9] m. **John Rice Miles,** son of *Alexander* and *Pollie Miles*; res. Miles Station, Ill.
- +90 Samuel,[9] b. 1832.
- —91 Beverly,[9] res. Pasadena, Cal.

71. JOHN STRATTON[8] (*Benjamin,*[7] *William,*[6] *Thomas*[5]) was born in 1820. Married **Martha Smith**, daughter of *Littleton Smith*.

Children:—*Born in Logan Co., Ky.*
- —92 Benjamin,[9] m. **Artie M. Ellis.**
- —93 John,[9] moved west.
- —94 Boon,[9] settled in Ill.
- +95 James W.,[9] b. 1850.
- —96 Robert,[9] m. **Florence Adams**; res. Olmstead, Ky.
- —97 Emma,[9] moved west, probably Ill.
- —98 Sarah,[9] moved west, probably Ill.
- —99 Ellen,[9] moved west, probably Ill.

88. THOMAS STRATTON[9] (*Robertson,*[8] *Benjamin,*[7] *Benjamin,*[6] *Thomas*[5]) married **Elizabeth Elsworthy** and lived in Piasa, Ill.

Children:—*Born in Maconpin, Ill.*
- —100 Lily,[10] m. **Alonzo Florida,** of Jerryville, Ill.
- —101 William,[10] m. **Ada Gibbs.**
- —102 Charles,[10] m. **Harriet Appleton**; res. Pasadena, Cal.
- —103 Abner,[10] m. **Ada Jones**; Piasa, Ill.
- —104 Angie,[10] m. **Arthur Torward**; res. Alton, Ill.
- —105 Julia,[10] m. **Wm. Jones**; res. Delhi, Ill.
- —106 Thomas,[10] d. unm.
- —107 Eliza,[10] d. unm.

90. SAMUEL STRATTON[9] (*Robertson,*[8] *Benjamin,*[7] *Benjamin,*[6] *Thomas*[5]) was born in 1832 in Logan Co., Ky., and moved with his mother to Maconpin Co., Ill., while a small boy. He married **Mary B. Webster** and in 1882 removed from Illinois to Pasadena, Cal., where he now resides.

Children:—*Born in Montgomery Co., Ill.*
- —108 Samuel Wesley,[10] grad. of University of Illinois, 1884;

Prof. Physics and Electrical Eng'ring, University of Ill., 1885 to 1892; Prof. Phys., University of Chicago, 1892-1901; now head of Bureau of Standards, Wash., D. C. (See *Who's Who in America*.)

—109 Matie E.,[10] res. Pasadena, Cal.; artist.
—110 Olive,[10] m. **Arthur T. Newcomb**; res. Pasadena.
—111 Lucy,[10] m. **Glenn Hobbs**; res. Chicago.

95. JAMES W. STRATTON [9] (*John,*[8] *Benjamin,*[7] *William,*[6] *Thomas* [5]) was born in 1850. He married **Mary Ellis**, his second cousin, granddaughter of William Stratton.[7] They live on the old Stratton farm, wrested from the virgin forest by William Stratton.[6] They have a son, Alonzo Stratton,[10] who married **Myrtle Rust**, and lives at Ferguson, Ky., and has five children: Karl Murial,[11] Vera Genevive,[11] James Warren,[11] Kenneth Loyd [11] and Alonzo, Jr.[11]

EDWARD STRATTON OF BERMUDA HUNDRED

(*Chart F, Vol. I*)

"Thoughts and deeds not pedigree are passports to enduring fame."
                                                            SKOBELEFF.

BERMUDA HUNDRED, settled by Thomas Dale, was originally in Henrico Co., Virginia. In 1674 this part of Henrico was set off as Chesterfield County. Edward Stratton [1] was then living at Bermuda Hundred (see p. 213, *Vol. I*).

Henrico was one of the original shires into which Virginia was divided. It embraced all the land along the James River from Charles City to the Blue Ridge, including what is now the counties of Goochland, Fluvanna, Albermarle, Nelson, Amherst, Bedford, Campbell, Appomattox, Cumberland and Powhatan. The Strattons were early scattered throughout this section as shown by the records of these counties. In 1728 Chesterfield and Goochland were cut off from Henrico. In 1748 Cumberland was formed, and about 1777 the present line between Cumberland and Powhatan was surveyed. There were Stratton farms on either side of this line, in the "Muddy Creek" region. Many of the records of these counties were destroyed during the Civil War. In Goochland County many papers on file in the County Clerk's office were taken out by the soldiers and scattered over the floor. After the soldiers left they were gathered up and stored in the attic where some of them remain to this day, an undeveloped source of historic and genealogic knowledge.* The following deed recently discovered among unindexed papers at

---

* The following, copied from the records of Cumberland Co., are here given to show how the marriage license was recorded "in ye olden time" in Virginia:

"We Abner Seay and Reubin Seay acknowledge ourselves indebted to Rob rt Burk Esq., Governor of Virginia, in the sum of $15. to be paid to the said Governor and his successors, yet, if there be no lawful cause to obstruct a marriage intended to be had and solemnized between the said Abner Seay and Mary Stratton then this obligation to be void,

1. Stratton Spring; *Page 353.* 2. *See page 258.* 3. Ebenezer Stratton house (tavern) built about 1798; *Pages 45 and 81.*

Burial place of Zebulon and Jerusha Stratton; *Page 193.* Grave of Thomas Stratton; *Page 374.* Hillside cemetery on the bank of the Yangetse-Kiang, burial place of Owen Lovejoy Stratton; *Page 310.*

Richmond proves that Edward Stratton [3] of Bermuda Hundred, Virginia, had a son Henry, as well as the two sons, Thomas and William, given on page 218, Vol. I.*

Know all men by these presents, I, Edward Stratton of this parish County of Henrico, for and in consideration of the love and natural affection which I have to and for my son, Thomas Stratton, do freely and willingly give and grant unto my said son, Thomas Stratton, *one tract and parcel of land* situated in the County and parish aforesaid it being that land and plantation which I purchased of William Parker together with all the land in that tract and all houses and improvements of what nature or kind soever, the place being called and known by the name of Bakers unto him my said son, Thomas Stratton and his heirs forever but if he dies without issue lawfully begotten, then I give the aforesaid land and premises with the appurtenances unto my son Henry Stratton and his heirs forever.

In witness and testimony whereof I have hereunto set my hand and seal this day of   1729.

Edward Stratton. (SEAL.

Memoranum that on the 6th day of October, anno. Dom. 1729, quiet and peacable possession and seizure was had and taken in the land within mentioned in the presence of—

Edward Stratton.

Signed, sealed and delivered in the presence of us.
{ Jno. Redford Jr.
John Hutchins.
Mary Hutchins.

---

else to remain in full force. Given under my hand and seals, this 2nd day of April 1795.   "ABNER SEAY,
                                                                "REUBEN SEAY."

"Know all men by these presents, that we, Alex Cheatwood and Sam'l Hatcher, are held and firmly bound unto Tho's M. Randolph, Governor of Va., in the just and full sum of $150. good and lawful money of Va. to be paid to the said Governor or his successors upon these conditions, that if there is no lawful cause to obstruct a marriage intended to be had and solemnized between said Alex Cheatwood and Jane Stratton of this county—then this obligation to be void, or else to remain in full force and virtue; given under our hands and seals this 25th day of Sept. 1820.   "A. CHEATWOOD,
                                                            "SAM HATCHER."

* For the discovery of this deed, and for the collecting of much material on this line of Virginia Strattons, the author is indebted to the untiring efforts of the Hon. Thomas J. Stratton of Appomattox Co., who has rendered valuable aid in searching county records, interviewing many of the older Strattons, and soliciting records from others through correspondence.

This is probably the Henry Stratton who bought land of Richard Manning in Goochland Co., Va., by deed dated June 28, 1743. The compiler has found no other mention of a Henry Stratton at this date. The United States Census of 1785 gives a Henry Stratton, "head of a family of four," then living in Amherst Co. The books of that county contain no mention of him.

That Edward Stratton[3] had also other sons is quite certain although *proof* is still lacking. The above census gives a John Stratton then (1785) living in Amherst Co., "head of a family of twelve." The county books show that he was there as early as 1771. He belonged to the Virginia militia in June, 1781, and his name appears occasionally from that date to 1796, after which no mention of him has been found there. Also Suriah (or Seraiah) Stratton, "head of a family of seven," was living in Rockingham Co. in 1785. His name appears on a list of Revolutionary soldiers, Oct. 25, 1780. Of him the writer has no further knowledge.* It is not unlikely that these families migrated to Southwest Virginia and Kentucky.

On page 219, Vol. I, the compiler asked for information concerning William Stratton[4] (No. 10, Chart F), son of Edward Stratton.[3] This led to much correspondence and many hours of research. The records of many Virginia counties were searched, and many older Strattons interviewed. Finally, the will of

---

*These may be the ancestors of some of the yet unplaced Strattons who between 1790 and 1820 found their way to the newly settled regions in Southwestern Virginia, Kentucky and Tennessee. There was a William Stratton, b. in 1779, who married **Rhoda Bennett** about 1800 and settled in Shelby Co., Ky., at Clay Village, where he died July 16, 1853, and she three years later, Aug. 28, 1856. Their family Bible gives the births of twelve children:

  Daniel, b. Dec. 20, 1800 Asa Bennett, b. 1817
  Bernett, b. July 16, 1805 Jack, b. Oct. 15, 1819
  Charles, b. Sept. 2, 1808 William, b. Nov. 13, 1821
  Gabriel, b. Dec. 15, 1810 Martha, b. Feb. 10, 1824
  Henry Harrison, b. 1813 Nelson, b. Oct. 15, 1825
  Mary, b. Nov. 1815 Elizabeth, b. June 15, 1831

Mary, m. John Demaree.
Dr. Henry Harrison, m. **Julia Lively**; lived in Alton, Ky.; had one d., Margaret Ann, who m. R. H. PARRENT.
Asa Bennett, m. **Mary McDonald**; lived in Bagdad, Ky.; children: Wm. J., James C., Charles, Tyler E., Andrew J., Robert Y., Mary S., Elizabeth.
Charles (Asa B.), m. **Mary Thomas**; children: Mary L., Everett B., Wm. E., Joseph C., Robert, Tyler, Thomas.

William Stratton [4] was found recorded in Powhatan County, as well as other information concerning him and his family, and many of his descendants traced to the present generation. These are given on the following pages together with the descendants of his brother, Thomas Stratton.*

10. WILLIAM STRATTON [4] (*Edward,*[3] *Edward,*[2] *Edward*[1]) lived in Powhatan Co., Va., where he accumulated considerable property—owned many slaves and a large tract of land which was divided among his children, who, as they married, settled around the old home.[4] His will, a copy of which is given below, was made in 1760. No wife is mentioned, showing that she died before that date. The date of his death is not known, although in the will he describes himself as being "very sick and weak," he may have lived some years longer. Among his descendants it is understood that he "lived to a good old age," and was one of the prominent planters of that region. His will was not probated until 1780.

Children:—*Born in Powhatan Co., Va.*

+15a William.[5]

15b John,[5] one of the executors of his father's will in 1780. The U. S. Census of 1783 gives him as living in Powhatan Co., "the head of a family of six, and owning five slaves," and he seems to have been living there in 1795. The compiler found nothing more of him there, and has failed to definitely locate him elsewhere.

+15c Edward.[5]

15d Martha,[5] unm. in 1760.

+15e Richard.[5]

15f Sarah,[5] m. —— Rice before 1760.

+15g Peter.[5]

WILL OF WILLIAM STRATTON [4]

In the name of God, Amen:—

I William Stratton Sr. of the County of Powhatan being very sick and weak in body but of perfect mind and memory do make

---

* His land was in the northwestern part of Powhatan Co., just south of the James River in the "Muddy Creek" district, near the present line of Cumberland County. A large part, if not the whole, of Powhatan was once embraced in Chesterfield County. William Stratton [4] was deeded land on the south side of the James River by his mother in 1749 (see p. 218, Vol. I).

and ordain this my last will and testament, that is to say principally and first of all, I give and recommend my soul into the hands of almighty God that gave and for my body I commend it to the Earth to be buryed in a christian like and decent manner at the discretion of my executor, and as touching such worldly estate wherewith it hath been pleased God to bless me in this life with, I give and dispose of as follows, first I would that all my just debts and funeral charges be paid, also I give and bequeath to my beloved son William the place and house where I now live with two hundred Acres more or less of land adjoining and the remainder of the said tract of land that I now live on I give and bequeath to my two sons Richard & Peter to belong to them as the lines are already laid off to them and their heirs forever.

Item, I give and bequeath to my said son Peter one Negro boy named Sylex also a two year old bay Horse colt, also two cows and calves, two Ewes and lambs and four hoggs a Feather bed and furniture.

Item, I give and bequeath unto my daughter Martha a Negro Girl named Judith and her two children named Tom and David with her future increase also two cows and calves two ewes and lambs and a two year old mare (dark bay) also a feather bed and furniture and a weiving loom.

Item, I give and bequeath unto my daughter Sarah Rice a negro girl named Betty also a Cow and calf.

Item, I give and bequeath unto Mary Stratton daughter of Henry Stratton a feather bed & furniture.

Item, It is my desire that none of the negroes that are not mentioned to the children should be sold out of the family but appraised and equally divided among my children excepting only the two negroes George and Kate, George at my death I give to my son John Stratton and Kate I give and bequeath to my son Edward Stratton.

Item, I give and bequeath my still an equal part to each of my five sons, (Viz) William, John, Edward, Richard and Peter

Item, It is my desire that the remainder of my estate should be appraised and equally divided among my children provided only that if any of them should die before having lawfully increased he or she is exempted from a share of the last mentioned devisee.

I likewise constitute and appoint my son William and John Stratton and Robert Murray Executors of this my last will and testament and I do hereby utterly dis-annul all other former wills and legacies by me before named will'd ratified and confirmed this and no other to be my last Will and Testament.

In witness whereof I have hereunto set my hand and seal this thirtieth day of August 1760.

William Stratton (L. S.)

Signed sealed in the presence of
>Jesse Tucker,
>John Tucker,
>Thomas Tucker,

It is my further will and desire that my daughter Martha Stratton shall have possession of the old room of my new dwelling house during her living a single life also the privilege of tending forty acres of land convenient to the said house during the aforesaid term of her living single, It is also my will and desire that my son Peter shall have my dark bay Feasnought Mare instead of the Bay Horse Colt mentioned in the will and the said Bay horse colt to be disposed of and divided as the other articles.

15a. WILLIAM STRATTON [5] (*William*,[4] *Edward*,[3] *Edward*,[2] *Edward*[1]) was bequeathed the homestead on Muddy Creek, and two hundred acres of land by his father's will, and was one of the executors of this will in 1780. The U. S. Census of 1783 gives him as the head of a family of nine and owning thirteen slaves. The names of only six of his children are known to the writer. No will or settlement of his estate has been found, nor the date of his death.

Children:
- —38* Peter,[6] m. **Polly Street** in 1807.
- —39 Edward.[6] Probably this is the Edward who married **Polly Flippen**, d. of *Philip Flippen*, Aug. 17, 1807.
- +40 James,[6] settled in Tennessee about 1805.
- —41 Richard,[6] of whom information is desired.†
- —42 Frances,[6] m. **James Hix**, Oct. 20, 1788.
- —43 Sarah.[6]

---

* From here the numbers are continued from No. 37, page 224, *Vol. I.*

† This may have been the Richard Stratton who married **Jane Mary Daniel** July 5, 1814, and who died in 1817, leaving a daughter, Ann Richard, who inherited from her father a farm on "Muddy Creek," and who married **Dr. A. M. Cantrell** Sept. 3, 1834. Peter Stratton, as her guardian, gave his consent to this marriage. Jane was daughter of *Leonard and Mary (Spears) Daniel.* Three years after Richard's death

15c. EDWARD STRATTON [5] (*William,*[4] *Edward,*[3] *Edward,*[2] *Edward* [1]) married **Sarah Ligon** about 1778. She was the daughter of *William* and *Ann Ligon* of Cumberland Co. They lived in Powhatan Co. on a farm that was a part of his father's original estate. Here he was a prosperous planter, owning many slaves. His will, made in 1817 and proved the following year, is given below.

Children:—*Born in Powhatan Co., Va.*
+44 Thomas,[6] b. 1782.
+45 William.[6]
—46 Edward.[6]
+47 John Robert.[6]
—48 George,[6] m. **Savannah** ——.
—49 Sarah,[6] m. **Stokes Tunstill.**
+50 Moseley Ligon.[6]
—51 Elizabeth Ann,[6] m. **Wm. A. Martin.**
—52 David T.,[6] m. —— **Parker.**

John Robert and Moseley Ligon were known by these double names, and so wrote the names themselves though the father's will does not give the middle initials. The will indicates that the older sons had already received their portion of the estate. Thomas is known to have settled in Tennessee before his father's death. What became of Edward,[6] George [6] and David T.[6]?

WILL OF EDWARD STRATTON [5]

In the name of God, Amen:

I Edward Stratton Sr. of the County of Powhatan, State of

---

she married Alexander Montague. Her brother, Robert Daniel, married Mary, daughter of Robert Stratton (No. 34, Chart F, *Vol. I*).

The census of 1783 gives a Martha Stratton of Powhatan Co. as head of a family of three, and owning five slaves. She was probably a widow with two children. Whose widow was she? Her daughter Judith married **Rev. Daniel Montague** Feb. 6, 1787.

Other Stratton marriage licenses recorded in Cumberland and Powhatan counties are as follows:

William Stratton and Nancy Stegar, d. of Hantz Stegar—1801.

Henry Stratton and Sally Russell, d. of William Russell, Oct. 15, 1820. This license is signed by William Stratton, James Stratton, and Joseph Stratton.

Edward Stratton and Jane B. Sanderson, May 1, 1826.

Peter Stratton and Ann T. Bendurant, d. of Geo. Bendurant, Feb. 28, 1815.

Also a will is found in Cumberland Co. of a Richard Stratton, dated March 3, 1814. He mentions only his mother and brother Joseph.

EARLY STRATTON HOMES IN EIGHT STATES
1. Built 1798 by Martin Stratton; *Page* 322. 2. By William Stratton in 1810; *Page* 69. 3. Albert G. Stratton, 1847; *Page* 113. 4. David D. Stratton; *Page* 459. 5. Nathan L. Stratton, 1817; *Page* 236. 6. Jonathan Stratton, 1730; *Page* 116, Vol. I. 7. Peter B. Stratton, 1790; *Page* 377. 8. Richard S. Stratton; *Page* 240.

Virginia, being low in health, but of perfect mind and memory do make this my last will and testament:

Item, I give and bequeath unto my son Thos. Stratton all that I have formerly given him, likewise Seventeen dollars current money of Virginia to him and his heirs forever.

Item, I give and bequeath unto my son William Stratton all that I have formerly given him likewise Seventeen dollars, current money of Virginia, to him and his heirs forever:

Item, I give and bequeath unto my son Edward Stratton all that I have formerly given to him, likewise Seventeen dollars current money of Virginia, to him and his heirs forever:

Item, I give and bequeath to my son John Stratton all that I have formerly given him, likewise and equal part of all my land, at the death of my wife Sally Stratton, which is to be his whole part, he is to have no part in any of my negroes, to him his heirs forever:

Item, I give and bequeath unto my son George Stratton, the following negroes, to-wit: Dinah, Henry, Hannah and her child, (named) Metilda, to have immediate possession of said negroes, likewise one feather bed and furniture, to him and his heirs forever, also and equal part of all my land, at the death of my wife, Sally Stratton, to him and his heirs forever:

Item, I give and bequeath unto Stokes Tunstill and Sally Tunstill, his wife, the negroes I have formerly given unto him and his wife, which is now in their possession, likewise five hundred dollars to be paid to them at the end of two years, also and equal part of all my land at the death of my wife Sally Stratton, to them and their heirs forever:

Item, I give and bequeath unto my son Moseley Stratton, when he arrives at the age of twenty-one years the sum of Fourteen Hundred dollars, in negroes valued to him, likewise and equal part of all my land at the death of my wife Sally Stratton, to him and his heirs forever:

Item, I give and bequeath unto my daughter Elizabeth Ann Stratton, at the age of twenty one years, or sooner, if she marries, the sum of Fourteen hundred dollars, in negroes valued to her, likewise and equal part in all my land, at the death of my wife Sally Stratton, to her and her heirs forever:

Item, I give and bequeath unto David T. Stratton when he arrives at the age of twenty-one years, the sum of fourteen hundred dollars, in negroes valued to him, likewise and equal part in all my land, at the death of my wife Sally Stratton to him and his heirs forever:

Item, To the use of my beloved wife Sally Stratton during her natural life, I wish her to have the benefit of my land, for her support, likewise the use of my negroes which has not been before given away, during her life, but in case she should live until Moseley becomes of age, she is to give up so many of the negroes left her as will satisfy his sum mentioned above; likewise if she should live until Elizabeth Ann marries or becomes of age, she is to give up so many of the negroes, left her during her life, as will satisfy the sum left Elizabeth Ann; likewise if she should live until David T. Stratton becomes of age, she is to give up so many of the negroes left her during her life, as will satisfy the sum before given him.

It is my wish, at the death of my wife, that John Stratton shall have and equal part in all my land, and to have no other part in any of my estate whatsoever:

Likewise I wish all my estate both real and personal that has not been before given away, at the death of my wife, to be equally divided between my children here named (that is to say,) George Stratton, Stokes Tunstill, and Sally Tunstill his wife, Moseley Stratton, Elizabeth Ann Stratton, and David T. Stratton, to them and their heirs forever:

I wish and do appoint my sons William and Edward Stratton my executors to this my last will:—

As witness my hand this thirty-first day of December One thousand eight hundred and seventeen.

his
Edward X Stratton Sr. (L. S.)
mark

Attest:
  P. Stratton
  Thomas Tucker
  James Amonett
  Wm. Stratton, Jr.

15e. RICHARD STRATTON [5] (*William,*[4] *Edward,*[3] *Edward,*[2] *Edward*[1]) was living in Powhatan Co. in 1783, the "head of a family of two" and owning three slaves. He is thought to have married **Frances Moseley**.

  Child:

—53 Nancy,[6] m. her cousin **William Stratton** (No. 45), Dec.

18, 1805. Her uncle William Stratton was her guardian, and signed her marriage license.*

If there were other children, data concerning them is much desired. The father probably died before 1805.

15g. PETER STRATTON [5] (*William,*[4] *Edward,*[3] *Edward,*[2] *Edward*[1]) was a well-to-do planter in Powhatan Co. He married **Jane Baugh** about 1760.†
Children:—*Born in Powhatan Co., Va.*
+54 Peter Baugh.
+55 William.

It is understood that there were other children, whose names the compiler has not yet been able to learn. Any information in regard to them would be gladly received.

SIXTH GENERATION ‡

19. WILLIAM STRATTON [6] (*Henry,*[5] *Thomas,*[4] *Edward,*[3] *Edward,*[2] *Edward*[1]) married **Mary Haynes**, Dec. 3, 1793. They were then living in Bedford Co.
Children:—*Born in Bedford Co., Va.*
—56 Elizabeth.[7]
—57 Henry.[7]
—58 Sarah.[7]
—59 William.[7]

Sept. 23, 1811, John Hampton Stratton (No. 20) made a deed of gift of four slaves to the above children of William and Mary Stratton. It is believed that their parents were then dead. What became of the children?

20. JOHN HAMPTON STRATTON [6] (*Henry,*[5] *Thomas,*[4] *Edward,*[3] *Edward,*[2] *Edward*[1]) married **Mary Ann Turner**, June 31, 1788, Rev. James Mitchell performing the ceremony. They lived in Bedford Co. until about 1816 when they removed to Montgomery Co. Between 1810 and 1819 he sold several tracts of

---

* Among her descendants her name was generally known as Ann, but the marriage license recorded in Cumberland Co. gives it Nancy Stratton.

† There are graves of several of the Baugh family in the old graveyard at Bermuda Hundred.

‡ Continued from page 221, *Vol. I.*

land in Bedford Co. amounting to about 600 acres for which he received $12,000. In 1807 he was Constable for the county, appointed by the Governor, and giving bond for $1,000. He died about 1838.

Children:—*Born in Bedford Co., Va.*
+60   Henry,[7] b. 1789.
−61   Sarah,[7] b. July 26, 1791; m. in 1810, **William Adams,** who was born Oct. 27, 1778; d. in Virginia Oct. 17, 1847. They were the parents of 9 children.
+62   Thomas,[7] b. 1793.
−63   Nancy,[7] b. Sept. 29, 1795; m. —— Cole.
−64   Milly,[7] b. June 20, 1797; m. **John Robertson;** moved to Mo.
−65   Jane,[7] b. Apr. 14, 1799; m. —— **Tennison.**
−66   Milton Lee,[7] b. Apr. 13, 1801.
+67   Admire T.,[7] b. 1803.
−68   Kitty,[7] b. Apr. 22, 1805; m. **Thomas Combs.**
−69   Mary H.,[7] b. Apr. 24, 1807; m. **Geo. Cloud.** Lived on a farm near Kingsport, Tenn., where she died Mar. 25, 1889.
−70   Julia Ann,[7] b. Oct. 26, 1809; m. **John Stover;** d. in Mo. Apr. 15, 1868.
−71   John Hampton,[7] b. July 25, 1811; d. in childhood.
−72   Lucy,[7] b. Feb. 20, 1814; m. **Thomas Barnett,** whose descendants have an old family Bible from which these names and dates were copied.
−73   Liensy,[7] b. Aug. 12, 1816; d. young.

21. THOMAS STRATTON [6] (*Henry,*[5] *Thomas,*[4] *Edward,*[3] *Edward,*[2] *Edward* [1]) married **Elizabeth Leftwich,** Dec. 2, 1775.*
They lived for a while in Richmond, and then returned to Bedford Co., where she died a widow in 1815.†

Children:
−74   Susan,[7] m. 1st, —— **Cary;** 2nd, **John Cyrus;** d. in Columbia, Tenn., Aug. 4, 1892.
−75   Willey S.,[7] d. in childhood. (?)
−76   Janette,[7] d. in childhood.

---

* She was a sister of Rev. W. H. Leftwich, a preacher of considerable renown in that part of Virginia.

† They are both buried in the graveyard on the old Stratton farm, about four miles from Bunker Hill, in Bedford Co., Va.

—77 John,⁷ of whom information is desired.*
—78 Thomas J.,⁷ a school teacher many years in Va. and Tenn. An officer in the Mexican war; m. **Mrs. Nannie Vorhees**; no children.
—79 Patsy,⁷ m. **Thomas Leftwich**, son of Rev. E. H. Leftwich, about 1820; d. in Columbia, Tenn., in 1878.†
—80 Frazier Otley,⁷ m. **Zalinda Lynch Davis**; had one child, Frazier Davis Stratton,⁸ who died unmarried.
—81 Parnelia,⁷ m. —— **Whiteby**.
—82 Virginia,⁷ m. **Jesse Leftwich**.

23. ARCHIBALD STRATTON ⁶ (*Henry*,⁵ *Thomas*,⁴ *Edward*,³ *Edward*,² *Edward* ¹) was born in Bedford Co., Va., Sept. 15, 1870. He settled in Montgomery Co., Va., where he was a farmer and a member of the Baptist Church. He owned several tracts of land in Bedford and Montgomery counties. He married **Edna Dickinson**, Oct. 13, 1793. She is remembered as a woman of more than usual intelligence, and a devoted wife and mother. She was a daughter of *Joseph* and *Elizabeth (Wooldridge) Dickinson*. She died in Kanawha Co., West Va., Jan. 7, 1842.

Children:—*Born in Montgomery Co., Va.*
+83 Joseph Dickinson,⁷ b. **1794**.
—84 Amerett,⁷ m. **Philips Bouseman**.
—85 Mecca,⁷ m. **Nathaniel Fuqua**; moved west.
—86 Henry,⁷ d. in infancy.
—87 Fanny,⁷ d. in childhood.

29. JOHN STRATTON ⁶ (*John*,⁵ *Thomas*,⁴ *Edward*,³ *Edward*,² *Edward* ¹) settled in that part of Campbell Co. which in **1810** became Appomattox Co., where he was a farmer and where he died about **1848**. He married **Sarah Ann Towler**, daughter of *Absolom Towler*, Nov. 20, 1800.

Children:—*Born in Campbell Co., Va.*
—88 Absolom,⁷ b. Jan. 19, 1802; d. unm.
—89 Louisa,⁷ b. Oct. 31, 1803; m. Dec. 24, 1820, **John Eddington** of Roanoke Co., Va.

---

* Was this the John Stratton who had a son, Wm. H. Stratton, who married a Miss Nowlin and had a son, John Nowlin Stratton, who graduated from the University of Virginia?

† A John Stratton, cousin of Patsey, with wife Rachel, lived for many years in Columbia, Tenn., and died there about twenty-five years ago, leaving no children. Whose son was he?

—90   John Bennett,[7] b. Oct. 13, 1805; m. —— **Brock,** and had but one son, John Francis,[8] who went to Miss. about 1859 and is believed to have lost his life in the Civil War.
—91   William Madison,[7] b. Dec. 13, 1807; m. **Mary Gough;** only child, Sarah,[8] married **Rob't White.**
—92   Robert D.,[7] b. Nov. 10, 1809; d. unm.
Born in Appomattox Co.
+93   James Pleasant,[7] b. 1812; d. 1883.
+94   Albon M.,[7] b. 1814; d. 1875.
—95   Edwin D.,[7] b. July 17, 1816; d. abt. 1854; m. **Ann Eliza Carson;** had two children, Mary Agnes,[8] d. in infancy; Wm. M.,[8] m. **Mary Horsley** and d. without issue.
+96   Burwell C.,[7] b. 1818; d. 1868.
—97   Sarah Ann,[7] b. Oct. 18, 1822; m. **Dr. Robt. H. Cox** of Amherst Co.

The will of John Stratton [5] (No. 15, Vol. I) has recently come into the compiler's hands through the kindness of Hon. T. J. Stratton (No. 231). It is dated Apr. 6, 1705. It names each of his nine children, leaving a legacy to each. No mention is made of his wife, which indicates that she died prior to date of will.

31. WILLIAM STRATTON [6] (*John,*[5] *Thomas,*[4] *Edward,*[3] *Edward,*[2] *Edward* [1]) was a farmer living in Powhatan Co., near Muddy Creek Baptist Church, where he died about 1843. He married, first, Nov. 19, 1800, **Mary Tucker,** daughter of *Thomas Tucker;* second, **Edith Tucker,** daughter of *Jesse Tucker,* Feb. 25, 1825.

Children:—*Born in Powhatan Co., Va.*
By first marriage.
— 98   William.[7] What became of him?
+ 99   Linnæus Bolling.[7]
+100   Thomas Jefferson.[7]
—101   Mildred Ann,[7] m. **Archibald Flippin.**
—102   Henderson,[7] d. young.
—103   Robert,[7] d. young.

32. JAMES F. STRATTON [6] (*John,*[5] *Thomas,*[4] *Edward,*[3] *Edward,*[2] *Edward* [1]) settled in Fluvanna Co., Va., where he was a well-to-do farmer. Nov. 7, 1807, he married **Mary Stegar,** daughter of *Capt. John P. Stegar.* The house which he built at the time of his marriage was burned during the Civil War.

Children:—*Born in Fluvanna Co., Va.*
- —104 John P.,⁷ b. 1807; d. 1856; m. **Annie Seay.**
- —105 William,⁷ b. 1809; d. 1870; unm.
- —106 Martha,⁷ b. 1811; d. 1875; m. **Rev. Pleasant Howard.**
- +107 James M.,⁷ b. 1813; d. 1874.
- +108 Richard Hale,⁷ b. 1814; d. 1887.
- —109 Emily,⁷ b. 1817; m. **John Harlan.**
- —110 Frances M.,⁷ b. 1819; d. 1898; m. **William Daniel Stratton.**
- —111 Mary Page,⁷ b. 1821; d. 1901; m. **Samuel Tillman.** Their daughter, Mary Etta Tillman,⁸ m. **German Stratton** of Goochland Co. Whose son was he?
- +112 Thomas C.,⁷ b. 1823; d. 1896.
- +113 Robert G.,⁷ b. 1825.
- +114 Peter L.,⁷ b. 1827.
- —115 Albert Fontaine,⁷ b. 1828; d. 1885; m. **Martha Layne,** and lived in Bedford Co. He was a Confederate soldier.

33. DAVID STRATTON ⁶ (*John,⁵ Thomas,⁴ Edward,³ Edward,² Edward ¹*) was born Apr. 25, 1788.* He was a Baptist minister of Cumberland and Powhatan counties, Va. He died Apr. 24, 1871, and is buried in Macon, Va. He married, first, **Susanna Norris,** daughter of *John Norris;* second, **Jordina Hopkins,** in 1833. She was born Dec. 5, 1809, and died March 2, 1868. They were members of the Peterville Baptist Church, Cumberland Co.

Children:—*Born in Cumberland Co., Va.*

By first marriage.
- —116 Ann,⁷ d. young.
- —117 Mary,⁷ m. **Henry R. Page;** d. in Chesterfield Co.
- —118 William D.,⁷ m. **Sara Hatten,** and went to Alabama to live.
- —119 Thomas J.,⁷ m. **Catharine Pennilk,** and went to Alabama.†
- —120 Robert J.,⁷ was killed in Alabama; unm.
- —121 Crawford,⁷ d. in childhood.

By second marriage.
- —122 Susan J.,⁷ d. unm. in Richmond.

---

*See page 223, *Vol. I*, where the minus (—) should be changed to the plus (+) sign.

† It is understood that the sons who settled in Alabama left descendants. The compiler has failed to get into communication with them.

—123 Louisa C.,⁷ m. **Robert F. Hogue**, who died Jan. 11, 1896; res. Macon, Va.
—124 Emily J.,⁷ m. **Frank Hogue**.
—125 David C.,⁷ d. during the war; unm.
—125a Annie E.,⁷ m. **Greenville Withall**; d. 1909 in Amelia Co.
—126 Edmonia,⁷ m. **LeRoy Wooldridge**.
—127 Douglass E.,⁷ never married.

34. ROBERT STRATTON ⁶ (*John,⁵ Thomas,⁴ Edward,³ Edward,² Edward* ¹) married, first, a **Miss Haden**, second, a **Miss Adams**. He lived in Cumberland Co. where he died in Feb., 1859. His will, dated a month before his death, mentions his five sons and two daughters. What became of them?
Children:—*Born in Cumberland Co., Va.*
   By first marriage.
—128 Robert.⁷
—129 Haden.⁷
—130 Nelson,⁷ not mentioned in father's will.
—131 Mary,⁷ m. **Robert Daniel**, brother of Jane Ann Daniel, who m. Richard Stratton.
   By second marriage.
—132 William Daniel,⁷ m. **Frances Stratton**.
—133 Hartwell,⁷ a lawyer, who while a young man went to Nashville, Tenn.
—134 Parmelia,⁷ m. —— **Jackson** of Cartersville, Va.

35. PETER STRATTON ⁶ (*John,⁵ Thomas,⁴ Edward,³ Edward,² Edward* ¹) married a **Miss Huddleston**, lived for a few years in Buckingham Co., Va., and then removed to Tenn.
Children:—*Born in Virginia.*
—135 James,⁷ d. in boyhood, in Va.
—136 Martha,⁷ m. **Anderson Davidson**.
—137 Lucy Jane,⁷ m. —— **Pettit**.
—138 Elvira.⁷
—139 Amanda.⁷

36. DANIEL STRATTON ⁶ (*John,⁵ Thomas,⁴ Edward,³ Edward,² Edward* ¹) lived in Appomattox Co., where he was a farmer. He married **Elizabeth Walker**. He died in the fall of 1874.
Children:—*Born in Appomattox Co., Va.*
+140 John W.⁷

—141 Lucy Douglass,⁷ m. **Ethelburt LeGrand**; she was the mother of eleven children, one of whom, Elizabeth Woodson LeGrand, m. Peter L. Stratton (No. 114); she d. in 1901.

—142 Richard,⁷ d. in infancy.

—143 Mary Walker,⁷ m. 1st, **Richard Wilburn**; 2nd, **Col. J. R. Gilliam**; d. in Buckingham Co., Va., 1903.

—144 Emeline,⁷ m. **Col. James A. Hamner**; d. in Lynchburg, 1904.

—145 William Daniel,⁷ Confederate soldier; d. in service.

—146 David W.,⁷ m. **Mary Ronton**. He was a Confederate soldier and died in the service in 1862.

—147 Virginia Buck,⁷ m. **Preston B. Stone**.

—148 Sarah L.,⁷ never married.

—149 Robert B.,⁷ d. unm. in Appomattox, 1903.

40. JAMES STRATTON ⁶ (*William*,⁵ *William*,⁴ *Edward*,³ *Edward*,² *Edward* ¹) was born in Powhatan Co., Va., about 1775. He married **Dinah Russell** in Cumberland Co., Va., by license dated Sept. 20, 1797.* About 1805 he settled in Sumner Co., Tenn., buying a tract of land about three miles west of the present town of Gallatin. Here he became a prosperous farmer, and here he died in 1851, and was buried in the family burial ground on his own farm, where a tombstone stands to his memory. He and most of his family were members of the Methodist Church. He was in the war of 1812, 1st Lieut. in Capt. Hamilton's company of Tennessee Volunteers, and was at the battle of New Orleans. For several years he was sheriff of Sumner Co. In his will he provides liberally for his wife and leaves the rest of his possessions to his children.

Children:

+150 William.⁷

—151 Edward,⁷ married and moved to LaFayette Co., Mo. (Did he leave children?)

—152 James,⁷ of whom information is desired.

—153 John L.,⁷ d. before 1851, leaving a widow and several children. What became of them?

—154 Richard,⁷ of whom information is desired.

+155 Thomas Jefferson.⁷

---

*In the family she was always called "Dicy," and is so called in her husband's will. But the marriage license gives her name as Dinah Russell.

—156 Frances,⁷ m. **Benjamin Ireland** and lived in Nashville.
—157 Lutitia Russell,⁷ m. **Thomas J. Stratton** (No. 100), his second wife.
—158 Martha Ann,⁷ m. —— **Adams.**

44. THOMAS STRATTON ⁶ (*Edward*,⁵ *William*,⁴ *Edward*,³ *Edward*,² *Edward* ¹) was one of the early settlers of Davidson Co., Tenn. He was born in Powhatan Co., Va., in 1782. Sept. 5, 1806, he married **Elizabeth Swan** in Powhatan Co. She died March 10, 1808. She was a daughter of *Thomas Swan*, deceased, and Ferguson Taylor was her guardian at the time of her marriage. Soon after her death Mr. Stratton went to Tennessee and remained about three years. Returning to Virginia he married, Mar. 25, 1812, **Elizabeth B. Swan,** a cousin of his first wife and daughter of *Willis S.* and *Elizabeth (McLaren) Swan.* Three years later they settled five miles north of Nashville on a plantation, a part of which is still in the possession of his descendants. In Spring Hill Cemetery, once a part of this Stratton farm, is a stone bearing this inscription:

> Sacred to the memory of
> Thomas Stratton
> who was born in Powhatan County, Va.,
> on the 31st day of July, 1782,
> and departed this life in Sumner County, Tenn.,
> on the 30th day of June, 1854,
> aged 71 years, 10 months and 20 days.
> Generous, honest and brave.
> God's best gift to man.

Mrs. Elizabeth B. Stratton died May 8, 1837, in the 38th year of her age. Late in life Mr. Stratton married **Mrs. Elizabeth (Green) Hudson** of Sumner Co. Genial, social and generous, he had many friends, and the hospitable home on the old Stratton plantation was the scene of many pleasant gatherings.

Children:—*Born in Powhatan Co., Va.*
  By second marriage.
+159 Madison,⁷ b. May 3, 1813.
—160 Elizabeth,⁷ b. Aug. 23, 1815; d. aged 9 years.
  Born in Davidson Co., Tenn.
—161 Sarah,⁷ b. Feb. 18, 1818; d. aged 17 years.
+162 Thomas Edward,⁷ b. Dec. 28, 1820.
—163 Catherine,⁷ b. Mar. 23, 1823; m. Dec. 12, 1839, **An-**

thony Johnson Snow, son of David Snow, a merchant of Nashville from Massachusetts.
—164 Jane M.,[7] b. Mar. 16, 1826; m. **Kindred Jackson Morris.**
+165 Willis Swan,[7] b. Jan. 16, 1829.
—166 Elizabeth,[7] b. Aug. 23, 1832; m. **George S. Bolling.**

45. WILLIAM STRATTON [6] (*Edward*,[5] *William*,[4] *Edward*,[3] *Edward*,[2] *Edward* [1]) married his cousin **Nancy (or Ann) Stratton,** daughter of Richard Stratton [5] (No. 53), Dec. 18, 1805. He lived in Cumberland Co., where he owned two estates, near Muddy Creek, and where he was familiarly known as "Creek Billy" to distinguish him from his uncle and cousin of the same name. He was also called "William, son of Edward." He was one of the executors of his father's will in 1817. He died in October, 1852, three months after making his own will, aged about 70 years. His wife died two years earlier. In his will he names the nine children given below. He was an active, energetic man, "big souled, entertaining largely, having many friends, owned many slaves, to whom he was a kind master." He was a regular attendant of the Baptist church. Later in life he became very corpulent and during his last years, being unable to get through his carriage doors, he rode to church every Sunday morning in his ox cart, attended by his devoted servant. The home in which his children were born is still standing, though in a delapidated condition. The home in which the family later lived, and from which the daughters were married, is still occupied by his descendants.

Children:—*Born in Cumberland Co., Va.*
—167 Frances Moseley,[7] b. June, 1809; m. **Barister White** in 1847; d. Oct., 1872.*
—168 Richard,[7] b. 1804; m. **Martha Moseley** and lived in Chesterfield Co. To them 14 ch. were born (3 sets of twins) 10 of whom lived to be grown, 4 sons and 6 daughters. Only two of the sons married: Moseley,[8] m. **Judette Crosby;** Robert A.,[8] capt. in Civil War, m. **Rosa Lee White** Nov. 21, 1866; chn. James M.,[9] William,[9] Robert B.[9] (lives in Richmond), Franklin,[9] Mary E.,[9] Goldie,[9] Lillian L.,[9] John A.,[9] m. **Indie E. Brooks,** June 16, 1898; res.

---

*Their daughter, Ann Jane White, m. William Toler Rudd.

Moseley's Junction, Va.; chn. Rachel E.,[10] Julian A.,[10] Mary E.[10]

—169 Martha Jane,[7] m. **Thomas W. Lepford.**
—170. Peter A.,[7] b. abt. 1815; m. his cousin **Frances Stratton** (No. 178) and settled in Texas.
+171 Edward T.,[7] m. **Martha Tunstall.**
—172 William S.,[7] d. unmarried.
—173 James A.,[7] d. unm.
—174 Sally Ann,[7] m. **William Anderson.**
—175 Daniel W.[7]

47. JOHN ROBERT STRATTON [6] (*Edward,[5] William,[4] Edward,[3] Edward,[2] Edward*[1]) married Mary Frances Stegar and lived on a farm near "Muddy Creek Church," where he was a man of considerable prominence.*

Children:—*Born in Powhatan Co., Va.*
—176 Elizabeth,[7] m. **Richard Aston** and moved to Texas.
—177 Ann Bradley,[7] m. **Linnaeus B. Stratton** (No. 99), May 4, 1843.
—178 Frances,[7] m. **Peter Stratton** (No. 170), her cousin, and moved to Texas.
—179 Samuel,[7] m. **Sarah Jordan** and lived on the old homestead, where he died in Dec., 1810, aged 85 years.
—180 Martha Hobson,[7] became the second wife of **Linnaeus B. Stratton** (No. 99), Dec. 10, 1850.
—181 John,[7] m. **Callie Scrugs** and moved to Texas.
—182 Elvira,[7] m. **Ira Williams**; lived in Texas.

50. MOSELEY LIGON STRATTON [6] (*Edward,[5] William,[4] Edward,[3] Edward,[2] Edward*[1]) was born at the old homestead in Powhatan Co. in 1802. In 1830 he married **Mary J. Bass** of Chesterfield Co. After his marriage he lived for awhile in Cumberland Co. and then moved to Richmond, where he was the first Auditor of the city and where he died June, 1862.

Children:
—183 Mary Astoria,[7] b. 1838; d. aged 10 mos.
—184 Thomas Emmett, b. 1840; a physician of Richmond; Confederate veteran; president of State Board of Health; m. **C. Astoria Bass.**

---

*This little church (Baptist) was long a landmark in the northwestern part of Powhatan Co. and many Strattons worshiped there. A large brick church now stands on the same site.

—185 Edwin Melvin,⁷ b. 1840; d. 1897; a lawyer; served as reading clerk in state senate; Confederate veteran.
—186 Henry Clay,⁷ b. 1845; d. 1845.
—187 James Taylor,⁷ b. 1845 (twin); res. Richmond; unm.; member City Council, 1888-1904; mem. Legislature, 1901-2; mem. City School Board, 1901-3; Clerk Engineers Dept. City of Richmond; served in 20th Va. Batt. Artillery, C. S. A.
—188 Ida M., b. 1848; d. 1849.
—189 Frank Moseley, b. 1850; d. 1852.

54. PETER BAUGH STRATTON ⁶ (*Peter,*⁵ *William,*⁴ *Edward,*³ *Edward,*² *Edward* ¹) was born in Powhatan County, July 11, 1761; married, Dec. 6, 1787, **Mary N. Stegar,** who was born Sept. 2, 1764. They removed to Buckingham Co., Va., and owned a large and valuable landed estate known as Red Oak, a part of which is still in possession of descendants. He was a Revolutionary soldier, known as "Fighting Peter," and according to family tradition was present at the surrender of Yorktown and saw Cornwallis's sword handed to Washington. He died June 18, 1835. He and his wife are both buried in the family graveyard at Red Oak. His old house at Red Oak is still standing. It was remodeled in 1854 and has always been kept in good repair. It is owned by D. M. Ganaway, a great grandson of Peter Stratton. The house was originally built entirely of lumber hewed and sawed by hand and hand-made shingles.

Children:—*Born in Powhatan Co., Va.*
—190 Hantz,⁷ b. Sept. 2, 1788; d. unm.
—191 Mary,⁷ b. Dec. 31, 1792; m. **Barnett Booker,** owner of the Buckingham gold mine.
—192 Jane Baugh,⁷ b. June 15, 1797; m. **David Malloy;** d. Aug. 29, 1830.
—193 James Harvey,⁷ b. Sept. 17, 1801; d. in boyhood.
+194 Peter Baugh,⁷ b. Jan. 1, 1807.
+195 John,⁷ b. Jan. 2, 1808.
—196 William,⁷ b. Aug. 7, 1811; moved to Missouri in 1843 and died there Sept. 19, 1846, unm.
+197 Richard,⁷ b. Sept. 14, 1815, in Buckingham Co.

55. WILLIAM STRATTON ⁶ (*Peter,*⁵ *William,*⁴ *Edward,*³ *Edward,*² *Edward* ¹) lived near Peterville Baptist church, in Cumberland Co., where he was known as "Capt. William." He married **Frances Stegar.**

Children:
+198 Moses.⁷
—199 Mosely,⁷ moved west.
—200 German,⁷ a lawyer of Powhatan Co.; m. **Martha Denom.**
+201 John C.⁷
—202 Frances,⁷ m. Creed Taylor.

60. HENRY STRATTON ⁷ (*John H.,⁶ Henry,⁵ Thomas,⁴ Edward,³ Edward,² Edward ¹*) was born in Bedford Co., Mo., May 18, 1789. He married **Margaret McCrary Rayburn** and moved first to Franklin Co., Ky., then to Holly Springs, Marshall Co., Miss., and in 1846 to Memphis, Tenn., where he died Sept. 10, 1849.

Children:—*Born in Bedford Co., Va.*
—203 Mary Jane,⁸ b. Aug. 19, 1811; m. **Edgar McDavitt**; d. in Memphis July 26, 1876.
—204 Eliza Green,⁸ m. **J. H. Goodlett.**
—205 Nancy T.,⁸ b. Jan. 20, 1815; m. **Edgar McDavitt**; d. Aug. 22, 1844.
—206 Helen,⁸ m. —— **Burgess.**
Born in Franklin Co., Ky.
—207 Henrietta,⁸ m. —— **Goodlett.**
+208 John Thomas,⁸ b. 1824.
—209 Margrett Miranda,⁸ m. **C .W. Alexander**; d. near Auburn, Ky., Oct. 23, 1879.
—210 Sarah,⁸ d. aged 16, in Memphis, 1846.
—211 Augusta V.,⁸ b. Feb. 1833; m. **Ben T. Fleming.**

62. THOMAS STRATTON ⁷ (*John H.,⁶ Henry,⁵ Thomas,⁴ Edward,³ Edward,² Edward ¹*) was born in Bedford Co., Va., Oct. 29, 1793. He married **Nancy Donald** of Roanoke Co. in 1841 and moved to Missouri in 1852, settling near Otterville in Cooper Co. on a large farm.

Children:—*Born in Roanoke Co., Va.*
—212 Mary Agnes,⁸ b. Nov. 21, 1842, m. Nov. 5, 1861, **Hon. John D. Storke,** one of the most prominent men of the county, having served as state senator, collector of revenue, and in several other offices.
—213 Elizabeth R.,⁸ b. 1844; m. **M. E. Murphy.**
Born in Kanawha Co., W. Va.
—214 Pauline,⁸ b. 1846.

+215 John C.,[8] b. 1849.
  Born in Cooper Co., Mo.
+216 Thomas Henry,[8] b. 1858.

67. ADMIRE T. STRATTON[7] (*John H.,*[6] *Henry,*[5] *Thomas,*[4] *Edward,*[3] *Edward,*[2] *Edward*[1]), born in Bedford Co., Va., Apr. 29, 1803; went south while a young man, married in New Orleans and lived some years in Eufaula, Ala., where his wife died. Soon after her death he went west, taking his two boys with him, and was last heard from in California.

Children:

—217 Thomas,[8] of whom information is desired.
—218 Henry,[8] of whom information is desired.
—219 Louise,[8] an infant when her mother died; adopted by Dr. Dunn of Eufaula; m. **James Milton**; died in Eufaula, Apr. 25, 1877.

83. JOSEPH DICKINSON STRATTON[7] (*Archibald,*[6] *Henry,*[5] *Thomas,*[4] *Edward,*[3] *Edward,*[2] *Edward*[1]) was born in Montgomery Co., Va., in 1794; in the war of 1812, serving one year in Co. H, 22d Va. Infantry, and from that time to the surrender he was in the cavalry service. He was in the battle of Tuckwilles Hill, Gordensville, Liberty Hill, and others on the soil of the old Dominion. He married, first, **Theresa Gray,** about 1815, who died 6 months later; married, second, Oct. 30, 1832, **Mary Ann Buster,** daughter of *Claudius* and *Annie Buster* of Kanawha Co., West Va. She was born Apr. 25, 1812, and died in 1890. Mr. Stratton was engaged in mercantile business and while on a business trip in the west as agent for several large salt companies was thrown from his horse at Perryville, Ind., receiving injuries from which he died July 6, 1843.

Children:—*Born in Kanawha Co., W. Va.*
  By second marriage.
—220 Theresa Gray,[8] d. in Staunton, Va., May 17, 1893.
—221 Julia Ellen,[8] graduated with honors from Virginia Female Institution, Staunton, in 1857; m. May 10, 1865, **A. A. McAllister,** a leading citizen of Covington, Ky.* She died Nov. 23, 1906.†
+222 James Henry Steptoe.[8]

---

* Son of Capt. Thompson and Lydia Miller (Addams) McAllister and descendant of Hugh McAllister, Scotch Protestant, who emigrated to America in 1730.

† She left six sons to honor her memory and do credit to her teaching:

93. JAMES PLEASANT STRATTON [7] (*John*,[6] *John*,[5] *Thomas*,[4] *Edward*,[3] *Edward*,[2] *Edward* [1]) was born Jan. 8, 1812, and lived in his native county, Appomattox, where he was a farmer, and where he died in 1883. He married **Mary Ann Plunkett.**

Children:—*Born in Appomattox Co., Va.*

—223 Louisa M.[8]
—224 Nannie W.,[8] m. **Edward H. Moore.**
—225 Henrietta M.,[8] d. in infancy.
—226 Robert C.,[8] moved to Ky.; m. —— Shields; a Confederate soldier, 20th Va. Batt. Artillery.
—227 Ann E.[8]
—228 Mary Alice.[8]
—229 Ida W.,[8] m. Capt. **James W. Carson.**

94. ALBON M. STRATTON [7] (*John*,[6] *John*,[5] *Thomas*,[4] *Edward*,[3] *Edward*,[2] *Edward* [1]) was a farmer of Appomattox Co., Va. He was born Jan. 3, 1814, and died July 18, 1875. He married, May 6, 1840, **Sarah Ann Woodson,** only child of *Capt. Edson Woodson* of Campbell Co.

Children:—*Born at Spanish Oaks, Va.*

—230 Mary Agnes,[8] b. July 27, 1841; m. **John O. Thornhill** Nov. 14, 1864.
+231 Thomas John,[8] b. 1843.
—232 Sarah Elizabeth,[8] b. Feb. 18, 1845; m. Oct. 31, 1866, **Rev. Josiah Thornhill** of Campbell Co.
—233 James Madison,[8] b. Feb. 1, 1847; a Confederate soldier; d. unm.
—234 Emma Martha,[8] b. June 14, 1849; m. **Thomas O. Davidson** Nov. 17, 1880; d. Mar. 12, 1889.
—235 Sterling Crawford,[8] b. Aug. 27, 1851; member Va. leg-

Joseph T. McAllister, attorney of Hot Springs, Va., author of several books on Virginia History; Wm. M. McAllister of Covington, Ky., merchant, vice president of Va. Fruit Growers Association, director Covington National Bank, etc.; Dr. J. Gray McAllister, Professor of Biblical Theology in Presby. Theological Seminary, Louisville, Ky.; Adams Stratton McAllister, graduate Penn. State College, received degree Ph.D. from Cornell, author of several works on scientific subjects, editor of *Electrical World,* New York City; Hugh M. McAllister, writer and business man of Covington; Julian R. McAllister, a successful merchant of Covington. To Drs. J. G. and A. S. McAllister the writer is indebted for much help on this branch of Strattons. The former is the author of an admirable pamphlet on McAllister-Stratton family history; the latter has contributed much to genealogical lore by his "Descendants of John Thompson" and other compilations.

STRATTONS: 1. David G; *Page* 316. 2. Richard H.; *Page* 382. 3. Henry B.; *Page* 70. 4. Zaccheus; *Page* 440. 5. William F.; *Page* 110. 6. Benjamin; *Page* 412. 7. Horace (b 1806); *Page* 32. 8. Asa B.; *Page* 216. 9. William (No. 62); *Page* 354.

islature 1893-1898; for 8 years member Board of Supervisors of Appomattox Co.; served 8 years as clerk in State Dept. Agriculture; m. **Lena M. Myers** in 1896; their only child, John Myers,[9] died in infancy.

—236 Gillette Whitfield,[8] b. Aug. 3, 1855.

96. BURWELL CHURCHILL STRATTON[7] (*John,*[6] *John,*[5] *Thomas,*[4] *Edward,*[3] *Edward,*[2] *Edward*[1]) was born June 27, 1818. He was a Methodist minister. He married, first, **Demarius Branch**; second, **Emily Wilson**. He died about 1868.
Children:
—237 Roberta F.,[8] m. **Rev. S. T. Thornhill**.
+238 Richard Whitfield.[8]

99. LINNÆUS BOLLING STRATTON[7] (*William,*[6] *John,*[5] *Thomas,*[4] *Edward,*[3] *Edward,*[2] *Edward*[1]), b. Dec., 1805; d. 1883; lived on his father's homestead in Powhatan Co., Va. He married, first, **Ann Bradley Stratton**, Apr. 27, 1841; second, **Martha Hobson Stratton**, both daughters of *John R. Stratton* (No. 47).
Children:—*Born in Powhatan Co., Va.*
By first marriage.
—239 Marcella Jane,[8] d. unm.
—240 Mary Hobson,[8] m. **Spencer Carter Palmore**; res. Trenholm, Va.
By second marriage.
—241 Adda Bolling,[8] m. **Shelby Smith** of Richmond.
—242 Lelia Martha,[8] d. unm.
+243 William Robert.[8]

100. THOMAS JEFFERSON STRATTON[7] (*William,*[6] *John,*[5] *Thomas,*[4] *Edward,*[3] *Edward,*[2] *Edward*[1]) was born in Powhatan Co., Va., about 1800. In 1823 he married **Nancy Dillon**, daughter of *John Dillon*, and the following year moved to Tennessee, settling in Smith Co., about 40 miles up the Cumberland river from Nashville. Here he became a well-to-do farmer. Here his wife died and in 1843 he married **Latitia Russell Stratton** (No. 157) and in 1852 sold his farm and removed to Shelby Co., Tenn., near Memphis, where he died in 1870.
Children:—*Born in Smith Co., Tenn.*
—244 Winston Henderson,[8] m. **Sallie Waldron** in 1857; d. in Memphis in 1864.

—245 Thomas Tucker,[8] d. in Memphis about **1902**.
—246 William Dillon,[8] res. Birmingham, Ala.
—247 James Henry,[8] m. **Marcie Childs**, **1872**; d. in Memphis about **1877**.
+248 Beaumont Macon.[8]
—249 Martin Van Buren,[8] m. **Mary Smith**, **1875**; d. in Capleville, Tenn., **1903**.
—250 Cylias,[8] killed at the battle of Atlanta, July 22, **1864**.
—251 Venora Ann,[8] m. **Dr. Edwin D. Mitchell**, **1869**.
Born in Shelby Co.
—252 Frank Malone,[8] m. **Della Beeker**, **1884**; d. in Memphis, **1904**.
—253 Linnie Donaldson,[8] m. **Alton F. Thompson**, **1879**.
—254 Robert Lee,[8] m. **Daisy Steel**, **1887**.
—255 Elizabeth,[8] m. **Joseph H. Turner**, **1897**.

107. JAMES MONROE STRATTON [7] (*James,*[6] *John,*[5] *Thomas,*[4] *Edward,*[3] *Edward,*[2] *Edward* [1]), born in **1813**; died March 13, **1889**, in Fluvana Co., Va. He married **Annie Snoddy**, who died Sept. 11, **1894**.

Children:—*Born near Columbia, Fluvana Co., Va.*
—256 Jennie Ann,[8] m. **Robert Bowles** of Fluvana Co.; res. New York City.
—257 Philip James,[8] m. **Nannie Martin**; d. at Howardville, Va., Sept. 6, **1902**; child, Philip.[9]
—258 Charles Wesley,[8] m. **Emma Woodruff** Sept. 6, **1882**; child, Maud Elizabeth.[9]
+259 Lewis Bransford.[8]
—260 Mary,[8] m. **J. Willard McGhee**.
—261 Joseph P.,[8] conductor on C. & O. Rd.
—262 Edward L.,[8] b. July 5, **1867**; m. **Lennie Carter** Apr. 23, **1896**; res. Richmond, Va.; no children.

108. RICHARD HALE STRATTON [7] (*James,*[6] *John,*[5] *Thomas,*[4] *Edward,*[3] *Edward,*[2] *Edward* [1]) was born Apr. 10, **1814**. Dec. 9, **1838**, he married **Annie Eliza Brown**, who was born in Amelia Co., Va., Dec. 15, **1810**. They lived in Lexington, Va., for a few years, then in Staunton, and then removed to Albemarle Co. where he owned considerable property and was a well-to-do farmer and contractor. He died in Gordansville, Va., June 4, **1887**. His wife died in January of the same year.

Children:
- −263 Mary Ella, m. **Joseph Jackson Hopkins** Dec., 1857; he was b. in York, Pa., in 1831.
- −264 John James,[8] d., unm., in Lynchburg, in R. R. service; a Confederate soldier serving through the entire period of the war.
- +265 Richard Henry, b. 1844.
- −266 Susie Alice, m. **John M. Coulter** Nov. 14, 1871, and resides in Clarksville, Tenn.
- −267 Annie Eliza, m. **S. L. Fulks**, May 5, 1870; res. Manchester, Va.
- +268 Maurice Anderson.

112. THOMAS C. STRATTON[7] (*James,*[6] *John,*[5] *Thomas,*[4] *Edward,*[3] *Edward,*[2] *Edward*[1]) was born in 1823 and died in Buena Vista, Va., Sept. 30, 1893. He married in 1847 **Elizabeth MacKey McCorkle,** daughter of *John* and *Sarah* (*Cunningham*) *McCorkle,* who died Feb. 12, 1893. He was a soldier in the Confederate army.

Children:—*Born in Oakland, Rockbridge Co., Va.*
- −269 Sarah Harris,[8] m. **James Tate McClung** in 1873; res. Buena Vista.
- −270 John William,[8] m. **Annie Lease** of Burlington, Iowa, and died without issue in Springfield, Ill., in 1878.
- −271 Staunton Field,[8] d. in infancy.
- −272 James Francis,[8] m. **Mattie E. Dixon**; res. Buena Vista, Va.; child, Edith Miller.[9]
- +273 Albert Waggoner.[8]
- +274 Harry Harlan.[8]
- +275 George Baxter.[8]
- −276 Lucy Anna,[8] m. **Wm. F. Pettyjohn** of Lynchburg.

113. ROBERT G. STRATTON[7] (*James,*[6] *John,*[5] *Thomas,*[4] *Edward,*[3] *Edward,*[2] *Edward*[1]), born in 1825; married **Virginia C. Ast**, and resided in Staunton, Va., where he died in 1904.

Children:—*Born in Staunton, Va.*
- −277 James Edward,[8] m. **Annie Lee Deal**; res. McKinney, Texas; ch: Elmer,[9] Virginia Margaret,[9] Robert G.[9]
- +278 Robert L.[8]
- −279 Fannie M.,[8] m. **Rev. Robert Lee Fultz.**

114. PETER LEE STRATTON[7] (*James,*[6] *John,*[5] *Thomas,*[4] *Edward,*[3] *Edward,*[2] *Edward*[1]), born Apr. 24, 1827; m. Dec. 22,

1853, Elizabeth Woodson LeGrand, whose mother was *Lucy Douglass Stratton* (No. 141); resided at Spanish Oaks, Va., where he died Jan. 21, 1910, and his wife Oct. 5, 1911. He was a Confederate soldier, provost guard at Lynchburg.

Children:—*Born in Appomattox Co., Va.*
- −280 Laura A.,[8] b. June 18, 1856; m. **D. D. Isbell** of Lynchburg.
- +281 Chesley Melvin.[8]
- −282 Mary Lucy,[8] m. **John B. Drinkard** Dec. 25, 1880; res. Lynchburg.
- +283 Ethelbert Marshall,[8] m. **Bruce Robertson** Dec. 16, 1891.
- −284 Jas. Albert,[8] m. **Besse W. Le Grand** June 29, 1904; child, Frances Walker.[9]
- −285 Della H.[8]
- −286 H. Hartwell.[8]

140. JOHN W. STRATTON [7] (*Daniel,*[6] *John,*[5] *Thomas,*[4] *Edward,*[3] *Edward,*[2] *Edward*[1]) was a farmer of Appomattox Co. He married **Martha Woodson**. He was a Confederate soldier in 19th Va. Battalion Artillery.

Children:—*Born in Appomattox Co., Va.*
- −287 William Walker,[8] m. **Ann Hughes**; resided in Buckingham Co.; no children.
- −288 John Daniel,[8] d. unm.
- −289 Jacob Woodson,[8] a Confederate soldier; wounded at the battle of Seven Pines.
- −290 Lesley Combs.[8]
- −291 Henry.[8]
- −292 Richard,[8] Confederate soldier; killed at the battle of the Wilderness.
- −293 Robert M.,[8] went to Missouri and married there.
- −294 Scott.[8]

150. WILLIAM STRATTON [7] (*James,*[6] *William,*[5] *William,*[4] *Edward,*[3] *Edward,*[2] *Edward*[1]) was born in Powhatan Co., Va., and moved with his parents to Sumner Co., Tenn., while a small boy. He married **Bettie** —— and lived at Gallatin, where he owned considerable property.

Children:
- +295 John Armfield.[8]
- −296 Moseley H.[8]

—297 Thomas.[8]
—298 Cherry.[8]
—299 Mary.[8]

The author would be glad to get into communication with some one of this family.

155. THOMAS JEFFERSON STRATTON [7] (*James,*[6] *William,*[5] *William,*[4] *Edward,*[3] *Edward,*[2] *Edward* [1]) was born in Sumner Co., Tenn., Aug. 5, 1817. He was a soldier in the Florida war. May 10, 1838, he married **Caroline M. Golladay.** They were married by Rev. Geo. Donnell in the Cumberland Presbyterian Church at Lebanon, Tenn. She was born Mar. 16, 1813, and died Aug. 15, 1865. She was a daughter of *Isaac* and *Elizabeth* (*Shall*) *Golladay,* who were married in 1804 in Greensburg, Westmoreland Co., Pa. In August, 1869, Mr. Stratton married **Mrs. Fannie (Watkins) Helm,** widow of Henry Helm. She died in Nashville, Mar. 23, 1909. Mr. Stratton was a merchant of Lebanon. Coming there in early manhood, by his energy and integrity he built up an extensive trade, reaching far into the country around Lebanon. He bought large quantities of goods, going East to Philadelphia, New York and other cities for them. There being no railroads in that section, the goods were brought down the Ohio River and up the Cumberland to Nashville, and then by wagon or stage to Lebanon. The old red stage coach which brought passengers, mail and express from Nashville, with its driver on top blowing his bugle and driving four, six and sometimes eight horses, was a picturesque scene of those pioneer days. Later Mr. Stratton, in connection with his son, Samuel G. Stratton, organized the Bank of Lebanon and was its president until his death, Jan. 18, 1885.

Children:—*Born in Lebanon, Tenn.*

By first marriage.

+300   Isaac Golladay.[8]
+301   James Edward.[8]
+302   Samuel Golladay.[8]
+303   Henry Thomas.[8]

By second marriage.

—304   Florence Russell,[8] b. July 4, 1870; m. Mar. 30, 1892, **Fontaine De G. Daniel.**

159. MADISON STRATTON [7] (*Thomas,*[6] *Edward,*[5] *William,*[4] *Edward,*[3] *Edward,*[2] *Edward* [1]) was born in Powhatan Co., Va., May

3, 1813. He was but two years old when his parents moved to Tennessee. He was a merchant and lumber dealer in Nashville, where he died Dec. 15, 1898. He married, first, **Mary Snow,** daughter of *David Snow;* second, **Elizabeth Hawks**; third, **Anna Whiterker.**

Children:—*Born in Nashville, Tenn.*
By first marriage.

- —305   Amanda Elizabeth,[8] m. **Hampton J. Cheney**; res. Nashville, Tenn.
- +306   David Thomas,[8] b. 1838.
- +307   William Oliver,[8] b. 1840.
- —308   Katherine,[8] m. **W. C. Dibrell** Nov. 11, 1868; res. Nashville.
- —309   Madison, Jr.,[8] m. **Ellen McKenney**; res. Nashville; child, Beverly McKenney.[9]
- —310   George,[8] m. **Louise Lanier** Feb. 13, 1883; no children.
- —311   Benjamin Frank,[8] res. Nashville; Dep. Sheriff; m. Oct. 9, 1883, **Mary Garrett.** They have one child, Mary,[9] who married **Rufus Payne.**

162. THOMAS EDWARD STRATTON [7] (*Thomas,*[6] *Edward,*[5] *William,*[4] *Edward,*[3] *Edward,*[2] *Edward*[1]) married **Sarah Mourning Morris** Nov. 6, 1844. He was a business man of Nashville.

Children:—*Born in Nashville, Tenn.*
- +312   Moseley Thomas.[8]
- —313   Adeene,[8] m. **John Kennedy** Feb. 15, 1877.
- —314   Carrie,[8] m. **William Burnet** Feb. 19, 1880.

165. WILLIS SWAN STRATTON [7] (*Thomas,*[6] *Edward,*[5] *William,*[4] *Edward,*[3] *Edward,*[2] *Edward*[1]) was born in Nashville Jan. 16, 1829. He married **Susan E. Hopson.** He died in 1873.

Children:—*Born in Hopkinsville, Ky.*
- —315   Susie,[8] m. **Joseph Richmond.**
  Born in Nashville.
- —316   Josephine Holeman,[8] b. June 28, 1882; m. **Henry Collier Benargh,** grandson of *Gov. Collier* of Alabama; res. Nashville.
  Born in Knoxville, Tenn.
- —317   Annie Kate,[8] m. 1st, in Nashville, Nov. 13, 1878, **Charels K. Hudson;** 2d, in Los Angeles, Aug. 26, 1901, **Geo. W. Bayley.**
  Born in Hopkinsville, Ky.
- —318   T. Matt,[8] m. **Elizabeth Cree** of Detroit, Mich.

171. EDWARD T. STRATTON [7] (*William*,[6] *Edward*,[5] *William*,[4] *Edward*,[3] *Edward*,[2] *Edward*[1]) lived in Cumberland Co. where he was a farmer. He married **Martha Ann Baldwin Tunstill** Oct. 6, 1841.

Children:—*Born in Cumberland Co., Va.*

—319 Virginia Ann,[8] b. Mar. 12, 1842; d., unm., Aug. 12, 1893.
—320 Thomas Henry,[8] m. **Bettie James Catterton** May 17, 1890; a farmer of Charlottesville, Va., where he died Aug. 3, 1902.
—321 Martha Alice,[8] resides at Free Union, Va.
—322 Sarah Elizabeth,[8] resides at Free Union, Va.
—323 Edward Emmett,[8] m. **Henrietta Phillips**, Sept. 14, 1831.

194. PETER BAUGH STRATTON [7] (*Peter B.*,[6] *Peter*,[5] *William*,[4] *Edward*,[3] *Edward*,[2] *Edward*[1]) was born in Powhatan Co., Va., Jan. 1, 1807. He married **Jane E. Swan,** daughter of *Thos. T. Swan* of Cumberland Co., whose wife was *Annie Taylor*, daughter of *George Taylor* of Phila., one of the signers of the Declaration of Independence. He moved to Missouri about 1843, where he became a prominent lawyer. He died at Sedalia, Mo., in March, 1892. He and his family were Methodists.

Children:—*Born in Curdsville, Va.*

—324 Henry M.,[8] d., unm., in 1874; soldier in Confederate army.
—325 John W.,[8] m. **Martha Miller**; Confederate veteran; res. Angola, Va. Has children, Jane,[9] Martha[9] and John.[9]

Born in Lexington, Mo.

—326 Thomas F.,[8] m. **Sue E. Zenley**; res. Wanaucher, Mo.; Confederate soldier.

Born in Bates Co., Mo.

—327 Ella J.,[8] m. **C. B. Patterson**; res. Henrietta, Texas.
—328 Mary R.,[8] m. **Rev. E. G. Frazier**; d. in 1902 at Sedalia, Mo.
—329 Sarah Ann Taylor,[8] m. **Dr. J. P. Wagner**; res. Sedalia, Mo.
—330 Peter Baugh,[8] editor *Sedalia Democrat*.
—331 Elizabeth B.,[8] d. in infancy.

Born in Butler Co., Mo.

—332 Richard S.,[8] unm.; res. Sedalia.
—333 Catherine P.,[8] m. **Dr. O. P. Kernodle**.

195. JOHN STRATTON [7] (*Peter B.,*[6] *Peter,*[5] *William,*[4] *Edward,*[3] *Edward,*[2] *Edward*[1]) was born in Powhatan Co. June 2, 1808. He married **Julia Holman** Mar. 24, 1841. Moved to Missouri before 1860. Was killed by Union soldiers.

Children:
—334 Peter,[8] b. Jan. 6, 1842.
—335 William A.,[8] b. Jan. 26, 1844.
—336 Julia E.,[8] b. Oct. 2, 1845.
—337 Archie C.,[8] b. Nov. 10, 1847; removed to Indian Territory.
—338 Martha Ann,[8] b. Sept. 3, 1849.
—339 John A.,[8] b. July 24, 1851.

Records of these children desired.

197. RICHARD BAUGH STRATTON [7] (*Peter B.,*[6] *Peter,*[5] *William,*[4] *Edward,*[3] *Edward,*[2] *Edward*[1]) married, Feb. 10, 1836, **Eliza Michaux McLaurane**; moved to Missouri in 1843; he was a Baptist minister.

Children:
—340 Mary,[8] m. **T. B. Cummings**.
—341 Olivia,[8] m. **Elbert Blackwell**.
+342 John Emmett,[8] served in the C. S. Army.

198. MOSES STRATTON [7] (*William,*[6] *Peter,*[5] *William,*[4] *Edward,*[3] *Edward,*[2] *Edward*[1]) married **Jane Wilburn**.

Children:
—343 William Daniel.[8]
—344 Thomas Jefferson.[8]
—345 German L.,[8] represented Goochland Co. in the Legislature; m. **Etta Tillman**. Left a daughter, Jane,[9] who married **Handley Gallagher**.
—346 Catherine.[8]
—347 Melvin P.,[8]
—348 Amanda.[8]

201. JOHN C. STRATTON [7] (*William,*[6] *Peter,*[5] *William,*[4] *Edward,*[3] *Edward,*[2] *Edward*[1]) married Dec. 30, 1838, **Mary P. Drake**, daughter of *Col. Samuel Drake*, and lived in Powhatan Co.

Children:
—349 John C., Jr.,[8] m. **Alice Owen**.
—350 Pocahontas,[8] m. **Wallace Farres**.

208. JOHN THOMAS STRATTON [8] (*Henry*,[7] *John H.*,[6] *Henry*,[5] *Thomas*,[4] *Edward*,[3] *Edward*,[2] *Edward*[1]) was born June 12, 1824, in Franklin Co., Ky. He married **Emma P. Ferguson** in 1851 and lived in Memphis, where he died July 26, 1876.

Children:—*Born in Memphis, Tenn.*
- —351 Kate Gasler,[9] m. **William Bibb Leedy**, 1873; res. Birmingham, Ala.
- —352 Margaret Jane,[9] m. **Edward P. Cloaker**; d. in Memphis, 1880.
- —353 Henry,[9] res. Memphis.
- —354 Emma,[9] m. **Charles M. Cole**, 1882; res. Memphis.
- —355 Eliza Ferguson,[9] d. in infancy.
- —355a Manetta D.,[9] m. **Hugh Pettit**, 1890.
- —356 Lillian Lee,[9] m. **Frank Bates Fowlkes**, 1894; res. Birmingham, Ala.
- —357 Annie Rayburn,[9] m. **Joseph Hamlin Deaderick**, 1901; res. Memphis.

215. JOHN C. STRATTON [8] (*Thomas*,[7] *John H.*,[6] *Henry*,[5] *Thomas*,[4] *Edward*,[3] *Edward*,[2] *Edward*[1]), born Feb. 24, 1849; married Oct. 24, 1867, **Sarah P. Storke**, who was born Feb. 24, 1849. They reside at Otterville, Mo.

Children:
- —358 Bertha Agnes,[9] d. Apr. 29, 1872, aged 4 years.
- —359 Effie Prior,[9] m. **Leonard Spilers**, Mar. 8, 1893.
- —360 Dryden Calvin,[9] m. **Alice Knowles**, Apr. 29, 1906.
- —361 Sallie H.,[9] d. Dec. 18, 1877, aged 2 years.
- —362 John Leslie,[9] d. Oct. 12, 1889.
- —363 Henry Jefferson,[9] m. **Mima Rogers** Mar. 4, 1909.
- —364 Elmer Donald,[9] m. **Anna May Moon**, Apr. 26, 1903.
- —365 Lena Elsie,[9] d. Oct. 15, 1908.
- —366 Dorsey N.[9]
- —367 Thomas William.[9]

216. THOMAS HENRY STRATTON [8] (*Thomas*,[7] *John H.*,[6] *Henry*,[5] *Thomas*,[4] *Edward*,[3] *Edward*,[2] *Edward*[1]) was born in Cooper Co., Mo., Jan. 7, 1858, and has lived in Colorado since 1879, where he is widely known politically, having served two terms in the state senate. He resides at Rocky Ford, where he has been mayor for two terms and president of the First National Bank. He married **Laura Witherspoon** Oct. 24, 1889.

Children:—*Born in Colorado.*
—368 Robert Donald.[9]
—369 Fannie Pauline,[9] d. Apr., 1905, aged 1 year.

222. JAMES HENRY STEPTOE STRATTON [8] (*Joseph D.,*[7] *Archibald,*[6] *Henry,*[5] *Thomas,*[4] *Edward,*[3] *Edward,*[2] *Edward* [1]) was born June 12, 1840, and his home was in Lewisburg, West Va., where he died Feb. 3, 1895. He was a member of Co. H, 22d Va. Infantry and then in cavalry service to the close of the war. For twenty-five years Maj. Stratton followed the river as clerk and captain on Ohio steamers. During the later years of his life he had charge of the Lewisburg hotel. He married **Mary Anna Nelson Handley**, Dec. 9, 1869. She was a daughter of *Harvey* and *Mary Caroline Lockhart* (B*ell*) *Handley*.
Children:—*Born in Lewisburg, West Va.*
—370 Joe Harvey,[9] d. Jan. 9, 1899.
—371 Mary Theresa,[9] m. **Henry Hunter** Nov. 19, 1896; res. Lewisburg.
—372 Carrie Bell,[9] res. Lewisburg.
—373 John Handley.[9]
—374 Henry Nelson,[9] d. May 4, 1884.
—375 Willie Thomas,[9] m. **George Nettleton**; res. Coal Creek, Tenn.
—376 James Marion.[9]

231. THOMAS JOHN STRATTON [8] (*Albon M.,*[7] *John,*[6] *John,*[5] *Thomas,*[4] *Edward,*[3] *Edward,*[2] *Edward* [1]) was born at Spanish Oak, Va., Apr. 29, 1843, and lives on a farm not far from the old homestead, where he is interested in various branches of agriculture. May 27, 1867, he married **Mary E. Harris**, daughter of *John Armstead* and *Ann M.* (*Jordon*) *Harris* of Bedford Co. She died Oct. 9, 1917. He is a Confederate veteran, having served during the war as 1st Corporal in Co. A, 20th Va. Battalion Artillery. He was Assessor of real estate in 1885; Public School Trustee of Appomattox Co. and Clerk of the School Board for twenty-two years; Chairman of Board of Supervisors for four years; Register and Judge of elections for twenty years; clerk of the State Dept. of Agriculture eleven years; represented Appomattox in the Legislature in 1908-10-12.
Children:—*Born in Appomattox Co.*
—377 James Earnest,[9] m. **Nannie Louise Jennings** Jan. 18, 1905; res. Appomattox Co.

—378   John Albon,[9] res. Allen's Creek, Amherst Co., Va.
—379   Thomas Carbon,[9] res. Appomattox Co.; m. Elizabeth Burnett, Dec. 13, 1913; chn. Mary Lena,[10] Thomas James.[10]
+380   Frank Woodson.[9]
—381   Walter Harris,[9] Pine Bluff, Ark.
—382   Sarah Elizabeth,[9] m. **Wm. Rice Scott** Oct. 12, 1904.

238. RICHARD WHITFIELD STRATTON [8] (*Burwell C.,*[7] *John,*[6] *John,*[5] *Thomas,*[4] *Edward,*[3] *Edward,*[2] *Edward*[1]) married **Nina Hilldrop** and lives in Campbell Co., Va.

Children:—*Born in Campbell Co., Va.*
—383   Annie Wilson.[9]
—384   Burwell Hilldrop.[9]
—385   Virginia Churchill.[9]
—386   Richard Whitfield.[9]

243. WILLIAM ROBERT STRATTON [8] (*Linnæus B.,*[7] *William,*[6] *John,*[5] *Thomas,*[4] *Edward,*[3] *Edward,*[2] *Edward*[1]) lives at the old Stratton homestead near Trenholm, Va. He married in Dec., 1897, **Amanda Wilburn.**

Children:—*Born in Powhatan Co., Va.*
—387   Zelma Lee.[9]
—388   Robert Stuart.[9]
—389   Paul.[9]

248. BEAUMONT MACON STRATTON [8] (*Thomas J.,*[7] *William,*[6] *John,*[5] *Thomas,*[4] *Edward,*[3] *Edward,*[2] *Edward*[1]) was born Feb. 10, 1842. He married **Blythe Avery,** daughter of *Wm. Avery,* Sept. 21, 1876; res. in Memphis.

Children:—*Born in Memphis, Tenn.*
—390   Florence C.,[9] m. **Charles W. Thompson.**
—391   Thomas Avery.[9]
—392   Beaumont Macon.[9]
—393   Blythe Avery.[9]
—394   Avery Weaver.[9]
—395   Rebecca Louisana.[9]

259. LEWIS BRANSFORD STRATTON [8] (*James M.,*[7] *James,*[6] *John,*[5] *Thomas,*[4] *Edward,*[3] *Edward,*[2] *Edward*[1]) is a conductor and lives in Richmond, Va. He married, first, **Martha Minerva Stratton,** daughter of *John Stratton of* Goochland Co., second, Mary Fran-

ces Davis, third, **Lillian W. Brown,** Apr. 14, 1904. She was daughter of *J. Henry Brown* of Richmond.
Children:
>By second marriage.
—396   Louise Lyndan.[9]
—397   Andrew Lewis.[9]
>By third marriage.
—398   J. Henry Brown.[9]

261. JOSEPH P. STRATTON [8] (*James M.,*[7] *James,*[6] *John,*[5] *Thomas,*[4] *Edward,*[3] *Edward,*[2] *Edward*[1]) married **Annie Orndorff** Jan. 30, 1889, and resided in Hinton, West Va. He was killed in a railroad accident at Sandstone, Va., Feb. 21, 1905. He was conductor on the C. & O. Rd. for twenty-three years.
Children:
—399   Fannie,[9] m. **L. A. Capell,** Sept. 28, 1911.
—400   Earl.[9]

265. RICHARD HENRY STRATTON [8] (*Richard H.,*[7] *James,*[6] *John,*[5] *Thomas,*[4] *Edward,*[3] *Edward,*[2] *Edward*[1]) was a druggist at Gordansville, where he was one of the leading business men of the town, and where his family still reside. He was born in Staunton, Va., Feb. 13, 1844. He married, Nov. 3, 1867, **Mary Elizabeth Atkins,** who died Apr. 30, 1897. He died Sept. 29, 1903. He was a Confederate soldier, beginning service at the age of 17 in the field hospital. The following year, 1864, he enlisted as a private in Co. I of the 5th Va. cavalry and gave faithful, gallant service until he was paroled at Appomattox.
Children:—*Born in Gordansville, Va.*
—401   Susie Catharine,[9] m. **Wm. Fenton Jacobs** Jan 23, 1890.
—402   George Elmer,[9] d. Feb. 23, 1881, aged 9 years.
—403   Samuel Edgar.[9]
—404   Lindsey Case.[9]
—405   Joseph Haywood.[9]
—406   Mary Elizabeth.[9]
—407   Maurice Anderson.[9]
—408. Richard Henry.[9]

268. MAURICE ANDERSON STRATTON [8] (*Richard H.,*[7] *James,*[6] *John,*[5] *Thomas,*[4] *Edward,*[3] *Edward,*[2] *Edward*[1]) was a merchant at Clarksville, Tenn., where he settled in 1871. He married **Rachel Tucker** in Jan., 1879.

Children:—Born in Clarksville, Tenn.
—409   Maurice Anderson, Jr.[9]
—410   Charles Tucker.[9]

273. ALBERT WAGGONER STRATTON [8] (*Thomas C.,*[7] *James,*[6] *John,*[5] *Thomas,*[4] *Edward,*[3] *Edward,*[2] *Edward*[1]) married **Mary Jane Coffey** of Amherst Co. and resides in Buena Vista.

Children:—Born in Buena Vista, Va.
—411   Hattie McClung,[9] m. **Lewis Dawson.**
—412   John Albert.[9]
—413   Charles Coffey.[9]
—414   Mary Louisa.[9]
—415   Thomas C.[9]
—416   James Francis.[9]

274. HARRY HARLAN STRATTON [8] (*Thomas C.,*[7] *James,*[6] *John,*[5] *Thomas,*[4] *Edward,*[3] *Edward,*[2] *Edward*[1]) married **Belle Vickers** of Radford, Va., in 1884. He died in Knoxville, Tenn., Feb. 26, 1896.

Children:
—417   Della McClung.[9]
—418   Harry Harlan, Jr.[9]

275. GEORGE BAXTER STRATTON [8] (*Thomas C.,*[7] *James,*[6] *John,*[5] *Thomas,*[4] *Edward,*[3] *Edward,*[2] *Edward*[1]) married **Ella C. Coffey** of Amherst Co. He died at River Home, Va., Feb. 26, 1896.

Children:
—419   Ethel McClung.[9]
—420   Mary Simpson.[9]
—421   George Baxter.[9]

278. ROBERT L. STRATTON [8] (*Robert G.,*[7] *James,*[6] *John,*[5] *Thomas,*[4] *Edward,*[3] *Edward,*[2] *Edward*[1]) married **Mary Wheeler Powell,** Oct. 21, 1884. He was a wholesale grocer at Staunton for nearly 30 years. He died June 2, 1916. His business is being carried on by his sons.

Children:—Born in Staunton, Va.
—422   Powell Goodman,[9] m. **Irma S. Lang,** Oct. 10, 1914; ch. Margaret Wheeler.[10]
—423   Jane.[9]
—424   Charles Lewis,[9] d. Sept. 24, 1896.
—425   Mary Frances.[9]

—425a Richard Haygood.[9]
—425b Eleanor Page.[9]

281. CHESLEY MELVIN STRATTON [8] (*Peter L.,*[7] *James,*[6] *John,*[5] *Thomas,*[4] *Edward,*[3] *Edward,*[2] *Edward*[1]) was born in Appomattox Co., Va., Aug. 13, 1858. He married **Jennie W. Drinkard** Dec. 18, 1886.

Children:
—426 Chesley Melvin, Jr.,[9] m. **Eula Mae Carson,** Apr. 29, 1916; res. Concord, Va.
—427 Aubrey Hunter.[9]
—428 Mary Winnifred,[9] m. **Clarence Price.**
—429 Ethelbert Douglass.[9]
—430 Elizabeth Drinkard,[9] m. **Dr. David A. Christian.**
—431 Sarah Mildred.[9]
—432 Charles Legrand.[9]
—433 Alice Virginia.[9]

283. ETHELBERT MARSHALL STRATTON [8] (*Peter L.,*[7] *James,*[6] *John,*[5] *Thomas,*[4] *Edward,*[3] *Edward,*[2] *Edward*[1]) of Appomattox married **P. Bruce Robertson** Dec. 16, 1891.

Children:
—434 Paul Brent.[9]
—435 Willie Robertson.[9]
—436 Elva.[9]
—437 Ruth Douglass.[9]
—438 Ethelbert Marshall, Jr.[9]

295. JOHN ARMFIELD STRATTON [8] (*William,*[7] *James,*[6] *William,*[5] *William,*[4] *Edward,*[3] *Edward,*[2] *Edward*[1]) married **Chenty Elizabeth Horn,** and lived in Sumner Co., Tenn.

Children:
—439 Minnie.[9]
—440 Prudence.[9]
—441 Alice.[9]
—442 Jasper.[9]
—443 Jackson Allen.[9]
—444 Patona.[9]
—445 Dicey.[9]
—446 James Edward.[9]
—447 Armfield.[9]

Data of this family is desired.

300. ISAAC GOLLADAY STRATTON [8] (*Thomas J.,*[7] *James,*[6] *William,*[5] *William,*[4] *Edward,*[3] *Edward,*[2] *Edward*[1]) was a merchant of Lebanon, where he died Oct. 6, 1894. He was born Nov. 14,

1829. He was a Confederate soldier, serving four years in the 7th Tenn. Regt. He married, June 12, 1866, **Louisa Norman**, daughter of *Dr. Thomas* and *Elizabeth* (*Clay*) *Norman*, and granddaughter of *Archibald* and *Elizabeth* (*High*) *Clay*.

Children:—*Born in Lebanon, Tenn.*

—444 Thomas Fite,[9] m. **Leila Harrison West**, in McMinnville, Tenn., July 2, 1888; a merchant in Memphis, Tenn.
—445 Samuel Edward,[9] a lawyer at Waco, Texas; m. **Kate Thomas**, 1891; chn. Lucille,[10] Katherine.[10]
—446 Arthur M.,[9] b. Aug. 6, 1870; d. Dec. 6, 1891.
—447 Louise Norman,[9] m. **Edgar Bird**; res. Gainesville, Tex.
—448 Mattie L.,[9] m. in 1898 **Rev. Charles Moore Collins**, son of *Ambros Collins*. He is now pastor of Court Street Presbyterian Church at Memphis.
+449 Golladay.[9]
+450 Leslie M.[9]
—451 Andrew C.,[9] b. Nov. 24, 1884; d. unm.

301. JAMES EDWARD STRATTON [8] (*Thomas J.*,[7] *James*,[6] *William*,[5] *William*,[4] *Edward*,[3] *Edward*,[2] *Edward* [1]) was born in Lebanon Feb. 27, 1842, and died in Nashville Aug. 7, 1904. He married, first, **Mary A. Grimes**, Mar. 24, 1864; second, **Addie Harrington**, Dec., 1888.

Children:
 By first marriage.
—452 James Grimes.[9]
—453 Thomas Edward Golladay.[9]
—454 Caroline May,[9] m. **Richard C. Everett**.
 By second marriage.
—455 Truman Randolph.[9]
—456 Mary Lou.[9]
—457 Earl Harold.[9]

302. SAMUEL GOLLADAY STRATTON [8] (*Thomas J.*,[7] *James*,[6] *William*,[5] *William*,[4] *Edward*,[3] *Edward*,[2] *Edward* [1]) was born in Lebanon, Tenn., Jan. 3, 1844. He was one of the leading business men of his native town, where he was Mayor in 1873. He was Circuit Court Clerk for eleven years; represented Davidson and Wilson counties in the General Assembly in 1902-3; state Senator in 1904-5. He helped to organize the bank of Lebanon, of which for years he was cashier and which he was instrumental in converting into the Lebanon National Bank, of which he was president at the time of his death. He was a strong temperance man, prominent in prohibition movements, a member of the Methodist Church, where for many years he taught a Sunday school class. He married, first, Nov. 9, 1865, **Alice A. Fisher,** daughter of *Houston* and *Ann (Cossett) Fisher*; second, Dec. 1, 1881, **Lelia Owen,** a lady prominent throughout the state as a W. C. T. U. lecturer and worker. He died Aug. 3, 1909.

Children:—*Born in Lebanon, Tenn.*
    By first marriage.
+458 Houston Fisher.^{9}
+459 Franceway Cossett.^{9}
    By second marriage.
—460 Mildred Owen,^{9} m. **Dr. J.R. Bone** in 1902.
—461 Julia Matilda,^{9} m. **W. A. Hall** in 1906.
—462 Mary Owen.^{9}
—463 Elizabeth.^{9}

303. HENRY THOMAS STRATTON^8 (*Thomas J.,^{7} James,^{6} William,^{5} William,^{4} Edward,^{3} Edward,^{2} Edward^1*) is cashier in bank at Springfield, Tenn. He married, first, **Irene Hopkins**; second, **Mrs. Elizabeth Morehouse.**

Child:
—464 Henry Thomas, Jr.,^{9} resides in Springfield, Tenn.

306. DAVID THOMAS STRATTON^8 (*Madison,^{7} Thomas,^{6} Edward,^{5} William,^{4} Edward,^{3} Edward,^{2} Edward^1*) was born Dec. 18, 1838; died in Nashville Nov. 6, 1896; married **Agnes Taylor** Nov. 22, 1860. She was daughter of *John* and *Agnes (Walker) Taylor.*

Children:—*Born in Nashville, Tenn.*
+465 John Taylor.^{9}
—466 Agnes Walker,^{9} m. **William Caine.**

307. WILLIAM OLIVER STRATTON^8 (*Madison,^{7} Thomas,^{6} Edward,^{5} William,^{4} Edward,^{3} Edward,^{2} Edward^1*) was born in Davidson Co., Tenn., Oct. 16, 1840. He married **Elizabeth T. Hall** Jan. 23, 1866, in Nashville. He died in Trousdale Co., Tenn., Oct. 6, 1908. He was a farmer; member of the Methodist Church.

Children:—*Born in Davidson Co.*
—467 Carrie M.,^{9} b. Dec. 16, 1866; d. Dec. 29, 1877.

—468 Walter M.,[9] m. **Elizabeth Irwin,** Oct. 27, 1897; chn. Nellie,[10] Wm. O.[10]
+469 William Frank.[9]

312. MOSELEY THOMAS STRATTON [8] (*Thomas E.,*[7] *Thomas,*[6] *Edward,*[5] *William,*[4] *Edward,*[3] *Edward,*[2] *Edward*[1]) lived at "Linn Lawn," the fine old Stratton homestead near Nashville, on Gallatin pike, and was long at the head of a leading wholesale grocery business of Nashville,—M. T. Stratton & Co. He married **Laura Sumner,** May 19, 1874.
Children:—*Born in Davidson Co., Tenn.*
—470 Nina Bess,[9] m. **Edgar Foster;** res. Nashville.
—471 Moseley Thomas, Jr.,[9] in Colorado.
+472 Thomas Edward.[9]
—473 Laura Sumner,[9] m. **John M. Branham,** of Chicago, in 1909.
—474 Fred Love,[9] res. Little Rock, Ark.
—475 Wallace,[9] d. aged 5 yrs.

380. FRANK WOODSON STRATTON [9] (*Thomas J.,*[8] *Albon M.,*[7] *John,*[6] *John,*[5] *Thomas,*[4] *Edward,*[3] *Edward,*[2] *Edward*[1]) married **Pearl Brant Taylor,** Dec. 20, 1897.
Children:
—476 Maude Elizabeth.[10]
—477 Claude Rice.[10]

449. GOLLADAY STRATTON [9] (*Isaac G.,*[8] *Thomas J.,*[7] *James,*[6] *William,*[5] *William,*[4] *Edward,*[3] *Edward,*[2] *Edward*[1]) married **Dessie Shear** in 1901 and moved to Waco, Texas, where he is a merchant; member of M. E. Church, South.
Children:—*Born in Mephis, Tenn.*
—478 Leslie Martin.[10]
Born in Waco, Tex.
—479 Martha Louisa.[10]
—480 Golladay.[10]
—481 Dessie Shear.[10]

450. LESLIE M. STRATTON [9] (*Isaac G.,*[8] *Thomas J.,*[7] *James,*[6] *William,*[5] *William,*[4] *Edward,*[3] *Edward,*[2] *Edward*[1]) is a merchant of Memphis; a prominent man in business and public affairs; an active member of the Southern Methodist Church. He married **Kate White** in 1902.

Children:—*Born in Memphis, Tenn.*
—482　Frances White.[10]
—483　Andrew Cavitt.[10]
—484　Alice White [10] (twin).
—485　Louise Norman [10] (twin).

458. HOUSTON FISHER STRATTON [9] (*Samuel G.,*[8] *Thomas J.,*[7] *James,*[6] *William,*[5] *William,*[4] *Edward,*[3] *Edward,*[2] *Edward* [1]) is an attorney at law, and Clerk of the Circuit Court at Lebanon, Tenn. July 11, 1902, he married **Emma (McAuley) Stockard**, at Erin, Tenn.

Child:—*Born at Lebanon, Tenn.*
—486　Samuel Golladay.[10]

459. FRANCEWAY COSSETT STRATTON [9] (*Samuel G.,*[8] *Thomas J.,*[7] *James,*[6] *William,*[5] *William,*[4] *Edward,*[3] *Edward,*[2] *Edward* [1]) has been in the banking business in Lebanon, Tenn., for twenty-six years. He is cashier of the Lebanon National Bank which was organized by his father and grandfather over fifty years ago, and is vice-president of the Tennessee Banker's Association. He married **May Brown**, March 14, 1889.

Children:—*Born in Lebanon, Tenn.*
—487　Curry K.[10]
—488　Austin.[10]
—489　Franceway C.[10]
—490　Albert Fite.[10]
—491　Gerald Brown.[10]
—492　Alice Fisher.[10]

465. JOHN TAYLOR STRATTON [9] (*David T.,*[8] *Madison,*[7] *Thomas,*[6] *Edward,*[5] *William,*[4] *Edward,*[3] *Edward,*[2] *Edward* [1]) is a prominent business man of Nashville, Chairman of the Davidson Co. Board of Education, Superintendent of Spring Hill Cemetery. He married **Katie Gray**, Oct. 11, 1887, a daughter of *Wm. F.* and *Mary (Winbourn) Gray.*

Children:—*Born in Nashville, Tenn.*
—493　Annie Lanier.[10]
—494　Mary Winbourn.[10]

469. WILLIAM FRANK STRATTON [9] (*William O.,*[8] *Madison,*[7] *Thomas,*[6] *Edward,*[5] *William,*[4] *Edward,*[3] *Edward,*[2] *Edward* [1]) married **Davie Pursley**, daughter of *R. J. L.* and *Virginia (Hall) Pursley*, June 9, 1896; res. Nashville.

Children:—*Born in Nashville, Tenn.*
—495 Carrie Hall.[10]
—496 Susie Belle.[10]
—497 William Pursley.[10]
—498 Nina.[10]

472. THOMAS EDWARD STRATTON [9] (*Moseley T.,*[8] *Thomas E.,*[7] *Thomas,*[6] *Edward,*[5] *William,*[4] *Edward,*[3] *Edward,*[2] *Edward*[1]) married **Loulie McGavock** in 1906. He is in the wholesale grocery business in Nashville.
Children:*Born in Nashville, Tenn.*
—499 Thomas McGavock.[10]
—500 Moseley Edward.[10]

STRATTONS OF EASTERN KENTUCKY

As early as 1790 there were Strattons living in Floyd and Pike counties, Kentucky.* One of the earliest of these was Col. Harry Stratton. He died about 1850, aged nearly ninety years. He was a member of the State Legislature, and for many years an officer in the State Militia. His second wife was the widow of Maj. Spencer Atkins of Kentucky. With him was a Richard Stratton who died about 1833, at an advanced age, and a Joel Stratton, a surveyor.† Of their families we have no authentic records. Hiram, Tandy, Cornelius and John Stratton (whose descendants are given on the following pages) may have been younger brothers of the above, but no *proof* has been found of their relationship, or parentage, or even to which line of Strattons they belonged. They are here placed with the Bermuda Hundred line, but future research may prove that they are descended

---

* Among their descendants are many "traditions" as to their Virginia ancestors—of a Solomon Stratton who had ten sons and was known among his neighbors as "King Solomon"; a Henry Stratton who lived to a great age and had sons and grandsons in the Revolution; a John Stratton who came from Amherst Co. and had many sons; of intermarriages with many prominent Virginia families; of "unsettled estates" from which legacies are due the descendants to-day, etc., etc. But no authentic records have been found.

† Taylor and Garrard, who from 1794 to 1800 made large land surveys for the government in the section now covered by McDowell, Mingo, Mercer, Wyoming and Logan counties, West Virginia, and Floyd and Pike counties, Kentucky, speak of Joel Stratton as their pilot. He is said to have gone with George Roger Clark on his expedition to the Northwest.

from the Eastern Shore line, or from one of the New Jersey Quaker families of Strattons who early settled in Virginia. (See *Vol. I*, also first two pages of "Bermuda Hundred Strattons," in this volume.) Perhaps some reader may be able to give some clew to their classification. Perhaps what is given here may interest some other Stratton to make a more thorough research than has yet been made. Some court, or county records, family Bible, or grave stones may yet be found which will make the whole matter clear.* The following records are compiled from correspondence with many of their descendants:

[501.] HIRAM STRATTON came from Virginia to Floyd Co., Ky., while a boy. He married **Hannah Leslie**, and settled on a farm on the east side of Jobe's Creek, four miles from Prestonburg. She was a daughter of *Robert* and *Esther Leslie*, and was born in Tazewell Co., Va. He died of typhoid fever early in life, about **1816**, while his children were small. His wife survived him many years.

Children:
- —505 Mary, m. **William McGuire**.
- —506 Elizabeth, m. **William Kelly**.
- —507 Wilson, d. unm.
- —508 Solomon, m. 1st, **Nancy McGuire**; 2nd, **Mary Jones**; d. in Lexington, Ky.
- +509 Milton.

[502.] TANDY STRATTON was born in Virginia and settled in Floyd Co., Ky., in 1826. He married, first, **Nellie Layne**;

---

* Another, yet unplaced, Stratton, a Confederate soldier, was Franklin Stratton (or Benjamin Franklin) of South Carolina. He was born about 1812, and was one of three brothers. He was a planter near Columbia; an Episcopalian. He m. Marian (?) Marion, a granddaughter of Gen. Francis Marion of Revolutionary fame. She died while their two sons were small boys. He was with Hoke's North Carolians, C. S. A. He and his elder son George were killed at Gettysburg July 3, 1863. His other son, Frank, born Feb. 29, 1844, served in 2nd South Carolina, and 11th Mississippi, Haygood's Brigade. He m. Ida Alice Dill Dec. 28, 1873. He is a civil engineer. Has lived in Pittsburg, Springfield, Ill. (where his two children were born), San Francisco and Brooklyn. Children: Ida Marian, m. Herman L. Ericksen; Charles Stonewall, m. Marguerite Anna Heene Dec. 21, 1907; children, Walter Robert and Charles Howard; residence, Richmond Hill, L. I. Perhaps some reader of this may know where to place this family.

Also, the names D. P. H. Stratton and Peter A. Stratton of Kentucky appear on the Mexican War Rolls. To what family do they belong?

second, **Mary Preast**. He owned a large farm and was a man of considerable prominence among his neighbors.

Children:—*Born at Cedar Bluff, Tazewell Co., Va.*
By first marriage.
+510 Solomon Hunter, b. 1796.
−511 William Layne, b. June 26, 1799.
Born in Floyd Co., Ky.
−512 Cynthia, b. Feb. 4, 1801; m. **Stephen Hamilton**.
−513 Nancy, b. Nov. 18, 1802; m. **Wm. Brown**.
By second marriage.
−514 Lewis P., b. Feb., 1807.
−515 Richard P., b. Nov. 7, 1814; d. July 12, 1847.
−516 Elizabeth Price, b. June 4, 1816; m. **Wm. Mayo**.
+517 John Jackson, b. 1818; d. 1906.
−518 Lettie B., m. **Harman Hager**.
−519 Mary Jane, m. **John W. Smith**.

[503.] CORNELIUS STRATTON was born in Virginia and died in Floyd Co., Ky., in 1832. He married **Margaret Davis**, who was born in North Carolina in 1797, and who moved to Lawrence Co., Ky., after the death of her husband.

Children:
+520 James.
−521 Cornelius, m. **Catherine (Rice) Todd**.
+522 Burwell.
+523 Henry Charles.

[504.] JOHN STRATTON was born in Virginia in 1787, and came with his parents to Floyd Co., Ky., a young boy. Jan. 31, 1808, he married **Dicie Mayo**.*[1] In 1812 they left Floyd Co. for "the west," stopping for awhile in Shelby and Jefferson counties, Ky., where he had relatives. Crossing the Ohio at Louisville, after a trip of nearly 300 miles, they reached Fort Harrison (now Terre Haute). Here Mr. Stratton left his family until the Indians, then extremely hostile, became sufficiently quiet to warrant his taking them any further in safety. Then in the spring of 1817, in company with Col. Mayo, Remember Black-

---

* One descendant writes that Dicie was a daughter of John Mayo; another that her parents were Rev. William and Elizabeth Mayo of Patrick Co., Va. She had a brother, Jonathan Mayo, born in Patrick Co. March 25, 1793. In some family records the name is written Dicea. Their descendants say that John Stratton's ancestors intermarried with the Wilkins family in Virginia (see pp. 146-149, Vol. I).

man, Robin Brown, and Mr. Whitley, he crossed the Wabash, and "took up" land 12 miles east of the present town of Paris, Edgar Co., Ill., in what was later called Stratton township. They were in time to prepare the land and plant small crops of corn, and a few months later brought their families over, becoming the first white settlers in that part of Illinois. John Stratton is said to have been the "first white man that ate his dinner in his own house west of the Wabash," and his daughter Charlotte was the first white child born in Edgar Co. For several years these brave pioneers, surrounded by hostile Indians, suffered many hardships and deprivations. The settlement was known as "Clay Prairie." Henry Clay owned a large tract of land there and was instrumental in bringing these Kentucky and Virginia families there. Among them were the Hunters, McGuires, Whitleys, Buntains, Martins, Lesleys, Mayos and Blackmans, with all of whom the Strattons intermarried. Henry Clay, being a warm friend, visited among them several times. John Stratton was one of the first to plant an orchard in the county, and he and Col. Mayo introduced sheep raising into the county in 1822, purchasing 130 head of sheep in Kentucky, driving them across the country about 600 miles into Edgar Co. and selling them to people who wished to embark in the new industry. "Mr. Stratton was a man of sterling integrity; progressive, enterprising, yet quiet and unassuming, fond of reading in days when reading matter was not easily obtained, and a man of much more than ordinary intelligence. He gave to his large family of children the best educational advantages the new country afforded, and they were all rather above the average in intellectual ability." He died in April, 1871, at the home of his son, W. J. Stratton, in Momence, Ill. In the cemetery at Union Corners is a monument to his memory. His wife died several years earlier and is buried at Paris, Ill. They were members of the Methodist Church.

Children:—*Born in Floyd Co., Ky.*
—524   Elizabeth, b. Oct. 18, 1809; m. **John Walker.**
—525   Bethena, b. Sept. 4, 1811; m. **John Stratton Brown.**[22]
—526   Sarah M., b. Apr. 20, 1813; m. **William Whitney.**
+527   William James, b. Aug. 1, 1815.
      Born in Edgar Co., Ill.
—528   Charlotte, b. Aug. 24, 1817; m. **Andrew Hunter.**

---
[22] They were cousins. His mother, a sister of John Stratton, married Robin Brown in Floyd Co., Ky.

—529 Minerva, b. 1819; m. **Andrew Bradley.**
—530 Sarulda, b. 1821; m. **Thomas** J. **Buntain,** Apr. 23, 1837, his second wife; he m. 1st, Sarah Gist, in Ky., Aug. 28, 1824.
+531 Jonathan Perry, b. Jan. 12, 1823.
+532 John F., b. Feb. 28, 1826.
+533 Henry J., b. June 23, 1828.
+534 Mayo E., b. Feb. 23, 1832.

509. MILTON STRATTON (*Hiram*) was born in Floyd Co., Ky., Jan. 27, 1811. Settled as a farmer in Wayne Co., West Va. He married **Martha Buchanan Leslie,** Sept., 1827.* He was killed by a falling tree, Oct. 30, 1841. After his death his family returned to Floyd Co., Ky. His widow married John Carson.

Children:
—535 Hiram Russell, b. Oct. 4, 1830; d. Oct. 17, 1898. A Baptist minister for many years in Pike and Floyd counties.
+536 John Buren.
—537 Harrison Strother, b. June 28, 1835; m. **Elizabeth Lesley** in 1854.
—538 James Wickliffe, b. Feb. 8, 1837; m. **Sarah Cox** in 1865; d. in Spooner, Wis.
—539 Amos Lafayette, b. 1839.
—540 Harriet Louisa, b. Nov. 15, 1840; m. 1st, **Harmon Wilson,** in 1858; 2nd, **Hugh Willis,** in 1876.

510. SOLOMON HUNTER STRATTON (*Tandy*) was a farmer of Floyd Co., Ky., and for some time lived in Louisville. In 1820 he married **Jennie S. Layne,** daughter of *James Layne;* died in 1883.

Children:—*Born in Louisville, Ky.*
—541 James Washington, b. Dec., 1820; a farmer; m. **Nancy Hunt;** d. at Laynesville.
+542 Tandy Louis, b. 1823.
—543 Catherine, b. 1825; m. **Wm. Brandon.**
—544 Mary Jane, b. 1827; m. **Harvey Lesley.**
—545 John Layne, b. 1829; m. **Eliza Burk,** and lived in Portsmouth, Ohio.

---

*She was a daughter of John Leslie (or Lesley) and her mother is said to have been a relative of President Buchanan. John Leslie was a soldier in the Revolution, and later with Gen. Clark helped to found the town of Vincennes, Ind.

—546 William Henry, d. in boyhood.
+547 Lindsey, b. 1832.
—548 Thomas Jefferson, d. in boyhood.
—549 Solomon Porter, b. 1836; d. in Ironton, Ohio.
—550 Samuel George (or George Samuel), b. 1840; m. **Nancy Williams**; d. in Seneca, Ore.
—551 Allen Monroe, b. 1842; m. **Mary Williams**; d. in Banner, Floyd Co., Ky.

517. JOHN JACKSON STRATTON (*Tandy*) was born Nov. 1, 1818. He married **Catherine Gayhart**. He was a farmer and lived all his life in Floyd Co., Ky., where he died June 28, 1907. He was a member of the Methodist Church.
Children:—*Born in Floyd Co., Ky.*
—552 Rody S., m. **John E. Helens** in 1868; res. Everett, Mo.
—553 Maria J., m. **Micheal Tarter**, 1872.
—554 Henel V., m. **Newton Harris**, 1876.
—555 Abram J., m. **Mary Layne** in 1882; res. Tram, Texas.
—556 Tandy L., m. **Sarah ——**, 1887; res. Cooper, Texas.
—557 John J., m. **Mary May**, 1893; res. Pikeville, Ky.
—558 Catherine.
—559 Richard P., m. 1st, **Henen J. Williams**; 2nd, **Louise Roberts**; res. Tram, Texas.

520. JAMES STRATTON (*Cornelius, Richard*) was born in 1827. He married **Louisa Millions**, and lived in Trimble, Ohio.
Children:
—560 William, a merchant at Nelsonville, O.; m. his cousin, **Lizzie Stratton**.
—561 Charles Henry, m. **Sallie McHenry**.
—562 Ephraim, m. **Mary Robinson**.
—563 Mary I., m. **G. A. Sayre**.
—564 John, d. unm.
—565 Samuel, m. **Dora Witzel**.

522. BURWELL STRATTON (*Cornelius*) married **Nancy Cox**, and lived in Louisa, Ky.
Children:
—566 Lizzie, m. her cousin, **Wm. Stratton** (No. 560).
—567 Cornelius M.
—568 Ira.
—569 Emerson.

—570 Lucy.
—571 Emma, m. **William Sharon**; res. Nelsonville, O.
—572 John B.
—573 Charles H., res. High Bridge, Ky.
—574 Goldie Lee.

523. HENRY CHARLES STRATTON (*Cornelius*) married **Jennie Steele**, and lived in Stewart, O.
Children:
—575 George, m. **Dora Morgan.**
—576 Frank, m. **Victor Shields.**
—577 Burwell, m. **Margaret Woody.**

527. WILLIAM JAMES STRATTON (*John*) married **Margaret Patrick** in Dec., 1838. He lived and died in Momence, Ill.
Children:
—578 Ellen, m. —— Worcester.
—579 Cordelia, m. **A. E. Wikstrom.**
—580 John, d. in 1864.
—581 Thomas, lives in Oregon.
—582 Charlotte.
—583 Mary, m. **O. B. Hewlett.**

531. JONATHAN PERRY STRATTON (*John*) married, first, **Memory Ann Seager**; second, **Sarah Daniel**. He died in Momence, Ill.
Children:
—584 Elizabeth, d. in infancy.
—585 Achsah Dicie, res. Momence, Ill.
—586 Emma, m. **Franklin C. Freeman.**
—587 Ida Belle, m. **L. F. Woody.**
—588 Jonathan Perry, Jr., m. **Edna Moore.**
—589 John W.

532. JOHN F. STRATTON (*John*) married **Susan H. Patrick**. He lived in Neodesha, Kan., where he was a hardware merchant, and member of the Methodist Church.
Children:—*Born in Edgar Co., Ill.*
+590 John T.
+591 George W.
—592 Benjamin F., b. Dec. 4, 1850; m. **Kate Arnold**; res. Ingalls, Kan.

—593 Emma J., m. **W. F. Baird** in 1872; res. Neodesha, Kan.
—594 Mary E., m. **Perry G. Penney**; res. Buffalo, Kan.

533. HENRY J. STRATTON (*John*) married **Nancy Jane Macy** in 1850. He died in Hartford, Kan., in 1897.
Children:—*Born in Hartford, Kan.*
—595 John W., m. **Mary V. Hortox** in 1884; res. in Hartford, Kan.; has son, Fred.
—596 James L., m. **Della Myers**, 1887; res. Hartford, Kan.

534. MAYO E. STRATTON (*John*) married, in Paris, Ill., Jan. 14, 1854, Catherine Elizabeth Wilkins, daughter of *William S.* and *Elizabeth (Mayo) Wilkins.** Four years later they moved to Greenwood Co., Kansas. He taught school for a while, then studied law and was admitted to the Bar. He volunteered for service in the Union army and was made lieutenant of his company. The company, however, was never mustered in, the State having sent its full quota of troops. Later he had large interests as a cattle dealer and ranchman in Kansas and Oklahoma. Mrs. Sratton died in Hamilton, Kan., Oct. 27, 1866. Mr. Stratton married, second, Dec. 24, 1871, **Agnes M. Shepard,** daughter of *Mark* and *Eliza T. (Ingalls) Shepard.*† She was born Oct. 30, 1848 and died Sept. 4, 1907. He died Aug. 1, 1914.
Children:
  By first marriage.
—597 Clara Etta, m. 1st, **William Saling**; 2nd, **David Burt.**
—598 Orlando Corden, b. 1860; d. 1878.
—599 Eugene Rose, d. in infancy.
—600 Willie, d. in infancy.
—601 Henry Ellsworth.
—602 Jennie Isabella, m. **James Wilson Augustus**; res. Kansas City, Kan.‡
—603 Ida Kate, m. **Asbrey Neer.**
  By second marriage.

---

* William Wilkins was born in North Carolina, but his father was a native of Virginia.

† Mark Shepard (or Shepherd) was from Sullivan, Me., where at one time he was half owner of a shipyard near Mt. Desert. He was in the state senate in 1855. His wife was a descendant of Edmund Ingalls, one of the founders of Lynn, Mass.

‡ The compiler is indebted to Mrs. Augustus for help on this branch of Strattons.

—604 Albert Mayo, res. Phœnix, Ariz.

—605 Zoe Agnes, m., July 15, 1903, **Senator William M. Tilghman,** a descendant of Richard Tilghman, who came over with Cecil Calvert; res. Ingalls, Okla.

536. JOHN BUREN STRATTON (*Milton, Hiram*) was born in Floyd Co., Ky., in 1833. While a young man he went west; settled at Shell Lake, Wis. He married **Annie Anderson,** of Tayler's Falls, Minn., in 1854.

Children:

—606 Milton Solomon, m. **Nellie Raberge** in 1881; d. in Redlands, Cal., in 1888.

—607 Harriet M., m. **Malcome Dobie;** res. Portland, Oregon.

—608 Clara, m. **J. M. Custard;** d. in Clark Co., Wash.

—609 Ella, m. **Judge L. A. Mead;** d. in 1885.

—610 Elizabeth Low, m. **J. W. Knapp, Jr.;** res. Shell Lake, Wis.

—611 Wickliffe Buren, m. **Georgina Irving Rodd** in 1894; res. Seattle. He is Attorney-General of Washington.

542. TANDY LOUIS STRATTON (*Solomon H., Tandy*), born in 1823; lived in Prestonburg, Ky., where he died in 1900. He married **Martha S. Burchett** in 1848. He was a farmer; member of the Methodist Church.

Children:—**Born in Prestonburg, Ky.**

—612 Nellie Jane, m. **R. P. Frazier;** res. Ford City, Kan.

—613 Thomas J., m. **Mary Roberts.**

—614 Lewis, d. in 1878.

—615 Granville R., m. **Edith Brown** in 1877.

—616 Dollie, m. **John S. Lowe;** res. Prestonburg, Ky.

—617 Angeline, m. **W. D. Ferguson;** res. Laynesville, Ky.

547. LINDSEY STRATTON (*Solomon H., Tandy*) was born in Floyd Co., Ky., Mar. 15, 1832. In 1853 he married **Mary Susan Robins** of Bath Co., Ky. In 1869 they went to Cass Co., Mo. A year later removed to Marshall Co., Kan., where they remained five years. In 1875 they settled on a farm near Belone, Pottawatomie Co., Kan., where they spent the remainder of their lives. Mrs. Stratton died Feb. 2, 1890. "Graupa Stratton," as he was affectionately called by a large circle of friends and neighbors, died Mar. 10, 1910, leaving five children, thirteen grandchildren, and nineteen great grandchildren. He had always

understood that his great grandfather was a Revolutionary soldier.

Children:—*Born in Bath Co., Ky.*
- —618 Bellvadora, m. **William McKinnon**, Dec. 28, 1891; d. in Kansas Oct. 9, 1896.
- —619 Eliza Jane, m. **John W. Weddle**, Dec. 25, 1877.
- +620 John Spencer.
- —621 Callie May, m. **Lincoln Esteps**, Dec. 13, 1888; res. Belone, Kan.
- —622 George Greeley, res. Belone, Kan.
- —623 Hattie Florence, m. **Wm. Little**, Aug. 6, 1896.

590. JOHN T. STRATTON (*John F., John*) was born in 1846. He married **Keziah Drake** in 1866, and died in Oak Valley, Kan., in 1878. After his death his family moved to Kokomo, Ind.

Children:
- —624 John Anderson, m. **Alice Coffinbery** in 1899; res. Chicago.
- —625 George Henry, m. **Dilola Young** in 1897.
- —626 Nora Alma, m. **Bert T. Hale** in 1903; res. Oakland, Ind.

591. GEORGE W. STRATTON (*John F., John*) was born July 12, 1848. He married **Armintha R. Stuart**. He was a real estate dealer in Kansas City, Kan. He died in 1913.

Children:
- —627 Harry G., res. Kansas City.
- —628 Vernon.
- —629 Pearl.
- —630 Beatrice.
- —631 Oda A., d. in Elk City, Kan., 1890.
- —632 Willie H., d. in Montgomery Co., Kan., 1881.
- —633 Sylvia, d. in Oak Valley, Kan., 1887.

620. JOHN SPENCER STRATTON (*Lindsey, Solomon H., Tandy*) married **Emma M. Taylor**, Feb. 15, 1882; resides at Hartford, Kan.

Children:—*Born in Pottawatomie Co., Kan.*
- —634 Virgie Lea, m. **Marcus Leppencott**, Sept. 15, 1898.
- —635 Charles Milton, m. **Ida Hall**, Mar. 6, 1905; res. Pottawatomie Co., Kan.
- —636 Bessie Lena, m. **Stephen McCoy**, Mar. 5, 1911.

—637 Walter Raymond.
—638 George Clifford.
—639 Frank Taylor.

NOTE. Among yet unplaced Strattons are the following:

A Capt. Thomas owned a farm of 2,000 acres at Point Rock in Chesterfield Co. On the farm is an old "Stratton Graveyard," so called by his descendants to-day. He had no sons, but several daughters. One m. Dr. J. A. Stracham, a Baptist minister. A part of the old farm is in possession of her descendant to-day. Another, Catherine, b. 1800, m. G. W. Ladd, a portrait painter of some note in Richmond. She is said to have designed the first Confederate flag.

Arthur Thomas Stratton owned a farm nearby, on Appomattox River. He m. Deborah Ladd in 1805. They had three sons, John, Richard and Henry T.

A John Stratton m. Nancy Lightfoot, d. of Daniel and Mary (Hines) Lightfoot. Their son James, 1793, lived in Fluvanna Co.; had three children: Mary Ann, m. C. B. Davis; Bettie C., m. Peter V. Foland of Scottsville; James W. d. aged 27 years.

The following marriage licenses are recorded in Amherst County:

1789, April 24, Jacob Stratton to Elizabeth Whittle.

1794, July 24, Wm. Stratton to Milly Wright, d. of Jesse Wright.

1799, Feb. 19, James Stratton to Elizabeth Blair.

1800, Sept. 17, Elizabeth Stratton to John Savage.

1802, Nov. 5, Abram Stratton to Mary Lavandor.

Perhaps some one who reads this may know where to place these people.

STRATTONS OF NEW JERSEY
MARK STRATTON OF EVESHAM

(Chart M, Vol. I)

*"There's a feeling within us that loves to revert
To the old, old times that are past."*
                                    PRENTICE.

IN 1914, in repairing and putting in order the old orthodox "Friends' Burial Ground" at Medford, N. J., in preparation for the centennial celebration (one hundred years since the present meeting house was built), a brick was found below the ground near a grave with "M. S. 1754" marked on it. It is suggested that this marks the grave of Mark Stratton, as his was the first burial there. At any rate, this is interesting in connection with "Grandmother Cowperthwaite's Sketch" given on page 240, *Vol. I*, of this work. This would put his birth back to 1687, as he was sixty-seven years old when he died. Headstones were not permitted by Quakers at that date. If, as Grandmother Cowperthwaite's Sketch indicates, Mark and Emanuel Stratton "came out of Old England in 1702," a research among the many sources of information in England would be quite likely to discover their ancestry there and perhaps show some connection between them and the early Boston Strattons, who were also Quakers, one of whom, it will be remembered, married a granddaughter of the eminent Ann Hutchinson. Mark Stratton was a man of some prominence in the Quaker community in which he lived and was quite well to do for that time and place. More than a thousand of his descendants are traced in this volume. Emanuel Stratton died early in 1725, twelve years after his marriage to Hannah Hancock. His son Jacob may be the ancestor of the Strattons who, a generation later, were living in Northern New Jersey.

FIFTH GENERATION

120. DAVID QUINN STRATTON [5] (*Joseph,*[4] *Joseph,*[3] *David,*[2] *Mark*[1]) was born in Campbell Co., Va., Mar. 23, 1793, and

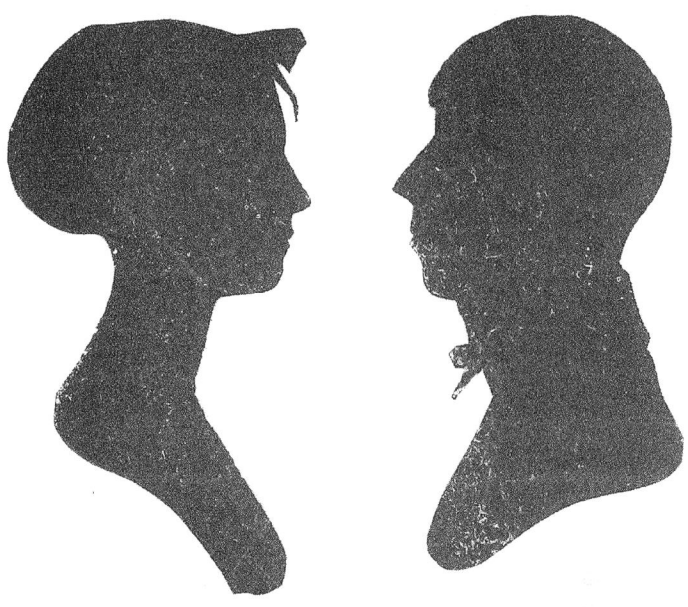

Isaiah and Anna (Green) Stratton; *Page* 289, *Vol.* I. Silhouettes made about time of their marriage, 1804. Parents of Isaiah G. Stratton; *Page* 431.

George Wooley Stratton, aged 80, and little grand-daughter, Ruth Stratton, aged 1 year; *Page* 428.

moved while a boy with his parents to Clinton, O. He married, first, **Ruth Thatcher** in 1816. She died at Wilmington in 1825. In 1826 he married **Harriet Hinman**, who died at Mt. Vernon, Ill., in 1879. He died at West Liberty, Iowa, June 14, 1876.*

Children:—*Born in Wilmington, O.*

By first marriage.

+266 Stephen Thatcher,[6] b. 1818.

By second marriage.

—267 Amanda M.,[6] b. Oct. 21, 1827; m. Azariah W. Doan in 1847; d. Aug. 6, 1854.

+268 Edward L.,[6] b. 1829.

+269 Oliver H.,[6] b. 1832.

—270 Letitia E.,[6] b. July 29, 1835; m. Edward Tellinghast in 1852; d. Aug. 4, 1854.

—271 Martha Emily,[6] b. Mar. 31, 1837; d. aged two years.

+272 Joseph D.,[6] b. 1839.

+273 Benjamin C.,[6] b. 1841.

—274 William David,[6] b. Apr. 10, 1843; d. Oct. 22, 1851.

—275 Carrie O.,[6] b. Aug. 3, 1845; m. Wm. G. Brooke in 1866, res Kalona, Iowa.

—276 John Hadley,[6] b. Nov. 24, 1849; d. Aug. 10, 1854.

—277 Isabella J.,[6] b. Feb. 28, 1852; d. in childhood.

Four children died of cholera at Wilmington in Aug., 1854.

123. JOSEPH PARMER STRATTON[5] (*Joseph,*[4] *Joseph,*[3] *David,*[2] *Mark*[1]) was born in Campbell Co., Va., Feb. 2, 1800, and moved from Clinton, O., to Wayne Co., Ind., while a young man and engaged in the mercantile business at Richmond, where he resided for over fifty years, one of the prominent business men of the town. He died Oct. 14, 1879. He was a lifelong member amongst Friends, belonging to the Hicksite branch, and a man greatly respected by all who knew him. He married at Richmond, July 1, 1830, **Martha W. Jefferis**, daughter of *Abraham* and *Anna Jefferis*. She died at the home of her daughter, Anna J. Wilson, in 1901.

Children:—*Born in Richmond, Ind.*

—278 Anna J.,[6] b. Apr. 2, 1831; m. **Stephen B. Wilson**, son of Mark L. and Mary (Brock) Wilson. Lived at Louisville, Ind.

+279 Benjamin W.[6]

---

*David Quinn and many of his descendants still spell the name "Strattan."

+280 Elwood H.⁶
—281 Theodocia M.,⁶ b. Dec. 17, 1839; m. **Wm. S. Wooten**, inventor of the Wooten Desk and other patents, and minister in Friends' Church.
+282 Abraham S.⁶
—283 Lydia J.,⁶ b. Nov. 17, 1842; m. **Daniel W. Wooten**.
—284 Mary Emily,⁶ b. July 31, 1844; m. **Wm. P. Hutton,** 1865.
—285 Joseph M.,⁶ b. Dec. 8, 1846; m. **Kate Hutchens**, Jan. 1, 1870.
—286 Charles Elwood,⁶ b. Jan. 3, 1850; m. **Amy V. Mitchell,** Nov. 15, 1878. No children.

124. MICAJAH STRATTON⁵ (*Joseph,⁴ Joseph,³ David,² Mark¹*) was born in Virginia, Jan. 22, 1802, and moved with his parents to Clinton Co., O., before he was twelve years old, where he lived the rest of his life on a farm at Lytle's Creek, near Wilmington. He married **Mary E. Haines** in 1830. He died May 12, 1857. His wife lived two years longer, dying in 1859.

Children:—*Born in Clinton Co., O.*
+287 John Haines.⁶
—288 Joseph,⁶ b. 1834; d. 1859.
—289 Ruth Ann,⁶ b. Mar. 1837; m. **Thomas Hazzard,**⁶ 1867; res. Wilmington, O.
—290 Mary Elizabeth,⁶ b. 1840; d. aged two years.
—291 Micajah Israel,⁶ b. 1843; d. 1855.
—292 Emma Marcissa,⁶ b. 1850; d. 1874.

126. BENJAMIN STRATTON⁵ (*Joseph,⁴ Joseph,³ David,² Mark¹*) was born in Clinton Co., O., Apr. 26, 1812, about two years after his parents moved there from Virginia. His mother died when he was eleven years old. While a young man he went to Richmond, Ind., where his two older brothers had previously settled. Here he became a dry goods merchant, and one of the prominent business men of the place, noted for his strict integrity and fair dealing. He was one of the directors of the State Bank of Indiana and held other positions of public trust and honor. Mr. Stratton was a prominent and active member of the Friends' Society and for many years recorder of Hicksite yearly meetings, and had charge of the large safe and all the valuable documents of that body. June 4, 1834, he married **Emily Lathrop**, only child of *Dr. Martin* and *Rebecca* (*Wright*) *Lathrop*, a lady of much refinement and intelligence, with a sweet, cheerful disposition and possessing a tender melodious voice.* Later she became a dearly beloved minister of the Society of Friends. She died May 17, 1879.[2] Mr. Stratton died Dec. 12, 1897, in the town where he had spent more than sixty years of his life.

Children:—*Born in Richmond, Ind.*
- —293 Rebecca D.,[6] b. July 7, 1836; m. **Prof. Jesse S. Wilson**; d. in St. Elmo, Tenn., at the home of her son, Dr. Wilson.
- +294 Joseph H.[6]
- —295 Esther Ann,[6] m. **Joseph S. Wallace.**
- —296 Martin Lathrop,[6] b. July 1, 1845; m. **Sarah S. Perry**, Aug. 3, 1865; d. Oct. 8, 1879. City Treasurer of Richmond for many years.
- —297 Mary Emily,[6] m. **Richard Shute**; res. Richmond, Ind.
- +298 Horace B.[6]

128. EDWARD KINLEY STRATTON[5] (*Joseph*,[4] *Joseph*,[3] *David*,[2] *Mark*[1]) was born Apr. 13, 1831, about two months after his father's death. He married **Hannah Bond**, Aug. 1, 1855. He is a well-to-do farmer, living on a farm five miles southeast of New Castle, Henry Co., Ind. He is a member of the Friends' Society.

Children:—*Born in Henry Co., Ind.*
- +299 Albert.[6]
- —300 William E.,[6] b. 1857; d. aged 2 years.
- —301 Jesse Arthur,[6] b. 1860; d. 1882.
- —302 Ella,[6] m. **Alonzo C. Hodson**, 1903.
- —303 Benjamin,[6] m. **Ella Moore**, Aug. 4, 1897.
- —304 Minnie B.,[6] m. **Milton Stafford**, Sept. 7, 1898.

131. LEVI STRATTON[5] (*Benjamin*,[4] *Joseph*,[3] *David*,[2] *Mark*[1]) was born in 1800 in Virginia, and while a small boy went with his parents to Ohio and later to Indiana. He married **Ruth Crews**, who was born in 1803 and died July 11, 1897. Their home was in Henry Co., Ind., where he died in 1885.

Children:—*Born in Richmond, Ind.*
- —305 Lucinda,[6] m. **Charles Rock.**
- —306 Albert.[6]
- —307 Hannah,[6] m. **Joseph C. Deem.**
- —308 Luama.[6] (?)

---

*Martin Lathrop was a son of *Simeon and Hannah Lathrop*. Rebecca Wright, a daughter of *Jonathan and Susannah Wright*.

Born in Knightstown, Ind.

—309   Joseph.[6]
—310   Milton.[6]
+311   Franklin.[6]
—312   Emma (or Amy),[6] m. **Wm. H. Harden.**

132. Ephraim Stratton[5] (*Benjamin,*[4] *Joseph,*[3] *David,*[2] *Mark*[1]) was born in 1803. Married, first, **Lavina Leonard**, near Lisbon, Iowa, and, second, at Spiceland, Iowa, **Edith Cope Elliott**, Jan., 1840. He moved to Story Co., Iowa, in 1854, one of the very early settlers of that region. There were only a few houses in the county and they of logs. He died Apr. 13, 1873. He was a farmer.

Children:—*Born in Henry Co., Ind.*
  By first marriage.
—313   Louisa Jane,[6] b. Oct. 28, 1828; m. **James Henley**; res. Straughns, Ind.
—314   Nathaniel,[6] d. in infancy.
—315   Benjamin Leander,[6] b. Sept. 9, 1832; died in the army during the Civil War.
—316   Nancy Ann,[6] d. in infancy.
—317   Esther Anna,[6] d. in infancy.
—318   Levina Ann,[6] d. in infancy.
  By second marriage.
—319   Luama,[6] m. **John May**, 1862.
—320   Levi,[6] lost his life in the Civil War, aged 19 years.
+321   Simon Cope.[6]
—322   Edith,[6] d. aged 6 years.
—323   Melinda,[6] b. 1848; m. **Jordan Ballard**, Jan. 7, 1872; res. Cambridge, Iowa.
—324   Lucinda,[6] d. aged two years.

133. Benjamin Stratton[5] (*Benjamin,*[4] *Joseph,*[3] *David,*[2] *Mark*[1]) married **Martha Carey**, Jan. 26, 1832. Lived and died in Knightstown. They had four children. Three died in infancy. The fourth, Nancy,[6] married —— **Hudelson** and moved to Iowa.

137. Joseph Stratton[5] (*Benjamin,*[4] *Joseph,*[3] *David,*[2] *Mark*[1]) was a farmer and carpenter. He married **Ann Hawley**, daughter of *Richard* and *Rachel Hawley*. They were married in Hopewell Church, Dudley Township, Henry Co., Ind. Ann was born Nov. 1, 1819, and died Dec. 6, 1877. Joseph died in 1889.

Children:—*Born in Henry Co., Ind.*

—325 Richard Hawley,⁶ b. Jan. 13, 1841; m. **Luama Hall**, daughter of *Moses* and *Anna (Newberry) Hall;* resided in Straughns, Ind.; died 1911.

+326 Benjamin,⁶ b. Nov. 13, 1842.

—327 Melinda,⁶ 1944; d. aged 3 years.

—328 Mary Jane,⁶ b. 1846; d. aged 17 years.

—329 Isaac Newton,⁶ b. July 5, 1848; d. Aug. 18, 1875.

—330 Eli Franklin,⁶ b. June 11, 1850; m. 1st, **Elmira Bell**, 2nd, **Sarah Henshaw**.

—331 Rebecca Ann,⁶ Nov. 28, 1855; d. Aug. 29, 1863.

145. LEVI STRATTON⁵ (*Mahlon,⁴ Daniel,³ David,² Mark¹*) was born in Campbell Co., Va., Aug. 5, 1799. Came with his parents to Clinton Co., O., when he was ten years old. He married **Mary S. Batton**, Jan. 21, 1858. He was a mechanic. In 1888 he moved to Logan Co., O. He died in Pickereltown, O., June 9, 1894.

Child:—*Born in Clinton Co., O.*

—332 Dolly B.,⁶ res. Pickereltown, O.

146. DAVID STRATTON⁵ (*Mahlon,⁴ Daniel,³ David,² Mark¹*) was born in Virginia, May 7, 1801, and came to Clinton Co., O., at the age of 8 years. He married **Lydia Baker** and lived in Clinton County.

Children:

—333 Sarah.⁶

—334 Hannah.⁶

—335 James M.⁶

—336 Eliza.⁶

—337 Alfred.⁶

—338 Albert.⁶

—339 Mortemer.⁶

—340 Virginia.⁶

150. MAHLON STRATTON⁵ (*Mahlon,⁴ Daniel,³ David,² Mark¹*) was born in Virginia, Sept. 25, 1809. In the fall of the same year his parents immigrated to Ohio. He married, first, **Mary J. Connely**, and, second, **Mrs. Harriet (Jenks) Osborn**, who died Dec. 5, 1887. After the death of his first wife he moved with his children to Paris, Ill. Some years after he married the second time, and moved back to Clinton Co., O., where he died Jan. 25, 1882. He was a farmer and a member of the Friends' Society.

Children:—*Born in Old Town, Green Co., O.*
By first marriage.
—341 Cynthia Ann,⁶ b. Apr. 15, 1833, m. **John H. Connely,** Sept. 22, 1853. She died in Paris, Ill., Feb. 28, 1914.
+342 David Williamson.⁶
Born at Ogden, Clinton Co., O.
—343 Martha J.,⁶ d., unm., at Ogden, O.
—344 Rebecca A.,⁶ d. in infancy.
—345 Nancy Ervin,⁶ d., unm., at Paris, Ill.
—346 Henry M.,⁶ d. in infancy.
—347 Sarah E.,⁶ m. **David Osborn**; res. Blanchester, O.
—348 John A.,⁶ m. **Amanda Turner**; d. at Ogden, O. They have one daughter, Nettie.⁷
+349 Robert A.⁶
—350 Samuel C.⁶
By second marriage.
—351 Clara E.⁶
—352 Mary E.⁶
—353 Florence A.⁶
—354 Almira A.⁶
—355 Charles,⁶ d. in childhood.

159. DAVID STRATTON⁵ (*John,*⁴ *Daniel,*³ *David,*² *Mark*¹) was born in Fairfield township, Columbiana Co., O., June 28, 1816. In 1838 he married **Susanna Betz**. He died in Leetonia, O., in Feb., 1898. He was a farmer and carpenter.
Children:—*Born near Leetonia, O.*
+356 John R.⁶
—357 Simon C.,⁶ m. **Velma F. Newhouse**, 1866. Soldier in the Civil War.
—358 George W.,⁶ m. **Precella Dickerson**, 1808; soldier in the Civil War.
—359 Artimus L.,⁶ soldier in the Civil War; received injuries from which he is totally blind.
—360 Mary,⁶ m. **Joseph Hollaway** in 1880.
—361 Lorenzo,⁶ d. in 1855.

167. WILLIAM I. STRATTON⁵ (*Elias,*⁴ *Daniel,*³ *David,*² *Mark*¹) was born in Union Co., O., Oct. 11, 1826, and died in Logan Co., O., Dec. 5, 1883. He married **Anne Predmore**, June 18, 1847. By trade he was a carpenter. He served three years in the Civil War as corporal.

Children:—*Born in Union Co., O.*
+362 John A., m. **Julia Smith**; d. in Bellefontaine, O., Oct. 27, 1900.
—363 Mary L., m. **George Craig**.
Born in Logan Co., D.
—364 Rosetta, m. **David Wiand**; res. Bellefontaine, O.

169. DANIEL M. STRATTON [5] (*Elias,*[4] *Daniel,*[3] *David,*[2] *Mark* [1]) was born in 1833. He married **Elizabeth Thompson** and lived near West Lebanon, Warren Co., Ind.
Child:—*Born in Warren Co., O.*
—365 Nancy.[6]

171. ELIAS J. H. STRATTON [5] (*Elias,*[4] *Daniel,*[3] *David,*[2] *Mark* [1]) was born in Logan Co., O., May 20, 1844. Soldier in the Civil War, enlisted in Bellefontaine, O., in 1862; discharged at Mobile, Ala., in 1865. Married, first, June 20, 1869, **Martha E. Bush**, who died Dec. 26, 1871; second, Nov. 29, 1877, **Louisa Dear**, who died May 24, 1885; third, Feb. 8, 1886, **Julia Thompson Archer**, who died Sept., 1902; fourth, July 4, 1907, **Mrs. Mary (Combs) Day**. He is a carpenter and resides in Harrisonville, O., in a nice home which he built almost entirely with his own hands at the age of sixty-eight.
Children:—*Born in Logan Co., O.*
By first marriage.
—366 Floyd S.[6]
By second marriage.
+367 Henry W.[6]
—368 Roy B.,[6] m. **Martha Walker**, Oct. 9, 1906; res. Springfield, O.
—369 Edith Augusta,[6] m. **Joseph Wade**.
—370 Louisa,[6] m. **J. J. Reynolds**.

174. AARON STRATTON [5] (*Aaron,*[4] *Joshua,*[3] *Daniel,*[2] *Mark* [1]) was born in 1799 at Great Egg Harbor, N. J., and was but seven years old when his parents moved to Ohio, settling at Salem.* He learned the cabinet-makers' trade, but later was a miller by occupation. On his farm near Salem he built and operated a large grist and saw mill.

---

*Salem, and much of the surrounding country, was settled by Quakers, who brought with them true ideas of human freedom, and habits of frugal industry, which they instilled into the minds of their children.

He married **Hannah Townsend** Mar. 17, 1821. They were lifelong Friends. He died in 1851.

Children:—*Born near Salem, O.*
- —371   Lewis,[6] b. 1822; d. 1827.
- +372   Joel,[6] b. 1824.
- —373   Emily,[6] b. 1825; d. 1902; m. **John M. Holmes**, 1852.
- —374   Edwin,[6] b. 1827; d. 1831.
- —375   Rachel,[6] b. 1829; d. 1862; m. **George Adams**.
- —376   Martha,[6] b. 1831; d. 1860.
- —377   Rebecca,[6] b. 1833; educated at the Friends' Boarding School at Mt. Pleasant, as were her older brothers and sisters; m. **Alexander S. Latty**, in 1856. He died in 1895, she is living with her devoted son and daughter, in Defiance, O.
- —378   Lydia,[6] b. 1835; d. 1860.
- —379   Jerusha,[6] b. 1837; m. 1st, **Jacob Houns**; 2nd, **Joseph Jenkins**.
- —380   Sina,[6] b. 1840; d. 1901; m. **Thomas Hooper**.
- —381   Louise,[6] b. 1842; m. Capt. **Joseph Ice**.
- —382   J. Whittier,[6] b. Mar. 10, 1848; m. **Jane Crawford**; d. in Masterville, O., in 1877. Chn. Ethel,[7] d. 1875; Donald,[7] m. *Bessie Moyers*, 1903.

175.   JOSIAH STRATTON[5] (*Michael,*[4] *Joshua,*[3] *Daniel,*[2] *Mark*[1]) was born Gloucester Co., N. J., Feb. 21, 1788. When a young man he came with the rest of his father's family to Columbiana Co., O. He died at Augusta, O., Nov. 13, 1846. He married **Deborah Schooley**, who died in 1862 in Oskaloosa, Iowa.

Children:—*Born in Salem, O.*
- +383   Ross,[6] b. 1813.
- +384   Elisha,[6] b. 1814.
- —385   Ellen,[6] b. Jan. 30, 1817; m. **Thomas Leach**, 1840; d. 1853.
- —386   Ann,[6] b. Feb. 8, 1819; m. **David Dean**, 1850; d. 1902.
- —387   Sarah,[6] b. Mar. 22, 1822; m. **Cyrenus Emmons**, 1844.
- —388   Lydia,[6] b. Jan. 3, 1826; d. 1888; m. **Benjamin Curlson**, Jan. 30, 1848.
- +389   Charles,[6] b. 1828.
- —390   Rhoda,[6] b. Sept. 7, 1832; d. in infancy.

176.   CHARLES STRATTON[5] (*Michael,*[4] *Joshua,*[3] *Daniel,*[2] *Mark*[1]) was born near Haddenfield, N. J., May 6, 1890, and was twenty years old when he settled in Columbiana Co., O. In 1811 he married **Hannah Mickle**. He died in Salem, O., in 1852.

Children:—*Born in Salem, O.*
- −391 Rhoda,[6] b. 1815; d., unm., in Salem, 1886.
- +392 James,[6] b. 1818.
- −393 Michael,[6] b. 1818; d. 1818.
- −394 Martha,[6] b. 1821; m. **William Daniel**; d. 1902.
- +395 John M.,[6] b. 1827.

177. JOSEPH STRATTON [5] (*Michael,*[4] *Joshua,*[3] *Daniel,*[2] *Mark* [1]) was born near Haddenfield, Gloucester (now Camden) Co., N. J., Apr. 15, 1792, and came to Columbiana Co., O., in the spring of 1810. He married **Sarah Test,** and settled on a farm near Salem, where he died in 1843 and is buried in Elk Run graveyard near the northwest corner of the meeting house.*

Children:—*Born near Salem, O.*
- −396 Rebecca,[6] b. Mar. 29, 1816; m. **Edwin Holloway**; d. Nov., 1884.
- −397 Anna M.,[6] b. Sept. 1, 1817; m. 1st, **John Brantingham**, 2nd, **James (or Joseph) Edgerton**; d. Jan. 28, 1897.
- −398 Abi,[6] b. Oct. 4, 1819; m. **James Heald**; d. Oct. 11, 1879.
- +399 Mark,[6] b. 1821.
- +400 Zaccheus,[6] b. 1824.
- −401 Joseph,[6] b. Oct. 9, 1825; d. Mar. 8, 1882; m. **Rachel Brantingham.**
- −402 Rhoda,[6] b. Mar. 7, 1827; d., unm., Nov. 5, 1830.
- −403 Michael,[6] b. Jan. 30, 1829; d., unm., Dec. 14, 1854.
- −404 Sarah,[6] b. June 13, 1830; m. **David Lupton**; d. Aug. 2, 1888.
- −405 Isaac,[6] b. July 17, 1832; d., unm., Dec. 4, 1952.
- +406 Josiah,[6] b. 1833.

180. JOSHUA STRATTON [5] (*Michael,*[4] *Joshua,*[3] *Daniel,*[2] *Mark* [1]) was born July 1, 1796, in Gloucester Co., N. J., and came to Columbiana Co., O., in 1810. He married **Rachael Townsend,**

---

* Elk Run graveyard and meeting house, so closely connected with the early Strattons, are still well cared for.

Headstones have only recently been permitted, and so the old Stratton graves are unmarked, as are nine-tenths of the graves within the yard, save by the carefully elevated mounds corresponding in size to the age of the one interred.

Mar. 4, 1819, and lived in Salem, where he was a faithful member of the Friends' Society. He died Aug. 23, 1843.

Children:—*Born in Salem, O.*
—407   Sina,[6] b. May 27, 1820; m. **Wilson Hall**.
+408   Edward,[6] b. 1822.
—409   Francis,[6] b. 1825; drowned in a pond near Salem, June 25, 1842.
—410   Joshua,[6] b. 1826; drowned in a pond near Salem, June 25, 1842.

181. DANIEL STRATTON[5] (*Michael,*[4] *Joshua,*[3] *Daniel,*[2] *Mark*[1]) was born Aug. 12, 1799, near Haddenfield, N. J., and came to Columbiana Co., O., when he was eleven years old. In 1823 he married **Abigail Borton**. Their home was in Salem, O. He died in Winona, O., Feb. 6, 1872.

Children:—*Born in Salem, O.*
—411   Michael,[6] b. May 7, 1824, a physician; m. **Martha Williams**, daughter of *Jos. Williams;* d. May 10, 1847; his wife died Sept. 8, 1851.
+412   Benjamin D., b. 1825.
—413   John, b. Jan. 9, 1827; was drowned, aged 17 years.
+414   Barklay, b. 1829.
—415   Esther, b. May 9, 1833; m. **Joseph Masters**.

183. AARON STRATTON[5] (*Michael,*[4] *Joshua,*[3] *Daniel,*[2] *Mark*[1]) was born in New Jersey, Oct. 31, 1801. Came to Ohio at the age of nine years. He married **Unity Crews**. He died in Salem, May 27, 1885.

Children:—*Born in Salem, O.*
+416   Simeon, b. Oct. 3, 1828.
—417   Rachel, b. June 27, 1830; d., unm., in Salem in 1909.
—418   Eliza, Jan. 19, 1834.
+419   Lewis, b. Nov. 21, 1836.
—420   Evi, b. Nov. 3, 1841; m. **Ann Strong**; d. in the army from wounds received in battle, Oct. 8, 1862; no children.
—421   Francis, b. Feb. 14, 1844; m. **Jennie Walton**; no children.

187. GEORGE STRATTON[5] (*Michael,*[4] *Joshua,*[3] *Daniel*[2] *Mark*[1]) was born Nov. 27, 1809, in Gloucester Co., N. J., and died Mar. 17, 1887, in Columbus, O. In 1834 he married **Susannah Evans**.

1. Samuel E. Stratton; *Page* 317. 2. David D. Stratton; *Page* 459.
3. Seth Le Grand Stratton; *Page* 318. 4. Nancy (Stratton) Hunter;
Page 458. 5. Hannah (Stratton) Wheeler; *Page* 40.

Children:—*Born at Goshen, O.*
—422 Mary,⁶ b. Nov. 7, 1836; m. **Jos. Shinn** in 1854; d. in Stringdale, Iowa, 1899.
—423 Elizabeth,⁶ b. 1842; d. Nov. 4, 1856.
—424 Rhoda,⁶ b. Sept. 26, 1844; m. **Joseph Ong.**
—425 Esther,⁶ b. Oct. 10, 1847; m. **Lorenzo Akin.**
—426 Anna,⁶ m. **Stewart Todd;** res. Lisbon, O., R. F. D. No. 6.

192. Daniel Stratton ⁵ (*Stacy*,⁴ *Joshua*,³ *Daniel*,² *Mark* ¹) was born Nov. 13, 1804, in Gloucester Co., N. J., and was six years old when his father's family moved to Ohio. By trade he was a cabinet maker. He married, first, **Angelina Phillips**, June 4, 1832, daughter of *John* and *Nancy Phillips*. She died Sept. 6, 1857. He married **Mary A. Rakestraw**, Apr. 27, 1859. He died in Salem, O., Mar. 18, 1884.

Children:—*Born in Pittsburg, Pa.*
—427 John,⁶ b. Apr. 26, 1836; d. in infancy.
—428 Elvira P.,⁶ b. Dec. 27, 1841; m. **Emmer Templin**, Aug. 9, 1867.
+429 William H.,⁶ b. Aug. 17, 1845.

195. Stacy Lippincott Stratton ⁵ (*Stacy*,⁴ *Joshua*,³ *Daniel*,² *Mark* ¹) was born Sept. 3, 1811, the year after his parents moved from New Jersey to Ohio, and passed his boyhood on his father's farm. Jan. 24, 1833, he married **Margaret Grimmesey**, who was born in County Tyrone, Ireland. He was raised a Quaker but became a Methodist, of which church both he and his wife were members to the time of their deaths. They lived near Salem until about 1848, when they moved to Peru, Ind.; from there to Mt. Hope, Wis., in 1854, and to Clay Center, Kan., in 1870. Mrs. Stratton died Sept. 28, 1890; Mr. Stratton, Oct. 11, 1891.

Children:—*Born near Salem, O.*
—430 Hannah Anne,⁶ b. Oct. 19, 1833; d. June 1, 1892.
—431 Anness Lucinda,⁶ b. June 30, 1835.
—432 Eliza Adeline,⁶ b. Jan. 8, 1838; d. June 15, 1803.
+433 Alcinous L.,⁶ b. Apr. 23, 1840; d. Mar. 29, 1897.
—434 Mary Catherine,⁶ b. Nov. 1, 1842; d. May 17, 1881.
+435 Gilmore M.,⁶ b. July 9, 1845.
—436 Albert P.,⁶ b. Apr. 3, 1847; d. Aug. 27, 1847.
—437 Lemon E.,⁶ b. Aug. 31, 1850; d. Oct. 2, 1852.

196. William C. Stratton[5] (*Stacy*,[4] *Joshua*,[3] *Daniel*,[2] *Mark*[1]) was born near Salem, O., Oct. 28, 1813. In May, 1835, he married **Julia Ann Woolf**. He died May 30, 1875.

Children:—*Born in Goshen Township, Mahoning Co., O.*

—438 Stacy W.,[6] b. Mar. 13, 1837; d. aged 8 mos., 12 days.
—439 Elizabeth S.,[6] b. Nov. 13, 1838; d. aged 1 year, 1 mo., 13 days.
—440 Elma E.,[6] b. Dec. 18, 1839; m. **Samuel Weaver**, Mar. 17, 1867; d. Dec. 12, 1909.
—441 Maria H.,[6] b. May 12, 1841; m. **Prof. Gershone B. Horner*** June 1, 1885. They worked together as evangelists, speaker and singer for nearly twenty years.
—442 Martha K.,[6] b. Aug. 6, 1843; m. **David H. Venable**, Oct. 30, 1864; d. Jan. 28, 1912.
+443 Job L.,[6] b. Feb. 4, 1845.
—444 John D.,[6] b. Feb. 1, 1847; d. aged 1 year, 7 mos., 27 days.
+445 George W.[6]
+446 Preston D.,[6] b. Dec. 28, 1852.
+447 Walter S.,[6] b. Sept. 16, 1856.

199. Simri Stratton[5] (*Job*,[4] *Jonathan*,[3] *Daniel*,[2] *Mark*[1]) was born in Evesham Township, N. J., Sept. 12, 1807. When he was about thirteen years old his parents moved with their family of five children to Warren Co., O. He went from Waynesville, O., to Richmond, Ind., in 1826, and the following year, Oct. 15, 1827, he married **Elizabeth Baker**, daughter of Hugh Baker. She died Nov. 3, 1832. Nov. 29, 1833, Mr. Stratton married **Hannah Osborn**. He died in Richmond Feb. 15, 1873. Mrs. Hannah Stratton died July 20, 1901. By trade he was a blacksmith. He was a member in good standing of the Orthodox branch of the Friends' Society.

Children:—*Born in Richmond, Ind.*

---

* One who knew Mrs. Horner well writes: "Among those who have attended the Patmos school, no one has occupied a larger place in the hearts and lives of the people with whom she came in contact than did Maria Stratton Horner, who was known throughout the states of Ohio and Pennsylvania not only for her beautiful life and excellent Christian character, but by the thousands of men and women who, under the influence of her earnest pleadings, became followers of the Lord Jesus Christ during the twenty-five years she spent in evangelistic work."

By first marriage.
+448 Daniel B.,[6] b. 1828.
+449 Stephen,[6] b. 1831.
By second marriage.
−450 Ellen Maria,[6] b. June 27, 1835; d. aged 17 years.
−451 Charles W.[6] His daughter Ann[7] m. **Arthur James**; res. Richmond, Ind.
−452 Joseph Isaac,[6] d. a soldier on Chilo battlefield May 8, 1862.
Born in Hagerstown, Ind.
−453 Samuel F.,[6] m. **Laura Paxson**; d. Sept. 27, 1902.
Born in Richmond, Ind.
−454 Sarah Elizabeth,[6] res. Cincinnati, O.

206. CHARLES STRATTON[5] (*Owen*,[4] *Jonathan*,[3] *Daniel*,[2] *Mark*[1]) was born near Medford, N. J., Aug. 11, 1811. He married, first, **Mary W. Troth**, daughter of *Levi* and *Sarah* (*Hills*) *Troth*. They lived on the farm inherited from his father, and later moved into Marlton, N. J., where he died in 1866. His wife died in 1853, and he married, second, **Rebecca Ann Hawkins**, in 1873.

Children:—*Born near Marlton, N. J.*
+455 Joseph Owen,[6] b. Oct. 12, 1835.
+456 Francis Shreve,[6] b. May 28, 1837.
+457 Charles W.,[6] b. Mar. 7, 1839.
−458 John W.,[6] b. Apr. 12, 1841.
+459 Amos Haines,[6] b. June 20, 1845.
+460 Benjamin Irvin,[6] b. Dec. 20, 1847.
−461 Mary Clementine,[6] b. June 23, 1850; m. **Richard Leeds**; d. in Marlton, N. J., Jan. 17, 1901.

211. JONATHAN DALLAS STRATTON[5] (*Eli*,[4] *Jonathan*,[3] *Daniel*,[2] *Mark*[1]) was born in Evesham, N. J., Nov. 8, 1804. He moved with his father's family to Preble, Ohio, about 1820. Oct. 1, 1828, he married **Prudence Edgerton**, daughter of *Samuel Edgerton*. In 1849 they moved to Rush Co., Ind., settling on a farm. Jonathan died near Kokomo, Ind., June 8, 1879. Prudence died a few years earlier at the same place.*

---

*Eunice Dallas, the mother of Jonathan Dallas Stratton, was a relative of George M. Dallas, Vice-President under James K. Polk.

A daughter of Jonathan Stratton writes that her grandfather, Eli Stratton, left New Jersey as early as 1816 and went to Philadelphia,

Children:—*Born in Preble Co., O.*
- —462 William,⁶ b. 1829; d. in infancy.
- —463 Jonathan,⁶ b. 1830; d. in infancy.
- —464 Millicent Ann,⁶ b. July 8, 1831; m. —— **Wright**; d. in Iowa Jan. 8, 1867.
- —465 Samuel Edgerton,⁶ b. Aug. 30, 1833; m. **Sarah Hollingworth** in 1832; d. at Kokomo, Ind., Oct. 10, 1884.
- +466 Joseph L.⁶
- +467 Eli B.,⁶ b. 1838.
- —468 Eunice,⁶ b. 1840; d. in childhood.

212. WILLIAM LOVE STRATTON⁵ (*Eli,⁴ Jonathan,³ Daniel,² Mark¹*) was born Mar. 14, 1808. He attended school at an academy in Philadelphia. At the age of fifteen years he went with his father to Preble Co., O., where for some years he clerked in his father's store. June 6, 1832, he married **Bathsheba Brown.** They located in Richmond, Ind., where he opened a shoe store. His health failing, he returned to Preble Co., O., and bought a farm. Here he resided until his death, Apr. 22, 1885, and was buried at the Friends' cemetery near his home. He belonged to Westfield Monthly Meeting, and Indiana yearly meeting of Friends. He was firm in the faith of his Society, and kind and generous to those in need.

Children:—*Born in Richmond, Ind.*
- —469 Sarah B.,⁶ b. Apr. 11, 1833; m. **Lewis Underwood,** and lived at Sheridan, Ind.; d. Aug. 3, 1908.
- —470 John B.,⁶ b. Jan. 30, 1835; d. in infancy.
- —471 Eunice D.,⁶ b. May 30, 1836; d. unm. Apr., 1876.
- —472 Ann Eliza,⁶ b. Oct. 2, 1840; m. **Egbert Higby.**
- —473 Mary M.,⁶ b. July 30, 1845; m. **Isaac H. Browne**; res. Camden, O.

213. JOSEPH ELKINGTON STRATTON⁵ (*Eli,⁴ Jonathan,³ Daniel,² Mark¹*) was born Sept. 2, 1811, in New Jersey. He was a birthright member of the Friends' Society. Was a farmer most of his life. He married, first, **Nancy Morrow,** Oct. 30, 1838, who died Nov. 21, 1843; second, **Martha Henley,** Mar. 4, 1846, who died Jan. 25, 1864; third, **Ann Eliza Brown,** Sept. 9, 1868. She

---

where he engaged in business as a merchant and where his children attended school. About six years later he removed to Preble Co., O., locating on Four-Mile-Creek, where he built a grist mill and storehouse and engaged in milling and general merchandising.

died at Long Beach, Cal., Feb. 8, 1914. Mr. Stratton died at Carmel, Ind., Nov. 24, 1878. All his children had birthrights in the Friends' Church.

Children:
    By first marriage.
+474 Edward Dallas,[6] b. Oct. 11, 1839.
—475 Caroline Elizabeth,[6] b. Mar. 25, 1841; m. **George H. Johnson**; d. in Monrovia, Ind., June 17, 1879.
—476 Charles William,[6] b. Feb. 10, 1843; d. in childhood.
    B*orn near Richmond, Ind.*
    By second marriage.
—477 Henry H.,[6] b. Aug. 31, 1847; m. **Rowena Fream**, Aug. 27, 1876. No children.
+478 Micajah H.,[6] b. Mar. 4, 1850; m. **Antonia B. Jerjius**, May 1, 1876. Res. Huntsville, Texas.
—479 Albert W.,[6] m. **Lizzie Wright**, 1882; d. July 19, 1888, at Shelbyville, Ind. No children.
+480 Eli L.,[6] b. Apr. 28, 1854.
+481 Oliver.[6]
—482 Eunice,[6] d. in childhood.
—483 Guliema (Elma),[6] m. 1st, —— **Kenzer**, Mar. 4, 1885; 2nd, **Ira Haines**, May 25, 1887; res. Carmel, Ind.

215. JOHN REEVES STRATTAN [5] (*John,*[4] *David,*[3] *Daniel,*[2] *Mark*[1]) was born at Port Elizabeth, N. J., in 1807, and moved to Clarion Co., Ohio, with his parents when about thirteen years old. He married, first, **Mary E. Barber**, Aug. 20, 1830; second, **Emma Ferguson**. His home was in Strattonville, where he built the fourth house on the town site after it was laid out by his father. He became one of the prominent men of that section, and accumulated considerable wealth. He was a farmer, a merchant, a lumber dealer and had interests in other enterprises in the building up of the community. He was one of the organizers of the First National Bank of Clarion, Pa., in 1865, and an officer and heavy stockholder. He was an active and influential member of the Methodist Church; in politics a Republican. He died Jan. 8, 1881.

Children:—*Born in Strattonville, Pa.*
    By first marriage.
+484 Charles B.[6]
    By second marriage.
—485 Harry Ferguson,[6] m. **Amanda Jane Rulofson**, May 9,

1901; grad. Allegheny College, 1898; mem. Σ A E Fraternity; mem. Masonic Lodge; asst. cashier 1st Nat. Bank at Clarion, Pa.

—486 Custer Ferguson,[6] m. **Acte Basim,** Jan. 20, 1900; supt. Strattonville Oil and Gas Co.; chn.: Cyril,[7] Harry, Jr.[7]

218. JOSEPH SHOUGH STRATTAN [5] (*John,*[4] *David,*[3] *Daniel,*[2] *Mark* [1]) was born in Burlington Co., N. J., Dec. 17, 1814, coming with his parents to Pennsylvania when he was about six years old. Sept. 10, 1836, he married **Lieucetta Wrhen,** daughter of *Samuel* (son of *Henry*) and *Sarah* (*White*) *Wrhen*. She was born Oct. 23, 1816. They lived at Strattonville, Pa., the town of which his father was one of the founders in 1826. He and his family have always been closely identified with the best interests of the town. He died Sept. 27, 1894.

Children:—*Born at Strattonville, Pa.*

—487 Dr. John Thomas,[6] b. 1837; resides Washington, D. C. Soldier in Civil War. Commissioned officer in 105th Pa. Vols., also the 3rd Pa. artillery at Fortress Monroe.

+488 Samuel R.,[6] b. 1839.

—489 Milton David,[6] b. 1841; assistant postmaster at Strattonville; private in 3rd Pa. Cavalry Vols.; m. **Sarah P. Williams.**

—490 Elizabeth,[6] b. 1844; m. 1st, **George W. Couser,** 1865; 2nd, **William Bean,** 1872.

—491 Grenfill Blake,[6] in government employ, Post Office Dept., Washington, D. C.

+492 Joseph C.[6]

219. DANIEL STRATTON [5] (*Joseph,*[4] *David,*[3] *Daniel,*[2] *Mark* [1]) was born in Culpeper, Va., Sept. 25, 1800. The following year his parents moved to Elkrun Township, Columbiana Co., O. Jan. 11, 1826, he married **Eliza Jenkins,** daughter of *David* and *Hannah* (*Doddridge*) *Jenkins*. He died Jan. 6, 1850, and was buried in Doddridge graveyard.

Children:—*Born in Columbiana Co., O.*

—493 Hannah A.,[6] b. Sept. 26, 1827; d. Mar. 5, 1896; unm.

—494 Helen M.,[6] b. June, 1830; d. aged 9 years.

—495 Rebecca N.,[6] b. Sept. 5, 1841; d. aged about 2 years.

—496 Laura L.,[6] b. Dec. 31, 1843; m. **John S. Stoddard,** Dec. 7, 1876.

220. JOHN STRATTON [5] (*Joseph,*[4] *David,*[3] *Daniel,*[2] *Mark*[1]) was born in Elkrun Township, Columbiana Co., O., Jan. 3, 1803. He married **Nancy A. Jackson,** daughter of *Lemuel* and *Mary (White) Jackson,* Sept. 3, 1854, and settled in Centerville, Ind., where he died July 26, 1882.
Child:
—497 Lucy L., b. July 26, 1856; m. 1st, Samuel Hiller, Nov. 26, 1874; 2nd, J. B. Easley, Mar. 1, 1893.

223. Dr. OWEN ROLEN STRATTON [5] (*Joseph,*[4] *David,*[3] *Daniel,*[2] *Mark*[1]) was a prominent physician of Wayne Co., Ind., for many years. He died Mar. 10, 1889, and is buried at Crown Hill Cemetery, near Centerville. He was never married.

224. ELWOOD STRATTON, m. **Hannah Gieberson**; d. Sept. 21, 1881; a druggist at Moorestown.

225. SAMUEL STRATTON,[5] m. **Mary Bird.**

226. REUBEN STRATTON,[5] m. **Adelia ——**; lived at Freehold, N. J.

229. RICHARD STRATTON,[5] m. **Isabella Hathaway.**

The above are sons of Reuben Stratton [4] (*Ephraim,*[3] *John,*[2] *Mark*[1]). The compiler has failed to obtain data or address of their descendants.

233. ENOCH BRANSON STRATTON [5] (*John,*[4] *Enoch,*[3] *John,*[2] *Mark*[1]) was born June 18, 1826, at the Stratton home between Medford and Crosskeys, N. J. Apr. 14, 1850, he married **Anna M. Rice,** who died in 1853. He died Apr. 26, 1893. Left no children.

235. WILLIAM STRATTON [5] (*John,*[4] *Enoch,*[3] *John,*[2] *Mark*[1]) was born Mar. 11, 1830. He married, Mar. 10, 1855, **Rachel (Halling) Clark,** widow, daughter of *Lawrence* and *Mary (Conrow) Halling.* They lived in Marlton, Glendale and Camden, N. J. He died Dec. 20, 1912.
Children:—*Born in Marlton, N. J.*
—498 Franklin,[6] b. Mar. 4, 1856; d. aged 8 years.
—499 Mary Ida,[6] m. **H. E. Vansceirt**; d. Nov. 7, 1903.

Born in Glendale, N. J.

+500   William H.⁶
+501   Howard B.⁶
—502   Anna C.,⁶ m. **Edward H. Fry.**

237. THEODORE STRATTON⁵ (*John*,⁴ *Enoch*,³ *John*,² *Mark*¹) was born July 14, 1835. In 1860 he went to Wilmington, Del.; returned to New Jersey two years later and enlisted in Co. A, 12th Reg., N. J. Volunteers. After the war he went back to Delaware. Jan. 1, 1866, he married **Eliza Sherry**, daughter of *John* and *Sarah Alice (Spear) Sherry* of Philadelphia. After their marriage they lived in Smyrna and Wilmington. He was a building contractor. He died Feb. 22, 1909.

Children:—*Born in Delaware.*
—503   John Sherry,⁶ b. Nov. 14, 1866; d. Mar. 12, 1881.
—504   Elizabeth Stokes,⁶ m. **John Cord Blizzard**, Oct. 30, 1893; res. Havre de Grace, Md.

238. JAMES LEANDER STRATTON⁵ (*John*,⁴ *Enoch*,³ *John*,² *Mark*¹) is a carpenter and lives in Camden. He was born Oct. 19, 1839. He was a soldier in the Civil War; Sergeant in 23rd N. J. Volunteers. Mar. 22, 1866, he married **Elizabeth Gosline**, daughter of *John* and *Lydia (Malsbury) Gosline.* She was born May 15, 1834, and died Feb. 5, 1883. He died Sept. 13, 1913.

Children:—*Born in Bristol, Pa.*
+505   John Gosline.⁶
—506   Hannah P.,⁶ d. July 10, aged 3 years.

241. GEORGE WOOLEY STRATTAN⁵ (*Enoch*,⁴ *Enoch*,³ *John*,² *Mark*¹) was born in Philadelphia Jan. 26, 1836.* When he was twelve years old his family moved to New York City. After attending the public school and Lexington Ave. Academy, he entered a wholesale hardware store. In March, 1856, in company with two other young men, he went west. At Chicago they purchased a farm wagon with oiled muslin cover, farm implements, and at Dubuque a yoke of oxen, all of which were shipped by river to St. Paul. Then began a three weeks' journey through a swampy country with bad roads (or no roads!) to a point fifty miles west of St. Paul. Here they staked out three quarter sections of prairie land and one of woods along the side of "High

---

*This family and several closely related families spell the name Strattan.

Island Lake" and built a log house; also a piece of land for a town site which they called "New Auburn," where they soon set up a portable saw-mill shipped out to them from Auburn, N. Y. While at work here Mr. Stratton cut his ankle so severely that he was unable to participate in further work connected with the farm and mill, so returned to New York. Later he went to Philadelphia and learned the trade of a machinist in the shops of Wm. Sellers & Co. In 1861 he entered the shops of the P. R. R. at Altoona, Pa., where he remained for more than forty years, as gang foreman, then assistant master mechanic, then master mechanic, where 6,000 men were employed. He entered largely into the various charitable, philanthropic and municipal affairs of Altoona, devoting time and means to their organization and development, and occupied many positions of trust and responsibility. In 1906 he retired from business and has since spent much time in travel, visiting nearly every country in Europe, Egypt, India, China, Japan, the Philippines, Hawaii, Panama and the West Indies. Sept 24, 1863, he married **Mary Virginia Satterthwaite,** who was born Sept. 30, 1833, in Middleburg, Va., and died at Altoona Feb. 10, 1897. She was a daughter of *Samuel* and *Hannah Satterthwaite* of Philadelphia. In 1906 he married **Margaret May Schneider.**

Children:—*Born in Altoona, Pa.*

—507 Charlotte Lewis,[6] m. **Clarence Elmer Postlethwaite,** Mar. 27, 1890.

—508 Clement Thorn,[6] b. May 29, 1868; d. Sept. 22, 1889.

—509 George Edmund,[6] graduate Swarthmore College, 1895; inspector of passenger equipment, Penn. R. R.; m. **Deborah Ferrier,** Nov. 20, 1914, daughter of *George Bartlett* and *Carrie (Arnold) Ferrier;* res. Moorestown, N. J. Ch. Ruth Ferrier.

244. WILLIAM IRVINE STRATTON [5] (*Enoch,*[4] *Enoch,*[3] *John,*[2] *Mark* [1]) was born in Philadelphia in 1845. June 15, 1875, he married **Elizabeth Onderdonk,** who was born in 1852. They live at Altoona, where he is in the employ of the Penn. R. R. They have no children.

245. EDWARD RANDOLPH STRATTON [5] (*Enoch,*[4] *Enoch,*[3] *John,*[2] *Mark* [1]) was born in Philadelphia in Mar. 19, 1850. Feb. 20, 1879, he married **Clara Hayes McCormick.** She was born Mar. 19, 1850, and died Mar. 2, 1888.

Children:—*Born in Altoona, Pa.*
—510 Lester Adams,[6] b. Aug. 29, 1880; d. aged 2 years, 4 mos.
—511 Ralph Thorn,[6] grad. of Williamson School of Mechanical Arts; draughtsman in Penn. R. R. shops at Altoona.
512 Mary Elizabeth,[6] m. **Charles Robert Hubbard**; res. Hamilton, Can.
512a Eleanor, d. in infancy.

246. ISAIAH STRATTON [5] (*Gideon,*[4] *Isaiah,*[3] *Enoch,*[2] *Mark*[1]) was born at Mt. Holly, N. J., Dec. 15, 1803. Apr. 21, 1828, he married **Esther D. Borton**, at Mt. Holly. She was daughter of *Obediah* and *Sarah Borton*. He died June 30, 1851. Three years later his widow and children moved to Richmond, Ind., where she died Oct. 30, 1855, at the age of 50 years.*

Children:—*Born at Mt. Holly, N. J.*
—513 Ann Maria,[6] m. **Nathan Hunt** in 1857, and lived on a farm near Richmond.
—514 Rebecca,[6] m. **Daniel B. Stratton** in 1855 (No. 448). They resided at Richmond, Ind.
—515 Job Henry [6] was 1st lieutenant in 69th Ind. Regiment. Was wounded at Vicksburg, in 1863, and died there, aged 27 years, 7 mos. and 16 days.
—516 Emma,[6] m. **John L. Rupe** in 1875. They reside in Richmond where he is prosecuting attorney and for several years was mayor of the city.

247. BENJAMIN STRATTON [5] (*Gideon,*[4] *Isaiah,*[3] *Enoch,*[2] *Mark*[1]) was born at Mt. Holly, N. J., Sept. 21, 1805. He married **Elizabeth Larrison**, and died in Philadelphia, Aug. 8, 1882. He was an wholesale and retail shoe merchant.

Children:—*Born in Philadelphia.*
—517 Sarah Jane,[6] b. Sept. 23, 1827.
+518 Charles,[6] b. July 25, 1829.

---

*Two cousins of Isaiah Green Stratton lived in Philadelphia and may have descendants there now: Benjamin, who had a son Levi, b. 1810, and William, who had three (perhaps more) sons: namely, John, who went to Cincinnati previous to 1850; Samuel, who was a starch manufacturer for many years prior to 1860; William, associated with his brother in the starch business, and who had two sons: George Washington, b. 1814, m. Frances Jane Elliot (chn. Henry Clay and Charles Elliot), and Samuel Torrance, m. Susan Lawrence (chn. Clara E., Anna May, Samuel T.).

Wm. L. Stratton: *Page* 424. John Stratton: *Page* 401. Eli Stratton: *Page* 284.
(1808-1885) (1787-1871) (1780-1860)

—519 Edwin Forest,⁶ b. Jan. 24, 1832; d. Mar. 28, 1852.
—520 Margaret Adelaide,⁶ b. Nov. 2, 1841; m. **Charles H. Gregg**, Nov. 20, 1862. Died Jan. 24, 1912, in West Philadelphia.
—521 Albert Gallatin,⁶ b. Apr. 17, 1875, a physician and druggist in Philadelphia, where he died Nov. 15, 1904. He never married.

248. CHARLES STRATTON ⁵ (*Gideon,*⁴ *Isaiah,*³ *Enoch,*² *Mark* ¹) was born in Mt. Holly, N. J., Aug. 30, 1809. He married **Mary Shinn**.

Children
—522 Howard F.,⁶ teacher of art in Philadelphia.
—523 Charles.⁶
—524 Sarah,⁶ m. **James R. Townsend** in Philadelphia, and lived and died in Salem, O.

255. ISAIAH GREEN STRATTON ⁵ (*Isaiah,*⁴ *Josiah,*³ *Enoch,*² *Mark* ¹) was born in Philadelphia June 3, 1813. Jan. 3, 1839, he married **Mary Ann Lamb**. They lived in Philadelphia where he was a merchant, member of the city council, tax collector, and inspector of customs. He was active in promoting the good government of his city, and interested in politics. A proof of his interest is shown in the names he gave two of his sons. He died in Philadelphia Feb. 8, 1887.

Children:—Born *in Philadelphia.*
—525 Isaiah Harrison,⁶ b. on the inauguration day of President Harrison, Mar. 4, 1840. Served in the Civil War, enlisting as private in 1862, in Anderson Cavalry, Philadelphia, which operated in Tennessee. Promoted for gallantry on the field to 1st sergeant. Died in army hospital, Murfreesboro, from pneumonia brought on through exposure and exhaustion in the battle of Stone River.
+526 Joel Van Meter,⁶ b. 1842.
—527 Theodore Freylinghuysen,⁶ b. Sept. 20, 1844. Enlisted at beginning of Civil War in 69th Penn. Infantry. Contracted disease in wilderness campaign, and was discharged. Upon recovery of health re-enlisted to close of war. When discharged held commission as captain.

—528 Anna Elizabeth,[6] b. Feb. 22, 1847; unm.; res. Pittsburgh, Pa.
—529 Sarah Jane,[6] b. 1849; d. 1850.

258. JOHN STRATTON,[5] b. 1819; d. unm. at Silvertown, N. J.

259. CHARLES STRATTON,[5] b. 1822; m. **Mary Thompson**; lived at Lakewood, N. J.

262. GEORGE B. STRATTON,[5] b. 1830; m. **Margaret Guice**; res. Long Branch, N. J.

263. LOVEMAN B. STRATTON,[5] b. 1833; m. **Susan Adams**.

The above are sons of Josiah Stratton[4] (*Josiah*,[3] *Enoch*,[2] *Mark*[1]) and were born in Manchester, N. J. The compiler has not succeeded in tracing their descendants.

265. EBENEZER STRATTON[5] (*Bradford*,[4] *Thomas*,[3] *Isaac*,[2] *Mark*[1]) was born Sept. 15, 1816. He married **Mary Brown**. Died in Philadelphia June 11, 1879.
Children:
+530 Jacob Brown.[6]
—531 Anna.[6]
—532 Charles.[6]
—533 William,[6] lived in Ambler, Pa.

266. STEPHEN THATCHER STRATTON[6] (*David Q.*,[5] *Joseph*,[4] *Joseph*,[3] *David*,[2] *Mark*[1]) was born Oct. 1, 1818. He married, first, **Mary Lauder**, in 1840; second, **Isabella J. Pavey**, 1849; third, **Eliza Koser**. He died in Mt. Vernon, Ill., Dec. 18, 1898.
Children:
+534 David F.[7]
—535 Rynd L.,[7] m. **Mary Jones**; chn. Keith,[8] Olivia,[8] Chancey.[8]
—536 Augusta M.[7]
—537 Ruth,[7] m. **A. C. Johnson**.
—538 Charles.[7]
—539 Emma,[7] m. **James Copeland**.
—540 Anna.[7]
—541 Mary.[7]

268. EDWARD LYNCH STRATTON[6] (*David Q.*,[5] *Joseph*,[4] *Joseph*,[3] *David*,[2] *Mark*[1]) was born Sept. 17, 1829, and resides in Buda, Ill. Sept. 16, 1862, he married **Caroline Robbins**.

Children:
- —542 Alice.[7]
- —543 Benjamin.[7]
- —544 Arthur R.,[7] res. Greenville, Iowa.
- —545 Eugene J.,[7] res. Molene, Ill.
- —546 Fred.[7]
- —547 Hattie.[7]

269. OLIVER HINMAN STRATTON[6] (*David Q.,*[5] *Joseph,*[4] *Joseph,*[3] *David,*[2] *Mark*[1]), born Aug. 8, 1832, and went from Ohio to Illinois in 1854, and from Illinois to Kansas in 1869. He married **Ruth H. Huestus** of Jersey City, N. J., Mar. 27, 1856. He is a carpenter and resides now in Vermilion, Kan.

Children:—*Born in Middlesburg, Ill.*
- +548 William D.[7]
- +549 Azariah D.[7]

Born in West Liberty, Iowa.
- —550 John H.,[7] m. **Grace Young** in Missouri in 1892; chn.: Oliver,[8] Bessie,[8] Marie.[8]

272. JOSEPH D. STRATTON[6] (*David Q.,*[5] *Joseph,*[4] *Joseph,*[3] *David,*[2] *Mark*[1]) was born Apr. 9, 1839. He married, first, **Frances E. Merryman**, in 1862; second, **Adella Turner**. Resides in Kewanee, Ill.

Children:
- —551 Ora,[7] m. **E. D. Sweet**.
- +552 Frank P.[7]
- —553 George C.,[7] m. **Bessie Palmer**; res. Kewanee; chn.: Frank P.,[8] Prudence F.,[8] Genevieve,[8] Lois.[8]

273. BENJAMIN C. STRATTON[6] (*David Q.,*[5] *Joseph,*[4] *Joseph,*[3] *David,*[2] *Mark*[1]) was born Apr. 23, 1841. In 1866 he married **Adelia M. Gregg**. Resides in Mt. Vernon, Ill.

Children:
- —554 Ed. D., m. **Minnie Bigelow**; chn. Russell, Grace B.
- —555 Roy, m. **Blanche Musgrave**.
- —556 Charles, m. **Lucy Seibert**; chn. Gregg, Gertrude.
- —557 Fred, m. **Hattie Ellis**; chn. Ruth, Leonard.
- —558 Kate, m. **William Edwards**.

279. BENJAMIN W. STRATTON[6] (*Joseph,*[5] *Joseph,*[4] *Joseph,*[3] *David,*[2] *Mark*[1]) was born Aug. 13, 1834. He married, first,

Rosaline Thomas, in 1867, daughter of *Stephen* and *Mary (Harlan) Thomas;* second, **Matilda F. Phillips**, in 1877, daughter of *Reuben Phillips*. For 21 years he was a drygoods salesman in New York. He died in 1806, at his home in Holbert, Ind.

Children:—*Born in Richmond, Ind.*
—559   Harlan T.[7]
—560   Oliver,[7] d. in Richmond, Ind., 1872.

280.   Elwood H. Stratton[6] (*Joseph P.*,[5] *Joseph*,[4] *Joseph*,[3] *David*,[2] *Mark*[1]) was born in Dublin, Ind., July 8, 1838. Married **Mary H. Lliff**, May 4, 1865, in Richmond. He was a bookkeeper. For many years Deputy County Recorder. He died Apr. 21, 1889.

Children:—*Born in Richmond, Ind.*
—561   Roy O.,[7] m. **Grace Flemming**; res. Richmond.
          Born in Indianapolis, Ind.
—562   Herbert E.,[7] res. Richmond.

282.   Abraham Sharpless Stratton[6] (*Joseph P.*,[5] *Joseph*,[4] *Joseph*,[3] *David*,[2] *Mark*[1]) was born May 8, 1841. He was a painter by trade but for many years was connected with a nursery and salesman for fruit trees. He married **Elizabeth M. Webb**, Jan. 19, 1870.

Children:—*Born in Richmond, Ind.*
—563   Stella.[7]
—564   Mary Emma.[7]
—565   Joseph Parmerlee,[7] m. 1888, **Elizabeth L. Powell**, d. of *Charles* and *Jane P. Powell*.

287.   John Haines Stratton[6] (*Micajah*,[5] *Joseph*,[4] *Joseph*,[3] *David*,[2] *Mark*[1]) was born near Wilmington, Ohio, at the Stratton farm, on Lytles Creek, May 12, 1831. He married **Judith Terrel**, Feb. 23, 1854.

Children:—*Born in Clinton Co., O.*
—566   John B.,[7] res. Hutchington, Kan.
—567   Joseph,[7] res. Paxico, Kan.; chn. Edward,[8] LeRoy,[8] Bertha,[8] Clara.[8]
—568   David J.,[7] res. Wilmington, O.
—569   Lorena [7] (twin).
—570   Irena [7] (twin).
—571   Clara.[7]
—572   Emma M.[7]

—573 Victor,[7] res. Xenia, O.
—574 Anna.[7]
—575 Mattie H.[7]

294. JOSEPH HENRY STRATTON [6] (*Benjamin*,[5] *Joseph*,[4] *Joseph*,[3] *David*,[2] *Mark* [1]), born May 13, 1838; married **Lydia Dawson** in 1861. He served through the Civil War in Co. I, 84th Reg. Ind. Vol. Was engaged in government employment at Reno, Indian Territory, where he died Oct. 26, 1884.

Children:—*Born in Richmond, Ind.*
—576 Josephine B.,[7] m. **Charles Bymaster**, Oct. 5, 1881.
—577 Russell W.,[7] m. **Ora I. Black**, Dec. 27, 1888.

298. HORACE B. STRATTON [6] (*Benjamin*,[5] *Joseph*,[4] *Joseph*,[3] *David*,[2] *Mark* [1]) was born Jan. 11, 1853, and died Apr. 21, 1899. He married **Emma Cooper**, daughter of *John Cooper*.

Children:
—578 John.[7]
—579 Benjamin.[7]

299. ALBERT STRATTON [6] (*Edward K.*,[5] *Joseph*,[4] *Joseph*,[3] *David*,[2] *Mark* [1]) married **Louisa Hobbs Unthank**, Feb. 27, 1884. She is a daughter of *John* and *Martha* (*Harvey*) *Unthanks*. Resides at Knightstown, Ind.

Children:—*Born in Knightstown, Ind.*
—580 Anna Mae.[7]
—581 Lois Emma.[7]
—582 John Myron.[7]

311. FRANKLIN STRATTON [6] (*Levi*,[5] *Benjamin*,[4] *Joseph*,[3] *David*,[2] *Mark* [1]) married **Melissa Dewey**, who died Oct. 6, 1812.

Child:—*Born in Knightsville, Ind.*
—583 Byron L.,[7] an electrician at Cambridge City, Ind.; m. **Catherine B. Higby**; chn. Everett F.,[8] George W.[8]

321. SIMON COPE STRATTON [6] (*Ephraim*,[5] *Benjamin*,[4] *Joseph*,[3] *David*,[2] *Mark* [1]) married **Anna Newkirk** in 1865, and settled on a farm near Ames, Iowa.

Children:—*Born in Ames, Iowa.*
—584 William F.,[7] m. **Lulu Smith**, 1893.
—585 Marion N.,[7] m. **Marie Helm**, 1896.
—586 Luella V.,[7] m. —— **Golden**.

—587 Simon C.⁷
—588 Ephraim,⁷ d. aged 2 years.
—589 Etta L.,⁷ m. **W. P. Hemstock**, 1902.
—590 Myrtle M.,⁷ m. **J. A. Ball**, 1898.
—591 Homer A.,⁷ m. **Lena Hagen**, 1906.
—592 Hattie M.⁷

326. BENJAMIN STRATTON⁶ (*Joseph*,⁵ *Benjamin*,⁴ *Joseph*,³ *David*,² *Mark*¹) married **Margaret Gilbert**, daughter of *Aaron* and *Margaret* (*Bell*) *Gilbert*.
Children:
—593 Charles Hawley,⁷ m. **Esther Ogle**.
—594 Marietta.⁷

342. DAVID WILLIAMSON STRATTON⁶ (*Mahlon*,⁵ *Mahlon*,⁴ *Daniel*,³ *David*,² *Mark*¹) was born in Old Town, Green Co., O., Sept. 17, 1863. He married **Mary Reynolds**. He was in business in Chicago for some time. Now resides in Holly Wood, Cal.
Children:—*Born in Paris, Ill.*
—595 Oliver R.,⁷ m. **Edith M. Clark**; res. Holly Wood, Cal.
—596 Herman,⁷ d. in Edgar Co., Ill., in 1869, aged 3 years.
Born in Olothe, Kan.
—597 Minnie Estella.⁷
—598 Arthur C.,⁷ m. **Kate Vogal**; res. Chicago.
—599 Nellie D.⁷

349. ROBERT A. STRATTON⁶ (*Mahlon*,⁵ *Mahlon*,⁴ *Daniel*,³ *David*,² *Mark*¹) was born in Ogden, Clinton Co., O. He married **Caroline Gaskill**, Oct. 12, 1874. He moved to Springfield, O., in 1881 where he is now in the grocery business.
Children:—*Born in Clinton Co., O.*
—600 Wilber Ervin,⁷ m. **Clara Grace** Clay, June 20, 1900. He is a photographer in Bellefontaine, O.
—601 Charles Arthur,⁷ d. Mar. 2, 1893.

356. JOHN R. STRATTON⁶ (*David*,⁵ *John*,⁴ *Daniel*,³ *David*,² *Mark*¹) married **Maria A. Newhouse**, June 9, 1864. He is a carpenter and joiner, and resides in Leetonia, O. He was in military service during three years of the Civil War, and is charter member of Burnside Post, G. A. R. No. 137 of Leetonia. Member of Pioneer Lodge No. 539, I. O. O. F. Taught school

seven terms; township trustee three years; notary public twelve years; trustee of water works three years; clerk of the Board of Health of Leetonia.

Children:
—602 William D.,⁷ m. **Laura Evens**; res. Salem, O.
—603 Alva M.,⁷ m. **Dora Warden**; res. Topeka, Kan.
—604 Manda V.,⁷ m. **E. Marshall**; res. Weeping Water, Nev.
—605 Addie M.,⁷ m. **J. O. Smith**; res. Leetonia, O.

362. JOHN A. STRATTON⁶ (*William I.,⁵ Elias,⁴ Daniel,³ David,² Mark¹*) married **Julia Smith**. He was a farmer near Bellefontaine, O., where he died Oct. 27, 1900.

Children:
—606 Susan.⁷
—607 Gertrude.⁷
—608 Benjamin.⁷

367. HENRY W. STRATTON⁶ (*Elias J. H.,⁵ Elias,⁴ Daniel,³ David,² Mark¹*) married **Catherine Wade**, June 17, 1901. Resides in Lake View, O.

Children:—*Born in Lake View.*
—609 Earnest S.⁷
—610 Floyd A.⁷
—611 Walter.⁷

372. JOEL STRATTON⁶ (*Aaron,⁵ Aaron,⁴ Joshua,³ Daniel,² Mark¹*) was born on a farm three and one-half miles northwest of Salem, O., Jan. 5, 1824. He married **Abby Kellogg** in 1854. She was daughter of *Oliver* and *Lydia (Maule) Kellogg*. His entire life of more than 82 years was spent in the vicinity of Salem, and the last 43 years on his farm on Franklin Road, where he passed peacefully away Sept. 16, 1906, "as a shock of wheat fully ripe and ready for the harvest." He was a man of unimpeachable character and respected by all who knew him. He was a faithful and consistent member of the Friends' Church, having a birthright membership. "Joel Stratton was always found on the right side of every great moral question, and never hesitated to let his opinions be known. He was of a cheerful, genial disposition and had many personal friends."

Children:—*Born in Salem, O.*
—612 Emma,⁷ m. **David Crew** in 1878.
—613 Cora,⁷ m. **John Benfield**.

—614 Lewis,[7] m. **Mary Stark**; res. Winona, O.; chn. **Paul**,[8] m. **Mamie Pierce**; chn. Marguerite Elizabeth,[9] Paul Lewis;[9] Abbie,[8] m. **Carl Marshall**.

—615 Laura,[7] m. **Stewart Marshall**.

383. Ross Stratton [6] (*Josiah*,[5] *Michael*,[4] *Joshua*,[3] *Daniel*,[2] *Mark* [1]) was born Sept. 13, 1813, and married **Mary Painter** in 1837. He died at the age of 35, his wife surviving him many years, dying Dec. 24, 1900.

Children:

—616 Deborah Ann,[7] b. Aug. 11, 1840; m. **Joel Smith** of Davenport, Iowa.

—617 Cynthia,[7] b. 1843; d. in infancy.

—618 John E.,[7] b. 1844 (twin); m. **Priscella Bailey**, 1871; res. W. Branch, Iowa. Chn. Ruth A.,[8] (m. **J. H. Cook**), Ross,[8] Charles.[8]

—619 William M.,[7] b. 1844; d. 1844.

384. Elisha Stratton [6] (*Joseph*,[5] *Michael*,[4] *Joshua*,[3] *Daniel*,[2] *Mark* [1]) was born Dec. 15, 1814, and married **Elizabeth Painter** in 1839. They lived in Salem, O., until about 1855 and then moved to Springdale, Iowa. He died in 1884.

Children:—*Born in Salem, O.*

+620 David Painter.[7]

—621 Martha E.,[7] b. 1842; d. 1843.

+622 William,[7] b. 1847.

—623 Mary Ann,[7] m. **John T. Painter**.

Born in Springdale, Iowa.

—624 Deborah, m. 1st, **Edward Hathaway**, 1870; 2nd, **Isaac W. Haines**; res. West Branch.

389. Charles Stratton [6] (*Josiah*,[5] *Michael*,[4] *Joshua*,[3] *David*,[2] *Mark* [1]) was born Jan. 29, 1828. Married **Mary Agnes Ball** in 1849.

Children:—*Born in Ohio.*

—625 Elizabeth Ann,[7] b. 1854; res. Chicago.

—626 Frank Charles,[7] m. **Joanna F. Long**, 1884. Chn.: Edith Agnes,[8] Donald Francis [8]; res. Chicago.

Born in Iowa.

—627 Nellie,[7] m. **William Henderson**.

—628 Mae,[7] m. **Wm. McFadden**, 1894.

392. JAMES STRATTON⁶ (*Charles,*⁵ *Michael,*⁴ *Joshua,*³ *Daniel,*² *Mark* ¹) was born May 23, 1818. He married, in 1843, Louisa Davis, who was born Sept. 4, 1823, and settled on a farm near Salem, where he lived for 56 years, and where he died Jan. 4, 1902. Mrs. Stratton died Aug. 3, 1909. Both were life-long members of the Friends' Society.

Children:—*Born near Salem, O.*
- —629   Hannah,⁷ b. Apr. 4, 1844; m. Nov., 1865, Joseph Lannan.
- —630   Martha,⁷ b. Oct. 23, 1846; m. Feb. 22, 1866, Henry Bonsall.
- —631   William D.,⁷ b. May 13, 1850; m. Nov. 21, 1882, Maggie Bradshaw.
- —632   Charles,⁷ b. Sept. 20, 1867; m. Aug. 19, 1891, Martha Whinney.

395. JOHN MICKLE STRATTON⁶ (*Josiah,*⁵ *Michael,*⁴ *Joshua,*³ *Daniel,*² *Mark* ¹) was born July 2, 1827, on a farm north of Salem, O. He married **Rachel W. Bonsall** in 1853. In 1865 he entered the lumber business in which he continued until 1901, when he retired from business. He became one of the substantial business men of Salem, operating a planing mill and lumber yard of prominence throughout that section. "A noticeable characteristic of Mr. Stratton was his unfailing loyalty to his friends, and home town; his local patriotism was marked. He was of that type of citizenship that constitutes the best element in any community." He was a life-long member of the Friends' Church and held offices of trust and confidence in the town government.*

Children:—*Born in Salem, O.*
- —633   Anna M.,⁷ b. Nov. 13, 1854; d. Aug. 3, 1860.
- —634   Martha D.⁷
- —635   Ella B.,⁷ b. 1864; d. 1867.

399. MARK STRATTON⁶ (*Joseph,*⁵ *Michael,*⁴ *Joshua,*³ *Daniel,*² *Mark* ¹) was born on a farm near Salem, O., Oct. 20, 1821. A carriage builder by trade, an elder in Friends' Church, he lived an active, consistent life, visited many of the churches and held

---

*A relative of John M. Stratton, writing of the 26th Stratton Reunion, says: "We shall greatly miss him at our reunions, for he was one of our most faithful attendants, and always had a kind word and hearty handshake for all who came."

gospel services, though he was not a minister. In 1845 he married **Mary Heald**, daughter of *James* and *Mary (Wilson) Heald*. He died Jan. 12, 1900.

Children:

+636   Charles H.[7]
—637   Anna Eliza,[7] b. Nov. 25, 1847; d. aged 15 mos.
+638   Franklin,[7] b. 1849.
—639   Joseph Henry, b. Apr. 6, 1852; m. Esther T. Stanley, 1870; d. at Beloit, O., 1900. One child, Margaret,[8] m. **Bismark Thompson**.
—640   Rev. Isaac,[7] b. July 14, 1854; m. **Sarah B. Halderman**, Aug. 24, 1880, a daughter of *Joseph* and *Esther (Crew) Halderman*. He has been an acknowledged minister of the Friends' Church since August, 1880. Spent three years in Canada in evangelistic work, and has been pastor of several churches in Ohio.

400. ZACCHEUS STRATTON [6] (*Joseph*,[5] *Michael*,[4] *Joshua*,[3] *Daniel*,[2] *Mark* [1]) was born on the Stratton farm near Salem, O., May 10, 1824. In his youth he learned the carpenter's trade. Apr. 5, 1849, he married **Rebecca Harris**, of an old Salem family. Although brought up a Quaker, after his marriage he united with the Christian Church, of which his wife was a member. In the last year of the war he enlisted in Co. B, 176th Ohio Volunteers Infantry. In April, 1876, he moved with his family to Lincoln, Neb. In 1880 he obtained in Hitchcock Co., Neb., several thousand acres of land for a cattle ranch, and on this tract the town of Stratton, Neb., was founded. Mr. Stratton was a man of quiet manners, enterprising and industrious. He died in Lincoln May 6, 1893. Mrs. Stratton died Nov. 14, 1904. On their farm near Lincoln, "a great farmhouse with some fifteen rooms on the ground floor alone, full of relics and keepsakes," was built with a view of some time converting it into a home for aged ladies. For years they planned for this, and in Oct., 1891, corporation papers were filed, under the laws of Nebraska, and a deed of trust was made to four trustees, but before the matter was settled Mr. Stratton's health failed; he grew worse, and on May 6, 1893, he died.

After his death Mrs. Stratton's one aim in life was to carry out the plans to found a "Stratton Home for aged gentlewomen," but death came before her earnest efforts had met with success.

1. "Forest Home," built by Benjamin Stratton; *Page* 412. 2. "Old Mansion"; *Page* 53. 3. Stratton home at Strattonville, Pa.; *Page* 426. 4. Stacy Stratton house in which have occurred fourteen Stratton births, two marriages and nine deaths; *Page* 284, *Vol.* I. 5. Stratton home near Plattsburg, N. Y.; *Page* 282.

Children:—*Born in Columbiana Co., O.*

—641 Myrtle,[7] b. June 25, 1853; m. **H. S. Gunter**, Feb. 22, 1882; res. Long Beach, Cal.

—642 Thomas A.,[7] b. May 18, 1856; m. **Mrs. Sarah A. Raub**, Apr. 26, 1896; res. Lincoln, Neb.; ch: Ashley T.[8]

406. JOSIAH STRATTON[6] (*Joseph,*[5] *Michael,*[4] *Joshua,*[3] *Daniel,*[2] *Mark*[1]) was born on a farm near Salem, O., Dec. 22, 1832. He was 10 years old when his father died. He was educated in a Friends' Boarding School at Mt. Pleasant, O. He learned the carpenter's trade. In 1855 he went to Iowa, and the following year married **Elizabeth Bundy**. In 1886 he removed to Pasadena, Cal., where he died Jan. 29, 1901.

Children:—*Born in Iowa.*

—643 Sarah T.,[7] b. 1857; d. aged 3 years.

+644 Willoughby,[7] b. 1859.

—645 Lucinda,[7] m. **Frank Simpson**, 1898.

—646 Alica A.,[7] res. Pasadena, Cal.

—647 Lydia,[7] m. **Joseph Floyd**, 1891.

—648 Anna,[7] m. **Renaldo Bufkin**, 1895.

—649 Elizabeth R.[7]

408. EDWARD STRATTON[6] (*Joshua,*[5] *Michael,*[4] *Joshua,*[3] *Daniel,*[2] *Mark*[1]), born May 20, 1822. He married, first, **Mary James**, in 1842, who died in 1869; second, **Mary H. Raley**, 1871. A faithful and influential member of the Friends' Society. He was always interested in family history, and was one of those to suggest and help to plan the first "Stratton Reunion," which his branch of the family have held annually for 28 years. He lived and died in Salem, O.

Children:—*Born in Salem, O.*

By first marriage.

—650 Semira,[7] b. June 5, 1844; m. **Jesse Edgerton**.

—651 Joshua,[7] b. Mar. 2, 1847; m. **Bertha Holcomb**. They have one child, Helen,[8] born in Albion, Iowa, now a teacher in Lenar, Ark.

By second marriage.

—652 Alfred H.,[7] b. 1872; res. Salem.

—653 Joseph R.,[7] b. 1874; m. **Anna M. Bunday**; res. Salem; chn. Mary E.,[8] Paul C.,[8] Joseph Russell,[8] Deborah A.[8]

—654 Edward Francis,[7] m. **Clara E. Frame**; res. Salem; chn. Frances R.,[8] Alice S.[8]

412. BENJAMIN D. STRATTON [6] (*Daniel,*[5] *Michael,*[4] *Joshua,*[3] *Daniel,*[2] *Mark*[1]) was born June 5, 1825. He married **Ellen Stanley**, and lived in Salem, O., until 1853, when he moved to Winona, O., where he died Jan. 19, 1879.

Children:—*Born in Salem, O.*
—655 Ruthanna,[7] b. June 4, 1849; m. **Joseph H. Branson.**
—656 Abigail,[7] m. **Elisha Llewllyn.**
—657 John F.,[7] b. Feb. 11, 1852; m. **Dorothy Hobson.**
Born in Winona, O.
—658 Charles,[7] m. **Mary French**; res. Flushing, O.
—659 Abram,[7] b. 1857; m. **Hannah Branlington.**
—660 Mary E.,[7] a trained nurse in Philadelphia.
—661 Sina,[7] a physician, Philadelphia.

414. BARKLAY STRATTON [6] (*Daniel,*[5] *Michael,*[4] *Joshua,*[3] *Daniel,*[2] *Mark*[1]) was born Dec. 22, 1829, and died July 21, 1892. He married **Hannah Hobson** in 1854, daughter of *Joseph* and *Ruth Hobson*. She was born Dec. 1, 1826, and died Dec. 5, 1903. She was a beloved minister of the Friends' Society.

Children:—*Born in Columbiana Co., O.*
+662 Joseph C.[7]
—663 Elizabeth B.[7]
+664 Dillwyn.[7]

416. SIMEON STRATTON [6] (*Aaron,*[5] *Michael,*[4] *Joshua,*[3] *Daniel,*[2] *Mark*[1]) was born Oct. 3, 1828. He married **Lavina Kirk**, Apr. 27, 1854. He lived in Salem, where he died Mar. 17, 1892.

Children:—*Born in Salem, O.*
—665 James M.,[7] m. **Ada White**; res. Salem, O.
—666 Sarah,[7] m. **Harvey Blackburn.**

419. LEWIS STRATTON [6] (*Aaron,*[5] *Michael,*[4] *Joshua,*[3] *Daniel,*[2] *Mark*[1]) was born May 21, 1837. He married **Elizabeth Holderman**, Aug. 28, 1862. Resides in Salem.

Children:—*Born in Salem, O.*
—667 Ella L.[7]
—668 Alpharetta.[7]
—669 Florence.[7]
—670 Lucy L.,[7] b. Aug. 8, 1870; d. aged 8 years.
—671 Warren B.,[7] m. **Mary Garthwaite**, Dec. 24, 1901; chn.: Lewis R.,[8] Katherine E.[8]

429. WILLIAM H. STRATTON[6] (*Daniel S.*,[5] *Stacy*,[4] *Joshua*,[3] *Daniel*,[2] *Mark*[1]) was born Aug. 17, 1845. He was in the Civil War from Apr. 18, 1864, to the close of the war. He married **Edith Townsend**, Aug. 8, 1867, daughter of *Jonathan* and *Ann (Fall) Townsend*. Before her marriage she was a teacher in Goshen Township—a teacher well remembered for the universal excellence of her work. Mr. and Mrs. Stratton belong to the Methodist church, their children to the Methodist and Presbyterian churches. He is a carpenter and farmer living in Salem.

Children:—*Born near Salem, O.*

—672 Charles D.,[7] d. at Youngstown, O., Oct. 26, 1903.

—673 Jonathan J.,[7] m. **Emma Stratton** (No. 690); res. Alliance, O.; chn. Homer E.,[8] Rachel E.[8]

—674 Henry Louis,[7] m. **Rebecca E. Bradshaw**, Dec. 1, 1879; ch.: Wm. E.,[8] Abraham L.[8]

—675 Sarah A.,[7] m. **Freeman G. Hively**, June 18, 1896.

—676 Marion F.,[7] m. **Ida Grace Coy**, July 25, 1901; chn. Lucile,[8] Herman C.,[8] Olive,[8] Paul L.[8]

—677 Mary G.,[7] m. **Delmer D. Baird**, Nov. 27, 1900.

433. ALCINOUS L. STRATTON[6] (*Stacy L.*,[5] *Stacy*,[4] *Joshua*,[3] *Daniel*,[2] *Mark*[1]) was born June 20, 1835, in Salem, O., and moved while a boy with his parents to Indiana, and then to Wisconsin, where he remained until 1889, and then moved to Kansas. He married **Emma Casler**, Feb. 22, 1862. She was daughter of *John* and *Jane (Gulick) Casler*. He died in Clay Center, Kan., Apr., 1897.

Children:—*Born in Mt. Hope, Wis.*

+678 Dan J.[7]

+679 Peter T.[7]

Born in Clay Center, Kan.

—680 Ola E.,[7] m. **Margaret Rea**; Res. Clay Center; chn. Everett R.,[8] Lama G.,[8] Warren L.,[8] Emma E.[8]

—681 Albert E.,[7] m. **Lorena B. Smith**, May 10, 1893, daughter of *Philo David* and *Lydia (Rogers) Smith*. They have one child, Lorena Alberta,[8] born at Lincoln, Neb., where they lived until recently, when they moved to Medford, Oregon.

435. GILMORE M. STRATTON[6] (*Stacy L.*,[5] *Stacy*,[4] *Joshua*,[3] *Daniel*,[2] *Mark*[1]) was born in Salem, O., July 9, 1845. He married **Mary E. Snyder**, daughter of *Jacob* and *Julia A. Snyder* of Mt. Hope, Wis., Jan. 10, 1867. In 1870 he moved to Kansas, taking up a government homestead. Five years later he settled in Clay Center, Kan., where he now resides and is secretary of the Triple Tie Benefit Association.*

Children:—*Born at Mt. Hope, Wis.*
—682 Nellie Lenord,[7] m. **E. A. Simes**, Jan. 15, 1890.
  Born at Clay Center, Kan.
—683 Addie Elizabeth,[7] m. **Dan. J. Stratton**, July, 1891.
—684 Allie Turner.[7]
—685 Margaret Ann,[7] m. **Henry E. Simes**, Mar. 5, 1896.
—686 Lottie Viola,[7] m. **Eugene W. Cross**, June 26, 1911.

443. Rev. JOB L. STRATTON [6] (*William C.*,[5] *Stacy*,[4] *Joshua*,[3] *Daniel*,[2] *Mark* [1]) was born in the Stacy Stratton homestead, Mahoning Co., O., Feb. 4, 1845. He married, first, **Ella Slutz**, daughter of *William* and *Anna Slutz*, Sept. 26, 1872, who died Feb. 10, 1881, at Waterloo, Pa.; second, **Mary McFall**, daughter of *John* and *Susan McFall*, Oct. 26, 1882. Mr. Stratton was educated in the school at Patmos, and at Mt. Union College, O., a graduate of the class of 1872. He was ordained as a Methodist minister at Titusville, Pa., and has held many charges in Ohio and Penn. He has spent forty-two years in the regular work of the ministry, during twelve of which he held charges in the city of New Castle, where he is now located.

Children:—*Born in Harlansburg, Pa.*
—687 Ruliff V.,[7] m. **Jesee Holmes** in 1896. She died in 1897. Nov. 18, 1902, he m. **Alice R. Blanton** of Frank-

---

* January 1, 1864, he left the schoolroom and enlisted in Company C, 2d Wis. Infantry, and served until the close of the Civil War. He participated in all the battles of the Army of the Potomac from the Wilderness to Appomattox and was present at Lee's surrender. He was discharged July 29, 1865, at the age of twenty years and twenty days. The second Wisconsin was a part of the famous "Iron Brigade."

Upon moving into Clay Center he engaged in the mercantile business, and has taken an active part in the politics of the County, District and State, serving several terms as chairman of the Congressional Committee. In April 1878 he was appointed postmaster at Clay Center, and reappointed in 1882.

He has served on the City Council, Board of Education and Board of Trustees of the county High School, and for about ten years was president of the Commercial Club of the city.

He is a Mason, having attained the degree of Knight Templar; also a member of the Knights of Pythias and the Grand Army of the Republic.

fort, Ky. He is professor of vocal and instrumental music.

—688 William A.,⁷ m. July, 1897, Mary Regal, daughter of *Benjamin* and *Sarah Regal*.

445. GEORGE W. STRATTON⁶ (*William C.*,⁵ *Stacy*,⁴ *Joshua*,³ *Daniel*,² *Mark*¹) was born Feb. 14, 1849. He married Rachel H. Wickersham, Dec. 26, 1872. He died in Alliance, O., Jan. 17, 1909.

Children:

—689 Emmor⁷ (twin), m. Maybelle McClintock; res. Alliance, O.

—690 Emma⁷ (twin), m. Jonathan R. Stratton, son of *William H.* and *Edith T. Stratton* (No. 673).

446. PRESTON D. STRATTON⁶ (*William C.*,⁵ *Stacy*,⁴ *Joshua*,³ *Daniel*,² *Mark*¹) was born at the Stacy Stratton homestead in Mahoning Co., O., six miles northwest of Salem, Dec. 28, 1852, and passed his boyhood on the farm. He was educated at the Patmos school, and at Mt. Union College, and taught for a few years. He married Mary E. Protheroe, daughter of *Francis* and *Rachel Protheroe*, Mar. 15, 1877, and is a prominent business man of Akron, Ohio. He is the founder of the "Protected Home Circle," the first fraternal insurance order to have a fixed monthly payment and reserve fund, and is now Past Supreme President of the order, and Supreme Chaplain, having charge of the Order's interests and work throughout the state of Ohio. He has been closely connected with church and Sunday school work all his life, is a deacon of the First Baptist Church of Akron, and was the first president of the men's Bible class and of the League of Men's Clubs of the city.*

Children:—*Born in Salem, O.*

—691 Florence C.,⁷ m. A. Loyd Baumgartner, Oct. 7, 1908.

—692 Delbert P.,⁷ m. Laura E. Lukesh, June 10, 1908.

—693 Raymond F.⁷

447. WALTER S. STRATTON⁶ (*William C.*,⁵ *Stacy*,⁴ *Joshua*,³ *Daniel*,² *Mark*¹) was born Sept. 16, 1856. He married Naomi L. Dean, Dec. 30, 1875. They live at Sioux City, Iowa.

---

* The author would here return thanks to Mr. Preston D. Stratton for his kind help on the Strattons of his line.

Children:
—694 Alvin D.,⁷ res. Kansas City, Mo.
—695 Anna Minerva,⁷ m. Prof. **Frank Seymore Watson** of Woonsocket, R. I. Both are teachers in New Eng. Conservatory of Music, Boston, of which school both are graduates.

448. DANIEL B. STRATTON ⁶ (*Simri,⁵ Job,⁴ Jonathan,³ Daniel,² Mark ¹*) was born Sept. 18, 1828. He married **Rebecca Stratton** (No. 514) May 30, 1855, and settled on a farm near Richmond, Ind., and later moved into Richmond. By trade he was a carriage smith and for many years was a member of the firm of "Parry and Stratton," manufacturers of carriages. He was a Methodist, and for a long time was trustee of Grove M. E. Church. He died in Richmond Jan. 10, 1910.

Children:—*Born in Richmond, Ind.*
—696 Ida Lee,⁷ d. Mar. 16, 1869, in her 13th year.
—697 Henry Clay,⁷ d. May 20, 1869, aged 6 years and 2 mos.

449. STEPHEN S. STRATTON ⁶ (*Simri,⁵ Job,⁴ Jonathan,³ Daniel,² Mark ¹*), born Apr. 13, 1831; married, Nov. 5, 1856, **Matilda Elderkin**, daughter of *John Elderkin*. By trade a carriage trimmer, he was for many years a manufacturer of carriages and other vehicles, and one of the prominent business men of his native town. For four years he was treasurer of Wayne Co. He was a regular attendant for many years of the Episcopal church. He died May 17, 1912.

Children:—*Born in Richmond, Ind.*
+698 Stephen S., Jr.⁷
—699 Ida,⁷ m. **Henry C. Bentlage**, Dec. 12, 1899.
—700 Mary,⁷ d. aged 15 years.

455. JOSEPH OWEN STRATTON ⁶ (*Charles,⁵ Owen,⁴ Jonathan,³ Daniel,² Mark ¹*) married **Anna Eliza Kay**, Nov., 1857.

Children:—*Born near Haddenfield, N. J.*
—701 Mary Wills,⁷ b. Sept. 29, 1859; m. **George Ed. Johnson**; d. May, 1860.
—702 Henry K.,⁷ b. May 29, 1860; m. 1st, **Katherine Morgan**; 2nd, **Cora A. Devendorf**; res. San Bernardino, Cal.

456. FRANCIS SHREVE STRATTON ⁶ (*Charles,⁵ Owen,⁴ Jonathan,³ Daniel,² Mark ¹*) married, Feb., 1859, **Eliza Henlings**, and lived on a farm near Marlton, N. J.

Children:—*Born in Marlton, N. J.*
—703 Florence B.,[7] b. Oct. 23, 1859; m. **James C. DeWitt** in 1882.
—704 Walter E.,[7] m. **Eunice C. Fowler,** Nov. 22, 1887; ch.: Frank W.,[8] m. **Marion E. Hills**; res. Haddenfield, N. J.; ch. Walter.[9]
—705 Thomas H.,[7] d. in Camden, N. J., Jan. 27, 1884, aged 27 years.
—706 Sara R.,[7] to whom the compiler is indebted for much help on this line; res. Mt. Holly, N. J.
—707 Mary Ella,[7] m. **Charles W. Lear,** July 4, 1885.

457. CHARLES W. STRATTON [6] (*Charles,*[5] *Owen,*[4] *Jonathan,*[3] *Daniel,*[2] *Mark*[1]) is a carpenter. He married **Anna Cowperthwaite** in 1864.

Children:—*Born near Medford, N. J.*
—708 Clarence,[7] b. Sept., 1864; m. **Sallie Mulholland** in 1887; res. Haddenfield.
—709 Sarah C.,[7] m. **Henry C. French.**
—710 George C.,[7] m. **Salome Danbert** in 1902; chn. b. Chestnut Hill, Pa., Edith,[8] Joseph,[8] Irene.[8]

458. JOHN W. STRATTON [6] (*Charles,*[5] *Owen,*[4] *Jonathan,*[3] *Daniel,*[2] *Mark*[1]) married **Mary Wilson,** about 1864. A farmer near Marlton.

Children:—*Born near Marlton, N. J.*
—711 Amos W.,[7] b. 1865; d. 1883.
+712 Schuyler C.[7]
—713 Lydia,[7] b. 1875; d. 1890.
—714 Thomas W.,[7] m. **Laura May Lees,** 1908, daughter of *Thomas* and *Anna Eliza Lees;* res. in Kennett Square, Pa.; ch. Herbert Evans.[8]

459. AMOS HAINES STRATTON [6] (*Charles,*[5] *Owen,*[4] *Jonathan,*[3] *Daniel,*[2] *Mark*[1]) married **Mary Martha Collins Kay** in Feb., 1869. He is a farmer; res. Haddenfield.

Children:—*Born near Haddenfield, N. J.*
—715 Leona Mary,[7] m. **Alonzo C. Stafford** in Oct., 1896.
—716 Job Kay [7] is a merchant, m. **Georgiana Newkirk,** Aug., 1899; chn. Herbert K.[8] and Clara S.[8]; res. Haddenfield, N. J.
+717 Levi Troth.[7]
—718 Helen Rachel.[7]

+719 Amos Collins.[7]
−720 Howard Isaac.[7]

460. BENJAMIN IRVIN STRATTON[6] (*Charles*,[5] *Owen*,[4] *Jonathan*,[3] *Daniel*,[2] *Mark*[1]) married **Mary Jane Repon,** and resides in Camden.

Children:—*Born in Camden, N. J.*
+721 Irvin R.[7]
−722 Mabel M.[7]
−723 Dorothy.[7]
−724 Ellen.[7]

466. JOSEPH LOVE STRATTON[6] (*Jonathan D.*,[5] *Eli*,[4] *Jonathan*,[3] *Daniel*,[2] *Mark*[1]) was born in Carthage, Ind., in 1836. He married **Jane Thomas,** daughter of *Snead* and *Mariam Thomas*, in 1857. He died in West Middleton, Ind., in 1901.

Children:—*Born in New London, Ind.*
−725 Charles E.,[7] m. **Abbie Duncan**; res. W. Middletown, Ind.; chn. Mabel A.,[8] m. **Howard Ramseyer** in 1902. Ethel E.,[8] d. 1888, aged 3 yrs.; Ina F.[8]
−726 Jonathan E.,[7] b. 1860; d. unm. 1890.
−727 William A.,[7] m. **Emergene Delon**; res. Middletown, Ind.; chn. Kate,[8] Maude,[8] Joseph J.[8]
−728 Eli A.,[7] m. **Adda Taylor**; res, Middletown; chn. Hazel L.,[8] Florence,[8] Rachel A.[8]
−729 Lilian J.,[7] m. **John W. Johnson.**
−730 Anna M.,[7] m. **John M. Middleton.**
−731 Sherley Fred,[7] d. unm. in 1904, aged 24 years.

467. ELI B. STRATTON[6] (*Jonathan D.*,[5] *Eli*,[4] *Jonathan*,[3] *Daniel*,[2] *Mark*[1]) was born Aug. 6, 1838. He married **Rebecca Moat** in 1857. He died Apr. 28, 1864.

Children:
−732 Susan,[7] m. **Jared Butler**; res. Russiaville, Ind.
−733 Rachel,[7] m. **Arthur Oyler**; res. Russiaville, Ind.
−734 Arthur.[7]

474. EDWARD DALLAS STRATTON[6] (*Joseph E.*,[5] *Eli*,[4] *Jonathan*,[3] *Daniel*,[2] *Mark*[1]) was born in Richmond, Ind., Aug. 11, 1839. He was educated at Earlham College, Richmond. He married **Louisa Hobbs,** Sept. 12, 1861.* He was a farmer the

---

* She was a daughter of *Elisha and Deborah Harvey Hobbs*. Elisha was born in Guilford Co., N. C., in 1805, brother of Barnabas Hobbs,

most of his life and he and his family were all Friends. He died in Indianapolis Mar. 16, 1911.

Children:—*Born in Plainfield, Ind.*
—735 Harvey Hobbs,[7] m. **Cecilia** ——; Aug., 1800. He is foreman of a packing plant, St. Joseph, Mo.
—736 Martha,[7] m. **Warren Oliver**, Sept. 21, 1894; res. Spokane, Wash.

478. MICAJAH H. STRATTON [6] (*Joseph E.,*[5] *Eli,*[4] *Jonathan,*[3] *Daniel,*[2] *Mark*[1]) was born near Richmond, Ind. He married **Antonia B. Jergius**, May 1, 1876, and resides in Huntsville, Texas.

Children:—*Born in Huntsville, Texas.*
—737 Joseph E.[7]
Born in Byron, Texas.
—738 Eva Beatrice.[7]

480. ELI L. STRATTON [6] (*Joseph E.,*[5] *Eli,*[4] *Jonathan,*[3] *Daniel,*[2] *Mark*[1]) married **Lorena A. Judd**, Sept. 7, 1879. He is a farmer residing in Carmel, Ind.

Children:
—739 Frank,[7] m. **Anna McGee**, Jan. 14, 1902.
—740 Fred.[7]
—741 Elmer.[7]

481. OLIVER STRATTON [6] (*Joseph E.,*[5] *Eli,*[4] *Jonathan,*[3] *Daniel,*[2] *Mark*[1]) was born Apr. 23, 1857. He married **Armittie Williams**, Nov. 3, 1878, and lived in Champaign, Ill. In Feb., 1881, they moved to Longjack, Mo. He died June 15, 1898. He was a Friend, but his family are Methodists.

Children:—*Born in Jackson Co., Mo.*
—742 Robert O.,[7] a farmer of Pleasant Hill, Mo.
—743 Anna E.,[7] a teacher at Raton, N. M.

484. CHARLES BARBER STRATTAN [6] (*John R.,*[5] *John,*[4] *David,*[3] *Daniel,*[2] *Mark*[1]) was a successful physician for many years at Strattonville, Pa., where he was born Sept. 24, 1831. He gradu-

---

the Quaker minister, who was Superintendent of Public Instruction in Indiana, and teacher in Earlham College. Isaac Harvey laid out the town of Harveysburg, O., and later he and his wife were missionaries to the Shawnee Indians in Indiana, and his twin daughters, Deborah and Martha, acted as interpreters for the traveling ministers preaching to the Indians. Martha married John Nothanks.

ated from the Penn. Medical College in 1855. In 1862 he raised a company and went into the army as captain of Co. H, 149th Regt., Pa. Vols. Aug. 13, 1853, he married **Rose A. Gray**, who died Aug. 10, 1890. May 26, 1893, he married **Rebecca A. Ledbetter**. He died Dec. 12, 1911.

Children:—*Born in Strattonville, Pa.*
  By first marriage.
+744 Francis G.,[7] a druggist at Philadelphia; chn. Sara,[8] George,[8] Marie,[8] Elizabeth,[8] Rose,[8] Eva.[8]
—745 John R.,[7] m. **Emma Foster**; res. Donara, Pa.
—746 Max M.,[7] m. **Lawrence George**; ch. Charles B.[8]
+747 Howard G.[7]
—748 Mary Ida,[7] m. **Louis Streng**.
—749 Carrie A.,[7] m. **Winfield Trainor**.
—750 Eva,[7] m. **James W. Jones**.
  By second marriage.
—751 LeRoy.[7]
—752 Paul C.[7]

488. SAMUEL RIDGEWAY STRATTAN [6] (*Joseph S.,[5] John,[4] David,[3] Daniel,[2] Mark [1]*) was born in Strattonville, Pa., in 1837. He married **Priscella J. Rulofson**, Aug. 7, 1866. He enlisted in Co. H., 11th Penn. Reserves, in May, 1861. Mustered out under general order Aug., 1862; re-enlisted Jan., 1864, in Co. 11, Penn. Cavalry. Mustered out at Richmond at close of war. Was 1st Lieutenant, then Adjutant, then commissioned as Captain. Employed in Post Office Dept., Washington, D. C.

Children:—*Born in Strattonville, Pa.*
—753 Ruloff R.,[7] m. **Susie Hutchenson**; in civil service commission at Washington, D. C.
  Born in Franklin, Pa.
—754 Mabel L.[7]
  Born in Emlenton, Pa.
+755 George W.[7]
  Born in Strattonville.
—756 Edith A.[7]

492. JOSEPH C. STRATTAN [6] (*Joseph S.,[5] John,[4] David,[3] Daniel,[2] Mark [1]*) is Post Master at Strattonville, Pa. He married **Anna M. Trainer** in 1879.

Children:—*Born in Strattonville, Pa.*
—757 Grace E.[7]

MARK STRATTON
Page 482.
Father of Gene Stratton-Porter.

JOHN REEVES STRATTON
Page 425.

—758 Maurice T.⁷
—759 C. Lieucella.⁷
—760 Mark R.⁷
—761 Donald M.⁷
—762 John J.,⁷ d. 1898, aged 7 years.

500. WILLIAM H. STRATTON ⁶ (*William,*⁵ *John,*⁴ *Enoch,*³ *John,*² *Mark* ¹) is a blacksmith in Camden, N. J. He married **Mabel Hill,** Jan. 1, 1885.
Children:—*Born in Camden, N. J.*
—763 William.⁷
—764 Henry C.⁷
—765 Raymond.⁷
—766 Mabel Eva.⁷
—767 Charles Hill.⁷

501. HOWARD B. STRATTON ⁶ (*William,*⁵ *John,*⁴ *Enoch,*³ *John,*² *Mark* ¹) married, Feb. 19, 1896, **Lizzie A. Shade,** daughter of *Henry* and *Anna May Shade.* He is a farmer.
Children:
—768 Mary Lillian.⁷
—769 Henry Shade.⁷

505. JOHN GOSLINE STRATTON ⁶ (*James L.,*⁵ *John,*⁴ *Enoch,*³ *John,*² *Mark* ¹) married **Rae Harker,** June 6, 1892, daughter of *Enos* and *Susan* (*Chambers*) *Harker.* He lives in Camden, N. J., and is Secretary of a Piano Manufacturing Corporation and President of Action Piano Co.
Children:—*Born in Camden, N. J.*
—770 Mildred Harker.⁷
—771 Dorothy Gosline.⁷

518. CHARLES STRATTON ⁶ (*Benjamin,*⁵ *Gideon,*⁴ *Isaiah,*³ *Enoch,*² *Mark* ¹) was a soldier in the Civil War, first in a company of West Virginia Volunteers, and then in the Hospital Corps. He married, first, **Martha Lord;** second, **Charlissa Talbot,** Nov. 9, 1870. They resided in Washington, D. C., where he was a clerk in the Bureau of Statistics. He died Oct. 27, 1910.
Children:—*Born in Washington, D. C.*
   By second marriage.
—772 Ella Gregg, b. in 1872; d. in childhood.

—773 Ethel Anna, m. 1st, **Charles A. Weaver,** in 1898; 2nd, **Norman N. Nock.**
—774 Charles Warren, a dentist in Washington, D. C.; died June 17, 1906.
—775 Caroline Chandler, teacher in Eldridge, Cal.; graduate from Pennington Seminary, valedictorian of class.

526. JOEL VAN METER STRATTON [6] (*Isaiah G.,*[5] *Isaiah,*[4] *Josiah,*[3] *Enoch,*[2] *Mark* [1]) was born May 10, 1842. Educated in the public schools of Philadelphia and University of Lewisburg, Pa. (now Bucknell University), ordained a Baptist minister at the age of twenty-two and became pastor of the Fourth Baptist Church of Pittsburg, Nov., 1864. Nov. 15, 1866, he married **Elizabeth Reese,** daughter of *William* and *Elizabeth L. Reese,* who came to the United States from Wales in 1832.* Mr. Stratton has been successively pastor at Sheron, Pa., 1867; Byron, O., 1869; Columbus, Wis., 1870; Roselle, N. J., 1873; Morristown, N. J., 1877; Waltham, Mass., 1880; Scottsdale, Pa., 1893. Moved to Pittsburg, Pa., in 1899, where he now resides.

Children:—*Born in Columbus, Wis.*
—776 William Cooper,[7] educated at Philips Academy, Andover, Mass., class 1890, and Brown University, Providence, R. I., 1894. Civil and mining engineer.
—777 Anna Reese,[7] graduate Mt. Holyoke, S. Hadley, Mass., 1892.

530. JACOB BROWN STRATTON [6] (*Ebenezer,*[5] *Bradford,*[4] *Thomas,*[3] *Isaac,*[2] *Mark* [1]) was born in Camden, N. J. He married **Maria Kathrine Williams.** He died in Philadelphia in 1882.
Children:—*Born in Philadelphia.*
—778 Clarence,[7] res. St. Louis, Mo.
—779 Kate,[7] m. **Wm. P. Smith;** res. Jordsville, N. J.
—780 Jacob Bradford.[7]

534. DAVID FRANCIS STRATTON [7] (*Stephen T.,*[6] *David Q.,*[5] *Joseph,*[4] *Joseph,*[3] *David,*[2] *Mark* [1]) married twice. His first wife was **Harriet E. Cooper.** He married 2nd **Lucy Deichman.**

---

* Elizabeth Reese belongs to a family of inventors, best known among them being Jacob Reese, to whom is attributed the discovery in this country of the Bessemer process, revolutionizing the steel industry. Another brother, Joseph Reese, lost his life in the Battle of Stone River in the Civil War. Another brother, Benjamin Reese, attached to the ambulance corps, serving through the war.

Children:
> By first marriage.
—781 Frank Stephen,[8] res. Chicago.
—782 Susan Isabella.[8]
—783 Josephine.[8]
—784 James Cooper,[8] res. Chicago.
—785 Ruth Lander.[8]
—786 Mary Louise,[8] m. —— White; res. Upper Alton, Ill.
> By second marriage.
—787 Evelyn Rynd,[8] res. Cedar Valley, Mo.

548. WILLIAM D. STRATTON [7] (*Oliver H.,*[6] *David Q.,*[5] *Joseph,*[4] *Joseph,*[3] *David,*[2] *Mark* [1]) married, first, **Alice Healy,** in Iowa in 1879; second, **Mamie Trobridge,** in Nebraska, 1891.
Children:
> By first marriage.
—788 Oliver.[8]
—789 Ephraim.[8]
> By second marriage.
—790 Harry.[8]
—791 Ross D.[8]

549. AZARIAH D. STRATTON [7] (*Oliver H.,*[6] *David Q.,*[5] *Joseph,*[4] *Joseph,*[3] *David,*[2] *Mark* [1]) married **Jessie McCune** in Missouri. Died in Mt. Vernon, Kan., Apr. 8, 1901.
Children:
—792 James Roy.[8]
—793 Mabel.[8]
—794 Goldie.[8]
—795 Charles E.[8]
—796 Nettie Amanda.[8]

552. FRANK P. STRATTON [7] (*Joseph D.,*[6] *David Q.,*[5] *Joseph,*[4] *Joseph,*[3] *David,*[2] *Mark* [1]) married **Bird Marquis,** Oct. 23, 1895; moved from Aledo, Ill., to Twin Falls, Idaho, in 1907; from there to Corning, Cal., where they now reside in 1910. He is a farmer and fruit grower.
Children:—*Born in Aledo, Ill.*
—797 Frances Jean.[8]
—798 George Marquis.[8]

620. DAVID PAINTER STRATTON [6] (*Elisha,*[5] *Josiah,*[4] *Michael,*[3] *Daniel,*[2] *Mark* [1]) was born in Salem, O., Aug. 22, 1840. He married **Sarah Ann Todd** in 1864 and resided at (or near) Portland, Oregon.

Children:
- —799   Robert E.,[8] m. 1st, **Rosalie** ——, 2nd, **Mary M. Franklin**.
- —800   Emma L.[8]
- —801   Walter,[8] m. **Elsie May Ferguson**; res. Washington.
- —802   Herbert,[8] m. **Myrtle Dofflemeyer**.
- —803   Clara R.,[8] m. **Henry H. Heltzel**.
- —804   Laura,[8] b. 1883; d. 1884.

622. WILLIAM STRATTON [7] (*Elisha,[6] Josiah,[5] Michael,[4] Joshua,[3] Daniel,[2] Mark [1]*) was born Nov. 8, 1847, in Columbiana Co., O. He married **Ella E. Briggs**, and resides in Newburg, Oregon, to which place they moved from Ohio in 1891. He is a farmer.

Children:—*Born in West Branch, Iowa.*
- —805   Martha,[8] m. **Charles Hodson**, Oct. 14, 1897; res. Newberg, Oregon.
- —806   Edna,[8] m. **Geo. B. Lamb**, Dec., 1903.
- —807   Joseph LeRoy,[8] m. **Augusta DeForest**, Dec., 1911.
- —808   Olive,[8] m. **Archie C. Seely**, Oct. 1, 1908.
- —809   Irving E.,[8] d. Oct. 25, 1906.

636. CHARLES H. STRATTON [7] (*Mark,[6] Joseph,[5] Michael,[4] Joshua,[3] Daniel,[2] Mark [1]*) was born Apr. 4, 1846. He married, at Richmond, Ind., **Anna O. Williams**, Sept. 1, 1870, daughter of *Thomas Williams* of Fontaine City, Ind. He is a carriage builder by trade and an ordained minister in the Protestant Methodist church.

Child:—*Born in Salem, O.*
- —810   Harold C.,[8] city engineer at Alliance, O.; m. **Nita Gilson** in 1893; chn. Donald G.,[9] William H.[9]

638. FRANKLIN STRATTON [7] (*Mark,[6] Joseph,[5] Michael,[4] Joshua,[3] Daniel,[2] Mark [1]*) was born Dec. 30, 1849, in Columbus, O. He is a member of the Friends' church. He married, first, **Philena Shreve**, who died Nov. 24, 1903; second, **Amelia Misselback**. By trade he is a carriage builder and is the inventor and patentee of the "Stratton rotating engine" and several other labor-saving machines; resides in Chicago.

Children:—*Born near Salem, O.*
- —811   Oliver B.,[8] m. **Agnes C. Birmingham**; res. Kansas City; chn. Leonard W.,[9] Clarence F.,[9] Mildred P.[9]

—812   Willis T.,[8] a lawyer in Oklahoma City, Okla.
—813   Hannah May,[8] res. Buffalo, N. Y.
—814   Albert,[8] a grain inspector at Buffalo, N. Y.

644. WILLOUGHBY STRATTON [7] (*Josiah*,[6] *Joseph*,[5] *Michael*,[4] *Joshua*,[3] *Daniel*,[2] *Mark* [1]) was born in Iowa in 1859. In 1882 he married **Sarah Lewis**.

Children:
—815   Eva May,[8] m. **Jas. Hawkins** in 1902.
—816   Nellie,[8] m. **Paul DeWolf**, 1907.
—817   William.[8]
—818   Mary R.,[8] res. Buffalo, N. Y.
—819   Emma,[8] res. Buffalo, N. Y.
—820   Charles.[8]

662. JOSEPH C. STRATTON [7] (*Barkley*,[6] *Daniel*,[5] *Michael*,[4] *Joshua*,[3] *Daniel*,[2] *Mark* [1]) was born Oct. 10, 1855. He married, Nov. 2, 1882, **Elizabeth Brantingham**, daughter of *Alfred* and *Ann* (*Dean*) Br*antingham*. They are superintendents of the Friends' Boarding School at Barnsville, O., a school established in 1837, in which many Strattons have received instruction.

Children:
—821   Mary,[8] m., Jan. 31, 1908, **Walter B. Edgerton**, son of Jesse and Susan Edgerton.
—822   Walter,[8] b. Dec. 31, 1908; m., May 6, 1910, **Atta Elizabeth Cope**, daughter of *Dr. A. L.* and *Rachel G. Cope* of Winona. They have one daughter, Esther.[9]

664. DILLWYN STRATTON [7] (*Barkley*,[6] *Daniel*,[5] *Michael*,[4] *Joshua*,[3] *Daniel*,[2] *Mark* [1]) was born Feb. 7, 1861. He married **Elizabeth Hall** of Harrisonville, O., and their home is in Winona, O. He has long been actively connected with the agricultural interests of his section and is president of the Ohio State Dairymen's Association. Mrs. Stratton died Mar. 18, 1911, in her forty-seventh year.

Children:—*Born in Winona, O.*
—823   Barkley W.[8]
—824   Lucinda.[8]
—825   Debora.[8]
—826   Laura M.[8]
—827   Rebecca H.,[8] d. June 10, 1907, aged 8 mos. 3 days.

678. DAN J. STRATTON [7] (*Alcinous,*[6] *Stacy L.,*[5] *Stacy,*[4] *Joshua,*[3] *Daniel,*[2] *Mark* [1]) married **Addie E. Stratton**, July 10, 1891 (No. 683). In Mar., 1907, they moved from Clay Center to Kingfisher, Oklahoma, where they now reside on a farm.

Children:—*Born at Clay Center, Kan.*
—828 Gilmore M.[8]
—829 Stacy B.[8]
—830 Carl D.[8]
—831 Kenneth C.[8]
—832 Don J.[8]
—833 Emmett L.[8]
—834 Alice Laurine.[8]

679. PETER T. STRATTON [7] (*Alcinous,*[6] *Stacy L.,*[5] *Stacy,*[4] *Joshua,*[3] *Daniel,*[2] *Mark* [1]) was born Aug. 25, 1866. He married **Lilian Miles**, daughter of *Enos P.* and *Mary Ellen Miles*, Feb. 22, 1896. In 1910 they moved to Colorado and took up a homestead at Abbott, which they have proved. It is 40 miles from a railroad with the mail three times a week.

Children:—*Born at Clay Center, Kan.*
—835 Alcinous L.[8]
—836 Lowell Miles.[8]

Born at Prairie Home, Neb.
—837 Clarence Enos.[8]
—838 Dorothy Lucile.[8]

698. STEPHEN S. STRATTON [6] (*Stephen S.,*[5] *Simri,*[4] *Job,*[3] *Jonathan,*[2] *Mark* [1]) for many years a business man of Richmond, Ill. Secretary Gaar, Scott & Co., the largest manufacturing establishment in the town, manufacturers of thrashers, engines and agricultural implements. Was director of the Richmond Bank; President of the School Board. May 4, 1892, he married **Nellie Ruby Gaar**. Resides in Chicago and is President of a Credit and Discount Company.

Child:—*Born in Richmond, Ind.*
—839 Abram Gaar.[7]

712. SCHUYLER C. STRATTON [7] (*John W.,*[6] *Charles,*[5] *Owen,*[4] *Jonathan,*[3] *Daniel,*[2] *Mark* [1]) married **Helen Barton**, 1893, daughter of *Aaron* and *Deborah Barton*, and resides in Moorestown.

Children:—*Born in Moorestown, N. J.*
—840 Harold.[8]

—841 Roland.[8]
—842 Aaron E.[8]
—843 Florence.[8]
—844 Arthur.[8]

717. LEVI TROTH STRATTON [7] (*Amos H.,*[6] *Charles,*[5] *Owen,*[4] *Jonathan,*[3] *Daniel,*[2] *Mark* [1]) married **Blanch Hillman** in Jan., 1900. He is a farmer living near Haddenfield, N. J.
Children:
—845 Ruth Hillman.[8]
—846 Myra Kelton.[8]
—847 Bessie Stokes.[8]
—848 Edna Collins.[8]
—849 Lawrence.[8]
—850 Hannah Ellis.[8]

719. AMOS COLLINS STRATTON [7] (*Amos H.,*[6] *Charles,*[5] *Owen,*[4] *Jonathan,*[3] *Daniel,*[2] *Mark* [1]) married **Georgiana** Crowell, Nov., 1906. He is a clerk and bookkeeper at Collinswood.
Children:—*Born in Collinswood, N. J.*
—851 George Amos,[8] twin.
—852 James Franklin,[8] twin.
—853 Dorothey Virginia.[8]

721. IRVIN R. STRATTON [7] (*Benjamin I.,*[6] *Charles,*[5] *Owen,*[4] *Jonathan,*[3] *Daniel,*[2] *Mark* [1]) married **Sophia F. Homer** and lives in Camden, N. J.
Children:
854 Richard,[8] m. **Mary C. Leeds**; res. Camden; chn. Howard C.,[9] Clara M.,[9] Charles H.,[9] m. Hannah D. Hilton; ch. Marion D.[10]
—855 Levaine.[8]

747. HOWARD G. STRATTAN [7] (*Charles B.,*[6] *John R.,*[5] *John,*[4] *David,*[3] *Daniel,*[2] *Mark* [1]) is a professor of music at Dubois, Pa. He was educated at Bucknell University. He married **Sarah Jane Young**, June 18, 1891. All his children are musical, playing on various instruments. Members of Methodist church.
Children:—*Born in Strattonville, Pa.*
—856 Pauline.[8]
—857 Mary Ruth.[8]
—858 Helen Cirrue.[8]

Born at Falls Creek, Pa.
—859 Howard Kenneth.[8]
—860 Eugine Judson,[8] m. **Alma Josephine Lowe**, Dec. 24, 1913; ch: Jean Lowe.[9]

755. George W. Strattan [7] (*Samuel R.*,[6] *Joseph S.*,[5] *John*,[4] *David*,[3] *Daniel*,[2] *Mark* [1]) married **Eva Pruden** and resides in Washington, where he is connected with the Treasury Department. He was sent to Europe in 1908 as Secretary of the Tariff Commission.

Child:—*Born in Washington, D. C.*
—861 Howard Worrell.[8]

SETH STRATTON OF FREDERICK COUNTY

[862] Seth Stratton [4] was a grandson of Mark Stratton of Evesham, N. J. He was a Revolutionary soldier. The military records of Virginia show that he was allotted 200 acres of land Apr. 29, 1785, but does not show where the land was located.

For a record of him and a list of his children, see page 296, Vol. I. The following are his descendants.*

863. William Stratton [5] (*Seth* [4]) was born in Virginia in 1788. When about 17 years old he moved with his parents to Shelby Co., Ky. He married **Nancy Wasson** in 1812. He was a farmer, owning a farm near Finchville. He and his family were members of the Baptist church. He died Sept. 17, 1835.

Children:—*Born in Shelby Co., Ky.*
—864 Mary Greenway,[6] b. Apr. 9, 1813; m. **Thomas C. Hunter**, Dec. 10, 1840; d. Feb. 18, 1892, in Campbellsburg, Ind.
+865 David Devoe,[6] b. 1814.
—866 Eliza Ann,[6] b. Sept. 1, 1816; m. **Elisha Carr** in 1846; d. Jan. 4, 1854, at Nebo, Ind.
—867 Nancy Jane,[6] b. Dec. 24, 1819; m. **William Hunter**; d. Apr., 1861, in Kentucky.
—868 Martha,[6] b. Feb. 12, 1822; m. **David Hunter**; d. Apr. 9, 1895, in Kentucky.
—869 Harriet Amanda,[6] b. Sept. 14, 1825; d. aged 10 years.

---

*Caleb Stratton (probably a great-grandson of Mark Stratton [1]) settled in Green Co., Ky., about 1820 (see Vol. I, pp. 298-299). His son, Jesse Falkner Stratton, married, first, Mary A. Walters; second, Marion G. Hagaman. He died in Emporia, Kan., aged about seventy-six years; chn. Rosecrans (m. Minnie Martin, 1891), Luella, Cora A., and Minnie M.

870. JOSEPH STRATTON [5] (*Seth* [4]) was born in Virginia in 1792 and came to Shelby Co., Ky., with his parents when he was about 12 years old. He married **Katie Wason** in 1815. He lived and died (in 1864) in his native county. He was in the war of 1812 and received a pension.

Children:—*Born in Shelby Co., Ky.*

—871   George W.,[6] b. Jan. 14, 1816; m. Catherine M. Hunter, Jan. 18, 1849; living in Bloomfield, Ky., in 1905.

—872   Harriet,[6] m. **John Orndorff**.

873. SETH STRATTON [5] (*Seth* [4]) was born Aug. 25, 1797, in Virginia, probably Frederick Co. July 4, 1800, he married **Susanna Ellis** in Shelby Co., Ky. She was born July 4, 1800. About 1825 they moved to Jennings Co., Ind., where Mr. Stratton died, Jan. 8, 1860, and Mrs. Stratton, June 7, 1876, both in Butlerville, Ind.*

Children:—*Born in Shelby Co., Ky.*

—874   Elenor,[6] b. Nov. 25, 1821; m. 1st, **Porter Town**, Oct. 31, 1842; 2nd, **John Ross**, 1845; 3rd, **William Eott**, 1875.

—875   William,[6] b. Aug. 3, 1823; m. **Tolitha Moncrief**, May 12, 1845; d. Nov. 24, 1900, in Ill.; no children.

—876   Mary Greenway,[6] b. Sept. 27, 1824; m. **James Butler**.

Born in Jennings Co., Ind.

+877   Ellis Garner,[6] b. 1827.

—878   Isaac Ellis,[6] b. Apr. 27, 1829; d. aged 6 years.

+879   Joseph Seth,[6] b. 1832.

—880   Susan Elizabeth,[6] b. Nov. 28, 1835; d. in infancy.

—881   Joseph Jacob,[6] b. Feb. 22, 1840; m. 1st, **Eliza Stanley**, 2nd, **Maggie Miller**; no children.

865. DAVID DEVOE STRATTON [6] (*William,*[5] *Seth* [4]) was born Dec. 22, 1814. He married **Martha A. Shanks**, Dec. 21, 1837. In 1875 they moved to Washington, Ind., near Campbellsburg. In 1887 they celebrated their golden wedding at the old homestead one mile south of Campbellsburg. All their children were present—all married and living in several different states. Mr. Stratton died June 24, 1901.

---

* In the old family Bible in the possession of a great-grandson of Seth Stratton, Sr., is this record: "Francis Washington Stratton was born May 21st, 1814." The compiler has not been able to place him.

Children:—*Born in Shelby Co., Ky.*

—882 William,[7] b. 1838; m. **Amanda Case** in 1860; d. in Fairfield, Ill., Feb. 24, 1902; he was a Federal soldier in the Civil War.
+883 Samuel,[7] b. 1840.
+884 George D.,[7] b. 1842.
—885 Serepta,[7] b. 1843; m. **William Peters**, 1865.
Born in Washington Co., Ill.
+886 Seth,[7] b. 1845.
—887 James,[7] b. 1847; m. **Desdemonia Letterman**; ch. Nora.[8]
+888 John,[7] b. 1849.
—889 Katherine,[7] b. 1851; m. **Jerome Stanley**, 1878.
—890 Lewis H.,[7] b. 1853; m. **Ella E. Semms**, 1878; res. Peabody, Kan.
—891 Eliza,[7] b. 1856; m. **Uriah Glover**, 1884; res. Franklin, Ind.

877. ELLIS GARNER STRATTON[6] (*Seth*,[5] *Seth*[4]) was born Mar. 1, 1827, and died in Holton, Ill., Jan. 26, 1895. He married **Mary A. Davidson**, Dec. 14, 1852. He died June 6, 1895.

Children:—Born in Holton, Ind.

—892 William James,[7] d. Feb. 10, 1854, aged about 1 year.
+893 John Seth,[7] b. Feb. 13, 1855.
+894 George Jacob.[7]
—895 Susannah,[7] b. Jan. 29, 1860; d. aged 20 years.
—896 Elizabeth J.,[7] m. **Theodore McClure**.
—897 Joseph T.,[7] d., unm., Mar. 7, 1913.
—898 Robert H.,[7] m. **Eliza Kiphart**.
—899 Mart E.,[7] m. **Oliver L. Beech**, Jan. 6, 1892.
—900 Martha A.,[7] m. **James Davis**, Nov. 8, 1899.

879. JOSEPH SETH STRATTON[6] (*Seth*,[5] *Seth*,[4]) was born July 22, 1832. He married **Minerva Monroe**, Jan. 12, 1859.

Children:—*Born in Buttlerville, Ind.*

—901 John W.,[7] d. in 1875.
—902 Joseph T.,[7] m. **Emma Harmon**, June 6, 1878; d. July 1, 1905; ch. Minerva.[8]

883. SAMUEL STRATTON[7] (*David D.*,[6] *William*,[5] *Seth*[4]) was born Aug. 17, 1840. He married, first, **Lydia Brown**, Apr. 7,

1864; second, **Rachael Arnold**, Aug. 22, 1882. Res. Newton, Kan. He was a Federal soldier.

Children:—*Born in Washington Co., Ind.*
By first marriage.
—903 Lorena.[8]
—904 Caskin David,[8] m. **Lizzie Riley**; res. Little York, Ill.
—905 Fannie Florence,[8] m. **O. L. Crawford**, Nov. 3, 1898.
—906 Charles L.,[8] m. **Pauline Roeder**, Feb. 20, 1900; res. Little York, Ill.
—907 Martha Ann,[8] m. **N. C. Golden**, Jan. 7, 1905.
Born in Henry Co., Kan.
By second marriage.
—908 Wallas William.[8]
—909 Irene L.[8]
—910 Melton Edward.[8]
—911 Grace M.[8]

884. GEORGE DUDLEY STRATTON [7] (*David D.,*[6] *William,*[5] *Seth* [4]) was born Mar. 19, 1842. He was 2nd Lieut. in the 66th Ind. Infantry, enlisting July 2, 1862, and serving four years. Nov. 5, 1865, he married **Camelia Russell**, who was born in Bardstown, Ky., Feb. 21, 1842.

Children:—*Born in Campbellsburg, Ind.*
—912 Nannie,[8] m. **Charles R. A. Marshall**, June 5, 1907; res. Stronghurst, Ill.
—913 Stella,[8] m. **Charles R. A. Marshall**, Oct. 1, 1891; d. May 21, 1905.
—914 Russell,[8] m. **Aura Carson**, Apr. 12, 1898; res. Trinchera, Cal.
—915 David,[8] m. **Cora Riddle**; res. Walton, Kan.
—916 William,[8] soldier in Spanish-American War.
—917 Guy,[8] soldier in Spanish-American War.
—918 Goldie,[8] m. **James Guthrie**; res. Walton, Kan.

886. SETH STRATTON [7] (*David D.,*[6] *William,*[5] *Seth* [4]) was born in 1845. He served in the Federal army. He married **Ella Teagarden**, 1870, and settled in Bromer, Orange Co., Ind. Res. Orleans, Ind.

Children:—*Born in Bromer, Ind.*
—919 -Hattie.[8]
—920 John C.[8]
—921 Henry S.[8]

—922 Roscoe D.[8]
—923 Louis.[8]
—924 Nellie S.[8]

888. JOHN STRATTON [7] (*David D.,*[6] *William,*[5] *Seth* [4]) was born in 1849. He married, first, **Margaret King**, 1872; second, **Ella Chastane**, 1883; res. Campbellsburg.
Children:—*Born in Campbellsburg, Ind.*
By first marriage.
—925 Celia,[8] m. **Robert Hayes**, 1898.
—926 Maude,[8] m. **Dr. L. W. Paynter**, 1894.
By second marriage.
—927 Golda Oscar.[8]

893. JOHN SETH STRATTON [7] (*Ellis G.,*[6] *Seth,*[5] *Seth* [4]) married **Sarah E. Fite**, Aug. 20, 1876; d. Sept. 20, 1904. He was a farmer living near Holton, Ind.
Children:
—928 Ethel.[8]
—929 William,[8] m. 1st, **Flora Davis**, chn. Rollie,[9] Carrie;[9] m. 2nd, **Nellie Raynor**, ch. Floyd.[9]
—930 Frank,[8] m. **Amy Edens**.
—931 Nettie.[8]

894. GEORGE JACOB STRATTON [7] (*Ellis G.,*[6] *Seth, Jr.,*[5] *Seth* [4]) married **Indiana Harmon**, Feb. 15, 1882. He is a deacon of the Baptist church; also Director and Vice-President of the bank at Holton, Ind.
Children:—*Born in Holton, Ind.*
—932 Stella,[8] m. **Ora E. Haines**.
—933 Gladys.[8]

WILLIAM STRATTON OF SPOTTSYLVANIA COUNTY

[934] William Stratton from Spottsylvania Co., Va., settled in Trimble Co., Ky., about 1803. See *Vol. I*, pp. 296-297. The following are some of his descendants:*

---

*It is not at all certain that William Stratton of Spottsylvania Co. and Absolom Stratton of Amherst Co. belong to this line. They may belong to one of the old Virginia lines. Some of their descendants spell the name Strattan, and among some of them is a tradition that their ancestor came to Virginia from New Jersey, which has led the compiler to place them here until further research may determine their rightful place.

935. JOHN A. STRATTON (*William*) was born in Trimble Co., Ky., in 1803. He married **Nancy Russell** about 1826 and settled in Jennings Co., Ind., near Madison. Like his father before him, he was a schoolmaster. He died in Jefferson Co., Ind., in 1833.

Children:—*Born in Jennings Co., Ind.*
- +936 Oliver H., b. 1827.
- —937 Rachel, m. **A. J. Tucker**, d. in Franklin, Ind., 1862.
- —938 James Wm., d. in childhood, about 1833.
- +939 Francis Marion.

940. ELISHA BOWMAN STRATTON (*William*), b. Oct. 29, 1811; m. 1st **Melinda Stewart**, Nov. 4, 1832; 2nd **Mary Antle**, March 27, 1839; 3rd **Mrs. Emma Briscoe**, 1864; d. May 7, 1875.

Children:—*Born in Campbellsburg, Ky.*
- —941 Joseph W., b. 1834; m. **Cora Forrester**, 1855; d. 1858; chn. Louisa M., Ida W.
- —942 William H., m. **Letitia Scott**; lived in Taylorsville, Ky.; chn. Scott, Elisha, Roy.
- —943 Garnett D. Federal soldier; d. in Texas; left chn.
- —944 Carrie D., m. **E. D. Briscoe**.
- —945-7 James, Nannie, Elisha, d. unm.; William, Frank, d. in infancy.
- +948 John Antle, b. 1854.

949. JAMES STRATTON (*William*) lived in Jeffersonville, Ky. He married **Delilah Finley**. He died in Louisville, Ky., in 1863. Chn. Florence, Cora, Chatty, Leonard, Samuel, Melissa.*

936. OLIVER H. STRATTON (*John A., William*) was born July 14, 1827, and died in Louisville, Ky., in 1905. His father died when he was six years old; his mother a few years later. The support of a brother and sister devolved on him when he was still but a boy. He prepared himself for Hanover College, but after two years of study there was forced to quit for want of funds. He entered the law office of Gen. Wm. O. Buttle at Carrollton, Ky. At the outbreak of the Mexican war he enlisted in the First Ky. Volunteer Regt. and served throughout the hostilities. At the close of the war he took up his residence at Louisville, obtaining a position at the Court House. He became actively

---

* A William Stratton married Susan Fish and had a son, James H. Stratton, born in Wirt, Ind., Jan. 8, 1828, who married Sarah Drydan. Does he belong to this family?

engaged in politics, affiliating with the old Whig party. He was the first clerk of the Board of Aldermen, Clerk of the City Court, City Auditor, Librarian of Heywood Library, and City Assessor. He was admitted to the bar in 1866, and when not holding public office practiced his profession. Mr. Stratton was always interested in the welfare of the city, and was instrumental in forming the Louisville School of Reform. He married, Mar. 1, 1853, **Mary Ellen Shyrock,** daughter of *Gideon* and *Elizabeth Pemberton (Bacon) Shyrock.*

Children:—*Born in Louisville, Ky.*

—950 Sophia, m. **Clarence W. Watkins,** Oct. 22, 1877, res. Louisville.

—951 Nellie, m. **William Thomas Shannon,** Sept. 27, 1882; res. Cincinnati.

—952 Lulu Belle, d. in 1876, aged 16 years.

939. Dr. Francis Marion Stratton (*John A., William*) married, first, **Harriet Maria Wadsworth** of Mass. She died June 17, 1859; second, **Lucinda Cave** in 1869; third, **Cinthia M. Bradbury,** in St. Louis, Mo., in 1875. She died Jan. 8, 1906. Dr. Stratton died in Forestville, Cal., 1901. He was a physician, a graduate of Ann Arbor.

Children:—*Born in Mill River, Mass.*

—953 John Augustus, b. 1857, a physician in Newman, Cal.; chn. John L., Frances B.

—954 Owen Tully, res. a physician and surgeon in Litchfield, Ill.; ch. Paul Vance.

—955 Francis Marion, res. San José, Cal.; chn. Richard O., Mary M.

948. John A. Stratton (*Elisha, William*) was a well known real estate dealer in Louisville, Ky. He was born Feb. 24, 1854. He married **Mamie C. Varble,** Dec. 16, 1874, daughter of *Capt. Pinkney Varble.*

At the time of his death, in 1905, he was one of the most prominent business men of his city and was rated as the best informed man on all questions connected with the history and the business affairs of Louisville. He studied law for its use in his business and became one of the best real estate lawyers in the city. He was instrumental in building up some of the most important parts of the Louisville of to-day. With a very limited early education he so improved the hours he had for study and reading that his conversation was a delight and his companionship enjoyed by every one he met. He collected a large library, and spent much time with his books. He was prominent in the Masonic orders. He was interested in politics and was elected to several offices in Louisville on the Republican ticket, and in 1901 made a good showing as Republican nominee for Mayor in that Democratic city. He died Sept. 4, 1906. By his will, after providing generously for his wife, son and several relatives, he bequeathed his business to his six employees, who, by their faithful service had helped him to build it up.

Child:

—956 Frank Leachman, res. New York City; grad. Cornell University, where he received degree M.E. in 1901.

ABSOLOM STRATTON OF AMHERST COUNTY

[957] Absolom Stratton married **Winnie Ennis** in Amherst Co., Va., Dec. 16, 1805, and settled in Logan Co., Ky., about 1809. He was a Revolutionary soldier (see records at Richmond). For all that is known of him, and a list of his children, see *Vol. I*, pp. 297-298. Those of his descendants who have been found are given below:

958. GEORGE VON STRATTON (*Absolom*) was born in Virginia, Dec., 1808, and died in July, 1861, in Parker Co., Texas. He married **Clara Logan** about 1830. He was a Missionary Baptist.

Children:

+959 Absolom Joshua, b. 1831.

—960 Lee Allen, m. **Theresa J. Brawley**; chn. Mary, m. James Beard, Cliessa E., m. James McCarther, Ruth F., m. J. W. Robinson.

961. JAMES DAVID STRATTON (*Absolom*) was born in Simpson Co., Ky., in 1825. He married **Mary Ann Buttler** in 1843 in Kentucky, and about three years later moved to Texas and lived near Richardson in Dallas Co. He served in the Confederate army two years.

Children:—*Born in Simson Co., Ky.*

—962 Eva, m. **G. B. Strait**; res. Richardson, Tex.

—963 George A., chn. George, Eva, Charles, Florence, Fannie.

—964 Mary E., m. **G. H. Mason**.

Born in Dallas Co., Tex.

—965 Charles F., res. Richardson, Tex.; chn. Nettie, James, Kenneth, William.
—966 Absolom.

967. JOSHUA P. STRATTON (*Absolom*) was born in Kentucky in 1827 and about 1846 went to Texas with his two brothers. He married **Mary Lane** and lived in Hamilton Co., Texas.

968. THOMAS JEFFERSON STRATTON (*Absolom*) served in Confederate army for three years and was wounded at the battle of Pleasant Hill, La. He married, first, **Georgia Ann Allen** in 1849; second, **Martha Huffhines**. He was born in Simpson Co., Ky., in 1829 and went to Texas in 1855. Belonged to the Missionary Baptist church.

Children:—*Born in Simpson Co., Ky.*
—969 George Knapp, m. **S. E. Huffhines**, 1870; res. Richardson, Texas.
—970 Melissie Jane, m. **Felix J. Judice**, 1867; res. Fort Worth, Texas.
—971 James Madison, m. **E. J. Huffhines**, 1873; res. Sangerm, Texas.

Born in Dallas Co., Texas.
—972 Texanna, m. **J. W. Larry**, 1874; res. Richardson, Texas.
—973 Isabell, m. **W. H. Stark**, 1876, res. Godley, Texas.
—974 Mary Catherine, m. **J. W. Breedlove**, 1880; res. Alpha, Texas.
—975 Thomas J., Jr., m. **Mary Westmoreland**; res. Gaymon, Okla.
—976 Richard D., m. **Lottie Stevans**, 1903; res. Dumas, Texas.

959. ABSOLOM JOSHUA STRATTON (*George V., Absolom*) was born in Kentucky, Feb. 28, 1831. He married **Dorras Emelia Beard**, daughter of *Sam Beard* of Tennessee, and lived in Arkansas and Texas.

Children:
+977 John M., b. 1852.
+978 Samuel Newton.
—979 Mary Ellen, m. —— Jones.
—980 Clara E., m. —— Blocker.
—981 George Van, m. **Lula Voyles**, 1891.
—982 Lee Allen, res. Advance, Tex.

—983 Louvenia A.
—984 James C., twin.
—985 Absolom J., twin.

977. JOHN M. STRATTON (*Absolom J., George V., Absolom*) was born at Columbia, Ark., in 1852; res. Carpenter, Okla. He married **Martha Hellums.**

Children:—B*orn in Texas.*

—986 Matilda, b. 1877.
—987 Lula.
—988 John C.
—989 Ollie.
—990 Clara.
—990a Eva May.
—991 Ruth.
—992 Venia.
—993 Fannie.
—994 Samuel.
—995 George W.
—996 Grace.

978. SAMUEL NEWTON STRATTON (*Absolom J., George V., Absolom*) was born in 1855. He married **Mary A. Brawley** in Parker C., Tex., July 3, 1879. She was born in Columbia, Ark., Aug. 8, 1858. He went to Texas from Kentucky in 1846. Res. Mangum, Okla.

Children:—B*orn in Peaster, Texas.*

— 997 Absolom F.
— 998 George V.
— 999 John L.
—1000 James C.
—1001 Effie M.
—1002 Samuel H.
—1003 Hazel.
—1004 Barney.

EMANUEL STRATTON OF EVESHAM

(Chart N, Vol. I)

That the generation to come might know them. PSALMS 78.6.

FIFTH GENERATION

15. SAMUEL STRATTON [5] (Jacob,[4] Samuel,[3] Emanuel,[2] Emanuel[1]) was born in Swedesboro, Gloucester Co., N. J., in 1796. He was a farmer and lived at Woodstown, in Salem Co., where he died in 1874. He married **Sarah Brown**.
Children:—*Born in Gloucester Co., N. J.*
+24 William.[6]
—25 Samuel,[6] m. **Ruth Titus**; resided in Camden.
—26 Mary,[6] m. —— **Cassaday**.
—27 Nathan,[6] m. **Beulah Gibson**, resided near Mullica Hill.
—28 Joseph[6] m. 1st, —— ——; 2nd, **Sarah Ashbrook**, resided at Mullica Hill.
—29 Sarah,[6] m. **Charles Gill**.
—30 Martha,[6] m. —— **Reese**.
—31 James P.[6]

More complete records of this family desired.

16. WILLIAM A. STRATTON [5] (Jacob,[4] Samuel,[3] Emanuel,[2] Emanuel[1]) was born in Swedesboro, N. J., in 1801. A country boy, raised on a farm, early in life Mr. Stratton went to Philadelphia where he established a reputation as a bright business man, rising from clerk to partner in the commission and transportation business ("Bingham, Dock and Stratton"), with branch business houses at Harrisburg and Pittsburg.* After his death the busi-

---

* Referring to this business, a daughter of William A. Stratton writes: "The Erie Canal was an important factor, the boats of this firm traversing the canal day and night, carrying not only grain but crowds of German settlers—and what a sight they were to us children, with their packs and wooden shoes and queer dressing. One of the first steamers that traversed the Ohio River was the *William A. Stratton.*"

To this branch of the New Jersey Strattons belongs Harrison D. Stratton, the inventor and designer of the Absorption Ice Machine, built for

ness was merged in the Adams Express. He married **Caroline Brown Strong**, daughter of *Capt. Mathew* and *Catherine (Brown) Strong*.* He and his family were Episcopalians, to which church he was a liberal supporter. Mrs. Stratton died in 1846. Soon after her death he retired from business and went to live on one of his properties at Mullica Hill, N. J. Two years later he moved to a larger farm which he owned near Swedesboro. Here in the following year he died, May, 1849, aged only 48 years.

Children:—*Born in Philadelphia.*

—32 Mary Catherine,[6] m. **Thomas C. Ware**; d. in Bridgeport.
—33 Elizabeth B.,[6] m. **John Keller**.
—34 Caroline S.,[6] m. **George Ford**; d. in Swedesboro, June, 1958.
—35 Martha S.,[6] m. **Lorenzo Mulford**, Aug. 3, 1858.
—36 Emeline L.,[6] d. in Cincinnati, O., Feb. 11, 1871.
—37 Josephine S.,[6] m. **William Heisler**; res. Camden.
—38 Arabella L.,[6] d. in New Jersey.
—39 Virginia R.,[6] d. in Cincinnati, Apr. 29, 1904.

17. THOMAS J. STRATTON[5] (*Jacob*,[4] *Samuel*,[3] *Emanuel*,[2] *Emanuel*[1]) was born on a farm near Swedesboro, N. J., in 1805. He married **Mary Hewett**, daughter of *Thomas Hewett*. He was an expert workman on fine edge tools; died at Mullica Hill in 1886.

Children:—*Born in Woodtown, N. J.*

+40 Jacob L.,[6] b. 1827.
—41 Susan,[6] b. 1829; m. **Richard Gosling**, 1846; res. at Woodtown.
—42 Elizabeth,[6] b. 1830; m. **Daniel Johnson** in 1850.
+43 Charles T.,[6] b. 1833.

---

many years by the Columbus Iron Works at Columbus, Ga. He married at Niagara Falls, N. Y., June 20, 1888, Alica Estella Liscom, daughter of Andrew and Caroline Deborah (Barber) Liscom. Since May 1891 they have resided at Philadelphia.

*Capt. Strong was a sea captain, owning his own vessel. Sailing from New York for South America, he died of yellow fever in Jamaica, leaving his wife, Catherine B. Strong, a widow at the age of twenty-seven. She was the eldest daughter of Col. Robert Brown, a Revolutionary soldier. At her father's death she inherited the colonial mansion at Swedesboro, and here, under her loving and tender care, were sheltered the children of William A. Stratton after the early death of both parents.

+44 Edward S.,⁶ b. 1835.
+45 Thomas C.,⁶ b. 1836, twin.
+46 David B.,⁶ b. 1838.
—47 Mary A.,⁶ b. 1842; m. **John P. Reese**, 1862. Born at Elbridge Hill, N. J.
+48 John B.,⁶ b. 1844.

19. Emanuel R. Stratton⁵ (*Jacob*,⁴ *Samuel*,³ *Emanuel*,² *Emanuel*¹) was born Sept. 12, 1807. He married **Elizabeth Smith**, daughter of *John* and *Margaret Smith*, Apr. 14, 1827. She was born in 1807 and died June 30, 1882. Mr. Stratton died Feb. 14, 1888. Four of his sons were in the army during the Civil War—two of them giving up their lives on the battlefield. Mr. and Mrs. Stratton and most of their family were Methodists.

Children:

—49 John,⁶ b. Aug. 11, 1828; d. Sept. 14, 1828.
—50 Margaret,⁶ b. Sept. 28, 1829; m. **Joshua Ashton**.
—51 Sarah,⁶ b. Jan. 18, 1831; m. **John F. Meley**, Feb. 19, 1853.
+52 Emanuel, Jr.,⁶ b. May 20, 1832.
—53 David F.,⁶ b. June 1, 1833; d. aged 19 years.
—54 Benjamin,⁶ b. July 6, 1834; d. Sept. 11, 1834.
—55 Anna Maria,⁶ b. Aug. 23, 1835; d. Sept. 7, 1835.
+56 William Henry,⁶ b. Sept. 21, 1836.
+57 Azariah,⁶ b. Jan. 14, 1838.
—58 Elizabeth,⁶ b. June 7, 1839; d. Sept. 23, 1839.
—59 Amos,⁶ b. July 22, 1840; d. Sept. 5, 1840.
—60 Isaac,⁶ b. Aug. 23, 1841; d. Sept. 17, 1841.
—61 Jacob,⁶ b. Oct. 8, 1842; d. Nov. 26, 1842.
—62 Mary Elizabeth,⁶ b. Jan. 11, 1844; m. **William Black**.
—63 Lucretia,⁶ b. May 7, 1845; d. Aug. 27, 1852.
—64 Charles C.,⁶ b. Aug. 26, 1846; enlisted at the age of sixteen with his three brothers in Co. F, 12th Reg. N. J. Vols.; lost in battle of Spottsylvania Court House, May 12, 1864.
—65 Caroline,⁶ b. Dec. 22, 1847; d. Aug. 14, 1848.
—66 Harriet,⁶ b. Feb. 11, 1851; d. July 13, 1851.
—67 Nathan,⁶ b. June 19, 1853; d. Aug. 14, 1853.

22. Hon. Nathan Taylor Stratton⁵ (*Jacob*,⁴ *Samuel*,³ *Emanuel*,² *Emanuel*¹) was born on a farm near Swedesboro in 1813. He married **Sarah M. Sherwin**, Feb. 11, 1836. She was a daughter of *Isaac* and *Sarah Sherwin,* who lived on a farm which they owned near Swedesboro. Mr. Stratton was a merchant for many years at Mullica Hill and owned considerable real estate in and near the town. He was a man of great force of character and fine ability. He was a member of Congress from New Jersey, 1854 to 1858, and occupied many positions of trust and responsibility in his state and county, and was sought by many who needed words of advice and council, and acted as executor and administrator in settling many estates. He died at his home in Mullica Hill, March 9, 1887.

Children:—*Born in Mullica Hill, N. J.*

+68 Isaac Sherwin.[6]

—69 Edward Livingston,[6] b. Mar. 4, 1839, was clerk and general manager in his father's store. When Co. F, 12th Regt., was formed in 1862 at the call for 300,000 men, he enlisted and was unanimously elected Captain and "entered upon his duties of that trying position with all the vigor and earnestness of his patriotic nature." He served faithfully until wounded at the battle of Chancellorsville. He married **Emma Norman** and lived at Mullica Hill where he has been postmaster, lay judge and held other positions of trust and honor.

—70 Mary Lucertia,[6] b. 1841; m. **Jacob J. Moore.**

—71 James Sherwin,[6] b. Dec. 11, 1843. Delighting in books and study, he passed through the common school, entered West Jersey Academy, and was looking forward to entering Princeton when the war broke out. With the same patriotic spirit which prompted his brothers and cousins, he enlisted in the same company, a boy of 18 years, was promoted to Sergeant, then 2nd Lieut., then 1st Lieut. He was killed in action at Reams Station, Aug. 25, 1864.

24. WILLIAM STRATTON[6] (*Samuel,*[5] *Jacob,*[4] *Samuel,*[3] *Emanuel,*[2] *Emanuel*[1]) was born Feb. 13, 1822. He married **Martha Titus** in Dec., 1842. He was a farmer and carpenter and lived most of his life in Gloucester Co. He died at Harrisonville, Sept. 9, 1901.

Children:—*Born in Mullica Hill, N. J.*

+72 Lemuel E.,[7] b. 1843.

—73 Rhoda T.,[7] m. **Richard Dawson;** res. Bridgeport, N. J.

—74 Sarah B.,⁷ d., unm., Oct. 4, 1885.
    Born in Wilmington, Del.
—75 William S.,⁷ d. near Mullica Hill, Oct. 3, 1860.
    Born near Mullica Hill.
—76 Samuel B.,⁷ res. Hancocks Bridge, N. J.
—77 Anna M. A.,⁷ m. 1st, **Thomas Munyan**, 2nd, **Frank Owens**.
—78 Hannah,⁷ m. **Edgar String**.
+79 Joseph T.,⁷ res. in California.
—80 Edwin R.,⁷ res. in Camden; m. **Sarah Akins**; chn. Clifton,⁸ Mary,⁸ Hazel.⁸
—81 Caroline B.,⁷ m. **Charles Franklin**.
—82 Ada F.,⁷ m. **Charles Wood**; d. Pittsgrove, N. J., June 2, 1887.
—83 Laura C.,⁷ m. **Robert Gunn**; res. Clayton, N. J.

40. JACOB L. STRATTON ⁶ (*Thomas J.,⁵ Jacob,⁴ Samuel,³ Emanuel,² Emanuel¹*) was born in 1827; married **Sarah Murphy** in 1846; died in Gloucester Co., N. J., in 1900.
    Children:—*Born in Mullica Hill, N. J.*
—84 John Murphy,⁷ m. **Ella Stout** in 1871; res. Odd Fellows Temple, Philadelphia, Pa.
—85 Thomas J.,⁷ m. **Mary Summers** in 1875; res. Mt. Royal, N. J.

43. CHARLES T. STRATTON ⁶ (*Thomas J.,⁵ Jacob,⁴ Samuel,³ Emanuel,² Emanuel¹*) was born in Woodstown, N. J., in 1833. He married **Sarah Fenimore** in 1865. She died in 1880 and in 1894 he married **Sophronia Jordon**. He was teacher of music, then civil engineer. He built the cliff wharf on Chester River and was agent for the Chester River Steamboat Co. at Chestertown, Md.
    Children:—*Born in Swedesboro, N. J.*
—86 Sarah,⁷ m. **Wm. F. Stoop**, 1897.
    Born in Odessa, Del.
—87 J. Fenimore.⁷
    Born in Chestertown, Md.
—88 Margaret,⁷ m. **Clark Stoop** in 1901.

44. EDWARD S. STRATTON ⁶ (*Thomas J.,⁵ Jacob,⁴ Samuel,³ Emanuel,² Emanuel¹*) was born in 1835. He married **Mary**

Summerset in 1855. He was a soldier in the Civil War. Attorney-at-law at Mullica Hill, where he died in 1879.
Children:
—89 William.[7]
—90 Samuel.[7]
—91 Clara.[7]
—92 Susan.[7]

45. THOMAS C. STRATTON [6] (*Thomas J.,*[5] *Jacob,*[4] *Samuel,*[3] *Emanuel,*[2] *Emanuel*[1]) married **Rose Diamond** in 1859. He was a farmer near Mullica Hill, where he died in 1902.
Children:
—93 Charles T.[7]
—94 Clementine.[7]

46. DAVID B. STRATTON [6] (*Thomas J.,*[5] *Jacob,*[4] *Samuel,*[3] *Emanuel,*[2] *Emanuel*[1]) was born in 1840 in Woodstown, N. J. In 1866 he married **Mary Sickler**.
Children:
—95 Delia,[7] m. **Albert Riggins**; res. Woodbury, N. J.
—96 William,[7] a physician in Woodbury.

48. JOHN B. STRATTON [6] (*Thomas J.,*[5] *Jacob,*[4] *Samuel,*[3] *Emanuel,*[2] *Emanuel*[1]) married **Mary S. Skinner** in 1868.
Children:
—97 Hester.[7]
—98 Florence.[7]
—99 David Barton.[7]

52. EMANUEL STRATTON, JR.[6] (*Emanuel R.,*[5] *Jacob,*[4] *Samuel,*[3] *Emanuel,*[2] *Emanuel*[1]), married, first, **Amanda Meley**, Dec. 25, 1854, daughter of *George* and *Mary Meley*. She died Aug. 29, 1858, aged 26 years. He married, second, **Sarah Story**, Dec. 1, 1861. He was a farmer near Swedesboro until he enlisted in the army, Co. F, 12th Regt. N. J. Vols., Aug. 11, 1862. He was the tallest man in the company. He gave faithful and courageous service under all circumstances until he was severely wounded in that "whirlpool of death" at Chancellorsville, May 3, 1863. After the war he was given a position in connection with Public Parks in Philadelphia, which he held until his death in 1906.

Children:—*Born in Swedesboro.*
>   By first marriage.
- —100   Theodore,⁷ b. Aug. 3, 1836; res. Millville, N. J.; chn. Louisa,⁸ George,⁸ Erma.⁸
>   By second marriage.
- —101   Sarah H.⁷

56. William Henry Stratton ⁶ (*Emanuel R.*,⁵ *Jacob*,⁴ *Samuel*,³ *Emanuel*,² *Emanuel* ¹) married **Helen Borradale**, June 10, 1858. They lived on a farm near Swedesboro. In July, 1862, when 26 years of age, he enlisted in Co. F, 12th Regt. N. J. Vols. After just one year of faithful service, July 3, 1863, he gave his life for his country in that famous charge on the "Bliss Barn" at Gettysburg.

Children:—*Born near Swedesboro, N. J.*
- —102   Lillian,⁷ b. Mar. 6, 1859; m. 1st, Frank Faucett, 2nd, **John J. Robinson**.
- —103   Lizzie,⁷ b. June 24, 1861; m. **Owen L. Guest**.

57. Capt. Azariah Stratton ⁶ (*Emanuel R.*,⁵ *Jacob*,⁴ *Samuel*,³ *Emanuel*,² *Emanuel* ¹) was born Jan. 14, 1838. In 1862, with his three brothers, he enlisted in Co. F., 12th Regt. N. J. Vols., was in the service three years, "taking part in every battle and skirmish of the company. Was never sick, never wounded enough to keep him off duty (though his clothing was pierced with bullets many times); filled every office of the company from private to Captain, and came home with the love and respect of every man who ever served with or under him." He was discharged July 15, 1865. Dec. 18, 1866, he married **Sarah Holdcroft**. They lived on a farm two miles out from Swedesboro, and later moved to Beesly's Point, N. J.

Children:—*Born in Swedesboro, N. J.*
- —104   John H.,⁷ b. Oct. 1, 1867; m. **Vinnie Gandy**, Jan. 21, 1897. Served 10 years on Life Saving Service at Longport, N. J.; res. Palermo, N. J., where he is a merchant; no children.
- —105   Charles H.,⁷ b. Jan. 27, 1870. Killed at a railroad crossing near Pitman Grove, N. J. He was a high school teacher.
- —106   Dwight R.,⁷ a farmer at Marmore, Cape Cod Co., N. J.

—107 Edgar A.,[7] m. **Maude Corson**, June 13, 1901; postmaster at Marmora, N. J.; ch. Helen Florence.[8]

—108 Mary Elizabeth,[7] d. Oct. 24, 1884, aged 1 year.

68. Isaac Sherwin Stratton[6] (*Nathan T.*,[5] *Jacob*,[4] *Samuel*,[3] *Emanuel*,[2] *Emanuel*[1]) was born at Mullica Hill, N. J., July 23, 1837. He married, Aug. 3, 1858, **Catherine L. Wright**, who was born in Green Co., N. Y. They both belong to the Baptist church. Mr. Stratton is one of the most prominent men of Swedesboro, having been in business since 1850—general store, coal and lumber business, first as "N. T. Stratton & Son," then "Stratton and Garrison," then "Stratton Brothers."

Children:—*Born in Swedesboro, N. J.*

+109 Horatio Mulford.[7]

—110 Laura Wright,[7] m. Apr. 21, 1887, **Howard W. Miller** of Paulsboro, N. J.

—111 Irene Henrietta,[7] m. Dec. 12, 1889, **George W. Hannold** of Swedesboro.

—112 Kate L.,[7] m. June 1, 1893, **George L. Barker**, an evangelist.

+113 Isaac Sherwin.[7]

72. Lemuel E. Stratton[7] (*William*,[6] *Samuel*,[5] *Jacob*,[4] *Samuel*,[3] *Emanuel*,[2] *Emanuel*[1]) was born in Harrisonville, N. J., Oct. 29, 1843. He was a farmer and lived in Gloucester and Salem counties. He married **Evaline V. Mead**, Nov. 18, 1871. He died at Daretown, N. J., Sept. 9, 1891. His widow lives at Wildwood, N. J.

Children:

—114 Franklin M.,[8] m. **Viola Benson**, Sept. 8, 1904; res. Philadelphia.

—115 Lizzie M.,[8] m. **Frank Dorrell**, May 12, 1901; res. Wildwood.

—116 Walter E.,[8] res. Woodstown.

—117 Fowler H.,[8] a plumber in Colon, Panama.

—118 Lemeta C.,[7] graduate Woodstown high school, 1909.

79. Joseph T. Stratton[7] (*William*,[6] *Samuel*,[5] *Jacob*,[4] *Samuel*,[3] *Emanuel*,[2] *Emanuel*[1]) married, first, —— **Simkins**; second, **Helen Cramer**; third, **Sarah Cramer**; moved to California in 1905.

Children:—*Born in Harrisonville, N. J.*
By second marriage.
—119   Pitman.[8]
By third marriage.
—120   Bernice.[8]
—121   Leslie Lemuel.[8]
—122   Helen.[8]
—123   Harry.[8]

109. HORATIO MULFORD (*Isaac S.,[6] Nathan T.,[5] Jacob,[4] Samuel,[3] Emanuel,[2] Emanuel[1]*) was born in Swedesboro, N. J., Jan. 16, 1860. He married, Jan. 17, 1883, **Maria L. Miller** of Paulsboro. He died May 16, 1910. He was engaged in the wholesale lumber business in New York at the time of his death.

Children:—*Born in Paulsboro, N. J.*
—124   Rose Miller,[8] m. **Paul E. Carroll,** June 27, 1912; res. Dennisville, N. J.
Born in Camden, N. J.
—125   Howard Walter,[8] m. **Catherine Simpson,** Apr. 22, 1913. In the lumber business; res. Collinswood, N. J.
—126   Carl[8] (twin), d. in infancy.
—127   Leon Dupree[8] (twin), m. **Laura Bruce,** July 29, 1913. Chemist in Droxtel Institute, Philadelphia.
Born in Paulsboro, N. J.
—128   Rachel G., d. in infancy.
—129   Stephen Miller, d. in infancy.

113. ISAAC SHERWIN STRATTON, JR.[7] (*Isaac S.,[6] Nathan T.,[5] Jacob,[4] Samuel,[3] Emanuel,[2] Emanuel[1]*), was born in Swedesboro, N. J., Jan. 29, 1870. He married **Lelah Keys** of Des Moines, Iowa, June 29, 1905. She died Mar. 29, 1911. He is in the insurance business in Des Moines.

Children:—*Born in Des Moines, Iowa.*
—130   Lorenzo D.[8]
—131   Lelah[8] (twin).
—132   Irene[8] (twin), both d. in infancy.

~~John~~ Daniel AND RACHEL (LOGAN) STRATTON AND THEIR CHILDREN
Margaret, Catherin, Elizabeth, Helen,
David, Daniel, John,
Thomas, Nathan.
See pages 484-486. *Also page* 295, *Vol.* I

STRATTONS OF SUSSEX COUNTY

(*Chart O, Vol. I*)

"*Strong are the ties of kindred.*" ÆSCHYLUS.

THE homes of Daniel and Thomas Stratton were in Vernon township, not far from the line dividing Sussex Co., New Jersey, from Orange Co., New York. When Capt John Sanford organized his regiment of Orange County men in April, 1777, Thomas Stratton enlisted in his company, but was soon transferred to Col. Oliver Spencer's 4th New Jersey Volunteers, and the papers granting his pension in 1820 are on file at Trenton. He was then living in Beaver Co., Pa., while Daniel Stratton settled in Hancock Co., O. No authentic record of their parentage has been found, though diligent search has been made for it. It seems most probable that they are descended either from Mark Stratton or Emanuel Stratton of Evesham, N. J., but we have no proof of it.

CONTINUED FROM PAGE 291, VOL. I.

5. DAVID STRATTON (*Daniel*) was born in Sussex Co., N. J.; went from New Jersey to Greensburgh, Beaver Co., Pa., and then settled in Richland Co., Ohio. His will, recorded in the Probate Office of Richland Co., was made June 15, 1843, and he died a a few days later. He married **Mary Logan,** daughter of *James Logan,* in Beaver Co.*

---

*"James Logan was President of the Colonial Council of Pennsylvania in 1736. When Gov. Gorden died, in August of that same year, Logan acted as Governor for two years until a successor arrived from England. John Logan (son of James) and his only son were drowned in the Ohio River, in Beaver Co., Pa., in 1800. His wife died from the shock of this terrible bereavement, leaving three daughters, Rachel, Mary and Catherine, the eldest seven years and the youngest but a few days old. Their maternal grandfather, James Parks, in whose house the most of their youth was spent, fought in the French and Indian wars, and in the Revolution, and lived to the great age of one hundred and eleven years. Rachel became the wife of Daniel Stratton (No. 15, Vol. I), and her memory is revered by over two hundred descendants. Mary mar-

Children:—*Born in Adario, Richland Co., O.*
—48 Lucinda, m. **Vincent Dancer.**
—49 Sarah Ann, m. **Jesse Dancer.**
+50 John Rigdon.
—51 Daniel G., twin (see data under James Logan Stratton), m. **Emma Dawson**; d. at Colorado Springs; left two daughters, Minnie and Josephine.
—52 Thomas Jefferson, twin, m. **Mary Dyke**; d. in Los Angeles, Cal. Federal soldier, 1863 to 1865. Only child, Daniel, d. 1885.
—53 George Washington, d. in camp at Dalo, Oregon, Aug. 1, 1852; unm.
+54 James Logan, b. 1833.
—55 Elizabeth, m. **Charles Malcolm**; res. Cambridge, Ill.
—56 Mary, m. **George Robinson.**
—57 Rachel, m. **Josiah Chamberlain.**
—58 Nancy Jane, m. **T. K. Jacobs.**

14. SAMUEL STRATTON (*Thomas*) was born in Sussex Co., N. J., Oct. 16, 1802, and came to Beaver Co., Pa., while a boy, with his parents. In 1824 he married **Jane Wood**, who was born Sept. 16, 1802. He was a farmer and a member of the Methodist Church.

Children:—*Born in Beaver Co., Pa.*
—59 Elazer, b. Sept. 4, 1825; m. **Jonah Platt.**
—60 Eveline, d. in infancy.
—61 Amanda, b. Dec. 10, 1829; m. **Joel Gould.**
—62 Adaline, b. Jan. 29, 1832; m. **James A. Cook.**
—63 Melissa, b. Dec. 9, 1835; m. Sept. 17, 1857, **John D. Marlin**, a soldier, who served through the Civil War; res. Clarenda, Page Co., Iowa.
—64 Joseph, d. in infancy.
—65 Hiram, d. in childhood.
—66 Samuel Colwell, b. Jan. 13, 1842. Was in college studying for the ministry in 1862 when he enlisted in the army; d. soon after the close of the war from the effects of several months in Andersonville prison.

---

ried David Stratton, and their son married the eldest granddaughter of Rachel and Daniel Stratton—and their children have grown gray in trying to figure out their exact relationship to the rest of the Strattons."—*Daniel Stratton.* Catherine married Sidney Rigdon, who for many years was an eloquent and widely known Presbyterian clergyman in the middle west.

—67 John Wesley, d. in childhood.
+68 Andrew, b. Aug. 19, 1847.

18. DAVID STRATTON (*Daniel, Daniel*) was born May 1, 1810, in Sussex Co., N. J. He was about ten years old when his parents moved, with their family of seven children to Wayne Co., O. Here, on a farm, David spent his youth, attending the district school during the winter months. In 1834 he married **Nancy A. Wade,** daughter of *Isaac* and *Sallie (Jones) Wade,* and two years later settled on a farm in Union Township, Handcock Co. In 1851 he moved to Fayette Co., Iowa, where he bought 80 acres of land and was one of the first settlers of that region. Mar. 13, 1858, Mrs. Stratton died, and the family became scattered for a time. In 1861 Mr. Stratton enlisted in the 16th U. S. Infantry. After a few months' service he was taken sick and discharged. In 1864 he sold his farm and went with his two younger sons to Dunn Co., Wis., and took up a homestead, where he spent the remainder of his life. He died at the home of his youngest son at the age of 94 years.

Children:—*Born in Wayne Co., O.*
+69 Isaac, b. 1835.
  Born in Hancock Co., O.
—70 Daniel, b. Jan. 23, 1837; went to California in 1859; was last heard of there in 1866.
+71 Nial, b. 1840.
+72 Cyrus, b. 1849.
  Born in Fayette Co., Iowa.
+73 Henry James, b. 1854.

19. WILLIAM STRATTON (*Daniel, Daniel*) was born Mar. 5, 1812. He married at the age of eighteen and lived on a farm in Wayne Co., O. He died in 1837 of quick consumption, the result of a cold.

Children:—*Born in Wayne Co., O.*
—74 James Allen, b. 1831; went West, and in 1865 was living in Story Co., Iowa.
—75 Charlotte.
—76 Adelaide.

20. JOSEPH STRATTON (*Daniel, Daniel*) was born Jan. 4, 1814. In 1836 he married Peggy Karnes, and lived in Wayne Co., O.,

until 1844, when he moved to Hancock Co. In 1865 he bought a farm in Dunn Co., Wis., and took his family there. Mrs. Stratton died in 1890, and the following year Mr. Stratton, with his sons Simeon and Joseph, went to Spokane Co., Wash., where he died in 1892. With little school education he was a great reader, a well informed man, a fine story teller, a favorite with young people, and well liked by all who knew him. He held several public offices, was Township Assessor, Chairman Board of Trustees.

Children:—*Born in Wayne Co., O.*
+77 John, b. 1837.
—78 Simon, b. 1839; res. Rockford, Wash.
—79 Sarah Ann, m. **Wm. Barnes,** 1864.
—80 Sophronia, m. Cyrus **Decker,** 1872.
—81 Elizabeth Ann, m. Jacob **Shultz.**
+82 Joseph, b. 1849.
—83 Phœbe, m. William **Sanderson.**
—84 Julia, m. Joseph **Phellps.**

21. JOHN STRATTON (*Daniel, Daniel*) was born Jan. 8, 1816. In 1838 he went to New Orleans, remained two years, and then returned to Ohio. In 1841 he married **Martha McCue,** and settled in Allen Co., Ohio. His wife died about 1846, and in 1848 he married **Mrs. Betsey Meeds,** who died in the following year. Mr. Stratton then went South again, and when the war broke out he joined the southern army, became a colonel, and was killed on the field of battle. He was a man of fine appearance, full six feet tall.

Children:—*Born in Ohio.*
    By first wife.
—85 William James passed his boyhood and youth among his father's people, a soldier in the Union army. Settled somewhere in Wisconsin.
—86 Philip, an infant when his mother died, brought up by his mother's people and lost track of by the Strattons.

22. HENRY STRATTON (*Daniel, Daniel*) was born Dec. 3, 1817. He married **Martha Wade** in 1841, and lived on a farm in Hancock Co., Ohio. Mrs. Stratton died in 1863, and about three years later Mr. Stratton married **Harriet Koonts.** He died in Blufton, Ohio, in 1896. Kind and generous, ready to offer a helping hand to all with whom he came in contact, he had many friends.

Children:
By first marriage.
- —87 Sarah J., m. J. V. Steinman.
- +88 Joseph.
- +89 Harmon.
- —90 Julia A., m. W. H. Brunk, 1872.
- —91 Maria C., m. W. H. Burns, 1872.
- +92 Jacob.
- —93 Andrew J., never married.

By second wife.
- —94 Myron, res. Bluffton, O.
- —95 Kerwin.
- —96 Sina, m. —— Morrison.

26. WILLIAM STRATTON (*Joseph, Daniel*) was born Oct. 8, 1810. When he was seven years old his parents moved to Beaver Co., Pa., and two years later to Canaan Township, Wayne Co., O., where he lived for nearly thirty-five years, and then moved to Hancock Co., O. July 4, 1837, he married **Elizabeth Demming**, who was born Sept. 23, 1818. He and his family were Methodists. He was a farmer, and for many years Justice of the Peace. He died Dec. 4, 1857.

Children:—*Born in Wayne Co., O.*
- — 97 Jasper, b. Sept. 2, 1838; d. aged 4 years.
- — 98 Joseph, b. 1840; m. **Magdalena Reiter**; res. Lichfield, Hinsdale Co., Mich.
- + 99 Asa, b. Sept. 2, 1841.
- —100 Robert, b. Aug. 19, 1843; m. **Nancy Ann Hews**; d. in Hancock Co., O. Left two daughters, Gertrude and Estella, who reside in Blufton, O.
- +101 Isaac, b. Apr. 4, 1845; m. **Sarah J. George**; res. Warrensburg, Mo.
- —102 Anne, b. Jan. 12, 1847; m. **Hiram McDowell**, Nov. 19, 1869.
- —103 William Oliver, b. Dec. 23, 1848; m. **Mary Ann George**; res. Findlay, O.; chn. Leyman M., m. **Eva Smith**; Netta, d. in infancy.
- —104 Elizabeth, b. July 27, 1851; m. **William Hough**, July 9, 1870; d. Feb. 24, 1887.
- —105 Cyrus, b. 1853; res. Mammoth Springs, Ark.
- —106 Emma, b. Aug. 4, 1855; m. **Isaac Quinn**, Apr. 8, 1877; res. Maples, Ind.

27. MARK STRATTON (*Joseph, Daniel*) was born Sept. 27, 1812, in Sussex Co., N. J., and passed his boyhood on his father's farm in Wayne Co., Ohio. Dec. 24, 1835, he married **Mary Shellenberger** of Beaver Co., Pa., daughter of *John* and *Mary (Miller) Shellenber*ger. She was born Mar. 11, 1816, and died Feb. 3, 1875. In 1848 they settled on a farm of 240 acres in Wabash Co., Ind., which he called "Hopewell Farm." Here he built a commodious country house, and here he spent the remainder of his long, useful life. At fifteen he joined the Methodist Episcopal church and was a licensed preacher in that church from early manhood. Although not holding a pastorate, he often conducted meetings in country churches, and did much mission work. He was several times elected to county offices. All his life he was a student, both of books and of nature and possessed a wonderful memory. He died Jan. 10, 1890.

Children:—*Born in Wayne Co., Ohio.*

107 Catherine Elizabeth,[6] m. **Mathew Samuel Marshall**, Feb. 25, 1857; resides in California.

108 Anastasia Lucella,[6] m. **Alva Taylor**.

Born at "Hopewell Farm," Ind.

109 Mary Ann, m. **John Oliver**; d. Feb. 19, 1872.

110 Louisa Jane, d. Oct. 16, 1851.

111 Jerome Quesnal, m. **Victoria Haskins**, Oct., 1868; chn. DeWitt and Herbert, d. in infancy; Cosette, m. **Lee Patrick**; Constance, m. **J. H. White**; Gertrude.

112 Samira Ellen, d. Nov., 1882.

113 Irvin Franklin, m. **Sarah Fitch**; killed by electric cars in San Bernardo, Cal., Apr. 3, 1902; chn. Leander, Harold, Helen, Margueritte.

114 Florence Shellenberger, m. **W. H. Compton**, Oct. 3, 1885; resides in Coldwater, Mich.

115 Leander Elliott, drowned in Wabash River, July 6, 1872, aged 19 yrs.

116 Lemon Mark, m. 2nd, Lillie **J. Haehl**; lived in Manilla and Waldron, Ind.; d. Jan. 3, 1916; left a daughter, Leah Mary.

117 Ada May, m. **Franklin Pierce Wilson**.

118 Gene, m. **Charles D. Porter**; res. "Limberlost Cabin," Rome City, Ind.; author of *The Song of the Cardinal, Freckles, The Limberlost Girl, The Harvester,* etc.

28. THOMAS STRATTON (*Joseph, Daniel*) was born Aug. 24, 1815. Coming to Hancock Co. from New Jersey when a small child, he was all his life closely identified with the country's best interests. He was Justice of the Peace for many years. In 1837 he married **Celia Jones**. He died May 30, 1864.

Children:—*Born in Hancock Co., Ohio.*
- —119 Elizabeth A., b. Nov. 11, 1841; m. **Dr. Virgil**, 1871; d. June 5, 1899, in Hancock Co.
- —120 Margaret J., m. **Samuel Burns**, 1863; res. Beverdam, O.
- —121 Katherine M., m. **Calvin Marshall**, 1890; res. Hennessey, Okla.
- —122 William A., m. **Josephine Bailey**, 1895; res. Lake City, Ark.
- —123 Lucinda S., b. Nov. 5, 1852; d. in 1853.
- —124 Almira Z., m. **William Cornwell**, 1871; res. Findlay, O.
- —125 Sylvester S., m. **Princella Cookson**, 1880; res. Hennessey, Okla.
- —126 John W., m. **Clara B. Hastings**, 1884; res. Rogers, Ark.
- —127 James C., b. 1861; d. July 29, 1865.

29. DANIEL STRATTON (*Joseph Daniel*) was born July 20, 1817. He married **Christina Myers**, Mar. 8, 1843, and lived on the old homestead in Canaan township, Wayne Co., O., where he was a farmer. They were members of the Methodist Church, and in the pleasant, genial atmosphere of their Christian home their seven sons grew to manhood, two of them becoming ministers of the gospel, the others successful farmers and business men. He died Nov. 2, 1890. She died July 18, 1884, aged 63 years.

Children:—*Born in Wayne Co., O.*
- +128 Cyrus L., b. 1843.
- +129 Lemuel, b. 1845.
- +130 Jefferson B., b. Mar. 13, 1848.
- +131 Albert A. Farmer, b. Nov. 13, 1850; m. **Mary Johnson**; res. Charlotte, Mich.
- —132 Joseph S., b. Dec. 30, 1854; res. San Diego, Cal.; m. Sept. 18, 1912, **Mrs. Frances Ada Stratton**.
- +133 William D., b. June 30, 1858; m. **Alice Taylor**; res. Grand Rapids, Mich.
- —134 Benjamin F., b. 1860; a farmer in W. Salem, O.; July 5, 1884, m. **Susan Muir**; chn. Earnest, Gladys.

31. CYRUS STRATTON (*Joseph, Daniel*) was born May 5, 1823. He lived in Wayne Co., O., where he married **Sarah Myers**, and where he died May 4, 1896.

Children:—*Born in Wayne Co., O.*
- —135 Clara E., b. Apr. 13, 1847; d. Feb., 1905; m. **William Frank**, Oct. 21, 1871.
- —136 Frances M., b. Jan. 3, 1849; d. aged 17 years.
- +137 Daniel B.
- —138 Alfred P., b. Feb. 5, 1853; d. aged 18 years.
- —139 Sara A., m. **John Hurst**, Mar. 24, 1875; d. in Mich. June 8, 1882.
- —140 Joseph W., b. Jan. 26, 1861; d. unm. in California.
- —141 Frank B.

40. THOMAS STRATTON (*Daniel, Thomas*) was born in Norwalk, Huron Co., O., July 26, 1821. He married **Mary Ann Manahan**, Feb. 29, 1844. He purchased a farm near his father's and built a substantial frame house and occupied it with his bride immediately after his marriage, and lived continuously in the same house until his death, Dec. 27, 1910.

Children:—*Born in Norwalk, O.*
- —142 Augusta, b. Oct. 17, 1847; m. **Henry Robbins**, June 18, 1838. Resides in the Stratton homestead.
- —143 John T., b. June 3, 1853; d. Jan. 31, 1856.
- +144 DeForest, b. Nov. 22, 1854.

41. NATHAN TANNER STRATTON (*Daniel, Thomas*) was born at Norwalk, Ohio, Oct. 20, 1823. He married **Jane Ann Smith**, daughter of *Benjamin Smith*, Feb. 22, 1848. They were married in Erie Co., O. She died in Wood Co., O., Aug. 4, 1884. Mr. Stratton died in 1909.

Children:—*Born in Erie Co., O.*
- —145 Frank Whitford, b. Feb. 13, 1849; m. June 27, 1873, **Hattie Caswell**; chn. Fred G., Charles H., Lena M., Howard O.
- —146 Sarah Jane, b. July 30, 1852; d. in infancy.
- —147 Charles Tanner, b. Feb. 7, 1854; d. in childhood.
- —148 Fannie L., b. Sept. 5, 1856; d. in infancy.
- —149 Benjamin P., b. Aug. 18, 1858; m. **Hattie J. Avery**, Mar. 11, 1880; res. Bowling Green, O.; chn. Pearle B., Harold B., d. Oct. 4, 1908, aged 20 yrs.

Born in Wood Co., O.

—150 John W., b. Aug. 5, 1861; m. Aug. 4, 1880, **Anna E. Ayers**; res. Yale, Mich.; chn. Jennie M., Hattie H., Nina L.

—151 Hattie Jane, b. Dec. 6, 1863; m. **Harvey A. Higgins**, Mar. 14, 1880.

—152 Nellie T., b. May 20, 1866; m. **Frank Grisnold**, Aug. 4, 1883.

—153 Burt Smith, b. Feb. 6, 1869; m. at Shephard, Mich., Dec. 16, 1887, **Cora Belle Cogswell**; chn. Pearl E., Earl B., Naomi, Robert C.

—154 Louis T., b. Mar. 28, 1871; m. **Olive Belle Ford**; ch. Donald B.

44. DAVID STRATTON (*Daniel, Thomas*) was born in Norwalk, Huron Co., O., Mar. 9, 1829, and died in Tonawanda, N. Y., Mar. 12, 1892, and is buried in the old cemetery, two miles south of Norwalk, O. He married **Mary E. Hedges**, Feb. 17, 1852. He served in the war of the rebellion, first as captain, and then as major, in the 10th Regiment, Ohio Cavalry.

Children:—*Born in Huron Co., O.*

—155 Inez, b. Feb. 1, 1853; d. Oct. 17, 1856.

Born in Kent, Mich.

+156 Ed, b. Nov. 23, 1854.

—157 Fred, b. Aug. 1, 1857; m. **Emma Staubuck**; ch. Gladys, Henry, Raymond, Victor, Maud, Fred, Edward.

—158 Helen, b. Mar. 9, 1862; d. Aug. 3, 1864.

45. JOHN LOGAN STRATTON (*Daniel, Thomas*) was born in Norwalk, Huron Co., O., Aug. 22, 1831. He married, Feb. 11, 1857, at Ripley, Ohio, **Helen Dorlisca Taft,** daughter of *Rev. Austin Taft,* a prominent minister of the M. E. Church.* She was a teacher before her marriage. She died Sept. 26, 1915. Mr. Stratton was a soldier during the war in the 10th Ohio Cavalry, Sergeant of Co. G, serving three years. In 1867 he moved from Norwalk to Wood Co., O., and in 1878 settled on a farm in Hollenberg precinct, Kansas. He served fourteen years as Justice of the Peace, and twenty-five years on the Board of Education. A member of the Methodist church. In 1901 he moved to Washington City, Kan.

---

* He was a third cousin of President William H. Taft.

Children:—*Born in Enterprise, O.*
+159 Archie Dorlisca, b. Sept. 18, 1859.
Born at Norwalk, O.
—160 Cora M., m. Frank E. Gwinn, Mar. 10, 1887; living on a 660-acre farm in Washington Co., Kan.

46. DANIEL STRATTON, JR., (*Daniel, Thomas*) was born Oct. 10, 1833. He married **Augusta E. Brooks**, Mar. 10, 1858. He served during the war of the Rebellion, first as lieutenant, and then as captain, in the 124th Regt., Ohio Vol. Infantry, and is a member of the G. A. R.* Res. Long Beach, Cal.†

Children:—*Born in Brecksville, O.*
—161 E. Claire, b. Jan. 26, 1859; m. **Susie C. Chapman**, Apr. 13, 1886; res. Wamego, Kan.; ch. John Daniel.
Born at Wilmington, O.
—162 Mary Louise, b. Apr. 16, 1861.
Born at Cleveland, O.
+163 Everett Lincoln, b. Nov. 11, 1864.

50. JOHN RIGDON STRATTON (*David, Daniel*) married **Julia Tull**; served in the artillery in the Federal army from 1862 to 1865. He died in Henry Co., Ill.

Children:—*Born in Middle Grove, Ill.*
—164 Frank.
Born in West Jersey, Ill.
—165 Palmira.
—166 Mary.
Born in Stockton, Mo.
—167 Emma.
—168 Dewey.

54. JAMES LOGAN STRATTON (*David, Daniel*) was born in Adario, Richland Co., Ohio, Oct. 8, 1833. In 1852, with his three brothers, Daniel G., Thomas J. and George W. he went West. Leaving Illinois Apr. 1, 1852, they crossed the plains, driving five yokes of oxen and two cows, going by the way of Forts Kerney,

---

* Thomas Stratton was a soldier in the Revolution; his son Daniel (No. 15) fought for the government in the War of 1812. Daniel's three sons (David, John L. and Daniel), three of the sons of his elder daughter, the husband of his second daughter, and two of her sons were all soldiers in the War of the Rebellion, each acquitting himself well, winning frequent promotions.

† To this Mr. Daniel Stratton the compiler is indebted for much valuable help on his line and for the picture of his father's family.

Hall and Boise, and over the Cascade Mountains, arriving in Portland in September. Along the Platte River they encountered many Indians and saw thousands of buffalo. From Portland they took loads of provisions a hundred miles up the Willamette Valley, selling flour at $50.00 per 100 lbs., beans at 65 cts. per lb., and other things accordingly. George W. Stratton died in camp on the Columbia River. After spending some time in the California gold mines, Daniel G. and Thomas J. came East as far as Illinois where for many years they engaged in merchandising. John L. Stratton walked from Portland to Olympia, went down the sound in an Indian canoe to Seattle, then a little hamlet in the wilderness, boarded a lumber sailing vessel, the *Franklin*, bound for San Francisco, which place he reached in fifteen days. Traded along the coast of Mexico and South America, going as far as Chile, where he remained in port six weeks, obtaining "good board and lodging at $1.00 per week." Returning to California he spent some time at the Roses Barguba gold mines, and then sailed for New York, via Panama, Aspenwall and Havana, and reached his old home in Ohio after an absence of six years. He married **Priscella A. Mills** in Ohio in **1860**. She was daughter of *Galen A.* and *Elizabeth (Stratton) Mills*. In 1862 he enlisted in Co. C, 112th Inf., and served three years in Sherman's army. Was all through the Georgia campaign, took part in twenty-seven hard fought battles and received four gun-shot wounds. Mrs. Stratton died in **1895**. Mr. Stratton is living in Colorado with his children and grandchildren.

Children:—*Born in Berea, O.*
—169 Frank Leon, m. **Jeane L. Hensley**, Oct. 13, 1887; res. Cope, Col.; chn. Hazel E., Judson C., Naomi P., Priscella J., Audrey M.

Born in Adario, O.
—170 Mae L., d. in Wood Co., O., in 1876.
—171 Fred Mills, m. **Mae Parks**, May 20, 1896; has two children born in Yampa, Col.; chn. James Beryl and Rex.

68. ANDREW STRATTON (*Samuel, Thomas*) was born Aug. 19, 1849. He was a farmer and lived in Beaver Co., Pa. He married **Jane Godard.**

Children:—*Born in Beaver Co., Pa.*
—172 John, res. Beaver Falls, Pa.
—173 Samuel, res. Beaver Falls, Pa.

69. Rev. Isaac Stratton [6] (*David,*[5] *Daniel,*[4] *Daniel*[3]) was born May 13, 1835. At twenty he united with the United Brethren Church and later became a minister, preaching in eastern Indiana, and in Clark, Hancock, and other counties in Ohio. He married **Margret Fox** in 1860. Having now retired from the active ministry, but preaching occasionally, he resides in North Findlay, O.

Children:—*Born in Hancock Co., O.*
- —174   Loren Lemuel, d. Dec. 27, 1865.
- —175   Cynthia Cindrella, m. **Marion Fox.**
  Born in Vanwort Co., O.
- —176   Emma Elizabeth, m. **John** Bird.
  Born in Adams Co., Ind.
- —177   Dora Derrell, m. **Nicholas Weirough.**
- —178   Mary Margret, d. Feb. 17, 1893.
  Born in Clark Co., O.
- —179   Ona Orpha.
  Born in Miami Co., O.
- —180   David Dary, res. Findlay, O.

71. Nial Stratton (*David, Daniel, Daniel*) was born Nov. 23, 1840, in Hancock Co., O., and was eleven years old when his parents moved to Fayette Co., Iowa. His school advantages in the new country were very limited, but he was fond of books, a diligent reader, and a student all his life, while he engaged in the many occupations common to pioneers,—and he was inately a pioneer, loving the woods and the wild. After spending some time in Colorado and Nebraska, in 1880, he settled in Dunn Co., Wis., buying 80 acres of land near his father and brothers. In 1880 he married **Florence Hevener.** In 1892 he moved to Ashland, Oregon, where the last years of his life were spent as an horticulturist, a grower of small fruits. Generous, genial and social, he had many friends. He was a member of the Congregational church. He died Feb. 4, 1908, of pneumonia. He gave the compiler much help in tracing this line.

Children:—*Born in Dunn Co., Wis.*
- —181   Percival Clement, res. Ashland, Ore.
- —182   Ethel Florence.
- —183   Lloyd William.
- —184   Reginold Wade.

72. Cyrus Stratton (*David, Daniel, Daniel*) was born Aug. 17, 1849, in Hancock Co., O. In 1864 he went to Dunn Co., Wis.

He married **Lavernia Eaton** in 1872; two years later he settled on a farm which he bought near his father's and on which he lived for nearly twenty-five years. In 1895 Mrs. Stratton died, and two years later Mr. Stratton moved to Jim Falls, Chippewa Co., Wis., where he is now living.

Children:—*Born in Dunn Co., Wis.*

—185 Nancy Maria, m. **Albert Knopps**; living in Idaho.
—186 Thomas Elmer, m. 1st, **Lilly A. Kaye**, in 1895; 2nd, **Adde Mullen**; lives in Idaho and has two sons.
—187 Ida May, m. 1st, **Luke Blank**; 2nd, **Mr. Tallman**, in 1902.
—188 Paul Jones, m. **Fay Hathaway**, 1901; res. Jim Falls, Wis.
—189 Jennie Laverrina, m. **Richard Gilbert**.
—190 Lottie Ruth, m. **Hugh Tallman**.
—191 Willis.
—192 Edwin.
—193 Hersey.

73. HENRY JAMES STRATTON (*David, Daniel, Daniel*) was born in Fayette Co., Iowa, July 16, 1854, and went to Wisconsin with his father in 1864. In spite of the very limited educational advantages of his boyhood and youth in a newly settled country, he managed to get a good education, and became a teacher. In 1877 he married **Nellie Burton**. He died Nov. 12, 1888.

Children:—*Born in Dunn Co., Wis.*

—194 Ella.
—195 Guy, m. **Sadie F. Higby** in Sioux City; a printer by trade; lives in Oregon.
—196 Myrtle, m. **Frank Duxberry**.
—197 Earl, after his father's death, was adopted into another family, and took the name of his adopted parents, Babcock.

77. JOHN STRATTON (*Joseph, Daniel, Daniel*) married **Catherine Mull** in 1858. He died in Menomonie, Wis.

Children:

—198 Simeon, res. Cœur d'Alene, Idaho.
—199 John, res. Menomonie, Wis.
—200 Daisy.

82. JOSEPH STRATTON (*Joseph, Samuel, Daniel*) was born in Ohio, 1849. Went to Wisconsin in 1865; married **Clara Phillips**

in 1877. In 1891 they removed to a farm near Spokane, Wash.
Children:—*Born in Dunn Co., Wis.*
—201 Nellie.
—202 Albert, d. in infancy.
—203 Delmer.
  Born in Spokane Co., Wash.
—204 Albert.   —209 Ernest.
—205 Glenn.   —210 Hazel.
—206 Norma.   —211 Simeon.
—207 Alice.   —212 Joseph, Jr.
—208 Clara.

The address of this family is desired.

88. JOSEPH STRATTON (*Henry, Daniel, Daniel*) enlisted in the Federal army in 1861 and served through the war. He was with Sherman in his "March to the Sea." In 1868 he married **Caroline Mull,** and the following year moved to Dunn Co., Wis., bought a farm, and lived there until 1883 when he moved to Dennison, Texas, where he is now superintendent of the city water works.
Children:—*Born in Ohio.*
—213 Serena.
  Born in Dunn Co., Wis.
—214 Lena.

89. HARMON STRATTON (*Henry, Daniel, Daniel*) enlisted in the Federal army in 1862. In 1873 he married **Abby Mull,** and moved from Ohio to Wisconsin. His health failing from disease caused from exposure during the war, he returned to Ohio, where he died in 1900.
Children:—*Born in Dunn Co., Wis.*
—215 Victor.
—216 Harry.

92. JACOB STRATTON (*Henry, Daniel, Daniel*) is a farmer near Menomonie, Wis., where he went from Ohio about 1869. He married **Matilda Denning** about 1875.
Children:—*Born in Wisconsin.*
—217 Olive.   —220 Susan.
—218 Chester.   —221 Effie.
—219 Pearl.   —222 Milton.

99. ASA STRATTON (*William, Joseph, Daniel*) is a farmer and lives at Blufton, Ohio. He was born Sept. 7, 1841. He married **Frances J.** Cromwell, Oct. 7, 1865, daughter of *Anderson* and *Eliza Jane (Coulter) Cromwell*.

Children:—*Born in Wayne Co., O.*
- —223 Lizzie Jane, twin, m. **Daniel Matter.**
- —224 Eliza Ann, twin, m. **John Felt,** Sept. 27, 1887.
- —225 Horace Eaton, m. **Ida Deihl**; chn. Ruth, Eva, Leuella Cristel.
- —226 Orton Lake, twin, m. **Arnelia Arras** in 1908; chn. Raymond, Frances, Catherine J.
- —227 Orland, twin, d. aged 2 years.
- —228 Christena, m. **John Zoll.**
- —229 John Anderson, m. **Nellie M. Cunningham**; chn. Geo. B., Forest, Doyet D., Margery I.
- —230 Charles Frederick, m. **Fairy Dale Deifendefer**; chn. Rhoda, Walter A., Donoven B.
- —231 George Clifford, hardware merchant at Blufton, O.; chn. Frances F., Donald C., Rolland L.
- —232 Jesse Ray, m. **Mozell Troup,** Apr., 1911.

101. ISAAC STRATTON (*William, Joseph, Daniel*) was born in Wayne Co., O., Apr. 4, 1845. He married, first, **Sarah J. George,** Oct. 10, 1871; second, **Lydia J.** Crawford, Jan. 14, 1886. He was a farmer in Hancock Co., O., and after 1877 removed with his family to Johnson Co., Mo. He died in Aug., 1908.

Children:—*Born in Hancock Co., O.*
- +233 William E.
- +234 Edgar C.
- +235 Henry B.
- —236 Waldo E., d. in infancy.

Born in Johnson Co., Mo:
- —237 Jasper C., d. aged 2 years, 6 mos.

128. Rev. CYRUS L. STRATTON (*Daniel, Joseph, Daniel*) was born Dec. 18, 1843. He married **Rebecca J. Sommers,** Aug. 29, 1863. He resides on a farm near Red Oak, Iowa, where he settled in 1872 from Ohio. He has been a local Methodist Episcopal minister for forty-eight years; served two terms in the Iowa General Assembly. All his family belong to the M. E. Church, and a little church building near his home is named for

him, "Stratton's Chapel." Mrs. Stratton died July 27, 1897. She was daughter of *Joseph* and *Catherine Sommers.*

Children:—*Born in Wayne Co., O.*
- —238   Charles Edwin, b. Aug. 16, 1866; d. in infancy.
- +239   William Jones.

    Born in Madison, Ohio.
- —240   Hattie Gertrude, now a teacher in Iowa.

    Born in Montgomery Co., Iowa.
- —241   Dora Christina, m. **J. M. Sanders**, Jan. 1, 1895.
- —242   Frank Paul, m. **Gertrude Abbott**, Feb. 14, 1907; chn. Paul L., Donald S.
- —243   Bertha Ellen, m. **Roye Shaffer**, Apr. 3, 1907.
- —244   Carrie Edith, d. Feb. 28, 1887.

129. LEMUEL STRATTON (*Daniel, Joseph, Daniel*) was born Sept. 18, 1845, in Wayne Co., O. He married **Susan Cockrell**, and resides in Albany, Oregon.

Children:—*Born in Medina, O.*
- —245   Mary Etta, m. **Frank D. Breckinridge**, 1892; res. San Diego, Cal.

    Born in Red Oak, Iowa.
- —246   Cora C., b. 1873; d. 1898.

    Born at Albany, Oregon.
- —247   Pearl F.
- —248   Clarence B.

130. JEFFERSON B. STRATTON (*Daniel, Joseph, Daniel*) married **Jane Clark** in Wayne Co., O., Jan. 24, 1871. The following year they moved to Iowa, where he engaged in farming until 1885. Since that time they have lived in Ohio, Kansas, New Mexico, Missouri. In Gerard, Kan., he owned and operated an electric light plant for several years. In New Mexico he and his sons took up and proved homesteads under the "Three Year Act." Mr. and Mrs. Stratton now live in Aurora, Mo., where they have a nice home and where their sons have mining interests.

Children:—*Born in Montgomery Co., Iowa.*
- —249   Albert Clark, m. Aug. 10, 1897, **Belle Long**. Sec'y of large mining plant at Aurora, Mo. Chn. Lloyd L., Royal E., James J., Albert C.
- —250   George Daniel, m. Apr. 28, 1899, **Jessie Vancil**. He is superintendent of a mine at Zinc, Ark.; res. Aurora, Mo. Chn. Mary J. and Laurence G.

Born in Wayne Co., O.

—251 Leo Everett, m. Apr. 12, 1902, **Minnie M. Gates.** Has been engaged in mining in Black Bear, Idaho, and Aurora, Mo. Now resides in Lawton, Kan. Chn. Leonard, Leon, Mabel, d. Jan. 14, 1907, aged 8 months.

Born in Red Oak, Iowa.

—252 Earl Jefferson, m. Sept. 24, 1905, **Laura Elizabeth Watson.** Spent several years in the mining industry in Idaho, Missouri and New Mexico; now a farmer and dairyman on a large farm near Richland, New Mexico. Chn. Fern E., Alice Helen, Wayne Jefferson.

—253 Richard Rowland, m. 1st, June 3, 1906, **Pearl Brooks,** who died the following year; m. 2nd, Aug. 3, 1912, **Gertha Hudson;** res. Aurora, Mo. Ch. Richard Hudson.

Born in Aurora, Mo.

—254 Dudley Dean, res. Aurora.

131. ALBERT A. STRATTON (*Daniel, Joseph, Daniel*) married, first, **Mary A. Johnson,** Jan. 1, 1879. She died at the age of thirty-five years, and he married, second, **Mrs. Sarah J. (Snyder) Taylor,** Oct. 16, 1894. Res. Charlotte, Mich.

Children:

By first marriage.

—255 Franklin D.
—256 Glycene E., m. J. W. Clements, Nov. 12, 1902.
—257 Hazel D.
—258 Mary Mae, m. Dec. 12, 1912, **Leon Ells.**

133. WILLIAM DANIEL STRATTON (*Daniel, Joseph, Daniel*) was born June 30, 1858, brought up on his father's farm, graduated from Ohio Normal University in 1878, and received the degree of A.M. from this institution in 1890. He has also received degrees from several other institutions. In 1886 he was licensed to preach by the Methodist Protestant Church. Held pastorates at Sunfield, Charlotte and Grand Rapids. In 1896 was elected Presiding Elder of the District Conference, and served in this capacity for nine years. He married, first, **Sarah Alice Taylor,** daughter of *Joseph* and *Lucinda Taylor,* of Wayne Co., O. She died Nov. 9, 1899. He married, second, **Rosa A. Taylor.** Res. Grand Rapids, Mich.

Children:
  By first marriage.
259 Taylor, d. Sept. 19, 1882.
260 Eva May, m. **Glenn D. Spafford**, Feb. 22, 1906; res. Hillsboro, O.
261 Althea Pearl.
  By second marriage.
262 Royal Rex.
263 Christina Alice.

137. DANIEL B. STRATTON (*Cyrus, Joseph, Daniel*) was born Mar. 11, 1851. He was a farmer and business man living near Lodi, Ohio. He was a deacon in the Congregational Church and held in high esteem by all who knew him. Jan. 14, 1875, he married **Frances Ada Shilling**. He died Mar. 23, 1908.

Children:
264 Olive Blanch, m. **S. R. Auble**; res. Lodi, O.
265 William J., d. in infancy.
266 Ira G., m. June 2, 1912, **Louise Conrad**; res. San Diego, Cal.

144. DEFOREST STRATTON (*Thomas, Daniel, Thomas*) was born Nov. 22, 1854. He is a merchant at Norwalk, O. He married Jan. 21, 1876, **Ina Jane Filkins**.

Children:
267 Ralph Ward, m. **Elsie Hall**; res. Campaign, Ill.; chn. Ruth E., Lucile H., Elizabeth.
268 Loyd Benjamin, m. **Isabel M. Ress**; res. Canton, O.
269 Archie Thayer, res. Pomona, Cal.

156. ED STRATTON (*David, Daniel, Thomas*) married at Rock Island, Ill., Feb. 11, 1880, **Florence May Cook**, who was born in Clearfield Co., Pa. Resides in Meridian, Miss.

Children:—*Born in Lyons, Iowa.*
—270 DeForest, m. **Eva Guy**, July 5, 1903; chn. Ora T., Ed. G., Forest B.
—271 Inez, b. Feb. 5, 1885; d. Apr. 15, 1886.
—272 Eunice Eliza.

159. ARCHIE DORLISCA STRATTON (*John L., Daniel, Thomas*) married, in Washington Co., Kan., Feb. 19, 1885, **Mary Alice Blackstone**, who was born in Louis Co., Iowa.

Children:—*Born in Washington, Kan.*
—273 Maude, m. **C. A. Totten**, Sept. 22, 1909; res. Throop, Kan.
—274 Mabel Claire, m. **H. H. McCleary**, Apr. 14, 1909; res. San Diego, Cal.
—275 John William, m. **Blanche Kinnan**, Apr. 21, 1912; ch. Jeannette.
—276 Frank Blackstone, m. **Elizabeth Burnett**, Dec. 24, 1914.
—277 Helen Florence.

163. EVERETT LINCOLN STRATTON (*Daniel, Daniel, Thomas*) married **Maude E. Ramsoner**, July 19, 1889; resides in Chicago. Colonization agent for the Southern Land Co.
Children:—*Born in Topeka, Kan.*
—278 Hazel M.
—279 Marguerite L.
Born in Wichita, Kan.
—280 Cecelia Marie.
Born in Chicago.
—281 Everett Lincoln, Jr.

233. WILLIAM E. STRATTON (*Isaac, William, Joseph, Daniel*) was born in Hancock Co., O., where, with his brother, he received a good common school education, and attended the Second District State Normal for two years. He is now a successful general contractor at Warrensburg, Mo. Apr. 13, 1908, he married **Maude Surbaugh**. He and his wife are members of the M. E. Church.
Children:—*Born in Johnson Co., Mo.*
—282 Frances Geraldine.
—283 Lena May.
—284 Georgia Lerison.

234. EDGAR C. STRATTON (*Isaac, William, Joseph, Daniel*) is a farmer and thresherman near Epping, N. Dakota. He married **Libbie May Deeter**, Mar. 13, 1898, in Warrensburg, Mo. She is a daughter of *John M.* and *Rachel A.* (*Swinger*) *Deeter*, of Ohio. They moved from Johnson Co., Mo., to Cavalier Co., Dakota, in 1904, and four years later moved to Williams Co., Dakota, where they proved up a claim upon which they are still living. They are members of the German Baptist Church.

Children:—*Born in Johnson Co., Mo.*
—285 Rachel Jane.
—286 Agnes Lucile.
—287 John Isaac, d. in infancy.
Born in N. Dakota.
—288 Dora May.
—289 Atta Bernice.
—290 Edgar C., Jr.

235. HENRY B. STRATTON (*Isaac, William, Joseph, Daniel*) married, first, **Virginia L. Coats**, Jan. 1, 1900; married, second, **Dessa Stanley**, Sept. 1, 1909. He lives on a ranch near Santa Rosa, Cal.

Children:—*Born in Johnson Co., Mo.*
By first marriage.
—291 Gladys Velma.
Born in Walla Walla Co., Wash.
—292 Archer Emerson.
Born in Santa Rosa, Cal.
—293 Pauline.

239. Rev. WILLIAM JONES STRATTON (*Cyrus L., Daniel, Joseph, Daniel*) was pastor of the Methodist Episcopal Church at Menden, Neb. He married **Ella E. Youtz**, June 20, 1894, daughter of *Reuben* and *Elizabeth Youtz*. He died May 3, 1908.

Children:
—294 Marian Esther.
—295 Frank Kenneth.
—296 Ruth Elizabeth.

"That ye may tell it to the generation following." PSALMS XLVIII, 13.

INDEXES

INDEX TO SUBJECTS*

A Charleston company, 191
A "good roads" movement, 67
An "after-planter," 321
An ancient parish charity, 12
An experiment with the American elk, 221
An old family Bible, 193
An old New Testament, 89
A Stratton deed, 1729, Va., 359-60
A "Pastor Emeritus," 245
A pastor's valedictory, 245
A "place-name," 3
A Quaker sea-captain, 187
A Stratton patent, Va., 351
Bryant and Stratton Colleges, 2
Committee of Safety, 38
Court of Canterbury, 3
Division of Counties, Va., 351
Earl of Northbrook, 11
"Elmwood," 20
Friends' burial ground, 410
Kirketon Manor, 9
Marriage license in "ye olden time," 358
Money values in 1798, 72
"Myron Stratton Home," 335
Nantucket Strattons, 176
New Jersey Volunteers, 277
"Oath of Fidelity," 20
Orange county men, 477
Some colonial heroes, 22
Some quaint Stratton epitaphs, 46, 194

Some unclassified Strattons, 32, 33, 35, 177
"Stratton Chapel," 245, 492
Stratton coat-of-arms, 321
"Stratton Falls," 280
"Stratton's Folly," 13
Stratton motto, 202, 214
Stratton park, 335
Stratton's mill, 66
Stratton Wills
  In England, 4, 7
  In America
    Benjamin, 1818, Philadelphia, 267
    Edward, 1817, Va., 364
    John, 1705, Va., 370
    Levi, 1792, N. J., 252
    William, 1760, Va., 361
"Street-towns," 3, 12
The Canadian expedition, 192
The "Fighting Sixteenth," 161
The "Flag of Our Country," 219
The "Great Ice Freshet," 109
The Hatton house, 232
The John Stratton Bible, 274
The Millville Strattons, 256
The novelty iron works, 181
Thurkolton manor, 10
"Warning out," 31
Washington's lifeguards, 39
Watertown's train-band, 20
"Woodchuck Lodge," 280

---

* For index to other subjects see *Contents,* pages ix and x.

INDEX TO PLACES*

Amherst, N. H., 204
Amherst Co., Va., 465
Athol, Mass., 56, 57, 96, 192-197
Barren Co., Mich., 33
Barrington, N. H., 34
Bedford Co., Va., 368
Bennington, 52, 91-93
Bradford Co., Pa., 322
Bradford, N. H., 57
Bridgeport, Conn., 320
Brighton, Ill., 151
Brookfield, 32, 45, 82, 130
Boylston, 110
Cambridge, 120
Cavendish, 90
Chester, Me., 109
Clark Co., O., 328
Clinton Co., O., 412
Concord, 21-26
Craftsbury, Vt., 32
Cummingsville, O., 324
Eastern Shore, Va., 349
Easthampton, 273-277
Edgar Co., Ill., 402
Fairfield, Conn., 278-279
Fairlee, Vt., 35, 61
Fallsburgh, 288
Floyd Co., Ky., 399
Foxboro, Mass., 229
Gill, Mass., 86, 97, 133
Glastonbury, Conn., 34, 60
Greenwich, Mass., 35
Guilford, Vt., 97
Hancock, Me., 102-3
Hardwick, 27
Harvard, 76
Hebron, Ill., 143
Henrico Co., Va., 358
Holden, Mass., 45, 63, 80
Holyoke, 215
Jeffersonville, 236
Jeffrey, N. H., 43, 79
Lincoln, 49
Lineville, Pa., 122

Lynchburg, Va., 138
Malden, Mass., 75
Marlboro, 30, 57
Meadville, Pa., 120
Medford, N. J., 410
Milford, Conn., 315
Montpelier, Vt.,
Nashua, N. H., 83
Natick, 29, 94, 145
New Bedford, 100
Newfane, Vt., 112
New Epswich, 38, 83, 128
Northfield, 84, 87, 88, 135
Northumberland Co., 343
Oswego, 60
Pawlet, Vt., 62
Philadelphia, 265
Phillipston, 74
Pike Co., Ky., 399
Plattsburg, N. Y., 282
Portland, 128
Portsmouth, Va., 341
Princeton, Mass., 43, 79
Richland, Mich., 140
Rindge, N. H., 43, 78, 112
Roxbury, 279
Rutland, 22, 81, 130
Sandisfield, Mass., 241
Saratoga Co., N. Y., 238
Sharon, Mass., 93
Shelburne, 46
Shelby Co., Ky., 360
Shotley, Eng., 10
Swanzey, N. H., 53, 93, 144
Tenterden, Eng., 6
Thompsonville, 287
Towanda, Pa., 330
Trimble Co., Ky., 462
West Chazy, 282
Weston, Mass., 41, 76
Williamstown, 50, 89
Wiltshire, 11
Winslow, Me., 39, 69
Woburn, Mass., 75

*This is by no means a complete index to places named in this volume. It contains only those which may aid in identifying and locating various branches of Strattons. See also *Contents,* pages ix and x.

INDEX OF NAMES

A

Abbott, 130, 215, 492
Aber, 305
Abley, 33
Ackley, 82
Adams, 17, 37, 40, 58, 63, 76, 78, 92, 95, 96, 99, 106, 112, 150, 172, 181, 260, 333, 353, 356, 368, 372, 374, 418, 432
Adamson, 306
Addams, 379
Akerley, 219
Akers, 226
Akin, 421
Albertin, 125
Aldrich, 126, 130
Aldridge, 292
Aldritch, 138
Alexander, 24, 25, 93, 200, 378
Alger, 89
Allaben, 278, 285
Allchin, 129
Allen, 22, 24, 36, 111, 157, 466
Allison, 134, 333
Almy, 241
Altman, 299
Ames, 95, 310
Amonett, 366
Amsworth, 56
Anderson, 256, 270, 272, 355, 376, 407
Andrews, 34, 152, 295
Angell, 304
Annis, 216
Antle, 463
Appleton, 356
Archer, 254, 417
Armistead, 349
Arnaelsteen, 175
Arnold, 95, 117, 331, 405, 429, 461
Arras, 491
Ashbrook, 468
Ashman, 248
Ashton, 470
Ast, 383
Aston, 376
Atherton, 153
Atkins, 392, 399, 472
Atkinson, 238, 334

Atwell, 286
Auble, 494
Augustus, 406
Austin, 69, 91, 186, 271
Avery, 299, 391, 484
Axtell, 198
Ayres, 90, 143, 485

B

Babcock, 164
Bachelor, 196
Bacon, 94, 464
Badlam, 276
Badger, 71
Baehr, 129
Baggs, 304
Bahr, 249
Bailey, 79, 112, 121, 323, 438, 483
Baird, 406, 443
Bagley, 33
Baker, 40, 76, 98, 127, 166, 224, 317, 415, 422
Baldwin, 314, 352
Ball, 44, 202, 209, 436, 438
Ballagh, 171
Ballard, 95, 280, 414
Ballou, 153
Banks, 136, 225, 270, 280
Barber, 425, 469
Bradley, 92
Bardwell, 56
Bark, 297
Barker, 104, 163, 475
Barlow, 156
Barnard, 191
Barnes, 30, 64, 84, 123, 130, 159, 252, 480
Barney, 91
Barnett, 368
Barnum, 300, 314
Barr, 253
Barrett, 70, 93
Barsham, 191
Barthey, 301
Bartlett, 66, 157
Barton, 182, 209, 219, 456
Basim, 426
Bass, 352, 367, 376
Bassett, 87, 106, 186, 196, 319

Batchelor, 48, 197
Bate, 261
Bateman, 237, 257, 258
Bates, 131
Battles, 217
Batton, 415
Baugh, 367
Baumgartner, 445
Baxley, 71
Baxter, 64
Bayless, 151
Bayley, 386
Beach, 315, 460
Beacher, 95
Beadle, 303
Beal, 101
Bean, 426
Beard, 62, 465, 466
Beatty, 233
Beavers, 307
Beck, 170
Beckett, 70
Beckner, 337
Beem, 413
Beeman, 52, 91, 97, 99
Belding, 54
Belknap, 48
Belknap, 82
Bell, 240, 328, 390, 415, 436
Bellis, 262
Bemis, 21, 42, 133, 185
Benargh, 386
Bendickson, 256
Bendurant, 364
Benfield, 437
Benjamin, 48
Bennett, 136, 360
Benson, 475
Bentlage, 446
Berthelet, 184
Berry, 114
Berry, 209, 278
Berray, 185
Betz, 416
Biddle, 271
Bidwell, 34
Biersley, 314
Biggs, 224
Bigham, 208
Biglow, 31, 36, 224, 333,
Billings, 231
Bingham, 238

INDEX

Bird, 230, 395, 427, 488
Birmingham, 454
Bishop, 81, 110
Bixby, 208
Black, 118, 435, 470
Blackburn, 355, 442
Blackman, 402
Blackmer, 91
Blackstone, 494
Blackwell, 388
Blair, 50, 409
Blake, 118
Blank, 489
Blanton, 444
Blarcum, 289
Blasius, 225
Blazer, 295, 307
Blekkingh, 180
Blizzard, 428
Blocker, 466
Blodgett, 223
Bloom, 167, 322
Bloomer, 201
Bloss, 320
Boleyn, 29
Bolles, 272
Bolling, 375
Bond, 164, 413
Bone, 396
Bonell, 159
Bonsall, 439
Bonton, 298
Bouton, 285
Booker, 377
Boone, 297
Booth, 319
Borradale, 474
Borton, 420, 430
Boseman, 226
Bostwick, 315
Bosworth, 211
Bouseman, 369
Boutwell, 201
Bowels, 382
Bowen, 216
Bower, 171, 318
Bowers, 299
Bowman, 28
Bowker, 73
Boyd, 336
Brace, 121
Brackman, 122
Bradbury, 464
Bradford, 65
Bradish, 193, 198
Bradley, 120, 279, 403
Bradshaw, 439, 443
Bradstreet, 117
Brancroft, 118
Branch, 381
Brandon, 403
Brandiff, 261

Brandith, 270
Branham, 397
Brantingham, 419, 455
Branlington, 442
Branson, 442
Brawley, 465, 467
Brecher, 158
Breckinridge, 492
Breed, 114
Breedlove, 466
Brescoe, 188
Brewster, 150
Brickley, 70
Bridge, 163
Briggs, 24, 155, 454
Brigham, 31, 44, 57, 59
Briscoe, 463
Britton, 253
Broad, 63, 68, 117
Brock, 213
Bronson, 113
Brock, 411
Brooks, 25, 30, 97, 112, 375, 411, 486
Brown, 49, 75, 88, 130, 132, 155, 157, 168, 189, 201, 202, 206, 211, 215, 270, 271, 288, 352, 382, 392, 398, 401, 402, 407, 424, 432, 460, 468, 469
Bruce, 133, 138, 167, 207, 476
Brumhall, 128
Brundage, 305
Brunk, 481
Brunsworth, 337
Bryan, 200, 213
Bryant, 64, 109, 203, 217
Buck, 106, 154, 234, 236
Buckhout, 316
Buckly, 168
Budd, 106
Buckmaster, 180
Bufkin, 441
Bugbee, 93
Bull, 44, 117
Bullard, 40, 54
Bump, 319
Bunday, 122
Bundy, 441
Bunker, 87, 102
Buntain, 403
Burchett, 407
Burdett, 225
Burk, 254, 403
Burlew, 272
Burlock, 320
Burgess, 75, 164, 378
Burnap, 55
Burns, 481, 483
Burnet, 386
Burnett, 127, 390, 391, 495
Burnsides, 261
Buroughs, 218

Burr, 135, 329
Burrill, 65
Burritt, 314
Burroughs, 280, 314
Burwell, 349
Burt, 92, 135, 406
Burton, 489
Butler, 110, 215, 448, 459
Butters, 228
Buttler, 465
Butts, 248, 296
Bush, 137, 417
Busby, 258
Buster, 379
Bymaster, 435
Bythers, 117

C

Caldwell, 123, 207
Caine, 121, 396
Call, 85
Calver, 295
Campbell, 26, 180, 202, 294, 312, 317, 354
Canfield, 251, 299
Cantrell, 363
Capell, 392
Capen, 136
Carey, 414
Carlisle, 259
Carlton, 163
Carmer, 32
Carpenger, 51
Carpenter, 168, 233
Carr, 458
Carroll, 280, 305, 476
Carson, 33, 260, 264, 370, 380, 394, 461, 475
Carter, 43, 101, 125, 382
Case, 212, 241, 321, 460
Casler, 443
Cass, 32
Cassaday, 468
Caswell, 484
Cate, 126
Catterton, 387
Chadbourne, 155
Challand, 255
Chamberlain, 124, 176, 211, 326, 478
Chambers, 159, 323, 352, 451
Champ, 339
Champney, 28
Chandler, 69
Chalmers, 71
Chapin, 63, 210
Chapman, 141, 486
Chappelear, 135
Charleston, 190
Charter, 157
Chase, 32, 65, 90, 93, 132, 206, 218

Index

Chastane, 462
Cheesbrough, 115
Cheney, 37, 42, 386
Chesterman, 161
Child, 77, 81, 110
Childs, 55, 382
Chisholm, 200
Christensen, 126
Christian, 394
Christie, 248
Church, 27, 100, 160
Churchill, 61
Chute, 167
Clark, 59, 69, 95, 126, 132, 142, 165, 241, 247, 282, 316, 329, 427, 436, 492
Clarke, 76, 162
Clapp, 123, 134
Clay, 395, 402, 436
Clemmons, 177
Clements, 297, 493
Clifford, 204
Clift, 318
Cline, 326
Clinton, 160
Cloaker, 389
Clobert, 317
Cloud, 368
Coats, 496
Cave, 464
Cobb, 326
Cochran, 297
Cockrell, 492
Codding, 168
Cody, 201
Coe, 276
Coffey, 393
Coffin, 146, 178
Coffinbery, 408
Coggin, 41, 55
Cogswell, 60, 585
Colborn, 21, 217
Cole, 167
Cole, 87, 114, 167, 303, 389
Collins, 188, 395
Colvin, 303
Combs, 368, 417
Comee, 230
Compton, 482
Comrike, 303
Comstock, 238
Condit, 215
Cone, 23, 46
Conger, 36
Congar, 103
Conklin, 283
Conn, 171
Connely, 120, 415, 416
Conner, 260
Conrad, 494
Conrow, 427
Converse, 51

Conway, 227
Cook, 57, 72, 74, 82, 88, 148, 240, 255, 320, 329, 438, 478, 494
Cookson, 483
Coombs, 109
Coolidge, 27, 28, 120
Cooper, 246, 301, 305, 435, 452
Cope, 455
Copeland, 116, 160, 432
Corbin, 276
Corden, 406
Cordray, 295
Corley, 26
Corney, 147
Cornwell, 295, 483
Cossett, 124, 396
Cotton, 74
Couger, 313
Coulter, 383, 491
Courser, 151
Cousen, 426
Cowbry, 136
Cowperthwaite, 447
Cox, 118, 190, 293, 370, 403, 404, 443
Coyle, 265
Cozine, 149
Craig, 417
Crain, 154
Crammer, 475
Cranford, 238
Crawford, 118, 197, 461, 491
Cray, 25
Cree, 386
Crew, 437, 440
Crews, 226, 413, 420
Crichett, 36
Creighton, 232
Cramer, 475
Cromwell, 491
Cronkite, 186
Crosby, 164, 289, 375
Cross, 226, 444
Crowell, 457
Culner, 276
Cummings, 303, 388
Cunningham, 154, 383, 491
Curlson, 418
Curtis, 315, 316, 319, 328, 347
Curtiss, 212
Cushing, 208
Cushman, 23
Custard, 407
Cutler, 75
Cutting, 45, 129, 202
Cyrus, 368

D

Dakin, 21
Dallas, 260, 423

Damon, 127, 201, 225
Dana, 77
Danbert, 477
Dancer, 478
Daniel, 363, 364, 372, 385, 405, 419, 486
Daniels, 33, 158, 272
Darling, 186, 284
Darrow, 279
Davidson, 32, 237, 272, 380, 460
Davis, 37, 42, 43, 44, 64, 96, 132, 165, 166, 185, 217, 237, 253, 271, 277, 283, 299, 355, 369, 392, 401, 409, 439, 460, 462
Dawson, 393, 435, 471, 478
Day, 96, 204, 417
Dayton, 60, 238, 255, 277
Deaderick, 389
Deal, 137, 383
Dean, 418, 445, 455
Deane, 209, 250
Dear, 417
Dearborn, 324
Decker, 480
Deeter, 495
DeForest, 454
Deidrick, 307
Deifendefer, 491
Deihl, 491
Delon, 448
Demis, 55
Demming, 481
Denis, 91, 224
Denneston, 288
Denning, 490
Denom, 378
Dent, 114
Denton, 293
Desing, 227
Devendorf, 446
Devenport, 191
Devoll, 55
Dewey, 142, 213, 284, 435
DeWitt, 447
DeWolf, 455
Diamond, 473
Dibrell, 386
Dickinson, 59, 173, 369
Digges, 349
Dillon, 331, 337, 381
Dilts, 284
Dixon, 239, 383
Doan, 411
Doddridge, 426
Dodge, 144
Dodd, 161
Dofflemeyer, 454
Dolen, 249
Donald, 378
Donnelson, 137

504 INDEX

Donovan, 338
Doolittle, 133
Dormer, 26
Dorrell, 475
Dorsett, 302
Doty, 293
Douglas, 137, 333
Dow, 40
Dowell, 236
Downing, 148
Drake, 69, 70, 132, 388, 408
Dresenberre, 316
Dressler, 174
Drinkard, 384, 394
Dryden, 463
Dudgin, 107
Dudley, 25, 57, 74, 96, 104
Duff, 237
Duffield, 292
Duncan, 448
Dunham, 72
Dunkle, 215
Dunn, 332
Durhan, 290
Dusing, 170
Duxberry, 489
Dyke, 198, 478

E

Eagan, 186
Eager, 31
Earl, 78
Earle, 64, 74, 146
Easley, 427
Eaton, 22, 116, 489
Eddington, 369
Eddy, 128, 226
Edens, 462
Edgerton, 419, 423, 441, 455
Edson, 81
Edwards, 17, 249, 433
Egan, 166
Eiseminger, 299
Elderkin, 446
Eldred, 123
Eldridge, 132, 259
Ellenwood, 133, 209
Ellinger, 107
Elliot, 238, 414, 430
Ellis, 80, 100, 328, 354, 356, 357, 433, 459
Ellsworth, 316
Elmer, 260
Elsrode, 318
Elsworth, 71, 356
Emerson, 305
Emery, 33
Emmons, 418
Ennis, 465
Ensign, 120
Eott, 459

Ericksen, 400
Erwin, 397
Ess, 152
Esteps, 408
Esterbrook, 145
Estes, 156
Eustis, 53
Evans, 155, 196, 310, 324, 420, 437
Eveleth, 105
Everett, 395
Everton, 216
Ewing, 336
Ezell, 201

F

Fairbanks, 211
Fairchild, 287, 330
Falconer, 109
Fall, 443
Fargo, 219
Farmer, 203
Farnham, 117
Farnum, 166
Farres, 388
Farwell, 63
Faucett, 474
Fay, 110, 191, 194, 292
Feaster, 330
Fellows, 147, 218
Felt, 491
Felton, 263
Fenimore, 472
Fenton, 166
Ferguson, 250, 389, 407, 425, 454
Ferrier, 429
Ferris, 292
Fessenden, 98
Field, 25, 45, 47, 48, 87
Fife, 79
Filkins, 494
Fillibrown, 61
Fine, 264
Fish, 93, 463
Fisher, 174, 259, 396
Fiske, 41
Fitch, 89, 323, 482
Fite, 462
Fithian, 233, 275
Fitzgerald, 290
Fleming, 378
Flemming, 434
Flint, 127
Flippen, 363, 370
Florida, 356
Flournoy, 251
Floyd, 242, 441
Fogg, 70
Foland, 409
Folsom, 165

Fontone, 153
Foote, 140
Ford, 140, 240, 248, 331, 469, 485
Forest, 250
Forrester, 463
Fosgate, 164
Foskett, 94
Fossen, 260
Foster, 26, 30, 39-50, 93, 140, 206, 207, 218, 219, 262, 322, 397, 450
Fowler, 271, 336, 447
Fowlkes, 389
Fox, 49, 221, 488
Foy, 221
Frame, 441
Frank, 484
Franklin, 219, 251, 454, 472
Frantz, 183, 308
Frazier, 108, 141, 387, 407
Fream, 425
Freeman, 230, 405
French, 75, 126, 314, 324, 442, 447
Friar, 212
Frink, 66, 93, 140, 143
Frost, 160
Fry, 428
Fulkert, 265
Fulks, 383
Fuller, 53, 94, 97, 116, 134, 289, 302
Fulsom, 84
Fultz, 383
Funchion, 332
Fuqua, 369

G

Gaar, 456
Gage, 32, 135, 147
Gallagher, 388
Gallaspy, 254
Galusha, 92
Gandy, 474
Gardner, 176, 184
Garfield, 41, 191, 197
Garrett, 386
Garthwaite, 442
Gaskill, 436
Gaston, 203, 257
Gates, 65, 110, 493
Gavitt, 123
Gayhart, 404
George, 203, 450, 481, 491
Gerry, 227
Gibbons, 200
Gibbs, 63, 105, 356
Gibson, 43, 124, 468
Gieberson, 427
Gifford, 152

INDEX

Gift, 183
Giles, 195
Gilbert, 436, 489
Gill, 225, 468
Gilliam, 373
Gillison, 103
Gillman, 318
Gilman, 61, 79, 97, 266
Gilmore, 265
Gilson, 454
Gipson, 112
Girard, 236
Gist, 403
Gleason, 30
Glessner, 256
Glezen, 131
Glover, 460
Godard, 487
Goddard, 151
Godfrey, 277
Golden, 435, 461
Golder, 263
Goldsmith, 283
Gole, 261
Golladay, 385
Good, 302
Goodale, 201
Gooden, 216
Goodlett, 378
Goodman, 27
Goodnough, 21
Goodrich, 60
Goodridge, 222
Goodrow, 66
Goodwin, 155
Gordon, 324, 350
Gorger, 298
Gorman, 104
Gosline, 428
Gosling, 469
Goodyear, 129
Gough, 96, 370
Gould, 189, 285, 289, 478
Gragg, 433
Graham, 136, 282
Granger, 322
Grant, 102, 231, 239, 253
Grassier, 148
Graves, 82, 353
Gray, 331, 379, 398, 452
Gregg, 431
Green, 91, 143, 223, 320, 334, 374
Gregory, 290, 309
Greeley, 222, 314
Greenleaf, 137
Greenwood, 54, 80, 170
Griffeth, 255, 285
Griffin, 149, 172
Grimes, 395
Grimmesey, 421
Grindle, 249

Grisnold, 485
Groover, 239
Grover, 154
Groves, 128
Guest, 474
Guice, 432
Gulick, 443
Gunn, 472
Gunter, 441
Gustin, 186
Guthrie, 461
Guy, 55, 346, 494
Guyant, 89
Gwinn, 486

H

Hack, 299
Hackett, 282
Hadden, 31
Hadley, 204, 355
Haehl, 482
Hagaman, 458
Hagen, 436
Hager, 228, 401
Haight, 287
Haines, 236, 412, 425, 438, 462
Hakes, 131
Hagely, 296
Halderman, 440
Hale, 125, 150, 408
Hall, 117, 124, 174, 188, 282, 283, 294, 319, 396, 398, 408, 415, 420, 455, 494
Halleburton, 260
Halling, 427
Hallock, 106
Halstead, 325
Halter, 271
Hamblin, 326
Hamilton, 401
Hammett, 153
Hammond, 300
Hamner, 373
Hampton, 32, 259
Hanchett, 291
Hancock, 243, 410
Hand, 239, 249
Handley, 390
Hanks, 178
Hann, 261
Hanna, 248, 299
Hannold, 475
Hanver, 295
Harbey, 71
Harden, 414
Hardon, 240
Hardy, 47, 303
Harker, 451
Harlan, 371, 434
Harlow, 201
Harmon, 460, 462

Harmanson, 347
Harpool, 299
Harriman, 156, 171
Harrington, 32, 52, 73, 92, 197, 395
Harris, 76, 99, 125, 150, 231, 232, 252, 390, 404, 440
Harrison, 89
Harshbarger, 100
Hartwell, 25, 217
Harvey, 99, 140, 216, 306, 435, 449
Hasbrook, 299
Haskell, 60
Haskens, 238
Haskill, 148
Haskins, 99, 148, 211, 482
Hassell, 202
Hastings, 133, 222, 483
Hatch, 31, 109
Hathaway, 91, 427, 438, 489
Hartshorne, 201
Hatten, 371
Hawkes, 137
Hawkins, 423, 455
Hawks, 107, 386
Hawley, 414
Hayes, 135, 315, 462
Hayford, 36
Hayne, 254
Haynes, 168, 367
Hayward, 228
Hazlet, 266
Hazzard, 412
Heacock, 308
Heald, 419
Heald, 440
Healy, 23, 184, 453
Heath, 134
Hedges, 255, 485
Heene, 400
Heisler, 469
Helens, 404
Hellums, 467
Helm, 385, 435
Helmer, 312
Hemstock, 436
Henderson, 438
Hendricks, 154, 328
Henlings, 446
Heltzel, 454
Henry, 347
Henshaw, 44, 415
Henley, 414, 424
Hensley, 487
Herrick, 85
Herring, 22
Hervey, 57
Hess, 329, 330
Hevener, 488
Hewett, 63
Hewlett, 405

Index

Hewitt, 469
Hews, 481
Heywood, 223
Hiatt, 336
Hickey, 170
Hicks, 363
Higby, 297, 424, 435, 489
Higgins, 485
High, 252, 395
Hildreth, 78, 87
Hill, 42, 55, 96, 160, 200, 214, 219, 220, 261, 300, 451
Hilldrop, 391
Hiller, 427
Hillman, 457
Hills, 75, 423, 447
Hilton, 457
Him, 290
Hines, 161, 409
Hiney, 323
Hinman, 319, 411
Hinkle, 328, 329
Hively, 443
Hobbs, 77, 357, 448
Hobson, 413, 442, 454
Hodge, 114, 130
Hodgman, 25, 217
Hodkins, 103
Hogan, 271
Hogben, 263
Hodgkins, 103
Hogue, 372
Holcomb, 72, 326, 441
Holdcroft, 474
Holden, 325
Holderman, 442
Hollister, 34, 35, 60, 424
Holladay, 159, 248, 416, 419
Holmes, 159, 418, 444
Holman, 99, 124, 125, 388
Holt, 82, 126, 186
Holton, 82, 83, 86, 128
Homes, 68, 120
Homer, 457
Hood, 240, 262
Hooper, 108, 292
Hoosear, 280
Hoover, 311
Hopkins, 309, 311, 371, 383, 392
Hopper, 418
Hopson, 386
Horigan, 248
Horn, 394
Horrocks, 154
Horsley, 370
Horton, 142
Hortox, 406
Hosly, 207
Hotchkiss, 119, 121
Hoton, 47
Hough, 481

Houghton, 94
Houghtaling, 295
Houns, 418
Hogue, 372
House, 123
Houser, 161
Houston, 296
Hover, 261, 328
Howard, 61, 69, 93, 110, 121, 187, 371
How, 41
Howe, 58, 80, 101, 148, 203
Howse, 300
Hoxie, 185
Hoyt, 294
Hubbard, 21, 60, 80, 81, 163, 238, 241, 276, 430
Hubbell, 319, 320
Hubley, 153
Huddleston, 372
Hudelson, 414
Hudson, 374, 386
Huestus, 433
Huffhines, 466
Hughs, 384
Hughes, 72, 331
Hull, 71, 114, 173, 280, 308
Hultz, 171
Hamilton, 136
Humlong, 296
Hummer, 336
Hammett, 153
Humphrey, 73, 196
Hungerford, 320
Hunt, 91, 146, 172, 346, 403, 430
Hunter, 254, 402, 458, 390, 459
Huntley, 164, 295
Huntting, 277
Hurd, 42, 77, 110
Hurst, 484
Hutchens, 105, 412
Hutchenson, 450
Hutchins, 153
Hutchings, 164
Hutchinson, 270
Hutton, 412
Hyde, 95, 124, 290

I

Ice, 418
Ingalls, 406
Ingersol, 307
Ingraham, 165
Ingrain, 165
Ireland, 160, 374
Isbell, 384

J

Jacobs, 184, 392, 478
Jackman, 57

Jackson, 89, 90, 427
James, 423, 441
Jaquette, 253
Jay, 189
Jefferis, 411
Jenkins, 111, 296, 418, 426
Jenks, 415
Jennings, 121, 150, 283, 390
Jepson, 265
Jergius, 449
Jett, 36
Jewell, 108
Jewett, 148
Johnson, 51, 88, 100, 144, **154**, 214, 425, 432, 446, 448, 469, 493
Jolley, 354
Jones, 41, 62, 80, 170, 281, 310, 356, 400, 450, 466, **479**, 483
Jordan, 376, 390, 472
Judd, 449
Judice, 466
Juliand, 113

K

Karnes, 479
Katcham, 288
Kay, 446, 447
Kaye, 489
Kea, 82
Kealing, 83
Keefoner, 174
Keeler, 294
Keeley, 162
Keen, 299
Keep, 81
Keethler, 237
Keller, 469
Kellogg, 60, 437
Kellum, 284
Killworth, 156
Kelly, 331, 400
Kelley, 131
Kendall, 54, 144, 222, 350
Kennard, 348
Kennedy, 263, 386
Kenzer, 425
Kernodle, 387
Kerr, 142, 241
Keyes, 127
Keys, 44, 289, 476
Kidder, 40, 70
Kilburn, 225
Killborne, 22
Kimball, 58, 94, **145**
Kimble, 159
Kincard, 261
Kindall, 356
Kinder, 319
Kinerk, 334

INDEX

King, 149, 157, 218, 297, 462
Kingman, 163
Kingsbury, 244, 322
Kinnan, 495
Kinne, 121
Kinney, 158
Kiphart, 460
Kirk, 442
Kirkland, 170, 214
Kirkpatrick, 300
Kitt, 310
Kivess, 292
Kline, 334
Knapp, 287, 407, 466
Knopps, 489
Knowles, 389
Knox, 24, 127
Koonts, 480
Koser, 432
Kragler, 272
Krum, 148

L

Ladd, 169, 409
LaFollette, 327
Lake, 70, 339
Lamb, 431, 454
Lambert, 260
Lander, 432
Landy, 254
Lane, 23, 94, 137, 327, 466
Lang, 393
Langley, 118
Le Grand, 384
Lanier, 386
Lannan, 439
Lansdowne, 170
Larabee, 195, 336
Larrison, 430
Larry, 466
Larvis, 208
Lathrop, 412, 413
Latty, 418
Lavandor, 409
Lawerence, 238, 269
Lawson, 202, 286, 305
Layne, 371, 400, 403, 404
Leach, 418
Leake, 233
League, 323
League, 331
Lear, 447
Learned, 29, 77
Lease, 383
Ledbetter, 450
Leeds, 423, 457
Leffel, 328
Lee, 32, 286, 309
Leedy, 389
Lees, 447
Legge, 130

Leftwich, 368, 369
LeGrand, 373, 384
Leggett, 226, 334
Lehr, 36
Lemmermen, 142
Leland, 43, 198
Leonard, 250, 414
Lepford, 376
Leppencott, 408
Lesley, 403
Leslie, 400, 403
Letterman, 460
Lewis, 67, 96, 137, 168, 177, 230, 444
Libberton, 310
Libby, 71
Lidzy, 147
Liele, 88
Lightfoot, 409
Ligon, 364
Like, 197
Lint, 155, 172
Liscom, 469
Litchfield, 147
Little, 291, 408
Littlefield, 57, 65, 97
Lively, 360
Livingston, 247, 271
Lliff, 434
Llewellyn, 442
Lockwood, 155, 295, 314
Loder, 237
Lombard, 144
Loomis, 136, 207
Logan, 465, 477
Long, 148, 324, 438
Louge, 61
Longly, 153
Loper, 259
Lord, 78, 84, 88, 128, 451
Losie, 27
Louder, 432
Love, 119
Loving, 138
Lowe, 335, 407, 458
Lowell, 20
Luce, 26
Lunt, 69
Lull, 183
Ludlam, 290
Lupton, 419
Lukesh, 445
Lyle, 163
Lyman, 24, 47
Lynch, 104, 119
Lyon, 171
Lyons, 93, 133, 162

M

Macgill, 247
MacKinney, 247

Macrery, 253
Macy, 179, 406
Malcom, 478
Mallory, 121
Malloy, 377
Malsbury, 428
Maltby, 24
Manahan, 484
Manette, 299, 300
Manford, 79
Manly, 33
Mann, 83, 99, 133, 145, 150, 204, 230, 303
Manning, 202
Mansfield, 210
Mario, 244
Marion, 400
Marks, 210, 319
Marlin, 478
Marquis, 453
Marsh, 123, 222, 340
Marshall, 159, 225, 299, 437, 438, 461, 482, 483
Martin, 98, 144, 150, 162, 291, 337, 364, 382, 458
Marvin, 53, 238
Mason, 98, 142, 160, 465
Masters, 336, 420
Matlack, 233
Matter, 491
Matterson, 177
Maul, 271
Maule, 437
Maurel, 247
May, 19, 137, 150, 230, 404, 414
Maynard, 59, 64, 293
Mayo, 401, 406
Mayhew, 64
McAllister, 379, 380
McAlpine, 174
McAuley, 398
McCarther, 465
McCasly, 324
McClain, 189
McCleary, 495
McClelland, 251
McClintock, 445
McClung, 383
McClure, 460
McCorkle, 383
McCormick, 429
McCornick, 263
McCoy, 408
McCue, 480
McCullock, 308
McCune, 453
McDavitt, 378
McDonald, 360
McDowell, 481
McFadden, 438
McFall, 444

McFarland, 116, 158, 168, 339
McGavock, 399
McGee, 449
McGhee, 382
McGlasson, 296
McGouldrick, 354
McGowan, 286
McGregor, 254
McGuire, 400
McHenry, 404
McIntire, 131
McKeage, 260
McKenney, 386
McKinze, 45
McKinney, 307
McKinnon, 408
McLaren, 374
McLaughlin, 129, 253
McLaughling, 143
McLaurance, 388
McMaster, 256
McMillen, 302
McNeil, 158
McPherson, 140
Meacham, 56, 99
Mead, 178
Mead, 178, 407, 475
Meader, 118
Meeds, 480
Meeker, 103
Meley, 470, 473
Melvin, 333
Menter, 330
Merrick, 87
Merrifield, 112
Merriman, 87
Merryman, 433
Merrill, 73, 117
Messick, 258
Metcalfe, 154
Meyers, 264
Mickle, 419
Middleton, 448
Miller, 33, 36, 40, 47, 104, 114, 116, 121, 122, 123, 129, 154, 156, 211, 249, 255, 271, 276, 283, 302, 382, 459, 475, 476-482
Miles, 99, 111, 355, 356, 457
Millions, 404
Mills, 271, 294, 315, 487
Milner, 71
Milton, 379
Miner, 285
Minkler, 298
Minnis, 123
Misselback, 454
Mitchell, 382, 412
Moat, 448
Molter, 101
Moncrief, 459

Monroe, 164, 250, 460
Montague, 364
Montgomery, 336
Moon, 137, 389
Moore, 17, 64, 128, 177, 263, 334, 380, 405, 413, 471
Moorhouse, 280
Morehouse, 396
Morgan, 60, 86, 405, 446
Morris, 375, 386
Morrison, 481
Morrow, 424
Morse, 22, 29, 31, 54, 66, 111, 145, 157, 196, 199, 229
Morton, 23, 193, 221, 231
Moseley, 223
Moslander, 271
Mosley, 366, 375
Moulton, 108
Moyers, 418
Mulholland, 447
Muir, 483
Mulford, 262, 283, 293, 469
Mull, 489, 490
Mullen, 489
Munday, 284
Munyan, 472
Muncy, 322
Munsee, 92
Murdock, 33
Murphy, 70, 378, 472
Murry, 309, 337
Musgrave, 433
Mutter, 282
Muzzy, 81
Myers, 381, 406, 483, 484

N

Narcross, 28, 169
Nash, 314
Nason, 239
Neal, 331
Neer, 406
Negus, 106
Neilson, 306
Nelson, 150
Nettleton, 390
Newberry, 415
Newbold, 235, 244
Newcomb, 357
Newell, 40
Newhouse, 416, 436
Newkirk, 435, 447
Newton, 198, 225, 304
Nicholas, 207
Nichols, 75, 97, 343
Nickel, 147
Night, 62
Niles, 65
Nine, 161
Nivison, 344

Nixon, 337
Noble, 50
Nock, 452
Norman, 395, 471
Norris, 371
Norton, 53
Norwood, 310
Nothanks, 449
Noyes, 182
Nutting, 86, 166, 317

O

Oatman, 180
Ober, 217, 282
O'Brian, 264
Ogle, 436
Olin, 91
Oliver, 56, 449, 482
Olophant, 338
Onderdonk, 429
O'Neal, 306
O'Neill, 300
O'Neille, 299
Ong, 421
Orndorff, 392, 459
Orr, 175, 276, 303, 330
Orric, 88
Osborn, 104, 282, 319, 415, 416, 422
Osborne, 320
Osburn, 91
Osterhoudt, 286
Ostler, 257
Otis, 149
Owen, 68, 163, 388, 396
Owens, 472
Oyler, 448

P

Page, 108, 210, 371
Paine, 69, 231
Painter, 438
Pallam, 286
Palmer, 28, 61, 169, 287, 340, 433
Palmore, 381
Pamenter, 77
Park, 302
Parke, 264
Parker, 31, 32, 55, 79, 90, 130, 143, 163, 266, 308, 309, 349
Parks, 64, 124, 477, 487
Parmalee, 140
Parmer, 320
Parrent, 360
Parsons, 88, 282, 347
Patridge, 86, 299
Patchen, 284, 289
Paterson, 299

INDEX

Patrick, 405, 482
Patterson, 295, 297, 387
Patton, 324
Pavey, 432
Paxson, 423
Payne, 239, 386
Paynter, 462
Payson, 230
Payton, 138
Peachie, 191
Peckingham, 320
Pearson, 111, 182, 200
Pease, 93, 337
Pellam, 101
Pellegrine, 166
Pendleton, 66
Penick, 296
Penn, 214
Pennilk, 371
Penny, 305, 406
Perkins, 45
Perley, 158
Perot, 247
Perry, 122, 413
Petequin, 250
Peters, 265, 460
Peterson, 85
Pettebone, 329
Pettee, 231
Pettit, 272, 372, 389
Pettyjohn, 383
Phelps, 50, 63
Philips, 434
Philley, 285
Phillips, 55
Phillips, 156, 387, 421, 480, 489
Phippen, 54
Philpot, 318
Pierce, 75, 130, 307, 438
Pike, 33, 125
Piper, 126, 195, 207
Platt, 100, 276, 478
Plumb, 89, 127, 178
Plundett, 380
Plympton, 230
Poindexter, 138
Pomroy, 24, 276
Porter, 186, 482
Posten, 189
Postlethwaite, 429
Potter, 123, 305, 316
Poulson, 270
Powel, 315
Powell, 298, 307, 333, 393, 434
Powers, 33, 157, 307
Pratt, 44, 86, 95, 132, 133, 201, 202
Preast, 401
Predmore, 416
Prentis, 269

Prentiss, 254
Prescott, 43, 180
Preston, 132, 257, 284
Price, 394
Prichard, 40
Pride, 246
Prindle, 74
Proctor, 40
Protheroe, 445
Pruden, 458
Pudney, 177
Puffer, 286
Pulman, 104
Punderson, 89
Pulsifer, 204
Pursley, 398
Purple, 131, 133
Putman, 84, 137
Putney, 130

Q

Quackenbush, 287
Quin, 138, 139
Quinn, 137, 481
Quint, 131

R

Raberge, 407
Race, 158
Rackliffe, 70
Rakestraw, 421
Raley, 441
Ramseyer, 448
Ramsoner, 495
Rancliffe, 250
Randall, 75
Rank, 330
Ranwold, 32
Rapeseloer, 250
Rapp, 334
Raub, 441
Rawson, 85
Rayburn, 378
Raymond, 307
Raynor, 462
Rea, 443
Read, 57, 75
Reece, 452
Reed, 71, 92, 240
Reese, 32, 468, 470
Regal, 445
Reid, 188
Reitenour, 336
Reiter, 481
Repon, 448
Ress, 494
Reuddock, 165
Reynold, 436
Reynolds, 19, 85, 99, 417
Rhodes, 142, 147, 162, 272

Rice, 41, 59, 88, 97, 102, 105, 152, 153, 209, 240, 401, 427
Rich, 194
Ritchie, 223
Richardson, 56, 75, 81, 125, 144, 195
Richards, 29, 87, 146
Richmond, 159, 386
Ricker, 118
Riddle, 461
Rigdon, 478
Riggins, 473
Riggs, 107
Riley, 461
Ripley, 83
Ritch, 308
Roach, 284
Roeder, 461
Robbins, 484
Robins, 29, 33, 195, 346, 407, 432
Roberts, 139, 144, 320, 404, 407
Robertson, 108, 368, 394
Robinson, 45, 115, 217, 271, 404, 465, 474, 478
Rocap, 260
Rock, 413
Rockwood, 93
Rodd, 407
Rogers, 56, 49, 97, 107, 389, 443
Romaine, 269
Rons, 250, 251
Ronton, 373
Rollins, 216
Roper, 44
Rood, 68
Root, 88
Rose, 135
Rosenkrans, 90
Ross, 336, 459
Rouse, 120
Routh, 246
Rowland, 255
Rudd, 375
Ruffane, 83
Ruggles, 86, 87
Rulofson, 425, 450
Rupe, 430
Rush, 285
Russell, 42, 75, 146, 220, 264, 294, 364, 373, 374, 461, 463
Rust, 357
Rutherford, 303
Rutledge, 70

S

Sackett, 104
Saling, 406
Saltmarsh, 31

510   INDEX

Sanders, 78, 492
Sanderson, 133, 364, 480
Sands, 162
Sanford, 289
Sargent, 211
Satterthwaite, 429
Savage, 129, 409
Saville, 217
Sawtell, 76
Saywer, 49, 86, 131
Sayre, 137, 494
Schneider, 429
Schooley, 418
Schreinen, 267
Schühle, 86
Schultz, 292
Scott, 33, 72, 95, 174, 297, 325, 343, 391, 463
Scrugs, 376
Scudder, 286
Scutt, 284
Seager, 405
Seaman, 289
Sears, 97
Seay, 371
Sebring, 170
Seeley, 236
Seely, 454
Seibert, 433
Semms, 460
Sessions, 111
Shade, 451
Shaffer, 492
Shall, 385
Shanks, 459
Shannon, 464
Sharp, 315
Shartel, 252
Shattuck, 122, 162, 164
Shaw, 19, 156, 189, 237
Shear, 397
Sheffer, 160
Sheldon, 207
Shellenberger, 482
Shellsmith, 168
Shephard, 27, 406
Shepherd, 88, 112, 229, 230, 240
Sherman, 84, 177, 248, 263
Sherry, 428
Sherwin, 470, 471
Sherwood, 49, 159
Shields, 380, 405
Shinn, 421
Shilling, 494
Shoals, 225
Shockley, 250
Shout, 298
Shreve, 454
Shryer, 140
Shufelt, 310
Shugart, 303

Shultz, 480
Shumway, 165
Shunway, 185
Shute, 413
Shyrock, 464
Sias, 227
Sibley, 69, 71, 148, 218
Simes, 444
Simkins, 147, 475
Sickler, 473
Simmons, 35, 62, 159, 322, 324
Silliman, 289
Simpson, 19, 84, 441, 476
Sinclair, 69
Sithens, 262
Simpson, 84, 441, 476
Skinner, 44, 330, 339, 473
Slack, 293
Slate, 86
Slavin, 143
Sloan, 49
Sloss, 65
Slutz, 444
Snow, 93, 97, 108, 155, 352, 375, 386
Snoddy, 382
Snyder, 444, 493
Sanford, 219
Smedley, 50
Small, 129
Smith, 17, 24, 32, 39, 42, 45, 60, 62, 74, 76, 81, 82, 84, 97, 105, 107, 129, 152, 156, 162, 185, 203, 206, 210, 212, 239, 246, 252, 288, 290, 300, 301, 302, 303, 338, 352, 356, 381, 382, 401, 434, 437, 438, 443, 444, 452, 470, 481, 484
Somers, 165
Sommers, 491, 492
Southland, 271, 472
Spafford, 494
Spalar, 334
Spaulding, 62, 68, 79
Spear, 128, 166, 428
Spilers, 389
Spiller, 152
Spofford, 127
Spooner, 153
Sprague, 98
Squire, 278, 280
Stafford, 320, 413, 447
Stanley, 440, 442, 459, 460, 496
Stark, 37, 438, 466
Starks, 89
Starkweather, 49
Starr, 279, 336
Staubuck, 485
Steames, 23
Stearns, 21, 43, 74, 132

Stebbins, 24, 30, 334
Stedman, 241
Steele, 337, 382, 405
Stegall, 336
Steger, 200, 364, 370, 376, 377
Steinman, 481
Stelson, 318
Stephens, 305
Sternes, 230
Stetson, 132
Stevens, 34, 56, 60, 79, 95, 154, 208, 213, 214, 260, 466
Stewart, 151, 155, 262, 312, 323, 328, 335, 342
Stickney, 62, 65
Stiles, 332
Stilson, 287
St. John, 123
Stith, 315
Stoakley, 343
Stockard, 398
Stockbridge, 318
Stocker, 151
Stoddard, 426
Stone, 30, 80, 92, 143, 148, 196, 373
Strong, 163
Stoop, 472
Storke, 378, 389
Story, 473
Stowell, 330
Stout, 472
Stover, 368
Strait, 465

Stratton (Strattan), Aaron, 30, 146, 237, 417, 420
  Aaron E., 457
  Aaron S., 196
  Abbie, 144, 438
  Abby N., 72
  Abby S., 87
  Abel, 196, 210
  Abi, 419
  Abigail, 26, 27, 29, 30, 33, 42, 51, 56, 61, 63, 196, 201, 237, 442
  Abijah, 29, 54, 94
  Abner, 50, 196, 356
  Abner G., 209
  Abraham, 280, 290
  Abraham L., 443
  Abraham N., 287
  Abraham S., 434
  Abram, 281, 304, 311, 409, 442
  Abram B., 312
  Abram G., 456
  Abram J., 404
  Abram L., 295, 311
  Abram M., 311
  Abram W., 304

INDEX 513

Stratton (Strattan), Carrie E., 155
  Carrie F., 96
  Carrie H., 399
  Carrie J., 143
  Carrie L., 159
  Carrie O., 411
  Carrie V., 101
  Carroll B., 333, 472
  Carroll I., 168
  Caskin D., 461
  Cassie, 292
  Catherine, 36, 260, 315, 374, 388, 403, 404, 409
  Catherine D., 145
  Catherine E., 482
  Catherine J., 491
  Catherine P., 387
  Cecelia M., 495
  Cecil C., 158
  Cecilia L., 299
  Celia, 462
  Chancey, 432
  Chandler, 240
  Charity S., 284
  Charles, 47, 49, 63, 70, 71, 75, 76, 79, 83, 87, 99, 119, 136, 145, 170, 174, 197, 202, 239, 248, 261, 294, 297, 305, 356, 360, 418, 423, 431, 432, 433, 438, 439, 442, 451, 455, 465
  Charles A., 129, 172, 184, 212, 226, 297
  Charles B., 106, 137, 248, 449, 450
  Charles C., 69, 74, 104, 107, 241, 303, 331, 393, 470
  Charles D., 74, 311
  Charles E., 68, 126, 168, 173, 212, 225, 227, 238, 249, 337, 412, 430, 448, 453
  Charles F. 253, 466, 491
  Charles G., 149, 299
  Charles H., 55, 81, 109, 128, 189, 197, 233, 240, 400, 404, 405, 436, 451, 454, 457, 474, 484
  Charles J., 158, 186
  Charles L., 165, 211, 226, 393, 394, 461
  Charles L. C., 226
  Charles M., 83, 111, 139, 217, 260, 408
  Charles N., 339
  Charles O., 140, 334
  Charley P., 152, 186, 227, 246, 253
  Charles R., 163, 168, 320

Stratton (Strattan), Charles S., 152, 318, 319, 338, 400
  Charles T., 149, 262, 393, 472, 473
  Charles W., 71, 96, 99, 118, 132, 224, 340, 382, 423, 447, 452
  Charlotte, 47, 69, 75, 91, 115, 187, 327, 402, 405, 479
  Charlotte A., 67, 96
  Charlotte E., 134
  Charlotte L., 429
  Charlotte S., 68, 131
  Chatty, 463
  Chauncey J., 337
  Cherry, 385
  Chesley M., 394
  Chester, 82, 135, 490
  Chester E., 145
  Chester H., 114
  Chloe, 65, 85
  Christina, 217, 491
  Christina A., 494
  Christopher, 237
  Claire, 486
  Clara, 49, 116, 121, 235, 289, 303, 407, 434, 467, 473, 490
  Clara A., 157, 160, 171, 300
  Clara C., 247
  Clara E., 124, 136, 254, 406, 416, 430, 466, 484
  Clara J., 100
  Clara M., 117, 186, 457
  Clara R., 454
  Clara S., 447
  Clarence, 167, 186, 447, 452
  Clarence B., 492
  Clarence E., 456
  Clarence F., 454
  Clarence M., 190
  Clarence R., 308
  Clarence W., 135
  Clark, 85
  Clark L., 114
  Clarica C., 92, 109
  Clarinda, 289
  Clarissa, 56, 60, 196, 240
  Clarity, 278
  Claude, 72
  Claude C., 160
  Claude L., 186, 187
  Claude R., 397
  Clementine, 473
  Clesson H., 150
  Cleve, 214
  Cliessa E., 465
  Clifford, 72

Stratton (Strattan), Clifford B., 320
  Clifford C., 174
  Clifton, 472
  Clifton J., 171
  Clifton M., 103
  Clinton, 292, 296
  Clyde R., 171
  Constance, 482
  Cora, 70, 437, 463
  Cora A., 458
  Cora B., 154, 216
  Cora C., 492
  Cora L., 150
  Cora M., 486
  Cora S., 221
  Cordelia, 32, 60, 154, 303, 309, 405
  Cornelia G., 180
  Cornelius, 294, 399, 401
  Cornelius A., 82
  Cornelius M., 404
  Cornet S., 319
  Cosette, 482
  Creed W., 333
  Cristel, 491
  Cryprian, 81
  Curena, 63
  Curry K., 398
  Curtis, 116
  Curtis D., 332
  Curtis P., 323
  Curtis W., 334
  Custer F., 426
  Cylias, 382
  Cyntha, 401
  Cynthia, 36, 75, 121, 178
  Cynthia A., 105, 416
  Cynthia C., 488
  Cyprian, 81
  Cyprian K., 129
  Cyrenius, 50, 282
  Cyrenius A., 305
  Cyril, 426
  Cyrus, 50, 481, 484, 488
  Cyrus J., 301
  Cyrus L., 491
  Cyrus M., 337
  Cyrus W., 211

D

  Daisy, 489
  Daisy C., 263
  Daisy D., 174
  Dan J., 444, 456
  Dana, 75
  Dana A., 157
  Dana P., 157
  Danforth D., 129

514 INDEX

Stratton (Strattan), Daniel, 18, 33, 37, 41, 50, 54, 56, 64, 65, 74, 124, 243, 360, 372, 420, 421, 426, 477, 478, 479, 483, 486
- Daniel B., 430, 446, 494
- Daniel C., 123
- Daniel G., 478
- Daniel H., 122, 325
- Daniel M., 417
- Daniel O., 112
- Daniel P., 233, 252
- Daniel S., 253, 302, 319
- Daniel W., 70, 156, 164, 172, 376
- David, 18, 27, 33, 36, 43, 50, 51, 154, 198, 204, 215, 231, 240, 241, 256, 284, 305, 314, 371, 415, 416, 461, 477, 479, 485
- David A., 72
- David B., 272, 473
- David C., 372
- David D., 459, 488
- David F., 324, 328, 452
- David G., 316
- David J., 434
- David P., 453
- David Q., 410
- David R., 98
- David T., 364, 396
- David W., 36, 154, 298, 308, 373, 436
- Debora, 455
- Deborah, 259, 438
- Deborah A., 438, 441
- DeForest, 494
- DeForest A., 158
- Delbert P., 445
- Delia, 141, 473
- Delia A., 127
- Delia C., 323
- Delia M., 69
- Delmer, 490
- Della, 138
- Della H, 384
- Della M., 159, 393
- Dennis C.
- Dessie S., 397
- Dewey, 214, 486
- DeWitt C., 334
- Dexter A., 166
- Diana, 136
- Dicey, 394
- Dillwyn, 455
- Dollie, 407
- Dolly, 38, 60, 215
- Dolly B., 415
- Don J., 456
- Donala, 104
- Donald, 418

Stratton (Strattan), Donald B., 485
- Donald C., 491
- Donald F., 438
- Donald G., 454
- Donald M., 451
- Donald S., 492
- Donna F., 133
- Donnald A., 36
- Donoven A., 491
- Dora, 295
- Dora C., 492
- Dora D., 488
- Dora M., 496
- Dorcas, 41
- Dorothy, 21, 143, 156, 236, 448
- Dorothy E., 173
- Dorothy G., 451
- Dorothy I., 173
- Dorothy L., 456
- Dorothy M., 157
- Dorothy V., 457
- Dorsey N., 389
- Douglas, 307
- Douglas E., 372
- Doyet D., 491
- Dryden C., 389
- Dudley B., 207
- Dudley D., 493
- Dwight F., 333
- Dwight R., 474
- D. P. H., 400

E

Earl, 78, 107, 212, 392, 489
- Earl B., 485
- Earl J., 493
- Earl H., 395
- Earl L., 320
- Earle C., 162
- Earle M., 151
- Earle P., 153
- Earnest, 135, 483
- Earnest A., 167
- Earnest D R., 167
- Earnest E., 132
- Earnest K., 272
- Earnest L., 108
- Earnest S., 437
- Ebenezer, 22, 42, 45, 50, 55, 70, 78, 89, 97, 432
- Ebenezer H., 136
- Ebenezer M., 157
- Ebenezer N., 111
- Ebenezer P., 138
- Ebenezer R., 116
- Edgar, 295, 306
- Edgar A., 475
- Edgar C., 495, 496

Stratton (Strattan), Edgar L., 150
- Edgar W., 97
- Edith, 354, 447
- Edith A., 132, 417, 438, 440
- Edith D., 260
- Edith E., 171
- Edith H., 110, 308
- Edith M., 150, 336, 340, 383
- Edith L., 121, 162, 225
- Edith O., 310
- Edith P., 127, 217
- Edmond B., 155
- Edmonia, 372
- Edna, 311, 454
- Edna C. 457
- Edna E., 150, 305
- Edna H., 159
- Edna I., 334
- Edna L., 163
- Edna M., 303
- Edson H., 107
- Edward, 17, 83, 138, 154, 187, 218, 271, 282, 350, 358, 359, 360, 363, 364, 366, 373, 434, 441, 485, 494
- Edward A., 222, 241, 301
- Edward B., 102, 151, 331
- Edward C., 250, 256
- Edward D., 320, 448
- Edward E., 255, 308, 387
- Edward F., 441
- Edward G., 433, 494
- Edward I., 154
- Edward J. 134, 175
- Edward K., 413
- Edward L., 160, 224, 308, 382, 432, 471
- Edward M., 161
- Edward P., 151, 210
- Edward R., 134, 429
- Edward S., 472
- Edward T., 387
- Edward W., 153, 184, 240
- Edwin, 93, 104, 133, 140, 215, 304, 489
- Edwin A., 131, 166, 216
- Edwin C., 107, 264
- Edwin D., 370
- Edwin E., 340
- Edwin F., 134, 143
- Edwin G., 272
- Edwin H., 217
- Edwin I. W., 144
- Edwin L., 147, 152, 303
- Edwin M., 377
- Edwin R., 472
- Edwin S., 32, 144

INDEX 515

Stratton (Strattan), Edwin W., 144
Effie, 467, 490
Effie P., 389
Elazer, 478
Elber E., 149
Eldridge, 68
Elbridge G., 239
Eleanor, 94, 98, 208, 282, 459
Eleanor L., 236
Eleanor F., 165
Eleanor H., 252
Eleanor N., 170
Eleanor P., 394
Eleazer, 24, 47, 84
Electa, 46, 60, 286
Electa M., 140
Elhanan, 91
Eli, 284, 297
Eli A., 448
Eli B., 158, 448
Eli F., 415
Eli L., 449
Elias, 30, 33, 56
Elias. J. H., 417
Elijah, 24, 59, 133
Eliphalet P., 291
Eliphalet W., 290
Elisha, 42, 77, 86, 97, 438, 463
Elisha T., 77
Elithalet, 24, 48, 280, 281, 286, 290, 299
Eliza, 49, 54, 68, 70, 95, 108, 154, 238, 259, 296, 304, 323, 331, 356, 415, 420, 460
Eliza A., 60, 66, 77, 178, 184, 210, 287, 421, 458, 491
Eliza B., 248
Eliza C., 295
Eliza F., 389
Eliza G., 378
Eliza J., 249, 288, 292, 408
Eliza M., 253, 289
Eliza R., 262
Eliza W., 268, 269
Elizabeth, 22, 23, 25, 31, 35, 38, 41, 44, 47, 54, 80, 87, 129, 139, 214, 238, 260, 279, 284, 289, 291, 295, 296, 305, 314, 343, 350, 354, 360, 367, 375, 376, 382, 396, 400, 402, 409, 426, 438, 450, 460, 469, 478, 481, 494
Elizabeth A., 364, 480, 483
Elizabeth B., 442, 469

Stratton (Strattan), Elizabeth D., 90, 394
Elizabeth G., 170
Elizabeth J., 64, 282
Elizabeth K., 199
Elizabeth L., 139, 286, 407
Elizabeth M., 183
Elizabeth O., 260
Elizabeth P., 262, 270, 401
Elizabeth R., 378, 441
Elizabeth S., 428
Elizabeth T., 143
Elma, 425
Elma E., 422
Elma M., 189
Elmer, 383, 449
Elmer B., 143, 227
Elmer C., 32
Elmer D., 389
Elmer E., 301
Ella, 70, 86, 91, 132, 154, 407, 413, 489
Ella B., 118, 256
Ella C., 226
Ella D., 334
Ella E., 159
Ella F., 134, 303
Elliot G., 238
Ella H., 99
Ella J., 110, 157, 307, 387
Ella L., 114, 121, 141, 186, 269, 442
Ella M., 101
Ella R., 112
Ellathier, 63
Ellen, 100, 102, 108, 125, 323, 356, 405, 418, 448
Ellen A., 147
Ellen C., 162
Ellen F., 306
Ellen M., 268, 269
Ellen O., 129
Elliott R., 164
Ellis G., 460
Elsie, 338
Elsie M., 130
Elsie P., 272
Elva, 394
Elvira, 79, 290, 372, 376
Elvira P., 421
Elwood, 20, 427
Elwood E., 320
Elwood H., 434
Emanuel, 17, 468, 473
Emanuel R., 470
Emeline, 33, 43, 239, 373, 469
Emerancy F., 166
Emerson, 404
Emerson O., 309

Stratton (Strattan), Emil H., 140
Emily, 60, 90, 237, 240, 285, 371, 418
Emily B., 213
Emily J., 372
Emily M., 82
Emily O., 69
Emily S., 251
Emma, 27, 91, 121, 130, 135, 295, 303, 115, 356, 389, 405, 414, 430, 432, 437, 445, 455, 481, 486
Emma A., 106, 145, 248
Emma C., 110, 114
Emma E., 443, 488
Emma F., 128, 250
Emma I., 163
Emma J., 117, 406
Emma L., 101, 454
Emma M., 380, 434
Emma S., 443
Emma V., 167, 260
Emmerson A., 150
Emmett A., 160
Emmett L., 456
Emmiline, 70
Emmor, 445
Emogene A., 128
Emogene F., 165
Emory A., 96
Emory W., 144
Enoch, 18, 33
Enoch B., 427
Enoch F., 117
Enoch V., 174
Enos W., 261
Ephraim, 33, 34, 237, 404, 414, 453
Erasmus, 50
Erastus W., 88, 103
Erma, 474
Erma W., 339
Ernest, 490
Ervin, 51
Erwin, 167
Erwin D., 107
Erwin R., 160
Essie, 270
Essie P., 161
Estella, 481
Estella H., 195
Estella L., 337
Esther, 116, 322, 420, 421, 455
Esther A., 413
Esther E. Stratton, 55
Esther R., 225
Esther T., 127, 283
Ethel, 116, 155, 418, 462
Ethel A., 452
Ethel C., 173

Stratton (Strattan),
  Ethel F., 488
  Ethel H., 159
  Ethel M., 147, 159, 189, 264, 311, 393
  Ethel W., 139
  Ethelbert D., 394
  Ethelburt M., 394
  Etta E., 32, 128
  Etta L., 346
  Eugene, 172
  Eugene B., 167
  Eugene C., 163, 334
  Eugene E., 134
  Eugene F., 242
  Eugene J., 251, 433, 458
  Eugenia, 135
  Eula I., 300
  Eunice, 24, 27, 45, 52, 64, 91, 108, 231, 292
  Eunice A., 36, 69
  Eunice E., 69, 494
  Eunice M., 284
  Eunice W., 88
  Euphema M., 328
  Eva, 255, 450, 465, 491
  Eva B., 449
  Eva M., 271, 455, 467, 494
  Evelyn, 309
  Evelyn R., 453
  Everett, 86, 133
  Everett B., 155, 360
  Everett F., 435
  Everett I., 166
  Everett L., 495
  Everett R., 443
  Evi, 420
  Ezra, 36, 196
  Ezra M., 289
  Ezra W., 278, 290

F

  Faith, 131
  Fannie, 265, 392, 465, 467
  Fannie B., 334
  Fannie E., 210
  Fannie F., 461
  Fannie H., 125
  Fannie L., 110
  Fannie M., 301, 307, 383
  Fannie T., 222
  Fanny, 239
  Fanny E., 223
  Fay, 339
  Fenimore, 472
  Fern B., 256
  Fern E., 493
  Fidelia F., 142
  Finley R., 328
  Fithian, 237

Stratton (Strattan),
  Flavel C., 120
  Flora E., 55
  Florence, 133, 170, 189, 213, 291, 323, 442, 448, 457, 463, 465, 473
  Florence A., 167, 416
  Florence B., 447
  Florence C., 391, 445
  Florence E., 129, 335
  Florence G., 163, 310
  Florence H., 129, 153, 159, 166
  Florence I., 55
  Florence L., 144, 168
  Florence M., 173, 256, 290, 308
  Florence R., 385
  Florence S., 129, 150, 482
  Florence T., 269
  Floyd, 462
  Floyd A., 437
  Floyd B., 139
  Floyd E., 161
  Floyd L., 333
  Floyd S., 417
  Floyd W., 139
  Forest, 491
  Foster A., 140
  Foweler H., 475
  Franceway C., 398
  Frances, 163, 233, 363, 374, 376, 378, 491
  Frances A., 120, 483
  Frances B., 464
  Frances C., 172, 288
  Frances D., 72
  Frances E., 137, 149, 260
  Frances F., 491
  Frances G., 495
  Frances J., 180, 238, 319, 453
  Frances M., 126, 163, 226, 371, 375
  Frances P., 63
  Frances R., 441
  Frances W., 398
  Francis, 26, 89, 126, 145, 221
  Francis A., 149, 150, 226
  Francis D., 75
  Francis E., 84
  Francis F., 446
  Francis G., 269, 450
  Francis J., 80, 137, 154
  Francis M., 238, 464
  Francis R., 209
  Francis W., 459
  Frank, 128, 165, 337, 400, 405, 449, 462, 486

Stratton (Strattan),
  Frank B., 110, 118, 338, 484, 495
  Frank C., 438
  Frank E., 110, 140, 150
  Frank H., 153, 168, 173
  Frank K., 118, 496
  Frank L., 19, 172, 465, 487
  Frank M., 382
  Frank N., 168
  Frank P., 163, 433, 453, 492
  Frank R., 124, 136, 174
  Frank S., 306, 453
  Frank T., 409
  Frank W., 130, 148, 304, 397, 447, 484
  Franklin, 119, 120, 248, 294, 375, 400, 435, 454
  Franklin A., 83
  Franklin B., 123
  Franklin D., 493
  Franklin M., 475
  Franklin S., 142
  Frazier O., 369
  Fred, 149, 311, 315, 406, 433, 449, 485
  Fred G., 484
  Fred J., 289
  Fred L., 223, 397
  Fred M., 487
  Fred S., 148
  Fred W., 155
  Frederick, 316
  Fredrick A., 80, 126, 159, 183, 197, 209, 263
  Frederick C., 166
  Frederick E., 151
  Frederick F., 183
  Fredrick G., 60, 184
  Frederick L., 160, 300
  Frederick N., 168
  Frederick S., 83, 263, 308, 318
  Fredrick W., 140
  Ferdinand P., 168
  Freeman, 92, 140, 141
  Freeman S., 140
  Fremont S., 110
  Frink, 37, 64

G

  Gabrella S., 329
  Gabriel, 360
  Gardner, 185, 186
  Garnett D., 463
  Gene, 482
  Genevieve, 183, 310, 433

INDEX 517

Stratton (Strattan),
  George, 19, 40, 60, 75, 77, 95, 102, 104, 105, 115, 116, 121, 122, 124, 127, 128, 131, 143, 162, 226, 230, 236, 255, 259, 263, 290, 301, 304, 305, 327, 364, 386, 400, 405, 420, 450, 465, 474
  George A., 106, 148, 159, 166, 177, 225, 227, 457, 465
  George B., 151, 163, 331, 393, 432, 491
  George B. M., 263
  George C., 223, 409, 433, 447, 491
  George D., 153, 183, 198, 256, 461, 492
  George E., 36, 149, 166, 429
  George F., 85, 124, 128, 162
  George G., 125, 408
  George H., 95, 97, 126, 155, 170, 256, 408
  George I., 186
  George J., 462
  George K., 222
  George L., 97, 140, 162, 163, 167, 250
  George M., 136, 184, 301
  George N., 249, 256
  George O., 148, 166, 185, 186, 311
  George R., 160, 166
  George S., 112, 287, 318, 319, 404
  George V., 300, 465, 466, 467
  George W., 57, 71, 79, 88, 106, 108, 138, 145, 153, 159, 169, 238, 302, 331, 408, 416, 428, 430, 435, 445, 458, 459, 467, 478
  Georgia A., 295
  Georgia L., 495
  Georgiana, 142, 299
  Gerald, 19
  Gerald B., 398
  Geraldine F., 170
  German, 371, 378, 388
  Gershone B., 422
  Gertrude, 102, 337, 433, 437, 481, 482
  Gertrude A., 338
  Gertrude E., 134
  Gertrude L., 332
  Gertrude N., 256
  Gertrude W., 225
  Gervas H., 272

Stratton (Strattan), Gilbert, 71
  Gilbert J., 114
  Gilford D., 156
  Gillette W., 381
  Gilmore M., 443, 456
  Gladys, 462, 483, 485
  Gladys C., 146
  Gladys E., 36
  Gladys I., 155
  Gladys V., 496
  Glenn, 490
  Glorianna C., 293
  Glycene E., 493
  Gold, 280
  Golda O., 462
  Goldie, 375, 453, 461
  Goldie L., 405
  Golladay, 397
  Gordon, 240
  Guliema, 425
  Guy, 461, 489
  Grace, 117, 163, 467
  Grace A., 110
  Grace B., 433
  Grace E., 140
  Grace E., 159, 174, 450
  Grace L., 151, 154
  Grace M., 118, 119, 161, 461
  Grace N., 172
  Grace P., 337
  Grace W., 124
  Granville R., 407
  Grata, 78
  Green B., 91
  Gregg, 433
  Grenfill B., 426
  Grenville W., 170
  Gretchen A., 312

H

Hadley F., 162
Hannah, 23, 26, 30, 34, 40, 49, 52, 53, 54, 56, 145, 197, 209, 215, 230, 261, 271, 276, 290, 322, 413, 415, 439, 472
Hannah A., 426
Hannah C., 264
Hannah E., 457
Hannah G., 88
Hannah J., 181
Hannah M., 80, 445
Hannah V., 326
Harlan T., 434
Harley LaR., 338
Harmon, 62, 490
Harold, 159, 306, 338, 456, 482
Harold B., 133, 272

Stratton (Strattan), Harold C., 454
  Harold G., 157
  Harold H., 110
  Harold M., 183
  Harold W., 162
  Harriet, 42, 44, 45, 68, 70, 75, 82, 93, 116, 233, 234, 293, 459
  Harriet A., 97, 318
  Harriet B., 109
  Harriet E., 73, 204, 295
  Harriet E. L., 123
  Harriet F., 57
  Harriet G., 223
  Harriet H., 284
  Harriet J., 107
  Harriet L., 403
  Harriet M., 236, 407
  Harriet N., 326
  Harriet R., 65, 221
  Harriet W., 292
  Harris, 56, 87, 88
  Harrison, 36, 249, 354
  Harrison D., 468
  Harrison S., 403
  Harrison W., 107
  Harry, 399, 426, 453, 476, 490
  Harry C., 153, 154, 163
  Harry E., 155
  Harry F., 425
  Harry G., 408
  Harry H., 393
  Harry J., 142
  Harry L., 255
  Hartwell, 372, 384
  Harver, 207
  Harvey, 50, 109, 196
  Harvey G., 332
  Harvey H., 449
  Harvey J., 160
  Harvey W., 173
  Hattie, 433, 461
  Hattie E., 110
  Hattie F., 408
  Hattie G., 492
  Hattie H., 485
  Hattie J., 485
  Hattie L., 151
  Hattie M., 136, 163, 392
  Hattie W., 250
  Hazel, 72, 467, 472, 490
  Hazel D., 493
  Hazel E., 487
  Hazel L., 448
  Hazel M., 495
  Hazel T., 161
  Henel V., 404
  Helen, 185, 241, 272, 317, 378, 441, 475, 482
  Helen A., 72, 159, 300

518   INDEX

Stratton (Strattan),
  Helen C., 457
  Helen E., 145, 167, 173
  Helen F., 221, 475, 495
  Helen H., 312
  Helen I., 164, 308
  Helen J., 173
  Helen L., 256, 333
  Helen M., 117, 236
  Helen R., 143, 300, 447
  Helena, 162
  Heman D., 296
  Henrietta, 34, 120, 287, 378
  Henrietta G., 253
  Henrietta N., 11
  Henry, 33, 34, 76, 88, 102, 120, 138, 162, 167, 197, 207, 238, 248, 259, 268, 282, 293, 327, 328, 341, 359, 360, 364, 367, 378, 379, 384, 389, 480, 485
  Henry A., 224
  Henry B., 70, 186, 300, 496
  Henry C., 55, 110, 173, 224, 238, 405, 430, 451
  Henry D., 217, 249
  Henry E., 250, 297, 303, 406
  Henry F., 165, 254
  Henry G., 189
  Henry H., 99, 107, 162, 171, 221, 360, 425
  Henry J., 389, 406, 489
  Henry J. W., 110
  Henry K., 446
  Henry L., 443
  Henry M., 160, 265, 355, 387
  Henry O., 112, 121
  Henry P., 133, 269
  Henry S., 256, 328, 451, 461
  Henry T., 129, 315, 396, 409
  Henry V., 243
  Henry W., 222, 224, 225, 271, 300, 316, 437
  Herbert, 106, 165, 264, 306, 454
  Herbert C., 168
  Herbert E., 174, 223, 434, 447
  Herbert K., 447
  Herbert P., 157
  Herbert R., 150
  Herbert S., 150, 223
  Herbert W., 306
  Herman C., 337, 443
  Herman J., 140, 339
  Hersey, 489

Stratton (Strattan), Hervey, 217
  Hester, 473
  Hezekiah, 20, 24, 37, 38, 39, 48, 74, 88, 117
  Hezekiah M., 64
  Hezekiah O., 135
  Hilda H., 271
  Hiram, 27, 33, 36, 323, 399, 400
  Hiram H., 80
  Hiram R., 403
  Hiram V., 174
  Hiram W., 97
  Homer, 74, 93, 127
  Homer A., 436
  Homer E., 443
  Homer J., 210
  Honour, 35
  Horace, 32, 58
  Horace B., 435
  Horace D., 32
  Horace E., 491
  Horace F., 151, 332
  Horace H., 81, 150, 252
  Horace J., 146
  Horace M., 150
  Horatio, 87, 95
  Horatio M., 476
  Hortence A., 172
  Houston F., 398
  Howard, 140, 261
  Howard B., 190, 451
  Howard C., 189, 190, 457
  Howard E., 294
  Howard F., 431
  Howard G., 160, 457
  Howard H., 175
  Howard I., 448
  Howard K., 458
  Howard M., 103
  Howard O., 484
  Howard R., 299
  Howard W., 189, 458
  Hubbard B., 108
  Hugh E., 55
  Hulda, 59
  Huldah, 49
  Huldah M., 325

I

  Ichabod, 27
  Ida, 128, 142, 185, 302, 320, 446
  Ida A., 186, 298
  Ida B., 405
  Ida E., 171
  Ida F., 131
  Ida K., 406
  Ida M., 155, 251, 302, 400, 489

Stratton (Strattan), Ida P., 272
  Ida S., 318
  Ida W., 380, 463
  Ina F., 448
  Ina V., 141
  Independence C., 141
  Ira, 36, 114, 120, 122, 404
  Ira F., 109
  Ira G., 494
  Irena, 434
  Irene, 447
  Irene C., 334
  Irene F., 309
  Irene H., 324, 475
  Irene L., 461
  Irvin, 165, 457, 482
  Irving E., 454
  Irwin H., 166
  Isaac, 18, 28, 35, 36, 41, 49, 74, 79, 122, 143, 201, 327, 440, 488, 491
  Isaac C., 215
  Isaac G., 103, 153, 394
  Isaac H., 328
  Isaac J., 89, 136
  Isaac N., 336
  Isaac S., 475, 476
  Isaac W., 260
  Isabel H., 293
  Isabell, 466
  Isabella, 233
  Isabella C., 147
  Isabelle C., 149
  Isadora, 329
  Isadore, 70
  Isiah, 430, 431
  Israel, 64, 260, 259
  Issacher, 105
  Issoline M., 318
  Izaak H., 336

J

  Jack, 360
  Jackson, 354, 394
  Jacob, 33, 409, 490
  Jacob B., 452
  Jacob L., 472
  Jacob M., 99
  Jacob S., 106
  Jacob W., 384
  Jabez, 35, 55, 57, 60, 62
  James, 19, 27, 33, 63, 70, 96, 103, 154, 194, 201, 204, 229, 231, 238, 239, 241, 242, 244, 251, 267, 268, 290, 350, 354, 364, 373, 404, 409, 439, 460, 463, 466
  James A., 36, 272, 276, 299, 384, 479

INDEX 519

Stratton (Strattan),
 James B., 79, 210, 281, 305, 487
 James C., 121, 303, 360, 453, 467
 James D., 159, 465
 James E., 151, 200, 212, 227, 317, 383, 390, 394, 395
 James F., 370, 383, 393, 457
 James G., 72, 297, 395
 James H., 36, 207, 208, 235, 307, 334, 382, 463
 James H. S., 390
 James J., 492
 James L., 76, 147, 187, 256, 406, 428, 486
 James M., 81, 107, 171, 375, 380, 382, 390, 415, 442, 466
 James N., 118, 299
 James O., 185, 307
 James P., 254, 380, 468
 James R., 453
 James S., 128, 471
 James T., 213, 214, 301, 377
 James W., 55, 182, 357, 403, 409
 Jane, 21, 33, 39, 68, 71, 95, 108, 320, 354, 368, 387, 388, 393
 Jane A., 94, 120, 200
 Jane B., 377
 Jane E., 241
 Jane E. L., 184
 Jane M., 375
 Jane S., 71
 Jannette, 101
 Jared O., 148
 Jason, 207
 Jason G., 212
 Jason W., 298, 308
 Jasper, 394
 Javius L., 171
 Jay W., 171
 Jean L., 458
 Jeane, 265
 Jeanette, 159, 495
 Jeanne, 302
 Jeanneth M., 162
 Jefferson, 52, 492
 J. Ford, 140
 J. Henry, 392
 Jennie, 106, 135, 251, 290, 305, 336
 Jennie A., 382
 Jennie C., 293
 Jennie E., 134
 Jennie F., 217
 Jennie I., 406

Stratton (Strattan), Jennie L., 292, 489
 Jennie M., 263, 318, 485
 Jennie R., 121, 134
 Jeremiah, 68, 258, 259, 263
 Jeremiah B., 263
 Jerial R., 285
 Jerome B., 130
 Jerome Q., 482
 Jerusha, 25, 418
 Jesse, 198, 289
 Jesse A., 413
 Jesse D. T., 214
 Jesse F., 148, 458
 Jesse K., 210, 211
 Jesse R., 99, 491
 Jessie A., 173
 Jessie B., 263
 Jessie L., 158
 Jessie M., 142
 Jessie O., 299
 Joanna, 296
 Joanna D., 297
 Joanna E., 296
 Job H., 430
 Job K., 447
 Job L., 444
 Joe H., 390
 Joel, 52
 Joel, 91, 98, 399, 437
 Joel A., 146, 147
 Joel B., 224
 Joel D., 96
 Joel H., 146
 Joel V., 452
 Joel W., 150
 John, 17, 18, 26, 27, 28, 29, 33, 34, 42, 45, 51, 61, 66, 78, 79, 93, 95, 102, 104, 105, 113, 144, 145, 177, 203, 228, 236, 237, 238, 239, 259, 260, 273, 274, 275, 276, 277, 279, 294, 297, 313, 314, 341, 344, 348, 350, 351, 353, 356, 361, 369, 376, 387, 388, 391, 399, 401, 405, 409, 427, 430, 432, 435, 462, 480, 485, 487, 489
 John A., 114, 143, 375, 388, 391, 393, 394, 408, 416, 437, 463, 464, 491
 John B., 69, 74, 95, 263, 270, 313, 323, 370, 405, 407, 434, 473
 John C., 36, 95, 144, 177, 337, 339, 388, 389, 461, 467
 John D., 133, 484

Stratton (Strattan), John E., 146, 224, 287, 438
 John F., 144, 183, 294, 405, 442
 John G., 346, 451
 John H., 33, 58, 64, 65, 151, 170, 295, 320, 328, 367, 390, 433, 434, 474
 John J., 137, 174, 317, 383, 404
 John L., 107, 234, 235, 244, 311, 373, 403, 464, 467
 John M., 138, 157, 435, 439, 467
 John N., 114, 254, 349, 369, 472
 John P., 101, 153, 236, 271, 371
 John R., 19, 334, 376, 425, 436, 450, 486
 John S., 157, 303, 408, 462
 John T., 146, 293, 389, 398, 408, 426
 John V., 305
 John W., 170, 314, 383, 384, 387, 405, 406, 423, 447, 483, 485, 494
 Jonas, 21, 25, 49, 62, 71, 203, 215, 292
 Jonah B., 31, 101
 Jonas M., 225
 Jonas S., 49
 Jonathan, 21, 30, 33, 36, 41, 51, 58, 73, 94, 95, 98, 170, 238, 265, 277, 283, 287, 289, 306, 307
 Jonathan C., 239
 Jonathan D., 423
 Jonathan E., 448
 Jonathan F., 237
 Jonathan J., 300, 443
 Jonathan M., 142, 255
 Jonathan P., 405
 Jonathan R., 123, 445
 Jonathan W., 79, 150
 Joseph, 18, 25, 56, 59, 99, 164, 178, 228, 231, 278, 295, 314, 364, 414, 419, 434, 447, 459, 468, 479, 481, 489, 490
 Joseph A., 143, 150
 Joseph B., 91, 244, 247, 253
 Joseph C., 360, 450, 455
 Joseph D., 379, 433
 Joseph E., 424, 449
 Joseph F., 112
 Joseph H., 261, 345, 392, 440

Stratton (Strattan), Joseph I., 423
  Joseph J., 318, 448, 459
  Joseph L., 98, 448, 454
  Joseph M., 265, 412
  Joseph O., 99, 446
  Joseph P., 231, 382, 392, 411, 434
  Joseph R., 441
  Joseph S., 426, 460, 483
  Joseph T., 460, 475
  Joseph W., 463, 484
  Joseph W. B., 142
  Josephine, 144, 260, 453, 478
  Josephine B., 435
  Josephine H., 386
  Josephine S., 148, 469
  Josephine W., 162
  Joshua, 27, 419, 441
  Joshua P., 466
  Joshua S., 98
  Josiah, 37, 64, 75, 78, 105, 125, 127, 418, 441
  Josiah B., 110
  Josiah H., 99
  Josiah J., 125
  Judith, 144, 176, 237
  Judith T., 434
  Judson B., 308
  Judson C., 487
  Julia, 43, 50, 60, 68, 71, 74, 79, 87, 137, 297, 302, 480
  Julia A., 284, 330, 368, 481
  Julia B., 285
  Julia E., 297, 379, 388
  Julia M., 188, 396
  Julia O., 117
  Julian, 80
  Julian A., 158, 376
  Julias, 79
  Julius, 329
  Julius A., 333
  Justina, 264
  Justine, 165

K

Karl E., 159
Karl M., 357
Kate, 433, 448, 452
Kate C., 171
Kate G., 389
Kate I., 297
Kate L., 118, 478
Kate M., 336
Katherine, 249, 290, 306, 322, 368, 386, 395, 442, 460
Katherine E., 442
Katherine M., 175, 483

Stratton (Strattan), Katherine N., 295
  Katherine W., 126
  Keith, 432
  Keneth L., 159
  Kendall, 212
  Kennie, 323
  Kenneth, 466
  Kenneth C., 456
  Kenneth L., 357
  Kerwin, 481

L

Lama G., 443
Lambert, 57
Latham, 178
Latsom W., 158
Laura, 137, 197, 279, 438
Laura A., 384
Laura C., 472
Laura E., 288
Laura G., 164
Laura J., 301
Laura M., 210, 455
Laura L., 328, 426
Laura S., 397
Laurena, 315
Laurence J., 159
Laurinda, 49
Levinia, 139
Lawerence, 457
Lawerence G., 492
Leah E., 189
Leah M., 482
Leander, 218, 482
Leander G., 196
Lee A., 465, 466
Lee N., 253, 254
Lemon M., 482
Lemeta C., 475
Lemira D., 195
Lemuel, 34, 57, 135, 230, 492
Lemuel P., 100, 152
Lena, 50, 490
Lena D., 69
Lena E., 162, 389
Lena L., 132
Lena M., 172, 484, 495
Lelia A., 330
Leo E., 493
Leon, 167, 493
Leon E., 493
Leon D., 476
Leona, 211
Leona M., 186, 447
Leonard, 202, 433, 463, 493
Leonard B., 300
Leonard T., 174
Leonard W., 132, 454

Stratton (Strattan), LeRoy, 434, 450
  LeRoy B., 224
  Leslie C., 328, 384
  Leslie E., 172
  Leslie L., 476
  Leslie M., 397
  Leslie W., 148
  Leta M., 265
  Letitia, 102
  Letitia E., 411
  Lettie B., 401
  Leulla, 491
  Levaine, 457
  Levina, 237
  Levinea A., 320
  Lavinia J., 290
  Levi, 36, 59, 78, 195, 196, 204, 236, 237, 252, 258, 413, 414, 415, 430
  Levi L., 270, 299
  Levi P., 457
  Levi W., 101
  Lewis, 107, 125, 154, 201, 237, 286, 295, 437, 442
  Lewis A., 173
  Lewis B., 391
  Lewis D., 159
  Lewis E., 337
  Lewis F., 121, 155, 336
  Lewis H., 460
  Lewis L., 172, 336
  Lewis P., 401
  Lewis R., 442
  Leyman M., 481
  Lieucella, 451
  Lila J., 255
  Lilian J., 448
  Lillian, 182, 251, 263, 474
  Lillian E., 110
  Lillian L., 187, 375, 389
  Lillian M., 293
  Lily, 356
  Lily V., 174
  Lindsey, 407
  Lindsey C., 392
  Linnaeus B., 381
  Linnie D., 382
  Lizzie, 311, 404, 474
  Lizzie A., 146
  Lizzie E., 132
  Lizzie J., 491
  Lizzie M., 475
  Lloyd, 488, 492
  Lodema, 337
  Lois, 33, 62, 69, 70, 71, 93, 176, 196, 433
  Lois E., 435
  Lois M., 310
  Lora G., 334
  Lorena, 434, 461
  Lorena A., 443

INDEX 521

Stratton (Strattan), Lorenzo, 87, 124, 164, 219, 286, 416, 476
Lorenzo D., 258
Loretta, 144
Lossena, 315
Lot, 237
Lotta, 295
Lottie R., 489
Lottie V., 444
Louannie, 214
Louella, 224
Louie M., 150
Louis, 42, 354, 462
Louis T., 485
Louisa, 42, 61, 69, 206, 237, 244, 248, 369, 417, 474
Louisa C., 372
Louisa J., 104, 414
Louisa M., 380, 463
Louisa W., 213
Louise, 104, 136, 312, 379, 418
Louise F., 69
Louise J., 118
Louise L., 392
Louise M. H., 123
Louise N., 395, 398
Louman, 106
Louvenia A., 467
Loveman B., 432
Lovilla, 93
Lovina, 44
Lowell M., 456
Loyd B., 494
Luama, 413, 414
Luana, 206
Lucas, 140
Lucele E., 186
Lucetta, 71
Lucella A., 150
Luella, 458
Luella V., 435
Lucelle E., 308
Lucettia, 51
Lucia, 82
Lucile, 395
Lucile, 443
Lucile H., 494
Lucile M., 339
Lucinda, 51
Lucinda, 64, 79, 95, 237, 238, 286, 413, 441, 455, 478
Lucinda S. 483
Lucius, 106, 137
Lucretia, 217, 280, 315
Lucy, 21, 25, 26, 28, 31, 36, 44, 48, 51, 54, 57, 58, 59, 64, 196, 202, 354, 357, 368, 405

Stratton (Strattan), Lucy A., 97, 104, 203, 340, 383
Lucy B., 198
Lucy D., 373
Lucy E., 105
Lucy J., 188, 372
Lucy L., 86, 427
Lucy M., 84, 101, 123, 331
Lucy N., 231
Lucy P., 210
Lucy T., 201
Luke, 44
Lula, 467
Lulu N., 247
Luna K., 222
Lura M., 324
Lurenda W., 96
Luther A., 140
Luverne, 160
Lydia, 24, 26, 29, 31, 33, 50, 51, 56, 58, 59, 74, 85, 89, 90, 121, 136, 178, 195, 257, 418
Lydia E., 82
Lydia J., 412
Lydia L., 66
Lydia R., 75, 98
Lydia V., 203
Lyle W., 159
Lyman, 43, 57, 71, 99, 217
Lyman F., 133
Lyman L., 167

M

Mabel, 50, 131, 137, 144, 310, 453
Mabel A., 209, 448
Mabel C., 495
Mabel E., 167, 451
Mabel I., 81
Mabel M., 222, 448
Mabel L., 140, 450
Mabel R., 122
Mabel S., 121, 174
Mabelle, 320
Madelyn G., 170
Madison, 385, 386
Mae, 438
Mae S., 162
Mahlon, 415
Malcome D., 407
Malinda, 286
Malvina C., 171
M. Louise, 217
Manda V., 437
Manetta D., 389
Marcellus D., 136
Marcia H., 112
Marcia I., 306

Stratton (Strattan), Marcus, 315
Margaret, 75, 138, 186, 440, 470, 472
Margaret A., 151, 224, 360, 431, 444
Margaret B., 306
Margaret E., 315
Margaret J., 389, 483
Margaret M., 248, 378
Margaret S., 138
Margaret W., 393
Margery I., 491
Marguerite E., 438
Margueritte, 482
Marguerite L., 495
Maria, 32, 63, 78, 202, 207, 233, 283
Maria C., 481
Maria H., 422
Maria J., 404
Maria L., 160
Maria S., 102
Mariah, 47, 48, 93
Marian, 311
Marian A., 173
Marian F., 496
Marian T., 183
Marianna, 57
Marianne, 44
Marie, 433, 450
Marie L., 182
Marietta, 75, 198, 225, 287, 436
Marina, 59
Marion, 99
Marion A., 103
Marion D., 457
Marion F., 443
Marion N., 345
Marjorie B., 222
Marjorie M., 174
Marjory H., 173
Mark, 17, 410, 439, 482
Mark R., 451
Marshall, 84
Marshall H., 355
Mart E., 460
Martha, 27, 42, 54, 70, 77, 82, 87, 91, 99, 108, 120, 204, 284, 322, 360, 371, 372, 387, 419, 439, 449, 454, 458, 468
Martha A., 86, 137, 227, 374, 387, 388, 360, 361
Martha B., 80
Martha C., 111
Martha D., 439
Martha E., 295
Martha F., 264
Martha H., 325, 376, 381
Martha I., 145

Stratton (Strattan).
  Martha J., 80, 130, 376
  Martha K., 422
  Martha L., 397
  Martha M., 250, 391
  Martha S., 173, 469
  Martha W., 79
  Martin, 27, 103, 325
  Martin G., 162
  Martin L., 413
  Martin S., 323
  Martin V., 238, 382
  Martin W., 147
  Mary, 21, 22, 24, 27, 28, 30, 33, 34, 37, 41, 42, 43, 44, 45, 47, 48, 49, 50, 51, 54, 55, 56, 57, 60, 63, 64, 67, 69, 70, 74, 75, 76, 79, 87, 92, 98, 99, 104, 105, 125, 135, 185, 201, 229, 230, 237, 238, 241, 248, 251, 258, 266, 267, 276, 277, 280, 286, 290, 292, 315, 322, 338, 346, 354, 360, 371, 372, 377, 382, 385, 386, 388, 400, 405, 416, 421, 432, 455, 465, 472, 478, 486
  Mary A., 74, 86, 89, 108, 137, 147, 185, 187, 188, 209, 215, 240, 260, 288, 378, 380, 409, 438, 470, 482
  Mary B., 126
  Mary C., 421, 423, 466, 469
  Mary D., 65
  Mary E., 32, 111, 114, 127, 130, 154, 157, 164, 197, 200, 202, 212, 224, 303, 316, 319, 330, 332, 375, 376, 383, 392, 406, 412, 413, 416, 430, 434, 441, 442, 447, 465, 466, 470, 492
  Mary F., 131, 207, 393
  Mary G., 263, 284, 458, 459, 443
  Mary H., 268, 368, 381
  Mary I., 404, 427, 450
  Mary J., 76, 78, 81, 84, 138, 208, 260, 306, 329, 355, 378, 401, 403, 492
  Mary L., 180, 246, 255, 339, 360, 384, 390, 391, 393, 395, 417, 451, 453, 471, 486
  Mary M., 255, 301, 330, 424, 464, 493
  Mary O., 283, 396
  Mary P., 70, 371
  Mary R., 387, 455, 457

Stratton (Strattan), Mary S., 360, 393
  Mary T., 36, 86, 133, 196, 390
  Mary V., 244, 300
  Mary W., 64, 88, 95, 145, 373, 394, 398, 446
  Mary Y., 198
  Mason, 135
  Matilda, 51, 467
  Matilda C., 76
  Matie E., 357
  Mattie H., 435
  Mattie L., 395
  Maud 305, 485
  Maud L., 131, 140
  Maude, 149, 154, 382, 448, 462, 495
  Maude E., 171, 186, 397
  Maude G., 129
  Maurice, 32, 451
  Maurice A., 392, 393
  Max M., 450
  May, 305, 312
  May G., 164
  May W., 133
  Maybelle G., 228
  Maynard N., 55
  Mayo E., 406
  Mecca, 369
  Meda E., 82
  Mehitable, 40, 60
  Mehitable H., 98
  Melanda, 196
  Melinda, 207, 414
  Melissa, 44, 355, 463, 478
  Melissa E., 92
  Melissie J., 466
  Melton E., 461
  Melvin, 307
  Melvin B., 339
  Melvin P., 388
  Melville N., 170
  Melville O., 169
  Menzies E., 143
  Mercy E., 130
  Merle D., 214
  Merle J., 110
  Merritt, 239
  Merton O., 340
  Metta, 302
  Micajah, 412
  Micajah H., 449
  Michael, 420
  Mila F., 156
  Mildred A., 370
  Mildred G., 130, 136
  Mildred H., 451
  Mildred L., 45
  Mildred O., 396
  Millicent, 30, 368
  Millicent A., 424

Stratton (Strattan), Milo, 91, 240
  Milton, 230, 403, 414, 490
  Milton A., 297, 301, 333
  Milton D., 295, 426
  Milton G., 254
  Milton J., 158
  Milton L., 328, 333, 368
  Milton M., 285
  Milton S., 407
  Milton W., 102
  Milville B., 158
  Minnie, 394, 478
  Minnie B., 159, 330, 413
  Minnie C., 214
  Minnie E., 436
  Minnie L., 300
  Minnie M., 458
  Minerva E., 299
  Minerva, 354, 403, 460
  Minor A., 175
  Miranda, 50
  Miriam C., 145
  Mirrian E., 103
  Montana, 337
  Morgan, 307, 329
  Morgan C., 340
  Morris H., 251
  Morrison W., 296, 297
  Mortemer, 415
  Morton, 91
  Moseley E., 399
  Moseley T., 397
  Mosley, 375, 378
  Mosley H., 384
  Mosley L., 376
  Moses, 51, 57, 145, 388
  Moses B., 129
  Murrell E., 186
  Myra, 215
  Myra A., 209
  Myra K., 457
  Myranda, 41
  Myron, 325, 481
  Myron A., 331
  Myron L., 330, 337
  Myron T., 209
  Myrtle, 307, 441, 489
  Myrtle E., 331
  Myrtle G., 224
  Myrtle I., 171, 340
  Myrtle M., 436

N

Nabby, 58, 231, 280
Nahum, 75, 214
Nancy, 40, 41, 43, 44, 61, 104, 195, 196, 230, 237, 238, 296, 354, 366, 368, 375, 401, 417
Nancy E., 170, 294, 322

INDEX 523

Stratton (Strattan),
  Nancy J., 458, 478
  Nancy M., 287, 489
  Nancy T., 378
  Nancy W., 380
  Nannie, 461
  Naomi, 485
  Naomi P., 487
  Napolian B., 238
  Nathan, 25, 29, 32, 43, 55, 74, 281, 291, 468
  Nathan J., 152
  Nathan L., 235, 247
  Nathan R., 208
  Nathan T., 470, 484
  Nathan W., 202
  Nathaniel, 28, 33, 34, 195, 262, 264, 346, 350
  Nathaniel A., 318
  Nathaniel F., 262
  Nathaniel H., 130
  Nathaniel M., 180
  Nathaniel W., 350
  Nehemiah, 39
  Nellie, 107, 129, 315, 397, 438, 455, 464, 490
  Nellie A., 110, 127
  Nellie B., 302, 337
  Nellie D., 436
  Nellie E., 299
  Nellie G., 336
  Nellie J., 407
  Nellie L., 444
  Nellie M., 140, 145, 146
  Nellie R., 157
  Nellie S., 462
  Nellie T., 485
  Nelson, 88, 360, 372
  Nettie, 416, 462, 466
  Nettie A., 453
  Nettie B., 298
  Nettie F., 117
  Nettie M., 221
  Neva I., 186
  Nevada M., 337
  Newell, 72
  Newton H., 254
  Nina, 399
  Nina B., 307
  Nina B., 397
  Nina L., 485
  Nial, 488
  Noah, 237
  Nona, 337
  Norma, 490
  Nora A., 408
  Nora J., 247
  Norman, 91
  Norman, 238
  Norman C., 338
  Norman P., 265
  Norris, 195

Stratton (Strattan), Norwood S., 312
  Norval O., 338

O

  Ola ., 443
  Olive, 49, 52, 165, 357, 443, 454, 490
  Olive B., 494
  Olive H., 312
  Olive J., 172
  Olive P., 323
  Oliver, 291, 294, 303, 311, 433, 434, 449, 453
  Oliver B., 454
  Oliver H., 433, 463
  Oliver O., 299
  Oliver R., 436
  Oliver W., 309
  Olivia, 388, 432
  Olivia A., 137
  Ollie, 467
  Ona O., 488
  Onita W., 167
  Ora, 433
  Ora E., 172
  Ora T., 494
  Orlando M., 112
  Orange, 324
  Orin, 36
  Orleana, 329
  Orson, 289
  Orton L., 491
  Orville G., 334, 338
  Otis J., 107
  Otis L., 300
  Oscar, 74, 145
  Oscar B., 288
  Oscar D., 302
  Oscar G., 83
  Owen L., 310
  Owen R., 427
  Owen T., 464

P

  Palmira, 486
  Pamelia, 62, 372
  Parnelia, 60, 369
  Patience M., 294
  Patona, 394
  Patsy, 369
  Patty, 43
  Paul, 63, 103, 171, 264, 265, 338, 391, 438
  Paul B., 394
  Paul C., 441, 450
  Paul J., 489
  Paul L., 438, 443, 492
  Paul R., 339
  Paul V., 464

Stratton (Strattan),
  Pauline, 165, 378, 457, 469
  Pauline E., 236
  Pearl, 135, 408, 490
  Pearl E., 485, 492
  Pearl H., 334
  Pearle B., 484
  Peleg, 197
  Percivial C., 488
  Percy F., 114
  Peter, 363, 364, 367, 372, 388
  Peter A., 400
  Peter B., 377, 383, 387
  Peter T., 456
  Philada, 52
  Philena, 93
  Philander, 293
  Philip, 176, 382, 480
  Philip D., 198
  Philip G., 131
  Philip H., 306
  Philip J., 382
  Philo, 85
  Phineas, 33, 321
  Phoebe, 26, 31, 36, 49, 51, 91, 177, 480
  Phoebe A., 58, 184
  Phoebe J., 181
  Pitman, 476
  Platt, 281
  Pocahontas, 388
  Polina, 142
  Porter, 330
  Porter R., 148
  Powell G., 393
  Prescott B., 183
  Preston, 257, 261, 263, 265
  Preston D., 445
  Priscilla, 42, 487
  Prudence, 394
  Prudence F., 433
  Purbot H., 153

R

  Rachel, 26, 49, 260, 284, 418, 420, 448, 463, 478
  Rachel A., 448
  Rachel E., 294, 443
  Rachel G., 476
  Rachel J., 496
  Rachel M., 160
  Ralph, 338
  Ralph E., 173
  Ralph H., 55
  Ralph O., 36
  Ralph R., 118
  Ralph W., 494
  Ramond, 43
  Ray, 339
  Ray H., 162

Stratton (Strattan), Raymond, 127
  Raymond, 166, 451, 485, 491
  Raymond F., 445
  Raymond O., 320
  Rebecca, 21, 34, 52, 54, 71, 237, 248, 260, 418, 419, 430, 446
  Rebecca B., 253
  Rebecca D., 413
  Rebecca F., 209
  Rebecca M., 265
  Rebecca L., 391
  Rebecca V., 215
  Reginold W., 488
  Relief, 32, 41
  Reuben, 56, 209, 427
  Rex, 487
  Rhoda, 25, 52, 91, 93, 419, 421, 491
  Rhoda H., 91
  Rhoda S., 404
  Rhoda T., 471
  Richard, 17, 26, 53, 89, 94, 229, 240, 253, 294, 363, 364, 373, 375, 384, 399, 409, 427, 457
  Richard A., 50
  Richard B., 388
  Richard D., 466
  Richard C., 247
  Richard H., 382, 392, 394
  Richard H., 415
  Richard O., 464
  Richard P., 401, 404
  Richard R., 493
  Richard S., 102, 387
  Richard T., 307
  Richard V., 130
  Richard W., 391
  Rienzie H., 308
  Riley, 27, 324
  Robert, 167, 187, 230, 350, 356, 360, 372, 481
  Robert A., 254, 375, 436
  Robert B., 138, 168, 373, 375
  Robert C., 151, 167, 314, 380, 485
  Robert D., 390
  Robert E., 171, 454
  Robert F., 118
  Robert G., 383
  Robert H., 223, 460
  Robert J., 371
  Robert L., 187, 327, 336, 382, 393
  Robert M., 118, 179, 300, 384
  Robert O., 449

Stratton (Strattan), Robert S., 151, 391
  Robert T., 309
  Robert W., 309
  Robert Y., 360
  Roberta F., 381
  Robertson, 355
  Rodney J., 166
  Rodney W., 166
  Ronald, 19, 190, 265, 457
  Rolland A., 151
  Rolland L., 491
  Rollie, 462
  Rollis A., 186
  Rosaline, 70
  Rosaline S., 123
  Rosamond F., 170
  Rosana R., 74
  Roscoe D., 462
  Roscoe W., 154
  Rose, 106, 450
  Rose B., 156
  Rose M., 476
  Rosecrans, 458
  Rosella E., 159
  Rosella H., 113
  Rosetta, 417
  Ross, 438
  Ross D., 453
  Roswell, 82
  Rowena, 27
  Roxey, 45, 62, 40
  Roxey A., 71
  Roy, 433, 463
  Roy B., 417
  Roy H., 156
  Roy L., 251
  Roy O., 434
  Royal A., 74, 162
  Royal E., 492
  Royal K., 338
  Royal R., 494
  Ruby, 93, 167, 186
  Rudolph M., 123
  Rufus, 48, 86, 124, 142, 143
  Rufus W., 134
  Ruloff R., 450
  Ruloff V., 271, 444
  Rupert E., 307
  Russell, 312, 461
  Russell S., 339
  Russell W., 435
  Ruth, 22, 26, 35, 44, 46, 51, 55, 60, 93, 104, 154, 166, 233, 283, 296, 317, 432, 467, 491
  Ruth A., 291, 306, 412, 438
  Ruth D., 394
  Ruth E., 494, 496

Stratton (Strattan), Ruth F., 429, 465
  Ruth G., 306
  Ruth H., 142, 162, 457
  Ruth L., 453
  Ruth W., 336
  Ruthanna, 442
  Rynd L., 432

S

  Sadie A., 155
  Salinda, 75
  Samira E., 482
  Samuel, 20, 22, 23, 27, 31, 32, 33, 34, 41, 43, 47, 55, 58, 59, 62, 68, 69, 79, 80, 81, 85, 97, 98, 102, 128, 141, 224, 261, 270, 277, 279, 281, 282, 322, 356, 376, 404, 427, 430, 460, 463, 467, 468, 473, 478, 487
  Samuel A., 63, 78, 79
  Samuel B., 318, 472
  Samuel C., 24, 241, 416, 478
  Samuel D., 19, 255
  Samuel E., 255, 256, 312, 314, 317, 392, 395, 424
  Samuel F., 310, 423
  Samuel G., 395, 398, 404
  Samuel H., 65, 467
  Samuel I., 214
  Samuel M., 171, 394
  Samuel N., 467
  Samuel O., 331
  Samuel P., 132
  Samuel R., 133, 209, 272, 450
  Samuel S., 154
  Samuel T., 238, 293, 430
  Samuel W., 32, 84, 117, 178, 312, 356
  Sanford, 237
  Sara, 450, 484
  Sara R., 447
  Sarah, 21, 22, 24, 25, 30, 33, 40, 41, 43, 45, 47, 48, 51, 55, 57, 60, 64, 65, 66, 83, 94, 104, 124, 131, 201, 230, 237, 257, 259, 270, 278, 279, 283, 289, 344, 350, 356, 361, 363, 364, 367, 368, 370, 415, 418, 419, 431, 442, 468, 470, 472
  Sarah A., 33, 68, 79, 83, 89, 98, 137, 161, 280, 370, 376, 387, 443, 478, 480
  Sarah B., 86, 203, 283, 424

INDEX 525

Stratton (Strattan),
  Sarah C., 330, 447
  Sarah D., 113, 172, 177, 325
  Sarah E., 100, 200, 208, 286, 319, 356, 380, 387, 391, 416, 423
  Sarah F., 288
  Sarah H., 84, 233, 383, 389, 474
  Sarah J., 112, 430, 481
  Sarah M., 198, 402
  Sarah R., 140
  Sarah S., 88
  Sarah W., 194, 262
  Sarulda, 403
  Schuyler, 107, 231, 250, 251
  Schuyler C., 456
  Scott, 384, 463
  Semira, 441
  Sepio, 119
  Serena, 490
  Serepta, 460
  Seth, 62, 83, 184, 458, 459, 461
  Seth H., 78
  Seth L., 318, 320
  Seth S., 315
  Seth V., 117
  Sewell, 202, 203
  Sheldon, 90, 91
  Shelton, 315
  Sherley F., 448
  Sherwood E., 319
  Shirley S., 337
  Shubael C., 72, 73, 121
  Sibyl, 69
  Sibyl Q, 139
  Sidney, 283
  Sidney H., 283
  Sidney P., 182
  Sidney V., 246, 253
  Silas A., 87
  Silas C., 281
  Silas S., 339
  Silvanus, 50
  Simeon, 442, 480, 489, 490
  Simon, 45
  Simon C., 416, 435
  Simon D., 37
  Simon P., 106
  Simri, 422
  Sina, 418, 420, 442, 481
  Solomon, 399, 400
  Solomon H., 403
  Solomon P., 126
  Solon, 328
  Solon C., 328
  Solon G., 209
  Sophia, 328, 464

Stratton (Strattan),
  Sophia H., 111, 236
  Sophia M., 88
  Sophrona, 45, 231
  Sophronia, 480
  Stacy B., 456
  Stella, 434, 461, 462
  Stella A., 248
  Stella G., 148
  Stella M., 151
  Stanley C., 223
  Stanley H., 147
  Stephen, 33, 102, 195, 207, 248, 279
  Stephen A., 196, 336
  Stephen C., 326
  Stephen B., 87
  Stephen J., 100
  Stephen S., 445, 456
  Stephen T., 432
  Stephen W., 207, 338
  Sterling C., 380
  Stewart C., 330
  Stillman, 127
  Submit, 24
  Sue V., 334
  Sumner, 88, 133
  Sumner W., 97
  Sprage, 71
  Squire D., 285
  Susan, 33, 42, 52, 54, 71, 92, 93, 237, 238, 354, 368, 437, 448, 469, 473, 490
  Susan A. 166
  Susan B., 74
  Susan E., 81, 126, 145
  Susan F., 207
  Susan G., 195
  Susan I., 453
  Susan J., 128, 207
  Susan M., 43, 184
  Susan V., 324
  Susanna, 61
  Susannah, 28
  Susie, 386
  Susie A., 383
  Susie B., 399
  Susie C., 392
  Sylvester S., 483

T

  Tabitha, 43
  Tabithia, 64
  Tandy, 399, 400
  Tandy L., 404, 407
  Temperance, 102
  Texanna, 466
  Thankful, 27, 46
  Theodocia M., 412
  Theodore, 33, 164, 428, 474

Stratton (Strattan), Theodore A., 240
  Theodore F., 431
  Theodore M., 249
  Theodore W., 215
  Theron A., 303
  Thomas, 17, 45, 76, 104, 122, 187, 191, 194, 288, 313, 314, 341, 343, 350, 351, 352, 356, 359, 360, 368, 374, 378, 379, 385, 405, 409, 477, 483, 484, 486
  Thomas A., 391, 441
  Thomas B., 133, 238, 258, 263, 264
  Thomas C., 19, 383, 391, 393, 473
  Thomas D., 76, 263
  Thomas E., 376, 386, 395, 399, 489
  Thomas F., 387, 395
  Thomas H., 387, 389, 447
  Thomas J., 177, 369, 371, 381, 385, 388, 390, 391, 407, 466, 472, 478
  Thomas M., 101, 399
  Thomas S., 163
  Thomas T., 214, 382
  Thomas W., 129, 389, 477
  Thurman, 308
  Thurlow W., 309
  Timothy, 327
  Timothy L., 328
  T. Matt. 386
  Tolman, 146
  Tracy F., 116
  Tracy M., 175
  Truman 36
  Truman R., 395
  True. 70
  Triphena. 51, 85, 351
  Tryphose E., 81
  Tyler. 230, 360

U

  Ulysses G., 175
  Uriah, 279
  Ursula, 63

V

  Valentine, 290
  Vasleti, H., 81
  Vaughn, H., 171
  Veda, 168
  Venlory, 51
  Venora A., 382
  Velna, 467
  Vera G., 357

INDEX

Stratton (Strattan), Vernon, 408
  Vernon D., 168
  Victor, 435, 485
  Viola M., 340
  Virgie L., 408
  Virginia, 369, 415
  Virginia B., 373
  Virginia C., 391
  Virginia M., 383
  Virginia R., 469
  Virginia S., 133
  Vivian, 190
  Vivian H., 153

W

Waitstill, 229
Wallace, 283
Wallace C., 146, 263
Wallace E., 144
Wallace H., 242
Wallas W., 461
Walter, 19, 96, 262, 285, 292, 311, 437, 447, 454, 455
Walter A., 166, 491
Walter D., 164, 308
Walter E., 302, 447, 475
Walter F., 290, 305
Walter H., 391
Walter J., 288
Walter L., 158, 164
Walter M., 172, 397
Walter P., 295
Walter R., 400, 409
Walter S., 153, 297, 318, 445
Ward, 154
Warren, 102, 207
Warren B., 442
Warren L., 443
Warren W., 166
Wayland W., 305
Wayne J., 493
Welcome, 239
Wellington, 135
Wendell W., 305
Wesley, 162
Wesley A., 162
Wesley L., 174
Whitman, 159
Wickliffe B., 407
Wilber E., 436
Wilber F., 104
Wilber R., 109, 172
Wilder, 97, 117
Wilder L., 227
Will B., 141
Willard E., 227
Willard G., 156
Willard O., 105

Stratton (Strattan), Willard P., 216
  Willard S., 80
  William, 17, 18, 28, 33, 35, 59, 60, 62, 64, 68, 69, 71, 78, 95, 102, 104, 144, 146, 153, 154, 177, 179, 187, 208, 224, 237, 238, 248, 261, 270, 279, 281, 307, 311, 321, 327, 350, 351, 352, 353, 354, 356, 359, 360, 361, 363, 364, 366, 367, 370, 371, 377, 384, 404, 409, 427, 430, 432, 451, 454, 458, 459, 460, 461, 462, 463, 466, 471, 473, 479, 481
  William A., 91, 115, 148, 162, 163, 173, 288, 352, 388, 445, 448, 468, 469, 483
  William B, 166, 272, 299
  William C., 123, 311, 422, 452
  William D., 111, 163, 177, 299, 302, 348, 371, 372, 373, 382, 388, 437, 439, 453, 493
  William E., 102, 291, 320, 360, 443, 495
  William F., 110, 115, 173, 345, 398
  William H., 110, 114, 135, 150, 161, 167, 184, 208, 249, 254, 264, 265, 291, 294, 327, 369, 381, 404, 443, 451, 454, 458, 463, 474
  William I., 416, 429
  William J., 19, 80, 251, 323, 331, 360, 405, 480, 496
  William L., 401, 424
  William M., 195, 242, 250, 251, 270, 271
  William O., 187, 396, 397, 481
  William P., 152, 296, 399
  William R., 256, 391, 394
  William S., 318
  William T., 130, 339, 390, 455
  William W., 116, 161, 384
  Williamson, 352
  Willis, 133, 135, 136, 489
  Willis G., 165
  Willis R., 330
  Willis S, 386
  Willoughby, 455
  Winella, W., 225
  Winifred A., 312

Stratton (Strattan), Winfield S., 335
  Winsor, 58
  Wright, 88

Z

Zaccheus, 440
Zacharias, 146
Zebulon, 192, 221
Zelma L., 391
Zoe A., 407
Zerviah B., 262

S

Street, 363
Streeter, 78
Streng, 450
String, 472
Strome, 250
Strong, 46, 122, 420, 469
Stowell, 136
Stuart, 227, 408
Sturtevant, 104
Styles, 288
Sudden, 250
Sullivan, 110
Summer, 28, 94, 184, 226, 397, 444, 472, 473, 495
Swan, 374, 387
Sweet, 282, 433
Sweetland, 240
Swift, 175
Swinger, 495
Symonds, 115, 116

T

Taft, 56, 98, 135, 485
Tafts, 268
Tagart, 242
Taintor, 47
Talbot, 129, 249, 491
Tales, 239
Tallman, 489
Talmage, 275
Tartar, 404
Taylor, 110, 118, 122, 146, 157, 212, 224, 254, 294, 295, 321, 322, 378, 387, 396, 397, 408, 448, 482, 493
Tazwell, 344, 345
Teagarden, 461
Tellinghast, 411
Tempany, 106
Temple, 31
Templin, 421
Ten Broeck, 67
Tenny, 80
Terrill, 36
Test, 419
Thatcher, 411

INDEX 527

Thayer, 41, 94
Thom, 349
Thomas, 40
Thomas, 96, 174, 260, 262, 340, 360, 395, 434, 448
Thompson, 109, 131, 141, 142, 158, 161, 254, 287, 288, 307, 311, 319, 382, 391, 417, 432, 440
Thorn, 430
Thornhill, 380, 381
Thorpe, 74, 300, 302, 320
Tiffany, 116
Tight, 299
Tilghman, 407
Tillman, 371, 388
Tilton, 163
Titus, 468, 471
Todd, 286, 401, 421, 454
Tolman, 94, 174
Tompkin, 303
Tooms, 142
Torward, 356
Totten, 283
Totten, 495
Town, 43, 459
Tower, 194
Towle, 156
Towler, 369
Townsend, 75, 106, 173, 259, 418, 419, 431, 443
Tower, 229
Trainer, 450
Trainor, 450
Trask, 74
Travis, 140
Treadwell, 276, 292, 314
Trembly, 251
Trime, 149
Trombridge, 149, 453
Troth, 423
Troter, 182
Troup, 491
Troy, 70
Tuck, 40
Tucker, 125, 318, 363, 370, 392, 463
Tunstill, 364, 387
Turk, 296
Turner, 36, 110, 143, 151, 226, 298, 367, 382, 416, 433
Tuttle, 288
Twinning, 223, 306
Twitchell, 196
Tyler, 48, 124, 127, 262, 236

U

Underhill, 264
Underwood, 302, 303, 424
Unthank, 435
Updike, 170
Upshur, 349

Vail, 260
Valentine, 121, 145, 290
Van Bushkirk, 143
Vance, 159
Vancil, 492
Vankirk, 104
Vanneman, 152
Vansceirt, 427
Van Winkle, 122, 324
Vanuxem, 246
Varble, 464
Varger, 336
Varmeyer, 251
Varney, 117
Venable, 422
Vian, 166
Vickers, 160, 393
Viles, 42
Virgil, 483
Vogal, 436
Vorhees, 369
Vosburg, 140
Voyles, 466

W

Wade, 191, 417, 437, 479, 480
Wadsword, 198
Wadsworth, 464
Waite, 59
Wagner, 387
Wagy, 71
Waldmann, 212
Waldo, 110, 143
Waldron, 381
Wales, 126
Walker, 40, 55, 137, 141, 167, 180, 186, 304, 309, 325, 332, 334, 372, 384, 396, 402, 417
Wallace, 413
Walling, 131
Walsh, 158
Walters, 145, 254, 458, 476
Walton, 420
Ward, 98, 144, 146, 194, 195, 199
Warden, 437
Wardner, 94
Ware, 469
Warner, 38, 86, 89, 137, 330
Warren, 32, 37, 254, 287
Warrener 38
Washington, 347
Washburn, 46, 138
Wasson, 458, 459
Waterman, 114, 219
Watkins, 143, 385, 464
Watson, 145, 149, 354, 446, 493
Wax, 251

Weaver, 422, 452
Webb, 40, 121, 159, 434
Webber, 38, 248
Webster, 164, 172, 247, 250, 283, 356
Weddle, 408
Wedge, 159
Weirough, 488
Weed, 303
Weeks, 62, 185
Welch, 260
Wellington, 163
Wellman, 52, 91
Wells, 88, 135, 265, 288
Wentworth, 153
Wert, 295
Wessels, 114
Wesson, 255
West, 97, 99, 141, 395
Westmoreland, 466
Westcott, 260
Wetherill, 244
Wetmore, 225
Wheat, 53
Wheatley, 45
Wheeler, 36, 40, 56, 101, 116, 128, 204, 212, 218, 253, 323
Whitaker 103, 386
Whitcome, 54, 93, 143
Whithall, 244
White, 33, 47, 70, 84, 163, 177, 189, 204, 224, 240, 248, 291, 370, 375, 397, 426, 427, 442, 453, 482
Whitehead, 90, 128
Whitemore, 324
Whithed, 46
Whitman, 33, 135
Whitmore, 25, 219, 249
Whitney, 32, 92, 96, 145, 217, 271, 402, 439
Whitney, 95, 145
Whittlesey, 188
Whyte, 268
Wiand, 417
Wick, 160
Wickersham, 445
Wikstrom, 405
Wilcox, 112, 177
Wilberforce, 107
Wilburn, 373, 388, 391
Wilcox, 112, 114, 116, 219
Wilder, 55, 117, 129, 193, 227
Wilds, 37
Wilker, 78
Wilkins, 350, 401, 406
Willard, 141
Willette, 135, 283
Willey, 207, 325
Williams, 71, 136, 288, 315, 333, 254, 376, 404, 420, 426, 449, 452, 454

Willis, 81, 96, 263, 310, 324, 403
Willoughby, 113, 114
Wilson, 179, 242, 261, 262, 267, 289, 293, 307, 309, 350, 381, 403, 411, 413, 440, 447, 482
Winbourn, 398
Winch, 68
Wing, 156
Winn, 201
Winship, 222
Winslow, 100
Wise, 347
Witherspoon, 389
Withington, 210
Withal, 372
Witherill, 305
Witzel, 404
Wolverton, 336
Womback, 352

Wood, 37, 58, 84, 95, 115, 136, 173, 191, 200, 318, 333, 339, 472, 478
Woodard, 159
Woodbridge, 60
Woodbury, 47
Woodcock, 128
Woodhull, 60, 292
Woodman, 333
Woodruff, 257, 276, 382
Woodson, 380, 384
Woodward, 92, 104
Woody, 25, 405
Wooley, 35, 290, 318
Woolley, 223
Woolf, 422
Woolridge, 369, 272
Wooster, 103
Wooten, 171, 412
Worcester, 405
Wormeley, 349

Worry, 128
Wrann, 102
Wright, 23, 26, 35, 46, 48, 82, 90, 143, 186, 204, 225, 409, 412, 413, 424, 425, 426, 475
Wrhen, 426
Wyman, 80, 128
Wynkoop, 19

Y

York, 85, 89
Young, 140, 162, 272, 292, 408, 433, 457
Youtz, 496

Z

Zenley, 387
Zimmerman, 301
Zoll, 491